PHILO

Introducing Philosophy

Questions of Knowledge and Reality

Revised Second Edition

SOPHY

Edited by Peter Atterton
San Diego State University

Bassim Hamadeh, CEO and Publisher

Kassie Graves, Director of Acquisitions

Jamie Giganti, Senior Managing Editor

Jess Estrella, Senior Graphic Designer

Carrie Montoya, Acquisitions Editor

Natalie Lakosil, Senior Licensing Manager

Allie Kiekhofer and Kaela Martin, Associate Editors

Kat Ragudos, Interior Designer

Cover image copyright © 2015 iStockphoto LP/Frederic Grosse.

Printed in the United States of America

ISBN: 978-1-5165-1062-7(pbk) / 978-1-5165-1063-4(br)

cognella® | ACADEMIC PUBLISHING

Dedicated to my students

And the end of all our exploring
Will be to arrive where we started
And know the place for the first time.
—T. S. Eliot, *Little Gidding*

CONTENTS

PART III 69

The Existence of God

PART IV   195

Knowledge of the External World

PART V   225

The Mind-Body Problem

PART VI   273

Personal Identity

PART VII   315

Free Will, Determinism, and Compatibilism

PART VIII   373

Modern Theories of Human Nature

INTRODUCTION

The unexamined life is not worth living.

—Plato, *Apology*

Everything you believe is questionable. How deeply have you questioned it? The uncritical acceptance of the beliefs handed down to you by parents, teachers, politicians, and religious leaders is dangerous. Many of the beliefs are false. Some of them are lies to control you. Even when what has been handed down is true, it is not your truth. To merely accept anything without questioning it is to be somebody else's puppet, a second-hand person. Beliefs can be handed down. Knowledge can perhaps be handed down. Wisdom can never be handed down. The goal of philosophy is wisdom. Trying to hand down philosophy is unphilosophical. Wisdom requires questioning what is questionable. Since everything is questionable, wisdom requires questioning everything. That is what philosophy is: the art of questioning.

—Daniel Kolak and Raymond Martin, *The Experience of Philosophy*

According to tradition, the first person to describe himself as a philosopher was the Greek mathematician Pythagoras (570–495 BCE). He is reported to have said that there are three kinds of men and women, just as there are three classes of people who attend the Olympic Games. The lowest are those who go to the Games to buy and sell; next above them are those who go there to compete; and "the best people" are those who are content simply to be nonparticipating spectators. Philosophers resemble the third class. They are not lovers of money or honor. They are lovers of wisdom. Indeed, the Greek word philosophia literally means "the love of wisdom." Let us take a closer look at this definition.

1. Philosophy is the love of wisdom. This is not to claim that philosophy is wisdom. Wisdom is something the philosopher searches for, not something that she currently possesses. Plato (427–347 BCE) says,

"Love is always the love of something, and … that something is what one lacks" (Symposium, 200e). In other words, nobody desires what she already has. You do not desire the ability to read; you already have that ability. If you suffered a stroke that left you unable to read, then you would probably desire to read. Similarly, we typically only want health after we have fallen sick and lost our health. In such cases we say, "I want my health back." What about people who are already rich but who want to get richer? Don't they desire what they already have? Not in the least. What they seek is more money to increase their wealth, not the riches they currently possess. King Midas already possessed considerable wealth, but it was not enough for him; he wanted more (and paid a tragic price for it by inadvertently turning his daughter into gold!).

The implication is clear: the philosopher who seeks wisdom does not yet possess wisdom. This is what distinguishes the philosopher from the white-bearded sage of antiquity. The sage already has the wisdom, whereas the philosopher is still searching for it. The sage seems to have found a shortcut to wisdom; he has it by direct intuition or in the manner of inspired guesses, or else through some sort of mystical experience. The philosopher, in stark contrast, is essentially rational or critical; she is always in search of reasons for believing something is true, reasons that are clear and communicable.

The fact that the philosopher does not yet possess true wisdom is not meant to imply that she is ignorant. Indeed, it might be that the very recognition that one does not yet possess wisdom is the wisest thing of all! The first of the great philosophers, Socrates (470–399 BCE), did not claim to have any special wisdom or insight. On the contrary, he repeatedly claimed to know nothing. Many people at the time found this hard to believe. Socrates was intellectually superior to his contemporaries, and, moreover, was fond of irony. Naturally, people assumed he did not mean it when he claimed to be ignorant. There is a story in Plato's *Apology* (21a–d) about a loyal friend of Socrates, Chaerephon, who went one day to consult Apollo, the god of truth, at the oracle at Delphi, asking if there were anyone wiser than Socrates. The answer was no. When Chaerephon returned to Athens and told Socrates what the oracle had said, Socrates was taken aback. How could it be true that he was the wisest person when he knew himself to be so bereft of wisdom? So, he decided to test the wisdom of the oracle. This might seem like a very impious thing to do, since Socrates was, in effect, calling into question the god of truth himself! (Socrates would later be placed on trial and executed for alleged impiety.[1]) Thus, he proceeded to engage all manner of people to see what they knew. He questioned, for example, politicians, poets, and artisans, only to find to his dismay that they too knew nothing! It was at this point that the light bulb switched on. He was able to reconcile his claim that he was ignorant with the oracle's claim that he was the wisest, because he knew at least one thing more than those he had questioned, namely, he *knew* that he knew nothing. The god Apollo had spoken the truth after all.

This is an extremely important tale. The wisest person is the one "who, like Socrates, knows that his wisdom is in truth worth nothing" (*Apology*, 21d). Socrates was so concerned that others would not be motivated to seek wisdom if they thought they had all the answers that he set about the thankless task of showing them that they, too, were ignorant. This is why, for the most part, we do not have a body of positive philosophical knowledge (positions, views, etc.) from Socrates himself, only a catalogue of negative assaults on the dogmatic opinions and beliefs of others. He tried to bring others to the same realization that wisdom is something we do not yet possess, but something all of us need to strive for.

2. Philosophy is the love of *wisdom*. Wisdom is not the same as mere "knowledge of facts" or "information." The Greeks had a word for such knowledge, which they called *episteme*, but they drew a distinction between it and a true philosophical wisdom (*sophia*). The Greeks would have considered someone who is good at *Jeopardy!* to have *episteme*, but not necessarily *sophia*. To gain a better understanding of the difference between the two, consider the following questions:

1. What is a byproduct of photosynthesis?
2. What does *cephalalagia* mean?
3. Who shot and killed the American rapper Biggie Smalls?
4. What is the best way to win friends and influence people?
5. What is the good life?

Only question five is a philosophical question. To answer it requires one to possess wisdom. The rest are nonphilosophical questions. To answer them, knowledge of facts alone suffices. If you study plant biology or do a simple experiment using an elodea plant, a jar containing water, and a toothpick, you will know that plants release oxygen as a by-product in photosynthesis. A good English dictionary will tell you that a *cephalalagia* is a headache. We do not know who murdered Mr. Wallace. Was it the result of a bicoastal rap rivalry? We will probably never know. However, this is not because we lack wisdom but because it is often very difficult to know the truth about events that occurred in the past, perhaps the very distant past, which we cannot directly observe and whose footprint becomes fainter as time goes by. Now, you might think that question four is different from the rest because we probably will not be able to agree on how best to win friends and influence people. Is it better to give honest and sincere appreciation to someone, or never say, "You're wrong" (when you know the person clearly is)? What is more important when meeting somebody for the first time? Remembering to smile or remembering her name? But even if we cannot agree about these things, presumably there is an answer to be found somewhere. If we knew enough about human psychology and about the person's cultural background, then we would know the answer. We just can't say in the abstract whether smiling is more important than remembering someone's name if we want that person to like us.

"What is the good life?" is truly a philosophical question. Not only is there no obvious answer to the question, we won't be able to find the answer by simply doing an experiment, reading the dictionary, extracting a confession, examining various cultures, studying human psychology, or taking an opinion poll. To attempt to answer the question requires us to think philosophically. To ask "What is the good life?" is equivalent to asking: "What is the right way to live?" or "What things should I strive toward?" This question has spawned a wide range of competing answers and arguments: knowledge (Plato), happiness (Aristotle), pleasure (Epicurus), reason and virtue (Stoicism), love (Augustine), moral duty (Kant), faith (Kierkegaard), freedom (Marx), creativity (Nietzsche), and authenticity (existentialism). Only someone who has formulated a clear, articulate, discussable, rational system of ideas and principles will be able to convince us that any one of these answers is correct. Only a person who is able to give reasons that will stand up to cross-examination will stand any chance of being taken seriously by people who think about such issues. That is a philosopher! One thing we can say for sure is that a truly good indication of a truly philosophical question is that the answer is not at all easy to come by. Nor will it win immediate acceptance by people who are not used to thinking philosophically, that is to say, people who from childhood have grown accustomed to certain ways of seeing things and who know particular facts or skills that allow them to carry out a specific task or plan, but never stand back from what they are doing to reflect on why they are doing it.

WHY STUDY PHILOSOPHY?

Philosophy requires slow judgment and laborious thinking. In such contexts, the philosopher may well look just the opposite of someone who is clever and intelligent. And studying philosophy almost certainly will not make you rich. So why bother? It will not always make you popular because it forces you to question not only your own but also other people's beliefs (for which they may not thank you). It will occasionally keep you awake at night when you should be sleeping. Indeed, there are a number of reasons not to bother with philosophy. But there is one reason why we *should* bother that outweighs them all: Philosophy will free or liberate your mind. Bertrand Russell (1872–1970), one of the most famous philosophers of the twentieth century, had this to say about the study of philosophy:

Philosophy is to be studied, not for the sake of any definite answers to its questions, since no definite answers can, as a rule, be known to be true, but rather for the sake of the questions themselves; because these questions enlarge our conception of what is possible, enrich our intellectual imagination and diminish the dogmatic assurance which closes the mind against speculation.[2]

If we want to free ourselves from prejudice—from "prejudgments" that seem to infiltrate our minds without our even knowing it—then we must stand back and reflect on what we believe and why.

Indeed, as human beings we cannot avoid asking philosophical questions. As Aristotle said in the very first line of his great work *Metaphysics*, "All human beings by nature desire to know." Philosophical questioning comes naturally to us; it is part of our essential makeup. The Greeks offered two famous definitions of human being (*anthropos*):

A human being is a rational animal. By this the Greeks meant that unlike other animals, we have the ability to think and make rational judgments. We can ask questions and theorize about things, formulate ideas, and generate hypotheses. We can use reason to unlock the secrets of the universe, discover laws of cause and effect, explain the workings of the atom, and devise new technology.

A human being is a moral being. What also makes us special as human beings is our ability to make moral judgments. For the Greeks, this is a consequence of our ability to reason. Unlike other animals, human beings do not merely live, they do not merely have a life, but they also have a conception of life. That means they can ask questions about what is the right way to live, what things should be striven for, whether life has any meaning, and, if so, what that meaning is.

Why study philosophy? Because as human beings we cannot help but ask questions that we cannot hope to answer without training. Philosophy provides that training, and in the process frees the mind from prejudice while opening us up to new ways of thinking and new experiences. In this type of questioning, nothing is taken for granted. Nothing is accepted as true unless it has run the gauntlet of argument. Philosophy is thus radically opposed to dogma, the acceptance of things on the basis or authority or faith. It is a matter of thinking for oneself. Another word we could use is *criticism*, not in the negative sense of faultfinding, but as a questioning of the hidden assumptions, beliefs, and opinions behind what is said. Why do we say the things we say? Why do we assume that we're right to say them? Are the reasons for believing something to be true *my* reasons?

This is, of course, what a college education is—or should be—all about. Albert Einstein once said, "The value of a college education is not the learning of many facts but the training of the mind to think."[2] Philosophy trains the mind to think. It is a strenuous, intellectual workout in which concepts and ideas are "muscles of the mind." It will not only get you to question all the stock responses that have been handed down from generation to generation, from tradition and the Church, from the television and the internet, from politicians and one's parents, from one's Sunday School teachers and one's high school teachers; it will not only get you to question yourself because it suspects that you are dreaming, sleeping, or naively accepting as true what may turn out to be false; but it will also help you to think clearly and rationally, as well as critically and independently.

FIELDS OF PHILOSOPHY

Unlike other disciplines, philosophy does not have a well-defined subject matter. In contrast to a discipline such as biology, which is the science of life, or sociology, which is the study of society, philosophy cannot be defined in terms of any particular object of inquiry. This is because everything you believe is questionable from a philosophical point of view—*everything*, that is to say, nothing in particular. There is a philosophy of mathematics (Do numbers exist independently of the mind?), a philosophy of science (How do you distinguish science from non-science?), a philosophy of history (*If* history can be said to progress, what, if anything, is the driving force of that progress?), a philosophy of law (What is the origin and justification of legal systems?), a philosophy of art (What is art?), and even a philosophy of cooking (Can anybody do it?). Indeed, some philosophers (called "postmodernists") are currently asking a philosophical question about philosophy itself: Has philosophy basically said all that it has to say?

There are, however, various fields or divisions within philosophy, each with their own particular focus and set of questions. The major divisions are logic, epistemology, ethics, and metaphysics. Here is a brief sketch of each.

Logic (from Greek *logos,* meaning "speech," "account," or "reason") is the discipline that studies the procedures by which we distinguish good from bad reasoning and discover when our thinking is muddled or confused. Logic helps us to assess whether a person is rationally justified in drawing the conclusion she wishes to draw; it also examines general forms that arguments may take (which arguments are strong, which are fallacies, and which forms are valid). In addition, logic helps us to unearth assumptions we did not know we were making and forces us to makes explicit what must be the case if our reasoning is sound or cogent.

Epistemology (from Greek *episteme,* meaning "knowledge," and *logos*) is the study of the nature and scope of knowledge. It includes these questions and many others: What is the difference between knowledge and opinion? What does it mean to know something is true? What is the nature of truth itself? What kinds of things can be known? How is knowledge acquired? Is there knowledge beyond the reach of science? What is the difference between knowing something is true (e.g., Everest is the tallest mountain) and knowing *how* to do something (e.g., ride a bike)?

Ethics (from Greek ethos, meaning "character," "habitual way of life") is the study of the nature of goodness in the area of human conduct. It examines questions to do with right behavior, obligation, and duty. What do we mean when we say, "You ought to give money to help the poor"? What criteria are appropriate for deeming something morally right or good? Is goodness objectively part of the universe? Or is it the case that, as Hamlet says, "There is nothing either good or bad, but thinking makes it so" (Shakespeare, *Hamlet* 2.2)? How are we to formulate principles to guide moral actions and decisions? What are our moral obligations to others? How can moral disagreements be rationally settled? What rights must a just society accord its citizens?

But why so much emphasis on Greece? Not every culture has produced philosophers. Many cultures have saints, prophets, religious experts, and so on, but no philosophers. True, there were other peoples of antiquity who came close to philosophy as it is understood in the West. The Chinese, Hebrews, the people of India, and the Persians produced some great thinkers. But these thinkers were chiefly concerned with religious or mystical systems of thinking, rather than the impartial judgments of reason. Their philosophy, if they had one, played second fiddle to their worship and religion. Philosophy in Greece marks a departure for the religious mindset. It was in this spirit that the Greeks were enabled quite early on to recognize their religion and gods (Zeus, Aphrodite, Apollo, etc.) for what they actually were—strikingly beautiful creations of their own artistic imagination, but not possessing one iota of truth. This was all part of what is sometimes called the "Greek miracle." How did the Greeks become so independently minded? Nobody really knows.

Notice I said "independently minded;" I did not say "learned" or "knowledgeable." The Egyptians and Babylonians were very learned and knowledgeable. The Egyptians, for example, calculated the length of the solar year in 4000 BCE and developed a breathtaking skill in mathematics. But their knowledge was always useful or pragmatic—never knowledge for its own sake—and was linked to utilizing the flood waters of the Nile. One needed to know when the floods were going to occur so as to manipulate water levels for irrigation purposes. One needed a sophisticated geometry to determine the size of irregular grain growing lands, etc. But the idea of pure speculation for its own sake was altogether foreign to the Egyptians. They knew about the "3–4–5 triangle," which they used for land surveying and to help design their pyramids, but Pythagoras's famous theorem ($a^2 + b^2 = c^2$) was a thoroughly Greek invention.

ABOUT THIS BOOK

Introducing Philosophy: Questions of Knowledge and Reality contains a broad selection of some of the best works—both classical and modern—on many of the central issues in philosophy. It purposely omits topics of ethics, which is a course unto itself. Aimed at the freshman–sophomore level, the collection presupposes no familiarity with the concepts it addresses and offers a well-balanced and accessible approach to the field, while avoiding the Scylla and Charybdis of either "dumbing down" the material or having unrealistic expectations of today's college students. The readings vary in difficulty, but all of them are—with effort—comprehensible if the student applies herself.

ACKNOWLEDGMENTS

My thanks to the team at Cognella—especially Seidy Cruz, Senior Field Acquisitions Editor; Jennifer Bowen, Academic Production Coordinator; Jessica Knott, Project Editor; and Brent Hannify, Production Assistant—who put the book on a fast-track production schedule, and Stephen Milano, Graphic Designer, for the beautiful book cover. It has been a delight to work with such a talented team. Thanks also to Christopher Burden, who offered useful suggestions for improving the introduction.

Peter Atterton
San Diego State University
July 2010

NOTES

1. Another capital charge brought against Socrates and of which he was found guilty was corrupting the youth. See Plato's *Euthyphro*, included in this volume.
2. Bertrand Russell, *The Problems of Philosophy* (New York: Galaxy, 1959), p. 161 (included in this volume).
3. Taken from Walter Isaacson, *Einstein: His Life and Universe*, (New York: Simon & Schuster, 2007), p. 299.

THE VALUE OF PHILOSOPHY

By Bertrand Russell

HAVING now come to the end of our brief and very incomplete review of the problems of philosophy, it will be well to consider, in conclusion, what is the value of philosophy and why it ought to be studied. It is the more necessary to consider this question, in view of the fact that many men, under the influence of science or of practical affairs, are inclined to doubt whether philosophy is anything better than innocent but useless trifling, hair-splitting distinctions, and controversies on matters concerning which knowledge is impossible.

This view of philosophy appears to result, partly from a wrong conception of the ends of life, partly from a wrong conception of the kind of goods which philosophy strives to achieve. Physical science, through the medium of inventions, is useful to innumerable people who are wholly ignorant of it; thus the study of physical science is to be recommended, not only, or primarily, because of the effect on the student, but rather because of the effect on mankind in general. Thus utility does not belong to philosophy. If the study of philosophy has any value at all for others than students of philosophy, it must be only indirectly, through its effects upon the lives of those who study it. It is in these effects, therefore, if anywhere, that the value of philosophy must be primarily sought.

But further, if we are not to fail in our endeavour to determine the value of philosophy, we must first free our minds from the prejudices of what are wrongly called 'practical' men. The 'practical' man, as this word is often used, is one who recognizes only material needs, who realizes that men must have food for the body, but is oblivious of the necessity of providing food for the mind. If all men were well off, if poverty and disease had been reduced to their lowest possible point, there would still remain much to be done to produce a valuable society; and even in the existing world the goods of the mind are at least as important as the goods of the body. It is exclusively among the goods of the mind that the value of philosophy is to be found; and only those who are not indifferent to these goods can be persuaded that the study of philosophy is not a waste of time.

Philosophy, like all other studies, aims primarily at knowledge. The knowledge it aims at is the kind of knowledge which gives unity and system to the body of the sciences, and the kind which results from a critical examination of the grounds of our convictions, prejudices, and beliefs. But it cannot be maintained that philosophy has had any very great measure of success in its attempts to provide definite answers to its questions. If you ask a mathematician, a mineralogist, a historian, or any other man of learning, what definite body of truths has been ascertained by his science, his answer will last as long as you are willing to listen. But if you put the same question to a philosopher, he will, if he is candid, have to confess that his study has not achieved positive results such as have been achieved by other sciences. It is true that this is partly accounted for by the fact that, as soon as definite knowledge concerning any subject becomes possible, this subject ceases to be called philosophy, and becomes a separate science. The whole study of the heavens, which now belongs to astronomy, was once included in philosophy; Newton's great work was called 'the mathematical principles of natural philosophy'. Similarly, the study of the human mind, which was a part of philosophy, has now been separated from philosophy and has become the science of psychology. Thus, to a great extent, the uncertainty of philosophy is more apparent than real: those questions which are already capable of definite answers are placed in the sciences, while those only to which, at present, no definite answer can be given, remain to form the residue which is called philosophy.

This is, however, only a part of the truth concerning the uncertainty of philosophy. There are many questions—and among them those that are of the profoundest interest to our spiritual life—which, so far as we can see, must remain insoluble to the human intellect unless its powers become of quite a different order from what they are now. Has the universe any unity of plan or purpose, or is it a fortuitous concourse of atoms? Is consciousness a permanent part of the universe, giving hope of indefinite growth in wisdom, or is it a transitory accident on a small planet on which life must ultimately become impossible? Are good and evil of importance to the universe or only to man? Such questions are asked by philosophy, and variously answered by various philosophers. But it would seem that, whether answers be otherwise discoverable or not, the answers suggested by philosophy are none of them demonstrably true. Yet, however slight may be the hope of discovering an answer, it is part of the business of philosophy to continue the consideration of such questions, to make us aware of their importance, to examine all the approaches to them, and to keep alive that speculative interest in the universe which is apt to be killed by confining ourselves to definitely ascertainable knowledge.

Many philosophers, it is true, have held that philosophy could establish the truth of certain answers to such fundamental questions. They have supposed that what is of most importance in religious beliefs could be proved by strict demonstration to be true. In order to judge of such attempts, it is necessary to take a survey of human knowledge, and to form an opinion as to its methods and its limitations. On such a subject it would be unwise to pronounce dogmatically; but if the investigations of our previous chapters have not led us astray, we shall be compelled to renounce the hope of finding philosophical proofs of religious beliefs. We cannot, therefore, include as part of the value of philosophy any definite set of answers to such questions. Hence, once more, the value of philosophy must not depend upon any supposed body of definitely ascertainable knowledge to be acquired by those who study it.

The value of philosophy is, in fact, to be sought largely in its very uncertainty. The man who has no tincture of philosophy goes through life imprisoned in the prejudices derived from common sense, from the habitual beliefs of his age or his nation, and from convictions which have grown up in his mind without the co-operation or consent of his deliberate reason. To such a man the world tends to become definite, finite, obvious; common objects rouse no questions, and unfamiliar possibilities are contemptuously rejected. As soon as we begin to philosophize, on the contrary, we find, as we saw in our opening chapters, that even the most everyday things lead to problems to which only very incomplete answers can be given. Philosophy, though unable to tell us with certainty what is the true answer to the doubts which it raises, is able to suggest many possibilities which enlarge our thoughts and free them from the tyranny of custom. Thus, while diminishing our feeling of certainty as to what things are, it greatly increases our knowledge as to what they may be; it removes the somewhat arrogant dogmatism of those who have never travelled into the region of liberating doubt, and it keeps alive our sense of wonder by showing familiar things in an unfamiliar aspect.

Apart from its utility in showing unsuspected possibilities, philosophy has a value—perhaps its chief value—through the greatness of the objects which it contemplates, and the freedom from narrow and personal aims resulting from this contemplation. The life of the instinctive man is shut up within the circle of his private interests: family and friends may be included, but the outer world is not regarded except as it may help or hinder what comes within the circle of instinctive wishes. In such a life there is something feverish and confined, in comparison with which the philosophic life is calm and free. The private world of instinctive interests is a small one, set in the midst of a great and powerful world which must, sooner or later, lay our private world in ruins. Unless we can so enlarge our interests as to include the whole outer world, we remain like a garrison in a beleagured fortress, knowing that the enemy prevents escape and that ultimate surrender is inevitable. In such a life there is no peace, but a constant strife between the insistence of desire and the powerlessness of will. In one way or another, if our life is to be great and free, we must escape this prison and this strife.

One way of escape is by philosophic contemplation. Philosophic contemplation does not, in its widest survey, divide the universe into two hostile camps—friends and foes, helpful and hostile, good and bad—it views the whole impartially. Philosophic contemplation, when it is unalloyed, does not aim at proving that the rest of the universe is akin to man. All acquisition of knowledge is an enlargement of the Self, but this enlargement is best attained when it is not directly sought. It is obtained when the desire for knowledge is alone operative, by a study which does not wish in advance that its objects should have this or that character, but adapts the Self to the characters which it finds in its objects. This enlargement of Self is not obtained when, taking the Self as it is, we try to show that the world is so similar to this Self that knowledge of it is possible without any admission of what seems alien. The desire to prove this is a form of self-assertion and, like all self-assertion, it is an obstacle to the growth of Self which it desires, and of which the Self knows that it is capable. Self-assertion, in philosophic speculation as elsewhere, views the world as a means to its own ends; thus it makes the world of less account than Self, and the Self sets bounds to the greatness of its goods. In contemplation, on the contrary, we start from the not-Self, and through its greatness the boundaries of Self are enlarged; through the infinity of the universe the mind which contemplates it achieves some share in infinity.

For this reason greatness of soul is not fostered by those philosophies which assimilate the universe to Man. Knowledge is a form of union of Self and not-Self; like all union, it is impaired by dominion, and therefore by any attempt to force the universe into conformity with what we find in ourselves. There is a widespread philosophical tendency towards the view which tells us that Man is the measure of all things, that truth is man-made, that space and time and the world of universals are properties of the mind, and that, if there be anything not created by the mind, it is unknowable and of no account for us. This view, if our previous discussions were correct, is untrue; but in addition to being untrue, it has the effect of robbing philosophic contemplation of all that gives it value, since it fetters contemplation to Self. What it calls knowledge is not a union with the not-Self, but a set of prejudices, habits, and desires, making an impenetrable veil between us and the world beyond. The man who finds pleasure in such a theory of knowledge is like the man who never leaves the domestic circle for fear his word might not be law.

The true philosophic contemplation, on the contrary, finds its satisfaction in every enlargement of the not-Self, in everything that magnifies the objects contemplated, and thereby the subject contemplating. Everything, in contemplation, that is personal or private, everything that depends upon habit, self-interest, or desire, distorts the object, and hence impairs the union which the intellect seeks. By thus making a barrier between subject and object, such personal and private things become a prison to the intellect. The free intellect will see as God might see, without a here and now, without hopes and fears, without the trammels of customary beliefs and traditional prejudices, calmly, dispassionately, in the sole and exclusive desire of knowledge—knowledge as impersonal, as purely contemplative, as it is possible for man to attain. Hence also the free intellect will value more the abstract and universal knowledge into which the accidents of private history do not enter, than the knowledge brought by the senses, and dependent, as such knowledge must be, upon an exclusive and personal point of view and a body whose sense-organs distort as much as they reveal.

The mind which has become accustomed to the freedom and impartiality of philosophic contemplation will preserve something of the same freedom and impartiality in the world of action and emotion. It will view its purposes and desires as parts of the whole, with the absence of insistence that results from seeing them as infinitesimal fragments in a world of which all the rest is unaffected by any one man's deeds. The impartiality which, in contemplation, is the unalloyed desire for truth, is the very same quality of mind which, in action, is justice, and in emotion is that universal love which can be given to all, and not only to those who are judged useful or admirable. Thus contemplation enlarges not only the objects of our thoughts, but also the objects of our actions and our affections: it makes us citizens of the universe, not only of one walled city at war with all the rest. In this citizenship of the universe consists man's true freedom, and his liberation from the thralldom of narrow hopes and fears.

Thus, to sum up our discussion of the value of philosophy; Philosophy is to be studied, not for the sake of any definite answers to its questions since no definite answers can, as a rule, be known to be true, but rather for the sake of the questions themselves; because these questions enlarge our conception of what is possible, enrich our intellectual imagination and diminish the dogmatic assurance which closes the mind against speculation; but above all because, through the greatness of the universe which philosophy contemplates, the mind also is rendered great, and becomes capable of that union with the universe which constitutes its highest good.

PART I

Historical Background

THE PRE-SOCRATES

By Louis Pojman

INTRODUCTION

Philosophy begins with wonder, and even now it is wonder that causes philosophers to philosophize. At first they wondered about the obvious difficulties and then they gradually progressed to puzzle about the greater ones, for example, the behavior of the moon and sun and stars and the coming to be of the universe. Whoever is puzzled and in a state of wonder believes he is ignorant (this is why the lover of myths is also in a way a philosopher, since myths are made up of wonders). And so, if indeed they pursued philosophy to escape ignorance, they were obviously pursuing scientific knowledge in order to know and not for the sake of any practical need.[1]

(aristotle)

They looked into the heavens and wondered how the universe had come about. They pondered the structure of the world. Is there one fundamental substance that underlies all of reality or are there many substances? What is the really *real,* and not just a matter of appearance?

The first philosophers were Greeks of the sixth century B.C. living on the Ionian coast of the Aegean Sea, in Miletus, Colophon, Samos, and Ephesus. Other people in other cultures had wondered about these questions, but usually religious authority or myth had imposed an answer. Typically, as in the Hebrews' Genesis 1 or the Greek Hesiod's *Theogony* the world order was said to have arisen from God or the gods. Now a break occurred. Here for the first time a pure philosophical and scientific inquiry was allowed to flourish. The Great Civilizations of Egypt, China, Assyria, Babylon, Israel, and Persia, not to mention those of the Incas, Mayans, and Africans, had produced art and artifacts and government of advanced sorts, but nowhere, with the possible exception of India, was anything like philosophy or science developed. Ancient India was the closest civilization to produce philosophy, but it was always connected with religion, with the question of salvation or the escape from suffering. Ancient Chinese thought, led by Confucius (551–475 B.C.), had a deep ethical dimension. But no epistemology or formulated logic. Now Greek philosophy, especially from Socrates on, also had a practical bent and was concerned with ethics, but it went deeper and further than ethics, asking for the nature of all things, aiming at knowledge and understanding for its own sake, seeking systematic understanding of metaphysics, and using experiment and logical argument, rather than religion or intuition alone, to reach its conclusions. Indeed, Socrates was the first to develop dialectical argument (the "Socratic Method") and Aristotle invented formal logic, the system of syllogisms.

The first Greek philosophers were materialists and naturalists, sometimes called *Hylicists* (from the Greek *hule,* which means matter), for they rejected spiritual and religious causes and sought naturalistic explanations of reality. The standard date for the beginning of philosophy is May 28, 585 B.C., when, according to Herodotus, Thales of Miletus (625–545 B.C.) on the coast of Asia Minor (then called Ionia, now Turkey) predicted a solar eclipse.[2] What has the prediction of an eclipse to do with philosophy? Thales used mathematical and astronomical investigation to make his prediction. In this sense he may have been the first scientist, and since at this early stage of development science cannot be separated from philosophy, the prediction of the solar eclipse serves as a clothespin holding one end of the long sheet of the history of philosophy to the clothesline of world history.

Thales, who was an engineer by training, asked, "What is the nature of reality? What is the ultimate explanation of all that is?" and speculated and experimented in order to come up with the answer. What was his answer? "Water." Water is necessary for the production and sustenance of life. Water is everywhere; look past the coastline and you'll find a sea of water, dig under the ground and you're bound to find water. It rises as mist from the sea and falls down to earth as rain. Heat water and it becomes a gas like air, freeze it and it becomes solid. So Thales concluded that earth was just especially solid water, a hard flat cork which floated in a sea of liquid of the same substance. It is the first recorded attempt to give a naturalistic answer to the question "What is reality?"

A simple beginning? No doubt, but it is worth quoting Friedrich Nietzsche here.

> Greek philosophy seems to begin with a preposterous fancy, with the proposition that water is the origin and mother-womb of all things. Is it really necessary to stop there and become serious? Yes, and for three reasons: Firstly, because the proposition does enunciate something about the origin of things; secondly, because it does so without figure and fable; thirdly,

because in it is contained, although only in the chrysalis state, the idea—Everything is one. The first-mentioned reason leaves Thales still in the company of religious and superstitious people; the second, however, takes him out of this company and shows him to us as a natural philosopher; but by virtue of the third, Thales becomes the first Greek philosopher.[3]

After Thales his fellow Ionian Anaximander (c. 612–545 B.C.) rejected the idea that water was the root substance and hypothesized that ultimate reality could not be equated with any one material substance, but was neutral between them, yet underlying all matter. It was an unknown boundless material substance (*Apeiron*), the *Infinite* or *Boundless.*

> Anaximander asserted that the source and elements of existing things is the *infinite.* He was the first to introduce this name for the source. He says that it is neither water nor any of the other so-called "elements," but of another nature which is infinite, from which all the heavens and the world-order in them arise.

No mention is made of the gods, nor of a beginning nor end of reality.

> Everything either is a beginning or has a beginning. But there is no beginning of the infinite; for if there were, it would limit it. Moreover, since it is a beginning, it is unbegotten and indestructible. For there must be a point at which what has come into being reaches completion, and a point at which all perishing ceases. Hence, as we say, there is no source of *the Infinite,* but it appears to be the source of all the rest and "encompasses all things" and "steers all things," as those assert who do not recognize other causes besides the infinite. And this, they say, is divine; for it is "deathless" and "imperishable" as Anaximander puts it, and most of the physicists agree with him.

The Infinite is externally in motion and the source of time, space, matter and mind. An opposition of forces keeps the world in its revolving place. These opposites "make reparation to one another for their injustice," creating an exterior homeostasis or equilibrium of forces.

> Into those things from which existing things have their coming into being, their passing away, too, takes place, according to what must be; for they make reparation to one another for their injustice according to the ordinance of time.[4]

Analogously, health is an inner homeostasis, an equilibrium of opposing forces within us. Our world is only one of many worlds produced by the Infinite in its eternal motion, a motion which is perpetually whirling. This Whirl separates as in a vortex or whirlpool in which heavy objects move to the bottom and light to the top. Hence the colder elements, earth and water, move downward and the lighter ones, fire and air, upward. This seems to be the beginning of the idea of Natural Law in which natural causes, blind and impersonal, replace the gods. Wind, not Zeus, causes lightning. He rejected Thales notion of a stationary flat earth and suggested that the earth was a revolving, cylindrical body, whose flat top was our home.[5]

Rejecting the anthropocentric notions of the religious and mythological explanations and anticipating Darwin by 2,500 years, Anaximander put forth a theory of evolution based on the need for species to adapt to their environment. Human beings evolved from fish or fish-like creatures who had to adapt to land and so developed the characteristics we now have.

Anaximander's disciple Anaximenes (585–528 B.C.) accepted his teacher's notion that reality is infinite, but observing evaporation and condensation and how breath animated both humans and animals, he posited air as the ultimate substance. "Just as our soul, being air, keeps us together in order, so also breath and air encompass the whole cosmos."

One other philosopher from the Ionian coast deserves mention. Xenophanes (c. 570–c. 478 B.C.) noted the anthropomorphic nature of the gods, their immorality, their stealings, adulteries, and deceivings, their ethnic qualities, suggesting that each culture creates its gods in its own image.

> The Ethiopians make their gods black and snub-nosed. The Thracians make theirs have grey-eyes and red-hair. And if oxen and horses and lions had hands and could paint with their hands, and produce works of art as men do, horses would paint the forms of the gods like horses, and oxen like oxen, and make their bodies in the image of their own.[6]

He argued that there was one God beyond all these mythological and anthropomorphic counterfeits, who seeks, hears and thinks all over. "He remains forever in the same place, without moving; nor is it fitting for him to go about from one place to another. But without labor he sets all things in motion by his intelligent willpower."

PYTHAGORAS

The first philosopher of which we have substantial information is Pythagoras of Samos (580–496 B.C.), who settled in Croton in southern Italy, where he founded the first community of philosophers. Pythagoras either visited Egypt himself or learned from those who did, since the Greek historian Herodotus points to similarities between his ideas and the Egyptians' (religious customs forbidding people to wear wool in temples and belief in an afterlife).[7] It could be argued that not Thales but Pythagoras was the father of philosophy, for with him a comprehensive study of the fundamental questions of philosophy first takes place: What is reality? How does one come to know the truth? How shall I live my life? Here is an early document on what he taught:

> First he said that the soul is immortal; second, that it migrates into other kinds of animals; third, that the same events are repeated in cycles, nothing being new in the strict sense; and finally, that all things with souls should be regarded as related to each other. Pythagoras seems to have been the first to introduce these ideas into Greece.[8]

Pythagoras rejected the Hylicist's materialism and opted for a refined spiritualism, a mathematical mysticism, aiming at the purification of the whole person, body and soul. Knowledge (or Science) and Music would purify the soul and Gymnastics and Medicine, the body. All living things (including plant life) had souls and were related to one another and involved in the transmigration of souls. Pythagoreans generally despised the body as inferior to the soul, which they sought to purify by ascetic practices. They were vegetarians, eating neither meat nor eggs nor beans, nor drinking wine. A story circulated in the ancient world that when Pythagoras noticed a man beating a dog, he cried to him to desist, claiming that he recognized in the dog the "voice of a dear friend."

Pythagoras related morality to the harmony of the soul. A good soul has a proper order of standards and impulses within itself like beautiful music and the sublime system of the heavens. Pythagoreans were renowned for their mutual friendship, altruism, integrity, devotion to duty. At the end of each day they asked themselves what wrongs they had committed, what duties they had neglected, what good they had done.

Pythagoras is the first person on record to hold the doctrine of universal brotherhood, which led him to provide equal opportunity for men and women. Two centuries before Plato's famous declaration of this doctrine in the *Republic* Pythagoras accepted women on an equal basis with men, admitting them into his school. He also called for, and himself practiced, humane treatment of slaves. He was reputed to have never chastised a slave.

Under the government of the Pythagoreans, Croton succeeded in establishing an intellectual aristocracy over a territory about four times the size of Attica, which was destroyed by the democratic party in the second half of the fifth century B.C. The democrats massacred the Pythagoreans, surrounding their assembly house, in which the leadership was lodged, and burning it to the ground.

Pythagoras's fundamental doctrine was that the world is really not material but made up of numbers. Numbers are things and constitute the essence of reality. The original "one," being fire, sets the surrounding cold air in motion, drawing it upon itself and limiting it. From numbers the world is created:

> From numbers points, from points lines, from lines plane figures, from plane figures solid figures, from these sensible bodies, of which the elements are four: fire, water, earth, and air.

These change and are wholly transformed; and from them arises a cosmos animate, intelligent, and spherical, embracing earth (itself spherical and inhabited all around) as its center.

Pythagoras was led to this doctrine by his musical studies. He recognized that the pitch of tones depends on the length of the strings on musical instruments and that musical harmony is determined by definite mathematical propositions. The recognition of this fact led the Pythagoreans to the soul, which was not contained in matter itself but was suprasensual. Thus the anthropological dualism of body and soul was extended to the cosmic dualism of matter and form, or, as they expressed it, of the unlimited and the limited. Hence number was for them something essentially different from water for Thales, or the Apeiron for Anaximander or air for Anaximenes; it was something opposed to matter and distinguished from it although closely connected with it, something which limits it and gives it shape. Matter, as such, was presupposed by the Pythagoreans, and they seem to have imagined it in a way that combined Anaximander's Unbounded and Anaximenes' air. Matter is unlimited breath, that is, the endless expanse of air beyond the cosmos from which the world draws its breath.

Now that number was established as a world-principle, they proceeded to make remarkable speculations on its nature. They drew distinctions between straight and not-straight, unity and duality, and thus derived two further pairs of opposites, whose number was later rather arbitrarily extended up to ten. Individual numbers were considered particularly sacred. One (1) is the paradoxical point, both the limited and the unlimited, 2 is the line, 3 the plane, 4 the solid, 5 physical qualities, 6 animation, 7 intelligence, 8 health, 9 love and wisdom, 10 the sacred Decad, by which they were accustomed to take oaths. From their experiments with numbers they were led to the discovery of the "Pythagorean Theorem" (the sum of the squares of the sides of a right angle triangle are equal to the square of the hypotenuse). Theophrastus tells us that the Pythagoreans were the first to speak of the spherical shape of the earth, the harmony of the spheres and planetary motion. Pythagoras supposed there to be a Central Fire around which the round earth revolved.

Mystic and mathematician, Pythagoras held that we are strangers and pilgrims in the world, that the body is the tomb of the soul, that the visible world of matter is appearance, which must be overcome if we are to know reality. In this life there are three types of people who come to the Olympic Games. The lowest class is made up of those who come to buy and sell, the next above them are those who compete. Best of all, however, are those who come simply to look on. These three types of people correspond to three parts of the soul: the love of gain, of honor, and of wisdom. We must aim at Purification from the world, which comes about through the disinterested pursuit of philosophy. We will meet all these ideas again in Plato, who seems to have been influenced by Pythagoras.

Pythagoras apparently wrote nothing, so we cannot study his writings.

THE ELEATICS

With Parmenides (540–470 B.C.) a further advance in philosophical discourse took place. Parmenides observed that nature is constantly changing and noted that such flux was inimical to the idea of knowledge: to have knowledge there must be permanence, something which is unchanging. He theorized that the real world was unchanging on the order of Pythagoras's number, whereas the apparent, illusory world was the world of change. The senses grasped the changing world of unreality or *Non-being*, whereas reason alone could grasp the real world of *Being*. Being never comes into existence, nor does it cease to be, for it always is. It cannot be divided or added onto, for it is whole and complete in itself, one. It is unmoved and undisturbed, for motion and disturbance are forms of becoming. Being is. It doesn't become. It is self-identical and uncaused. This view is sometimes called Absolute Idealism: there is an Absolute Idea which makes up all there is, and all change is illusory. All is One and Permanently at Rest.

Three theses can be identified in Parmenides' work.

1. That which is, is and cannot not-be; that which is not, is not and cannot be. The real is and cannot be nonexistent.
2. That which is can be thought or known and truly named. That which is not, cannot. Thinking and the thought that it is are the same thing.
3. That which is, is one and cannot be many. The real is unique. There is no second thing besides it. It is also indivisible. It does not contain a plurality of distinct parts.

Being or Reality is one, immaterial, continuous, indivisible, motionless, beginningless, imperishable, and everywhere. It is wholly indeterminate and can only be described in negative terms. It cannot be created nor pass away. It cannot be created, for if it were, it would have to be created from Nothing, which is impossible. It cannot be destroyed, for if it could, then something could become nothing, which is impossible. When thought has negated all that can be negated, it is Being which remains, the unique, godlike One.

Parmenides' most famous disciple was Zeno of Elea (c. 490–c. 430 B.C.), who defended the Eleatic Idealism against those who claimed that there were both multiplicity and motion. Zeno is the first philosopher we know of who self-consciously makes use of the law of noncontradiction to argue against his opponents. Using universally acceptable premises, he develops a series of paradoxes which leads to the conclusion that there is no motion or multiplicity. One of his paradoxes, *The Line,* attempts to show that motion does not exist.

The Eleatics held that a line was one, whereas their opponents held that it was divisible into parts, discrete units. Zeno argues that if a line was divisible into units, it must be divisible into an infinite number of discrete units, so that each unit must be infinitely small. But if there were an infinite number of these units, then if we multiplied them, we would get a line which was infinitely large, for the smallest magnitude multiplied by infinity becomes an infinite magnitude. So what started out as a finite line turns out to be infinitely long, which is a contradiction.

> A second paradox is his Arrow Paradox: the Argument Against Movement. If everything is at rest when it is in a place equal to itself, and if the moving object is always in the present and therefore in a place equal to itself, then the moving arrow is motionless.[9]

Consider an arrow flying from one place to another. Does it really move? No, movement is only an illusion. Consider.

1. The arrow could not move in the place in which it is not.
2. But neither could it move in the place where it is.
3. For this is "a place equal to itself."
4. Everything is always at Rest when it is "at a place equal to itself."
5. But the flying arrow is always at the place where it is.
6. Therefore the flying arrow is always at Rest and cannot move.

A body must either be moving in a place where it is or where it is not. It can't be moving in a place where it is not, for it is not there. But if it is in place, it cannot be moving. For the arrow is at rest at any point in the trajectory and what is at rest at any point cannot move. Therefore the flying arrow cannot be moving.

All of the paradoxes have the same form. Any quantity of space must either be indivisible or divisible ad infinitum. If it is composed of indivisible units, these must have magnitude which can't be divided. If it is composed of divisible units, it must be divisible ad infinitum and we are faced with the contradiction of supposing that an infinite number of parts can be added up to make a finite sum total.

Zeno's paradoxes were in part aimed at destroying Pythagorean doctrines that motion and plurality could be explained by mathematics and logic. He showed that logic led to paradoxes that undermined the notions of motion and plurality. In this he vindicated the Eleatic doctrine that Reality was One, immovable, eternal, and uncreated.

HERACLITUS

Heraclitus (535–475 B.C.) of Ephesus, a cynical, aloof, solitary aristocrat, sometimes called "the weeping philosopher," was contemptuous of democracy ("most men are bad") and scornful of the Pythagorean and Eleatic Idealism and set forth an opposing philosophy ("Pythagoras claimed for his own wisdom what was but a knowledge of many things and an art of mischief"). Rejecting the notion that only Being is, he posited that only Becoming is ("nothing ever is, everything is becoming"). All things are in perpetual flux (Greek *panta rhei*), and permanence is an illusion. There is a single principle at work in the universe. It is fire. "Mind is fire." Fire, an infinite mass of substance, uncreated and eternal, is identical with the universe.

> The world order was not made by a god or a man, but always was and is and will be an ever-living fire.[10]

Fire consumes fuel, thus changing all, but is in constant flux. Transforming all that it comes in contact with, fire replaces Anaximander's Unlimited. Reality is like a stream of fire in constant motion. Nothing is stable. All comes from fire and to fire it shall return. At the same time Heraclitus posited *logos* (reason) as the lawlike process which governed the world.

The world follows an orderly process, though one of conflict and survival of the fittest. Hence war is reason's way of justice in the world. It is the "father of all and the king of all."

The logos, as the rational principle of the universe, has independent existence and according to it all things come into existence. It perpetually confronts people, calling on them to awake from their sleep of illusion. "To those who are awake the world-order is one, common to all, but the sleeping turn aside each into a world of his own."

The logos is hidden in humanity. We become intelligent "by drawing in the divine logos when we breathe." In sleep we are separated from the source of our being and forget. Further, Heraclitus said that the laws of the city were but a reflection of the logos which runs through all things.

> It is necessary for men who speak with common sense to place reliance on what is common to all, as a city relies upon law, and even more firmly. For all human laws are nourished by the one divine law. For it governs as far as it will, and it is sufficient for all things and outlasts them.

THE PLURALISTS: EMPEDOCLES AND THE ATOMISTS

Three philosophers rejected both the absolute monism of the Eleatics and the spiritual dynamics of Heraclitus. The first was Empedocle's (ca. 450 B.C.) who argued that the world was made up of different combinations of four basic elements, water, earth, air, and fire. At the center of the universe there are two forces: attraction and repulsion, called "Love" and "Hate," which are in constant strife. When Love prevails, all things tend toward unity. When Hate prevails, all things separate, individuate. An eternal cosmological battle is waged, so that as one seems to be winning, the other experiences a resurgence.

According to Empedocle's it is literally the case that "Love makes the world go round." But, so does Hate.

The second reaction to the Eleatics was that of the materialists, who hearkened back to the Milesians. Leucippus (c. 450 B.C.) and his more famous disciple, Democritus (c. 460–370 B.C.) taught that the ultimate constituents of the world were atoms (from the Greek *a* for "not" and *tome* for "cut" or "separable"). They were simple, indestructible, internally solid, homogeneous particles which are perpetually in motion in the void of empty space. Their combination and interaction account for all that is. Materialists were hedonists who believed that the only thing that is good is pleasure and the only thing bad is pain. They did not believe in the gods or in immortality.

ANAXAGORAS OF CLAZOMENAE

Anaxagoras (500–428 B.C.) was the first philosopher to make his home in Athens. He reintroduced pluralism, going against the Eleatic stream of monism, but he also rejected Empedocles' notion of the four elements (earth, fire, air, and water) of which all things were composed. They failed to account for the infinite variety and differentiation of the world of experience. Instead Anaxagoras taught that all things contain a portion of everything else.

> In everything there is a portion of everything. For how else could hair come from what is not hair? or flesh from what is not flesh? unless hair and flesh as well as teeth, eyes, and bone, et cetera are contained in food?[11]

Nous is a material (airy) substance but it is the purest and most rarefied of things, having power over all else. As an efficient cause, Nous sets up a rotary motion in the undifferentiated mass of being and causes separation and differentiation.

Anaxagoras was accused of uttering blasphemy in saying that the sun was a red hot stone and the moon was made of earth, for the Athenians regarded the heavenly bodies as gods. He was condemned, tried, found guilty of blasphemy, but escaped Athens to another country.

Socrates heard someone reading from a book of Anaxagoras. He was struck by the phrase, "Mind orders all things," and got hold of the book. Although the book proved a disappointment, concerning itself mainly with mechanical causation, it was a catalyst in turning Socrates away from speculations about the physical world and toward the study of human existence.

NOTES

1. Aristotle, *Metaphysics* 1.2 982b.
2. Discussed and quoted in G. S. Kirk and J. E. Raven, *The Presocratic Philosophers* (Cambridge: Cambridge University Press, 1957), pp. 74–81.

3. Friedrich Nietzsche quoted in ed. L. Miller, *Questions That Matter* (New York: McGraw-Hill, 1987), p. 61.

4. Quoted by Simplicius in his *Physics*. Quoted in John Mansley Robinson, *An Introduction to Early Greek Philosophy* (New York: Houghton Mifflin Company, 1968), p. 34.

5. Alcameon developed this thought, applying it to health: The essence of health lies in the "equality" of the powers—moist, dry, cold, hot, bitter, sweet, and the rest—whereas the cause of sickness is the "supremacy of one" among these. For the rule of any one of them is a cause of destruction … while health is the proportionate mixture of the qualities. Quoted in Robinson, *Introduction,* p. 35.

6. Quoted in Robinson, *Introduction,* p. 52.

7. See Richard McKirahan, Jr., *Philosophy Before Socrates* (82–87) for a lucid discussion of this point.

8. Diogenes Laertius viii.5 quoted in Robinson, *Introduction,* p. 57.

9. *Aristotle*, Physics 6.9, 239.

10. This and the following quotations are from Diogenes Laertius ix.

11. Diels and Kranz, *Fragments of the Presocratic Philosophers* 59 B 11.

APOLOGY

By Plato

Trans. by Benjamin Jowett

SOCRATES' DEFENSE

How you have felt, O men of Athens, at hearing the speeches of my accusers, I cannot tell; but I know that their persuasive words almost made me forget who I was—such was the effect of them; and yet they have hardly spoken a word of truth. But many as their falsehoods were, there was one of them which quite amazed me;—I mean when they told you to be upon your guard, and not to let yourselves be deceived by the force of my eloquence. They ought to have been ashamed of saying this, because they were sure to be detected as soon as I opened my lips and displayed my deficiency; they certainly did appear to be most shameless in saying this, unless by the force of eloquence they mean the force of truth; for then I do indeed admit that I am eloquent. But in how different a way from theirs! Well, as I was saying, they have hardly uttered a word, or not more than a word, of truth; but you shall hear from me the whole truth: not, however, delivered after their manner, in a set oration duly ornamented with words and phrases. No indeed! but I shall use the words and arguments which occur to me at the moment; for I am certain that this is right, and that at my time of life I ought not to be appearing before you, O men of Athens, in the character of a juvenile orator—let no one expect this of me. And I must beg of you to grant me one favor, which is this—If you hear me using the same words in my defence which I have been in the habit of using, and which most of you may have heard in the agora, and at the tables of the money-changers, or anywhere else, I would ask you not to be surprised at this, and not to interrupt me. For I am more than seventy years of age, and this is the first time that I have ever appeared in a court of law, and I am quite a stranger to the ways of the place; and therefore I would have you regard me as if I were really a stranger, whom you would excuse if he spoke in his native tongue, and after the fashion of his country;—that I think is not an unfair request. Never mind the manner, which may or may not be good; but think only of the justice of my cause, and give heed to that: let the judge decide justly and the speaker speak truly.

And first, I have to reply to the older charges and to my first accusers, and then I will go to the later ones. For I have had many accusers, who accused me of old, and their false charges have continued during many years; and I am more afraid of them than of Anytus and his associates, who are dangerous, too, in their own way. But far more dangerous are these, who began when you were children, and took possession of your minds with their falsehoods, telling of one Socrates, a wise man, who speculated about the heaven above, and searched into the earth beneath, and made the worse appear the better cause. These are the accusers whom I dread; for they are the circulators of this rumor, and their hearers are too apt to fancy that speculators of this sort do not believe in the gods. And they are many, and their charges against me are of ancient date, and they made them in days when you were impressible—in childhood, or perhaps in youth—and the cause when heard went by default, for there was none to answer. And, hardest of all, their names I do not know and cannot tell; unless in the chance of a comic poet. But the main body of these slanderers who from envy and malice have wrought upon you—and there are some of them who are convinced themselves, and impart their convictions to others—all these, I say, are most difficult to deal with; for I cannot have them up here, and examine them, and therefore I must simply fight with shadows in my own defence, and examine when there is no one who answers. I will ask you then to assume with me, as I was saying, that my opponents are of two kinds—one recent, the other ancient; and I hope that you will see the propriety of my answering the latter first, for these accusations you heard long before the others, and much oftener.

Well, then, I will make my defence, and I will endeavor in the short time which is allowed to do away with this evil opinion of me which you have held for such a long time; and I hope I may succeed, if this be well for you and me, and that my words may find favor with you. But I know that to accomplish this is not easy—I quite see the nature of the task. Let the event be as God wills: in obedience to the law I make my defence.

I will begin at the beginning, and ask what the accusation is which has given rise to this slander of me, and which has encouraged Meletus to proceed against me. What do the slanderers say? They shall be my prosecutors, and I will sum up their words in an affidavit. "Socrates is an evil-doer, and a curious person, who searches into things under the earth and in heaven, and he makes the worse appear the better cause; and he teaches the aforesaid doctrines to others." That is the nature of the accusation, and that is what you have seen yourselves in the comedy of Aristophanes; who has introduced a man whom he calls Socrates, going about and saying that he can walk in the air, and talking a deal of nonsense concerning matters of which I do not pretend to know either much or little—not that I mean to say anything disparaging of anyone who is a student of natural philosophy. I should be very sorry if Meletus could lay that to my charge. But the simple truth is, O Athenians, that I have nothing to do with these studies. Very many of those here present are witnesses to the truth of this, and to them I appeal. Speak then, you who have heard me, and tell your neighbors whether any of you have ever known me hold forth in few words or in many upon matters of this sort. You hear their answer. And from what they say of this you will be able to judge of the truth of the rest.

As little foundation is there for the report that I am a teacher, and take money; that is no more true than the other. Although, if a man is able to teach, I honor him for being paid. There is Gorgias of Leontium, and Prodicus of Ceos, and Hippias of Elis, who go the round of the cities, and are able to persuade the young men to leave their own citizens, by whom they might be taught for nothing, and come to them, whom they not only pay, but are thankful if they may be allowed to pay them. There is actually a Parian philosopher residing in Athens, of whom I have heard; and I came to hear of him in this way:—I met a man who has spent a world of money on the Sophists, Callias the son of Hipponicus, and knowing that he had sons, I asked him: "Callias," I said, "if your two sons were foals or calves, there would be no difficulty in finding someone to put over them; we should hire a trainer of horses or a farmer probably who would improve and perfect them in their own proper virtue and excellence; but as they are human beings, whom are you thinking of placing over them? Is there anyone who understands human and political virtue? You must have thought about this as you have sons; is there anyone?" "There is," he said. "Who is he?" said I, "and of what country? and what does he charge?" "Evenus the Parian," he replied; "he is the man, and his charge is five minae." Happy is Evenus, I said to myself, if he really has this wisdom, and teaches at such a modest charge. Had I the same, I should have been very proud and conceited; but the truth is that I have no knowledge of the kind.

I dare say, Athenians, that someone among you will reply, "Why is this, Socrates, and what is the origin of these accusations of you: for there must have been something strange which you have been doing? All this great fame and talk about you would never have arisen if you had been like other men: tell us, then, why this is, as we should be sorry to judge hastily of you." Now I regard this as a fair challenge, and I will endeavor to explain to you the origin of this name of "wise," and of this evil fame. Please to attend then. And although some of you may think I am joking, I declare that I will tell you the entire truth. Men of Athens, this reputation of mine has come of a certain sort of wisdom which I possess. If you ask me what kind of wisdom, I reply, such wisdom as is attainable by man, for to that extent I am inclined to believe that I am wise; whereas the persons of whom I was speaking have a superhuman wisdom, which I may fail to describe, because I have it not myself; and he who says that I have, speaks falsely, and is taking away my character. And here, O men of Athens, I must beg you not to interrupt me, even if I seem to say something extravagant. For the word which I will speak is not mine. I will refer you to a witness who is worthy of credit, and will tell you about my wisdom—whether I have any, and of what sort—and that witness shall be the god of Delphi. You must have known Chaerephon; he was early a friend of mine, and also a friend of yours, for he shared in the exile of the people, and returned with you. Well, Chaerephon, as you know, was very impetuous in all his doings, and he went to Delphi and boldly asked the oracle to tell him whether—as I was saying, I must beg you not to interrupt—he asked the oracle to tell him whether there was anyone wiser than I was, and the Pythian prophetess answered that there was no man wiser. Chaerephon is dead himself, but his brother, who is in court, will confirm the truth of this story.

Why do I mention this? Because I am going to explain to you why I have such an evil name. When I heard the answer, I said to myself, What can the god mean? and what is the interpretation of this riddle? for I know that I have no wisdom, small or great. What can he mean when he says that I am the wisest of men? And yet he is a god and cannot lie; that would be against his nature. After a long consideration, I at last thought of a method of trying the question. I reflected that if I could only find a man wiser than myself, then I might go to the god with a refutation in my hand. I should say to him, "Here is a man who is wiser than I am; but you said that I was the wisest." Accordingly I went to one who had the reputation of wisdom, and observed to him—his name I need not mention; he was a politician whom I selected for examination—and the result was as follows: When I began to talk with him, I could not help thinking that he was not really wise, although he was thought wise by many, and wiser still by himself; and I went and tried to explain to him that he thought himself wise, but was not really wise; and the consequence was that he hated me, and his enmity was shared by several who were present and heard me. So I left him, saying to myself, as I went away: Well, although I do not suppose that either of us knows anything really beautiful and good, I am better off than he is—for he knows nothing, and thinks that he knows. I neither know nor think that I know. In this latter particular, then, I seem to have slightly the advantage of him. Then I went to another, who had still higher philosophical pretensions, and my conclusion was exactly the same. I made another enemy of him, and of many others besides him.

After this I went to one man after another, being not unconscious of the enmity which I provoked, and I lamented and feared this: but necessity was laid upon me—the word of God, I thought, ought to be considered first. And I said to myself, Go I must to all who appear to know, and find out the meaning of the oracle. And I swear to you, Athenians, by the dog I swear!—for I must tell you the truth—the result of my mission was just this: I found that the men most in repute were all but the most foolish; and that some inferior men were really wiser and better. I will tell you the tale of my wanderings and of the "Herculean" labors, as I may call them, which I endured only to find at last the oracle irrefutable. When I left the politicians, I went to the poets; tragic, dithyrambic, and all sorts. And there, I said to myself, you will be detected; now you will find out that you are more ignorant than they are. Accordingly, I took them some of the most elaborate passages in their own writings, and asked what was the meaning of them—thinking that they would teach me something. Will you believe me? I am almost ashamed to speak of this, but still I must say that there is hardly a person present who would not have talked better about their poetry than they did themselves. That showed me in an instant that not by wisdom do poets write poetry, but by a sort of genius and inspiration; they are like diviners or soothsayers who also say many fine things, but do not understand the meaning of them. And the poets appeared to me to be much in the same case; and I further observed that upon the strength of their poetry they believed themselves to be the wisest of men in other things in which they were not wise. So I departed, conceiving myself to be superior to them for the same reason that I was superior to the politicians.

At last I went to the artisans, for I was conscious that I knew nothing at all, as I may say, and I was sure that they knew many fine things; and in this I was not mistaken, for they did know many things of which I was ignorant, and in this they certainly were wiser than I was. But I observed that even the good artisans fell into the same error as the poets; because they were good workmen they thought that they also knew all sorts of high matters, and this defect in them overshadowed their wisdom—therefore I asked myself on behalf of the oracle, whether I would like to be as I was, neither having their knowledge nor their ignorance, or like them in both; and I made answer to myself and the oracle that I was better off as I was.

This investigation has led to my having many enemies of the worst and most dangerous kind, and has given occasion also to many calumnies, and I am called wise, for my hearers always imagine that I myself possess the wisdom which I find wanting in others: but the truth is, O men of Athens, that God only is wise; and in this oracle he means to say that the wisdom of men is little or nothing; he is not speaking of Socrates, he is only using my name as an illustration, as if he said, He, O men, is the wisest, who, like Socrates, knows that his wisdom is in truth worth nothing. And so I go my way, obedient to the god, and make inquisition into the wisdom of anyone, whether citizen or stranger, who appears to be wise; and if he is not wise, then in vindication of the oracle I show him that he is not wise; and this occupation quite absorbs me, and I have no time to give either to any public matter of interest or to any concern of my own, but I am in utter poverty by reason of my devotion to the god.

There is another thing:—young men of the richer classes, who have not much to do, come about me of their own accord; they like to hear the pretenders examined, and they often imitate me, and examine others themselves; there are plenty of persons, as they soon enough discover, who think that they know something, but really know little or nothing: and then those who are examined by them instead of being angry with themselves are angry with me: This confounded Socrates, they say; this villainous misleader of youth!—and then if somebody asks them, Why, what evil does he practise or teach? they do not know, and cannot tell; but in order that they may not appear to be at a loss, they repeat the ready-made charges which are used against all philosophers about teaching things up in the clouds and under the earth, and having no gods, and making the worse appear the better cause; for they do not like to confess that their pretence of knowledge has been detected—which is the truth: and as they are numerous and ambitious and energetic, and are all in battle array and have persuasive tongues, they have filled your ears with their loud and inveterate calumnies. And this is the reason why my three accusers, Meletus and Anytus and

Lycon, have set upon me; Meletus, who has a quarrel with me on behalf of the poets; Anytus, on behalf of the craftsmen; Lycon, on behalf of the rhetoricians: and as I said at the beginning, I cannot expect to get rid of this mass of calumny all in a moment. And this, O men of Athens, is the truth and the whole truth; I have concealed nothing, I have dissembled nothing. And yet I know that this plainness of speech makes them hate me, and what is their hatred but a proof that I am speaking the truth?—this is the occasion and reason of their slander of me, as you will find out either in this or in any future inquiry.

I have said enough in my defence against the first class of my accusers; I turn to the second class, who are headed by Meletus, that good and patriotic man, as he calls himself. And now I will try to defend myself against them: these new accusers must also have their affidavit read. What do they say? Something of this sort:—That Socrates is a doer of evil, and corrupter of the youth, and he does not believe in the gods of the state, and has other new divinities of his own. That is the sort of charge; and now let us examine the particular counts. He says that I am a doer of evil, who corrupt the youth; but I say, O men of Athens, that Meletus is a doer of evil, and the evil is that he makes a joke of a serious matter, and is too ready at bringing other men to trial from a pretended zeal and interest about matters in which he really never had the smallest interest. And the truth of this I will endeavor to prove.

Come hither, Meletus, and let me ask a question of you. You think a great deal about the improvement of youth?

Yes, I do.

Tell the judges, then, who is their improver; for you must know, as you have taken the pains to discover their corrupter, and are citing and accusing me before them. Speak, then, and tell the judges who their improver is. Observe, Meletus, that you are silent, and have nothing to say. But is not this rather disgraceful, and a very considerable proof of what I was saying, that you have no interest in the matter? Speak up, friend, and tell us who their improver is.

The laws.

But that, my good sir, is not my meaning. I want to know who the person is, who, in the first place, knows the laws.

The judges, Socrates, who are present in court.

What do you mean to say, Meletus, that they are able to instruct and improve youth?

Certainly they are.

What, all of them, or some only and not others?

All of them.

By the goddess Here, that is good news! There are plenty of improvers, then. And what do you say of the audience,—do they improve them?

Yes, they do.

And the senators?

Yes, the senators improve them.

But perhaps the members of the citizen assembly corrupt them?—or do they too improve them?

They improve them.

Then every Athenian improves and elevates them; all with the exception of myself; and I alone am their corrupter? Is that what you affirm?

That is what I stoutly affirm.

I am very unfortunate if that is true. But suppose I ask you a question: Would you say that this also holds true in the case of horses? Does one man do them harm and all the world good? Is not the exact opposite of this true? One man is able to do them good, or at least not many;—the trainer of horses, that is to say, does them good, and others who have to do with them rather injure them? Is not that true, Meletus, of horses, or any other animals? Yes, certainly. Whether you and Anytus say yes or no, that is no matter. Happy indeed would be the condition of youth if they had one corrupter only, and all the rest of the world were their improvers. And you, Meletus, have sufficiently shown that you never had a thought about the young: your carelessness is seen in your not caring about matters spoken of in this very indictment.

And now, Meletus, I must ask you another question: Which is better, to live among bad citizens, or among good ones? Answer, friend, I say; for that is a question which may be easily answered. Do not the good do their neighbors good, and the bad do them evil?

Certainly.

And is there anyone who would rather be injured than benefited by those who live with him? Answer, my good friend; the law requires you to answer—does anyone like to be injured?

Certainly not.

And when you accuse me of corrupting and deteriorating the youth, do you allege that I corrupt them intentionally or unintentionally?

Intentionally, I say.

But you have just admitted that the good do their neighbors good, and the evil do them evil. Now is that a truth which your superior wisdom has recognized thus early in life, and am I, at my age, in such darkness and ignorance as not to know that if a man with whom I have to live is corrupted by me, I am very likely to be harmed by him, and yet I corrupt him, and intentionally, too;—that is what you are saying, and of that you will never persuade me or any other human being. But either I do not corrupt them, or I corrupt them unintentionally, so that on either view of the case you lie. If my offence is unintentional, the law has no cognizance of unintentional offences: you ought to have taken me privately, and warned and admonished me; for if I had been better advised, I should have left off doing what I only did unintentionally—no doubt I should; whereas you hated to converse with me or teach me, but you indicted me in this court, which is a place not of instruction, but of punishment.

I have shown, Athenians, as I was saying, that Meletus has no care at all, great or small, about the matter. But still I should like to know, Meletus, in what I am affirmed to corrupt the young. I suppose you mean, as I infer from your indictment, that I teach them not to acknowledge the gods which the state acknowledges, but some other new divinities or spiritual agencies in their stead. These are the lessons which corrupt the youth, as you say.

Yes, that I say emphatically.

Then, by the gods, Meletus, of whom we are speaking, tell me and the court, in somewhat plainer terms, what you mean! for I do not as yet understand whether you affirm that I teach others to acknowledge some gods, and therefore do believe in gods and am not an entire atheist—this you do not lay to my charge; but only that they are not the same gods which the city recognizes—the charge is that they are different gods. Or, do you mean to say that I am an atheist simply, and a teacher of atheism?

I mean the latter—that you are a complete atheist.

That is an extraordinary statement, Meletus. Why do you say that? Do you mean that I do not believe in the godhead of the sun or moon, which is the common creed of all men?

I assure you, judges, that he does not believe in them; for he says that the sun is stone, and the moon earth.

Friend Meletus, you think that you are accusing Anaxagoras; and you have but a bad opinion of the judges, if you fancy them ignorant to such a degree as not to know that those doctrines are found in the books of Anaxagoras the Clazomenian, who is full of them. And these are the doctrines which the youth are said to learn of Socrates, when there are not unfrequently exhibitions of them at the theatre (price of admission one drachma at the most); and they might cheaply purchase them, and laugh at Socrates if he pretends to father such eccentricities. And so, Meletus, you really think that I do not believe in any god?

I swear by Zeus that you believe absolutely in none at all.

You are a liar, Meletus, not believed even by yourself. For I cannot help thinking, O men of Athens, that Meletus is reckless and impudent, and that he has written this indictment in a spirit of mere wantonness and youthful bravado. Has he not compounded a riddle, thinking to try me? He said to himself:— I shall see whether this wise Socrates will discover my ingenious contradiction, or whether I shall be able to deceive him and the rest of them. For he certainly does appear to me to contradict himself in the indictment as much as if he said that Socrates is guilty of not believing in the gods, and yet of believing in them—but this surely is a piece of fun.

I should like you, O men of Athens, to join me in examining what I conceive to be his inconsistency; and do you, Meletus, answer. And I must remind you that you are not to interrupt me if I speak in my accustomed manner.

Did ever man, Meletus, believe in the existence of human things, and not of human beings? I wish, men of Athens, that he would answer, and not be always trying to get up an interruption. Did ever any man believe in horsemanship, and not in horses? or in flute-playing, and not in flute-players? No, my friend; I will answer to you and to the court, as you refuse to answer for yourself. There is no man who ever did. But now please to answer the next question: Can a man believe in spiritual and divine agencies, and not in spirits or demigods?

He cannot.

I am glad that I have extracted that answer, by the assistance of the court; nevertheless you swear in the indictment that I teach and believe in divine or spiritual agencies (new or old, no matter for that); at any rate, I believe in spiritual agencies, as you say and swear in the affidavit; but if I believe in divine beings, I must believe in spirits or demigods;—is not that true? Yes, that is true, for I may assume that your silence gives assent to that. Now what are spirits or demigods? are they not either gods or the sons of gods? Is that true?

Yes, that is true.

But this is just the ingenious riddle of which I was speaking: the demigods or spirits are gods, and you say first that I don't believe in gods, and then again that I do believe in gods; that is, if I believe in demigods. For if the demigods are the illegitimate sons of gods, whether by the Nymphs or by any other mothers, as is thought, that, as all men will allow, necessarily implies the existence of their parents. You might as well affirm the existence of mules, and deny that of horses and asses. Such nonsense, Meletus, could only have been intended by you as a trial of me. You have put this into the indictment because you had nothing real of which to accuse me. But no one who has a particle of understanding will ever be convinced by you that the same man can believe in divine and superhuman things, and yet not believe that there are gods and demigods and heroes.

I have said enough in answer to the charge of Meletus: any elaborate defence is unnecessary; but as I was saying before, I certainly have many enemies, and this is what will be my destruction if I am destroyed; of that I am certain;—not Meletus, nor yet Anytus, but the envy and detraction of the world, which has been the death of many good men, and will probably be the death of many more; there is no danger of my being the last of them.

Someone will say: And are you not ashamed, Socrates, of a course of life which is likely to bring you to an untimely end? To him I may fairly answer: There you are mistaken: a man who is good for anything ought not to calculate the chance of living or dying; he ought only to consider whether in doing anything he is doing right or wrong—acting the part of a good man or of a bad. Whereas, according to your view, the heroes who fell at Troy were not good for much, and the son of Thetis above all, who altogether despised danger in comparison with disgrace; and when his goddess mother said to him, in his eagerness to slay Hector, that if he avenged his companion Patroclus, and slew Hector, he would die himself—"Fate," as she said, "waits upon you next after Hector;" he, hearing this, utterly despised danger and death, and instead of fearing them, feared rather to live in dishonor, and not to avenge his friend. "Let me die next," he replies, "and be avenged of my enemy, rather than abide here by the beaked ships, a scorn and a burden of the earth." Had Achilles any thought of death and danger? For wherever a man's place is, whether the place which he has chosen or that in which he has been placed by a commander, there he ought to remain in the hour of danger; he should not think of death or of anything, but of disgrace. And this, O men of Athens, is a true saying.

Strange, indeed, would be my conduct, O men of Athens, if I who, when I was ordered by the generals whom you chose to command me at Potidaea and Amphipolis and Delium, remained where they placed me, like any other man, facing death; if, I say, now, when, as I conceive and imagine, God orders me to fulfil the philosopher's mission of searching into myself and other men, I were to desert my post through fear of death, or any other fear; that would indeed be strange, and I might justly be arraigned in court for denying the existence of the gods, if I disobeyed the oracle because I was afraid of death: then I should be fancying that I was wise when I was not wise. For this fear of death is indeed the pretence of wisdom, and not real wisdom, being the appearance of knowing the unknown; since no one knows whether death, which they in their fear apprehend to be the greatest evil, may not be the greatest good. Is there not here conceit of knowledge, which is a disgraceful sort of ignorance? And this is the point in which, as I think, I am superior to men in general, and in which I might perhaps fancy myself wiser than other men,—that whereas I know but little of the world below, I do not suppose that I know: but I do know that injustice and disobedience to a better, whether God or man, is evil and dishonorable, and I will never fear or avoid a possible good rather than a certain evil. And therefore if you let me go now, and reject the counsels of Anytus, who said that if I were not put to death I ought not to have been prosecuted, and that if I escape now, your sons will all be utterly ruined by listening to my words—if you say to me, Socrates, this time we will not mind Anytus, and will let you off, but upon one condition, that you are not to inquire and speculate in this way any more, and that if you are caught doing this again you shall die;—if this was the condition on which you let me go, I should reply: Men of Athens, I honor and love you; but I shall obey God rather than you, and while I have life and strength I shall never cease from the practice and teaching of philosophy, exhorting anyone whom I meet after my manner, and convincing him, saying: O my friend, why do you who are a citizen of the great and mighty and wise city of Athens, care so much about laying up the greatest amount of money and honor and reputation, and so little about wisdom and truth and the greatest improvement of the soul, which you never regard or heed at all? Are you not ashamed of this? And if the person with whom I am arguing says: Yes, but I do care; I do not depart or let him go at once; I interrogate and examine and cross-examine him, and if I think that he has no virtue, but only says that he has, I reproach him with undervaluing the greater, and overvaluing the less. And this I should say to everyone whom I meet, young and old, citizen and alien, but especially to the citizens, inasmuch as they are my brethren. For this is the command of God, as I would have you know; and I believe that to this day no greater good has ever happened in the state than my service to the God. For I do nothing but go about persuading you all, old and young alike, not to take thought for your persons and your properties, but first and chiefly to care about the greatest improvement of the soul. I tell you that virtue is not given by money, but that from virtue come money and every other good of man, public as well as private. This is my teaching, and if this is the doctrine which corrupts the youth, my influence is ruinous indeed. But if anyone says that this is not my teaching, he is speaking an untruth. Wherefore, O men of Athens, I say to you, do as Anytus bids or not as Anytus bids, and either acquit me or not; but whatever you do, know that I shall never alter my ways, not even if I have to die many times.

Men of Athens, do not interrupt, but hear me; there was an agreement between us that you should hear me out. And I think that what I am going to say will do you good: for I have something more to say, at which you may be inclined to cry out; but I beg that you will not do this. I would have you know that, if you kill such a one as I am, you will injure yourselves more than you will injure me. Meletus and Anytus will not injure me: they cannot; for it is not in the nature of things that a bad man should injure a better than himself. I do not deny that he may, perhaps, kill him, or drive him into exile, or deprive him of civil rights; and he may imagine, and others may imagine, that he is doing him a great injury: but in that I do not agree with him; for the evil of doing as Anytus is doing—of unjustly taking away another man's life—is greater far. And now, Athenians, I am not going to argue for my own sake, as you may think, but for yours, that you may not sin against the God, or lightly reject his boon by condemning me. For if you kill me you will not easily find another like me, who, if I may use such a ludicrous figure of speech, am a sort of gadfly, given to the state by the God; and the state is like a great and noble steed who is tardy in his motions owing to his very size, and requires to be stirred into life. I am that gadfly which God has given the state and all day long and in all places am always fastening upon you, arousing and persuading and reproaching you. And as you will not easily find another like me, I would advise you to spare me. I dare say that you may feel irritated at being suddenly awakened when you are caught napping; and you may think that if you were to strike me dead, as Anytus advises, which you easily might, then you would sleep on for the remainder of your lives, unless God in his care of you gives you another gadfly. And that I am given to you by God is proved by this:—that if I had been like other men, I should not have neglected all my own concerns, or patiently seen the neglect of them during all these years, and have been doing yours, coming to you individually, like a father or elder brother, exhorting you to regard virtue; this I say, would not be like human nature. And had I gained anything, or if my exhortations had been paid, there would have been some sense in that: but now, as you will perceive, not even the impudence of my accusers dares to say that I have ever exacted or sought pay of anyone; they have no witness of that. And I have a witness of the truth of what I say; my poverty is a sufficient witness.

Someone may wonder why I go about in private, giving advice and busying myself with the concerns of others, but do not venture to come forward in public and advise the state. I will tell you the reason of this. You have often heard me speak of an oracle or sign which comes to me, and is the divinity which

Meletus ridicules in the indictment. This sign I have had ever since I was a child. The sign is a voice which comes to me and always forbids me to do something which I am going to do, but never commands me to do anything, and this is what stands in the way of my being a politician. And rightly, as I think. For I am certain, O men of Athens, that if I had engaged in politics, I should have perished long ago and done no good either to you or to myself. And don't be offended at my telling you the truth: for the truth is that no man who goes to war with you or any other multitude, honestly struggling against the commission of unrighteousness and wrong in the state, will save his life; he who will really fight for the right, if he would live even for a little while, must have a private station and not a public one.

I can give you as proofs of this, not words only, but deeds, which you value more than words. Let me tell you a passage of my own life, which will prove to you that I should never have yielded to injustice from any fear of death, and that if I had not yielded I should have died at once. I will tell you a story—tasteless, perhaps, and commonplace, but nevertheless true. The only office of state which I ever held, O men of Athens, was that of senator; the tribe Antiochis, which is my tribe, had the presidency at the trial of the generals who had not taken up the bodies of the slain after the battle of Arginusae; and you proposed to try them all together, which was illegal, as you all thought afterwards; but at the time I was the only one of the Prytanes who was opposed to the illegality, and I gave my vote against you; and when the orators threatened to impeach and arrest me, and have me taken away, and you called and shouted, I made up my mind that I would run the risk, having law and justice with me, rather than take part in your injustice because I feared imprisonment and death. This happened in the days of the democracy. But when the oligarchy of the Thirty was in power, they sent for me and four others into the rotunda, and bade us bring Leon the Salaminian from Salamis, as they wanted to execute him. This was a specimen of the sort of commands which they were always giving with the view of implicating as many as possible in their crimes; and then I showed, not in words only, but in deed, that, if I may be allowed to use such an expression, I cared not a straw for death, and that my only fear was the fear of doing an unrighteous or unholy thing. For the strong arm of that oppressive power did not frighten me into doing wrong; and when we came out of the rotunda the other four went to Salamis and fetched Leon, but I went quietly home. For which I might have lost my life, had not the power of the Thirty shortly afterwards come to an end. And to this many will witness.

Now do you really imagine that I could have survived all these years, if I had led a public life, supposing that like a good man I had always supported the right and had made justice, as I ought, the first thing? No, indeed, men of Athens, neither I nor any other. But I have been always the same in all my actions, public as well as private, and never have I yielded any base compliance to those who are slanderously termed my disciples or to any other. For the truth is that I have no regular disciples: but if anyone likes to come and hear me while I am pursuing my mission, whether he be young or old, he may freely come. Nor do I converse with those who pay only, and not with those who do not pay; but anyone, whether he be rich or poor, may ask and answer me and listen to my words; and whether he turns out to be a bad man or a good one, that cannot be justly laid to my charge, as I never taught him anything. And if anyone says that he has ever learned or heard anything from me in private which all the world has not heard, I should like you to know that he is speaking an untruth.

But I shall be asked, Why do people delight in continually conversing with you? I have told you already, Athenians, the whole truth about this: they like to hear the cross-examination of the pretenders to wisdom; there is amusement in this. And this is a duty which the God has imposed upon me, as I am assured by oracles, visions, and in every sort of way in which the will of divine power was ever signified to anyone. This is true, O Athenians; or, if not true, would be soon refuted. For if I am really corrupting the youth, and have corrupted some of them already, those of them who have grown up and have become sensible that I gave them bad advice in the days of their youth should come forward as accusers and take their revenge; and if they do not like to come themselves, some of their relatives, fathers, brothers, or other kinsmen, should say what evil their families suffered at my hands. Now is their time. Many of them I see in the court. There is Crito, who is of the same age and of the same deme with myself; and there is Critobulus his son, whom I also see. Then again there is Lysanias of Sphettus, who is the father of Aeschines—he is present; and also there is Antiphon of Cephisus, who is the father of Epignes; and there are the brothers of several who have associated with me. There is Nicostratus the son of Theosdotides, and the brother of Theodotus (now Theodotus himself is dead, and therefore he, at any rate, will not seek to stop him); and there is Paralus the son of Demodocus, who had a brother Theages; and Adeimantus the son of Ariston, whose brother Plato is present; and Aeantodorus, who is the brother of Apollodorus, whom I also see. I might mention a great many others, any of whom Meletus should have produced as witnesses in the course of his speech; and let him still produce them, if he has forgotten—I will make way for him. And let him say, if he has any testimony of the sort which he can produce. Nay, Athenians, the very opposite is the truth. For all these are ready to witness on behalf of the corrupter, of the destroyer of their kindred, as Meletus and Anytus call me; not the corrupted youth only—there might have been a motive for that—but their uncorrupted elder relatives. Why should they too support me with their testimony? Why, indeed, except for the sake of truth and justice, and because they know that I am speaking the truth, and that Meletus is lying.

Well, Athenians, this and the like of this is nearly all the defence which I have to offer. Yet a word more. Perhaps there may be someone who is offended at me, when he calls to mind how he himself, on a similar or even a less serious occasion, had recourse to prayers and supplications with many tears, and how he produced his children in court, which was a moving spectacle, together with a posse of his relations and friends; whereas I, who am probably in danger of my life, will do none of these things. Perhaps this may come into his mind, and he may be set against me, and vote in anger because he is displeased at this. Now if there be such a person among you, which I am far from affirming, I may fairly reply to him:

My friend, I am a man, and like other men, a creature of flesh and blood, and not of wood or stone, as Homer says; and I have a family, yes, and sons. O Athenians, three in number, one of whom is growing up, and the two others are still young; and yet I will not bring any of them hither in order to petition you for an acquittal. And why not? Not from any self-will or disregard of you. Whether I am or am not afraid of death is another question, of which I will not now speak. But my reason simply is that I feel such conduct to be discreditable to myself, and you, and the whole state. One who has reached my years, and who has a name for wisdom, whether deserved or not, ought not to debase himself. At any rate, the world has decided that Socrates is in some way superior to other men. And if those among you who are said to be superior in wisdom and courage, and any other virtue, demean themselves in this way, how shameful is their conduct! I have seen men of reputation, when they have been condemned, behaving in the strangest manner: they seemed to fancy that they were going to suffer something dreadful if they died, and that they could be immortal if you only allowed them to live; and I think that they were a dishonor to the state, and that any stranger coming in would say of them that the most eminent men of Athens, to whom the Athenians themselves give honor and command, are no better than women. And I say that these things ought not to be done by those of us who are of reputation; and if they are done, you ought not to permit them; you ought rather to show that you are more inclined to condemn, not the man who is quiet, but the man who gets up a doleful scene, and makes the city ridiculous.

But, setting aside the question of dishonor, there seems to be something wrong in petitioning a judge, and thus procuring an acquittal instead of informing and convincing him. For his duty is, not to make a present of justice, but to give judgment; and he has sworn that he will judge according to the laws, and not according to his own good pleasure; and neither he nor we should get into the habit of perjuring ourselves—there can be no piety in that. Do not then require me to do what I consider dishonorable and impious and wrong, especially now, when I am being tried for impiety on the indictment of Meletus. For if, O men of Athens, by force of persuasion and entreaty, I could overpower your oaths, then I should be teaching you to believe that there are no gods, and convict myself, in my own defence, of not believing in them. But that is not the case; for I do believe that there are gods, and in a far higher sense than that in which any of my accusers believe in them. And to you and to God I commit my cause, to be determined by you as is best for you and me.

The jury finds Socrates guilty.

SOCRATES' PROPOSAL FOR HIS SENTENCE

There are many reasons why I am not grieved, O men of Athens, at the vote of condemnation. I expected it, and am only surprised that the votes are so nearly equal; for I had thought that the majority against me would have been far larger; but now, had thirty votes gone over to the other side, I should have been acquitted. And I may say that I have escaped Meletus. And I may say more; for without the assistance of Anytus and Lycon, he would not have had a fifth part of the votes, as the law requires, in which case he would have incurred a fine of a thousand drachmae, as is evident.

And so he proposes death as the penalty. And what shall I propose on my part, O men of Athens? Clearly that which is my due. And what is that which I ought to pay or to receive? What shall be done to the man who has never had the wit to be idle during his whole life; but has been careless of what the many care about—wealth, and family interests, and military offices, and speaking in the assembly, and magistracies, and plots, and parties. Reflecting that I was really too honest a man to follow in this way and live, I did not go where I could do no good to you or to myself; but where I could do the greatest good privately to everyone of you, thither I went, and sought to persuade every man among you that he must look to himself, and seek virtue and wisdom before he looks to his private interests, and look to the state before he looks to the interests of the state; and that this should be the order which he observes in all his actions. What shall be done to such a one? Doubtless some good thing, O men of Athens, if he has his reward; and the good should be of a kind suitable to him. What would be a reward suitable to a poor man who is your benefactor, who desires leisure that he may instruct you? There can be no more fitting reward than maintenance in the Prytaneum, O men of Athens, a reward which he deserves far more than the citizen who has won the prize at Olympia in the horse or chariot race, whether the chariots were drawn by two horses or by many. For I am in want, and he has enough; and he only gives you the appearance of happiness, and I give you the reality. And if I am to estimate the penalty justly, I say that maintenance in the Prytaneum is the just return.

Perhaps you may think that I am braving you in saying this, as in what I said before about the tears and prayers. But that is not the case. I speak rather because I am convinced that I never intentionally wronged anyone, although I cannot convince you of that—for we have had a short conversation only; but if there were a law at Athens, such as there is in other cities, that a capital cause should not be decided in one day, then I believe that I should have convinced you; but now the time is too short. I cannot in a moment refute great slanders; and, as I am convinced that I never wronged another, I will assuredly not wrong myself. I will not say of myself that I deserve any evil, or propose any penalty. Why should I? Because I am afraid of the penalty of death which Meletus proposes? When I do not know whether death is a good or an evil, why should I propose a penalty which would certainly be an evil? Shall I say imprisonment? And why should I live in prison, and be the slave of the magistrates of the year—of the Eleven? Or shall the penalty be a fine, and imprisonment until the fine is paid? There is the same objection. I should have to lie in prison, for money I have none, and I cannot pay. And if I say exile (and this may possibly be the penalty which you will affix), I must indeed be blinded by the love of life if I were to consider that when you, who are my own citizens, cannot endure my discourses and words, and have found them so grievous and odious that you would fain have done with them, others are likely to endure me. No, indeed, men of

Athens, that is not very likely. And what a life should I lead, at my age, wandering from city to city, living in ever-changing exile, and always being driven out! For I am quite sure that into whatever place I go, as here so also there, the young men will come to me; and if I drive them away, their elders will drive me out at their desire: and if I let them come, their fathers and friends will drive me out for their sakes.

Someone will say: Yes, Socrates, but cannot you hold your tongue, and then you may go into a foreign city, and no one will interfere with you? Now I have great difficulty in making you understand my answer to this. For if I tell you that this would be a disobedience to a divine command, and therefore that I cannot hold my tongue, you will not believe that I am serious; and if I say again that the greatest good of man is daily to converse about virtue, and all that concerning which you hear me examining myself and others, and that the life which is unexamined is not worth living—that you are still less likely to believe. And yet what I say is true, although a thing of which it is hard for me to persuade you. Moreover, I am not accustomed to think that I deserve any punishment. Had I money I might have proposed to give you what I had, and have been none the worse. But you see that I have none, and can only ask you to proportion the fine to my means. However, I think that I could afford a minae, and therefore I propose that penalty; Plato, Crito, Critobulus, and Apollodorus, my friends here, bid me say thirty minae, and they will be the sureties. Well then, say thirty minae, let that be the penalty; for that they will be ample security to you.

The jury condemns Socrates to death.

SOCRATES' COMMENTS ON HIS SENTENCE

Not much time will be gained, O Athenians, in return for the evil name which you will get from the detractors of the city, who will say that you killed Socrates, a wise man; for they will call me wise even though I am not wise when they want to reproach you. If you had waited a little while, your desire would have been fulfilled in the course of nature. For I am far advanced in years, as you may perceive, and not far from death. I am speaking now only to those of you who have condemned me to death. And I have another thing to say to them: You think that I was convicted through deficiency of words—I mean, that if I had thought fit to leave nothing undone, nothing unsaid, I might have gained an acquittal. Not so; the deficiency which led to my conviction was not of words—certainly not. But I had not the boldness or impudence or inclination to address you as you would have liked me to address you, weeping and wailing and lamenting, and saying and doing many things which you have been accustomed to hear from others, and which, as I say, are unworthy of me. But I thought that I ought not to do anything common or mean in the hour of danger: nor do I now repent of the manner of my defence, and I would rather die having spoken after my manner, than speak in your manner and live. For neither in war nor yet at law ought any man to use every way of escaping death. For often in battle there is no doubt that if a man will throw away his arms, and fall on his knees before his pursuers, he may escape death; and in other dangers there are other ways of escaping death, if a man is willing to say and do anything. The difficulty, my friends, is not in avoiding death, but in avoiding unrighteousness; for that runs faster than death. I am old and move slowly, and the slower runner has overtaken me, and my accusers are keen and quick, and the faster runner, who is unrighteousness, has overtaken them. And now I depart hence condemned by you to suffer the penalty of death, and they, too, go their ways condemned by the truth to suffer the penalty of villainy and wrong; and I must abide by my award—let them abide by theirs. I suppose that these things may be regarded as fated,—and I think that they are well.

And now, O men who have condemned me, I would fain prophesy to you; for I am about to die, and that is the hour in which men are gifted with prophetic power. And I prophesy to you who are my murderers, that immediately after my death punishment far heavier than you have inflicted on me will surely await you. Me you have killed because you wanted to escape the accuser, and not to give an account of your lives. But that will not be as you suppose: far otherwise. For I say that there will be more accusers of you than there are now; accusers whom hitherto I have restrained: and as they are younger they will be more severe with you, and you will be more offended at them. For if you think that by killing men you can avoid the accuser censuring your lives, you are mistaken; that is not a way of escape which is either possible or honorable; the easiest and noblest way is not to be crushing others, but to be improving yourselves. This is the prophecy which I utter before my departure, to the judges who have condemned me.

Friends, who would have acquitted me, I would like also to talk with you about this thing which has happened, while the magistrates are busy, and before I go to the place at which I must die. Stay then awhile, for we may as well talk with one another while there is time. You are my friends, and I should like to show you the meaning of this event which has happened to me. O my judges—for you I may truly call judges—I should like to tell you of a wonderful circumstance. Hitherto the familiar oracle within me has constantly been in the habit of opposing me even about trifles, if I was going to make a slip or error about anything; and now as you see there has come upon me that which may be thought, and is generally believed to be, the last and worst evil. But the oracle made no sign of opposition, either as I was leaving my house and going out in the morning, or when I was going up into this court, or while I was speaking, at anything which I was going to say; and yet I have often been stopped in the middle of a speech; but now in nothing I either said or did touching this matter has the oracle opposed me. What do I take to be the explanation of this? I will tell you. I regard this as a proof that what has happened to me is a good, and that those of us who think that death is an evil are in error. This is a great proof to me of what I am saying, for the customary sign would surely have opposed me had I been going to evil and not to good.

Let us reflect in another way, and we shall see that there is great reason to hope that death is a good, for one of two things:—either death is a state of nothingness and utter unconsciousness, or, as men say, there is a change and migration of the soul from this world to another. Now if you suppose that there is no consciousness, but a sleep like the sleep of him who is undisturbed even by the sight of dreams, death will be an unspeakable gain. For if a person were to select the night in which his sleep was undisturbed even by dreams, and were to compare with this the other days and nights of his life, and then were to tell us how many days and nights he had passed in the course of his life better and more pleasantly than this one, I think that any man, I will not say a private man, but even the great king, will not find many such days or nights, when compared with the others. Now if death is like this, I say that to die is gain; for eternity is then only a single night. But if death is the journey to another place, and there, as men say, all the dead are, what good, O my friends and judges, can be greater than this? If indeed when the pilgrim arrives in the world below, he is delivered from the professors of justice in this world, and finds the true judges who are said to give judgment there, Minos and Rhadamanthus and Aeacus and Triptolemus, and other sons of God who were righteous in their own life, that pilgrimage will be worth making. What would not a man give if he might converse with Orpheus and Musaeus and Hesiod and Homer? Nay, if this be true, let me die again and again. I, too, shall have a wonderful interest in a place where I can converse with Palamedes, and Ajax the son of Telamon, and other heroes of old, who have suffered death through an unjust judgment; and there will be no small pleasure, as I think, in comparing my own sufferings with theirs. Above all, I shall be able to continue my search into true and false knowledge; as in this world, so also in that; I shall find out who is wise, and who pretends to be wise, and is not. What would not a man give, O judges, to be able to examine the leader of the great Trojan expedition; or Odysseus or Sisyphus, or numberless others, men and women too! What infinite delight would there be in conversing with them and asking them questions! For in that world they do not put a man to death for this; certainly not. For besides being happier in that world than in this, they will be immortal, if what is said is true.

Wherefore, O judges, be of good cheer about death, and know this of a truth—that no evil can happen to a good man, either in life or after death. He and his are not neglected by the gods; nor has my own approaching end happened by mere chance. But I see clearly that to die and be released was better for me; and therefore the oracle gave no sign. For which reason also, I am not angry with my accusers, or my condemners; they have done me no harm, although neither of them meant to do me any good; and for this I may gently blame them.

Still I have a favor to ask of them. When my sons are grown up, I would ask you, O my friends, to punish them; and I would have you trouble them, as I have troubled you, if they seem to care about riches, or anything, more than about virtue; or if they pretend to be something when they are really nothing,—then reprove them, as I have reproved you, for not caring about that for which they ought to care, and thinking that they are something when they are really nothing. And if you do this, I and my sons will have received justice at your hands.

The hour of departure has arrived, and we go our ways—I to die, and you to live. Which is better God only knows.

WHERE ARE ALL THE WOMEN AND NON-WESTERN PHILOSOPHERS?

By Robert C. Solomon and Kathleen M. Higgins

PHILOSOPHY DISCOVERS "THE OTHER": THE QUESTION OF POSTMODERNISM

Simone de Beauvoir sparked an important question: Where are all the women? Western philosophy has historically discussed or included women only as an afterthought, if at all. Some feminists have suggested that philosophy has been based on a "masculine" style of disputation and confrontation exemplified by Socrates. But whatever else it may have been, philosophy has always been a refuge, a luxury enjoyed primarily by those who have (one way or another) been free from the demands of exhausting physical labor, earning a living, or cleaning and caring for a household. For that reason, it should not be surprising that most of the men we have discussed, and many of the greatest philosophers, were gentlemen bachelors (or, often, priests). Surprisingly few talk very much about the family, and interpersonal relationships in general play an embarrassingly minuscule role in the history of Western philosophy.

Then, again, making a name for yourself in philosophy depends not just on talent but on time, teachers, colleagues, an audience, publishers, readers, and one's students. The sad truth is that women have been shut out at virtually every level of philosophical success. Relatively few women have been allowed even to become interested in philosophy. Before this century, few women were admitted to the appropriate schools, and those who were allowed to study philosophy (some of the students of Plato and Pythagoras, for example) were rarely allowed to achieve stature. If a woman did manage to disseminate some ideas of her own and attract a following, she would rarely be recognized as "one of the boys," in all probability remaining unpublished and unknown. If she was published, her books did not survive. The absence of women in philosophy was not, we can be sure, due to lack of talent. But no woman philosopher ever found her Plato, as did Socrates, to carry her legend to posterity. (If there was such a Plato, she evidently never got published, either.).

Feminist philosophy challenges the entire Western tradition (and not only that tradition). While claiming to be universal and all-inclusive, philosophy has not even included or taken account of the woman next door. It certainly has not asked whether she sees things differently, or whether she would ask the same questions in the same way as male philosophers. Thus one of the most radical changes that feminism has provoked in contemporary philosophy is the centrality of the notion of a personal "standpoint"—what Nietzsche called a "perspective." Different people, in different positions, might "see" the world very differently. Thus, a plurality of perspectives might replace the competing demands for a singular "objectivity."

The same charge extends to the neglect of the rest of the world. Only recently have American and European philosophers generally started to take seriously the ancient philosophical traditions of Asia, and only more recently has there been even a glimmer of interest in the "Third World," despite an unprecedented degree of interaction, intermingling, and confrontation between cultural groups. As the world gets smaller, there are growing concerns about the way cultural groups can and should live together. Philosophy should become a major intermediary in this process.

The most successful philosophy for this purpose, at least until very recently, has been Marxism. Soon after the Second World War, Mao Zedong overthrew the traditional government of China with a "peasant revolt" that pricked up the ears of every oppressed people in the world. Marxism was aggressively synthesized with local traditions and concepts. One might argue that Marxism appropriated Confucianism, with its emphasis on supreme personal and family authority, now focussing on Mao the patriach. Like most revolutionary governments, Mao's new China took on many of the worst oppressive habits of its predecessors, but the Maoist revolution continues to beckon to poor and oppressed peoples across the world. An equally stunning contrast to Mao's violent revolution, however, was Mahatma Gandhi's "nonviolent resistance" against the British in India. As Asia gains in prominence and economic power in the modern world, and as Africa and the other Americas emerge to claim their heritage, modern philosophy cannot but be affected by this twin set of dramatic examples, a philosophy of revolution and the philosophy of nonviolence.

Philosophy, in the West, has until recently been treated as a uniquely Western tradition. We want to insist, to the contrary, that philosophy has appeared almost everywhere. There is no single philosophical perspective, no one "correct" philosophical method, no unique and "true" philosophy. The movement in modern philosophy that begins with the New Science and Descartes is but one set of claims among many.

Not surprisingly, this rejection of traditional "modern" philosophy has itself become a philosophy. Postmodernism is a rag-tag "movement" that insists that overly authoritarian, unapologetically Western philosophy has run its course. Feminism and multiculturalism, postmodernists argue, are two powerful pieces of evidence that this is so. Philosophy, the search for a single truth, no longer exists. There are only philosophies. Indeed, there is no longer Truth, only "discourses"—people talking, thinking, writing, broadcasting. There is no longer a center, a "mainstream" in philosophy, only rapidly expanding margins and numerous streams and puddles. Postmodernism, if its advocates are to be believed, signals the end of the Western philosophical tradition.

Nevertheless, we might, in closing, consider the phenomenon sometimes labeled New Age philosophy, an amazing collection of ideas from healthy whole-earth thinking to loony-tunes from the edge. But the evident hunger for philosophy that "New Age" phenomena reveal does suggest an important prognosis for philosophy, despite the doomsday warnings from the postmodernists and the desiccation that has come to define so much of academic philosophy. What remains is a need for philosophy complicated by a new global awareness. As philosophers, we cannot help being excited by the bewildering variety of ideas, the dynamism of ongoing confrontations. But at the same time, we are disturbed by the fact that the old ideal of philosophy, as a search for wisdom rather than a peculiar professional skill or a merely clever game, has gotten lost.

Philosophy has always been representative of what is most human about us. Perhaps what we need is not more sophistication but more openness. We need to be not more clever but, rather, better listeners. What philosophy is, after all, is a thoughtful openness to the world, a passion for wisdom.

PART II

Introduction
to Logic

ARGUMENTS, PREMISES,
CONCLUSIONS, AND FALLACIES

By Patrick Hurley

ARGUMENTS, PREMISES, AND CONCLUSIONS

Logic may be defined as the organized body of knowledge, or science, that evaluates arguments. All of us encounter arguments in our day-to-day experience. We read them in books and newspapers, hear them on television, and formulate them when communicating with friends and associates. The aim of logic is to develop a system of methods and principles that we may use as criteria for evaluating the arguments of others *and* as guides in constructing arguments of our own. Among the benefits to be expected from the study of logic is an increase in confidence that we are making sense when we criticize the arguments of others and when we advance arguments of our own,

An **argument**, in its most basic form, is a group of statements, one or more of which (the premises) are claimed to provide support for, or reasons to believe, one of the others (the conclusion). All arguments may be placed in one of two basic groups; those in which the premises really do support the conclusion and those in which they do not, even though they are claimed to. The former are said to be good arguments (at least to that extent), the latter bad arguments. The purpose of logic, as the science that evaluates arguments, is thus to develop methods and techniques that allow us to distinguish good arguments from bad.

As is apparent from the given definition, the term *argument* has a very specific meaning in logic. It does not mean, for example, a mere verbal fight, as one might have with one's parent, spouse, or friend. Let us examine the features of this definition in greater detail First of all, an argument is a group of statements. A **statement** is a sentence that is either true or false—in other words, typically a declarative sentence or a sentence component that could stand as a declarative sentence. The following sentences are statements:

> Chocolate truffles are loaded with calories.
> Melatonin helps relieve jet lag.
> Political candidates always tell the complete truth.
> No wives ever cheat on their husbands.
> Tiger Woods plays golf and Maria Sharapova plays tennis.

The first two statements are true, the second two false. The last one expresses two statements, both of which are true. Truth and falsity are called the two possible **truth values** of a statement. Thus, the truth value of the first two statements is true, the truth value of the second two is false, and the truth value of the last statement, as well as that of its components, is true.

Unlike statements, many sentences cannot be said to be either true or false. Questions, proposals, suggestions, commands, and exclamations usually cannot, and so are not usually classified as statements. The following sentences are not statements:

Where is Khartoum?	(question)
Let's go to a movie tonight.	(proposal)
I suggest you get contact lenses.	(suggestion)
Turn off the TV right now.	(command)
Fantastic!	(exclamation)

The statements that make up an argument are divided into one or more premises and one and only one conclusion. The **premises** are the statements that set forth the reasons or evidence, and the **conclusion** is the statement that the evidence is claimed to support or imply. In other words, the conclusion is the statement that is claimed to follow from the premises. Here is an example of an argument:

> All film stars are celebrities.
> Halle Berry is a film star.
> Therefore, Halle Berry is a celebrity.

The first two statements are the premises; the third is the conclusion. (The claim that the premises support or imply the conclusion is indicated by the word "therefore.") In this argument the premises really do support the conclusions and so the argument is a good one. But consider this argument:

> Some film stars are men.
> Cameron Diaz is a film star.
> Therefore, Cameron Diaz is a man.

In this argument the premises do not support the conclusion, even though they are claimed to, and so the argument is not a good one.

One of the most important tasks in the analysis of arguments is being able to distinguish premises from conclusions. If what is thought to be a conclusion is really a premise, and vice versa, the subsequent analysis cannot possibly be correct. Many arguments contain indicator words that provide clues in identifying premises and conclusion. Some typical **conclusion indicators** are:

therefore	accordingly	entails that
wherefore	we may conclude	hence
thus	it must be that	it follows that
consequently	for this reason	implies that
we may infer	so	as a result

Whenever a statement follows one of these indicators, it can usually be identified as the conclusion. By process of elimination the other statements in the argument are the premises. Example:

> Tortured prisoners will say anything just to relieve the pain. Consequently torture is not a reliable method of interrogation.
> The conclusion of this argument is "Torture is not a reliable method of interrogation," and the premise is "Tortured prisoners will say anything just to relieve the pain."

If an argument does not contain a conclusion indicator, it may contain a premise indicator. Some typical premise indicators are:

since	in that	seeing that
as indicated	may be	for the
by	inferred from	reason that

| because | as | inasmuch as |
| for | given that | owing to |

Any statement following one of these indicators can usually be identified as a premise. Example:

Expectant mothers should never use recreational drugs, since the use of these drugs can jeopardize the development of the fetus.

The premise of this argument is "The use of these drugs can jeopardize the development of the fetus," and the conclusion is "Expectant mothers should never use recreational drugs."

In reviewing the list of indicators, note that "for this reason" is a conclusion indicator, whereas "for the reason that" is a premise indicator. "For this reason" (except when followed by a colon) means for the reason (premise) that was just given, so what follows is the conclusion. On the other hand, "for the reason that" announces that a premise is about to be stated.

Sometimes a single indicator can be used to identify more than one premise. Consider the following argument:

It is vitally important that wilderness areas be preserved, for wilderness provides essential habitat for wildlife, including endangered species, and it is a natural retreat from the stress of daily life.

The premise indicator "for" goes with both "Wilderness provides essential habitat for wildlife, including endangered species," and "It is a natural retreat from the stress of daily life." These are the premises. By method of elimination, "It is vitally important that wilderness areas he preserved" is the conclusion.

Some arguments contain no indicators. With these, the reader/listener must ask such questions as: What single statement is claimed (implicitly) to follow from the others? What is the arguer trying to prove? What is (t)he main point in the passage? The answers to these questions should point to the conclusion. Example:

The space program deserves increased expenditures in the years ahead. Not only does the national defense depend on it, but the program will more than pay for itself in terms of technological spinoffs. Furthermore, at current funding levels the program cannot fulfill its anticipated potential.

The conclusion of this argument is the first statement, and all of the other statements are premises. The argument illustrates the pattern found in most arguments that lack indicator words: the intended conclusion is stated first, and the remaining statements are then uttered in support of this first statement. When the argument is restructured according to logical principles, however, the conclusion is always listed *after* the premises:

P_1: The national defense is dependent on the space program.
P_2: The space program will more than pay for itself in terms of technological spinoffs.
P_3: At current funding levels the space program cannot fulfill its anticipated potential.
C: The space program deserves increased expenditures in the years ahead.

When restructuring arguments such as this, one should remain as close as possible to the original version, while at the same time attending to the requirement that premises and conclusion be complete sentences that are meaningful in the order in which they are listed.

Note that the first two premises are included within the scope of a single sentence in the original argument. For the purposes of this chapter, compound arrangements of statements in which the various components are all claimed to be true will be considered as separate statements.

Passages that contain arguments sometimes contain statements that are neither premises nor conclusions. Only statements that are actually intended to support the conclusion should be included in the list of premises. If, for example, a statement serves merely to introduce the general topic, or merely makes a passing comment, it should not be taken as part of the argument. Examples:

> The claim is often made that malpractice lawsuits drive up the cost of health care. But if such suits were outlawed or severely restricted, then patients would have no means of recovery for injuries caused by negligent doctors. Hence, the availability of malpractice litigation should be maintained intact.
>
> Currently 47 million Americans are without health insurance. When these people go to a hospital, they are routinely charged two to three times the normal cost for treatment This practice, which covers the cost of treating indigent patients, is clearly unfair. For these reasons, a national health insurance program should be adopted. Politicians who oppose this change should be ashamed of themselves.

In the first argument the opening statement serves merely to introduce the topic, so it is not part of the argument. The premise is the second statement, and the conclusion is the last statement. In the second argument, the final statement merely makes a passing comment, so it is not part of the argument. The premises are the first three statements, and the statement following "for these reasons" is the conclusion.

Closely related to the concepts of argument and statement are those of inference and proposition. An **inference**, in the narrow sense of the term, is the reasoning process expressed by an argument. In the broad sense of the term, "inference" is used interchangeably with "argument." Analogously, a **proposition,** in the narrow sense, is the meaning or information content of a statement. For the purposes of this book, however, "proposition" and "statement" are used interchangeably.

DEDUCTION AND INDUCTION

In the previous section we saw that every argument involves an inferential claim—the claim that the conclusion is supposed to follow from the premises. The question we now address has to do with the strength of this claim. Just how strongly is the conclusion claimed to follow from the premises? If the conclusion is claimed to follow with strict certainty or necessity, the argument is said to he deductive; but if it is claimed to follow only probably, the argument is inductive.

Stated more precisely, a **deductive argument** is an argument incorporating the claim that it is *impossible* for the conclusion to be false given that the premises are true. Deductive arguments are those that involve necessary reasoning. On the other hand, an **inductive argument** is an argument incorporating the claim that it is *improbable* the conclusion be false given that the premises are true. Inductive arguments involve probabilistic reasoning. Here are two examples:

> The meerkat is closely related to the suricat.
> The suricat thrives on beetle larvae.
> Therefore, probably the meerkat thrives on beetle larvae.

> The meerkat is a member of the mongoose family.
> All members of the mongoose famliy are carnivores.
> Therefore, it necessarily follows that the meerkat is a carnivore.

The first of these arguments is inductive, the second deductive.

In deciding whether an argument is inductive or deductive, we look to certain objective features of the argument. These features include (1) the occurrence of special indicator words. (2) the *actual* strength of the inferential link between premises and conclusion, and (3) the form or style of argumentation. However, we must acknowledge at the outset that many arguments in ordinary language are incomplete, and because of this, deciding whether the argument should best be interpreted as deductive or inductive may he impossible.

The occurrence of special indicator words is illustrated in the examples we just considered. The word "probably'" in the conclusion or the first argument suggests that the argument should he taken as inductive, and the word "necessarily" in the conclusion of the second suggests that the second argument be taken as deductive. Additional inductive indicators are "improbable," plausible," "likely," "unlikely," and "reasonable to conclude." Additional deductive indicators are certainly, "absolutely," and "definitely." (Note that the phrase "it must be the case that" is simply a conclusion indicator that can occur in either deductive or inductive arguments.)

Inductive and deductive indicator words often suggest the correct interpretation. However, if they conflict with one of the other criteria (discussed shortly), we should probably ignore them. Arguers often use phrases such as "it certainly follows that" for rhetorical purposes to add impact to their conclusion and not to suggest that the argument be taken as deductive. Similarly, some arguers, not knowing the distinction between inductive and deductive, will claim to "deduce" a conclusion when their argument is more correctly interpreted as inductive.

The second factor that bears on our interpretation of an argument as inductive or deductive is the *actual* strength of the inferential link between premises and conclusion. If the conclusion actually does follow with strict necessity from the premises, the argument is clearly deductive. In such an argument it is impossible for the premises to be true and the conclusion false. On the other hand, if the conclusion does not follow with strict necessity but does follow probably, it is often best to consider the argument inductive. Examples:

All entertainers are extroverts.
David Letterman is an entertainer.
Therefore, David Letteman is an extrovert.

The vast majority of entertainers are extroverts.
David Letterman is an entertainer.
Therefore, David Letterman is an extrovert.

In the first example, the conclusion follows with strict necessity from the premises. It we assume that all entertainers are extroverts and that David Letterman is an entertainer, then it is impossible that David Letterman not be an extrovert. Thus, we should interpret this argument as deductive. In the second example, the conclusion does not follow from the premises with strict necessity, but it does follow with some degree of probability. It we assume that the premises are true, then based on that assumption it is probable that the conclusion is true. Thus, it is best to interpret the second argument as inductive.

Occasionally an argument contains no special indicator words, and the conclusion does not follow either necessarily or probably from the premises; in other words, it does not follow at all. This situation points the need for the third factor to be taken into account, which is the character or form of argumentation the arguer uses.

Many arguments have a distinctive character or form that indicates that the premises are supposed to provide absolute support for the conclusion. Five examples of such forms or kinds of argumentation are arguments based on mathematics, arguments from definition, and categorical, hypothetical and disjunctive syllogisms.

An **argument based on mathematics** is an argument in which the conclusion depends on some purely arithmetic or geometric computation or measurement. For example, a shopper might place two apples and three oranges into a paper bag and then conclude that the bag contains five pieces of fruit. Or a surveyor might measure a square piece of land and, after determining that it is 100 feet on each side, conclude that it contains 10,000 square feet. Since all arguments in pure mathematics are deductive, we can usually consider arguments that depend on mathematics to be deductive as well. A noteworthy exception, however, is arguments that depend on statistics. Such arguments are usually best interpreted as inductive.

An **argument from definition** is an argument in which the conclusion is claimed to depend merely on the definition of some word or phrase used in the premise or conclusion. For example, someone might argue that because Claudia is mendacious, it follows that she tells lies, or that because a certain paragraph is prolix, it follows that it is excessively wordy. These arguments are deductive because their conclusions follow with necessity from the definitions of "mendacious" and "prolix."

A *syllogism*, in general, is an argument consisting of exactly two premises and one conclusion. A **categorical syllogism** is a syllogism in which each statement begins with one of the words "all, " no," or "some." Example:

> All ancient forests are sources of wonder.
> Some ancient forests are targets of the timber industry.
> Therefore, some sources of wonder are targets of the timber industry.

Arguments such as these are nearly always best treated as deductive.

A **hypothetical syllogism** is a syllogism having a conditional statement for one or both of its premises. Examples:

> If estate taxes are abolished, then wealth will accumulate disproportionately.
> If wealth accumulates disproportionately, then democracy will be threatened.
> Therefore, if estate taxes were abolished, then democracy will be threatened.

If Fox News is a propaganda machine, then it misleads its viewers.

Fox News is a propaganda machine.

Therefore, Fox News misleads its viewers.

Although certain tones of such arguments can sometimes he interpreted inductively, the deductive interpretation is usually the most appropriate.

A **disjunctive syllogism** is a syllogism having a disjunctive statement (i.e., an "either ... or ..." statement) to one of its premises. Example:

Either global warming will be arrested, or hurricanes will become more intense.

Global warming will not be arrested.

Therefore, hurricanes will become more intense.

As with hypothetical syllogisms, such arguments are usually best taken as deductive.

In general inductive arguments are such that the content of the conclusion is in some way intended to "go beyond" the content of the premises. The premises of such an argument typically deal with some subject that is relatively familiar, and the conclusion then moves beyond this to a subject that is less familiar or that little is known about. Such an argument may take any of several forms: predictions about the future, arguments from analogy, inductive generalizations, arguments from authority, arguments based on signs, and causal inferences, to name just a few.

A **prediction** is an argument that proceeds from our knowledge of the past to a claim about the future. For example, someone might argue that because certain meteorological phenomena have been observed to develop over a certain region of central Missouri, a storm will occur there in six hours. Or again, one might argue that because certain fluctuations occurred in the prime interest rate on Friday the value of the dollar will decrease against foreign currencies on Monday. Nearly everyone realizes that the future cannot be known with certainty; thus, whenever an argument makes a prediction about the future, one is usually justified in considering the argument inductive.

An **argument from analogy** is an argument that depends on the existence of an analogy, or similarity, between two things or states of affairs. Because of the existence of this analogy, a certain condition that affects the better-known thing or situation is concluded to affect the similar, lesser-known thing or situation. For example, someone might argue that because Christina's Porsche is a great handling car, it follows that Angela's Porsche must also be a great handling car. The argument depends on the existence of a similarity or analogy between the two cars. The certitude attending such an inference is probabilistic at best.

A **generalization** is an argument that proceeds from the knowledge of a selected sample to some claim about the whole group. Because the members of the sample have a certain characteristic, it is argued that all the members of the group have that same characteristic. For example, one might argue that because three oranges selected from a certain crate were especially tasty and juicy, all the oranges from that crate are especially tasty and juicy. Or again, one might argue that because six out of a total of nine members sampled from a certain labor union intend to vote for Johnson for union president, two-thirds of the entire membership intend to vote for Johnson, These examples illustrate the use of statistics in inductive argumentation.

An **argument from authority** is an argument that concludes something is true because a presumed expert or witness has said that it is. For example, a person might argue that earnings for Hewlett-Packard Corporation will be up in the coming quarter because of a statement to that effect by an investment counselor. Or a lawyer might argue that Mack the Knife committed the murder because an eyewitness testified to that effect under oath. Because the investment counselor and the eyewitness could be either mistaken or lying, such arguments are essentially probabilistic.

An **argument based on signs** is an argument that proceeds from the knowledge a sign to a claim about the tiling or situation that the sign symbolizes. The word "sign," as it is used here, means any kind of message (usually visual) produced by an intelligent being. For example, when driving on an unfamiliar highway one might see a sign indicating that the road makes several sharp turns one mile ahead. Based on this information, one might argue that the road does indeed make several sharp turns one mile ahead. Because the sign might be misplaced or in error about the turns, the conclusion is only probable.

A **causal inference** is an argument that proceeds from knowledge of a cause to a claim about an effect, or, conversely, from knowledge or an effect to a claim about a cause. For example, from the knowledge that a bottle of wine had been accidentally left in the freezer overnight, someone might conclude that it had frozen (cause to effect). Conversely, after tasting a piece of chicken and finding it dry and tough, one might conclude that it had been overcooked (effect to cause). Because specific instances of cause and effect can never he known with absolute certainty, one may usually interpret such arguments as inductive.

Furter Considerations

It should be noted that the various subspecies of inductive arguments listed here are not intended to be mutually exclusive. Overlaps can and do occur. For example, many causal inferences that proceed from cause to effect also qualify as predictions. The purpose of this survey is not to demarcate in precise terms the various forms of induction but rather to provide guidelines for distinguishing induction from deduction.

Keeping this in mind, we should take care not to confuse arguments in geometry, which are always deductive, with arguments from analogy or inductive generalizations. For example, an argument concluding that a triangle has a certain attribute (such as a right angle) because another triangle, with which it is congruent, also has that attribute might be mistaken for an argument from analogy. Similarly, an argument that concludes that all triangles have a certain attribute (such as angles totaling two right angles) because any particular triangle has that attribute might be mistaken for an inductive generalization. Arguments such as these, however, are always deductive, because the conclusion follows necessarily and with complete certainty from the premises.

One broad classification of arguments not listed in this survey is scientific arguments. Arguments that occur in science can be either inductive or deductive, depending on the circumstances. In general, arguments aimed at the *discovery* of a law of nature are usually considered inductive. Suppose, for example, that we want to discover a law that governs the time required for a falling body to strike the earth. We drop bodies of various weights from various heights and measure the time it takes them to fall. Comparing our measurements, we notice that the time is approximately proportional to the square root of the distance. From this we conclude that the time required for any body to fall is proportional to the square root of the distance through which it falls. Such an argument is best interpreted as an inductive generalization.

Another type of argument that occurs in science has to do with the *application* of known laws to specific circumstances. Arguments of this sort are often considered to be deductive—but only with certain reservations. Suppose, for example, that we want to apply Boyle's law for ideal gases to a container of gas in our laboratory. Boyle's law states that the pressure exerted by a gas on the walls of its container is inversely proportional to the volume. Applying this law, we conclude that when we reduce the volume of our laboratory sample by half, the pressure will double. Considered purely as a mathematical computation, this argument is deductive. But if we acknowledge the fact that the conclusion pertains to the future and the possibility that Boyle's law may not work in the future, then the argument is best considered inductive.

A final point needs to be made about the distinction between inductive and deductive arguments. There is a tradition extending back to the time of Aristotle that holds that inductive arguments are those that proceed from the particular to the general, while deductive arguments are those that proceed from the general to the particular. (**A particular statement** is one that makes a claim about one or more particular members of a class, while a **general statement** makes a claim about *all* the members of a class.) It is true, of course, that many inductive and deductive arguments do work in this way; but this fact should not be used as a criterion for distinguishing induction from deduction. As a matter of fact, there are deductive arguments that proceed from the general to the general, from the particular to the particular, and from the particular to the general, as well as from the general to the particular; and there are inductive arguments that do the same. For example, here is a deductive argument that proceeds from the particular to the general:

> Three is a prime number
> Five is a prime number.
> Seven is a prime number.
> Therefore, all odd numbers between two and eight are prime numbers.

And here is one that proceeds from the particular to the particular:

> Gabriel is a wolf.
> Gabriel has a tail.
> Therefore, Gabriel's tail is the tail of a wolf.

Here is an inductive argument that proceeds from the general to the particular:

> All emeralds previously found have been green.
> Therefore, the next emerald to be found will be green.

The other varieties are easy to construct. Thus, the progression from particular to general, and vice versa, cannot be used as a criterion for distinguishing induction and deduction.

SUMMARY

To distinguish deductive arguments from inductive arguments, we attempt to evaluate the strength of the argument's inferential claim—how strongly the conclusion is claimed to follow from the premises. This claim is an objective feature of an argument, and it may or may not be related to the subjective intentions of the arguer.

To interpret an argument's inferential claim we look at three factors: special indicator words, the actual strength of the inferential link between premises and conclusion, and the character or form of argumentation. Given that we have more than one factor to look at, it is possible in a single argument for the occurrence of two of these factors to conflict with each other, leading to opposite interpretations. For example, in drawing a conclusion to a categorical syllogism (which is clearly deductive), an arguer might say "It probably follows that …" (which suggests induction). To help alleviate this conflict we can list the factors in order of importance:

1. Arguments in which the premises provide absolute support for the conclusion. Such arguments are always deductive.
2. Arguments having a specific deductive character or form (e.g., categorical syllogism). This factor is often of equal importance to the first, and, when present, it provides a clear-cut indication that the argument is deductive.
3. Arguments having a specific inductive character or form (e.g., a prediction). Arguments of this sort are nearly always best interpreted as inductive.

4. Arguments containing inductive indicator language (e.g., "It probably follows that ..."). Since arguers rarely try to make their argument appear weaker than it really is, such language can usually be trusted, but if this language conflicts with one of the first two factors, it should be ignored.

5. Arguments containing deductive indicator language (e.g., "It necessarily follows that ..."). Arguers occasionally use such language for rhetorical purposes, to make their argument appear stronger than it really is, so such language should be evaluated carefully.

6. Arguments in which the premises provide only probable support for the conclusion. This is the least important factor, and if it conflicts with any of the earlier ones, it should probably be ignored.

Unfortunately, many arguments in ordinary language are incomplete, so it often happens that none of these factors are clearly present. Determining the inductive or deductive character of such arguments may be impossible.

VALIDITY, TRUTH, SOUNDNESS, STRENGTH, COGENCY

This section introduces the central ideas and terminology required to evaluate arguments. We have seen that every argument makes two basic claims; a claim that evidence or reasons exist and a claim that the alleged evidence or reasons support something (or that something follows from the alleged evidence or reasons). The first is a factual claim, the second an inferential claim. The evaluation of every argument centers on the evaluation of these two claims. The more important of the two is the inferential claim, because if the premises fail to support the conclusion (that is, if the reasoning is bad), an argument is worthless. Thus we will always test the inferential claim first, and only if the premises do support the conclusion will we test the factual claim (that is, the claim that the premises present genuine evidence, or are true). The material that follows considers first deductive arguments and then inductive.

Deductive Arguments

The previous section defined a deductive argument as one incorporating the claim that it is impossible for the conclusion to be false given that the premises are true. If this claim is true, the argument is said to be valid. Thus, a **valid deductive argument** is an argument in which it is impossible for the conclusion to be false given that the premises are true. In these arguments the conclusion follows with strict necessity from the premises. Conversely, an **invalid deductive argument** is a deductive argument in which it *is* possible for the conclusion to be false given that the premises are true. In these arguments the conclusion does not follow with strict necessity from the premises, even though it is claimed to.

An immediate consequence of these definitions is that there is no middle ground between valid and invalid. There are no arguments that are "almost" valid and "almost" invalid. If the conclusion follows with strict necessity from the premises, the argument is valid; if not, it is invalid

To test an argument for validity we begin by assuming that all the premises are true, and then we determine if it is possible, in light of that assumption, for the conclusion to be false. Here is an example:

> All television networks are media companies.
> NBC is a television network.
> Therefore, NBC is a media company.

In this argument both premises are actually true, so it is easy to *assume* that they are true. Next we determine, in light or this assumption, if it is possible for the conclusion to be false. Clearly this is not possible. If NBC is included in the group of television networks (second premise) and if the group of television networks is included in the group of media companies (first premise), it necessarily follows that NBC is included in the group of media companies (conclusion). In other words, assuming the premises to be true and the conclusion false entails a strict *contradiction*. Thus, the argument is valid. Here is another example:

> All automakers are computer manufacturers.
> United Airlines is an automaker.
> Therefore, United Airlines is a computer manufacturer.

In this argument, both premises are actually false, but it is easy to assume that they are true. Every automaker could have a corporate division that manufactures computers. Also, in addition to flying airplanes, United Airlines could make cars. Next, in light of these assumptions, we determine if it is possible for the conclusion to be false. Again, we see that this is not possible, by the same reasoning as the previous example. Assuming the premises to be true and the conclusion false entails a contradiction. Thus, the argument is valid. Another example:

> All banks are financial institutions.
> Wells Fargo is a financial institution.
> Therefore, Wells Fargo is a bank.

As in the first example, both premises of this argument are true, so it is easy to assume they are true. Next we determine, in light of this assumption, if it is possible for the conclusion to be false. In this case it is possible. If banks were included in one part of the group or financial institutions and Wells Fargo were included in another part, then Wells Fargo would *not* be a bank. In other words, assuming the premises to be true and the conclusion false does not involve any contradiction, and so the argument is invalid. In addition to illustrating the basic idea of validity, these examples suggest an important point about validity and truth. In general, validity is not something that is uniformly determined by the actual truth or falsity of the premises and conclusion. Both the NBC example and the Wells Fargo example have actually true premises and an actually true conclusion, yet one is valid and the other invalid. The United Airlines example has actually false premises and an actually false conclusion, yet the argument is valid. Rather, validity is something that is determined by the *relationship* between premises and conclusion. The question is not whether the premises and conclusion are true or false, but whether the premises *support* the conclusion. In the examples of valid arguments the premises do support the conclusion, and in the invalid case they do not.

Nevertheless, there is *one* arrangement of truth and falsity in the premises and conclusion that does determine the issue of validity. Any deductive argument having actually true premises and an actually false conclusion is invalid. The reasoning behind this fact is fairly obvious. If the premises are actually true and the conclusion is actually false, then it certainly is *possible* for the premises to be true and the conclusion false. Thus, by the definition of invalidity the argument is invalid.

The idea that any deductive argument having actually true premises and a false conclusion is invalid may be the most important point in all of deductive logic. The entire system of deductive logic would be quite useless if it accepted as valid any inferential process by which a person could start with truth in the premises and arrive at falsity in the conclusion.

Table 1.1 presents examples of deductive arguments that illustrate the various combinations of truth and falsity in the premises and conclusion. In the examples having false premises, both premises are false, but it is easy to construct other examples having only one false premise. When examining this table, note that the only combination of truth and falsity that does not allow for *both* valid and invalid arguments is true premises and false conclusion. As we have just seen, any argument having this combination is necessarily invalid.

The relationship between the validity of a deductive argument and the truth or falsity of its premises and conclusion, as illustrated in Table 1.1, is summarized as follows:

Premises	Conclusion	Validity
T	T	?
T	F	Invalid
F	T	?
F	F	?

A **sound argument** is a deductive argument that is *valid* and has *all true premises*. Both conditions must be met for an argument to be sound; if either is missing the argument is unsound. Thus, an **unsound**

Table 1.1. Deductive Arguments

	Valid	Invalid
True premises **True conclusion**	All wines are beverages. Chardonnay is a wine. Therefore, chardonnay is a beverage. [sound]	All wines are beverages. Chardonnay is a beverage. Therefore, chardonnay is a wine. [unsound]
True premises **False conclusion**	None exist	All wines are beverages. Ginger ale is a beverage. Therefore, ginger ale is a wine. [unsound]
False premises **True conclusion**	All wines are soft drinks. Ginger ale is a wine. Therefore, ginger ale is a soft drink. [unsound]	All wines are whiskeys. Chardonnay is a whiskey. Therefore, chardonnay is a wine. [unsound]
False premises **False conclusion**	All wines are whiskeys. Ginger ale is a wine. Therefore, ginger ale is a whiskey. [unsound]	All wines are whiskeys. Ginger ale is a whiskey. Therefore, ginger ale is a wine. [unsound]

argument is a deductive argument that is invalid, has one or more false premises, or both. Because a valid argument is one such that it is impossible for the premises to be true and the conclusion false, and because, sound argument does in fact have true premises, it follows that every sound argument, by definition, will have a true conclusion as well. A sound argument, therefore, is what is meant by a "good" deductive argument in the fullest sense of the term.

In connection with this definition of soundness, a single proviso is required. For an argument to be unsound, the false premise or premises must actually be needed to support the conclusion. An argument with a conclusion that is validly supported by true premises but with a superfluous false premise would still be sound. By similar reasoning, no addition of a false premise to an originally sound argument can make the argument unsound. Such a premise would be superfluous and should not be considered part of the argument. Analogous remarks, incidentally, extend to inductive arguments.

Inductive Arguments

We defined an inductive argument as one incorporating the claim that it is improbable that the conclusion be false given that the premises are true. If this claim is true, the argument is said to be strong. Thus, a **strong inductive argument** is an inductive argument in which it is improbable that the conclusion be false given that the premises are true. In such arguments, the conclusion does in fact follow probably from the premises. Conversely, a **weak inductive argument** is an argument in which the conclusion does not follow probably from the premises, even though it is claimed to.

The procedure for testing the strength of inductive arguments runs parallel to the procedure for deduction. First we assume the premises are true, and then we determine whether, based on that assumption, the conclusion is probably true. Example:

> All dinosaur bones discovered to this day have been at least 50 million years old. Therefore, probably the next dinosaur bone to be found will be at least 50 million years old.

In this argument the premise is actually true, so it is easy to assume that it is true. Based on that assumption, the conclusion is probably true, so the argument is strong. Here is another example:

> All meteorites found to this day have contained sugar. Therefore, probably the next meteorite to be found will contain sugar.

The premise of this argument is obviously false. But if we assume the premise is true, then based on that assumption, the conclusion would probably be true. Thus, the argument is strong.

The next example is an argument from analogy:

> When a lighted match is slowly dunked into water, the flame is snuffed out. But gasoline is a liquid, just like water. Therefore, when a lighted match is slowly dunked into gasoline, the flame will be snuffed out.

In this argument the premises are actually true and the conclusion is probably false. Thus, if we assume the premises are true, then, based on that assumption, it is not probable that the conclusion is true. Thus, the argument is weak.

Another example:

> During the past fifty years, inflation has consistently reduced the value of the American dollar. Therefore, industrial productivity will probably increase in the years ahead.

In this argument, the premise is actually true and the conclusion is probably true in the actual world, but the probability of the conclusion is in no way based on the assumption that the premise is true. Because there is no direct connection between inflation and increased industrial productivity, the premise is irrelevant to the conclusion and it provides no probabilistic support for it. The conclusion is probably true independently of the premise. As a result, the argument is weak.

This last example illustrates an important distinction between strong inductive arguments and valid deductive arguments. If the conclusion of a deductive argument is necessarily true independently of the premises, the argument is still considered valid. But if the conclusion of an inductive argument is probably true independently of the premises, the argument is weak.

These four examples show that in general the strength or weakness of an inductive argument results not from the actual truth or falsity of the premises and conclusion, but from the probabilistic support the premises give to the conclusion. The dinosaur argument has a true premise and a probably true conclusion, and the meteorite argument has a false premise and a probably false conclusion: yet both are strong because the premise of each provides probabilistic support for the conclusion. The industrial productivity argument has a true premise and a probably true conclusion, but the argument is weak because the premise provides no probabilistic support for the conclusion. As in the evaluation of deductive arguments, the only arrangement of truth and falsity that establishes anything is true premises and probably false conclusion (as in the lighted match argument). Any inductive argument having true premises and a probably false conclusion is weak.

Table 1.2 presents the various possibilities of truth and falsity in the premises and conclusion of inductive arguments. Note that the only arrangement of truth and falsity that is missing for strong arguments is true premises and probably false conclusion.

The relationship between the strength of an inductive argument and the truth or falsity of its premises and conclusion, as illustrated in Table 1.2, is summarized as follows:

Premises	Conclusion	Strength
T	prob. T	?
T	prob. F	Weak
F	prob. T	?
F	prob. F	?

Unlike the validity and invalidity of deductive arguments, the strength and weakness of inductive arguments admit of degrees. To be considered strong, an inductive argument must have a conclusion that is more probable than improbable, in other words, given that the premises are true, the likelihood that the conclusion is true must be more than 50 percent, and as the probability increases, the argument becomes stronger. For this purpose, consider the following pair of arguments:

This barrel contains 100 apples.
Three apples selected at random were found to be ripe.
Therefore, probably all 100 apples are ripe.
This barrel contains 100 apples.
Eighty apples selected at random were found to be ripe.

Table 1.2. Inductive Arguments

	Strong	Weak
True premise Probably true conclusion	All previous U.S. presidents were older than 40. Therefore, probably the next U.S. president will be older than 40. [cogent]	A few U.S. presidents were lawyers. Therefore, probably the next U.S. president will be older than 40. [uncogent]
True premise Probably false conclusion	None exist	A few U.S. presidents were unmarried. Therefore, probably the next U.S. president will be unmarried.[uncogent]
False premise Probably true conclusion	All previous U.S. presidents were TV debaters. Therefore, probably the next U.S. president will be a TV debater. [uncogent]	A few U.S. presidents were dentists. Therefore, probably the next U.S. president will be a TV debater.[uncogent]
False premise Probably false conclusion	All previous U.S. presidents died in office. Therefore, probably the next U.S. president will die in office. [uncogent]	A few U.S. presidents were dentists. Therefore, probably the next U.S. president will be a dentist.[uncogent]

Therefore, probably all 100 apples are ripe.

The first argument is weak and the second is strong. However, the first is not absolutely weak nor the second absolutely strong. Both arguments would be strengthened or weakened by the random selection of a larger or smaller sample. For example, if the size of the sample in the second argument were reduced to seventy apples, the argument would be weakened. The incorporation of additional premises into an inductive argument will also generally tend to strengthen or weaken it. For example, if the premise "One unripe apple that had been found earlier was removed" were added to either argument, the argument would be weakened.

A **cogent argument** is an inductive argument that is strong and has *all true premises;* if either condition is missing, the argument is uncogent. Thus, an **uncogent argument** is an inductive argument that is weak, has one or more false premises, or both. A cogent argument is the inductive analogue of a sound deductive argument and is what is meant by a "good" inductive argument without qualification. Because the conclusion of a cogent argument is genuinely supported by true premises, it follows that the conclusion of every cogent argument is probably true.

There is a difference, however, between sound and cogent arguments in regard to the true premise requirement. In a sound argument it is necessary only that the premises be true and nothing more. Given such premises and good reasoning, a true conclusion is guaranteed. In a cogent argument, on the other hand, the premises must not only be true, but they must also not ignore some important piece of evidence that entails a quite different conclusion. This is called the *total evidence requirement.* As an illustration of the need for it, consider the following argument:

> Swimming in the Caribbean is usually lots of fun. Today the water is warm, the surf is gentle, and on this beach there are no dangerous currents. Therefore, it would be fun to go swimming here now.

If the premises reflect all the important factors, then the argument is cogent. But if they ignore the fact that several large dorsal fins are cutting through the water (suggesting sharks), then obviously the argument is not cogent. Thus, for cogency the premises must not only be true but also not overlook some important fact that requires a different conclusion.

SUMMARY

For both deductive and inductive arguments, two separate questions need to be answered: (1) Do the premises support the conclusion? (2) Are all the premises true?

To answer the first question we begin by *assuming* the premises to be true. Then, for deductive arguments we determine whether, in light of this assumption, it *necessarily* follows that the conclusion is true. If it does, the argument is valid; if not, it is invalid. For inductive arguments we determine whether it *probably* follows that the conclusion is true. If it does, the argument is strong; if not, it is weak. For inductive arguments we keep in mind the requirements that the premises actually support the conclusion and that they not ignore important evidence. Finally, if the argument is either valid or strong, we turn to the second question and determine whether the premises are actually true. If all the premises are true, the argument is sound (in the case of deduction) or cogent (in the case of induction). All invalid deductive arguments are unsound, and all weak inductive arguments are uncogent.

Note that in logic one never speaks of an argument as being "true" or "false," and one never speaks of a statement as being "valid," "invalid," "strong," or "weak."

FALLACIES IN GENERAL

A **fallacy** is a defect in an argument that consists of something other than false premises alone. The fallacies introduced in this chapter involve defective patterns of arguing that occur so often they have been given specific names. Such defects comprise either mistakes in reasoning or the creation of an illusion that makes a bad argument appear good. The term *non sequitur* ("it does not follow") is another name for fallacy. Both deductive and inductive arguments may contain fallacies; if they do, they are either unsound or uncogent, depending on the kind of argument. Conversely, if an argument is unsound or uncogent, it has one or more false premises or it contains a fallacy (or both).

Fallacies are usually divided into two groups; formal and informal. A formal fallacy is one that may be identified by merely examining the form or structure of an argument. Fallacies of this kind are found only in deductive arguments that have identifiable forms. Earlier we presented some of these forms: categorical syllogisms, disjunctive syllogisms, and hypothetical syllogisms. The following categorical syllogism contains a formal fallacy:

> All bullfights are grotesque rituals.
>
> All executions are grotesque rituals.
>
> Therefore, all bullfights are executions.

This argument has the following form:

> All A are B.
>
> <u>All C are B</u>
>
> All A are C.

By merely examining this form, one can see that it is invalid. The fact that A, B, and C stand respectively for "bullfights," "grotesque rituals," and "executions" is irrelevant in detecting the fallacy. The problem may be traced to the second premise. If the letters C and B are interchanged, the form becomes valid, and the original argument, with the same change introduced, also becomes valid (but unsound).

Here is an example of a formal fallacy that occurs in a hypothetical syllogism:

> If apes are intelligent, then apes can solve puzzles.
>
> Apes can solve puzzles.
>
> Therefore apes are intelligent.

This argument has the following form:

If *A* then *B*.
B.
A.

In this case, if *A* and *B* are interchanged in the first premise, the form becomes valid, and the original argument, with the same change, also becomes valid. In distinguishing formal from informal fallacies, remember that formal fallacies occur only in deductive arguments. Thus, if a given argument is inductive, it cannot contain a formal fallacy. Also, keep an eye out for standard deductive argument forms such as categorical syllogisms and hypothetical syllogisms. If such an argument is invalid because of an improper arrangement of terms or statements, it commits a formal fallacy.

Informal fallacies are those that can be detected only by examining the content of the argument. Consider the following example:

The Brooklyn Bridge is made of atoms.
Atoms are invisible.
Therefore, the Brooklyn Bridge is invisible.

To detect this fallacy one must know something about bridges—namely, that they are large visible objects, and even though their atomic components are invisible, this does not mean that the bridges themselves are invisible.

Or consider this example:

A chess player is a person.
Therefore, a bad chess player is a bad person.

To detect this fallacy one must know that the meaning of the word "bad" depends on what it modifies, and that being a bad chess player is quite different from being a bad person.

The various informal fallacies accomplish their purpose in so many different ways that no single umbrella theory covers them all. Some fallacies work by getting the reader or listener to feel various emotions, such as fear, pity, or camaraderie, and then attaching a certain conclusion to those emotions. Others attempt to discredit an opposing argument by associating it with certain pejorative features of its author. And then there are those that appeal to various dispositions on the part or the reader or listener, such as superstition or mental laziness, to get him or her to accept a conclusion. By studying the typical ways in which arguers apply these techniques, one is less likely to be fooled by the fallacious arguments posed by others or to stumble blindly into fallacies when constructing arguments for one's own use.

Since the time of Aristotle, logicians have attempted to classify the various informal fallacies. Aristotle himself identified thirteen and separated them into two groups. The work of subsequent logicians has produced dozens more, rendering the task of classifying them even more difficult. The presentation that follows divides twenty-two informal fallacies into five groups: fallacies of relevance, fallacies of weak induction, fallacies of presumption, fallacies of ambiguity, and fallacies of grammatical analogy.

SUMMARY OF INFORMAL FALLACIES

Fallacies of Relevance

Appeal to force: Arguer threatens reader/listener.

Appeal to pity: Arguer elicits pity from reader/listener.

Appeal to the people (direct): Arguer arouses mob mentality.

Appeal to the people (indirect): Arguer appeals to reader/listener's desire for security, love, respect, etc.

Argument against the person (abusive): Arguer verbally abuses other arguer.

Argument against the person (circumstantial): Arguer presents other arguer as predisposed to argue this way.

Argument against the person (*tu quoque*): Arguer presents other arguer as hypocrite.

Accident: General rule is applied to a specific case it was not intended to cover.

Straw man: Arguer distorts opponent's argument and then attacks the distorted argument.

Missing the point: Arguer draws conclusion different from that supported by premises.

Red herring: Arguer leads reader/listener off track.

Fallacies of Weak Induction

Appeal to unqualified authority: Arguer cites untrustworthy authority.

Appeal to ignorance: Premises report that nothing is known or proved, and then a conclusion is drawn.

Hasty generalization: Conclusion is drawn from an atypical sample.

False cause: Conclusion depends on nonexistent or minor causal connection.

Slippery slope: Conclusion depends on unlikely chain reaction.

Weak analogy: Conclusion depends on defective analogy.

Fallacies of Presumption

Begging the question: Arguer creates the illusion that inadequate premises are adequate by leaving out a key premise, by restating the conclusion as a premise, or by reasoning in a circle.

Complex question: Multiple questions are concealed in a single question.

False dichotomy: "Either … or …," statement hides additional alternatives.

Suppressed evidence: Arguer ignores important evidence that requires a different conclusion.

Fallacies of Ambiguity

Equivocation: Conclusion depends on a shift in meaning of a word or phrase.

Amphiboly: Conclusion depends on the wrong interpretation of a syntactically ambiguous statement.

Fallacies of Grammatical Analogy

Composition: Attribute is wrongly transferred from parts to whole.

Division: Attribute is wrongly transferred from whole to parts.

PART III

The Existence of God

EUTHYPHRO

By Plato
Trans. By Benjamin Jowett

Euthyphro. Why have you left the Lyceum, Socrates? and what are you doing in the Porch of the King Archon? Surely you cannot be concerned in a suit before the King, like myself?

Socrates. Not in a suit, Euthyphro; impeachment is the word which the Athenians use.

Euth. What! I suppose that some one has been prosecuting you, for I cannot believe that you are the prosecutor of another.

Soc. Certainly not.

Euth. Then some one else has been prosecuting you?

Soc. Yes.

Euth. And who is he?

Soc. A young man who is little known, Euthyphro; and I hardly know him: his name is Meletus, and he is of the deme of Pitthis. Perhaps you may remember his appearance; he has a beak, and long straight hair, and a beard which is ill grown.

Euth. No, I do not remember him, Socrates. But what is the charge which he brings against you?

Soc. What is the charge? Well, a very serious charge, which shows a good deal of character in the young man, and for which he is certainly not to be despised. He says he knows how the youth are corrupted and who are their corruptors. I fancy that he must be a wise man, and seeing that I am the reverse of a wise man, he has found me out, and is going to accuse me of corrupting his young friends. And of this our mother the state is to be the judge. Of all our political men he is the only one who seems to me to begin in the right way, with the cultivation of virtue in youth; like a good husbandman, he makes the young shoots his first care, and clears away us who are the destroyers of them. This is only the first step; he will afterwards attend to the elder branches; and if he goes on as he has begun, he will be a very great public benefactor.

Euth. I hope that he may; but I rather fear, Socrates, that the opposite will turn out to be the truth. My opinion is that in attacking you he is simply aiming a blow at the foundation of the state. But in what way does he say that you corrupt the young?

Soc. He brings a wonderful accusation against me, which at first hearing excites surprise: he says that I am a poet or maker of gods, and that I invent new gods and deny the existence of old ones; this is the ground of his indictment.

Euth. I understand, Socrates; he means to attack you about the familiar sign which occasionally, as you say, comes to you. He thinks that you are a neologian, and he is going to have you up before the court for this. He knows that such a charge is readily received by the world, as I myself know too well; for when I speak in the assembly about divine things, and foretell the future to them, they laugh at me and think me a madman. Yet every word that I say is true. But they are jealous of us all; and we must be brave and go at them.

Soc. Their laughter, friend Euthyphro, is not a matter of much consequence. For a man may be thought wise; but the Athenians, I suspect, do not much trouble themselves about him until he begins to impart his wisdom to others, and then for some reason or other, perhaps, as you say, from jealousy, they are angry.

Euth. I am never likely to try their temper in this way.

Soc. I dare say not, for you are reserved in your behaviour, and seldom impart your wisdom. But I have a benevolent habit of pouring out myself to everybody, and would even pay for a listener, and I am afraid that the Athenians may think me too talkative. Now if, as I was saying, they would only laugh at me, as you say that they laugh at you, the time might pass gaily enough in the court; but perhaps they may be in earnest, and then what the end will be you soothsayers only can predict.

Euth. I dare say that the affair will end in nothing, Socrates, and that you will win your cause; and I think that I shall win my own.

Soc. And what is your suit, Euthyphro? are you the pursuer or the defendant?

Euth. I am the pursuer.

Soc. Of whom?

Euth. You will think me mad when I tell you.

Soc. Why, has the fugitive wings?

Euth. Nay, he is not very volatile at his time of life.

Soc. Who is he?

Euth. My father.

Soc. Your father! my good man?

Euth. Yes.

Soc. And of what is he accused?

Euth. Of murder, Socrates.

Soc. By the powers, Euthyphro! how little does the common herd know of the nature of right and truth. A man must be an extraordinary man, and have made great strides in wisdom, before he could have seen his way to bring such an action.

Euth. Indeed, Socrates, he must.

Soc. I suppose that the man whom your father murdered was one of your relatives—clearly he was; for if he had been a stranger you would never have thought of prosecuting him.

Euth. I am amused, Socrates, at your making a distinction between one who is a relation and one who is not a relation; for surely the pollution is the same in either case, if you knowingly associate with the murderer when you ought to clear yourself and him by proceeding against him. The real question is whether the murdered man has been justly slain. If justly, then your duty is to let the matter alone; but if unjustly, then even if the murderer lives under the same roof with you and eats at the same table, proceed against him. Now the man who is dead was a poor dependent of mine who worked for us as a field labourer on our farm in Naxos, and one day in a fit of drunken passion he got into a quarrel with one of our domestic servants and slew him. My father bound him hand and foot and threw him into a ditch, and then sent to Athens to ask of a diviner what he should do with him. Meanwhile he never attended to him and took no care about him, for he regarded him as a murderer; and thought that no great harm would be done even if he did die. Now this was just what happened. For such was the effect of cold and hunger and chains upon him, that before the messenger returned from the diviner, he was dead. And my father and family are angry with me for taking the part of the murderer and prosecuting my father. They say that he did not kill him, and that if he did, the dead man himself was but a murderer, and I ought not to take any notice, for that a son is impious who prosecutes a father. Which shows, Socrates, how little they know what the gods think about piety and impiety.

Soc. Good heavens, Euthyphro! and is your knowledge of religion and of things pious and impious so very exact, that, supposing the circumstances to be as you state them, you are not afraid lest you too may be doing an impious thing in bringing an action against your father?

Euth. The best of Euthyphro, and that which distinguishes him, Socrates, from other men, is his exact knowledge of all such matters. What should I be good for without it?

Soc. Rare friend! I think that I cannot do better than be your disciple. Then before the trial with Meletus comes on I shall challenge him, and say that I have always had a great interest in religious questions, and now, as he charges me with rash imaginations and innovations in religion, I have become your disciple. You, Meletus, as I shall say to him, acknowledge Euthyphro to be a great theologian, and sound in his opinions; and if you approve of him you ought to approve of me, and not have me into court; but if you disapprove, you should begin by indicting him who is my teacher, and who will be the ruin, not of the young, but of the old; that is to say, of myself whom he instructs, and of his old father whom he admonishes and chastises. And if Meletus refuses to listen to me, but will go on, and will not shift the indictment from me to you, I cannot do better than repeat this challenge in the court.

Euth. Yes, indeed, Socrates; and if he attempts to indict me I am mistaken if I do not find a flaw in him; the court shall have a great deal more to say to him than to me.

Soc. And I, my dear friend, knowing this, am desirous of becoming your disciple. For I observe that no one appears to notice you—not even this Meletus; but his sharp eyes have found me out at once, and he has indicted me for impiety. And therefore, I adjure you to tell me the nature of piety and impiety, which you said that you knew so well, and of murder, and of other offences against the gods. What are they? Is not piety in every action always the same? and impiety, again—is it not always the opposite of piety, and also the same with itself, having, as impiety, one notion which includes whatever is impious?

Euth. To be sure, Socrates.

Soc. And what is piety, and what is impiety?

Euth. Piety is doing as I am doing; that is to say, prosecuting any one who is guilty of murder, sacrilege, or of any similar crime—whether he be your father or mother, or whoever he may be—that makes no difference; and not to prosecute them is impiety. And please to consider, Socrates, what a notable proof I will give you of the truth of my words, a proof which I have already given to others:—of the principle, I mean, that the impious, whoever he may be, ought not to go unpunished. For do not men regard Zeus as the best and most righteous of the gods?—and yet they admit that he bound his father (Cronos) because he wickedly devoured his sons, and that he too had punished his own father (Uranus) for a similar reason, in a nameless manner. And yet when I proceed against my father, they are angry with me. So inconsistent are they in their way of talking when the gods are concerned, and when I am concerned.

Soc. May not this be the reason, Euthyphro, why I am charged with impiety—that I cannot always agree with these stories about the gods? And therefore I suppose that people think me wrong. But, as you who are well informed about them approve of them, I cannot do better than assent to your superior wisdom. What else can I say, confessing as I do, that I know nothing about them? Tell me, for the love of Zeus, whether you really believe that they are true.

Euth. Yes, Socrates; and things more wonderful still, of which the world is in ignorance.

Soc. And do you really believe that the gods, fought with one another, and had dire quarrels, battles, and the like, as the poets say, and as you may see represented in the works of great artists? The temples are full of them; and notably the robe of Athene, which is carried up to the Acropolis at the great Panathenaea, is embroidered with them. Are all these tales of the gods true, Euthyphro?

Euth. Yes, Socrates; and, as I was saying, I can tell you, if you would like to hear them, many other things about the gods which would quite amaze you.

Soc. I dare say; and you shall tell me them at some other time when I have leisure. But just at present I would rather hear from you a more precise answer, which you have not as yet given, my friend, to the question, What is "piety"? When asked, you only replied, doing as you do, charging your father with murder.

Euth. And what I said was true, Socrates.

Soc. No doubt, Euthyphro; but you would admit that there are many other pious acts?

Euth. There are.

Soc. Remember that I did not ask you to give me two or three examples of piety, but to explain the general idea which makes all pious things to be pious. Do you not recollect that there was one idea which made the impious impious, and the pious pious?

Euth. I remember.

Soc. Tell me what is the nature of this idea, and then I shall have a standard to which I may look, and by which I may measure actions, whether yours or those of any one else, and then I shall be able to say that such and such an action is pious, such another impious.

Euth. I will tell you, if you like.

Soc. I should very much like.

Euth. Piety, then, is that which is dear to the gods, and impiety is that which is not dear to them.

Soc. Very good, Euthyphro; you have now given me the sort of answer which I wanted. But whether what you say is true or not I cannot as yet tell, although I make no doubt that you will prove the truth of your words.

Euth. Of course.

Soc. Come, then, and let us examine what we are saying. That thing or person which is dear to the gods is pious, and that thing or person which is hateful to the gods is impious, these two being the extreme opposites of one another. Was not that said?

Euth. It was.

Soc. And well said?

Euth. Yes, Socrates, I thought so; it was certainly said.

Soc. And further, Euthyphro, the gods were admitted to have enmities and hatreds and differences?

Euth. Yes, that was also said.

Soc. And what sort of difference creates enmity and anger? Suppose for example that you and I, my good friend, differ about a number; do differences of this sort make us enemies and set us at variance with one another? Do we not go at once to arithmetic, and put an end to them by a sum?

Euth. True.

Soc. Or suppose that we differ about magnitudes, do we not quickly end the differences by measuring?

Euth. Very true.

Soc. And we end a controversy about heavy and light by resorting to a weighing machine?

Euth. To be sure.

Soc. But what differences are there which cannot be thus decided, and which therefore make us angry and set us at enmity with one another? I dare say the answer does not occur to you at the moment, and therefore I will suggest that these enmities arise when the matters of difference are the just and unjust, good and evil, honourable and dishonourable. Are not these the points about which men differ, and about which when we are unable satisfactorily to decide our differences, you and I and all of us quarrel, when we do quarrel?

Euth. Yes, Socrates, the nature of the differences about which we quarrel is such as you describe.

Soc. And the quarrels of the gods, noble Euthyphro, when they occur, are of a like nature?

Euth. Certainly they are.

Soc. They have differences of opinion, as you say, about good and evil, just and unjust, honourable and dishonourable: there would have been no quarrels among them, if there had been no such differences—would there now?

Euth. You are quite right.

Soc. Does not every man love that which he deems noble and just and good, and hate the opposite of them?
Euth. Very true.

Soc. But, as you say, people regard the same things, some as just and others as unjust,—about these they dispute; and so there arise wars and fightings among them.

Euth. Very true.

Soc. Then the same things are hated by the gods and loved by the gods, and are both hateful and dear to them?

Euth. True.

Soc. And upon this view the same things, Euthyphro, will be pious and also impious?

Euth. So I should suppose.

Soc. Then, my friend, I remark with surprise that you have not answered the question which I asked. For I certainly did not ask you to tell me what action is both pious and impious: but now it would seem that what is loved by the gods is also hated by them. And therefore, Euthyphro, in thus chastising your father you may very likely be doing what is agreeable to Zeus but disagreeable to Cronos or Uranus, and what is acceptable to Hephaestus but unacceptable to Hera, and there may be other gods who have similar differences of opinion.

Euth. But I believe, Socrates, that all the gods would be agreed as to the propriety of punishing a murderer: there would be no difference of opinion about that.

Soc. Well, but speaking of men, Euthyphro, did you ever hear any one arguing that a murderer or any sort of evil-doer ought to be let off?

Euth. I should rather say that these are the questions which they are always arguing, especially in courts of law: they commit all sorts of crimes, and there is nothing which they will not do or say in their own defence.

Soc. But do they admit their guilt, Euthyphro, and yet say that they ought not to be punished?

Euth. No; they do not.

Soc. Then there are some things which they do not venture to say and do: for they do not venture to argue that the guilty are to be unpunished, but they deny their guilt, do they not?

Euth. Yes.

Soc. Then they do not argue that the evil-doer should not be punished, but they argue about the fact of who the evil-doer is, and what he did and when?

Euth. True.

Soc. And the gods are in the same case, if as you assert they quarrel about just and unjust, and some of them say while others deny that injustice is done among them. For surely neither God nor man will ever venture to say that the doer of injustice is not to be punished?

Euth. That is true, Socrates, in the main.

Soc. But they join issue about the particulars—gods and men alike; and, if they dispute at all, they dispute about some act which is called in question, and which by some is affirmed to be just, by others to be unjust. Is not that true?

Euth. Quite true.

Soc. Well then, my dear friend Euthyphro, do tell me, for my better instruction and information, what proof have you that in the opinion of all the gods a servant who is guilty of murder, and is put in chains by the master of the dead man, and dies because he is put in chains before he who bound him can learn from the interpreters of the gods what he ought to do with him, dies unjustly; and that on behalf of such a one a son ought to proceed against his father and accuse him of murder. How would you show that all the gods absolutely agree in approving of his act? Prove to me that they do, and I will applaud your wisdom as long as I live.

Euth. It will be a difficult task; but I could make the matter very dear indeed to you.

Soc. I understand; you mean to say that I am not so quick of apprehension as the judges: for to them you will be sure to prove that the act is unjust, and hateful to the gods.

Euth. Yes indeed, Socrates; at least if they will listen to me.

Soc. But they will be sure to listen if they find that you are a good speaker. There was a notion that came into my mind while you were speaking; I said to myself: "Well, and what if Euthyphro does prove to me that all the gods regarded the death of the serf as unjust, how do I know anything more of the nature of piety and impiety? for granting that this action may be hateful to the gods, still piety and impiety are not adequately defined by these distinctions, for that which is hateful to the gods has been shown to be also pleasing and dear to them." And therefore, Euthyphro, I do not ask you to prove this; I will suppose, if you like, that all the gods condemn and abominate such an action. But I will amend the definition so far as to say that what all the gods hate is impious, and what they love pious or holy; and what some of them love and others hate is both or neither. Shall this be our definition of piety and impiety?

Euth. Why not, Socrates?

Soc. Why not! certainly, as far as I am concerned, Euthyphro, there is no reason why not. But whether this admission will greatly assist you in the task of instructing me as you promised, is a matter for you to consider.

Euth. Yes, I should say that what all the gods love is pious and holy, and the opposite which they all hate, impious.

Soc. Ought we to enquire into the truth of this, Euthyphro, or simply to accept the mere statement on our own authority and that of others? What do you say?

Euth. We should enquire; and I believe that the statement will stand the test of enquiry.

Soc. We shall know better, my good friend, in a little while. The point which I should first wish to understand is whether the pious or holy is beloved by the gods because it is holy, or holy because it is beloved of the gods.

Euth. I do not understand your meaning, Socrates.

Soc. I will endeavour to explain: we speak of carrying and we speak of being carried, of leading and being led, seeing and being seen. You know that in all such cases there is a difference, and you know also in what the difference lies?

Euth. I think that I understand.

Soc. And is not that which is beloved distinct from that which loves?

Euth. Certainly.

Soc. Well; and now tell me, is that which is carried in this state of carrying because it is carried, or for some other reason?

Euth. No; that is the reason.

Soc. And the same is true of what is led and of what is seen?

Euth. True.

Soc. And a thing is not seen because it is visible, but conversely, visible because it is seen; nor is a thing led because it is in the state of being led, or carried because it is in the state of being carried, but the converse of this. And now I think, Euthyphro, that my meaning will be intelligible; and my meaning is, that any state of action or passion implies previous action or passion. It does not become because it is becoming, but it is in a state of becoming because it becomes; neither does it suffer because it is in a state of suffering, but it is in a state of suffering because it suffers. Do you not agree?

Euth. Yes.

Soc. Is not that which is loved in some state either of becoming or suffering?

Euth. Yes.

Soc. And the same holds as in the previous instances; the state of being loved follows the act of being loved, and not the act the state.

Euth. Certainly.

Soc. And what do you say of piety, Euthyphro: is not piety, according to your definition, loved by all the gods?

Euth. Yes.

Soc. Because it is pious or holy, or for some other reason?

Euth. No, that is the reason.

Soc. It is loved because it is holy, not holy because it is loved?

Euth. Yes.

Soc. And that which is dear to the gods is loved by them, and is in a state to be loved of them because it is loved of them?

Euth. Certainly.

Soc. Then that which is dear to the gods, Euthyphro, is not holy, nor is that which is holy loved of God, as you affirm; but they are two different things.

Euth. How do you mean, Socrates?

Soc. I mean to say that the holy has been acknowledged by us to be loved of God because it is holy, not to be holy because it is loved.

Euth. Yes.

Soc. But that which is dear to the gods is dear to them because it is loved by them, not loved by them because it is dear to them.

Euth. True.

Soc. But, friend Euthyphro, if that which is holy is the same with that which is dear to God, and is loved because it is holy, then that which is dear to God would have been loved as being dear to God; but if that which is dear to God is dear to him because loved by him, then that which is holy would have been holy because loved by him. But now you see that the reverse is the case, and that they are quite different from one another. For one (theophiles) is of a kind to be loved because it is loved, and the other (osion) is loved because it is of a kind to be loved. Thus you appear to me, Euthyphro, when I ask you what is the essence of holiness, to offer an attribute only, and not the essence—the attribute of being loved by all the gods. But you still refuse to explain to me the nature of holiness. And therefore, if you please, I will ask you not to hide your treasure, but to tell me once more what holiness or piety really is, whether dear to the gods or not (for that is a matter about which we will not quarrel) and what is impiety?

Euth. I really do not know, Socrates, how to express what I mean. For somehow or other our arguments, on whatever ground we rest them, seem to turn round and walk away from us.

Soc. Your words, Euthyphro, are like the handiwork of my ancestor Daedalus; and if I were the sayer or propounder of them, you might say that my arguments walk away and will not remain fixed where they are placed because I am a descendant of his. But now, since these notions are your own, you must find some other gibe, for they certainly, as you yourself allow, show an inclination to be on the move.

Euth. Nay, Socrates, I shall still say that you are the Daedalus who sets arguments in motion; not I, certainly, but you make them move or go round, for they would never have stirred, as far as I am concerned.

Soc. Then I must be greater than Daedalus: for whereas he only made his own inventions to move, I move those of other people as well. And the beauty of it is, that I would rather not. For I would give the wisdom of Daedalus, and the wealth of Tantalus, to be able to detain them and keep them fixed. But enough of this. As I perceive that you are lazy, I will myself endeavor to show you how you might instruct me in the nature of piety; and I hope that you will not grudge your labour. Tell me, then—Is not that which is pious necessarily just?

Euth. Yes.

Soc. And is, then, all which is just pious? or, is that which is pious all just, but that which is just, only in part and not all, pious?

Euth. I do not understand you, Socrates.

Soc. And yet I know that you are as much wiser than I am, as you are younger. But, as I was saying, revered friend, the abundance of your wisdom makes you lazy. Please to exert yourself, for there is no real difficulty in understanding me. What I mean I may explain by an illustration of what I do not mean. The poet (Stasinus) sings—

> Of Zeus, the author and creator of all these things,
> You will not tell: for where there is fear there is also reverence.

Now I disagree with this poet. Shall I tell you in what respect?

Euth. By all means.

Soc. I should not say that where there is fear there is also reverence; for I am sure that many persons fear poverty and disease, and the like evils, but I do not perceive that they reverence the objects of their fear.

Euth. Very true.

Soc. But where reverence is, there is fear; for he who has a feeling of reverence and shame about the commission of any action, fears and is afraid of an ill reputation.

Euth. No doubt.

Soc. Then we are wrong in saying that where there is fear there is also reverence; and we should say, where there is reverence there is also fear. But there is not always reverence where there is fear; for fear is a more extended notion, and reverence is a part of fear, just as the odd is a part of number, and number is a more extended notion than the odd. I suppose that you follow me now?

Euth. Quite well.

Soc. That was the sort of question which I meant to raise when I asked whether the just is always the pious, or the pious always the just; and whether there may not be justice where there is not piety; for justice is the more extended notion of which piety is only a part. Do you dissent?

Euth. No, I think that you are quite right.

Soc. Then, if piety is a part of justice, I suppose that we should enquire what part? If you had pursued the enquiry in the previous cases; for instance, if you had asked me what is an even number, and what part of number the even is, I should have had no difficulty in replying, a number which represents a figure having two equal sides. Do you not agree?

Euth. Yes, I quite agree.

Soc. In like manner, I want you to tell me what part of justice is piety or holiness, that I may be able to tell Meletus not to do me injustice, or indict me for impiety, as I am now adequately instructed by you in the nature of piety or holiness, and their opposites.

Euth. Piety or holiness, Socrates, appears to me to be that part of justice which attends to the gods, as there is the other part of justice which attends to men.

Soc. That is good, Euthyphro; yet still there is a little point about which I should like to have further information. What is the meaning of "attention"? For attention can hardly be used in the same sense when applied to the gods as when applied to other things. For instance, horses are said to require attention, and not every person is able to attend to them, but only a person skilled in horsemanship. Is it not so?

Euth. Certainly.

Soc. I should suppose that the art of horsemanship is the art of attending to horses?

Euth. Yes.

Soc. Nor is every one qualified to attend to dogs, but only the huntsman?

Euth. True.

Soc. And I should also conceive that the art of the huntsman is the art of attending to dogs?

Euth. Yes.

Soc. As the art of the ox herd is the art of attending to oxen?

Euth. Very true.

Soc. In like manner holiness or piety is the art of attending to the gods?—that would be your meaning, Euthyphro?

Euth. Yes.

Soc. And is not attention always designed for the good or benefit of that to which the attention is given? As in the case of horses, you may observe that when attended to by the horseman's art they are benefited and improved, are they not?

Euth. True.

Soc. As the dogs are benefited by the huntsman's art, and the oxen by the art of the ox herd, and all other things are tended or attended for their good and not for their hurt?

Euth. Certainly, not for their hurt.

Soc. But for their good?

Euth. Of course.

Soc. And does piety or holiness, which has been defined to be the art of attending to the gods, benefit or improve them? Would you say that when you do a holy act you make any of the gods better?

Euth. No, no; that was certainly not what I meant.

Soc. And I, Euthyphro, never supposed that you did. I asked you the question about the nature of the attention, because I thought that you did not.

Euth. You do me justice, Socrates; that is not the sort of attention which I mean.

Soc. Good: but I must still ask what is this attention to the gods which is called piety?

Euth. It is such, Socrates, as servants show to their masters.

Soc. I understand—a sort of ministration to the gods.

Euth. Exactly.

Soc. Medicine is also a sort of ministration or service, having in view the attainment of some object—would you not say of health?

Euth. I should.

Soc. Again, there is an art which ministers to the ship—builder with a view to the attainment of some result?

Euth. Yes, Socrates, with a view to the building of a ship.

Soc. As there is an art which ministers to the housebuilder with a view to the building of a house?

Euth. Yes.

Soc. And now tell me, my good friend, about the art which ministers to the gods: what work does that help to accomplish? For you must surely know if, as you say, you are of all men living the one who is best instructed in religion.

Euth. And I speak the truth, Socrates.

Soc. Tell me then, oh tell me—what is that fair work which the gods do by the help of our ministrations?

Euth. Many and fair, Socrates, are the works which they do.

Soc. Why, my friend, and so are those of a general. But the chief of them is easily told. Would you not say that victory in war is the chief of them?

Euth. Certainly.

Soc. Many and fair, too, are the works of the husbandman, if I am not mistaken; but his chief work is the production of food from the earth?

Euth. Exactly.

Soc. And of the many and fair things done by the gods, which is the chief or principal one?

Euth. I have told you already, Socrates, that to learn all these things accurately will be very tiresome. Let me simply say that piety or holiness is learning how to please the gods in word and deed, by prayers and sacrifices. Such piety, is the salvation of families and states, just as the impious, which is unpleasing to the gods, is their ruin and destruction.

Soc. I think that you could have answered in much fewer words the chief question which I asked, Euthyphro, if you had chosen. But I see plainly that you are not disposed to instruct me—clearly not: else why, when we reached the point, did you turn aside? Had you only answered me I should have truly learned of you by this time the nature of piety. Now, as the asker of a question is necessarily dependent on the answerer, whither he leads I must follow; and can only ask again, what is the pious, and what is piety? Do you mean that they are a sort of science of praying and sacrificing?

Euth. Yes, I do.

Soc. And sacrificing is giving to the gods, and prayer is asking of the gods?

Euth. Yes, Socrates.

Soc. Upon this view, then piety is a science of asking and giving?

Euth. You understand me capitally, Socrates.

Soc. Yes, my friend; the reason is that I am a votary of your science, and give my mind to it, and therefore nothing which you say will be thrown away upon me. Please then to tell me, what is the nature of this service to the gods? Do you mean that we profer requests and give gifts to them?

Euth. Yes, I do.

Soc. Is not the right way of asking to ask of them what we want?

Euth. Certainly.

Soc. And the right way of giving is to give to them in return what they want of us. There would be no meaning in an art which gives to any one that which he does not want.

Euth. Very true, Socrates.

Soc. Then piety, Euthyphro, is an art which gods and men have of doing business with one another?

Euth. That is an expression which you may use, if you like.

Soc. But I have no particular liking for anything but the truth. I wish, however, that you would tell me what benefit accrues to the gods from our gifts. There is no doubt about what they give to us; for there is no good thing which they do not give; but how we can give any good thing to them in return is far from being equally clear. If they give everything and we give nothing, that must be an affair of business in which we have very greatly the advantage of them.

Euth. And do you imagine, Socrates, that any benefit accrues to the gods from our gifts?

Soc. But if not, Euthyphro, what is the meaning of gifts which are conferred by us upon the gods?

Euth. What else, but tributes of honour; and, as I was just now saying, what pleases them?

Soc. Piety, then, is pleasing to the gods, but not beneficial or dear to them?

Euth. I should say that nothing could be dearer.

Soc. Then once more the assertion is repeated that piety is dear to the gods?

Euth. Certainly.

Soc. And when you say this, can you wonder at your words not standing firm, but walking away? Will you accuse me of being the Daedalus who makes them walk away, not perceiving that there is another and far greater artist than Daedalus who makes them go round in a circle, and he is yourself; for the argument, as you will perceive, comes round to the same point. Were we not saying that the holy or pious was not the same with that which is loved of the gods? Have you forgotten?

Euth. I quite remember.

Soc. And are you not saying that what is loved of the gods is holy; and is not this the same as what is dear to them—do you see?

Euth. True.

Soc. Then either we were wrong in former assertion; or, if we were right then, we are wrong now.

Euth. One of the two must be true.

Soc. Then we must begin again and ask, "what is piety?" That is an enquiry which I shall never be weary of pursuing as far as in me lies; and I entreat you not to scorn me, but to apply your mind to the utmost, and tell me the truth. For, if any man knows, you are he; and therefore I must detain you, like Proteus, until you tell. If you had not certainly known the nature of piety and impiety, I am confident that you would never, on behalf of a serf, have charged your aged father with murder. You would not have run such a risk of doing wrong in the sight of the gods, and you would have had too much respect for the opinions of men. I am sure, therefore, that you know the nature of piety and impiety. Speak out then, my dear Euthyphro, and do not hide your knowledge.

Euth. Another time, Socrates; for I am in a hurry, and must go now.

Soc. Alas! my companion, and will you leave me in despair? I was hoping that you would instruct me in the nature of piety and impiety; and then I might have cleared myself of Meletus and his indictment. I would have told him that I had been enlightened by Euthyphro, and had given up rash innovations and speculations, in which I indulged only through ignorance, and that now I am about to lead a better life.

DIVINE COMMAND THEORY
IN PLATO'S *EUTHYPHRO*

By Thomas Brickhouse and Nicholas Smith

The divine command theory of ethics introduced

In fact, it is not at all uncommon for monotheistic religious people to think that the very standard which Socrates and Euthyphro seek can be given in a formula philosophers call "the divine command theory of ethics." The precise formulation of this theory can be a matter of serious dispute among those inclined to it, but for our purposes a rather generic one will probably work best:

Divine command theory: Good (or goodness) is whatever is commanded (or recommended, or prescribed) by God.

Notice that this theory would not be significantly changed if we imagined it situated within a polytheism that supposed the gods all and always agreed on what they should command, recommend, or prescribe. But whether or not we situate this idea within such a polytheism or—as we encounter it more familiarly these days—in a monotheism, how does this do providing just the kind of reliable and objective standard Socrates and Euthyphro are trying to articulate?

In one way, Socrates and Euthyphro implicitly confront one problem with this conception of the ethical standard that most philosophers would notice first. Even if we ignore challenges to the theory from those who doubt the existence of God (or the gods), one obvious problem with the divine command theory of ethics is that we must first determine exactly what the god or gods to which the account refers actually do command, recommend, or prescribe. Contemporary monotheisms include many different sects of Judaism, Christianity, and Islam and there can be very sharp (even deadly) disputes among different sects of each of these general religions. So, even though the faithful among any one sect of any one religion might feel confident that their own is "the one true way," others of us—even if we are generally inclined to be religious—might feel some very real doubt as to which religion and which sect actually understands God's commands, recommendations, or prescriptions in exactly the right way. Now, it might seem as if Socrates and Euthyphro shouldn't have to face this same kind of problem, given that they are situated within the same culture. But as Socrates' reactions to Euthyphro's conceptions of the gods shows, even within the same culture there can be no presumption that the exact same beliefs about the gods and their preferences apply. So at the very least, the divine command theory of ethics must confront a serious problem of discerning what divine preferences or commands really are, or the formula it provides for determining what is good will be entirely useless.

Socrates' argument about piety and being loved by the gods (10a1–11b5)

This is not, however, the problem that Socrates identifies with this theory. Instead, Socrates shows that there is something inherently wrong with the divine command theory of ethics, and his objection against it works whether or not we attempt to situate the theory within a monotheistic or a polytheistic context— which is why this argument has become such a famous one in the history of philosophy. Once Euthyphro has plainly affirmed the new account, that piety is what all the gods love and impiety is what all the gods hate, Socrates asks a very subtle question: "Is the pious loved by the gods because it is pious, or is it pious because it is loved?" (10a2–3). At first, Euthyphro is puzzled by the question—he certainly does not recognize its importance to his view. But as Socrates eventually shows, the answer one gives to this question makes all the difference in the world. So let's go through Socrates' argument in stages. Socrates first begins to explain his important question by getting Euthyphro to get clear on the relationship between a thing's being loved by the gods and the gods loving it. The way in which Socrates establishes this relationship can seem quite confusing, however, so it will help if we consider an example of one of the general sort that Socrates gives. Socrates gives the examples of being carried, being led, and being seen (10a5–c5), but let's stick just to an example of carrying and being carried. Suppose we notice Mary carrying a telephone book. When we say that something is what it is, or is the way that it is, because of something else, we give an answer to a "why" question. Suppose we want to explain what it is that makes the telephone book a carried thing. So we might ask the "why" question, "Why is that telephone book a carried thing?" The answer seems straightforward: "That telephone book is a carried thing because Mary is carrying it." But now suppose we wanted to ask the "why" question about Mary carrying the telephone book: "Why is Mary carrying the telephone book?" What would we make of this answer: "Mary is carrying the telephone book because the telephone book is a carried thing"? Plainly, that can't be right. To answer the "why" question about Mary's carrying the telephone book we will need to know something more about Mary: what are her intentions, what is her goal, in carrying that telephone book? But even though the telephone book is certainly a carried thing, its being a carried thing is the *result* of Mary's acting on her intentions or goals—and not the explanation *for* Mary's actions, intentions, or goals. So the explanatory relationship between being a carried thing and carrying something only goes one way—we can explain being a carried thing in virtue of something or someone carrying it, but we cannot explain the carrying that *makes* it a carried thing in virtue of that thing *being* a carried thing. So, just as Socrates puts it to Euthyphro, it is never the case that someone's carrying something will be *because* it is carried by them—that, as it were, gets the explanatory "cart before the horse;" it will, however, always be the case that something is a carried thing *because* something or someone carries that thing.

So, in making this point to Euthyphro, Socrates is trying to allow Euthyphro to get clearer on what it means to say that something is what it is or the way it is *because* of something else. Well, then, in the case of loving and being a loved thing, something is a loved thing because something or someone loves that thing. In this case, what is loved by the gods is a loved-by-the-gods thing because the gods love it. But we cannot explain why the gods love it by saying that it is a loved-by-the-gods thing. Now, here is how Euthyphro stated his most recent explanation of what piety is:

> I'd say that the pious is what all of the gods love, and the opposite of this, what all of the gods hate, is the impious.
>
> (9e1–3)

It was this formulation of Euthyphro's position that led Socrates to ask whether it is loved because it is pious or pious because it is loved. The way this works with the earlier discussion should now be easier to see. What is pious is loved by the gods; so being pious is a loved thing. What is pious is a loved-by-the-gods thing *because* it is loved by the gods—it is not loved by the gods *because* it is a loved-by-the-gods thing. The question we must ask now is the "why" question: *why* do the gods love what is pious?

Now, it appears that to this question, there are three general possibilities:

1. The gods love what is pious *because* it is pious.
2. The gods love what is pious for no reason at all.
3. The gods love what is pious for some reason other than that it is pious.

When Socrates asks the "why" question (at 10d4), Euthyphro gives the first of the three possible answers: the gods love what is pious because it is pious (10d5). But this answer is ruinous to his earlier explanation of what piety is, because it shows that his earlier explanation gets the explanatory relationship between piety and being loved by the gods wrong. Recall that explanatory relationships are *one-way* relationships: if what explains the gods' loving what is pious is the piety of what is pious, then the gods' loving what is pious cannot be what explains the piety of what is pious. What makes something pious cannot be the fact that the gods love it—for it is the thing's being pious that makes it lovable to the gods in the first place. If it weren't pious, they wouldn't love it. So what makes it pious cannot be their loving it, since their loving it is the *result*—and not the explanation—of its being pious. So, if we think—as Euthyphro does—that the gods love what is pious *because* it is pious, then we cannot explain piety in terms of something's being loved by the gods. This is why Socrates scolds Euthyphro at the end of the argument for not explaining what piety is (11a6–b1).

It might occur to us at this point to wonder what would have happened if Euthyphro had chosen some other answer when Socrates asked him why the gods love what is pious (at 10d4). So let us try out each of the other two possible answers. Suppose Euthyphro gave answer (2): the gods love what is pious for no reason at all. If this were true, then there would be in principle no explanation for why the gods love what it pious. There wouldn't be *anything at all* about what is pious that *made* it lovable to the gods, and the *fact* that it is pious would be irrelevant to their loving it. But this raises an obvious problem: if the fact that what is pious *is* pious is irrelevant to why the gods love what is pious (and the fact that what is impious *is* impious is irrelevant to why the gods hate what is impious), then how could it be that the gods all agree about loving what is pious and hating what is impious? Why would there be such a complete unanimity and convergence among the gods about what they love and hate? Answer (2) insists that there is simply *no reason at all* for this! The gods love and hate things for absolutely no reason—they just do it. Of course, if this were true, their loves and hates would be completely senseless! Obviously, this is not at all what a serious theist who takes divine preferences to be reliable moral guides wants to say.

The third answer raises other problems. If the gods love what is pious for some reason *other* that its being pious, then the piety of the thing is really irrelevant to its being loved by the gods. But if so, then there is something fundamentally misleading even in saying that the gods love what is pious. To see this, imagine that John loves Barbara. On a whim, Barbara decides to dye her hair green. Now, if Barbara asked John about his preferences, let's imagine that John would say that he preferred her hair its natural color. But because he really loves Barbara so much, he also loves her hair no matter what color it is. Now, imagine further that many of Barbara's friends are actually quite vocal in disliking her new hair color, and—feeling somewhat defensive, Barbara tells her critical friends, "Well, John loves my green hair!" What do we say about Barbara's claim?

Even though it is technically true that John loves Barbara's green hair, to anyone interested in the question of whether her green hair is attractive or not, John's reaction, plainly, is entirely irrelevant. Indeed, if anything, John's actual judgment of the greenness of Barbara's hair is (however mildly, given his love for Barbara) actually negative. Anyone who knew this could quite rightly object to Barbara's claim by saying, "Look, Barbara, John loves your green hair only because it is *your* hair. He would love it any color at all, and so his loving it has nothing whatever to do with its being green. So don't try to fool us by saying that he loves it—he doesn't! In fact, he would prefer it if you did what we are telling you to do and put it back to your natural color!"

If the gods love what is pious, but it is not the piety of what is pious that they find lovable in what is pious, then *saying* that the gods love what is pious is just as misleading as Barbara's claim that John loves her green hair. The idea is that the piety of what is pious is completely irrelevant to why the gods love it, and so there is only an accidental connection between something's being pious and its being loved by the gods. To one who thinks that there is any *real* or *significant* connection between piety and something's being loved by the gods, this is an unacceptable consequence.

So when Euthyphro answers that the gods love what is pious *because* it is pious, he actually makes a very good—indeed, the only sensible—choice, given the options. But, again, this very choice shows that the explanation of piety Euthyphro offered—as what is loved by (all) the gods—is a failure. It fails because the actual explanation must go the other way around: the gods love what is pious *because* it is pious; but this means that it cannot be pious *because* the gods love it.

The applicability of Socrates' argument to monotheistic divine command theory

Once we understand how Socrates' argument works against Euthyphro's latest proposed account of piety, we can also see why this argument is so decisive against divine command theory even when it is applied to a conception of moral value in relation to a single god. The divine command theory of ethics, again, holds that the way to understand what moral goodness is, is to explain it in terms of whatever God commands (recommends, prescribes). Of one who might be attracted to such a theory, we can imagine Socrates asking, "Well, then, does God command such things because they are good, or are they good because God commands them?"

Now, the same sorts of options apply in response to this question as those Euthyphro faced:

1. God commands what He does *because* it is good.
2. God commands what He does for no reason at all.
3. God commands what He does for some reason other than that it is good.

If we are inclined to think that option (1) is the correct answer to such a Socratic question, we must admit that the divine command theory is thereby defeated: if whatever God commands is commanded by God because it is good, then its goodness is the explanation of *why* God commands it and that goodness thus cannot be explained *by* God's commanding it. It has to be good *in order* for God to command it—it doesn't *become* good by *being* commanded!

Think of it this way: if you go to the store to buy some bread, then your intention to buy bread explains your going to the store. If someone then asks, "Well, why did you buy the bread?" you can't then answer, "Well, because I went to the store!" This gets the explanation wrong. You didn't buy the bread because you went to the store—as if you went to the store for no reason and then, when there, it occurred to you to buy some bread; you went to that store for that purpose, to buy the bread. So you can't say that you bought the bread because you went to the store—it's the other way around: you went to the store because you wanted to buy some bread. So, similarly, if God commands something because it is good, then its goodness explains the command and not vice versa. But divine command theory holds that the explanation goes the other way around: it is good *because* God commands it.

Now suppose you still find yourself attracted to the divine command theory, but you understand that option (1) defeats your view, so you decide to defend the explanation the other way around: it is good, you claim, because God commands it. So now Socrates asks, "OK, then, why does God command it?" and now you must give one of the other two answers:

1. God commands what He does for no reason at all.
2. God commands what He does for some reason other than that it is good.

It is probably already obvious why these are not going to be satisfactory replies to such a question, but just to be very clear let us look at each one in order. Suppose (2) is your answer. This answer means that God's commands are inherently arbitrary and whimsical. God has no reason whatsoever for doing things one way or another. (Imagine God thinking about what to command, or even whether to command anything, and settling on what to command just by flipping coins.) Moreover, because God is fully in control of what is commanded (they are *God's* commands, after all!), God can decide to change commands from day to day or even minute to minute. Maybe it gets boring where God is, and so changing commands is a way to keep things interesting. "*Thou shalt not kill!* Oh! Wait a minute! It's Friday, isn't it? Oh, well, then, for today, *Thou shalt kill!* On second thought, we did that last Friday. This Friday, let's make it, *Thou shalt commit adultery.*" It really doesn't make any difference to *God* what is commanded, after all, since there is no reason for God to make any one command over another: nothing is good or bad, according to this account, except when (and only when, and then because) God commands it. "*Thou shalt burn and torture small children until I change my mind!*" Obviously, this would make God into a very irrational being, and would leave the moral order a matter of simple (albeit divine) whim.

And suppose we now ask, all right, by the divine command theory, things are good *because* God commands them. So, "good" just means "commanded by God." But now let's ask, *why* should we obey these commands? If the answer is that we should obey them because God commands them, we might ask, but what is it about God that deserves our obedience? Theists (or monotheists, at any rate) generally believe that God is a good being, even a perfect being. But consider what it means to call God good if the divine command theory were correct: "God is good" now means just that God commands you to say (or believe) that God is good; that's all. Of course, *any* being powerful enough to enforce its will over mere human beings might make such a command, but why should we accept it? Satan might make some command of this sort, but should we believe it—or if Satan commands us, should we obey, and if so why—or if not, why not? Notice that if we are committed to the divine command theory of ethics, we can't say that we should accept God's command to say (or believe) that God is good, because that's the good thing to do. If we should accept God's commands *because* they are good, we obviously are back to the first option again—the commands aren't good *because* God commands them; God commands them *because* they are good. Similarly, Satan's commands aren't good (or bad) because Satan commands them. We should not obey Satan's commands because *Satan* is bad. But Satan isn't bad simply because someone (or something) *says* Satan is bad—even God! If God says that Satan is bad, it is because Satan *is* bad. So, again, the goodness or badness of things explains why God commands what God commands, and not the other way around.

But we haven't yet considered option (3). Might it not be that God commands what He does for some reason other than that it is good? Now here we have two options: either (A) God commands only good things, or (B) God commands some things that are good and some that are bad. Obviously, if (B) is the case, then the divine command theory cannot be correct—if God commands some bad things, then it can't be that goodness *just is* whatever God commands! What if (A) is the case? Well, if God commands only good things, but God commands them for some reason other than that they are good, then we should suppose that God commands them because this other reason is what makes things good. Suppose, for example, that God commands things because they are conducive to the survival and flourishing of living things. Well, then, *this* is what makes things good—this is *why* things are good—and God knows this, and that's why God makes commands. But that shows that the divine command theory is wrong—after all, in this or any other version of option (3) in which God commands only good things, it is not, after all, God's commanding something that makes that thing good—it is, rather, that God commands it because it is conducive to the survival and flourishing of living things. And if *that* is what makes things good, then notice their goodness *does not depend* upon God's commanding them, but the other way around: God's commanding them depends on what makes things good (namely, the survival or flourishing of living things—or whatever else it might be that makes things good, which God recognizes). One way or another, then, divine command theory is shown to get the explanation of moral value (or any specific moral value, such a piety) exactly backwards: God commands (or loves) things *because* they are good (or pious), or else because of whatever it is that makes them good or pious; they are not good (or pious) just because God commands (or loves) them.

PROSLOGION

By Anselm

CHAPTER II.

Truly there is a God, although the fool has said in his heart, There is no God.

AND so, Lord, do you, who do give understanding to faith, give me, so far as you knowest it to be profitable, to understand that you are as we believe; and that you are that which we believe. And indeed, we believe that you are a being than which nothing greater can be conceived. Or is there no such nature, since the fool has said in his heart, there is no God? (Psalms xiv. 1). But, at any rate, this very fool, when he hears of this being of which I speak—a being than which nothing greater can be conceived—understands what he hears, and what he understands is in his understanding; although he does not understand it to exist.

For, it is one thing for an object to be in the understanding, and another to understand that the object exists. When a painter first conceives of what he will afterwards perform, he has it in his understanding, but be does not yet understand it to be, because he has not yet performed it. But after he has made the painting, he both has it in his understanding, and he understands that it exists, because he has made it.

Hence, even the fool is convinced that something exists in the understanding, at least, than which nothing greater can be conceived. For, when he hears of this, he understands it. And whatever is understood, exists in the understanding. And assuredly that, than which nothing greater can be conceived, cannot exist in the understanding alone. For, suppose it exists in the understanding alone: then it can be conceived to exist in reality; which is greater.

Therefore, if that, than which nothing greater can be conceived, exists in the understanding alone, the very being, than which nothing greater can be conceived, is one, than which a greater can be conceived. But obviously this is impossible. Hence, there is doubt that there exists a being, than which nothing greater can be conceived, and it exists both in the understanding and in reality.

CHAPTER III.

God cannot be conceived not to exist. God is that than which nothing greater can be conceived. That which can be conceived not to exist is not God.

AND it assuredly exists so truly, that it cannot be conceived not to exist. For, it is possible to conceive of a being which cannot be conceived not to exist; and this is greater than one which can be conceived not to exist. Hence, if that, than which nothing greater can be conceived, can be conceived not to exist, it is not that, than which nothing greater can be conceived. But this is an irreconcilable contradiction. There is, then, so truly a being than which nothing greater can be conceived to exist, that it cannot even be conceived not to exist; and this being you are, O Lord, our God.

So truly, therefore, do you exist, O Lord, my God, that you can not be conceived not to exist; and rightly. For, if a mind could conceive of a being better than you, the creature would rise above the Creator; and this is most absurd. And, indeed, whatever else there is, except you alone, can be conceived not to exist. To you alone, therefore, it belongs to exist more truly than all other beings, and hence in a higher degree than all others. For, whatever else exists does not exist so truly, and hence in a less degree it belongs to it to exist. Why, then, has the fool said in his heart, there is no God (Psalms xiv. 1), since it is so evident, to a rational mind, that you do exist in the highest degree of all? Why, except that he is dull and a fool?

CHAPTER IV.

How the fool has said in his heart what cannot be conceived. A thing may be conceived in two ways: (1) when the word signifying it is conceived; (2) when the thing itself is understood. As far as the word goes, God can be conceived not to exist; in reality he cannot.

BUT how has the fool said in his heart what he could not conceive; or how is it that he could not conceive what he said in his heart, since it is the same to say in the heart and to conceive.

But, if really, nay, since really, he both conceived, because he said in his heart; and did not say in his heart, because he could not conceive; there is more than one way in which a thing is said in the heart or conceived.

For, in one sense, an object is conceived, when the word signifying it is conceived; and in another, when the very entity, which the object is, is understood.

In the former sense, then, God can be conceived not to exist; but in the latter, not at all. For no one who understands what fire and water are can conceive fire to be water, in accordance with the nature of the facts themselves, although this is possible according to the words. So, then, no one who understands what God is can conceive that God does not exist; although he says these words in his heart, either without any or with some foreign, signification. For, God is that than which a greater cannot be conceived. And he who thoroughly understands this, assuredly understands that this being so truly exists, that not even in concept can it be non-existent. Therefore, he who understands that God so exists, cannot conceive that he does not exist.

I thank you, gracious Lord, I thank you; because what I formerly believed by your bounty, I now so understand by your illumination, that if I were unwilling to believe that you do exist, I should not be able not to understand this to be true.

CHAPTER V.

God is whatever it is better to be than not to be; and he, as the only self-existent being, creates all things from nothing.

WHAT are you, then, Lord God, than whom nothing greater can be conceived? But what are you, except that which, as the highest of all beings, alone exists through itself, and creates all other things from nothing? For, whatever is not this is less than a thing which can be conceived of. But this cannot be conceived of you. What good, therefore, does the supreme Good lack, through which every good is? Therefore, you are just, truthful, blessed, and whatever it is better to be than not to be. For it is better to be just than not just; better to be blessed than not blessed.

IN BEHALF OF THE FOOL, WITH ANSELM'S REPLY

By Gaunilo
Trans. by Sidney Norton Deane

But that this being must exist, not only in the understanding but also in reality, is thus proved to me:
    If it did not so exist, whatever exists in reality would be greater than it. And so the being which has been already proved to exist in my understanding, will not be greater than all other beings.

I still answer: if it should be said that a being which cannot be even conceived in terms of any fact, is in the understanding, I do not deny that this being is, accordingly, in my understanding. But since through this fact it can in no wise attain to real existence also, I do not yet concede to it that existence at all, until some certain proof of it shall be given.

For he who says that this being exists, because otherwise the being which is greater than all will not be greater than all, does not attend strictly enough to what he is saying. For I do not yet say, no, I even deny or doubt that this being is greater than any real object. Nor do I concede to it any other existence than this (if it should be called existence) which it has when the mind, according to a word merely heard, tries to form the image of an object absolutely unknown to it.

How, then, is the veritable existence of that being proved to me from the assumption, by hypothesis, that it is greater than all other beings? For I should still deny this, or doubt your demonstration of it, to this extent, that I should not admit that this being is in my understanding and concept even in the way in which many objects whose real existence is uncertain and doubtful, are in my understanding and concept.

For it should be proved first that this being itself really exists somewhere; and then, from the fact that it is greater than all, we shall not hesitate to infer that it also subsists in itself.

For example: it is said that somewhere in the ocean is an island, which, because of the difficulty, or rather the impossibility, of discovering what does not exist, is called the lost island. And they say that this island has an inestimable wealth of all manner of riches and delicacies in greater abundance than is told of the Islands of the Blest; and that having no owner or inhabitant, it is more excellent than all other countries, which are inhabited by mankind, in the abundance with which it is stored.

Now if someone should tell me that there is such an island, I should easily understand his words, in which there is no difficulty. But suppose that he went on to say, as if by a logical inference: "You can no longer doubt that this island which is more excellent than all lands exists somewhere, since you have no doubt that it is in your understanding. And since it is more excellent not to be in the understanding alone, but to exist both in the understanding and in reality, for this reason it must exist. For if it does not exist, any land which really exists will be more excellent than it; and so the island already understood by you to be more excellent will not be more excellent."

If a man should try to prove to me by such reasoning that this island truly exists, and that its existence should no longer be doubted, either I should believe that he was jesting, or I know not which I ought to regard as the greater fool: myself, supposing that I should allow this proof; or him, if he should suppose that he had established with any certainty the existence of this island. For he ought to show first that the hypothetical excellence of this island exists as a real and indubitable fact, and in no wise as any unreal object, or one whose existence is uncertain, in my understanding.

Anselm's reply to Gaunilo

CHAPTER II

The argument is continued. It is shown that a being than which a greater is inconceivable can be conceived, and also, in so far, exists.

I have said that if it [the being than which none greater can be conceived] is even in the understanding alone, it can be conceived also to exist in reality, which is greater. If, then, it is in the understanding alone, obviously the very being than which greater cannot be conceived is one than which a greater can be conceived. What is more logical? For if it exists even in the understanding alone, can it not be conceived also to exist in reality? And if it can be so conceived, does not he who conceives of this conceive of a thing greater than that being, if it exists in the understanding alone? What more consistent inference, then, can be made than this: that if a being than which a greater cannot be conceived is in the understanding alone, it is not that than which a greater cannot be conceived?

But, assuredly, in no understanding is a being than which a greater is conceivable a being than which a greater is inconceivable. Does it not follow, then, that if a being than which a greater cannot be conceived is in any understanding, it does not exist in the understanding alone? For if it is in the understanding alone, it is a being than which a greater can be conceived, which is inconsistent with the hypothesis.

CHAPTER III.

A criticism of Gaunilo's example, in which he tries to show that in this way the real existence of a lost island might be inferred from the fact of its being conceived.

But, you say, it is as if one should suppose an island in the ocean, which surpasses all lands in its fertility, and which, because of the difficulty, or the impossibility, of discovering what does not exist, is called a lost island; and should say that there be no doubt that this island truly exists in reality, for this reason, that one who hears it described easily understands what he hears.

Now I promise confidently that if any man shall devise anything existing either in reality or in concept alone (except that than which a greater be conceived) to which he can adapt the sequence of my reasoning, I will discover that thing, and will give him his lost island, not to be lost again.

But it now appears that this being than which a greater is inconceivable cannot be conceived not to be, because it exists on so assured a ground of truth; for otherwise it would not exist at all.

Hence, if any one says that he conceives this being not to exist, I say that at the time when he conceives of this either he conceives of a being than which a greater is inconceivable, or he does not conceive at all. If he does not conceive, he does not conceive of the non-existence of that of which he does not conceive. But if he does conceive, he certainly conceives of a being which cannot be even conceived not to exist. For if it could be conceived not to exist, it could be conceived to have a beginning and an end. But this is impossible.

He, then, who conceives of this being conceives of a being which cannot be even conceived not to exist; but he who conceives of this being does not conceive that it does not exist; else he conceives what is inconceivable. The non-existence, then, of that than which a greater cannot be conceived is inconceivable.

THE ONTOLOGICAL ARGUMENT

By Nicholas Everitt

When considered generally and impartially, this famous ontological proof is really a most delightful farce.

(Schopenhauer, *On the Fourfold Root of the Principle of Sufficient Reason*)

INTRODUCTION

We can begin our consideration of arguments for God's existence with the first of three large groups of arguments (the ontological, the cosmological and the teleological) which have gained a sort of classic status as arguments for God's existence. Just as Aquinas's Five Ways were once thought of as one significant cluster of arguments, so are these three. But there is only a historical reason for this. They are not as a group obviously any stronger than other arguments and there is no reason for separating them out for special treatment. The only reason that they are treated as a triumvirate is that Kant declared in his discussion of God's existence that they constituted the only three possible proofs for the existence of God (he did not include his own attempted proof from morality).

Of the three classic proofs, the ontological is in several ways the most peculiar. It would probably be true to say that of the purported proofs that we will consider, all but this one have functioned for at least some theists as the factor that initially convinced them of the intellectual defensibility of theism.

No doubt many people accept one or more of the arguments *after* they have already come to accept the existence of God. The arguments then function for them as a post hoc justification for what they already believe—and they are none the worse for that. But nevertheless for *some* people, the arguments probably function as what initially persuades them of the truth of theism. But it seems unlikely that the same could be said of the ontological argument: it is difficult to believe that anyone has been converted to theism simply by studying the ontological argument.

An ontological argument is typically one which starts from the mere idea or concept or notion of God, and, simply by examining the content of this idea, seeks to infer the existence of God. It thus proceeds wholly a priori, not using as a premise any assumptions about the existence or nature of the contingent universe or of its contents. And typically, the conclusion of the argument is not merely that God exists, but that he exists *necessarily*—that is to say, he not only does exist, he could not have failed to exist.

Overall, the argument has had a rather bad press philosophically. It was first propounded by St Anselm, an eleventh-century Archbishop of Canterbury. In the thirteenth century, it was rejected by St Thomas Aquinas. A different version of it was revived in the seventeenth century by Descartes, and different versions again were endorsed by Spinoza and by Leibniz. It was heavily and some would say conclusively criticised in the eighteenth century by Hume and Kant, attacks which were strengthened by the writings of Frege in the nineteenth century (although he did not discuss the ontological argument as such). In the twentieth century, it has had some able supporters, such as Norman Malcolm, Alvin Plantinga and Charles Hartshorne. But the balance of modern philosophical opinion would be heavily weighted against the argument, and the main dispute centres not on *whether* the argument fails, but on *where and how* it fails.

ANSELM'S VERSION

Anselm starts off with what he treats as a definition of God. He says that God is a being than which none greater can be thought. He does not tell us explicitly what he means by greatness, but we can take it that he is drawing on a Christian tradition which sees God as being the greatest in terms of knowledge, greatest in terms of power, greatest in terms of goodness, and so on. It is in this sense that God is a being than which a greater cannot be thought. Anselm now identifies his opponent with the fool mentioned in Psalms 14: 1 ('The fool has said in his heart "There is no God"'), and he continues as follows:

> When this same Fool hears what I am speaking about, namely 'something-than-which-no thing-greater-can-be-thought', he understands what he hears, and what he understands is in his mind, even if he does not understand that it actually exists. Even the Fool, then, is forced to agree that something-than-which-nothing-greater-can-be-thought exists in the

mind, since he understands this when he hears it, and whatever is understood is in the mind. And surely that-than-which-a-greater-cannot-be-thought cannot exist in the mind alone. For if it exists solely in the mind, it can be thought to exist in reality also, which is greater. If then that-than-which-nothing-greater-can-be-thought exists in the mind alone, this same that-than-which-a-greater-*cannot*-be-thought is that-than-which-a-greater-*can*-be-thought. But this is obviously impossible. Therefore there is absolutely no doubt that something-than-which-a-greater-cannot-be-thought exists both in the mind and in reality.

(Anselm 1998: 87–8)

The argument thus suggests that prima facie we might think that we can distinguish between the idea of God on the one hand, and God's reality on the other. After all, in general, we can distinguish between our ideas of things and the things themselves, and we know that in some cases there are no real things corresponding to our ideas. We can, for example, have the idea of unicorns and dragons, faster-than-light rockets and perpetual motion machines, although no such things exist. Why can't the atheist in a similar way agree that he has the idea of God but deny that there is a really existing God who corresponds to this idea?

Anselm's claim is that in the case of God, the idea and the reality *must* go hand in hand: the very content of the idea entails that God really exists. For, if we try to imagine a situation in which the idea exists but God does not, it would turn out that it was not the idea *of God* which we were thinking of. Given, then, that both the atheistical fool and the theist are contemplating the same idea (as they must be if the fool is to deny what the theist asserts), it follows that willy-nilly the fool *is* committed to the existence of God.

We can summarise the argument more formally as follows:

1. When the fool hears 'A being-than-which … etc.', he understands it (premise, which must be granted by a fool who tries to deny that there is such a being).
2. Whatever is understood is in the mind (premise—true by definition). So:
3. When the fool hears 'A being-than-which … etc.,' such a being exists at least in his mind (from (1) and (2)).
4. If 'A being-than-which … etc.' existed only in the fool's mind, it could also be thought of as existing in reality as well, and this is greater (premise). So:
5. If 'A being-than-which … etc.' existed only in the fool's mind, it would not after all be 'A being-than-which … etc.' (from (4)). So:
6. 'A being-than-which … etc.' cannot exist only in the mind (from (5)). So:
7. 'A being-than-which … etc.' exists both in the mind and in reality (from (6)).

Anselm's argument was famously criticised by one of his contemporaries, the monk Gaunilo, who produced what is usually called the 'lost island' objection. Gaunilo said that if Anselm's argument succeeded in proving the existence of God, a parallel argument would prove the existence of a perfect island, full of every conceivable delight. For we understand what is meant by speaking of such an island, so the island exists at least in our understanding. But if the island existed only in our understanding, we could think of such an island as existing in reality, and that would be better still. So this most marvellous island cannot exist only in our understanding but must exist in reality as well. Now, says Gaunilo, we can see that this 'lost island' argument does not really prove the existence of a perfect island, and since it has exactly the same structure as Anselm's argument for God, it follows that Anselm's argument is a failure too. (For a text of Gaunilo's objection, see Anselm 1998: 105–10; Davies 1993: 60; or Plantinga 1974: 89.)

One of the twentieth-century defenders of the ontological argument, Plantinga, has argued that Gaunilo's objection fails—and by implication that all similar attempts at reductio ad absurdum refutations of Anselm will likewise fail. Plantinga argues that the concept of a most perfect island is impossible. The very concept is self-contradictory, and hence no argument could succeed in proving the existence of such an island. The reason that the concept is self-contradictory is this: whatever features contribute to the perfection of an island (Plantinga suggests Nubian maidens, dancing girls, palm trees and coconuts), it is always possible to imagine an island with twice as many, and *that* island would be more perfect than the one we originally thought of (Plantinga 1977: 91). By contrast, there *is* an intrinsic maximum to the qualities in terms of which God is normally defined (knowledge, power, goodness). For once we have imagined a being who knows everything, can do *anything*, etc., we cannot imagine another being who has those powers to a higher degree.

But this objection to Gaunilo seems less than compelling. Given an island with a certain degree of F, where F is some desirable feature, there is no reason to accept that an island with twice as much would be any better. You *can* have too much of a good thing—and Plantinga's own examples neatly illustrate this. Even if we grant that an abundance of coconuts contributes to the perfection of an island, we cannot assume that doubling and redoubling repeatedly the number of coconuts would keep improving the island. Clearly there would come a point where the superabundance of coconuts became a positive nuisance. The same point surely goes for palm trees—and presumably at *some* point even for Nubian maidens and dancing girls.

So this rebuttal of Gaunilo's 'lost island' objection fails, and Anselm's argument seems to be exposed to the objection. But Anselm himself also offers a different line of reply to Gaunilo (Anselm 1965: 119–21; Hick 1964: 27). Like Plantinga, he tries to show that the concept of God and of a perfect island are different in a way which would undermine the parallel which Gaunilo has set up. He says that a being than which none greater can be conceived cannot be thought of as non-existent, since if it could be thought of as non-existent, it could be thought of as having a beginning and an end, which is impossible. Anselm does not say why it is impossible but his reasoning may have been that if something had a beginning, its coming into existence would be dependent on the creative action of something else; and if it could cease to exist, then its continued existence would be dependent on the refraining from action (action of an annihilating kind) of some other being; and each of these kinds of dependence would be incompatible with the nature of a being than whom none greater can be thought. The implicit contrast with the island seems to be this: an island is by its very nature the sort of thing which can be thought of as having a beginning and an end in time. It can therefore be thought of as non-existent. But if it can be thought of as non-existent, its existence cannot follow from the mere thought or idea of it. So, Anselm can say, there *is* a difference between Gaunilo's 'lost island' argument, and Anselm's original argument.

But this line of defence for Anselm in fact fails, for a reason which is best brought out by considering some remarks by Hume. Hume tells us that

> The idea of existence … is the very same with what we conceive to be existent. To reflect on anything simply, and to reflect on it as existent, are nothing different from each other. That idea [i.e. of existence], when conjoined with the idea of any object, makes no addition to it.
>
> (Hume 1960: 66–7)

Hume was not explicitly commenting on Anselm or the ontological argument when he made those remarks. But they clearly have a direct bearing on what Anselm is claiming. There are two ways in which we could interpret what Hume is saying, and both of them are fatal to Anselm. The first way would be to say that the idea of existence is conjoined to the idea of *everything*, not just to the idea of God. To think of God is certainly to think of God as existing, but equally to think of a table or a cloud or a unicorn is to think of the table, the cloud and the unicorn as existing. This is not to say that when we think of an x, or of an existent x, we must *believe* that x exists. We can certainly think of things which we know not to exist. The point is that when we think of them, we think of them *as* existing. It is rather that if told to think of a tiger, and then to think of it as existing, the second command adds nothing to the first. To comply with the first is necessarily to comply with the second.

But in that case, the contrast on which Anselm is relying must collapse. For he is assuming that in every case except when we are thinking of God, we *can* think of entities without thinking of them as existing. He assumes that it is only in the case of the maximally great being that when we think of it, we *have to* think of it as existing—from which Anselm wrongly infers that we must accept that it really does exist. But Hume's point shows that when we think of something, even if we have to think of it as existing (because thinking of anything is thinking of it as existing), it does not follow that we have to accept that it really exists. Thinking of God and thinking of unicorns are precisely on a par here, and if Anselm's argument proved the existence of God, it would also prove the existence of unicorns.

But there is a second way in which Hume might intend his remarks. Perhaps his point is not that the idea of existence is conjoined to every other idea, but that it is conjoined to *no* other idea. He does say, after all, 'that idea [i.e. of existence], when conjoined with the idea of any object, *makes no addition to it*' (my emphasis), and we might well think that an idea which 'makes no addition' to anything to which it is added is not a real idea at all. Interpreted this way, Anselm's contrast between thinking of a maximally great being, and thinking of it as existing would again collapse. If the 'as existing' makes no addition to the thought of the maximally great being, then clearly the thought of it as existing will be the same as the bare thought of it. Anselm wanted to use the 'as existing' as a bridge from the mere thought to the real existence of the maximally great being. What Hume's sharp little comment shows is that taken one way, it is a bridge which not just God but everything we can think of would have to cross; taken another way, it is a bridge that nothing, not even God, could cross. Either way, the underlying assumption which Anselm makes that an ontological argument will work for the concept of God and for that concept alone, is untenable.

But even if we were not persuaded by Hume's comments, Anselm's argument faces a further conclusive objection. It suffers from a crippling confusion about what is involved in existing in the understanding. Briefly, what Anselm is assuming is: (1) that there are two ways in which a thing might exist: either in the mind, or in reality, and (2) that existing in the mind is an inferior way of existing. Both of these assumptions are false.

Consider the first assumption. Something that exists *only* in the mind does not exist *at all*, just as a non-existent tiger is not one kind of tiger. I understand the phrase 'tenth planet of the Sun', so that to use Anselm's terminology, we could say that the tenth planet of the Sun 'exists in my mind'. But that is compatible with saying that the tenth planet of the sun does not exist *at all*—or more idiomatically, that there is no tenth planet. The situation is not, as it were, that astronomers have located the tenth planet in my mind, and then have the further task of locating it in the solar system. What is 'in my mind' is better described as a bit of linguistic competence, not a shadowy planet.

A parallel point applies to thinking of a being than whom none greater can be thought. That I understand the phrase does not show that such a being has at least one kind of existence, namely in my mind, and might possibly have another kind of existence, namely in reality. All it shows is that I have some linguistic competence.

So Anselm's first assumption about two kinds of existence is mistaken. And since there are not the two kinds of existence which he supposes, it follows that he is mistaken too in thinking that one kind of existence is superior to the other.

It might be thought that this is to attribute to Anselm a blunder of which he is not guilty. After all, his argument contrasts: (a) existing in the mind alone, and (b) being thought of as existing in reality. But the contrast which we have just attributed to him is that between (a) above and (c) existing in reality as well as in the mind. Even if the contrast between (a) and (c) is untenable, it might well be thought that the contrast between (a) and (b) is defensible, and hence that Anselm's argument can escape this attack.

However, this is a too kind reading of Anselm, for two reasons. First, it is clear that the conclusion which he thinks he can defend is that God exists, not just that he must be *thought of* as existing. The end of Chapter 1 of *Proslogion* says 'Without doubt, therefore, there exists, both in the understanding and in reality, something than which a greater cannot be thought'. Second, if Anselm were seeking to defend only the more modest claim that God must be thought of as existing, the Humean criticism which we mentioned earlier would bite. The fool will reply to Anselm, 'If you think of God, you think of him as existing, just as if you think of anything, you think of it as existing. But that does not show either that he does exist, or that if we think of him, we must believe that he exists.'

SUMMA THEOLOGICA

By Thomas Aquinas
Trans. by The Fathers of the English Dominican Province

WHETHER THE EXISTENCE OF GOD IS SELF-EVIDENT?

Objection 1: It seems that the existence of God is self-evident. Now those things are said to be self-evident to us the knowledge of which is naturally implanted in us, as we can see in regard to first principles. But as Damascene says (De Fide Orth. i, 1,3), "the knowledge of God is naturally implanted in all." Therefore the existence of God is self-evident.

Objection 2: Further, those things are said to be self-evident which are known as soon as the terms are known, which the Philosopher (1 Poster. iii) says is true of the first principles of demonstration. Thus, when the nature of a whole and of a part is known, it is at once recognized that every whole is greater than its part. But as soon as the signification of the word "God" is understood, it is at once seen that God exists. For by this word is signified that thing than which nothing greater can be conceived. But that which exists actually and mentally is greater than that which exists only mentally. Therefore, since as soon as the word "God" is understood it exists mentally, it also follows that it exists actually. Therefore the proposition "God exists" is self-evident.

Objection 3: Further, the existence of truth is self-evident. For whoever denies the existence of truth grants that truth does not exist: and, if truth does not exist, then the proposition "Truth does not exist" is true: and if there is anything true, there must be truth. But God is truth itself: "I am the way, the truth, and the life" (Jn. 14:6) Therefore "God exists" is self-evident.

On the contrary, No one can mentally admit the opposite of what is self-evident; as the Philosopher (Metaph. iv, lect. vi) states concerning the first principles of demonstration. But the opposite of the proposition "God is" can be mentally admitted: "The fool said in his heart, There is no God" (Ps. 52:1). Therefore, that God exists is not self-evident.

I answer that, A thing can be self-evident in either of two ways: on the one hand, self-evident in itself, though not to us; on the other, self-evident in itself, and to us. A proposition is self-evident because the predicate is included in the essence of the subject, as "Man is an animal," for animal is contained in the essence of man. If, therefore the essence of the predicate and subject be known to all, the proposition will be self-evident to all; as is clear with regard to the first principles of demonstration, the terms of which are common things that no one is ignorant of, such as being and non-being, whole and part, and such like. If, however, there are some to whom the essence of the predicate and subject is unknown, the proposition will be self-evident in itself, but not to those who do not know the meaning of the predicate and subject of the proposition. Therefore, it happens, as Boethius says (Hebdom., the title of which is: "Whether all that is, is good"), "that there are some mental concepts self-evident only to the learned, as that incorporeal substances are not in space." Therefore I say that this proposition, "God exists," of itself is self-evident, for the predicate is the same as the subject, because God is His own existence as will be hereafter shown (Q[3], A[4]). Now because we do not know the essence of God, the proposition is not self-evident to us; but needs to be demonstrated by things that are more known to us, though less known in their nature--namely, by effects.

Reply to Objection 1: To know that God exists in a general and confused way is implanted in us by nature, inasmuch as God is man's beatitude. For man naturally desires happiness, and what is naturally desired by man must be naturally known to him. This, however, is not to know absolutely that God exists; just as to know that someone is approaching is not the same as to know that Peter is approaching, even though it is Peter who is approaching; for many there are who imagine that man's perfect good which is happiness, consists in riches, and others in pleasures, and others in something else.

Reply to Objection 2: Perhaps not everyone who hears this word "God" understands it to signify something than which nothing greater can be thought, seeing that some have believed God to be a body. Yet, granted that everyone understands that by this word "God" is signified something than which nothing greater can be thought, nevertheless, it does not therefore follow that he understands that what the word signifies exists actually, but only that it exists mentally. Nor can it be argued that it actually exists, unless it be admitted that there actually exists something than which nothing greater can be thought; and this precisely is not admitted by those who hold that God does not exist.

Reply to Objection 3: The existence of truth in general is self-evident but the existence of a Primal Truth is not self-evident to us.

WHETHER IT CAN BE DEMONSTRATED THAT GOD EXISTS?

Objection 1: It seems that the existence of God cannot be demonstrated. For it is an article of faith that God exists. But what is of faith cannot be demonstrated, because a demonstration produces scientific knowledge; whereas faith is of the unseen (Heb. 11:1). Therefore it cannot be demonstrated that God exists.

Objection 2: Further, the essence is the middle term of demonstration. But we cannot know in what God's essence consists, but solely in what it does not consist; as Damascene says (De Fide Orth. i, 4). Therefore we cannot demonstrate that God exists.

Objection 3: Further, if the existence of God were demonstrated, this could only be from His effects. But His effects are not proportionate to Him, since He is infinite and His effects are finite; and between the finite and infinite there is no proportion. Therefore, since a cause cannot be demonstrated by an effect not proportionate to it, it seems that the existence of God cannot be demonstrated.

On the contrary, The Apostle says: "The invisible things of Him are clearly seen, being understood by the things that are made" (Rom. 1:20). But this would not be unless the existence of God could be demonstrated through the things that are made; for the first thing we must know of anything is whether it exists.

I answer that, Demonstration can be made in two ways: One is through the cause, and is called "a priori," and this is to argue from what is prior absolutely. The other is through the effect, and is called a demonstration "a posteriori;" this is to argue from what is prior relatively only to us. When an effect is better known to us than its cause, from the effect we proceed to the knowledge of the cause. And from every effect the existence of its proper cause can be demonstrated, so long as its effects are better known to us; because since every effect depends upon its cause, if the effect exists, the cause must pre-exist. Hence the existence of God, in so far as it is not self-evident to us, can be demonstrated from those of His effects which are known to us.

Reply to Objection 1: The existence of God and other like truths about God, which can be known by natural reason, are not articles of faith, but are preambles to the articles; for faith presupposes natural knowledge, even as grace presupposes nature, and perfection supposes something that can be perfected. Nevertheless, there is nothing to prevent a man, who cannot grasp a proof, accepting, as a matter of faith, something which in itself is capable of being scientifically known and demonstrated.

Reply to Objection 2: When the existence of a cause is demonstrated from an effect, this effect takes the place of the definition of the cause in proof of the cause's existence. This is especially the case in regard to God, because, in order to prove the existence of anything, it is necessary to accept as a middle term the meaning of the word, and not its essence, for the question of its essence follows on the question of its existence. Now the names given to God are derived from His effects; consequently, in demonstrating the existence of God from His effects, we may take for the middle term the meaning of the word "God."

Reply to Objection 3: From effects not proportionate to the cause no perfect knowledge of that cause can be obtained. Yet from every effect the existence of the cause can be clearly demonstrated, and so we can demonstrate the existence of God from His effects; though from them we cannot perfectly know God as He is in His essence.

WHETHER GOD EXISTS?

Objection 1: It seems that God does not exist; because if one of two contraries be infinite, the other would be altogether destroyed. But the word "God" means that He is infinite goodness. If, therefore, God existed, there would be no evil discoverable; but there is evil in the world. Therefore God does not exist.

Objection 2: Further, it is superfluous to suppose that what can be accounted for by a few principles has been produced by many. But it seems that everything we see in the world can be accounted for by other principles, supposing God did not exist. For all natural things can be reduced to one principle which is nature; and all voluntary things can be reduced to one principle which is human reason, or will. Therefore there is no need to suppose God's existence.

On the contrary, It is said in the person of God: "I am Who am." (Ex. 3:14)

I answer that, The existence of God can be proved in five ways.

The first and more manifest way is the argument from motion. It is certain, and evident to our senses, that in the world some things are in motion. Now whatever is in motion is put in motion by another, for nothing can be in motion except it is in potentiality to that towards which it is in motion; whereas a thing moves inasmuch as it is in act. For motion is nothing else than the reduction of something from potentiality to actuality. But nothing can be reduced from potentiality to actuality, except by something in a state of actuality. Thus that which is actually hot, as fire, makes wood, which is potentially hot, to be actually hot, and thereby moves and changes it. Now it is not possible that the same thing should be at once in actuality and potentiality in the same respect, but only in different respects. For what is actually hot cannot simultaneously be potentially hot; but it is simultaneously potentially cold. It is therefore impossible that in the same respect and in the same way a thing should be both mover and moved, i.e. that it should move itself. Therefore, whatever is in motion must be put in motion by another. If that by which it is put in motion be itself put in motion, then this also must needs be put in motion by another, and that by another again. But this cannot go on to infinity, because then there would be no first mover, and, consequently, no other mover; seeing that subsequent movers move only inasmuch as they are put in motion by the first mover; as the staff moves only because it is put in motion by the hand. Therefore it is necessary to arrive at a first mover, put in motion by no other; and this everyone understands to be God.

The second way is from the nature of the efficient cause. In the world of sense we find there is an order of efficient causes. There is no case known (neither is it, indeed, possible) in which a thing is found to be the efficient cause of itself; for so it would be prior to itself, which is impossible. Now in efficient causes it is not possible to go on to infinity, because in all efficient causes following in order, the first is the cause of the intermediate cause, and the intermediate is the cause of the ultimate cause, whether the intermediate cause be several, or only one. Now to take away the cause is to take away the effect. Therefore, if there be no first cause among efficient causes, there will be no ultimate, nor any intermediate cause. But if in efficient causes it is possible to go on to infinity, there will be no first efficient cause, neither will there be an ultimate effect, nor any intermediate efficient causes; all of which is plainly false. Therefore it is necessary to admit a first efficient cause, to which everyone gives the name of God.

The third way is taken from possibility and necessity, and runs thus. We find in nature things that are possible to be and not to be, since they are found to be generated, and to corrupt, and consequently, they are possible to be and not to be. But it is impossible for these always to exist, for that which is possible not to be at some time is not. Therefore, if everything is possible not to be, then at one time there could have been nothing in existence. Now if this were true, even now there would be nothing in existence, because that which does not exist only begins to exist by something already existing. Therefore, if at one time nothing was in existence, it would have been impossible for anything to have begun to exist; and thus even now nothing would be in existence—which is absurd. Therefore, not all beings are merely possible, but there must exist something the existence of which is necessary. But every necessary thing either has its necessity caused by another, or not. Now it is impossible to go on to infinity in necessary things which have their necessity caused by another, as has been already proved in regard to efficient causes. Therefore we cannot but postulate the existence of some being having of itself its own necessity, and not receiving it from another, but rather causing in others their necessity. This all men speak of as God.

The fourth way is taken from the gradation to be found in things. Among beings there are some more and some less good, true, noble and the like. But "more" and "less" are predicated of different things, according as they resemble in their different ways something which is the maximum, as a thing is said to be hotter according as it more nearly resembles that which is hottest; so that there is something which is truest, something best, something noblest and, consequently, something which is uttermost being; for those things that are greatest in truth are greatest in being, as it is written in Metaph. ii. Now the maximum in any genus is the cause of all in that genus; as fire, which is the maximum heat, is the cause of all hot things. Therefore there must also be something which is to all beings the cause of their being, goodness, and every other perfection; and this we call God.

The fifth way is taken from the governance of the world. We see that things which lack intelligence, such as natural bodies, act for an end, and this is evident from their acting always, or nearly always, in the same way, so as to obtain the best result. Hence it is plain that not fortuitously, but designedly, do they achieve their end. Now whatever lacks intelligence cannot move towards an end, unless it be directed by some being endowed with knowledge and intelligence; as the arrow is shot to its mark by the archer. Therefore some intelligent being exists by whom all natural things are directed to their end; and this being we call God.

Reply to Objection 1: As Augustine says (*Enchiridion* xi): "Since God is the highest good, He would not allow any evil to exist in His works, unless His omnipotence and goodness were such as to bring good even out of evil." This is part of the infinite goodness of God, that He should allow evil to exist, and out of it produce good.

Reply to Objection 2: Since nature works for a determinate end under the direction of a higher agent, whatever is done by nature must needs be traced back to God, as to its first cause. So also whatever is done voluntarily must also be traced back to some higher cause other than human reason or will, since these can change or fail; for all things that are changeable and capable of defect must be traced back to an immovable and self-necessary first principle, as was shown in the body of the Article.

THE COSMOLOGICAL ARGUMENT

By William Lane Craig

INTRODUCTION

I t has become conventional wisdom that in light of the critiques of Hume and Kant there are no good arguments for the existence of God. But insofar as we mean by a "good argument" an argument which is formally and informally valid and consists of true premises which are more plausible than their negations, there do appear to be good arguments for God's existence, and there are on the contemporary scene many philosophers who think so. Indeed, it would be fair to say that the rise of analytic philosophy of religion has been accompanied by a resurgence of interest in natural theology—that branch of theology which seeks to offer cogent arguments or reasons for God's existence apart from the resources of authoritative divine revelation. In this chapter I shall focus on the so-called cosmological argument for the existence of God.

The cosmological argument is a family of arguments which seeks to demonstrate the existence of a *sufficient reason* or *first cause* of the existence of the cosmos. The roll of the defenders of this argument reads like a *Who's Who* of Western philosophy: Plato, Aristotle, ibn Sina, al-Ghazali, Maimonides, Anselm, Aquinas, Scotus, Descartes, Spinoza, Leibniz, and Locke, to name but some. The arguments can be grouped into three basic types: the *kalam* cosmological argument for a First Cause of the beginning of the universe, the Thomist cosmological argument for a sustaining Ground of Being of the world, and the Leibnizian cosmological argument for a Sufficient Reason why something exists rather than nothing.

The *kalam* cosmological argument derives its name from the Arabic word designating medieval Islamic scholasticism, the intellectual movement largely responsible for developing the argument. It aims to show that the universe had a beginning at some moment in the finite past and, since something cannot come out of nothing, must therefore have a transcendent cause, which brought the universe into being. Classical proponents of the argument sought to demonstrate that the universe began to exist on the basis of philosophical arguments against the existence of an infinite, temporal regress of past events. Contemporary interest in the argument arises largely out of the startling empirical evidence of astrophysical cosmology for a beginning of space and time. Today, the controlling paradigm of cosmology is the standard Big Bang model, according to which the space-time universe originated *ex nihilo* about 15 billion years ago. Such an origin *ex nihilo* seems to many to cry out for a transcendent cause.

By contrast the Thomist cosmological argument, named for the medieval philosophical theologian Thomas Aquinas, seeks a cause which is first, not in the temporal sense, but in the sense of rank. Aquinas agreed that "If the world and motion have a first beginning, some cause must clearly be posited for this origin of the world and of motion."[1] But since he did not regard the *kalam* arguments for the past's finitude as demonstrative, he argued for God's existence on the more difficult assumption of the eternity of the world. On Aquinas's Aristotelian-inspired metaphysic, every existing finite thing is composed of essence and existence and is therefore radically contingent. A thing's essence is an individual nature which serves to define what that thing is. Now if an individual essence is to exist, there must be conjoined with that essence an act of being. This act of being involves a continual bestowal of being, or the thing would be annihilated. Essence is in potentiality to the act of being, and therefore without the bestowal of being the essence would not exist. For the same reason no substance can actualize itself; for in order to bestow being upon itself, it would have to be already actual. A pure potentiality cannot actualize itself but requires some external cause. Now although Aquinas argued that there cannot be an infinite regress of causes of being (because in such a series all the causes would be merely instrumental and so no being would be produced, just as no motion would be produced in a watch without a spring even if it had an infinite number of gears), and that therefore there must exist a First Uncaused Cause of being, his actual view was that there can be no intermediate causes of being at all, that any finite substance is sustained in existence immediately by the Ground of Being. This must be a being which is not composed of essence and existence and, hence, requires no sustaining cause. We cannot say that this being's essence includes existence as one of its properties, for existence is not a property but an act, the instantiating of an essence. Therefore, we must conclude that this being's essence just *is* existence. In a sense, this being has no essence; rather it is the pure act of being, unconstrained by any essence. It is, as Thomas says, *ipsum esse subsistens*, the act of being itself subsisting. Thomas identifies this being with the God whose name was revealed to Moses as "I AM" (Exodus 3:15).

The German polymath Gottfried Wilhelm Leibniz, for whom the third form of the argument is named, sought to develop a version of the cosmological argument from contingency without the Aristotelian metaphysical underpinnings of the Thomist argument. "The first question which should rightly be asked," he wrote, "is this: why is there something rather than nothing?"[2] Leibniz meant this question to be truly universal, not merely to apply to finite things. On the basis of his Principle of Sufficient Reason, that "no fact can be real or existent, no statement true, unless there be a sufficient reason why it is so and not otherwise,"[3] Leibniz held that this question must have an answer. It will not do to say that the universe (or even God) just exists as a brute fact. There must be an explanation why it exists. He went on to argue that the Sufficient Reason cannot be found in any individual thing in the universe, nor in the collection of such things which comprise the universe, nor in earlier states of the universe, even if these regress infinitely. Therefore, there must exist an ultra-mundane being which is metaphysically necessary in its existence, that is to say, its non-existence is impossible. It is the Sufficient Reason for its own existence as well as for the existence of every contingent thing.

THE LEIBNIZIAN COSMOLOGICAL ARGUMENT

In evaluating these arguments, let us consider them in reverse order. A simple statement of a Leibnizian cosmological argument might run as follows:[4]

1. Every existing thing has an explanation of its existence, either in the necessity of its own nature or in an external cause.
2. If the universe has an explanation of its existence, that explanation is God.
3. The universe is an existing thing.
4. Therefore the explanation of the existence of the universe is God.

Is this a good argument? One of the principal objections to Leibniz's own formulation of the argument is that the Principle of Sufficient Reason as stated in *The Monadology* seems evidently false. There cannot be an explanation of why there are any contingent states of affairs at all; for if such an explanation is contingent, then it, too, must have a further explanation, whereas if it is necessary, then the states of affairs explained by it must also be necessary.

Some theists have responded to this objection by agreeing that one must ultimately come to some explanatory stopping point which is simply a brute fact, a being whose existence is unexplained. For example, Richard Swinburne claims that in answering the question "Why is there something rather than nothing?" we must finally come to the brute existence of some contingent being. This being will not serve to explain its own existence (and, hence, Leibniz's question goes unanswered), but it will explain the existence of everything else. Swinburne argues that God is the best explanation of why everything other than the brute Ultimate exists because as a unique and infinite being God is simpler than the variegated and finite universe.

But the above formulation of the Leibnizian argument avoids the objection without retreating to the dubious position that God is a contingent being. For premise 1 merely requires any existing *thing* to have an explanation of its existence, either in the necessity of its own nature or in some external cause. This premise is compatible with there being brute *facts* or *states of affairs* about the world. What it precludes is that there could exist things—substances exemplifying properties—which just exist inexplicably. This principle seems quite plausible, at least more so than its contradictory, which is all that is required for a successful argument. On this analysis, there are two kinds of being: necessary beings, which exist of their own nature and so have no external cause of their existence, and contingent beings, whose existence is accounted for by causal factors outside themselves. Numbers might be prime candidates for the first sort of being, whereas familiar physical objects fall under the second kind of being.

Premise 2 is, in effect, the contrapositive of the typical atheist response to Leibniz that on the atheistic worldview the universe simply exists as a brute contingent thing. Atheists typically assert that, there being no God, it is false that everything has an explanation of its existence, for the universe, in this case, just exists inexplicably.[5] In so saying, the atheist implicitly recognizes that if the universe has an explanation, then God exists as its explanatory ground. This seems quite plausible, for if the universe, by definition, includes all of physical reality, then it is hard to see how it could have an explanation, or at least a better one, other than its being caused by God.

Finally, premise 3 states the obvious, that there is a universe.[6] Since the universe is obviously an existing thing (especially evident in its very early stages when its density was so extreme), possessing many unique properties such as a certain density, pressure, temperature, space–time curvature, and so on, it follows that God exists.

It is open to the atheist to retort that while the universe has an explanation of its existence, that explanation lies not in an external ground but in the necessity of its own nature; in other words, premise 2 is false. The universe is a metaphysically necessary being. This was the suggestion of David Hume, who demanded, "Why may not the material universe be the necessarily existent being …?" Indeed, "How can anything, that exists from eternity, have a cause, since that relation implies a priority in time and a beginning of existence?"[7]

This is an extremely bold suggestion on the part of the atheist. It runs precisely counter to the conviction driving the Swinburnian formulation of the argument, namely that there must be some ultimately inexplicable contingent being. Even if we reject that assumption, we have, I think we can safely say, a strong intuition of the universe's contingency. A possible world in which no concrete objects exist certainly seems conceivable. We generally trust our modal intuitions on other matters with which we are familiar;[8] if we are to do otherwise with respect to the universe's contingency, then the atheist needs to provide some reason for such scepticism other than his desire to avoid theism.

THE THOMIST COSMOLOGICAL ARGUMENT

Still, it would be desirable to have some stronger argument for the universe's contingency than our modal intuitions alone. Could the Thomist cosmological argument help us here? If successful, it would show that the universe is a contingent being, causally dependent upon a necessary being for its continued existence. The difficulty with appeal to the Thomist argument, however, is that it is very difficult to show that things are, in fact, contingent in the special sense required by the argument. Certainly, things are naturally contingent in that their continued existence is dependent upon a myriad of factors including particle masses and fundamental forces, temperature, pressure, entropy level, and so forth, but this natural contingency does not suffice to establish things' metaphysical contingency in the sense that being must continually be added to their essences lest they be spontaneously annihilated. Indeed, if Thomas's argument does ultimately lead to an absolutely simple being whose essence is existence, then one might well be led to deny that beings are metaphysically composed of essence and existence if the idea of such an absolutely simple being proves to be unintelligible.[9]

THE *KALAM* COSMOLOGICAL ARGUMENT

But what about the *kalam* cosmological argument? An essential property of a metaphysically necessary being is eternality, that is to say, being without beginning or end. It has been countered that a being with a temporal beginning or end could, nonetheless, be metaphysically necessary in that it is caused to exist in all possible worlds. But this understanding of metaphysical necessity fails to take tense seriously and is therefore inadequate. Metaphysicians have in recent years begun to appreciate the metaphysical importance of whether time is tensed or tenseless, that is to say, whether items in the temporal series are ordered objectively as past, present, or future, or whether, alternatively, they are ordered merely by tenseless relations of *earlier than*, *simultaneous with*, and *later than*.[10] Possible worlds semantics is a tenseless semantics and so is incapable of expressing the significance of one's view of time. In particular, it is evident that a truly necessary being, one whose non-existence is impossible, must exist at every moment in every world. It is not enough for it to exist at only some moment or moments in every possible world, for the fact that there exist moments in various worlds at which it fails to exist shows that its non-existence is not impossible. By the same token, a truly metaphysically necessary being must exist either timelessly or sempiternally in any tensed world in which it exists, for otherwise its coming into being or ceasing to be would again make it evident that its existence is not necessary.[11] If the universe is not eternal, then, it could not be, as Hume suggested, a metaphysically necessary being.

But it is precisely the aim of the *kalam* cosmological argument to show that the universe is not eternal but had a beginning. It would follow that the universe must therefore be contingent in its existence. Not only so; the *kalam* argument shows the universe to be contingent in a very special way: it came into existence out of nothing. The atheist who would answer Leibniz by holding that the existence of the universe is a brute fact, an exception to the Principle of Sufficient Reason, is thus thrust into the very awkward position of maintaining not merely that the universe exists eternally without explanation, but rather that for no reason at all it magically popped into being out of nothing, a position which might make theism look like a welcome alternative. Thus, the *kalam* argument not only constitutes an independent argument for a transcendent Creator but also serves as a valuable supplement to the Leibnizian argument.

The *kalam* cosmological argument may be formulated as follows:

1. Whatever begins to exist has a cause.
2. The universe began to exist.
3. Therefore, the universe has a cause.

Conceptual analysis of what it means to be a cause of the universe then helps to establish some of the theologically significant properties of this being.

Whatever begins to exist has a cause

Premise 5 seems obviously true—at the least, more so than its negation. It is rooted in the metaphysical intuition that something cannot come into being from nothing. Moreover, this premise is constantly confirmed in our experience. The conviction that an origin of the universe requires a causal explanation seems quite reasonable, for, on the atheistic view, there was not even the *potentiality* of the universe's existence prior to the Big Bang, since nothing is prior to the Big Bang. But then how could the universe become actual if there was not even the potentiality of its existence? It makes much more sense to say that the potentiality of the universe lay in the power of God to create it.

Nevertheless, a number of atheists, in order to avoid the argument's conclusion, have denied premise 5. Sometimes it is said that sub-atomic physics furnishes an exception to premise 5, since on the sub-atomic level events are said to be uncaused. In the same way, certain theories of cosmic origins are interpreted as showing that the whole universe could have sprung into being out of the sub-atomic vacuum. Thus the universe is said to be the proverbial "free lunch."

This objection, however, is based on misunderstandings. In the first place, not all scientists agree that sub-atomic events are uncaused. A great many physicists today are quite dissatisfied with this view (the so-called Copenhagen Interpretation) of sub-atomic physics and are exploring deterministic theories like that of David Bohm. Thus, sub-atomic physics is not a proven exception to premise 5. Second, even on the traditional, indeterministic interpretation, particles do not come into being out of nothing. They arise as spontaneous fluctuations of the energy contained in the sub-atomic vacuum, which constitutes an indeterministic cause of their origination. Third, the same point can be made about theories of the origin of the universe out of a primordial vacuum. Popular magazine articles touting such theories as getting "something from nothing" simply do not understand that the vacuum is not nothing but is a sea of fluctuating energy endowed with a rich structure and subject to physical laws. Thus, there is no basis for the claim that quantum physics proves that things can begin to exist without a cause, much less that universe could have sprung into being uncaused from literally nothing.

Other critics have said that premise 5 is true for things *in* the universe, but it is not true *of* the universe itself. But, first, this objection misconstrues the nature of the premise. Premise 5 does not state merely a physical law like the law of gravity or the laws of thermodynamics, which are valid for things within the universe. Premise 5 is not a physical principle. Rather, premise 5 is a metaphysical principle: being cannot come from non-being; something cannot come into existence uncaused from nothing. The principle therefore applies to all of reality, and it is thus metaphysically absurd that the universe should pop into being uncaused out of nothing.

NOTES

1. *Summa contra gentiles*, Vol. 1, Anton C. Pegis (trans.) (Notre Dame, IN: University of Notre Dame Press, 1975) 1.13.30.

2. G. W. Leibniz, "The Principles of Nature and of Grace, Based on Reason," in *Leibniz Selections*, P. Wiener (ed.) (New York: Charles Scribner's Sons, 1951),527.

3. Leibniz, "The Monadology," in *Leibniz Selections*, 539.

4. Cf. Stephen T. Davis, "The Cosmological Argument and the Epistemic Status of Belief in God," *Philosophia Christi* 1 (New series) (1999), 5–15.

5. Recall Russell's response to Copleston in their famous BBC exchange: "I should say the universe is just there, and that's all." Bertrand Russell and F. C. Copleston, "A Debate On The Existence of God," reprinted in *The Existence of God*, Introduction by John Hick (New York: Macmillan, 1964), 175.

6. I do not mean to pronounce here on ontological debates about what constitutes an object, but merely to claim that the universe is just as much a thing as are other familiar entities which we recognize to have causes, such as chairs, mountains, planets, and stars.

7. David Hume, *Dialogues concerning Natural Religion*, with an Introduction by Norman Kemp Smith, Library of Liberal Arts (Indianapolis: Bobbs-Merrill, 1947), pt. IX, 190.

8. See Charles Taliaferro's *Auseindersetzung* with Peter Van Inwagen's modal skepticism in Charles Taliaferro, "Sensibility and Possibilia: In Defense of Thought Experiments," *Philosophia Christi* 3, 2 (New series) (2001), 403–20. Especially noteworthy for the present discussion is Van Inwagen's own rejection of Spinozism. Taliaferro proposes the following principle: if one can conceive that a state of affairs obtain, and one has carefully considered whether the state of affairs is internally coherent (self-consistent at a minimum) and consistent with what one justifiably believes, then one has prima facie reason to believe it is possible for the state of affairs to obtain.

9. To say that God does not have distinct properties seems patently false: omnipotence is not the same property as goodness, for a being may have one and not the other. To respond that these properties differ in our conception only, as manifestations of a single divine property, just as, say, "the morning star" and "the evening star" have different senses but both refer to the same reality, namely Venus, is inadequate. For being the morning star and being the evening star are distinct properties both possessed by Venus; in the same way that being omnipotent and being good are not different senses for the same property (as are, say, being even and being divisible by two) but are clearly distinct properties. Moreover, if God is not distinct from His essence, then God cannot know or do anything different than what he knows and does, in which case everything becomes necessary. To respond that God is perfectly similar in all logically possible worlds which we can imagine but that contingency is real because God stands in no real relation to things is to make the existence or non-existence of creatures in various possible worlds independent of God and utterly mysterious. To say that God's essence just is His existence seems wholly obscure, since then there is in God's case no entity that exists; there is just the existing itself without any subject. For further critique, see Christopher Hughes, *On a Complex Theory of a Simple God* (Ithaca, NY: Cornell University Press, 199); Thomas V. Morris, *Anselmian Explorations* (Notre Dame, IN: University of Notre Dame Press, 1987), 98–123.

10. For discussion and bibliography see both Robin LePoidevin (ed.) *Questions of Time and Tense* (Oxford: Oxford University Press, 1998) and my companion volumes *The Tensed Theory of Time: A Critical Examination* (Dordrecht: Kluwer Academic Publishers, 2000) and *The Tenseless Theory of Time: A Critical Examination* (Dordrecht: Kluwer Academic Publishers, 2000).

11. Thus, considerations of tense disclose the inadequacy of possible worlds semantics for dealing with metaphysical questions related to necessary existence. One might also question whether true

metaphysical necessity is compatible with being caused to exist, even at all times in all possible worlds, for this leaves open the option that such a being is the causal product of some contingent being in one world and of another in another world, which seems incompatible with its being truly necessary. Only if the being were caused to exist by a truly necessary being could its being caused seem even plausibly compatible with its being metaphysically necessary. But even in such a case the demonstration that the universe began to exist shows that it is either contingent in its existence or else necessary *ab alio* in being necessarily caused by some greater necessary being. If, as Aquinas held, such a regress cannot go on to infinity, then there must be an absolutely necessary being that has its necessity per se. In a sense, then, the Thomist argument returns to supplement the *kalam* argument, just as the latter reinforces the Leibnizian argument.

NATURAL THEOLOGY

By William Paley

CHAPTER I. STATE OF THE ARGUMENT

In crossing a heath, suppose I pitched my foot against a *stone*, and were asked how the stone came to be there; I might possibly answer, that, for any thing I knew to the contrary, it had lain there for ever: nor would it perhaps be very easy to show the absurdity of this answer. But suppose I had found a *watch* upon the ground, and it should be inquired how the watch happened to be in that place; I should hardly think of the answer which I had before given, that, for any thing I knew, the watch might have always been there. Yet why should not this answer serve for the watch as well as for the stone? Why is it not as admissible in the second case, as in the first? For this reason, and for no other, viz. that, when we come to inspect the watch, we perceive (what we could not discover in the stone) that its several parts are framed and put together for a purpose, *e. g.* that they are so formed and adjusted as to produce motion, and that motion so regulated as to point out the hour of the day; that, if the different parts had been differently shaped from what they are, of a different size from what they are, or placed after any other manner, or in any other order, than that in which they are placed, either no motion at all would have been carried on in the machine, or none which would have answered the use that is now served by it. To reckon up a few of the plainest of these parts, and of their offices, all tending to one result: We see a cylindrical box containing a coiled elastic spring, which, by its endeavour to relax itself, turns round the box. We next observe a flexible chain (artificially wrought for the sake of flexure), communicating the action of the spring from the box to the fusee. We then find a series of wheels, the teeth of which catch in, and apply to, each other, conducting the motion from the fusee to the balance, and from the balance to the pointer; and at the same time, by the size and shape of those wheels, so regulating that motion, as to terminate in causing an index, by an equable and measured progression, to pass over a given space in a given time. We take notice that the wheels are made of brass in order to keep them from rust; the springs of steel, no other metal being so elastic; that over the face of the watch there is placed a glass, a material employed in no other part of the work, but in the room of which, if there had been any other than a transparent substance, the hour could not be seen without opening the case. This mechanism being observed (it requires indeed an examination of the instrument, and perhaps some previous knowledge of the subject, to perceive and understand it; but being once, as we have said, observed and understood), the inference, we think, is inevitable, that the watch must have had a maker: that there must have existed, at some time, and at some place or other, an artificer or artificers who formed it for the purpose which we find it actually to answer; who comprehended its construction, and designed its use.

I. Nor would it, I apprehend, weaken the conclusion, that we had never seen a watch made; that we had never known an artist capable of making one; that we were altogether incapable of executing such a piece of workmanship ourselves, or of understanding in what manner it was performed; all this being no more than what is true of some exquisite remains of ancient art, of some lost arts, and, to the generality of mankind, of the more curious productions of modern manufacture. Does one man in a million know how oval frames are turned? Ignorance of this kind exalts our opinion of the unseen and unknown artist's skill, if he be unseen and unknown, but raises no doubt in our minds of the existence and agency of such an artist, at some former time, and in some place or other. Nor can I perceive that it varies at all the inference, whether the question arise concerning a human agent, or concerning an agent of a different species, or an agent possessing, in some respects, a different nature.

II. Neither, secondly, would it invalidate our conclusion, that the watch sometimes went wrong, or that it seldom went exactly right. The purpose of the machinery, the design, and the designer, might be evident, and in the case supposed would be evident, in whatever way we accounted for the irregularity of the movement, or whether we could account for it or not. It is not necessary that a machine be perfect, in order to show with what design it was made: still less necessary, where the only question is, whether it were made with any design at all.

III. Nor, thirdly, would it bring any uncertainty into the argument, if there were a few parts of the watch, concerning which we could not discover, or had not yet discovered, in what manner they conduced to the general effect; or even some parts, concerning which we could not ascertain, whether they conduced to that effect in any manner whatever. For, as to the first branch of the case; if by the loss, or disorder, or decay of the parts in question, the movement of the watch were found in fact to be stopped, or disturbed, or retarded, no doubt would remain in our minds as to the utility or intention of these parts, although we should be unable to investigate the manner according to which, or the connexion by which, the ultimate effect depended upon their action or assistance; and the more complex is the machine, the more likely is this obscurity to arise. Then, as to the second thing supposed, namely, that there were parts which might be spared, without prejudice to the movement of the watch, and that we had proved this by experiment, these superfluous parts, even if we were completely assured that they were such, would not vacate the reasoning which we had instituted concerning other parts. The indication of contrivance remained, with respect to them, nearly as it was before.

IV. Nor, fourthly, would any man in his senses think the existence of the watch, with its various machinery, accounted for, by being told that it was one out of possible combinations of material forms; that whatever he had found in the place where he found the watch, must have contained some internal configuration or other; and that this configuration might be the structure now exhibited, viz. of the works of a watch, as well as a different structure.

V. Nor, fifthly, would it yield his inquiry more satisfaction to be answered, that there existed in things a principle of order, which had disposed the parts of the watch into their present form and situation. He never knew a watch made by the principle of order; nor can he even form to himself an idea of what is meant by a principle of order, distinct from the intelligence of the watch-maker.

VI. Sixthly, he would be surprised to hear that the mechanism of the watch was no proof of contrivance, only a motive to induce the mind to think so:

VII. And not less surprised to be informed, that the watch in his hand was nothing more than the result of the laws of *metallic* nature. It is a perversion of language to assign any law, as the efficient, operative cause of any thing. A law presupposes an agent; for it is only the mode, according to which an agent proceeds: it implies a power; for it is the order, according to which that power acts. Without this agent, without this power, which are both distinct from itself, the *law* does nothing; is nothing. The expression, "the law of metallic nature," may sound strange and harsh to a philosophic ear; but it seems quite as justifiable as some others which are more familiar to him, such as "the law of vegetable nature," "the law of animal nature," or indeed as "the law of nature" in general, when assigned as the cause of phænomena, in exclusion of agency and power; or when it is substituted into the place of these.

VIII. Neither, lastly, would our observer be driven out of his conclusion, or from his confidence in its truth, by being told that he knew nothing at all about the matter. He knows enough for his argument: he knows the utility of the end: he knows the subserviency and adaptation of the means to the end. These points being known, his ignorance of other points, his doubts concerning other points, affect not the certainty of his reasoning. The consciousness of knowing little, need not beget a distrust of that which he does know.

CHAPTER II. STATE OF THE ARGUMENT CONTINUED

Suppose, in the next place, that the person who found the watch, should, after some time, discover that, in addition to all the properties which he had hitherto observed in it, it possessed the unexpected property of producing, in the course of its movement, another watch like itself (the thing is conceivable); that it contained within it a mechanism, a system of parts, a mould for instance, or a complex adjustment of lathes, files, and other tools, evidently and separately calculated for this purpose; let us inquire, what effect ought such a discovery to have upon his former conclusion.

I. The first effect would be to increase his admiration of the contrivance, and his conviction of the consummate skill of the contriver. Whether he regarded the object of the contrivance, the distinct apparatus, the intricate, yet in many parts intelligible mechanism, by which it was carried on, he would perceive, in this new observation, nothing but an additional reason for doing what he had already done,—for referring the construction of the watch to design, and to supreme art. If that construction *without* this property, or which is the same thing, before this property had been noticed, proved intention and art to have been employed about it; still more strong would the proof appear, when he came to the knowledge of this further property, the crown and perfection of all the rest.

II. He would reflect, that though the watch before him were, *in some sense*, the maker of the watch, which was fabricated in the course of its movements, yet it was in a very different sense from that, in which a carpenter, for instance, is the maker of a chair; the author of its contrivance, the cause of the relation of its parts to their use. With respect to these, the first watch was no cause at all to the second: in no such sense as this was it the author of the constitution and order, either of the parts which the new watch contained, or of the parts by the aid and instrumentality of which it was produced. We might possibly say, but with great latitude of expression, that a stream of water ground corn: but no latitude of expression would allow us to say, no stretch of conjecture could lead us to think, that the stream of water built the mill, though it were too ancient for us to know who the builder was. What the stream of water does in the affair, is neither more nor less than this; by the application of an unintelligent impulse to a mechanism previously arranged, arranged independently of it, and arranged by intelligence, an effect is produced, viz. the corn is ground. But the effect results from the arrangement. The force of the stream cannot be said to be the cause or author of the effect, still less of the arrangement. Understanding and plan in the formation of the mill were not the less necessary, for any share which the water has in grinding the corn: yet is this share the same, as that which the watch would have contributed to the production of the new watch, upon the supposition assumed in the last section. Therefore,

III. Though it be now no longer probable, that the individual watch, which our observer had found, was made immediately by the hand of an artificer, yet doth not this alteration in anywise affect the inference, that an artificer had been originally employed and concerned in the production. The argument from design remains as it was. Marks of design and contrivance are no more accounted for now, than they were before. In the same thing, we may ask for the cause of different properties. We may ask for the cause of the colour of a body, of its hardness, of its head; and these causes may be all different. We are now asking for the cause of that subserviency to a use, that relation to an end, which we have remarked in the watch before us. No answer is given to this question, by telling us that a preceding watch produced it. There cannot be design without a designer; contrivance without a contriver; order without choice; arrangement, without any thing capable of arranging; subserviency and relation to a purpose, without that which could intend a purpose; means suitable to an end, and executing their office, in accomplishing that end, without the end ever having been contemplated, or the means accommodated to it. Arrangement, disposition of parts, subserviency of means to an end, relation of instruments to a use, imply the presence of intelligence and mind. No one, therefore, can rationally believe, that the insensible, inanimate watch, from which the watch before us issued, was the proper cause of the mechanism we so much admire in it; could be truly said to have constructed the instrument, disposed its parts, assigned their office, determined their order, action, and mutual dependency, combined their several motions into one result, and that also a result connected with the utilities of other beings. All these properties, therefore, are as much unaccounted for, as they were before.

IV. Nor is any thing gained by running the difficulty farther back, i.e. by supposing the watch before us to have been produced from another watch, that from a former, and so on indefinitely. Our going back ever so far, brings us no nearer to the least degree of satisfaction upon the subject. Contrivance is still unaccounted for. We still want a contriver. A designing mind is neither supplied by this supposition, nor dispensed with. If the difficulty were diminished the further we went back, by going back indefinitely we might exhaust it. And this is the only case to which this sort of reasoning applies. Where there is a tendency, or, as we increase the number of terms, a continual approach towards a limit, *there*, by supposing the number of terms to be what is called infinite, we may conceive the limit to be attained: but where there is no such tendency, or approach, nothing is effected by lengthening the series. There is no difference as to the point in question (whatever there may be as to many points), between one series and another; between a series which is finite, and a series which is infinite. A chain, composed of an infinite number of links, can no more support itself, than a chain composed of a finite number of links. And of this we are assured (though we never *can* have tried the experiment), because, by increasing the number of links, from ten for instance to a hundred, from a hundred to a thousand, &c. we make not the smallest approach, we observe not the smallest tendency, towards self-support. There is no difference in this respect (yet there may be a great difference in several respects) between a chain of a greater or less length, between one chain and another, between one that is finite and one that is infinite. This very much resembles the case before us. The machine which we are inspecting, demonstrates, by its construction, contrivance and design. Contrivance must have had a contriver; design, a designer; whether the machine immediately proceeded from another machine or not. That circumstance alters not the case. That other machine may, in like manner, have proceeded from a former machine: nor does that alter the case; contrivance must have had a contriver. That former one from one preceding it: no alteration still; a contriver is still necessary. No tendency is perceived, no approach towards a diminution of this necessity. It is the same with any and every succession of these machines; a succession of ten, of a hundred, of a thousand; with one series, as with another; a series which is finite, as with a series which is infinite. In whatever other respects they may differ, in this they do not. In all equally, contrivance and design are unaccounted for.

CHAPTER III. APPLICATION OF THE ARGUMENT

Every indication of contrivance, every manifestation of design, which existed in the watch, exists in the works of nature; with the difference, on the side of nature, of being greater and more, and that in a degree which exceeds all computation. I mean that the contrivances of nature surpass the contrivances of art, in the complexity, subtility, and curiosity of the mechanism; and still more, if possible, do they go beyond them in number and variety; yet, in a multitude of cases, are not less evidently mechanical, not less evidently contrivances, not less evidently accommodated to their end, or suited to their office, than are the most perfect productions of human ingenuity.

I know no better method of introducing so large a subject, than that of comparing a single thing with a single thing; an eye, for example, with a telescope. As far as the examination of the instrument goes, there is precisely the same proof that the eye was made for vision, as there is that the telescope was made for assisting it. They are made upon the same principles; both being adjusted to the laws by which the transmission and refraction of rays of light are regulated. I speak not of the origin of the laws themselves; but such laws being fixed, the construction, in both cases, is adapted to them. For instance; these laws require, in order to produce the same effect, that the rays of light, in passing from water into the eye, should be refracted by a more convex surface, than when it passes out of air into the eye. Accordingly we find that the eye of a fish, in that part of it called the crystalline lens, is much rounder than the eye of terrestrial animals. What plainer manifestation of design can there be than this difference? What could a mathematical-instrument-maker have done more, to show his knowledge of this principle, his application of that knowledge, his suiting of his means to his end; I will not say to display the compass or excellence of his skill and art, for in these all comparison is indecorous, but to testify counsel, choice, consideration, purpose?

CHAPTER IV. APPLICATION OF THE ARGUMENT CONTINUED

Every observation which was made in our first chapter, concerning the watch, may be repeated with strict propriety, concerning the eye; concerning animals; concerning plants; concerning, indeed, all the organized parts of the works of nature. As,

I. When we are inquiring simply after the *existence* of an intelligent Creator, imperfection, inaccuracy, liability to disorder, occasional irregularities, may subsist in a considerable degree, without inducing any doubt into the question: just as a watch may frequently go wrong, seldom perhaps exactly right, may be faulty in some parts, defective in some, without the smallest ground of suspicion from thence arising that it was not a watch; not made; or not made for the purpose ascribed to it. When faults are pointed out, and when a question is started concerning the skill of the artist, or dexterity with which the work is executed, then indeed, in order to defend these qualities from accusation, we must be able, either to expose some intractableness and imperfection in the materials, or point out some invincible difficulty in the execution, into which imperfection and difficulty the matter of complaint may be resolved; or if we cannot do this, we must adduce such specimens of consummate art and contrivance, proceeding from the same hand, as may convince the inquirer, of the existence, in the case before him, of impediments like those which we have mentioned, although, what from the nature of the case is very likely to happen, they be unknown and unperceived by him. This we must do in order to vindicate the artist's skill, or, at least, the perfection of it; as we must also judge of his intention, and of the provisions employed in fulfilling that intention, not from an instance in which they fail, but from the great plurality of instances in which they succeed. But, after all, these are different questions from the question of the artist's existence: or, which is the same, whether the thing before us be a work of art or not: and the questions ought always to be kept separate in the mind. So likewise it is in the works of nature. Irregularities and imperfections are of little or no weight in the consideration, when that consideration relates simply to the existence of a Creator. When the argument respects his attributes, they are of weight; but are then to be taken in conjunction (the attention is not to rest upon them, but they are to be taken in conjunction) with the unexceptionable evidences which we possess, of skill, power, and benevolence, displayed in other instances; which evidences may, in strength; number, and variety, be such, and may so overpower apparent blemishes, as to induce us, upon the most reasonable ground, to believe, that these last ought to be referred to some cause, though we be ignorant of it, other than defect of knowledge or of benevolence in the author.

DIALOGUES CONCERNING NATURAL RELIGION

By David Hume

PART II.

Cleanthes, addressing himself to Demea, much less in replying to the pious declamations of Philo; "I shall briefly explain how I conceive this matter. Look round the world: contemplate the whole and every part of it: you will find it to be nothing but one great machine, subdivided into an infinite number of lesser machines, which again admit of subdivisions to a degree beyond what human senses and faculties can trace and explain. All these various machines, and even their most minute parts, are adjusted to each other with an accuracy which ravishes into admiration all men who have ever contemplated them. The curious adapting of means to ends, throughout all nature, resembles exactly, though it much exceeds, the productions of human contrivance; of human designs, thought, wisdom, and intelligence. Since, therefore, the effects resemble each other, we are led to infer, by all the rules of analogy, that the causes also resemble; and that the Author of Nature is somewhat similar to the mind of man, though possessed of much larger faculties, proportioned to the grandeur of the work which he has executed. By this argument a posteriori, and by this argument alone, do we prove at once the existence of a Deity, and his similarity to human mind and intelligence."

"I shall be so free, Cleanthes," said Demea, "as to tell you, that from the beginning," I could not approve of your conclusion concerning the similarity of the Deity to men; still less can I approve of the mediums by which you endeavour to establish it. What! No demonstration of the Being of God! No abstract arguments! No proofs a priori! Are these, which have hitherto been so much insisted on by Philosophers, all fallacy, all sophism? Can we reach no further in this subject than experience and probability? I will not say that this is betraying the cause of a Deity: but surely, by this affected candour, you give advantages to Atheists, which they never could obtain by the mere dint of argument and reasoning.

"What I chiefly scruple in this subject," said Philo, "is not so much that all religious arguments are by Cleanthes reduced to experience, as that they appear not to be even the most certain and irrefragable of that inferior kind. That a stone will fall, that fire will burn, that the earth has solidity, we have observed a thousand and a thousand times; and when any new instance of this nature is presented, we draw without hesitation the accustomed inference. The exact similarity of the cases gives us a perfect assurance of a similar event; and a stronger evidence is never desired nor sought after. But wherever you depart, in the least, from the similarity of the cases, you diminish proportionably the evidence; and may at last bring it to a very weak analogy, which is confessedly liable to error and uncertainty. After having experienced the circulation of the blood in human creatures, we make no doubt that it takes place in Titius and Maevius. But from its circulation in frogs and fishes, it is only a presumption, though a strong one, from analogy, that it takes place in men and other animals. The analogical reasoning is much weaker, when we infer the circulation of the sap in vegetables from our experience that the blood circulates in animals; and those, who hastily followed that imperfect analogy, are found, by more accurate experiments, to have been mistaken.

If we see a house, Cleanthes, we conclude, with the greatest certainty, that it had an architect or builder; because this is precisely that species of effect which we have experienced to proceed from that species of cause. But surely you will not affirm, that the universe bears such a resemblance to a house that we can with the same certainty infer a similar cause, or that the analogy is here entire and perfect. The dissimilitude is so striking, that the utmost you can here pretend to is a guess, a conjecture, a presumption concerning a similar cause; and how that pretension will be received in the world, I leave you to consider."

"It would surely be very ill received," replied Cleanthes, "and I should be deservedly blamed and detested, did I allow, that the proofs of a Deity amounted to no more than a guess or conjecture. But is the whole adjustment of means to ends in a house and in the universe so slight a resemblance? The economy of final causes? The order, proportion, and arrangement of every part? Steps of a stair are plainly contrived, that human legs may use them in mounting; and this inference is certain and infallible. Human legs are also contrived for walking and mounting; and this inference, I allow, is not altogether so certain, because of the dissimilarity which you remark; but does it, therefore, deserve the name only of presumption or conjecture?"

"Good God!" cried Demea, interrupting him, "where are we? Zealous defenders of religion allow, that the proofs of a Deity fall short of perfect evidence! And you, Philo, … do you assent to all these extravagant opinions of Cleanthes? For what other name can I give them? or, why spare my censure, when such principles are advanced, supported by such an authority, before so young a man as Pamphilus?"

"You seem not to apprehend," replied Philo, "that I argue with Cleanthes in his own way;" and, by showing him the dangerous consequences of his tenets, hope at last to reduce him to our opinion. But what sticks most with you, I observe, is the representation which Cleanthes has made of the argument a posteriori; and finding that that argument is likely to escape your hold and vanish into air, you think it so disguised, that you can scarcely believe it to be set in its true light. Now, however much I may dissent, in other respects, from the dangerous principles of Cleanthes, I must allow that he has fairly represented that argument; and I shall endeavour so to state the matter to you, that you will entertain no further scruples with regard to it.

Were a man to abstract from every thing which he knows or has seen, he would be altogether incapable, merely from his own ideas, to determine what kind of scene the universe must be, or to give the preference to one state or situation of things above another. For as nothing which he clearly conceives could be esteemed impossible or implying a contradiction, every chimera of his fancy would be upon an equal footing; nor could he assign any just reason why he adheres to one idea or system, and rejects the others which are equally possible.

Again; after he opens his eyes, and contemplates the world as it really is, it would be impossible for him at first to assign the cause of any one event, much less of the whole of things, or of the universe. He might set his fancy a rambling; and she might bring him in an infinite variety of reports and representations. These would all be possible; but being all equally possible, he would never of himself give a satisfactory account for his preferring one of them to the rest. Experience alone can point out to him the true cause of any phenomenon.

Now, according to this method of reasoning, Demea, it follows, (and is, indeed, tacitly allowed by Cleanthes himself,) that order, arrangement, or the adjustment of final causes, is not of itself any proof of design; but only so far as it has been experienced to proceed from that principle. For ought we can know a priori, matter may contain the source or spring of order originally within itself as well as mind does; and there is no more difficulty in conceiving, that the several elements, from an internal unknown cause, may fall into the most exquisite arrangement, than to conceive that their ideas, in the great universal mind, from a like internal unknown cause, fall into that arrangement. The equal possibility of both these suppositions is allowed. But, by experience, we find, (according to Cleanthes,) that there is a difference between them. Throw several pieces of steel together, without shape or form; they will never arrange themselves so as to compose a watch. Stone, and mortar, and wood, without an architect, never erect a house. But the ideas in a human mind, we see, by an unknown, inexplicable economy, arrange themselves so as to form the plan of a watch or house. Experience, therefore, proves, that there is an original principle of order in mind, not in matter. From similar effects we infer similar causes. The adjustment of means to ends is alike in the universe, as in a machine of human contrivance. The causes, therefore, must be resembling.

I was from the beginning scandalized, I must own, with this resemblance, which is asserted, between the Deity and human creatures; and must conceive it to imply such a degradation of the Supreme Being as no sound Theist could endure. With your assistance, therefore, Demea, I shall endeavour to defend what you justly call the adorable mysteriousness of the Divine Nature, and shall refute this reasoning of Cleanthes, provided he allows that I have made a fair representation of it."

When Cleanthes had assented, Philo, after a short pause, proceeded in the following manner.

"That all inferences, Cleanthes, concerning fact, are founded on experience; and that all experimental reasonings are founded on the supposition that similar causes prove similar effects, and similar effects similar causes; I shall not at present much dispute with you. But observe, I entreat you, with what extreme caution all just reasoners proceed in the transferring of experiments to similar cases. Unless the cases be exactly similar, they repose no perfect confidence in applying their past observation to any particular phenomenon. Every alteration of circumstances occasions a doubt concerning the event; and it requires new experiments to prove certainly, that the new circumstances are of no moment or importance. A change in bulk, situation, arrangement, age, disposition of the air, or surrounding bodies; any of these particulars may be attended with the most unexpected consequences: and unless the objects be quite familiar to us, it is the highest temerity to expect with assurance, after any of these changes, an event similar to that which before fell under our observation. The slow and deliberate steps of Philosophers here, if anywhere, are distinguished from the precipitate march of the vulgar, who, hurried on by the smallest similitude, are incapable of all discernment or consideration.

But can you think, Cleanthes, that your usual phlegm and Philosophy have been preserved in so wide a step as you have taken, when you compared to the universe houses, ships, furniture, machines, and, from their similarity in some circumstances, inferred a similarity in their causes? Thought, design, intelligence, such as we discover in men and other animals, is no more than one of the springs and principles of the universe, as well as heat or cold, attraction or repulsion, and a hundred others, which fall under daily observation. It is an active cause, by which some particular parts of nature, we find, produce alterations on other parts. But can a conclusion, with any propriety, be transferred from parts to the whole? Does not the great disproportion bar all comparison and inference? From observing the growth of a hair, can we learn any thing concerning the generation of a man? Would the manner of a leaf's blowing, even though perfectly known, afford us any instruction concerning the vegetation of a tree?

But, allowing that we were to take the *operations* of one part of nature upon another, for the foundation of our judgment concerning the *origin* of the whole, (which never can be admitted,) yet why select so minute, so weak, so bounded a principle, as the reason and design of animals is found to be upon this planet? What peculiar privilege has this little agitation of the brain which we call *thought*, that we must thus make it the model of the whole universe? Our partiality in our own favour does indeed present it on all occasions; but sound Philosophy ought carefully to guard against so natural an illusion."

"So far from admitting," continued Philo, "that the operations of a part can afford us any just conclusion concerning the origin of the whole, I will not allow any one part to form a rule for another part, if the latter be very remote from the former. Is there any reasonable ground to conclude, that the inhabitants of other planets possess thought, intelligence, reason, or any thing similar to these faculties in men? When nature has so extremely diversified her manner of operation in this small globe, can we imagine that she incessantly copies herself throughout so immense a universe? And if thought, as we may well suppose, be confined merely to this narrow corner, and has even there so limited a sphere of action, with what propriety can we assign it for the original cause of all things? The narrow views of a peasant, who makes his domestic economy the rule for the government of kingdoms, is in comparison a pardonable sophism.

But were we ever so much assured that a thought and reason, resembling the human, were to be found throughout the whole universe, and were its activity elsewhere vastly greater and more commanding than it appears in this globe; yet I cannot see, why the operations of a world constituted, arranged, adjusted, can with any propriety be extended to a world which is in its embryo state, and is advancing towards that constitution and arrangement. By observation, we know somewhat of the economy, action, and nourishment of a finished animal; but we must transfer with great caution that observation to the growth of a foetus in the womb, and still more in the formation of an animalcule in the loins of its male parent. Nature, we find, even from our limited experience, possesses an infinite number of springs and principles, which incessantly discover themselves on every change of her position and situation. And what new and unknown principles would actuate her in so new and unknown a situation as that of the formation of a universe, we cannot, without the utmost temerity, pretend to determine.

A very small part of this great system, during a very short time, is very imperfectly discovered to us; and do we then pronounce decisively concerning the origin of the whole?

Admirable conclusion! Stone, wood, brick, iron, brass, have not, at this time, in this minute globe of earth, an order or arrangement without human art and contrivance; therefore the universe could not originally attain its order and arrangement, without something similar to human art. But is a part of nature a rule for another part very wide of the former? Is it a rule for the whole? Is a very small part a rule for the universe? Is nature in one situation, a certain rule for nature in another situation vastly different from the former?

And can you blame me, Cleanthes, if I here imitate the prudent reserve of Simonides, who, according to the noted story, being asked by Hiero, "What God was? or what God was, desired a day to think of it, and then two days more; and after that manner continually prolonged the term, without ever bringing in his definition or description? Could you even blame me, if I answered at first, *that I did not know*, and was sensible that this subject lay vastly beyond the reach of my faculties? You might cry out sceptic and rallier, as much as you pleased: but having found, in so many other subjects much more familiar, the imperfections and even contradictions of human reason, I never should expect any success from its feeble conjectures, in a subject so sublime, and so remote from the sphere of our observation. When two *species* of objects have always been observed to be conjoined together, I can *infer*, by custom, the existence of one wherever I see the existence of the other; and this I call an argument from experience. But how this argument can have place, where the objects, as in the present case, are single, individual, without parallel, or specific resemblance, may be difficult to explain. And will any man tell me with a serious countenance, that an orderly universe must arise from some thought and art like the human, because we have experience of it? To ascertain this reasoning, it were requisite that we had experience of the origin of worlds; and it is not sufficient, surely, that we have seen ships and cities arise from human art and contrivance."

PART IX

"But if so many difficulties attend the argument a posteriori," said Demea, "had we not better adhere to that simple and sublime argument a priori, which, by offering to us infallible demonstration, cuts off at once all doubt and difficulty? By this argument, too, we may prove the Infinity of the Divine attributes, which, I am afraid, can never be ascertained with certainty from any other topic. For how can an effect, which either is finite, or, for aught we know, may be so; how can such an effect, I say, prove an infinite cause? The unity too of the Divine Nature, it is very difficult, if not absolutely impossible, to deduce merely from contemplating the works of nature; nor will the uniformity alone of the plan, even were it allowed, give us any assurance of that attribute. Whereas the argument a priori …"

"You seem to reason, Demea," interposed Cleanthes, "as if those advantages and conveniences in the abstract argument were full proofs of its solidity. But it is first proper, in my opinion, to determine what argument of this nature you choose to insist on; and we shall afterwards, from itself, better than from its useful consequences, endeavour to determine what value we ought to put upon it."

"The argument," replied Demea, "which I would insist on," is the common one. Whatever exists must have a cause or reason of its existence; it being absolutely impossible for any thing to produce itself, or be the cause of its own existence. In mounting up, therefore, from effects to causes, we must either go on in tracing an infinite succession, without any ultimate cause at all; or must at last have recourse to some ultimate cause, that is necessarily existent: now, that the first supposition is absurd, may be thus proved. In the infinite chain or succession of causes and effects, each single effect is determined to exist by the power and efficacy of that cause which immediately preceded; but the whole eternal chain or succession, taken together, is not determined or caused by any thing; and yet it is evident that it requires a cause or reason, as much as any particular object which begins to exist in time. The question is still reasonable, why this particular succession of causes existed from eternity, and not any other succession, or no succession at all. If there be no necessarily existent being, any supposition which can be formed is equally possible; nor is there any more absurdity in Nothing's having existed from eternity, than there is in that succession of causes which constitutes the universe. What was it, then, which determined Something to exist rather than Nothing, and bestowed being on a particular possibility, exclusive of the rest? *External causes*, there are supposed to be none. *Chance* is a word without a meaning. Was it *Nothing*? But that can never produce any thing. We must, therefore, have recourse to a necessarily existent Being, who carries the reason of his existence in himself, and who cannot be supposed not to exist, without an express contradiction. There is, consequently, such a Being; that is, there is a Deity."

"I shall not leave it to Philo," said Cleanthes, "though I know that the starting objections is his chief delight, to point out the weakness of this metaphysical reasoning. It seems to me so obviously ill-grounded, and at the same time of so little consequence to the cause of true piety and religion, that I shall myself venture to show the fallacy of it.

I shall begin with observing, that there is an evident absurdity in pretending to demonstrate a matter of fact, or to prove it by any arguments a priori. Nothing is demonstrable, unless the contrary implies a contradiction. Nothing, that is distinctly conceivable, implies a contradiction. Whatever we conceive as existent, we can also conceive as non-existent. There is no being, therefore, whose non-existence implies a contradiction. Consequently there is no being, whose existence is demonstrable. I propose this argument as entirely decisive, and am willing to rest the whole controversy upon it.

It is pretended that the Deity is a necessarily existent being; and this necessity of his existence is attempted to be explained by asserting, that if we knew his whole essence or nature, we should perceive it to be as impossible for him not to exist, as for twice two not to be four. But it is evident that this can never happen, while our faculties remain the same as at present. It will still be possible for us, at any time, to conceive the non-existence of what we formerly conceived to exist; nor can the mind ever lie under a necessity of supposing any object to remain always in being; in the same manner as we lie under a necessity of always conceiving twice two to be four. The words, therefore, *necessary existence*, have no meaning; or, which is the same thing, none that is consistent.

But further, why may not the material universe be the necessarily existent being, according to this pretended explication of necessity? We dare not affirm that we know all the qualities of matter; and for aught we can determine, it may contain some qualities, which, were they known, would make its non-existence appear as great a contradiction as that twice two is five. I find only one argument employed to prove, that the material world is not the necessarily existent Being: and this argument is derived from the contingency both of the matter and the form of the world. "Any particle of matter," it is said, "may be conceived to be annihilated; and any form may be conceived to be altered. Such an annihilation or alteration, therefore, is not impossible." But it seems a great partiality not to perceive, that the same argument extends equally to the Deity, so far as we have any conception of him; and that the mind can at least imagine him to be non-existent, or his attributes to be altered. It must be some unknown, inconceivable qualities, which can make his non-existence appear impossible, or his attributes unalterable: and no reason can be assigned, why these qualities may not belong to matter. As they are altogether unknown and inconceivable, they can never be proved incompatible with it.

Add to this, that in tracing an eternal succession of objects, it seems absurd to enquire for a general cause or first author. How can anything, that exists from eternity, have a cause, since that relation implies a priority in time, and a beginning of existence?

In such a chain, too, or succession of objects, each part is caused by that which preceded it, and causes that which succeeds it. Where then is the difficulty? But the whole, you say, wants a cause. I answer, that the uniting of these parts into a whole, like the uniting of several distinct countries into one kingdom, or several distinct members into one body, is performed merely by an arbitrary act of the mind, and has no influence on the nature of things. Did I show you the particular causes of each individual in a collection of twenty particles of matter, I should think it very unreasonable, should you afterwards ask me, what was the cause of the whole twenty. This is sufficiently explained in explaining the cause of the parts."

THE TELEOLOGICAL ARGUMENT[1]

By Robin Collins

INTRODUCTION AND HISTORICAL BACKGROUND

My contention in this essay will be that discoveries in physics and cosmology, along with developments in philosophy, particularly in the logic of inference, have significantly bolstered the traditional teleological argument, or argument from design. Today, I contend, the evidence from physics and cosmology offers us significant, well-formulated reasons for believing in theism.

The design argument has a long history, probably being the most commonly cited argument for believing in a deity. Before the eighteenth century, design arguments typically appealed to the idea that the universe is orderly, or appears to be ordered toward some end. In ancient India, for instance, the argument from design was advanced by the so-called Nyāya (or logical-atomist) school (100–1000 CE), which argued for the existence of a deity based on the order of the world, which they compared both to human artifacts and to the human body.[2] In the West, the design argument goes back at least to Heraclitus, who attempted to account for the order in the universe by hypothesizing that the universe was directed by a principle of intelligence or reason. Related arguments were offered by Plato, Aristotle, and the Stoics. This sort of argument was further elaborated upon by Thomas Aquinas, in his famous Fifth Way. According to Aquinas, nature appears to be directed toward an end, yet it lacks knowledge to direct itself. Thus, Aquinas claimed, "some intelligent being exists by whom all natural things are directed to their end; and this being we call God." From the perspective of our modern scientific understanding of the world, one outstanding problem with Aquinas's argument is that it is unclear in what sense nature is "directed toward an end," other than that it simply appears to be orderly.

More generally, since the rise of the scientific revolution, these versions of the teleological argument that simply appealed to the orderliness of the universe lost much of their force as philosophers and scientists became increasingly contented with appealing to the laws of nature as a sufficient explanation of the regular operation of the universe, although God was still appealed to by some as the explanation of the existence of these laws. The version of the design argument that began to take its place was one based on the *intricate* ordering of various natural systems for some end, not the mere regularity of some aspect of the world. In William Paley's famous presentation of the design argument, the intricate organization of the organs of the body—such as an eye—is compared to the intricate ordering of the parts of a watch for the apparent purpose of telling of time. Since, Paley argues, upon finding such an object on a heath (or somewhere else), one would attribute it to some intelligence, the same should be done for the intricate structure of plants and animals. As skeptical philosophers such as David Hume pointed out, however, there is an important disanalogy between the universe or plants and animals and the case of watches that seems to undercut the argument: we know from experience that the watches are produced by minds, but we have no experience of animal life or universes being created by minds.

In the view of many, however, the real blow to Paley's argument came from a different quarter: Darwin's theory of evolution. Before Darwin, the problem facing atheists was to offer some alternative explanation for the extraordinarily complex and well-ordered biological systems in animal and plant life. One could raise philosophical doubts about the validity of the inference to design, as Hume did, but without an alternative explanation the impression of design remained overwhelming. After Darwin, however, one no longer needed to appeal to some transcendent intelligence as responsible for the apparent design of plants and animals, but could appeal to the "blind watchmaker" (to use one of Richard Dawkins's phrases) of evolution by chance plus natural selection. In his *Natural Theology*,[3] however, Paley presented another design argument that was not subject to the "evolution objection." This was the argument that in order for life to exist, the laws of nature and the physical environment of the earth must also be well designed. Partly because of the lack of detailed physical and astrophysical knowledge at the time, this version of Paley's argument was never considered particularly strong.

In recent decades, however, this version of the argument has become much more convincing. Scientists have increasingly come to realize how the initial conditions of the universe and the basic constants of physics must be balanced on a razor's edge for intelligent life to evolve—something known in the literature as the "fine-tuning" of the cosmos for (intelligent) life. Calculations show that if the constants of physics—such as the physical constant governing the strength of gravity—were slightly different, the evolution of complex, embodied life-forms of comparable intelligence to ourselves would be seriously inhibited, if not rendered impossible. These calculations added an important quantitative element to the argument from design: instead of simply appealing to a qualitative impression of the intricate ordering of nature for some end, as in Aquinas's Fifth Way, one could now give "hard" numerical content to these qualitative impressions. Because of this new quantitative data, along with developments in the logic of inference during the twentieth century, the design argument can be cast into a much more rigorous form then in the past, as I will now elaborate. We will begin by looking at the evidence for the fine-tuning of the cosmos for intelligent life.

THE EVIDENCE OF FINE-TUNING

Many examples of the fine-tuning for intelligent life can be given, a few of which we will briefly recount here.[4] One particularly important category of fine-tuning is that of the *constants* of physics. The constants of physics are a set of fundamental numbers that, when plugged into the laws of physics, determine the basic structure of the universe. An example of such a constant is the gravitational constant G that is part of Newton's law of gravity, $F = GM_1M_2/r^2$. G determines the strength of gravity between two masses. If one were to double the value of G, for instance, then the force of gravity between any two masses would double.

So far, physicists have discovered four forces in nature: gravity, the weak force, electromagnetism, and the strong nuclear force that binds protons and neutrons together in an atom. As measured in a certain set of standard dimensionless units,[5] gravity is the weakest of the forces, and the strong nuclear force is the strongest, being a factor of 10^{40}—or ten thousand billion, billion, billion, billion—times stronger than gravity.

Various calculations show that the strength of each of the forces of nature must fall into a very small life-permitting region for intelligent life to exist. As just one example, consider gravity. Compared with the total range of forces, the strength of gravity must fall in a relatively narrow range in order for complex life to exist. If we increased the strength of gravity a billion-fold, for instance, the force of gravity on a planet with the mass and size of the earth would be so great that organisms anywhere near the size of human beings, whether land-based or aquatic, would be crushed. (The strength of materials depends on the electromagnetic force via the fine-structure constant, which would not be affected by a change in the strength of gravity.) Even a much smaller planet of only 40 feet in diameter—which is not large enough to sustain organisms of our size—would have a gravitational pull of 1000 times that of earth, still too strong for organisms of our brain size, and hence level of intelligence, to exist. As astrophysicist Martin Rees notes, "In an imaginary strong gravity world, even insects would need thick legs to support them, and no animals could get much larger."[6] Other calculations show that if the gravitational force were increased by more than a factor of 3000, the maximum life-time of a star would be a billion years, thus severely inhibiting the probability of intelligent life evolving.[7] Of course, a 3000-fold increase in the strength of gravity is a lot, but compared with the total range of the strengths of the forces in nature (which span a range of 10^{40}, as we saw above), it is very small, being one part in a billion, billion, billion, billion.

Similarly, if the strong force were slightly increased or decreased, the existence of complex life would be seriously inhibited, if not rendered impossible. For instance, using the latest equations and codes for stellar evolution and nucleosynthesis, Heinz Oberhummer *et al.* showed that a small increase or decrease in the strong force—by as little as 1 percent—would drastically decrease, by 30- to 1000-fold, the total amount of either carbon or oxygen formed in stars.[8] Since the carbon and oxygen on planets comes from previous stars that have exploded or blown off their outer layers, this means that very little oxygen would be available for the existence of carbon-based life. At the very least, this would have a life-inhibiting effect given the many important, and seemingly irreplaceable, roles both carbon and oxygen play in living processes.[9]

There are other cases of the fine-tuning of the constants of physics besides the strength of the forces, however. Probably the most widely discussed—and esoteric—among physicists and cosmologists is the fine-tuning of what is known as the *cosmological constant*, which influences the expansion rate of the universe. If the cosmological constant were not fine-tuned to within one part in 10^{53} or even 10^{120} of its natural range of values, the universe would expand so rapidly that all matter would quickly disperse, and thus galaxies, stars, and even small aggregates of matter could never form.[10]

Besides the constants of physics, however, there is also the "fine-tuning" of the laws. If the laws of nature were not just right, life would probably be impossible. For example, consider again the four forces of nature. If gravity did not exist, masses would not clump together to form stars or planets; if the electromagnetic force did not exist, there would be no chemistry; if the strong force did not exist, protons and neutrons could not bind together and hence no atoms with atomic number greater than hydrogen would exist; and if the strong force were a long-range force (like gravity and electromagnetism) instead of a short range force that only acts between protons and neutrons in the nucleus, all matter would either almost instantaneously undergo nuclear fusion and explode or be sucked together forming a black hole. Each of these consequences would seriously inhibit, if not render impossible, the existence of complex intelligent life.

Similarly, other laws and principles are necessary for complex life: as prominent Princeton physicist Freeman Dyson points out,[11] if the Pauli-exclusion principle did not exist, which dictates that no two fermions can occupy the same quantum state, all electrons would occupy the lowest atomic orbit, eliminating complex chemistry; and if there were no quantization principle, which dictates that particles can only occupy certain discrete quantum states, there would be no atomic orbits and hence no chemistry, since all electrons would be sucked into the nucleus.

Finally, in his book *Nature's Destiny*, biochemist Michael Denton extensively discusses various higher-level features of the natural world, such as the many unique properties of carbon, oxygen, water, and the electromagnetic spectrum, that are conducive to the existence of complex biochemical systems. As one of many examples that Denton presents, both the atmosphere and water are transparent to electromagnetic radiation in a thin band in the visible region, but nowhere else except in radio waves. If, instead, either of them absorbed electromagnetic radiation in the visible region, the existence of terrestrial life would be seriously inhibited, if not rendered impossible.[12] These higher-level coincidences indicate a deeper-level fine-tuning of the fundamental laws and constants of physics.

As the above examples indicate, the evidence for fine-tuning is extensive, even if one has doubts about some individual cases. As philosopher John Leslie has pointed out, "clues heaped upon clues can constitute weighty evidence despite doubts about each element in the pile."[13] At the very least, these cases of fine-tuning show the truth of Freeman Dyson's observation that there are many "lucky accidents in physics,"[14] without which our existence as intelligent embodied beings would be impossible.

THE ARGUMENT FORMULATED

Now it is time to consider the way in which the fine-tuning supports theism. In this section, I will argue that the evidence of fine-tuning primarily gives us a reason for preferring theism over what could be called the atheistic single-universe hypothesis—that is, the hypothesis that there is only one universe, and it exists as a brute fact. We will examine the typical alternative explanation of the fine-tuning offered by many atheists—what I call the "many-universes hypothesis"—in the section 'The many-worlds hypothesis' below.

Although the fine-tuning argument against the atheistic single-universe hypothesis can be cast in several different forms—such as inference to the best explanation—I believe that the most rigorous way of formulating the argument is in terms of what I will call the *prime principle of confirmation* (PPC), and which Rudolph Carnap has called the "*increase in firmness*" principle, and others have simply called the *likelihood principle*.[15] The PPC is a general principle of reasoning that tells us when some observation counts as evidence in favor of one hypothesis over another. *Simply put, the principle says that whenever we are considering two competing hypotheses, an observation counts as evidence in favor of the hypothesis under which the observation has the highest probability (or is the least improbable).* (Or, put slightly differently, the principle says that whenever we are considering two competing hypotheses, H_1 and H_2, an observation, O, counts as evidence in favor of H_1 over H_2 if O is more probable under H_1 than it is under H_2.) Moreover, the degree to which the evidence counts in favor of one hypothesis over another is proportional to the degree to which the observation is more probable under the one hypothesis than the other.[16] To illustrate, consider a case of finding a defendant's fingerprints on the murder weapon. Normally, we would take such a finding as strong evidence that the defendant was guilty. Why? Because we judge that it would be *unlikely* for these fingerprints to be on the murder weapon if the defendant was innocent, but *not unlikely* if the defendant was guilty. Then by the prime principle of confirmation, we would conclude that the fingerprints offered significant evidence that the defendant was guilty.

Using this principle, we can develop the fine-tuning argument in a two-step form as follows:

1. The existence of the fine-tuning is not highly improbable under theism.
2. The existence of the fine-tuning is very improbable under the atheistic single-universe hypothesis.[17]

We can conclude from premises 1 and 2 and the prime principle of confirmation that the fine-tuning data provide significant evidence in favor of the design hypothesis over the atheistic single-universe hypothesis.

At this point, we should pause to note two features of this argument. First, the argument does not say that the fine-tuning evidence proves that the universe was designed, or even that it is likely that the universe was designed. Indeed, of itself it does not even show that we are epistemically warranted in believing in theism over the atheistic single-universe hypothesis. In order to justify these sorts of claims, we would have to look at the full range of evidence both for and against the theistic hypothesis—something I am not doing in this essay. Rather, the argument merely concludes that the fine-tuning significantly *supports* theism *over* the atheistic single-universe hypothesis. (I say significantly supports, because presumably the ratio of probabilities for the fine-tuning under theism versus the atheistic single-universe hypothesis is quite large. See note 16.)

In this way, the evidence of the fine-tuning argument is much like fingerprints found on a gun: although they can provide strong evidence that the defendant committed the murder, one could not conclude merely from them alone that the defendant is guilty; one would also have to look at all the other evidence offered. Perhaps, for instance, ten reliable witnesses claimed to see the defendant at a party at the time of the shooting. In this case, the fingerprints would still count as significant evidence of guilt, but this evidence would be counterbalanced by the testimony of the witnesses. Similarly the evidence of fine-tuning significantly supports theism over the atheistic single-universe hypothesis, but it does not itself show that, everything considered, theism is the most plausible explanation of the fine-tuning of the world.

The second feature of the argument we should note is that, given the truth of *the prime principle of confirmation,* the conclusion of the argument follows from the premises. Specifically, if the premises of the argument are true, then we are guaranteed that the conclusion is true: that is, the argument is what philosophers call *valid.* Thus, insofar as we can show that the premises of the argument are true, we will have shown that the conclusion is true. Our next task, therefore, is to attempt to show that the premises are true, or at least that we have good reasons to believe them.

Support for the premises

Support for premise 1

Premise 1 is easy to support and somewhat less controversial than premise 2. The argument in support of it can be simply stated as follows: *since God is an all good being, and it is good for intelligent, conscious beings to exist, it is not highly surprising or highly improbable that God would create a world that could support intelligent life.* Thus, the fine-tuning is not highly improbable under theism.

Support for premise 2

Upon looking at the data, many people find it very obvious that the fine-tuning is highly improbable under the atheistic single-universe hypothesis. And it is easy to see why when we think of the fine-tuning in terms of various analogies. In the "dart-board analogy," for example, the theoretically possible values for fundamental constants of physics can be represented as a dart-board that fills the whole galaxy, and the conditions necessary for life to exist as a small inch-wide target. Accordingly, from this analogy it seems obvious that it would be highly improbable for the fine-tuning to occur under the atheistic single-universe hypothesis—that is, for the dart to hit the target by chance.

Now some philosophers object to claim that the fine-tuning is highly improbable under the atheistic single-universe hypothesis by arguing that since there is only one universe, the notion of the fine-tuning of the universe being probable or improbable is meaningless. Ian Hacking, for instance, claims that a probability could only be meaningfully assigned to the fine-tuning if we had some model of universe generation which implied that a certain percentage of universes would turn out to be fine-tuned.[18] Given such a model, and given that a single-universe is generated, we could then assign the universe a certain probability of being fine-tuned. Keith Parsons raises similar objections.[19]

Although I do not have space to provide a full-scale response to this objection, I will briefly sketch an answer. The first is to note that the relevant notion of probability occurring in the fine-tuning argument is a widely recognized type of probability called *epistemic probability.*[20] Roughly, the epistemic probability of a proposition can be thought of as the degree of confidence or belief that we rationally should have in the proposition. Further, the conditional epistemic probability of a proposition R on another proposition S—written as $P(R/S)$—can be defined as the degree to which the proposition S *of itself* should rationally lead us to expect that R is true. Under the epistemic conception of probability, therefore, the statement that *the fine-tuning of the cosmos is very improbable under the atheistic single-universe hypothesis* is to be understood as making a statement about the degree to which the atheistic single-universe hypothesis would or should, *of itself,* rationally lead us to expect cosmic fine-tuning.

The phrase "*of itself*" is important here. The rational degree of expectation should not be confused with the degree to which one should expect the constants of physics to fall within the life-permitting range if one believed the atheistic single-universe hypothesis. For even those who believe in this atheistic hypothesis should expect the values of the constants of physics to be life-permitting since this follows from the fact that we are alive. Rather, the conditional epistemic probability in this case is the degree to which the atheistic single-universe hypothesis *of itself* should lead us to expect the values of the constants of physics to be life-permitting. This means that in assessing the conditional epistemic probability in this and other similar cases, one must exclude contributions to our expectations arising from other information that we have, such as that we are alive. In the case at hand, one way of doing this is by means of the following sort of thought experiment. Imagine a disembodied being with mental capacities and a knowledge of physics similar to that of the most intelligent physicists alive today, except that the being does not know whether the values of the constants of physics allow for embodied, intelligent life to arise. Further, suppose that this disembodied being believed in the atheistic single-universe hypothesis. Then, the degree that being should rationally expect the values of the constants of physics to be life-permitting would be equal to our conditional epistemic probability, since its expectation is solely a result of its belief in the atheistic single-universe hypothesis, not other factors such as its awareness of its own existence.

Given this understanding of the notion of conditional epistemic probability, it is not difficult to see that the conditional epistemic probability of a constant of physics having a life-permitting value under the atheistic single-universe hypothesis will be much smaller than under theism. The reason is simple when we think about our imaginary disembodied being. If such a being were a theist, it would have some reason to believe that the values of the constants would fall into the life-permitting region. (See the argument in support of premise 1 above.) On the other hand, if the being were a subscriber to the atheistic single-universe hypothesis, it would have no reason to think that the values would be in the life-permitting region instead of any other part of the "theoretically possible" range of values. Thus, the being has more reason to believe that the constants would fall into the life-permitting region under theism than the atheistic single-universe hypothesis—that is, the epistemic probability under theism is larger than under this atheistic hypothesis. How much larger? That depends on the degree of fine-tuning. Here, I will simply note that it seems obvious that in general the higher the degree of fine-tuning— that is, the smaller the width of the life-permitting range is to the "theoretically possible" range—the greater the surprise under the atheistic single-universe hypothesis, and hence the greater the ratio of the two probabilities. To go beyond these statements and to assign actual probabilities under the atheistic single-universe hypothesis—or to further justify these claims of improbability—would require appealing to the probabilistic principle of indifference, which is beyond the scope of this essay.

OBJECTIONS TO THE ARGUMENT

As powerful as the fine-tuning argument against the atheistic single-universe hypothesis is, several major objections have been raised to it by both atheists and theists. In this section, we will consider these objections in turn.

Objection 1: more fundamental law objection

One criticism of the fine-tuning argument is that, as far as we know, there could be a more fundamental law under which the constants of physics *must* have the values they do. Thus, given such a law, it is not improbable that the known constants of physics fall within the life-permitting range.

Besides being entirely speculative, the problem with postulating such a law is that it simply moves the improbability of the fine-tuning up one level, to that of the postulated physical law itself. As astrophysicists Bernard Carr and Martin Rees note, "even if all apparently anthropic coincidences could be explained [in terms of some grand unified theory], it would still be remarkable that the relationships dictated by physical theory happened also to be those propitious for life."[21] A similar sort of response can be given to the claim that the fine-tuning is not improbable because it might be *logically necessary* for the constants of physics to have life-permitting values. That is, according to this claim, the constants of physics must have life-permitting values in the same way that 2 + 2 must equal 4, or the interior angles of a triangle must add up to 180 degrees in Euclidian geometry. Like the "more fundamental law" proposal above, however, this postulate simply transfers the improbability up one level: of all the laws and constants of physics that conceivably could have been logically necessary, it seems highly improbable that it would be those that are life-permitting.[22]

Objection 2: other forms of life objection

Another objection people commonly raise against the fine-tuning argument is that, as far as we know, other forms of life could exist even if the constants of physics were different. So, it is claimed, the fine-tuning argument ends up presupposing that all forms of intelligent life must be like us. One answer to this objection is that many cases of fine-tuning do not make this presupposition. If, for example, the cosmological constant were much larger than it is, matter would disperse so rapidly that no planets, and indeed no stars could exist. Without stars, however, there would exist no stable energy sources for complex material systems of any sort to evolve. So, all the fine-tuning argument presupposes in this case is that the evolution of intelligent life requires some stable energy source. This is certainly a very reasonable assumption.

Of course, if the laws and constants of nature were changed enough, other forms of embodied intelligent life might be able to exist of which we cannot even conceive. But this is irrelevant to the fine-tuning argument since the judgment of improbability of fine-tuning under the atheistic single-universe hypothesis only requires that, given our current laws of nature, the life-permitting range for the values of the constants of physics (such as gravity) is small compared with the *surrounding* range of non-life-permitting values.

Objection 3: anthropic principle objection

According to the weak version of the so-called *anthropic principle*, if the laws of nature were not fine-tuned, we would not be here to comment on the fact. Some have argued, therefore, that the fine-tuning is not really *improbable or surprising* at all under atheism, but simply follows from the fact that we exist. The response to this objection is simply to restate the argument in terms of our existence: our existence as embodied, intelligent beings is extremely unlikely under the atheistic single-universe hypothesis (since our existence requires fine-tuning), but not improbable under theism. Then, we simply apply the prime principle of confirmation to draw the conclusion that *our existence* significantly confirms theism over the atheistic single-universe hypothesis.

To further illustrate this response, consider the following "firing-squad" analogy. As John Leslie points out, if fifty sharp shooters all miss me, the response "if they had not missed me I wouldn't be here to consider the fact" is not adequate. Instead, I would naturally conclude that there was some reason why they all missed, such as that they never really intended to kill me. Why would I conclude this? Because my continued existence would be very improbable under the hypothesis that they missed me by chance, but not improbable under the hypothesis that there was some reason why they missed me.[23] Thus, by the prime principle of confirmation, my continued existence strongly confirms the latter hypothesis.

Objection 4: the "Who designed God?" objection

Perhaps the most common objection that atheists raise to the argument from design, of which the fine-tuning argument is one instance, is that postulating the existence of God does not solve the problem of design, but merely transfers it up one level, to the question of who designed God. In fact, philosopher J. J. C. Smart claims that hypothesizing God as an explanation for the order and complexity of the universe makes us explanatorily worse off:

> If we postulate God in addition to the created universe we increase the complexity of our hypothesis. We have all the complexity of the universe itself, and we have in addition the at least equal complexity of God. (The designer of an artifact must be at least as complex as the designed artifact).… If the theist can show the atheist that postulating God actually reduces the complexity of one's total world view, then the atheist should be a theist. [24]

In response, we can first note that even if Smart is correct in claiming that God exhibits enormous internal complexity, it still would be the case that the fine-tuning provides evidence in favor of theism over the atheistic single-universe hypothesis. The reason is that the above argument only relies on comparison of probabilities of fine-tuning under the two different hypotheses, not on whether the new hypothesis reduces the overall complexity of one's worldview. As an analogy, if complex, intricate structures (such as aqueducts and buildings) existed on Mars, one could conclude that they would support the hypothesis that intelligent, extraterrestrial beings existed on Mars in the past, even if such beings are much more complex than the structures to be explained. Second, however, for reasons entirely independent of the argument from design, God has been thought to have little, if any, internal complexity. Indeed, medieval philosophers and theologians often went as far as advocating the doctrine of divine simplicity, according to which God is claimed to be absolutely simple, without any internal complexity. So, atheists who push this objection have a lot of arguing to do to make it stick.

THE MANY-WORLDS HYPOTHESIS

In response to the theistic explanation of the fine-tuning, many atheists have offered an alternative explanation, what I will call the *many-universes hypothesis,* but which in the literature goes under a variety of names, such as many-worlds hypothesis, the many-domains hypothesis, the world-ensemble hypothesis, the multi-universe hypothesis, etc. According to this hypothesis, there are a very large—perhaps infinite—number of universes, with the constants of physics varying from universe to universe.[25] Of course, in the vast majority of these universes, the constants of physics would *not* have life-permitting values. Nonetheless, in a small proportion of universes they would, and consequently it is no longer improbable that universes such as ours exist that have life-permitting values for their constants.

Further, usually these universes are thought to be produced by some sort of physical mechanism, which I call a many-universe generator. The universe generator can be thought of as analogous to a lottery ticket generator: just as it would be no surprise that a winning number is eventually produced if enough tickets are generated, it would be no surprise that a universe fine-tuned for life would occur if enough universes are generated.[26]

Most many-universes models are entirely speculative, having little basis in current physics. However, many physicists, such as Steven Weinberg, have proposed a model that does have a reasonable basis in current physics—namely, inflationary cosmology. Inflationary cosmology is a currently widely discussed cosmological theory that attempts to explain the origin of the universe, and which has recently passed some preliminary observational tests. Essentially, it claims that our universe was formed by a small area of pre-space being massively blown up by a hypothesized *inflation* field, in much the same way as a soap bubble would form in an ocean full of soap. In chaotic inflation models—widely considered the most plausible—various points of the pre-space are randomly blown up, forming an enormous number of bubble universes.[27]

In order to get the initial conditions and constants of physics to vary from universe to universe, as they must do if this scenario is going to explain the fine-tuning, there must be a further physical mechanism to cause the variation. Such a mechanism *might* be given by superstring theory, one of the most hotly discussed hypotheses about the fundamental structure of matter, but it is too early to tell. Other leading alternatives to string theory being explored by physicists, such as the currently proposed models for Grand Unified Theories (GUTs), do not appear to allow for enough variation (e.g. they only give a dozen or so different values for the constants, not the enormous number needed to account for the fine-tuning).[28]

Although at present these theories are highly speculative (for example, superstring theory has no experimental evidence in its favor),[29] I do not believe that simply rejecting the many-universe generator hypothesis is an adequate response. Not only does the inflationary/superstring scenario have some plausibility, but God could have created our universe via some many-universe generator, just as God created our planet by the Big Bang—a sort of many-planets generator. A better response is to note that the "many-universe generator" itself, whether that given by chaotic inflationary models or some other type, seems to need to be "well-designed" in order to produce life-sustaining universes. After all, even a mundane item like a bread machine, which only produces loaves of bread instead of universes, must be well designed to produce decent loaves of bread. If this is right, then, to some extent, invoking some sort of many-universe generator as an explanation of the fine-tuning only kicks the issue of design up one level, to the question of who designed the many-universe generator.

For example, the inflationary scenario discussed above only works to produce universes because of the prior existence of the inflation field, and the peculiar nature of the central equation of general relativity, that is Einstein's equation.[30] Without either factor, there would neither be regions of space that inflate nor would those regions have the mass–energy necessary for a universe to exist. If, for example, the universe obeyed Newton's theory of gravity instead of Einstein's, the inflation field would at best simply create a gravitational attraction causing space to contract, not to expand. Moreover, as mentioned above, one needs a special underlying physical theory—such as perhaps superstring theory—that allows for enough variation in the constants of physics among universes.

Further, the inflationary many-universe generator can only produce life-sustaining universes if the right background laws are in place. For example, without the Pauli-exclusion principle, electrons would occupy the lowest atomic orbit and hence complex and varied atoms would be impossible; or, without a universally attractive force between all masses, such as gravity, matter would not be able to form sufficiently large material bodies (such as planets) for life to develop or for long-lived stable energy sources such as stars to exist. The universe generator hypothesis, however, does not explain these background laws.

Finally, I would argue, the many-universes generator hypothesis cannot explain other features of the universe that seem to exhibit apparent design whereas theism can. For example, many physicists, such as Albert Einstein, have observed that the basic laws of physics exhibit an extraordinary degree of beauty, elegance, harmony, and ingenuity. Nobel Prize winning physicist Steven Weinberg, for instance, devotes a whole chapter of his book *Dreams of a Final Theory* (Chapter 6, "Beautiful Theories") to explaining how the criteria of beauty and elegance are commonly used to guide physicists in formulating the right laws.[31]

Indeed, one of most prominent theoretical physicists of this century, Paul Dirac, went so far as to claim that "it is more important to have beauty in one's equations than to have them fit experiment."[32] Now such beauty, elegance, and ingenuity make sense if the universe was designed by God; I would contend, however, that apart from some sort of design hypothesis, there is no reason to expect the fundamental laws to be elegant or beautiful. Thus theism makes more sense of this aspect of the world than atheism, whether that atheism is of the single-universe or many-universe variety.[33]

CONCLUSION

In this chapter, I argued that the fine-tuning of the cosmos for life provides strong evidence for preferring theism over the atheistic single-universe hypothesis. I then argued that although one can partially explain the fine-tuning of the constants of physics by invoking some sort of many-universes generator, we have good reasons to believe that the many-universe generator itself would need to be well designed, and hence that hypothesizing some sort of many-universes generator only pushes the case for design up one level. The arguments I have offered do not prove the truth of theism, or even show that theism is epistemically warranted or the most plausible position to adopt. To show this would require examining all the evidence both for and against theism, along with looking at all the alternatives to theism. Rather, the arguments in this essay were only intended to show that the fine-tuning of the cosmos offers us significant reasons for preferring theism over atheism (where atheism is understood as not simply the denial of theism but as also including the denial of any sort of intelligence behind the existence or structure of the universe). As with the design argument in general, by itself the fine-tuning argument cannot get one all the way to theism. Other arguments or considerations must be brought into play to do that. Thus, although quite significant, it only constitutes one part of the case for theism, other parts of which are explored in this book.

NOTES

1. A full-scale treatment of the fine-tuning argument, and related design arguments, will be presented in a book I am currently working on tentatively entitled *The Well-Tempered Universe: God, Fine-tuning, and the Laws of Nature*. Some parts of this paper were adapted from previous articles and book chapters: "The Fine-Tuning Design Argument" in *Reason for the Hope Within*, Michael Murray (ed.) (Grand Rapids, MI: Eerdmans, 1999); "The Argument from Design and the Many-Worlds Hypothesis," in *Philosophy of Religion: a Reader and Guide*, William Lane Craig (ed.) (Tronten: Rutgers University Press, 2001); "God, Design, and Fine-tuning" in *God Matters: Readings in the Philosophy of Religion*, Raymond Martin and Christopher Bernard (eds) (New York: Longman Press, 2002); "The Evidence for Fine-tuning," in *God and Design: The Teleological*

Argument and Modern Science, Neil Manson (ed.) (London: Routledge, 2003). Work on this topic was made possible by a yearlong fellowship from the Pew Foundation, several grants from the Discovery Institute, and a grant from Messiah College.

2. Ninian Smart, *Doctrine and Argument in Indian Philosophy* (London: George Allen and Unwin, 1964) 153–4.

3. Paley, William, *Natural Theology* (Boston: Gould and Lincoln, 1852 [1802])

4. For an up-to-date analysis of the evidence for fine-tuning, with a careful physical analysis of what I consider the six strongest cases, see my "The Evidence for Fine-Tuning," in *God and Design*, Neil Manson (ed.) (London: Routledge, forthcoming); more etailed treatments of the cases of fine-tuning cited below are presented in that chapter, along with more detailed references to the literature. Other useful references are John Barrow and Frank Tipler, *The Anthropic Cosmological Principle* (Oxford: Oxford University Press, 1986); Paul Davies, *The Accidental Universe* (Cambridge: Cambridge University Press, 1982); John Leslie, *Universes* (London: Routledge, 1989); B. J. Carr and M. J. Rees, "The Anthropic Cosmological Principle and the Structure of the Physical World," *Nature* 278 (1979), 605–12; Martin Rees, *Just Six Numbers: The Deep Forces that Shape the Universe* (New York: Basic Books, 2000).

5. Barrow and Tipler, *Anthropic Cosmological Principle*, 292–5.

6. Rees, *Just Six Numbers*, 30.

7. For the actual calculations, see my "The Evidence for Fine-tuning."

8. H. Oberhummer, A. Csoto, and H. Schlattl, "Fine-Tuning of Carbon Based Life in the Universe by Triple-Alpha Process in Red Giants," *Science* 289 (2000), 88.

9. Michael Denton, *Nature's Destiny: How the Laws of Biology Reveal Purpose in the Universe* (New York: The Free Press, 1998), 19–47, 117–40.

10. The fine-tuning of the cosmological constant is widely discussed in the literature. See Davies, *The Accidental Universe*, 105–9; Rees, *Just Six Numbers*, 95–102, 154–5. For an accessible, current discussion, see my "The Evidence for Fine-Tuning."

11. Freeman Dyson, *Disturbing the Universe* (New York: Harper and Row, 1979), 251.

12. Denton, *Nature's Destiny*, 56–7.

13. John Leslie, "How to Draw Conclusions From a Fine-Tuned Cosmos," in *Physics, Philosophy and Theology: A Common Quest for Understanding*, Robert Russell, Nancy Murphy, and C. J. Isham (eds) (Vatican City State: Vatican Observatory Press, 1988), 300.

14. Dyson, *Disturbing the Universe*, 251.

15. See Rudolph Carnap, *The Logical Foundations of Probability* (Chicago: University of Chicago Press, 1962). For a basic, but somewhat dated, introduction to confirmation theory and the prime principle of confirmation, see Richard Swinburne, *An Introduction to Confirmation Theory* (London:

Methuen and Co. Ltd, 1973). For literature specifically casting design arguments as likelihood comparisons, see A. W. F. Edwards, *Likelihood* (Baltimore: Johns Hopkins University Press, 1992).

16. For those familiar with the probability calculus, a precise statement of the degree to which evidence counts in favor of one hypothesis over another can be given in terms of the odds form of Bayes's Theorem: that is, $P(H_1/E)/P(H_2/E) = [P(H_1)/P(H_2)] \cdot [P(E/H_1)/P(E/H_2)]$. The general version of the principle stated here, however, does not require the applicability or truth of Bayes's theorem.

17. To be precise, the fine-tuning refers to the joint fact that the life-permitting values of the constants of physics are small compared with the "theoretically possible" ranges for those values *and* the fact that the values actually fall in the life-permitting range. It is only this latter fact that we are arguing is highly improbable under the atheistic single-universe hypothesis.

18. Ian Hacking, "Coincidences: Mundane and Cosmological," in *Origin and Evolution of the Universe: Evidence for Design*, John M. Robson (ed.) (Montreal: McGill-Queen's University Press, 1987), 128–30.

19. Keith Parsons, "Is There a Case for Christian Theism?" In *Does God Exist? The Great Debate*, J. P. Moreland and Kai Nielsen (eds) (Nashville: Thomas Nelson, 1990), 182.

20. For an in-depth discussion of epistemic probability, see Swinburne, *An Introduction to Confirmation Theory*; Ian Hacking, *The Emergence of Probability: A Philosophical Study of Early Ideas About Probability, Induction and Statistical Inference* (Cambridge: Cambridge University Press, 1975); and Alvin Plantinga *Warrant and Proper Function* (Oxford: Oxford University Press, 1993), Chapters 8 and 9.

21. Carr and Rees, "The Anthropic Cosmological Principle and the Structure of the Physical World," 612.

22. Those with some training in probability theory will want to note that the kind of probability invoked here is what philosophers call *epistemic probability*, which, as we discussed above, is a measure of the rational degree of belief that we should have in a proposition. Since our rational degree of belief in a necessary truth can be less than 1, we can sensibly speak of it being improbable for a given law of nature to exist necessarily. For example, we can speak of an unproven mathematical hypotheses—such as Goldbach's conjecture that every even number greater than 6 is the sum of two odd primes—as being probably true or probably false given our current evidence, even though all mathematical hypotheses are either necessarily true or necessarily false.

23. Leslie, "How To Draw Conclusions from a Fine-Tuned Cosmos," 304.

24. J. J. C. Smart, "Laws of Nature and Cosmic Coincidence," *The Philosophical Quarterly* 35 (1981), 275–6.

25. I define a "universe" as any region of space–time that is disconnected from other regions in such a way that the constants of physics in that region could differ significantly from the other regions.

A more thorough discussion of the many-universes hypothesis is presented in my essay, "The Argument from Design and the Many-Worlds Hypothesis," in *Philosophy of Religion: A Reader and Guide*, William Lane Craig (ed.) (Tronten: Rutgers University Press 2001).

26. Some have proposed what could be called a *metaphysical* many-universe hypothesis, according to which universes are thought to exist on their own without being generated by any physical process. Typically, advocates of this view—such as the late Princeton University philosopher David Lewis [*On the Plurality of Worlds* (New York: Basil Blackwell, 1986)] and University of Pennsylvania astrophysicist Max Tegmark ["Is 'the theory of everything' merely the ultimate ensemble theory?," *Annals of Physics* 270 (1998), 1–51]—claim that every possible world exists. According to Lewis, for instance, there exists a reality parallel to our own in which a duplicate of me is President of the United States and a reality in which objects can travel faster than the speed of light. Dream up a possible scenario, and it exists in some parallel reality, according to Lewis. Besides being completely speculative (and in many people's eyes, outlandish), a major problem with this scenario is that the vast majority of possible universes are ones that are chaotic, just as the vast majority of possible arrangements of letters of 1,000 characters would not spell a meaningful pattern. So, the only way that these metaphysical hypotheses can explain the regularity and predictability of our universe, and the fact that it seems to be describable by a few simple laws, is to invoke an "observer selection" effect. That is, Lewis and Tegmark must claim that only universes like ours in this respect could support intelligent life, and hence be observed. The problem with this explanation is that it is much more likely for there to exist local islands of the sort of order necessary for intelligent life than for the entire universe to have such an ordered arrangement. Thus, their hypotheses cannot explain why we, considered as generic observers, find ourselves in a universe that is highly ordered throughout.

    Among others, George Schlesinger has raised this objection against Lewis's hypothesis ["Possible Worlds and the Mystery of Existence" *Ratio* 26 (1984), 1–18]. This sort of objection was raised against a similar explanation of the high degree of order in our universe offered by the famous physicist Ludwig Boltzman, and has generally been considered fatal to Boltzman's explanation [Paul Davies, *The Physics of Time Asymmetry* (Berkeley, CA: University of California Press, 1974), 103].

27. For an accessible introduction to superstring theory, see Alan Guth, *The Inflationary Universe: The Quest for a New Theory of Cosmic Origins* (New York: Helix Books, 1997).

28. Andrei Linde, *Particle Physics and Inflationary Cosmology*, Marc Damashek (trans.) (Longhorne, PA: Harwood Academic Publishers, 1990), 3; *Inflation and Quantum Cosmology* (New York: Academic Press, 1990), 6.

29. Michio Kaku, *Introduction to Superstrings and M-Theory*, 2nd edn (New York: Springer-Verlag, 1999), 17.

30. John Peacock, *Cosmological Physics* (Cambridge, UK: Cambridge University Press, 1999), 24–6.

31. Steven Weinberg, *Dreams of a Final Theory* (New York: Vintage Books, 1992), Chapter 6.

32. P. A. M. Dirac, "The evolution of the physicist's picture of nature," *Scientific American* (May 1963), 47.

33. For a further development of this argument for design from the simplicity and beauty of the laws of nature, see Part II of my "Argument from Design and the Many-Worlds Hypothesis," in William Lane Craig (ed.) *Philosophy of Religion*.

REBELLION

By Fyodor Dostoyevsky
Trans. by Constance Garnett

"I must make you one confession," Ivan began. "I could never understand how one can love one's neighbors. It's just one's neighbors, to my mind, that one can't love, though one might love those at a distance. I once read somewhere of John the Merciful, a saint, that when a hungry, frozen beggar came to him, he took him into his bed, held him in his arms, and began breathing into his mouth, which was putrid and loathsome from some awful disease. I am convinced that he did that from 'self-laceration,' from the self-laceration of falsity, for the sake of the charity imposed by duty, as a penance laid on him. For any one to love a man, he must be hidden, for as soon as he shows his face, love is gone."

"Father Zossima has talked of that more than once," observed Alyosha; "he, too, said that the face of a man often hinders many people not practiced in love, from loving him. But yet there's a great deal of love in mankind, and almost Christ-like love. I know that myself, Ivan."

"Well, I know nothing of it so far, and can't understand it, and the innumerable mass of mankind are with me there. The question is, whether that's due to men's bad qualities or whether it's inherent in their nature. To my thinking, Christ-like love for men is a miracle impossible on earth. He was God. But we are not gods. Suppose I, for instance, suffer intensely. Another can never know how much I suffer, because he is another and not I. And what's more, a man is rarely ready to admit another's suffering (as though it were a distinction). Why won't he admit it, do you think? Because I smell unpleasant, because I have a stupid face, because I once trod on his foot. Besides, there is suffering and suffering; degrading, humiliating suffering such as humbles me—hunger, for instance—my benefactor will perhaps allow me; but when you come to higher suffering—for an idea, for instance—he will very rarely admit that, perhaps because my face strikes him as not at all what he fancies a man should have who suffers for an idea. And so he deprives me instantly of his favor, and not at all from badness of heart. Beggars, especially genteel beggars, ought never to show themselves, but to ask for charity through the newspapers. One can love one's neighbors in the abstract, or even at a distance, but at close quarters it's almost impossible. If it were as on the stage, in the ballet, where if beggars come in, they wear silken rags and tattered lace and beg for alms dancing gracefully, then one might like looking at them. But even then we should not love them. But enough of that. I simply wanted to show you my point of view. I meant to speak of the suffering of mankind generally, but we had better confine ourselves to the sufferings of the children. That reduces the scope of my argument to a tenth of what it would be. Still we'd better keep to the children, though it does weaken my case. But, in the first place, children can be loved even at close quarters, even when they are dirty, even when they are ugly (I fancy, though, children never are ugly). The second reason why I won't speak of grown-up people is that, besides being disgusting and unworthy of love, they have a compensation—they've eaten the apple and know good and evil, and they have become 'like gods.' They go on eating it still. But the children haven't eaten anything, and are so far innocent. Are you fond of children, Alyosha? I know you are, and you will understand why I prefer to speak of them. If they, too, suffer horribly on earth, they must suffer for their fathers' sins, they must be punished for their fathers, who have eaten the apple; but that reasoning is of the other world and is incomprehensible for the heart of man here on earth. The innocent must not suffer for another's sins, and especially such innocents! You may be surprised at me, Alyosha, but I am awfully fond of children, too. And observe, cruel people, the violent, the rapacious, the Karamazovs are sometimes very fond of children. Children while they are quite little—up to seven, for instance—are so remote from grown-up people; they are different creatures, as it were, of a different species. I knew a criminal in prison who had, in the course of his career as a burglar, murdered whole families, including several children. But when he was in prison, he had a strange affection for them. He spent all his time at his window, watching the children playing in the prison yard. He trained one little boy to come up to his window and made great friends with him…. You don't know why I am telling you all this, Alyosha? My head aches and I am sad."

"You speak with a strange air," observed Alyosha uneasily, "as though you were not quite yourself."

"By the way, a Bulgarian I met lately in Moscow," Ivan went on, seeming not to hear his brother's words, "told me about the crimes committed by Turks and Circassians in all parts of Bulgaria through fear of a general rising of the Slavs. They burn villages, murder, outrage women and children, they nail their prisoners by the ears to the fences, leave them so till morning, and in the morning they hang them—all sorts of things you can't imagine. People talk sometimes of bestial cruelty, but that's a great injustice and insult to the beasts; a beast can never be so cruel as a man, so artistically cruel. The tiger only tears and gnaws, that's all he can do. He would never think of nailing people by the ears, even if he were able to do it.

These Turks took a pleasure in torturing children, too; cutting the unborn child from the mother's womb, and tossing babies up in the air and catching them on the points of their bayonets before their mothers' eyes. Doing it before the mothers' eyes was what gave zest to the amusement. Here is another scene that I thought very interesting. Imagine a trembling mother with her baby in her arms, a circle of invading Turks around her. They've planned a diversion: they pet the baby, laugh to make it laugh. They succeed, the baby laughs. At that moment a Turk points a pistol four inches from the baby's face. The baby laughs with glee, holds out its little hands to the pistol, and he pulls the trigger in the baby's face and blows out its brains. Artistic, wasn't it? By the way, Turks are particularly fond of sweet things, they say."

"Brother, what are you driving at?" asked Alyosha.

"I think if the devil doesn't exist, but man has created him, he has created him in his own image and likeness."

"Just as he did God, then?" observed Alyosha.

"'It's wonderful how you can turn words,' as Polonius says in *Hamlet*," laughed Ivan. "You turn my words against me. Well, I am glad. Yours must be a fine God, if man created Him in his image and likeness. You asked just now what I was driving at. You see, I am fond of collecting certain facts, and, would you believe, I even copy anecdotes of a certain sort from newspapers and books, and I've already got a fine collection. The Turks, of course, have gone into it, but they are foreigners. I have specimens from home that are even better than the Turks. You know we prefer beating—rods and scourges—that's our national institution. Nailing ears is unthinkable for us, for we are, after all, Europeans. But the rod and the scourge we have always with us and they cannot be taken from us. Abroad now they scarcely do any beating. Manners are more humane, or laws have been passed, so that they don't dare to flog men now. But they make up for it in another way just as national as ours. And so national that it would be practically impossible among us, though I believe we are being inoculated with it, since the religious movement began in our aristocracy. I have a charming pamphlet, translated from the French, describing how, quite recently, five years ago, a murderer, Richard, was executed—a young man, I believe, of three and twenty, who repented and was converted to the Christian faith at the very scaffold. This Richard was an illegitimate child who was given as a child of six by his parents to some shepherds on the Swiss mountains. They brought him up to work for them. He grew up like a little wild beast among them. The shepherds taught him nothing, and scarcely fed or clothed him, but sent him out at seven to herd the flock in cold and wet, and no one hesitated or scrupled to treat him so. Quite the contrary, they thought they had every right, for Richard had been given to them as a chattel, and they did not even see the necessity of feeding him. Richard himself describes how in those years, like the Prodigal Son in the Gospel, he longed to eat of the mash given to the pigs, which were fattened for sale. But they wouldn't even give him that, and beat him when he stole from the pigs. And that was how he spent all his childhood and his youth, till he grew up and was strong enough to go away and be a thief. The savage began to earn his living as a day laborer in Geneva. He drank what he earned, he lived like a brute, and finished by killing and robbing an old man. He was caught, tried, and condemned to death. They are not sentimentalists there. And in prison he was immediately surrounded by pastors, members of Christian brotherhoods, philanthropic ladies, and the like. They taught him to read and write in prison, and expounded the Gospel to him. They exhorted him, worked upon him, drummed at him incessantly, till at last he solemnly confessed his crime. He was converted. He wrote to the court himself that he was a monster, but that in the end God had vouchsafed him light and shown grace. All Geneva was in excitement about him—all philanthropic and religious Geneva. All the aristocratic and well-bred society of the town rushed to the prison, kissed Richard and embraced him; 'You are our brother, you have found grace.' And Richard does nothing but weep with emotion, 'Yes, I've found grace! All my youth and childhood I was glad of pigs' food, but now even I have found grace. I am dying in the Lord.' 'Yes, Richard, die in the Lord; you have shed blood and must die. Though it's not your fault that you knew not the Lord, when you coveted the pigs' food and were beaten for stealing it (which was very wrong of you, for stealing is forbidden); but you've shed blood and you must die.' And on the last day, Richard, perfectly limp, did nothing but cry and repeat every minute: 'This is my happiest day. I am going to the Lord.' 'Yes,' cry the pastors and the judges and philanthropic ladies. 'This is the happiest day of your life, for you are going to the Lord!' They all walk or drive to the scaffold in procession behind the prison van. At the scaffold they call to Richard: 'Die, brother, die in the Lord, for even thou hast found grace!' And so, covered with his brothers' kisses, Richard is dragged on to the scaffold, and led to the guillotine. And they chopped off his head in brotherly fashion, because he had found grace. Yes, that's characteristic. That pamphlet is translated into Russian by some Russian philanthropists of aristocratic rank and evangelical aspirations, and has been distributed gratis for the enlightenment of the people. The case of Richard is interesting because it's national. Though to us it's absurd to cut off a man's head, because he has become our brother and has found grace, yet we have our own speciality, which is all but worse. Our historical pastime is the direct satisfaction of inflicting pain. There are lines in Nekrassov describing how a peasant lashes a horse on the eyes, 'on its meek eyes,' every one must have seen it. It's peculiarly Russian. He describes how a feeble little nag has foundered under too heavy a load and cannot move. The peasant beats it, beats it savagely, beats it at last not knowing what he is doing in the intoxication of cruelty, thrashes it mercilessly over and over again. 'However weak you are, you must pull, if you die for it.' The nag strains, and then he begins lashing the poor defenseless creature on its weeping, on its 'meek eyes.' The frantic beast tugs and draws the load, trembling all over, gasping for breath, moving sideways, with a sort of unnatural spasmodic action—it's awful in Nekrassov. But that's only a horse, and God has given horses to be beaten. So the Tatars have taught us, and they left us the knout as a remembrance of it. But men, too, can be beaten. A well-educated, cultured gentleman and his wife beat their own child with a birch-rod, a girl of seven. I have an exact account of it. The papa was glad that the birch was covered with twigs. 'It stings more,' said he, and so he began stinging his daughter. I know for a fact there are people who at every blow are worked up to sensuality, to literal sensuality, which increases progressively at every blow they inflict. They beat for a minute, for five minutes, for ten minutes, more often and more savagely. The child screams. At last the child cannot scream, it gasps, 'Daddy! daddy!' By some diabolical unseemly chance the case was brought into court. A counsel is engaged. The Russian people have long called a barrister 'a conscience for hire.' The counsel protests in his client's defense. 'It's such a simple thing,' he says, 'an everyday domestic event. A father corrects his child. To our shame be it said, it is brought into court.' The jury, convinced by him, give a favorable verdict. The public roars with delight that the torturer is acquitted. Ah, pity I wasn't there! I would have proposed to raise a subscription in his honor! Charming pictures.

"But I've still better things about children. I've collected a great, great deal about Russian children, Alyosha. There was a little girl of five who was hated by her father and mother, 'most worthy and respectable people, of good education and breeding.' You see, I must repeat again, it is a peculiar characteristic of many people, this love of torturing children, and children only. To all other types of humanity these torturers behave mildly and benevolently, like cultivated and humane Europeans; but they are very fond of tormenting children, even fond of children themselves in that sense. It's just their defenselessness that tempts the tormentor, just the angelic confidence of the child who has no refuge and no appeal, that sets his vile blood on fire. In every man, of course, a demon lies hidden—the demon of rage, the demon of lustful heat at the screams of the tortured victim, the demon of lawlessness let off the chain, the demon of diseases that follow on vice, gout, kidney disease, and so on.

"This poor child of five was subjected to every possible torture by those cultivated parents. They beat her, thrashed her, kicked her for no reason till her body was one bruise. Then, they went to greater refinements of cruelty—shut her up all night in the cold and frost in a privy, and because she didn't ask to be taken up at night (as though a child of five sleeping its angelic, sound sleep could be trained to wake and ask), they smeared her face and filled her mouth with excrement, and it was her mother, her mother did this. And that mother could sleep, hearing the poor child's groans! Can you understand why a little creature, who can't even understand what's done to her, should beat her little aching heart with her tiny fist in the dark and the cold, and weep her meek unresentful tears to dear, kind God to protect her? Do you understand that, friend and brother, you pious and humble novice? Do you understand why this infamy must be and is permitted? Without it, I am told, man could not have existed on earth, for he could not have known good and evil. Why should he know that diabolical good and evil when it costs so much? Why, the whole world of knowledge is not worth that child's prayer to 'dear, kind God'! I say nothing of the sufferings of grown-up people, they have eaten the apple, damn them, and the devil take them all! But these little ones! I am making you suffer, Alyosha, you are not yourself. I'll leave off if you like."

"Never mind. I want to suffer too," muttered Alyosha.

"One picture, only one more, because it's so curious, so characteristic, and I have only just read it in some collection of Russian antiquities. I've forgotten the name. I must look it up. It was in the darkest days of serfdom at the beginning of the century, and long live the Liberator of the People! There was in those days a general of aristocratic connections, the owner of great estates, one of those men—somewhat exceptional, I believe, even then—who, retiring from the service into a life of leisure, are convinced that they've earned absolute power over the lives of their subjects. There were such men then. So our general, settled on his property of two thousand souls, lives in pomp, and domineers over his poor neighbors as though they were dependents and buffoons. He has kennels of hundreds of hounds and nearly a hundred dog-boys—all mounted, and in uniform. One day a serf-boy, a little child of eight, threw a stone in play and hurt the paw of the general's favorite hound. 'Why is my favorite dog lame?' He is told that the boy threw a stone that hurt the dog's paw. 'So you did it.' The general looked the child up and down. 'Take him.' He was taken—taken from his mother and kept shut up all night. Early that morning the general comes out on horseback, with the hounds, his dependents, dog-boys, and huntsmen, all mounted around him in full hunting parade. The servants are summoned for their edification, and in front of them all stands the mother of the child. The child is brought from the lock-up. It's a gloomy, cold, foggy autumn day, a capital day for hunting. The general orders the child to be undressed; the child is stripped naked. He shivers, numb with terror, not daring to cry…. 'Make him run,' commands the general. 'Run! run!' shout the dog-boys. The boy runs…. 'At him!' yells the general, and he sets the whole pack of hounds on the child. The hounds catch him, and tear him to pieces before his mother's eyes!… I believe the general was afterwards declared incapable of administering his estates. Well—what did he deserve? To be shot? To be shot for the satisfaction of our moral feelings? Speak, Alyosha!"

"To be shot," murmured Alyosha, lifting his eyes to Ivan with a pale, twisted smile.

"Bravo!" cried Ivan, delighted. "If even you say so…. You're a pretty monk! So there is a little devil sitting in your heart, Alyosha Karamazov!"

"What I said was absurd, but—"

"That's just the point, that 'but'!" cried Ivan. "Let me tell you, novice, that the absurd is only too necessary on earth. The world stands on absurdities, and perhaps nothing would have come to pass in it without them. We know what we know!"

"What do you know?"

"I understand nothing," Ivan went on, as though in delirium. "I don't want to understand anything now. I want to stick to the fact. I made up my mind long ago not to understand. If I try to understand anything, I shall be false to the fact, and I have determined to stick to the fact."

"Why are you trying me?" Alyosha cried, with sudden distress. "Will you say what you mean at last?"

"Of course, I will; that's what I've been leading up to. You are dear to me, I don't want to let you go, and I won't give you up to your Zossima."

Ivan for a minute was silent, his face became all at once very sad.

"Listen! I took the case of children only to make my case clearer. Of the other tears of humanity with which the earth is soaked from its crust to its center, I will say nothing. I have narrowed my subject on purpose. I am a bug, and I recognize in all humility that I cannot understand why the world is arranged as it is. Men are themselves to blame, I suppose; they were given paradise, they wanted freedom, and stole fire from heaven, though they knew they would become unhappy, so there is no need to pity them. With my pitiful, earthly, Euclidian understanding, all I know is that there is suffering and that there are none guilty; that cause follows effect, simply and directly; that everything flows and finds its level—but that's only Euclidian nonsense, I know that, and I can't consent to live by it! What comfort is it to me that there are none guilty and that cause follows effect simply and directly, and that I know it?—I must have justice, or I will destroy myself. And not justice in some remote infinite time and space, but here on earth, and that I could see myself. I have believed in it. I want to see it, and if I am dead by then, let me rise again, for if it all happens without me, it will be too unfair. Surely I haven't suffered, simply that I, my crimes and my sufferings, may manure the soil of the future harmony for somebody else. I want to see with my own eyes the hind lie down with the lion and the victim rise up and embrace his murderer. I want to be there when every one suddenly understands what it has all been for. All the religions of the world are built on this longing, and I am a believer. But then there are the children, and what am I to do about them? That's a question I can't answer. For the hundredth time I repeat, there are numbers of questions, but I've only taken the children, because in their case what I mean is so unanswerably clear. Listen! If all must suffer to pay for the eternal harmony, what have children to do with it, tell me, please? It's beyond all comprehension why they should suffer, and why they should pay for the harmony. Why should they, too, furnish material to enrich the soil for the harmony of the future? I understand solidarity in sin among men. I understand solidarity in retribution, too; but there can be no such solidarity with children. And if it is really true that they must share responsibility for all their fathers' crimes, such a truth is not of this world and is beyond my comprehension. Some jester will say, perhaps, that the child would have grown up and have sinned, but you see he didn't grow up, he was torn to pieces by the dogs, at eight years old. Oh, Alyosha, I am not blaspheming! I understand, of course, what an upheaval of the universe it will be, when everything in heaven and earth blends in one hymn of praise and everything that lives and has lived cries aloud: 'Thou art just, O Lord, for Thy ways are revealed.' When the mother embraces the fiend who threw her child to the dogs, and all three cry aloud with tears, 'Thou art just, O Lord!' then, of course, the crown of knowledge will be reached and all will be made clear. But what pulls me up here is that I can't accept that harmony. And while I am on earth, I make haste to take my own measures. You see, Alyosha, perhaps it really may happen that if I live to that moment, or rise again to see it, I, too, perhaps, may cry aloud with the rest, looking at the mother embracing the child's torturer, 'Thou art just, O Lord!' but I don't want to cry aloud then. While there is still time, I hasten to protect myself, and so I renounce the higher harmony altogether. It's not worth the tears of that one tortured child who beat itself on the breast with its little fist and prayed in its stinking outhouse, with its unexpiated tears to 'dear, kind God'! It's not worth it, because those tears are unatoned for. They must be atoned for, or there can be no harmony. But how? How are you going to atone for them? Is it possible? By their being avenged? But what do I care for avenging them? What do I care for a hell for oppressors? What good can hell do, since those children have already been tortured? And what becomes of harmony, if there is hell? I want to forgive. I want to embrace. I don't want more suffering. And if the sufferings of children go to swell the sum of sufferings which was necessary to pay for truth, then I protest that the truth is not worth such a price. I don't want the mother to embrace the oppressor who threw her son to the dogs! She dare not forgive him! Let her forgive him for herself, if she will, let her forgive the torturer for the immeasurable suffering of her mother's heart. But the sufferings of her tortured child she has no right to forgive; she dare not forgive the torturer, even if the child were to forgive him! And if that is so, if they dare not forgive, what becomes of harmony? Is there in the whole world a being who would have the right to forgive and could forgive? I don't want harmony. From love for humanity I don't want it. I would rather be left with the unavenged suffering. I would rather remain with my unavenged suffering and unsatisfied indignation, *even if I were wrong*. Besides, too high a price is asked for harmony; it's beyond our means to pay so much to enter on it. And so I hasten to give back my entrance ticket, and if I am an honest man I am bound to give it back as soon as possible. And that I am doing. It's not God that I don't accept, Alyosha, only I most respectfully return Him the ticket."

"That's rebellion," murmured Alyosha, looking down.

"Rebellion? I am sorry you call it that," said Ivan earnestly. "One can hardly live in rebellion, and I want to live. Tell me yourself, I challenge you—answer. Imagine that you are creating a fabric of human destiny with the object of making men happy in the end, giving them peace and rest at last, but that it was essential and inevitable to torture to death only one tiny creature—that baby beating its breast with its fist, for instance— and to found that edifice on its unavenged tears, would you consent to be the architect on those conditions? Tell me, and tell the truth."

"No, I wouldn't consent," said Alyosha softly.

"And can you admit the idea that men for whom you are building it would agree to accept their happiness on the foundation of the unexpiated blood of a little victim? And accepting it would remain happy for ever?"

"No, I can't admit it. Brother," said Alyosha suddenly, with flashing eyes.

LEIBNIZ, THEODICY, AND THE BEST OF ALL POSSIBLE WORLDS

By Nicholas Jolley

In 1710 Leibniz published his one philosophical book, the *Essays in Theodicy on the Goodness of God, the Freedom of Man and the Origin of Evil*. The term 'theodicy' (*theos* = God; *dike* = justice) was Leibniz's own coinage; because of an ambiguity in the French, the word even misled some of Leibniz's earliest readers into supposing that it was the author's pseudonym; thus they interpreted the title to mean 'Essays by a Theodicean' (G II 428). But if the term was new, the project of the book was not; it marked a new departure neither in the history of philosophy nor in terms of Leibniz's philosophical career. Indeed, the *Theodicy* simply represents the culmination of Leibniz's lifelong concern with defending God's character and justice before the bar of reason. And (as the full title indicates), the project of the work is also continuous with that of the last chapter. As we have seen, central to the defence of divine freedom is the claim that God makes a contingent, spontaneous, and intelligent choice among an infinity of possible worlds. At the heart of the defence of God's character is the claim that the world which God freely chooses is the best.

Ever since Voltaire's devastating satire in *Candide* Leibniz's thesis that the actual world is the best of all possible worlds has been notorious; to many readers it has seemed to exhibit a callous disregard for the facts about sin and suffering in our world. Some philosophers, such as Nicholas Rescher, have accordingly attempted to come to Leibniz's defence by saying that Voltaire's critique is wide of the mark; they have argued that Leibniz's 'optimism' (the thesis that the actual world is the best of all possible worlds) is a technical thesis which has nothing to do with issues concerning human happiness (Rescher 1967: 19).

It is true that Leibniz does advance a criterion of value for possible worlds which seems to have no relevance for happiness, but the claim that Voltaire's satire is wide of the mark is itself wide of the mark. At least as early as the *Discourse on Metaphysics* Leibniz does wish to maintain that the happiness of minds is God's primary goal in creation, even if he seeks to realize other, possibly conflicting goods as well. Indeed, it should not surprise us that Leibniz's God makes the happiness of minds his principal goal, for this thesis is rooted in Leibniz's further thesis that minds are made in the image of God.

'EPICURUS'S OLD QUESTIONS' IN A NEW SETTING

The problem of evil—that is, the problem of reconciling the existence of evil in our world with the attributes of God—is an old one in the history of philosophy. In Hume's famous *Dialogues Concerning Natural Religion* Philo remarks that the problem has remained unsolved since the time of the Greeks: 'Epicurus's old questions are yet unanswered. Is [God] willing to prevent evil but not able? Then is he impotent. Is he able but not willing? Then is he malevolent. Is he both able and willing? Whence then is evil?' (Hume, *Dialogues*, Part X). (The last phrase recalls the full title of the *Theodicy*.) The difficulty can be formulated in terms of an apparently inconsistent triad of propositions. (For the sake of simplicity, we will assume that the subject term in the first two propositions denotes an existent entity.)

1. God is omnipotent.
2. God is just and benevolent.
3. Evil exists in the world.

In other words, for a theist such as Leibniz each of these propositions would seem to be intuitive, but it is difficult to see how all three of them can be true. The problem of consistency should be sharply distinguished, as it is by Hume himself, from the problem of inference: this is the problem of inferring moral attributes in a deity from the facts of our world which include such things as sin and suffering. The problem of consistency, by contrast, arises for a philosopher who is, as Hume says, antecedently convinced of the existence of a God who is at once omnipotent, just and benevolent. In his writings on theodicy Leibniz is almost exclusively concerned with the problem of consistency rather than the problem of inference.

In Leibniz's time the problem of evil (understood as the problem of consistency) became particularly pressing as a result of the Scientific Revolution. The new scientific picture of the world accustomed people to regard the universe as a vast and intricate machine governed by the laws of physics; the admirable order disclosed by Galileo, Descartes, and later Newton, seemed to provide clear evidence of intelligent design.

But when people reflected on the moral world they were struck by the appearance, not of order, but of chaos; in our world little children die of hideous diseases such as meningitis and leukemia, and in the words of the Psalmist, the ways of the wicked prosper. The very triumphs of the Scientific Revolution thus conspired to throw the problem of evil into relief.

At least by the time of Leibniz's maturity the problem of evil had acquired a new urgency for Christian philosophers as a result of the pointed challenge thrown down by Spinoza. In the *Ethics* Spinoza in effect dissolves the problem of evil in the same way in which he dissolves other philosophical problems; he denies at least one of the central assumptions which give rise to it. According to Spinoza, as we have seen, God is not a person but nature itself; he is thus not the sort of entity to which moral predicates such as 'is just' and 'is benevolent' can possibly apply. Thus in Spinoza's philosophy the traditional problem of reconciling the facts of evil in our world with the existence of an omnipotent, just and benevolent God simply cannot get off the ground. We can make the point by returning to the seemingly inconsistent triad of propositions. Spinoza's attitude to (1) and (3) is subtle and complex, but there is no doubt that he straightforwardly rejects (2). Thus Spinoza could claim that it was a great strength of his philosophy that it dissolves the problem of evil which had baffled Christian philosophers for centuries.

In Leibniz's time Christian philosophers tended to react to Spinoza's challenge in one of two very different ways. Fortunately for our purposes the contrasting approaches are represented in the writings of the two philosophers who did most to stimulate Leibniz's own interest in theodicy: the writings of Malebranche and Bayle embody the rationalist and fideist strategies respectively. As a rationalist in theodicy Malebranche refuses to concede to Spinoza that Christian philosophers are devoid of resources for solving the problem of evil; as we shall see, Malebranche in fact draws his inspiration from the Scientific Revolution itself by making the concept of law central to his whole project of theodicy. God acts through general laws not only in the natural world but also in the distribution of grace: the results may sometimes be less than fully optimal, but God is obliged by concern for his glory to act in accordance with laws. Bayle, by contrast, is prepared to concede to Spinoza that the problem of evil admits of no rational solution, but he insists that faith must lead us where reason cannot. As we should expect, Leibniz is far closer in spirit to Malebranche than he is to Bayle whose fideistic writings, as we have seen, provided the immediate stimulus for the composition of the *Theodicy*. But despite their common commitment to a broadly rationalist approach to the problem of theodicy, there are differences of emphasis between Leibniz and Malebranche. Neither philosopher of course would agree that the three propositions above constitute an inconsistent triad, but each is prepared to give ground a little, though in different places. It is fair to say that Malebranche tends to soft-pedal divine benevolence, whereas Leibniz tends to soft-pedal both divine omnipotence and the reality of evil.

THE KINDS OF EVILS

At the beginning of this chapter we noted that Leibniz's theodicy comes in several stages. The first stage consists in defending God's character by showing that he has done the best job open to him: he has created the best of all possible worlds. As we have seen, this stage of the defence requires an extended clarification of the criteria in terms of which possible worlds are to be evaluated. The second main stage consists in defending the thesis that God has created the best of all possible worlds against obvious objections; it is natural to protest, as Voltaire does, that, in view of all the evils it contains, this world surely cannot be the best of all possible worlds.

As God's defence attorney, as it were, Leibniz is prepared to make an initial concession: the world does contain three kinds of evil: metaphysical, physical, and moral. The first kind of evil—metaphysical—presents no problem for Leibniz at this stage of his theodicy, for metaphysical evil is simply the absence of absolute perfection which is incident to any world that God might create. Indeed, the presence of this kind of evil has been conceded at the first stage of Leibniz's theodicy. But the other two kinds of evil—physical (suffering) and moral (sin)—are in a different position, for they do not simply follow, as does metaphysical evil, from the very nature of creation. As Broad points out, there are possible worlds which are wholly devoid of both physical and moral evil: consider, for instance, a possible world which is constituted by bare monads, none of whose perceptions crosses the threshold of consciousness (Broad 1975: 160). And of course it is the presence of these evils—sin and suffering—which is most troubling to Voltaire in *Candide*; it is the experience of 'man's inhumanity to man' and of the pain inflicted by diseases and natural disasters such as earthquakes which comes to undermine Candide's confidence in his master's teaching that this is the best of all possible worlds.

The presence of physical and moral evils in our world thus demands a separate treatment, but in one way such evils are less problematic than they appear. We can see this by returning to the criteria in terms of which possible worlds are evaluated. On the interpretation proposed here Leibniz's God chooses the world in which there is the optimal balance between moral and physical perfection (as measured by happiness on the one hand and the variety/simplicity criterion on the other). Thus Leibniz is not committed to saying that the happiness of minds is strictly at a maximum in our world; he can concede to Voltaire that there are possible worlds that contain less sin and suffering than does our world.

Voltaire's objections, then, are not exactly irrelevant, as some scholars have supposed, but they do lose some of their sting. Moreover, Leibniz has further strategies available to him for showing how the presence of physical and moral evil in our world is consistent with its status as the best of all possible worlds. As we have seen, unlike Epicurus, Leibniz is not troubled by the suspicion that such evils are incompatible with divine benevolence and omnipotence, taken together. But it is still fair to say that the first of Leibniz's strategies tends to play down the reality of evil, whereas the third (in contrast to Malebranche) tends to play down divine omnipotence.

The tendency to play down the reality of evil is most evident in the first strategy: evil is something purely negative, or, in technical terms, it is a privation (DM 30, WF 82). This Augustinian doctrine arises naturally from reflection on the theme from the Book of Genesis: according to Genesis, God beheld his creation and saw that it was good. The philosophical moral, then, is that whatever God creates is good, and this is equivalent (by contraposition) to saying that whatever is not good is not created by God. If we add the further plausible premise that whatever is not created by God has no positive reality, the doctrine of the negativity of evil straightforwardly follows.

The doctrine of the negativity of evil fits certain facts rather well. Blindness is an evil, and it is an evil which is constituted by the lack of a certain property—namely vision—which certain creatures ought to have. On the other hand, in the light of modern medical science it may seem that there are other diseases which are more difficult to bring into line with the doctrine. We now know, for instance, that Down's syndrome is associated with the presence of an extra chromosome. Perhaps the defender of the doctrine is not without resources for replying to such objections. For it may be said that what constitutes the evil of Down's syndrome is not the presence of the extra chromosome but the absence of certain skills, and that this absence either supervenes on or is caused by the presence of the extra chromosome. Indeed, it could be said that in this respect Down's syndrome is on a par with blindness which may be caused by the presence of cataracts or by the pressure of fluid on the retina.

Leibniz's second strategy involves no such tendency to play down the reality of evil: it consists rather in the familiar ploy of saying that the presence of local evil is a necessary condition of, and indeed contributes to, the overall goodness of the world. As we might say, local imperfection is in the service of global perfection. This doctrine is typically illustrated by the analogy with 'shadows in a picture'. Taken by itself, in isolation, an area of shadow in a painting is less than optimally attractive, but in a work such as Rembrandt's *Night Watch* even large areas of shadow contribute in an essential way to the excellence of the whole painting. Leibniz is perhaps even more fond of a musical analogy:

> The great composers frequently mingle discords with harmonious chords so that the listener may be stimulated and pricked as it were, and become, in a way, anxious about the outcome; presently when all is restored to order he feels so much the more content.
>
> (P 142)

The dissonant chords thus give spice to many a musical composition, and thereby contribute to their excellence.

Leibniz sometimes employs the picture analogy to make a rather different point, which he does not carefully distinguish from the first: we do not know enough to make informed judgements about the whole universe. According to Leibniz, we are in the position of someone looking at a picture most of which is covered up. Now it would be rash for such a person to make a judgement about the quality of the whole composition on the evidence of the small part of the painting which is exposed. Similarly, it would be rash for us to judge the quality of the universe as a whole on the basis of our experience of a very small part of it. Leibniz seems to blur the distinction between this point and the previous one by saying that the spectator in this position will see only 'a kind of confused medley of colours, without selection, without art' (P 142). Now this of course may be true, but it is also conceivable that the exposed part of the painting might be extremely pleasing to the eye. Even if this were the case, however, it would still be true to say that the spectator would not be in a position to make an informed judgement about the quality of the whole or even to appreciate properly the small part of the painting which was exposed. Thus Leibniz's second point here does not depend in an essential way on a claim about local imperfection.

The first two strategies for reconciling physical and moral evil with the thesis that this is the best of all possible worlds are wholly conventional and traditional. The third strategy, by contrast, employs the distinctive resources of Leibniz's metaphysics: it draws on the theory of complete concepts and on the very conception of a possible world. We may set up this third strategy by considering a very natural line of objection in the spirit of Voltaire. Looking around the world, we are inclined to think that certain obvious improvements could be made. We notice, for example, that our world contains Adolf Hitler. We wonder, then, why an omnipotent and benevolent God did not edit Hitler out of our world and replace him, say, by Adolf Schmitler, a counterpart of Hitler's who is an admirable ruler of Germany between 1933 and 1945.

The distinctive resources of Leibniz's metaphysics allow him to offer two related arguments against objections of this sort. In the first place, Leibniz can exploit his thesis that individuals have complete concepts to mount a *reductio ad absurdum* argument to show why Adolf Hitler could not be edited out of our world while leaving intact, say, its more attractive individuals such as Mother Theresa. For it is part of the complete concept of Mother Theresa that she died fifty-two years after Hitler's death in the Berlin bunker; any individual to whom that predicate does not apply is not Mother Theresa but someone else. But if *per impossibile* Hitler were edited out of our world, then this predicate would no longer be true of her, for there would be no Hitler to whom she could be related. Thus a contradiction results: it is both true and not true of Mother Theresa that she died fifty-two years after the death of Hitler. It follows, then, that Hitler cannot be edited out of our world while leaving Mother Theresa or indeed any other individual intact. To say this is not to deny that all reference to Hitler can be deleted from the complete concept of Mother Theresa: for no contradiction results from doing so (Hacking 1982: 190). But in that case to conceive of such an individual is no longer to conceive of her or of this world, but rather of another possible individual in another possible world.

Leibniz can thus exploit the theory of complete concepts which express the whole world to show why Hitler could not be edited out of our world while leaving its good individuals intact. Leibniz can also invoke a further distinction which he sometimes draws to show specifically that the notion of replacing Hitler by Schmitler is incoherent. In places Leibniz stresses that not all individuals who are possible in themselves are compossible—that is, logically capable of co-existing in the same world (e.g. L 661–2). The point of Leibniz's distinction is easily explained. Suppose that Smith is 7 feet tall and that Jones is an even more towering 7 feet 6 inches tall; as described so far, these individuals are not merely possible in themselves but compossible as well. But if we suppose that each of these two possible individuals has the further, relational predicate 'is taller than any other human being', then they are no longer compossible. Now by virtue of his theory of complete concepts Leibniz holds that all possible individuals are partitioned off into possible worlds, each of which is incompossible with every other possible world. (A possible world, indeed, might be defined as a maximum set of compossible individuals.) Thus each possible individual is, as we might say, 'world-bound'; it is confined to its particular possible world. It follows, then, that whereas I am compossible with Adolf Hitler, I am not compossible with Adolf Schmitler in, say, possible world #747.

We are now in a position to see how Leibniz can defend God, his client, as it were, against the charges of Voltaire. Recall that Voltaire objects that the actual world cannot be the best of all possible worlds because it contains such monsters as Hitler. Surely, then, God could have created a better world by replacing Hitler; thus God has not done the best job of which he is capable. Leibniz can reply on behalf of his client that he would indeed like to replace Hitler by Schmitler but that his hands are tied by the laws of logic; and it is a fundamental feature of Leibniz's philosophy that divine omnipotence does not extend over logical laws. A possible world is a package deal, or to vary the metaphor, a *table d'hôte*; it is not an *à la carte* menu from which God can pick and choose the dishes that take his fancy.

This third strategy thus draws ingeniously on distinctive features of Leibniz's philosophy, and it is natural to ask how this final strategy is related to the more familiar second strategy. It may seem that the third strategy serves simply as a fall-back position; that is, according to the 'shadows in a picture' approach Leibniz argues that Hitler is like a dark patch in the *Night Watch* which contributes to the greater beauty of the whole; however offensive it may sound to say so, there is a sense in which this world is better for the presence of Hitler. According to the third strategy, by contrast, Leibniz concedes that the world is not better for the presence of Hitler: Hitler is simply the price to be paid for the moral and physical goods of our world. But this is perhaps a superficial view of the relationship between the second and third strategies. For in Leibniz's philosophy to say that this world would be better without Hitler is not coherent, for then we are no longer thinking about this world, but about another presumptively possible world. Thus it may be more correct to say that Leibniz's third strategy is a deep version of his second strategy.

FURTHER READING

D. Blumenfeld (1995) 'Perfection and Happiness in the Best Possible World,' Jolley (ed.), *The Cambridge Companion to Leibniz.* (A careful analytic treatment which is sometimes controversial.)

Broad (1975) *Leibniz: An Introduction*, Ch. 7. (A clear exposition of the main issues.)

Brown (1988) 'Leibniz's Theodicy and the Confluence of Worldly Goods'. (An important scholarly study which defends the overall coherence of Leibniz's position.)

Nadler (1994) 'Choosing a Theodicy: The Leibniz–Malebranche–Arnauld Connection'. (An illuminating account of Leibniz's theodicy in relation to Malebranche and Arnauld.)

Rescher (1967) *The Philosophy of Leibniz*, Ch 12. (A useful introductory account of the main themes of Leibniz's theodicy.)

Rutherford (1995a) *Leibniz and the Rational Order of Nature*, Chs. 1–3. (A scholarly discussion which critcizes the 'optimal balance' interpretation of Leibniz's theodicy).

Wilson (1983) 'Leibnizian Optimism'. (Examines Leibniz's views in the light of Voltaire's critique.)

Wilson (1989) *Leibniz's Metaphysics*, Ch. 8. (A valuable account of Leibniz's theodicy in its historical setting.)

CHILD HURBINEK

By Primo Levi
Trans. by Stuart Woolf

Hurbinek was a nobody, a child of death, a child of Auschwitz. He looked about three years old, no one knew anything of him, he could not speak and he had no name; that curious name, Hurbinek, had been given to him by us, perhaps by one of the women who had interpreted with those syllables one of the inarticulate sounds that the baby let out now and again. He was paralysed from the waist down, with atrophied legs, as thin as sticks; but his eyes, lost in his triangular and wasted face, flashed terribly alive, full of demand, assertion, of the will to break loose, to shatter the tomb of his dumbness. The speech he lacked, which no one had bothered to teach him, the need of speech charged his stare with explosive urgency: it was a stare both savage and human, even mature, a judgement, which none of us could support, so heavy was it with force and anguish.

None of us, that is, except Henek; he was in the bunk next to me, a robust and hearty Hungarian boy of fifteen. Henek spent half his day beside Hurbinek's pallet. He was maternal rather than paternal; had our precarious coexistence lasted more than a month, it is extremely probable that Hurbinek would have learnt to speak from Henek; certainly better than from the Polish girls who, too tender and too vain, inebriated him with caresses and kisses, but shunned intimacy with him.

Henek, on the other hand, calm and stubborn, sat beside the little sphinx, immune to the distressing power he emanated; he brought him food to eat, adjusted his blankets, cleaned him with skilful hands, without repugnance; and he spoke to him, in Hungarian naturally, in a slow and patient voice.

After a week, Henek announced seriously, but without a shadow of self-consciousness, that Hurbinek 'could say a word'. What word? He did not know, a difficult word, not-Hungarian: something like 'mass-klo', 'matisklo'. During the night we listened carefully: it was true, from Hurbinek's corner there occasionally came a sound, a word. It was not, admittedly, always exactly the same word, but it was certainly an articulated word; or better, several slightly different articulated words, experimental variations on a theme, on a root, perhaps on a name. Hurbinek continued in his stubborn experiments for as long as he lived. In the following days everybody listened to him in silence, anxious to understand, and among us there were speakers of all the languages of Europe; but Hurbinek's word remained secret. No, it was certainly not a message, it was not a revelation; perhaps it was his name, if it had ever fallen to his lot to be given a name; perhaps (according to one of our hypotheses) it meant 'to eat', or 'bread'; or perhaps 'meat' in Bohemian, as one of us who knew that language maintained.

Hurbinek, who was three years old and perhaps had been born in Auschwitz and had never seen a tree; Hurbinek, who had fought like a man, to the last breath, to gain his entry into the world of men, from which a bestial power had excluded him; Hurbinek, the nameless, whose tiny forearm—even his—bore the tattoo of Auschwitz; Hurbinek died in the first days of March 1945, free but not redeemed. Nothing remains of him: he bears witness through these words of mine.

THE PROBLEM OF EVIL

By Richard Swinburne

God is, by definition, omniscient, omnipotent, and perfectly good. By "omniscient" I understand "one who knows all true propositions." By "omnipotent" I understand "able to do anything logically possible."[1] By "perfectly good" I understand "one who does no morally bad action," and I include among actions omissions to perform some action. The problem of evil is then often stated as the problem whether the existence of God is compatible with the existence of evil. Against the suggestion of compatibility, an atheist often suggests that the existence of evil entails the nonexistence of God. For, he argues, if God exists, then being omniscient, he knows under what circumstances evil will occur, if he does not act; and being omnipotent, he is able to prevent its occurrence. Hence, being perfectly good, he will prevent its occurrence and so evil will not exist. Hence the existence of God entails the nonexistence of evil. Theists have usually attacked this argument by denying the claim that necessarily a perfectly good being, foreseeing the occurrence of evil and able to prevent it, will prevent it. And indeed, if evil is understood in the very wide way in which it normally is understood in this context, to include physical pain of however slight a degree, the cited claim is somewhat implausible. For it implies that if through my neglecting frequent warnings to go to the dentist, I find myself one morning with a slight toothache, then necessarily, there does not exist a perfectly good being who foresaw the evil and was able to have prevented it. Yet it seems fairly obvious that such a being might well choose to allow me to suffer some mild consequences of my folly—as a lesson for the future which would do me no real harm.

The threat to theism seems to come, not from the existence of evil as such, but rather from the existence of evil of certain kinds and degrees—severe undeserved physical pain or mental anguish, for example. I shall therefore list briefly the kinds of evil which are evident in our world, and ask whether their existence in the degrees in which we find them is compatible with the existence of God. I shall call the man who argues for compatibility the theodicist, and his opponent the antitheodicist. The theodicist will claim that it is not morally wrong for God to create or permit the various evils, normally on the grounds that doing so is providing the logically necessary conditions of greater goods. The antitheodicist denies these claims by putting forward moral principles which have as consequences that a good God would not under any circumstances create or permit the evils in question. I shall argue that these moral principles are not, when carefully examined, at all obvious, and indeed that there is a lot to be said for their negations. Hence I shall conclude that it is plausible to suppose that the existence of these evils is compatible with the existence of God.[2]

What then is wrong with the world? First, there are painful sensations, felt both by men, and, to a lesser extent, by animals. Second, there are painful emotions, which do not involve pain in the literal sense of this word—for example, feelings of loss and failure and frustration. Such suffering exists mainly among men, but also, I suppose, to some small extent among animals too. Third, there are evil and undesirable states of affairs, mainly states of men's minds, which do not involve suffering. For example, there are the states of mind of hatred and envy; and such states of the world as rubbish tipped over a beauty spot. And fourth, there are the evil actions of men, mainly actions having as foreseeable consequences evils of the first three types, but perhaps other actions as well—such as lying and promise breaking with no such foreseeable consequences. As before, I include among actions, omissions to perform some actions. If there are rational agents other than men and God (if he exists), such as angels or devils or strange beings on distant planets, who suffer and perform evil actions, then their evil feelings, states, and actions must be added to the list of evils.

I propose to call evil of the first type physical evil, evil of the second type mental evil, evil of the third type state evil, and evil of the fourth type moral evil. Since there is a clear contrast between evils of the first three types, which are evils that happen to men or animals or the world, and evils of the fourth type which are evils that men do, there is an advantage in having one name for evils of any of the first three types— I shall call these passive evils.[3] I distinguish evil from mere absence of good. Pain is not simply the absence of pleasure. A headache is a pain, whereas not having the sensation of drinking whiskey is, for many people, mere absence of pleasure. Likewise, the feeling of loss in bereavement is an evil involving suffering, to be contrasted with the mere absence of the pleasure of companionship. Some thinkers have, of course, claimed that a good God would create a "best of all (logically) possible worlds"[4] (i.e., a world than which no better is logically possible), and for them the mere absence of good creates a problem since it looks as if a world would be a better world if it had that good. For most of us, however, the mere absence of good seems less of a threat to theism than the presence of evil, partly because it is not at all clear whether any sense can be given to the concept of a best of all possible worlds (and if it cannot then of logical necessity there will be a better world than any creatable world) and partly because even if sense can be given to this concept it is not at all obvious that God has an obligation to create such a world[5]—to whom would he be doing an injustice if he did not? My concern is with the threat to theism posed by the existence of evil.

Now much of the evil in the world consists of the evil actions of men and the passive evils brought about by those actions. The antitheodicist suggests as a moral principle (P 1) that a creator able to do so ought to create only creatures such that necessarily they do not do evil actions. From this it follows that God would not have made men who do evil actions. Against this suggestion the theodicist naturally deploys the free-will defense, elegantly expounded in recent years by Alvin Plantinga.[6] This runs roughly as follows: it is not logically possible for an agent to make another agent such that necessarily he freely does only good actions. Hence if a being G creates a free agent, he gives to the agent power of choice between alternative actions, and how he will exercise that power is something which G cannot control while the agent remains free. It is a good thing that there exist free agents, but a logically necessary consequence of their existence is that their power to choose to do evil actions may sometimes be realized. The price is worth paying, however, for the existence of agents performing free actions remains a good thing even if they sometimes do evil. Hence it is not logically possible that a creator create free creatures "such that necessarily they do not do evil actions." But it is not a morally bad thing that he create free creatures, even with the possibility of their doing evil. Hence the cited moral principle is implausible.

All that the free-will defense has shown so far, however (and all that Plantinga seems to show) is grounds for supposing that the existence of moral evil is compatible with the existence of God. It has not given grounds for supposing that the existence of evil consequences of moral evils is compatible with the existence of God. In an attempt to show an incompatibility, the antitheodicist may suggest instead of (P1), (P2)—that a creator able to do so ought always to ensure that any creature whom he creates does not cause passive evils, or at any rate passive evils which hurt creatures other than himself. For could not God have made a world where there are humanly free creatures, men with the power to do evil actions, but where those actions do not have evil consequences, or at any rate evil consequences which affect others—e.g., a world where men cannot cause pain and distress to other men? Men might well do actions which are evil either because they were actions which they believed would have evil consequences or because they were evil for some other reason (e.g., actions which involved promise breaking) without them in fact having any passive evils as consequences. Agents in such a world would be like men in a simulator training to be pilots. They can make mistakes, but no one suffers through those mistakes. Or men might do evil actions which did have the evil consequences which were foreseen but which damaged only themselves.

I do not find (P2) a very plausible moral principle. A world in which no one except the agent was affected by his evil actions might be a world in which men had freedom but it would not be a world in which men had responsibility. The theodicist claims that it would not be wrong for God to create interdependent humanly free agents, a society of such agents responsible for each other's well-being, able to make or mar each other.

Fair enough, the antitheodicist may again say. It is not wrong to create a world where creatures have responsibilities for each other. But might not those responsibilities simply be that creatures had the opportunity to benefit or to withhold benefit from each other, not a world in which they had also the opportunity to cause each other pain? One answer to this is that if creatures have only the power to benefit and not the power to hurt each other, they obviously lack any very strong responsibility for each other. To bring out the point by a caricature—a world in which I could choose whether or not to give you sweets, but not whether or not to break your leg or make you unpopular, is not a world in which I have a very strong influence on your destiny, and so not a world in which I have a very full responsibility for you.

So then the theodicist objects to (*P2*) on the grounds that the price of possible passive evils for other creatures is a price worth paying for agents to have great responsibilities for each other. It is a price which (logically) must be paid if they are to have those responsibilities. Here again a reasonable antitheodicist may see the point. In bringing up our own children, in order to give them responsibility, we try not to interfere too quickly in their quarrels—even at the price, sometimes, of younger children getting hurt physically. We try not to interfere, first, in order to train our children for responsibility in later life and second because responsibility here and now is a good thing in itself. True, with respect to the first reason, whatever the effects on character produced by training, God could produce without training. But if he did so by imposing a full character on a humanly free creature, this would be giving him a character which he had not in any way chosen or adopted for himself. Yet it would seem a good thing that a creator should allow humanly free creatures to influence by their own choices the sort of creatures they are to be, the kind of character they are to have. That means that the creator must create them immature, and allow them gradually to make decisions which affect the sort of beings they will be. And one of the greatest privileges which a creator can give to a creature is to allow him to help in the process of education, in putting alternatives before his fellows.

Yet, though the antitheodicist may see the point in theory, he may well react to it rather like this, "Certainly some independence is a good thing. But surely a father ought to interfere if his younger son is really getting badly hurt. The ideal of making men free and responsible is a good one, but there are limits to the amount of responsibility which it is good that men should have, and in our world men have too much responsibility. A good God would certainly have intervened long ago to stop some of the things which happen in our world." Here, I believe, lies the crux—it is simply a matter of quantity. The theodicist says that a good God could allow men to do to each other the hurt they do, in order to allow them to be free and responsible. But against him the antitheodicist puts forward as a moral principle (*P3*) that a creator able to do so ought to ensure that any creature whom he creates does not cause passive evils as many and as evil as those in our world. He says that in our world freedom and responsibility have gone too far—produced too much physical and mental hurt. God might well tolerate a boy hitting his younger brother, but not Belsen.

The theodicist is in no way committed to saying that a good God will not stop things getting too bad. Indeed, if God made our world, he has clearly done so. There are limits to the amount and degree of evil which are possible in our world. Thus there are limits to the amount of pain which a person can suffer—persons live in our world only so many years and the amount which they can suffer at any given time (if mental goings-on are in any way correlated with bodily ones) is limited by their physiology. Further, theists often claim that from time to time God intervenes in the natural order which he has made to prevent evil which would otherwise occur. So the theodicist can certainly claim that a good God stops too much suffering—it is just that he and his opponent draw the line in different places.

But what of the passive evil apparently not due to human action? What of the pain caused to men by disease or earthquake or cyclone, and what too of animal pain which existed before there were men? There are two additional assumptions, each of which has been put forward to allow the free-will defense to show the compatibility of the existence of God and the existence of such evil. The first is that, despite appearances, men are ultimately responsible for disease, earthquake, cyclone, and much animal pain. There seem to be traces of this view in Genesis 3:16–20. One might claim that God ties the goodness of man to the well-being of the world and that a failure of one leads to a failure of the other. Lack of prayer, concern, and simple goodness lead to the evils in nature. This assumption, though it may do some service for the free-will defense, would seem unable to account for the animal pain which existed before there were men. The other assumption is that there exist humanly free creatures other than men, which we may call fallen angels, who have chosen to do evil, and have brought about the passive evils not brought about by men. These were given the care of much of the material world and have abused that care.

This defense has recently been used by, among others, Plantinga. This assumption, it seems to me, will do the job, and is not *clearly* false. It is also an assumption which was part of the Christian tradition long before the free-will defense was put forward in any logically rigorous form. I believe that this assumption may indeed be indispensable if the theist is to reconcile with the existence of God the existence of passive evils of certain kinds, e.g., certain animal pain. But I do not think that the theodicist need deploy it to deal with the central cases of passive evils not caused by men—mental evils and the human pain that is a sign of bodily malfunctioning. Note, however, that if he does not attribute such passive evils to the free choice of some other agent, the theodicist must attribute them to the direct action of God himself, or rather, what he must say is that God created a universe in which passive evils must necessarily occur in certain circumstances, the occurrence of which is necessary or at any rate not within the power of a humanly free agent to prevent. The antitheodicist then naturally claims, that although a creator might be justified in allowing free creatures to produce various evils, nevertheless (P4) a creator is never justified in creating a world in which evil results except by the action of a humanly free agent. Against this the theodicist tries to sketch reasons which a good creator might have for creating a world in which there is evil not brought about by humanly free agents. One reason which he produces is … that various evils are logically necessary conditions for the occurrence of actions of certain especially noble kinds give further opportunities for courage, patience, and tolerance. I shall consider here one further reason that, the theodicist may suggest, a good creator might have for creating a world in which various passive evils were implanted, which is another reason for rejecting (P4). It is, I think, a reason which is closely connected with some of the other reasons which we have been considering why a good creator might permit the existence of evil.

A creator who is going to create humanly free agents and place them in a universe has a choice of the kind of universe to create. First, he can create a finished universe in which nothing needs improving. Humanly free agents know what is right, and pursue it; and they achieve their purposes without hindrance. Second, he can create a basically evil universe, in which everything needs improving, and nothing can be improved. Or, third, he can create a basically good but half-finished universe—one in which many things need improving, humanly free agents do not altogether know what is right, and their purposes are often frustrated; but one in which agents can come to know what is right and can overcome the obstacles to the achievement of their purposes. In such a universe the bodies of creatures may work imperfectly and last only a short time; and creatures may be morally ill-educated, and set their affections on things and persons which are taken from them. The universe might be such that it requires long generations of cooperative effort between creatures to make perfect. While not wishing to deny the goodness of a universe of the first kind, I suggest that to create a universe of the third kind would be no bad thing, for it gives to creatures the privilege of making their own universe. Genesis 1 in telling of a God who tells men to "subdue" the earth pictures the creator as creating a universe of this third kind; and fairly evidently—given that men are humanly free agents—our universe is of this kind.

Now a creator who creates a half-finished universe of this third kind has a further choice as to how he molds the humanly free agents which it contains. Clearly he will have to give them a nature of some kind, that is, certain narrow purposes which they have a natural inclination to pursue until they choose or are forced to pursue others—e.g., the immediate attainment of food, sleep, and sex. There could hardly be humanly free agents without some such initial purposes. But what is he to do about their knowledge of their duty to improve the world—e.g., to repair their bodies when they go wrong, so that they can realize long-term purposes, to help others who cannot get food to do so, etc.? He could just give them a formal hazy knowledge that they had such reasons for action without giving them any strong inclination to pursue them. Such a policy might well seem an excessively laissez-faire one. We tend to think that parents who give their children no help toward taking the right path are less than perfect parents. So a good creator might well help agents toward taking steps to improve the universe. We shall see that he can do this in one of two ways.

An action is something done for a reason. A good creator, we supposed, will give to agents some reasons for doing right actions—e.g., that they are right, that they will improve the universe. These reasons are ones of which men can be aware and then either act on or not act on. The creator could help agents toward doing right actions by making these reasons more effective causally; that is, he could make agents so that by nature they were inclined (though not perhaps compelled) to pursue what is good. But this would be to impose a moral character on agents, to give them wide general purposes which they naturally pursue, to make them naturally altruistic, tenacious of purpose, or strong-willed. But to impose a character on creatures might well seem to take away from creatures the privilege of developing their own characters and those of their fellows. We tend to think that parents who try too forcibly to impose a character, however good a character, on their children, are less than perfect parents.

The alternative way in which a creator could help creatures to perform right actions is by sometimes providing additional reasons for creatures to do what is right, reasons which by their very nature have a strong causal influence. Reasons such as improving the universe or doing one's duty do not necessarily have a strong causal influence, for as we have seen creatures may be little influenced by them. Giving a creature reasons which by their nature were strongly causally influential on a particular occasion on any creature whatever his character, would not impose a particular character on a creature. It would, however, incline him to do what is right on that occasion and maybe subsequently too. Now if a reason is by its nature to be strongly causally influential it must be something of which the agent is aware which causally inclines him (whatever his character) to perform some action, to bring about some kind of change. What kind of reason could this be except the existence of an unpleasant feeling, either a sensation such as a pain or an emotion such as a feeling of loss or deprivation? Such feelings are things of which agents are conscious, which cause them to do whatever action will get rid of those feelings, and which provide reason for performing such action. An itch causally inclines a man to do whatever will cause the itch to cease, e.g., scratch, and provides a reason for doing that action. Its causal influence is quite independent of the agent—saint or sinner, strong-willed or weak-willed, will all be strongly inclined to get rid of their pains (though some may learn to resist the inclination). Hence a creator who wished to give agents some inclination to improve the world without giving them a character, a wide set of general purposes which they naturally pursue, would tie some of the imperfections of the world to physical or mental evils.

To tie desirable states of affairs to pleasant feelings would not have the same effect. Only an existing feeling can be causally efficacious. An agent could be moved to action by a pleasant feeling only when he had it, and the only action to which he could be moved would be to keep the world as it is, not to improve it. For men to have reasons which move men of any character to actions of perfecting the world, a creator needs to tie its imperfections to unpleasant feelings, that is, physical and mental evils.

There is to some considerable extent such tie-up in our universe. Pain normally occurs when something goes wrong with the working of our body which is going to lead to further limitation on the purposes which we can achieve; and the pain ends when the body is repaired. The existence of the pain spurs the sufferer, and others through the sympathetic suffering which arises when they learn of the sufferer's pain, to do something about the bodily malfunctioning. Yet giving men such feelings which they are inclined to end involves the imposition of no character. A man who is inclined to end his toothache by a visit to the dentist may be saint or sinner, strong-willed or weak-willed, rational or irrational. Any other way of which I can conceive of giving men an inclination to correct what goes wrong, and generally to improve the universe, would seem to involve imposing a character. A creator could, for example, have operated exclusively by threats and promises, whispering in men's ears, "unless you go to the dentist, you are going to suffer terribly," or "if you go to the dentist, you are going to feel wonderful." And if the order of nature is God's creation, he does indeed often provide us with such threats and promises—not by whispering in our ears but by providing inductive evidence. There is plenty of inductive evidence that unattended cuts and sores will lead to pain; that eating and drinking will lead to pleasure. Still, men do not always respond to threats and promises or take the trouble to notice inductive evidence (e.g., statistics showing the correlation between smoking and cancer). A creator could have made men so that they naturally took more account of inductive evidence. But to do so would be to impose character. It would be to make men, apart from any choice of theirs, rational and strong-willed.

Many mental evils too are caused by things going wrong in a man's life or in the life of his fellows and often serve as a spur to a man to put things right, either to put right the cause of the particular mental evil or to put similar things right. A man's feeling of frustration at the failure of his plans spurs him either to fulfill those plans despite their initial failure or to curtail his ambitions. A man's sadness at the failure of the plans of his child will incline him to help the child more in future. A man's grief at the absence of a loved one inclines him to do whatever will get the loved one back. As with physical pain, the spur inclines a man to do what is right but does so without imposing a character—without, say, making a man responsive to duty, or strong-willed.

Physical and mental evils may serve as spurs to long-term cooperative research leading to improvement of the universe. A feeling of sympathy for the actual and prospective suffering of many from tuberculosis or cancer leads to acquisition of knowledge and provision of cure for future sufferers. Cooperative and long-term research and cure is a very good thing, the kind of thing toward which men need a spur. A man's suffering is never in vain if it leads through sympathy to the work of others which eventually provides a long-term cure. True, there could be sympathy without a sufferer for whom the sympathy is felt. Yet in a world made by a creator, there cannot be sympathy on the large scale without a sufferer, for whom the sympathy is felt, unless the creator planned for creatures generally to be deceived about the feelings of their fellows; and that would be morally wrong.

So generally many evils have a biological and psychological utility in producing spurs to right action without imposition of character, a goal which it is hard to conceive of being realized in any other way. This point provides a reason for the rejection of (*P4*).

So, I have argued, there seem to be kinds of justification for the evils which exist in the world, available to the theodicist. Although a good creator might have very different kinds of justification for producing, or allowing others to produce, various different evils, there is a central thread running through the kind of theodicy which I have made my theodicist put forward. This is that it is a good thing that a creator should make a half-finished universe and create immature creatures, who are humanly free agents, to inhabit it; and that he should allow them to exercise some choice over what kind of creatures they are to become and what sort of universe is to be (while at the same time giving them a slight push in the direction of doing what is right); and that the creatures should have power to affect not only the development of the inanimate universe but the well-being and moral character of their fellows, and that there should be opportunities for creatures to develop noble characters and do especially noble actions.

NOTES

1. This account of omnipotence will do for present purposes. But a much more careful account is needed to deal with other well-known difficulties. I have attempted to provide such an account in my "Omnipotence," *American Philosophical Quarterly,* 10(1973), 231–237.

2. Some of what I have to say will not be especially original. The extensive writing on this subject has of course been well described in John Hick, *Evil and the God of Love* (London, 1966).

3. In discussion of the problem of evil, terminology has not always been very clear or consistent. See Gerald Wallace, "The Problems of Moral and Physical Evil,' *Philosophy,* 46 (1971), 349–351.

4. Indeed they have often made the ever stronger claim that a good God would create *the* best of all (logically) possible worlds—implying that necessarily there was just one possible world better than all others. There seem to me no grounds at all for adopting this claim.

5. That he has no such obligation is very well argued by Robert Merrihew Adams, "Must God Create the Rest?" *Philosophical Review*, 81 (1972), 317–332.

6. See Alvin Plantinga, "The Free Will Defence," in Max Black, ed., *Philosophy in America* (London, 1965); *God and Other Minds* (Ithaca, N.Y., and London, 1967), chaps. 5 and 6; and *The Nature of Necessity* (Oxford, 1974), chap. 9.

PART IV

Knowledge of the External World

THE ENLIGHTENMENT
AND THE AGE OF NEWTON

By William F. Lawhead

The historian of the eighteenth century does not have to search very far for an appropriate title for this period. The thinkers of this age presided at their own christening. The eighteenth-century writers spoke of their own time as the Age of Enlightenment. Their time was special, they thought, for reason had now made good on its promise. It had showed the way to progress in science, philosophy, religion, politics, and the arts. The pure, brilliant light of reason would vanquish once and for all the darkness in which humanity had previously labored and lived. What was this darkness? It was passion, prejudice, authority, and dogma. The pride shining through the self-proclaimed title of "Enlightenment" reveals the mood of the times. In any account you will read of this period, the words "hope," "optimism," "confidence," and "happiness" abound. As one writer aptly put it, "the eighteenth century is perhaps the last period in the history of Western Europe when human omniscience was thought to be an attainable goal."[1]

The Enlightenment did not, of course, suddenly spring into being. It was the culmination of many of the cultural and intellectual trends we have discussed in previous chapters. However, for our purposes, the overture began with the publishing of Sir Isaac Newton's great scientific work *Principia*

Mathematica in 1687.* The opening act was John Locke's *An Essay Concerning Human Understanding* (1690) and the beginning of the final scene was Immanuel Kant's *Critique of Pure Reason*, first published in 1781. By the time Kant published his 1784 essay "What is Enlightenment?" answering such a question was superfluous. No one had to be told by Kant that "Enlightenment is man's leaving his self-caused immaturity."

THE IMPACT OF NEWTON'S SCIENCE

It is impossible to appreciate the philosophy of the eighteenth-century philosophers without taking note of the enormous influence Newtonian science had on this period. It is interesting, that Newton was born in the year 1642, the same year that Galileo died. It is almost as though the earlier scientist passed on the torch of scientific inquiry to his successor as he left this world. This poetic coincidence would not have escaped Newton, for he was well aware of his debt to his predecessors. As he says in a letter, "If I have seen farther [than other scientists], it is because I have stood upon the shoulders of Giants."[2]

There is much we can learn from the case of Newton concerning the process of intellectual history. History is often made by the fortuitous combination of the right circumstances and the gifted genius. The work of Isaac Newton is a clear case of fertile intellectual soil accumulating for centuries, while being cultivated and seeded by previous thinkers, until it was finally brought to harvest by a great intellect. This was strikingly demonstrated by the fact that Newton and Leibniz both, independently, discovered the infinitesimal calculus. Newton's achievement in physics consisted in developing a single, comprehensive theory from which he could derive both Galileo's laws describing the motion of falling bodies and Kepler's laws of the planetary motions. It was as though previous scientists had each been working on parts of a jigsaw puzzle, one piecing together a field of wild flowers, the other piecing together some clouds, all with the hope that somehow they were working on the same picture. Along came Newton who showed that the contributions of previous scientists could indeed be integrated into a single coherent and beautiful picture of nature. Imagine yourself in the seventeenth century, standing on the beach under a moonlit sky, tossing pebbles into the waves as the tide rolls in. Would you have thought that the motion of the moon and the planets up there in the sky, the trajectory made by your pebbles as they fell back to earth, and the movement, of the approaching tide could all be explained by the same fundamental laws? So stupendous was Newton's achievement that it provided the framework for science for over two hundred years, until Albert Einstein provided a new model of the cosmos in the twentieth century.

*The full title is *Philosophiae Naturalis Principia Mathematica*, which means "Mathematical Principles of Natural Philosophy."

Newton's discoveries dealt the final blow to any lingering remnants of the Aristotelian science of the Middle Ages. Aristotle thought that there was a major gulf between earthly matters and celestial affairs. These two spheres operated according to completely different laws. For the medievals, this was reinforced by their theological distinction between heaven and earth. But after Newton it was absolutely clear there are no special, sacred spaces in the physical realm. The heavens and the earth are made of the same materials and follow the same laws. The universe became increasingly less mysterious and more open to human understanding, prediction, and even control. Earlier, Robert Boyle, the great chemist, had mused that the universe was like a great clock. Now Newton had given mathematical substance to this image.

By the time Newton published his *Principia*, it became clear that mathematical, experimental science was no longer the new kid on the block—it was now the "king of the mountain." All philosophy (and religion) hereafter had to come to terms with it in some way or another. To the Enlightenment, Newton was more than a great physicist, he was a cultural hero. Alexander Pope voiced the spirit of the age when he said,

Nature and Nature's laws lay hid in night:
God said, Let Newton be! and all was Light.

In his book on the rise of modern science, E. A. Burtt makes the ironic observation that "Newton enjoys the remarkable distinction of having become an authority paralleled only by Aristotle to an age characterized through and through by rebellion against authority."[3] Both the rationalists and the empiricists claimed Newton as their own. Indeed, the great synthesizing mind of Newton recognized the importance of both the deductive, mathematical approach favored by scientists and philosophers such as Galileo Galilei and René Descartes, as well as the inductive, experimental approach favored by those such as Francis Bacon and Robert Boyle. Nevertheless, the net effect of Newton's method was to tilt the scales more in the direction of the empiricists. Even though his remarks were not completely consistent with his practice, Newton ended the *Principia* by denouncing any speculative theories (which he called "hypotheses") that are not firmly rooted in the empirical data. As we will see in the next three chapters, this concern to trace the genealogy of all our affirmations back to the bedrock of experience played an important role in the epistemology of the British philosophers.

Newton, therefore, wanted to put science on a severe cognitive diet. This means that we must avoid the fatty and rich fare of speculative metaphysics and stick to the lean and unadulterated data of experience. For example, his law of gravitation states that the force of attraction (F) between any two bodies (M_1 and M_2) separated by distance R, where G is a universal constant, is as follows:

$$F = \frac{GM_1M_2}{R_2}$$

This law of gravitation describes the observable behavior of bodies and enables us to calculate future observations. However, it does not attempt to explain what gravity is or what causes the attraction between bodies. As Newton expressed it,

> Hitherto I have not been able to discover the cause of those properties of gravity from phenomena, and I frame no hypotheses: for whatever is not deduced from the phenomena is to be called an hypothesis; and hypotheses, whether metaphysical or physical whether of occult qualities or mechanical, have no place in experimental science.[4]

This represents a significant turning point in the history of thought, for Newton was telling scientists to give up all attempts to deal with essences and the underlying reality of things. Henceforth, science is to only describe the patterns of phenomena. The reality that lies behind, underneath, or beyond the phenomena cannot be scientifically comprehended. The implications of this methodological principle will become clearer step-by-step as we move in the next four chapters through the thought of John Locke, George Berkeley, David Hume, and finally Immanuel Kant. Philosophy began with the early Greeks' attempts to distinguish appearance and reality. After Newton, however, it gradually became apparent that the more science and experience were considered the sole basis of knowledge, the less we could know about reality in itself apart from the way it appears to us.

Philosophizing in a Newtonian Style

The philosophers of the time thought that just as Newton had resolved all mysteries concerning physical bodies, so now the task was to apply the same methods of experimental observation to the mysteries concerning human existence. The operations of the human mind, ethics, and politics were thought to be a collection of phenomena that could be explained in terms of descriptive laws. Hence, the philosophers of this time all aspired to be the "Newton" of the human sciences. The titles of the leading works of this period seemed to be permutations of the same set of interchangeable words concerned with epistemology. There was, for example, Locke's *An Essay Concerning Human Understanding*, Berkeley's *A Treatise Concerning the Principles of Human Knowledge*, and Hume's *An Enquiry Concerning Human Understanding*, as well as his *A Treatise of Human Nature*. The most extreme expression of this scientific approach to human nature was found in the works of Julien La Mettrie (1709–1751). Among his many controversial books was *Man the Machine* (1747). La Mettrie said that the true philosopher is an engineer who analyzes the apparatus of the human mind. Although his theory was crude, it was way ahead of its own time, for it pointed toward the twentieth-century theory that the brain is like an organic computer. However, unlike La Mettrie, most philosophers at this time did not fully understand the reductionists and deterministic implications of their own scientific and mechanistic approach to the human sciences. Instead (to exaggerate a bit), it almost seemed as though they saw scientific epistemology as a more efficient method for doing what the poets had always tried to do—provide us with an enriched self-understanding.

The model of Newtonian physics haunted the epistemology of this era. Corresponding to the physical particles whose laws of motion Newton unveiled, ideas were thought to be mental particles that could be analyzed down into fundamental, atomic units. Hence, all the ideas contained within the dialogues of Plato, the works of Shakespeare, and even the formulas of Newton, if they had any meaning at all, were considered complexes made up of simple ideas derived from experience. Corresponding to the outer space of the astronomer was the "inner space" of the mind, a container within which ideas floated and connected together according to psychological laws. Although this model of the mind assured philosophers that epistemology could duplicate the successes of physics, we have already seen in Descartes and will later see with Hume that this dichotomy between the inner, mental world and the outer, physical world created problems. If all mental awareness takes place within the container of the mind, how do we know that what appears on the inside represents what is going on in the outside world? As we have seen, Leibniz's idealism tried to get around that problem by rejecting the mental-physical dualism on which it rested. Berkeley, likewise, developed a metaphysical idealism to overcome the problem. In wrestling with epistemological and metaphysical puzzles created by the philosophies of their time, Leibniz and Berkeley were among the first thinkers to question the Newtonian model. The alternative view-points they launched would come to fruition in the twentieth century with the physics of Albert Einstein and the process philosophy of Alfred North Whitehead.

The Consequences for Religion

In addition to its impact on philosophy, Newtonian science made waves within the religious sensibilities of the age as well. At first, people feared that the new physics would undermine religion. After all, Newton provided natural explanations for a great deal of celestial phenomena once thought to result from the direct providence of God. The notion that the universe was a clockwork mechanism did not mesh well with the theology of the day, which still clung to many medieval assumptions. As one critic of the new science complained, if the universe is ruled by geometry and mechanical laws, "I cannot any way comprehend how God can do any miracles."[5] Many feared that materialism and atheism would ride in on the coattails of mechanistic science and take over the culture. Nevertheless, Newton himself was a deeply pious Christian and even wrote works on theology and biblical exposition. For him, science revealed a universe that was majestic and marvelous in its design, pointing to the greatness of its creator. Newton expressed his scientific piety in a letter to a friend:

> When I wrote my treatise about our system, I had an eye upon such principles as might work with considering men for the belief of a deity; and nothing can rejoice me more than to find it useful for that purpose.[6]

Newton's argument for God was based not only on the evidence of design, but also on the problems within his own physics. First, Newton could not explain why the gravitational attraction of the stars does not cause them to collapse together. Second, he observed what seemed to be irregularities in the universe that would eventually cause it to run down. Because he could not solve these problems scientifically, he assumed that God actively intervened to keep the world machine going. However, this created what is known as a "God-of-the-gaps." It is risky to use gaps within our scientific knowledge as evidence for the necessity of God. When these gaps are eventually filled as scientific knowledge expands, there seems to be less need to believe in God. This is exactly what happened in Newton's case. Eighteenth-century scientists showed that further developments of Newton's physics could explain all the problematic phenomena and that the planetary orbits were not as irregular as Newton had supposed. Accordingly, the story is told that when the French astronomer Laplace presented his 1796 work to Napoleon, the general asked about God's role in explaining planetary motion. Laplace is said to have replied, "Sire, I have no need of that hypothesis."

From the beginning of modern science all the way up to and through the twentieth century, many, if not the majority, of the leading scientists and philosophers have been theists of some sort. Nevertheless, the ability to explain physical events on the basis of natural causes made a secular view of the world more viable than at any previous stage in history. Historically, the emergence of unbelief went through several overlapping stages in the modern period. (1) Initially, most scientists and philosophers, such as Newton, saw religion and science as co-equal partners in the search for truth. Among the philosophers in this period, George Berkeley stands out as one who taught the perfect convergence of religion and science when both are properly understood. (2) Gradually the viewpoint emerged that the claims of revealed religion should be accepted, but only after they have been trimmed down to conform to the scientific outlook. Although John Locke could be identified with the previous position, he also fits in here, for he introduced the notion that the credentials of revelation must be approved by reason before we can believe it. (3) As science gained greater authority, the position of deism emerged. The deists claimed that the world machine is a perfectly ordered mechanism, understandable on its own terms. Hence, while they believed that God created the world, they thought it unreasonable to suppose that he needs to intervene in the processes of nature. Furthermore, they believed that autonomous human reason is self-sufficient to discover all truths about nature, religion, and morality without relying on revelation. Many of the key figures in the American Revolution such as Thomas Paine, Thomas Jefferson, and Benjamin Franklin were deists. (4) Agnosticism or religious skepticism began to appear in the works of such thinkers as David Hume. The agnostics urged that we must suspend judgment concerning God's existence, for reason does not give us any grounds for believing in a deity, although it cannot prove that one does not exist. Immanuel Kant agreed with Hume that we cannot have *knowledge* of God, because knowledge about what exists is to be found only in the sciences. However, he tempered this theoretical agnosticism with the notion that we still find it compelling to postulate a deity. (5) Finally, full- blown naturalism or atheism appeared. However, in terms of the major figures in philosophy, it would not have a strong voice until the nineteenth century. Its proponents claimed that the philosophical and scientific evidence is stacked against the God hypothesis. Therefore, the rational person will reject it, just as we have the flat earth theory and the theory that diseases have supernatural causes.

The French Enlightenment

It did not take long for the spirit of the Enlightenment to find its way to France. This spirit was embodied in a group of eighteenth-century French writers known as the *philosophes* (from the French term for philosopher). In spite of their name, they were primarily literary intellectuals rather than technical philosophers. Nevertheless, they used their considerable skill with words to popularize the Enlightenment among the educated public. Representing a wide range of talents, they used novels, poems, essays, historical studies, political writings, scientific treatises, dictionaries, and an encyclopedia to disseminate their philosophical and political ideas. They were popular guests at the French *salons*, the equivalent of elite cocktail parties where fashionable intellectuals mingled with European aristocracy to discuss the current (and often scandalous) ideas of the day. Leading *philosophes* were Montesquieu, Voltaire, La Mettrie, Rousseau, Diderot, Condillac, Helvétius, d'Alembert, Holbach, and Condorcet, among others. Their works were replete with social criticism that attacked bigotry, ignorance, the hypocrisy of organized religion, and oppressive political institutions. More positively, the *philosophes* believed in the power of reason, the ideal of progress, and the perfectibility of humanity. Although they continually clashed with established religion, many *philosophes*, such as Voltaire, were deists who held that belief in God supported morality and social order. However, their company also included materialists and atheists. Diderot, for example, said that a deist was a man who had not lived long enough—or wisely enough—to become an atheist.

The initial influx of fresh ideas were imported to France from across the English Channel. Montesquieu (1689–1755) and Voltaire (1694–1778) were enamored of English culture and thought. Newton and Locke were their heroes and the English system, with its ideals of freedom and tolerance, was their political ideal. Montesquieu's influential works included his early satirical attack on French culture and religion in the *Persian Letters* (1721) as well as his work on political science, *The Spirit of Laws* (1748). Voltaire's influential works ranged in style from a celebration of English philosophy and culture in *Lettres philosophiques* (1734) to his famous satirical novel *Candide* (1759).

One of the notable, accomplishments of the *philosophes* was the French *Encyclopédie*. Many writers contributed to it; however, the burden of editing it eventually fell on Diderot, who received some assistance from d'Alembert. In addition to scientific, mathematical, and technological subjects, it also included thinly veiled attacks on orthodox religion and prevailing social institutions. More than just a reference work, it was a manifesto of the Enlightenment. In a pithy statement of secular faith, one of its articles proclaimed, "Reason is to the *philosophe* what grace is to the Christian." Although there were many quarrels among the editors and continual battles with censorship, over three decades the work grew to thirty-five volumes. Recognizing its influence, alarmed conservatives attacked it for promoting deism, materialism, and irreligion. Indeed, compared with the attempts of present-day reference works to be objective and impersonal, the *Encyclopédie* had all the subjective style and polemical tone of a newspaper opinion page. Diderot bluntly acknowledges that the purpose of the project was not simply to impart information but "to change the general way of thinking." Despite attempts to suppress it, the work proved to be enormously popular and succeeded in disseminating the ideals of the Enlightenment among the reading public.

Summary of the Enlightenment

Although eighteenth-century philosophers differed on the details, the four pillars of Enlightenment thought were nature, reason, experience, and progress. Nature was viewed as orderly, governed by laws, and basically benevolent. Human nature was likewise seen as orderly, governed by laws, and basically benevolent, or at least it will be once we remove the distractions of passion and dogma and let reason prevail. Whether reason was understood as a source of *a priori* knowledge as the rationalists thought or simply as an instrument to organize experience as the empiricists claimed, it was thought to be the great equalizer among people. Everyone has the basic capacity to be reasonable, and by learning from experience and with the help of education our rational powers will be released. Hence all problems, theoretical or social, can be solved through science and concerted, rational effort. The Enlightenment's optimism and faith in progress was summarized in the words of Kant:

> *Do we live at present in an enlightened age? The answer is: No, but in an age of enlightenment.*

Already, Kant claimed, conditions were developing that would enable people to

> *work freely and reduce gradually the hindrances preventing a general enlightenment and an escape from self-caused immaturity. In this sense, this age is the age of enlightenment.*[7]

NOTES

1. Isaiah Berlin, ed., *The Age of Enlightenment* (New York: Mentor, The New American Library, 1956), 14.
2. In a letter to Robert Hooke, February 5, 1675/6, in *The Correspondence of Isaac Newton*, vol. 1, ed. H. W. Turnbull (Cambridge, England: Cambridge University Press, 1959), 416.

3. Edwin A. Bunt, *The Metaphysical Foundations of Modern Physical Science*, rev. ed. (Garden City, NY: Doubleday, 1932), 207.

4. Newton's Principia. vol. 2, *The System of the World*, trans. Andrew Motte, rev. Florian Cajori (Berkeley: University of California Press, 1962), 547.

5. Henry Stubbe, quoted in Richard S. Westfall, *Science and Religion in Seventeenth-Century England* (New Haven, CT: Yale University Press, 1958), 24.

6. Quoted in Richard Westfall, 193.

7. Immanuel Kant, "What Is Enlightenment?" trans. Carl J. Friedrich, in *The Philosophy of Kant: Immanuel Kant's Moral and Political Writings*, ed. Carl J. Friedrich (New York: The Modern Library, 1949), 138.

FIRST MEDITATION

By René Descartes

Of the things which may be brought within the sphere of the doubtful.

I t is now some years since I detected how many were the false beliefs that I had from my earliest youth admitted as true, and how doubtful was everything I had since constructed on this basis; and from that time I was convinced that I must once for all seriously undertake to rid myself of all the opinions which I had formerly accepted, and commence to build anew from the foundation, if I wanted to establish any firm and permanent structure in the sciences. But as this enterprise appeared to be a very great one, I waited until I had attained an age so mature that I could not hope that at any later date I should be better fitted to execute my design. This reason caused me to delay so long that I should feel that I was doing wrong were I to occupy in deliberation the time that yet remains to me for action. Today, then, since very opportunely for the plan I have in view I have delivered my mind from every care [and am happily agitated by no passions] and since I have procured for myself an assured leisure in a peaceable retirement, I shall at last seriously and freely address myself to the general upheaval of all my former opinions.

Now for this object it is not necessary that I should show that all of these are false. I shall perhaps never arrive at this end. But inasmuch as reason already persuades me that I ought no less carefully to withhold my assent from matters which are not entirely certain and indubitable than from those which appear to me manifestly to be false, if I am able to find in each one some reason to doubt, this will suffice to justify my rejecting the whole. And for that end it will not be requisite that I should examine each in particular, which would be an endless undertaking; for owing to the fact that the destruction of the foundations of necessity brings with it the downfall of the rest of the edifice, I shall only in the first place attack those principles upon which all my former opinions rested.

All that up to the present time I have accepted as most true and certain I have learned either from the senses or through the senses; but it is sometimes proved to me that these senses are deceptive, and it is wiser not to trust entirely to anything by which we have once been deceived.

But it may be that although the senses sometimes deceive us concerning things which are hardly perceptible, or very far away, there are yet many others to be met with as to which we cannot reasonably have any doubt, although we recognise them by their means. For example, there is the fact that I am here, seated by the fire, attired in a dressing gown, having this paper in my hands and other similar matters. And how could I deny that these hands and this body are mine, were it not perhaps that I compare myself to certain persons, devoid of sense, whose cerebella are so troubled and clouded by the violent vapours of black bile, that they constantly assure us that they think they are kings when they are really quite poor, or that they are clothed in purple when they are really without covering, or who imagine that they have an earthenware head or are nothing but pumpkins or are made of glass. But they are mad, and I should not be any the less insane were I to follow examples so extravagant.

At the same time I must remember that I am a man, and that consequently I am in the habit of sleeping, and in my dreams representing to myself the same things or sometimes even less probable things, than do those who are insane in their waking moments. How often has it happened to me that in the night I dreamt that I found myself in this particular place, that I was dressed and seated near the fire, whilst in reality I was lying undressed in bed! At this moment it does indeed seem to me that it is with eyes awake that I am looking at this paper; that this head which I move is not asleep, that it is deliberately and of set purpose that I extend my hand and perceive it; what happens in sleep does not appear so clear nor so distinct as does all this. But in thinking over this I remind myself that on many occasions I have in sleep been deceived by similar illusions, and in dwelling carefully on this reflection I see so manifestly that there are no certain indications by which we may clearly distinguish wakefulness from sleep that I am lost in astonishment. And my astonishment is such that it is almost capable of persuading me that I now dream.

Now let us assume that we are asleep and that all these particulars, e. g. that we open our eyes, shake our head, extend our hands, and so on, are but false delusions; and let us reflect that possibly neither our hands nor our whole body are such as they appear to us to be. At the same time we must at least confess that the things which are represented to us in sleep are like painted representations which can only have been formed as the counterparts of something real and true, and that in this way those general things at least, i. e. eyes, a head, hands, and a whole body, are not imaginary things, but things really existent. For, as a matter of fact, painters, even when they study with the greatest skill to represent sirens and satyrs by forms the most strange and extraordinary, cannot give them natures which are entirely new, but merely make a certain medley of the members of different animals; or if their imagination is extravagant enough to invent something so novel that nothing similar has ever before been seen, and that then their work represents a thing purely fictitious and absolutely false, it is certain all the same that the colours of which this is composed are necessarily real. And for the same reason, although these general things, to with, [a body], eyes, a head, hands, and such like, may be imaginary, we are bound at the same time to confess that there are at least some other objects yet more simple and more universal, which are real and true; and of these just in the same way as with certain real colours, all these images of things which dwell in our thoughts, whether true and real or false and fantastic, are formed.

To such a class of things pertains corporeal nature in general, and its extension, the figure of extended things, their quantity or magnitude and number, as also the place in which they are, the time which measures their duration, and so on.

That is possibly why our reasoning is not unjust when we conclude from this that Physics, Astronomy, Medicine and all other sciences which have as their end the consideration of composite things, are very dubious and uncertain; but that Arithmetic, Geometry and other sciences of that kind which only treat of things that are very simple and very general, without taking great trouble to ascertain whether they are actually existent or not, contain some measure of certainty and an element of the indubitable. For whether I am awake or asleep, two and three together always form five, and the square can never have more than four sides, and it does not seem possible that truths so clear and apparent can be suspected of any falsity [or uncertainty].

Nevertheless I have long had fixed in my mind the belief that an all-powerful God existed by whom I have been created such as I am. But how do I know that He has not brought it to pass that there is no earth, no heaven, no extended body, no magnitude, no place, and that nevertheless [I possess the perceptions of all these things and that] they seem to me to exist just exactly as I now see them? And, besides, as I sometimes imagine that others deceive themselves in the things which they think they know best, how do I know that I am not deceived every time that I add two and three, or count the sides of a square, or judge of things yet simpler, if anything simpler can be imagined? But possibly God has not desired that I should be thus deceived, for He is said to be supremely good. If, however, it is contrary to His goodness to have made me such that I constantly deceive myself, it would also appear to be contrary to His goodness to permit me to be sometimes deceived, and nevertheless I cannot doubt that He does permit this.

There may indeed be those who would prefer to deny the existence of a God so powerful, rather than believe that all other things are uncertain. But let us not oppose them for the present, and grant that all that is here said of a God is a fable; nevertheless in whatever way they suppose that I have arrived at the state of being that I have reached—whether they attribute it to fate or to accident, or make out that it is by a continual succession of antecedents, or by some other method—since to err and deceive oneself is a defect, it is clear that the greater will be the probability of my being so imperfect as to deceive myself ever, as is the Author to whom they assign my origin the less powerful. To these reasons I have certainly nothing to reply, but at the end I feel constrained to confess that there is nothing in all that I formerly believed to be true, of which I cannot in some measure doubt, and that not merely through want of thought or through levity, but for reasons which are very powerful and maturely considered; so that henceforth I ought not the less carefully to refrain from giving credence to these opinions than to that which is manifestly false, if I desire to arrive at any certainty [in the sciences].

But it is not sufficient to have made these remarks, we must also be careful to keep them in mind. For these ancient and commonly held opinions still revert frequently to my mind, long and familiar custom having given them the right to occupy my mind against my inclination and rendered them almost masters of my belief; nor will I ever lose the habit of deferring to them or of placing my confidence in them, so long as I consider them as they really are, i. e. opinions in some measure doubtful, as I have just shown, and at the same time highly probable, so that there is much more reason to believe in than to deny them. That is why I consider that I shall not be acting amiss, if, taking of set purpose a contrary belief, I allow myself to be deceived, and for a certain time pretend that all these opinions are entirely false and imaginary, until at last, having thus balanced my former prejudices with my latter [so that they cannot divert my opinions more to one side than to the other], my judgment will no longer be dominated by bad usage or turned away from the right knowledge of the truth. For I am assured that there can be neither peril nor error in this course, and that I cannot at present yield too much to distrust, since I am not considering the question of action, but only of knowledge.

I shall then suppose, not that God who is supremely good and the fountain of truth, but some evil genius not less powerful than deceitful, has employed his whole energies in deceiving me; I shall consider that the heavens, the earth, colours, figures, sound, and all other external things are nought but the illusions and dreams of which this genius has availed himself in order to lay traps for my credulity; I shall consider myself as having no hands, no eyes, no flesh, no blood, nor any senses, yet falsely believing myself to possess all these things; I shall remain obstinately attached to this idea, and if by this means it is not in my power to arrive at the knowledge of any truth, I may at least do what is in my power [i. e. suspend my judgment], and with firm purpose avoid giving credence to any false thing, or being imposed upon by this arch deceiver, however powerful and deceptive he may be. But this task is a laborious one, and insensibly a certain lassitude leads me into the course of my ordinary life. And just as a captive who in sleep enjoys an imaginary liberty, when he begins to suspect that his liberty is but a dream, fears to awaken, and conspires with these agreeable illusions that the deception may be prolonged, so insensibly of my own accord I fall back into my former opinions, and I dread awakening from this slumber, lest the laborious wakefulness which would follow the tranquility of this repose should have to be spent not in daylight, but in the excessive darkness of the difficulties which have just been discussed.

THE PROBLEM OF THE EXTERNAL WORLD

By Barry Stroud

Since at least the time of Descartes in the seventeenth century there has been a philosophical problem about our knowledge of the world around us.[1] Put most simply, the problem is to show how we can have any knowledge of the world at all. The conclusion that we cannot, that no one knows anything about the world around us, is what I call 'scepticism about the external world', so we could also say that the problem is to show how or why scepticism about the external world is not correct. My aim is not to solve the problem but to understand it. I believe the problem has no solution; or rather that the only answer to the question as it is meant to be understood is that we can know nothing about the world around us. But how is the question meant to be understood? It can be expressed in a few English words familiar to all of us, but I hope to show that an understanding of the special philosophical character of the question, and of the inevitability of an unsatisfactory answer to it, cannot be guaranteed by our understanding of those words alone. To see how the problem is meant to be understood we must therefore examine what is perhaps best described as its source—how the problem arises and how it acquires that special character that makes an unsatisfactory negative answer inevitable. We must try to understand the *philosophical* problem of our knowledge of the external world.

The problem arose for Descartes in the course of reflecting on everything he knows. He reached a point in his life at which he tried to sit back and reflect on everything he had ever been taught or told, everything he had learned or discovered or believed since he was old enough to know or believe anything.[2] We might say that he was reflecting on his knowledge, but putting it that way could suggest that what he was directing his attention to was indeed knowledge, and whether it was knowledge or not is precisely what he wanted to determine. 'Among all the things I believe or take to be true, what amounts to knowledge and what does not?'; that is the question Descartes asks himself. It is obviously a very general question, since it asks about everything he believes or takes to be true, but in other respects it sounds just like the sort of question we are perfectly familiar with in everyday life and often know how to answer.

For example, I have come to accept over the years a great many things about the common cold. I have always been told that one can catch cold by getting wet feet, or from sitting in a draught, or from not drying one's hair before going outdoors in cold weather. I have also learned that the common cold is the effect of a virus transmitted by an already infected person. And I also believe that one is more vulnerable to colds when over-tired, under stress, or otherwise in less than the best of health. Some of these beliefs seem to me on reflection to be inconsistent with some others; I see that it is very unlikely that all of them could be true. Perhaps they could be, but I acknowledge that there is much I do not understand. If I sit back and try to think about all my 'knowledge' of the common cold, then, I might easily come to wonder how much of it really amounts to knowledge and how much does not. What do I really know about the common cold? If I were sufficiently interested in pursuing the matter it would be natural to look into the source of my beliefs. Has there ever been any good reason for thinking that colds are even correlated with wet hair in cold weather, for example, or with sitting in a draught? Are the people from whom I learned such things likely to have believed them for good reasons? Are those beliefs just old wives' tales, or are they really true, and perhaps even known to be true by some people? These are questions I might ask myself, and I have at least a general idea of how to go about answering them.

Apart from my impression of the implausibility of all my beliefs about the common cold being true together, I have not mentioned any other reason for being interested in investigating the state of my knowledge on that subject. But for the moment that does not seem to affect the intelligibility or the feasibility of the reflective project. There is nothing mysterious about it. It is the sort of task we can be led to undertake for a number of reasons, and often very good reasons, in so far as we have very good reasons for preferring knowledge and firm belief to guesswork or wishful thinking or simply taking things for granted.

Reflection on or investigation of our putative knowledge need not always extend to a wide area of interest. It might be important to ask whether some quite specific and particular thing I believe or have been taking for granted is really something I know. As a member of a jury I might find that I have been ruling out one suspect in my mind because he was a thousand miles away, in Cleveland, at the time of the crime. But I might then begin to ask myself whether that is really something that I know. I would reflect on the source of my belief, but reflection in this case need not involve a general scrutiny of everything I take myself to know about the case. Re-examining the man's alibi and the credentials of its supporting witnesses might be enough to satisfy me. Indeed I might find that its reliability on those counts is precisely what I had been going on all along.

In pointing out that we are perfectly familiar with the idea of investigating or reviewing our knowledge on some particular matter or in some general area I do not mean to suggest that it is always easy to settle the question. Depending on the nature of the case, it might be very difficult, perhaps even impossible at the time, to reach a firm conclusion. For example, it would probably be very difficult if not impossible for me to trace and assess the origins of many of those things I believe about the common cold. But it is equally true that sometimes it is not impossible or even especially difficult to answer the question. We do sometimes discover that we do not really know what we previously thought we knew. I might find that what I had previously believed is not even true-—that sitting in draughts is not even correlated with catching a cold, for example. Or I might find that there is not or perhaps never was any good reason to believe what I believed—that the man's alibi was concocted and then falsely testified to by his friends. I could reasonably conclude in each case that I, and everyone else for that matter, never did know what I had previously thought I knew. We are all familiar with the ordinary activity of reviewing our knowledge, and with the experience of reaching a positive verdict in some cases and a negative verdict in others.

Descartes's own interest in what he knows and how he knows it is part of his search for what he calls a general method for 'rightly conducting reason and seeking truth in the sciences'.[3] He wants a method of inquiry that he can be assured in advance will lead only to the truth if properly followed. I think we do not need to endorse the wisdom of that search or the feasibility of that programme in order to try to go along with Descartes in his general assessment of the position he is in with respect to the things he believes. He comes to find his putative knowledge wanting in certain general respects, and it is in the course of that original negative assessment that the problem I am interested in arises. I call the assessment 'negative' because by the end of his *First Meditation* Descartes finds that he has no good reason to believe anything about the world around him and therefore that he can know nothing of the external world.

How is that assessment conducted, and how closely does it parallel the familiar kind of review of our knowledge that we all know how to conduct in everyday life? The question in one form or another will be with us for the rest of this book. It is the question of what exactly the problem of our knowledge of the external world amounts to, and how it arises with its special philosophical character. The source of the problem is to be found somewhere within or behind the kind of thinking Descartes engages in.

One way Descartes's question about his knowledge differs from the everyday examples I considered is in being concerned with *everything* he believes or takes to be true. How does one go about assessing all of one's knowledge all at once? I was able to list a few of the things I believe about the common cold and then to ask about each of them whether I really know it, and if so how. But although I can certainly list a number of the things I believe, and I would assent to many more of them as soon as they were put to me, there obviously is no hope of assessing everything I believe in this piecemeal way. For one thing, it probably makes no sense, strictly speaking, to talk of the number of things one believes. If I am asked whether it is one of my beliefs that I went to see a film last night I can truly answer 'Yes'. If I were asked whether it is one of my beliefs that I went to the movies last night I would give the same answer. Have I thereby identified two, or only one, of my beliefs? How is that question ever to be settled? If we say that I identified only one of my beliefs, it would seem that I must also be said to hold the further belief that going to see a film and going to the movies are one and the same thing. So we would have more than one belief after all. The prospects of arriving even at a principle for counting beliefs, let alone at an actual number of them, seem dim.

Even if it did make sense to count the things we believe it is pretty clear that the number would be indefinitely large and so an assessment of our beliefs one by one could never be completed anyway. This is easily seen by considering only some of the simplest things one knows, for example in arithmetic. One thing I know is that one plus one equals two. Another thing I know is that one plus two is three, and another, that one plus three is four. Obviously there could be no end to the task of assessing my knowledge if I had to investigate separately the source of each one of my beliefs in that series. And even if I succeeded I would only have assessed the things I know about the addition of the number one to a given number; I would still have to do the same for the addition of two, and then the addition of three, and so on. And even that would exhaust only my beliefs about addition; all my other mathematical beliefs, not to mention all the rest of my knowledge, would remain so far unexamined. Obviously the job cannot be done piecemeal, one by one. Some method must be found for assessing large classes of beliefs all at once.

One way to do this would be to look for common sources or channels or bases of our beliefs, and then to examine the reliability of those sources or bases, just as I examined the source or basis of my belief that the suspect was in Cleveland. Descartes describes such a search as a search for 'principles' of human knowledge, 'principles' whose general credentials he can then investigate (HR, 145). If some 'principles' are found to be involved in all or even most of our knowledge, an assessment of the reliability of those 'principles' could be an assessment of all or most of our knowledge. If I found good reason to doubt the reliability of the suspect's alibi, for example, and that was all I had to go on in my belief that he was in Cleveland, then what I earlier took to be my knowledge that he was in Cleveland would have been found wanting or called into question. Its source or basis would have been undermined. Similarly, if one of the 'principles' or bases on which all my knowledge of the world depends were found to be unreliable, my knowledge of the world would to that extent have been found wanting or called into question as well.

Are there any important 'principles' of human knowledge in Descartes's sense? It takes very little reflection on the human organism to convince us of the importance of the senses—sight, hearing, touch, taste, and smell. Descartes puts the point most strongly when he says that 'all that up to the present time I have accepted as most true and certain I have learned either from the senses or through the senses' (HR, 145). Exactly what he would include under 'the senses' here is perhaps somewhat indeterminate, but even if it is left vague many philosophers would deny what Descartes appears to be saying. They would hold that, for example, the mathematical knowledge I mentioned earlier is not and could not be acquired from the senses or through the senses, so not *everything* I know is known in that way. Whether Descartes is really denying the views of those who believe in the non-sensory character of mathematical knowledge, and whether, if he were, he would be right, are issues we can set aside for the moment. It is clear that the senses are at least very important for human knowledge. Even restricting ourselves to the traditional five senses we can begin to appreciate their importance by reflecting on how little someone would ever come to know without them. A person blind and deaf from birth who also lacked taste buds and a sense of smell would know very little about anything, no matter how long he lived. To imagine him also anaesthetized or without a sense of touch is perhaps to stretch altogether too far one's conception of a human organism, or at least a human organism from whom we can hope to learn something about human knowledge. The importance of the senses as a source or channel of knowledge seems undeniable. It seems possible, then, to acknowledge their importance and to assess the reliability of that source, quite independently of the difficult question of whether *all* our knowledge comes to us in that way. We would then be assessing the credentials of what is often called our 'sensory' or 'experiential' or 'empirical' knowledge, and that, as we shall see, is quite enough to be going on with.

Having found an extremely important 'principle' or source of our knowledge, how can we investigate or assess *all* the knowledge we get from that source? As before, we are faced with the problem of the inexhaustibility of the things we believe on that basis, so no piecemeal, one-by-one procedure will do. But perhaps we can make a sweeping negative assessment. It might seem that as soon as we have found that the senses are one of the sources of our beliefs we are immediately in a position to condemn all putative knowledge derived from them. Some philosophers appear to have reasoned in this way, and many have even supposed that Descartes is among them. The idea is that if I am assessing the reliability of my beliefs and asking whether I really know what I take myself to know, and I come across a large class of beliefs which have come to me through the senses, I can immediately dismiss all those beliefs as unreliable or as not amounting to knowledge because of the obvious fact that I can sometimes be wrong in my beliefs based on the senses. Things are not always as they appear, so if on the basis of the way they appear to me I believe that they really are a certain way, I might still be wrong. We have all found at one time or another that we have been misled by appearances; we know that the senses are not always reliable. Should we not conclude, then, that as a general source of knowledge the senses are not to be trusted? As Descartes puts it, is it not wiser never 'to trust entirely to any thing by which we have once been deceived' (HR, 145)? Don't we have here a quite general way of condemning as not fully reliable *all* of our beliefs acquired by means of the senses?

I think the answer to that question is 'No, we do not', and I think Descartes would agree with that answer. It is true that he does talk of the senses 'deceiving' us on particular occasions, and he does ask whether that is not enough to condemn the senses in general as a source of knowledge, but he immediately reminds us of the obvious fact that the circumstances in which the senses 'deceive' us might be special in certain ascertainable ways, and so their occasional failures would not support a blanket condemnation of their reliability.

Sometimes, to give an ancient example, a tower looks round from a distance when it is actually square. If we relied only on the appearances of the moment we might say that the distant tower is round, and we would be wrong. We also know that there are many small organisms invisible to the naked eye. If the table before me is covered with such organisms at the moment but I look at it and say there is nothing on the table at all, once again I will be wrong. But all that follows from these familiar facts, as Descartes points out, is that there are things about which we can be wrong, or there are situations in which we can get false beliefs, if we rely entirely on our senses at that moment. So sometimes we should be careful about what we believe on the basis of the senses, or sometimes perhaps we should withhold our assent from any statement about how things are—when things are too far away to be seen properly, for example, or too small to be seen at all. But that obviously is not enough to support the policy of never trusting one's senses, or never believing anything based on them. Nor does it show that I can never know anything by means of the senses. If my car starts promptly every morning for two years in temperate weather at sea level but then fails to start one morning in freezing weather at the top of a high mountain, that does not support the policy of never trusting my car to start again once I return to the temperate lower altitude from which I so foolishly took it. Nor does it show that I can never know whether my car will ever start again. It shows only that there are certain circumstances in which my otherwise fully reliable car might not start. So the fact that we are sometimes wrong or 'deceived' in our judgements based on the senses is not enough in itself to show that the senses are never to be trusted and are therefore never reliable as a source of knowledge.

Descartes's negative assessment of all of his sensory knowledge does not depend on any such reasoning. He starts his investigation, rather, in what would seem to be the most favourable conditions for the reliable operation of the senses as a source of knowledge. While engaging in the very philosophical reflections he is writing about in his *First Meditation* Descartes is sitting in a warm room, by the fire, in a dressing gown, with a piece of paper in his hand. He finds that although he might be able to doubt that a distant tower that looks round really is round, it seems impossible to doubt that he really is sitting there by the fire in his dressing gown with a piece of paper in his hand. The fire and the piece of paper are not too small or too far away to be seen properly, they are right there before his eyes; it seems to be the best kind of position someone could be in for getting reliable beliefs or knowledge by means of the senses about what is going on around him. That is just how Descartes regards it. Its being a best-possible case of that kind is precisely what he thinks enables him to investigate or assess at one fell swoop all our sensory knowledge of the world around us. The verdict he arrives at about his putative knowledge that he is sitting by the fire with a piece of paper in his hand in that particular situation serves as the basis for a completely general assessment of the senses as a source of knowledge about the world around us.

How can that be so? How can he so easily reach a general verdict about all his sensory knowledge on the basis of a single example? Obviously not simply by generalizing from one particular example to all cases of sensory knowledge, as one might wildly leap to a conclusion about all red-haired men on the basis of one or two individuals. Rather, he takes the particular example of his conviction that he is sitting by the fire with a piece of paper in his hand as representative of the best position any of us can ever be in for knowing things about the world around us on the basis of the senses. What is true of a representative case, if it is truly representative and does not depend on special peculiarities of its own, can legitimately support a general conclusion. A demonstration that a particular isosceles triangle has a certain property, for example, can be taken as a demonstration that all isosceles triangles have that property, as long as the original instance was typical or representative of the whole class. Whether Descartes's investigation of the general reliability of the senses really does follow that familiar pattern is a difficult question. Whether, or in precisely what sense, the example he considers can be treated as representative of our relation to the world around us is, I believe, the key to understanding the problem of our knowledge of the external world. But if it turns out that there is nothing illegitimate about the way his negative conclusion is reached, the problem will be properly posed.

For the moment I think at least this much can be said about Descartes's reasoning. He chooses the situation in which he finds himself as representative of the best position we can be in for knowing things about the world in the sense that, if it is impossible for him in that position to know that he is sitting by the fire with a piece of paper in his hand then it is also impossible for him in other situations to know anything about the world around him on the basis of his senses. A negative verdict in the chosen case would support a negative verdict everywhere else. The example Descartes considers is in that sense meant to be the *best* kind of case there could be of sensory knowledge about the world around us. I think we must admit that it is very difficult to see how Descartes or anyone else could be any better off with respect to knowing something about the world around him on the basis of the senses than he is in the case he considers. But if no one could be in any better position for knowing, it seems natural to conclude that any negative verdict arrived at about this example, any discovery that Descartes's beliefs in this case are not reliable or do not amount to knowledge, could safely be generalized into a negative conclusion about all of our sensory 'knowledge' of the world. If candidates with the best possible credentials are found wanting, all those with less impressive credentials must fall short as well.

It will seem at first sight that in conceding that the whole question turns on whether Descartes knows in this particular case we are conceding very little; it seems obvious that Descartes on that occasion does know what he thinks he knows about the world around him. But in fact Descartes finds that he cannot know in this case that he is sitting by the fire with a piece of paper in his hand. If the case is truly representative of our sensory knowledge in general, that will show that no one can know anything about the world around us. But how could he ever arrive at that negative verdict in the particular case he considers? How could anyone possibly doubt in such a case that the fire and the piece of paper are there? The paper is in Descartes's hand, the fire is right there before his open eyes, and he feels its warmth. Wouldn't anyone have to be mad to deny that he can know something about what is going on around him in those circumstances? Descartes first answers 'Yes'. He says that if he were to doubt or deny on that occasion that he is sitting by the fire with a piece of paper in his hand he would be no less mad than those paupers who say they are kings or those madmen who think they are pumpkins or are made of glass. But his reflections continue:

> At the same time I must remember that I am a man, and that consequently I am in the habit of sleeping, and in my dreams representing to myself the same things or sometimes even less probable things, than do those who are insane in their waking moments. How often has it happened to me that in the night I dreamt that I found myself in this particular place, that I was dressed and seated near the fire, whilst in reality I was lying undressed in bed! At this moment it does indeed seem to me that it is with eyes awake that I am looking at this paper; that this head which I move is not asleep, that it is deliberately and of set purpose that I extend my hand and perceive it; what happens in sleep does not appear so clear nor so distinct as does all this. But in thinking over this I remind myself that on many occasions I have in sleep been deceived by similar illusions, and in dwelling carefully on this reflection I see so manifestly that there are no certain indications by which we may clearly distinguish wakefulness from sleep that I am lost in astonishment. And my astonishment is such that it is almost capable of persuading me that I now dream. (HR, 145–6.)

With this thought, if he is right, Descartes has lost the whole world. He knows what he is experiencing, he knows how things appear to him, but he does not know whether he is in fact sitting by the fire with a piece of paper in his hand. It is, for him, exactly as if he were sitting by the fire with a piece of paper in his hand, but he does not know whether there really is a fire or a piece of paper there or not; he does not know what is really happening in the world around him. He realizes that if everything he can ever learn about what is happening in the world around him comes to him through the senses, but he cannot tell by means of the senses whether or not he is dreaming, then all the sensory experiences he is having are compatible with his merely dreaming of a world around him while in fact that world is very different from the way he takes it to be. That is why he thinks he must find some way to tell that he is not dreaming. Far from its being mad to deny that he knows in this case, he thinks his recognition of the possibility that he might be dreaming gives him 'very powerful and maturely considered' (HR, 148) reasons for withholding his judgement about how things are in the world around him. He thinks it is eminently reasonable to insist that if he is to know that he is sitting by the fire he must know that he is not dreaming that he is sitting by the fire. That is seen as a necessary condition of knowing something about the world around him. And he finds that that condition cannot be fulfilled. On careful reflection he discovers that 'there are no certain indications by which we may clearly distinguish wakefulness from sleep'. He concludes that he knows nothing about the world around him because he cannot tell that he is not dreaming; he cannot fulfil one of the conditions necessary for knowing something about the world.

The Cartesian problem of our knowledge of the external world therefore becomes: how can we know anything about the world around us on the basis of the senses if the senses give us only what Descartes says they give us? What we gain through the senses is on Descartes's view only information that is compatible with our dreaming things about the world around us and not knowing anything about that world. How then can we know anything about the world by means of the senses? The Cartesian argument presents a challenge to our knowledge, and the problem of our knowledge of the external world is to show how that challenge can be met.

When I speak here of the Cartesian argument or of Descartes's sceptical conclusion or of his negative verdict about his knowledge I refer of course only to the position he finds himself in by the end of his *First Meditation*. Having at that point discovered and stated the problem of the external world, Descartes goes on in the rest of his *Meditations* to try to solve it, and by the end of the *Sixth Meditation* he thinks he has explained how he knows almost all those familiar things he began by putting in question. So when I ascribe to Descartes the view that we can know nothing about the world around us I do not mean to suggest that that is his final and considered view; it is nothing more than a conclusion he feels almost inevitably driven to at the early stages of his reflections. But those are the only stages of his thinking I am interested in here. That is where the philosophical problem of our knowledge of the external world gets posed, and before we can consider possible solutions we must be sure we understand exactly what the problem is.

I have described it as that of showing or explaining how knowledge of the world around us is possible by means of the senses. It is important to keep in mind that that demand for an explanation arises in the face of a challenge or apparent obstacle to our knowledge of the world. The possibility that he is dreaming is seen as an obstacle to Descartes's knowing that he is sitting by the fire, and it must be explained how that obstacle can either be avoided or overcome. It must be shown or explained *how* it is possible for us to know things about the world, given that the sense-experiences we get are compatible with our merely dreaming. Explaining how something is nevertheless possible, despite what looks like an obstacle to it, requires more than showing merely that there is no impossibility involved in the thing—that it is consistent with the principles of logic and the laws of nature and so in that sense *could* exist. The mere possibility of the state of affairs is not enough to settle the question of how our knowledge of the world is possible; we must understand how the apparent obstacle is to be got round.

Descartes's reasoning can be examined and criticized at many different points, and has been closely scrutinized by many philosophers for centuries. It has also been accepted by many, perhaps by more than would admit or even realize that they accept it. There seems to me no doubt about the force and the fascination—I would say the almost overwhelming persuasiveness—of his reflections. That alone is something that needs accounting for. I cannot possibly do justice to all reasonable reactions to them here. In the rest of this first chapter I want to concentrate on deepening and strengthening the problem and trying to locate more precisely the source of its power.

There are at least three distinct questions that could be pressed. Is the possibility that Descartes might be dreaming really a threat to his knowledge of the world around him? Is he right in thinking that he must know that he is not dreaming if he is to know something about the world around him? And is he right in his 'discovery' that he can never know that he is not dreaming? If Descartes were wrong on any of these points it might be possible to avoid the problem and perhaps even to explain without difficulty how we know things about the world around us.

On the first question, it certainly seems right to say that if Descartes were dreaming that he is sitting by the fire with a piece of paper in his hand he would not then know that he is sitting by the fire with a piece of paper in his hand. When you dream that something is going on in the world around you, you do not thereby know that it is. Most often, of course, what we dream is not even true; no one is actually chasing us when we are lying asleep in bed dreaming, nor are we actually climbing stairs. But although usually what we dream is not really so, that is not the real reason for our lack of knowledge. Even if Descartes were in fact sitting by the fire and actually had a piece of paper in his hand at the very time he was dreaming that he is sitting by the fire with a piece of paper in his hand, he would not thereby know he was sitting there with that paper. He would be like a certain Duke of Devonshire who, according to G. E. Moore, once dreamt he was speaking in the House of Lords and woke up to find that he *was* speaking in the House of Lords.[4] What he was dreaming was in fact so. But even if what you are dreaming is in fact so you do not thereby know that it is. Even if we allow that when you are dreaming that something is so you can be said, at least for the time being, to think or to believe that it is so, there is still no real connection between your thinking or believing what you do and its being so. At best you have a thought or a belief which just happens to be true, but that is no more than coincidence and not knowledge. So Descartes's first step relies on what seems to be an undeniable fact about dreams: if you are dreaming that something is so you do not thereby know that it is so.

This bald claim needs to be qualified and more carefully explained, but I do not think that will diminish the force of the point for Descartes's purposes. Sometimes what is going on in the world around us has an effect on what we dream; for example, a banging shutter might actually cause me to dream, among other things, that a shutter is banging. If my environment affects me in that way, and if in dreams I can be said to think or believe that something is so, would I not in that case know that a shutter is banging?

It seems to me that I would not, but I confess it is difficult to say exactly why I think so. That is probably because it is difficult to say exactly what is required for knowledge. We use the term 'know' confidently, we quite easily distinguish cases of knowledge from cases of its absence, but we are not always in a position to state what we are going on in applying or withholding the term in the ways we do. I think that in the case of the banging shutter it would not be knowledge because I would be *dreaming*, I would not even be awake. At least it can be said, I think, that even if Descartes's sitting by the fire with a piece of paper in his hand (like the banging shutter) is what in fact causes him to dream that he is sitting by the fire with a piece of paper in his hand, that is still no help to him in coming to know what is going on in the world around him. He realizes that he could be dreaming that he is sitting by the fire even if he is in fact sitting there, and that is the possibility he finds he has to rule out.

I have said that if you are dreaming that something is so you do not thereby know that it is so, and it might seem as if that is not always true. Suppose a man and a child are both sleeping. I say of the child that it is so young it does not know what seven times nine is, whereas the grown man does know that. If the man happens at that very moment to be dreaming that seven times nine is sixty-three (perhaps he is dreaming that he is computing his income tax), then he is a man who is dreaming that something is so and also knows that it is so. The same kind of thing is possible for knowledge about the world around him. He might be a physicist who knows a great deal about the way things are which the child does not know. If the man also dreams that things are that way he can once again be said to be dreaming that something is so and also to know that it is so. There is therefore no incompatibility between dreaming and knowing. That is true, but I do not think it affects Descartes's argument. He is led to consider how he knows he is not dreaming at the moment by reflecting on how he knows at that moment that he is sitting by the fire with a piece of paper in his hand. If he knows that at all, he thinks, he knows it on the basis of the senses. But he realizes that his having the sensory experiences he is now having is compatible with his merely dreaming that he is sitting by the fire with a piece of paper in his hand. So he does not know on the basis of the sensory experiences he is having at the moment that he is sitting by the fire. Nor, of course, did the man in my examples know the things he was said to know on the basis of the sensory experiences he was having at that moment. He knew certain things to be so, and he was dreaming those things to be so, but in dreaming them he did not *thereby* know them to be so.

But as long as we allow that the sleeping man does know certain things about the world around him, even if he does not know them on the basis of the very dreams he is having at the moment, isn't that enough to show that Descartes must nevertheless be wrong in his conclusion that no one can know any-thing about the world around him? No. It shows at most that we were hasty or were ignoring Descartes's conclusion in conceding that someone could know something about the world around him. If Descartes's reasoning is correct the dreaming physicist, even when he is awake, does not really know any of the things we were uncritically crediting him with knowing about the way things are—or at least he does not know them on the basis of the senses. In order to know them on the basis of the senses there would have to have been at least some time at which he knew something about what was going on around him at that time. But if Descartes is right he could not have known any such thing unless he had established that he was not dreaming at that time; and according to Descartes he could never establish that. So the fact about dreams that Descartes relies on—that one who dreams that something is so does not thereby know that it is so—is enough to yield his conclusion if the other steps of his reasoning are correct.

When he first introduces the possibility that he might be dreaming Descartes seems to be relying on some knowledge about how things are or were in the world around him. He says 'I remind myself that on many occasions I have in sleep been deceived by similar illusions', so he seems to be relying on some knowledge to the effect that he has actually dreamt in the past and that he remembers having been 'deceived' by those dreams. That is more than he actually needs for his reflections about knowledge to have the force he thinks they have. He does not need to support his judgement that he has actually dreamt in the past. The only thought he needs is that it is now *possible* for him to be dreaming that he is sitting by the fire, and that if that possibility were realized he would not know that he is sitting by the fire. Of course it was no doubt true that Descartes had dreamt in the past and that his knowledge that he had done so was partly what he was going on in acknowledging the possibility of his dreaming on this particular occasion. But neither the fact of past dreams nor knowledge of their actual occurrence would seem to be strictly required in order to grant what Descartes relies on—the possibility of dreaming, and the absence of knowledge if that possibility were realized. The thought that he *might* be dreaming that he is sitting by the fire with a piece of paper in his hand, and the fact that if he were he wouldn't know he was sitting there, is what gives Descartes pause. That would worry him in the way it does even if he had never actually had any dreams exactly like it in the past—if he had never dreamt about fires and pieces of paper at all. In fact, I think he need never have actually dreamt of anything before, and certainly needn't know that he ever has, in order to be worried in the way he is by the thought that he might be dreaming now.

The fact that the possibility of dreaming is all Descartes needs to appeal to brings out another truth about dreams that his argument depends on—that anything that can be going on or that one can experience in one's waking life can also be dreamt about. This again is only a statement of possibility—no sensible person would suggest that we *do* at some time dream of everything that actually happens to us, or that everything we dream about does in fact happen sometime. But it is very plausible to say that there is nothing we *could* not dream about, nothing that could be the case that we *could* not dream to be the case. I say it is very plausible; of course I cannot prove it to be true. But even if it is not true with complete generality, we must surely grant that it is possible to dream that one is sitting by a fire with a piece of paper in one's hand, and possible to dream of countless other equally obvious and equally mundane states of affairs as well, and those possibilities are what Descartes sees as threatening to his knowledge of the world around him.

There seems little hope, then, of objecting that it is simply not possible for Descartes to dream that he is sitting by the fire with a piece of paper in his hand.

NOTES

1. It has been argued that the problem in the completely general form in which I discuss it here is new in Descartes, and that nothing exactly similar appears in philosophy before that time. See M. F. Burnyeat, 'Idealism and Greek Philosophy: What Descartes Saw and Berkeley Missed', *The Philosophical Review,* 1982.

2. See the beginning of the first of his *Meditations on First Philosophy* in *The Philosophical Works of Descartes,* edited and translated by E. S. Haldane and G. R. T. Ross (2 vols., New York, 1955), vol. I, p. 145. (Hereafter cited as HR.)

3. See his *Discourse on the Method of Rightly Conducting Reason and Seeking Truth in the Sciences* in HR. pp. 81 ff.

4. G. E. Moore, *Philosophical Papers* (London, 1959), p. 245.

PART V

The Mind-Body Problem

SECOND MEDITATION

By René Descartes

Of the Nature of the Human Mind; and that it is more easily known than the Body.

The Meditation of yesterday filled my mind with so many doubts that it is no longer in my power to forget them. And yet I do not see in what manner I can resolve them; and, just as if I had all of a sudden fallen into very deep water, I am so disconcerted that I can neither make certain of setting my feet on the bottom, nor can I swim and so support myself on the surface. I shall nevertheless make an effort and follow anew the same path as that on which I yesterday entered, i.e. I shall proceed by setting aside all that in which the least doubt could be supposed to exist, just as if I had discovered that it was absolutely false; and I shall ever follow in this road until I have met with something which is certain, or at least, if I can do nothing else, until I have learned for certain that there is nothing in the world that is certain. Archimedes, in order that he might draw the terrestrial globe out of its place, and transport it elsewhere, demanded only that one point should be fixed and immovable; in the same way I shall have the right to conceive high hopes if I am happy enough to discover one thing only which is certain and indubitable.

I suppose, then, that all the things that I see are false; I persuade myself that nothing has ever existed of all that my fallacious memory represents to me. I consider that I possess no senses; I imagine that body, figure, extension, movement and place are but the fictions of my mind. What, then, can be esteemed as true? Perhaps nothing at all, unless that there is nothing in the world that is certain.

But how can I know there is not something different from those things that I have just considered, of which one cannot have the slightest doubt? Is there not some God, or some other being by whatever name we call it, who puts these reflections into my mind? That is not necessary, for is it not possible that I am capable of producing them myself? I myself, am I not at least something? But I have already denied that I had senses and body. Yet I hesitate, for what follows from that? Am I so dependent on body and senses that I cannot exist without these? But I was persuaded that there was nothing in all the world, that there was no heaven, no earth, that there were no minds, nor any bodies: was I not then likewise persuaded that I did not exist? Not at all; of a surety I myself did exist since I persuaded myself of something [or merely because I thought of something]. But there is some deceiver or other, very powerful and very cunning, who ever employs his ingenuity in deceiving me. Then without doubt I exist also if he deceives me, and let him deceive me as much as he will, he can never cause me to be nothing so long as I think that I am something. So that after having reflected well and carefully examined all things, we must come to the definite conclusion that this proposition: I am, I exist, is necessarily true each time that I pronounce it, or that I mentally conceive it.

But I do not yet know clearly enough what I am, I who am certain that I am; and hence I must be careful to see that I do not imprudently take some other object in place of myself, and thus that I do not go astray in respect of this knowledge that I hold to be the most certain and most evident of all that I have formerly learned. That is why I shall now consider anew what I believed myself to be before I embarked upon these last reflections; and of my former opinions I shall withdraw all that might even in a small degree be invalidated by the reasons which I have just brought forward, in order that there may be nothing at all left beyond what is absolutely certain and indubitable.

What then did I formerly believe myself to be? Undoubtedly I believed myself to be a man. But what is a man? Shall I say a reasonable animal? Certainly not; for then I should have to inquire what an animal is, and what is reasonable; and thus from a single question I should insensibly fall into an infinitude of others more difficult; and I should not wish to waste the little time and leisure remaining to me in trying to unravel subtleties like these. But I shall rather stop here to consider the thoughts which of themselves spring up in my mind, and which were not inspired by anything beyond my own nature alone when I applied myself to the consideration of my being. In the first place, the, I considered myself as having a face, hands, arms, and all that system of members composed on bones and flesh as seen in a corpse which I designated by the name of body. In addition to this I considered that I was nourished, that I walked, that I felt, and that I thought, and I referred all these actions to the soul: but I did not stop to consider what the soul was, or if I did stop, I imagined that it was something extremely rare and subtle like a wind, a flame, or an ether, which was spread throughout my grosser parts. As to body I had no manner of doubt about its nature, but thought I had a very clear knowledge of it; and if I had desired to explain it according to the notions that I had then formed of it, I should have described it thus: By the body I understand all that which can be defined by a certain figure: something which can be confined in a certain place, and which can fill a given space in such a way that every other body will be excluded from it; which can be perceived either by thought, or by sight, or by hearing, or by taste, or by smell: which can be moved in many ways not, in truth, by itself, but by something which is foreign to it, by which it is touched [and from which it receives impressions]: for to have the power of self-movement, as also of feeling or of thinking, I did not consider to appertain to the nature of body: on the contrary, I was rather astonished to find that faculties similar to them existed in some bodies.

But what am I, now that I suppose that there is a certain genius which is extremely powerful, and, if I may say so, malicious, who employs all his powers in deceiving me? Can I affirm that I possess the least of all those things which I have just said pertain to the nature of body? I pause to consider, I revolve all these things in my mind, and I find none of which I can say that it pertains to me. It would be tedious to stop to enumerate them. Let us pass to the attributes of soul and see if there is any one which is in me? What of nutrition or walking [the first mentioned]? But if it is so that I have no body it is also true that I can neither walk nor take nourishment. Another attribute is sensation. But one cannot feel without body, and besides I have thought I perceived many things during sleep that I recognized in my waking moments as not having been experienced at all. What of thinking? I find here that thought is an attribute that belongs to me; it alone cannot be separated from me. I am, I exist, that is certain. But how often? Just when I think; for it might possibly be the case if I ceased entirely to think, that I should likewise cease altogether to exist. I do not now admit anything which is not necessarily true: to speak accurately I am not more than a thing which thinks, that is to say a mind or a soul, or an understanding, or a reason, which are terms whose significance was formerly unknown to me. I am, however, a real thing and really exist; but what thing? I have answered: a thing which thinks.

And what more? I shall exercise my imagination [in order to see if I am not something more]. I am not a collection of members which we call the human body: I am not a subtle air distributed through these members, I am not a wind, a fire, a vapour, a breath, nor anything at all which I can imagine or conceive; because I have assumed that all these were nothing. Without changing that supposition I find that I only leave myself certain of the fact that I am somewhat. But perhaps it is true that these same things which I supposed were non-existent because they are unknown to me, are really not different from the self which I know. I am not sure about this, I shall not dispute about it now; I can only give judgment on things that are known to me. I know that I exist, and I inquire what I am, I whom I know to exist. But it is very certain that the knowledge of my existence taken in its precise significance does not depend on things whose existence is not yet known to me; consequently it does not depend on those which I can feign in imagination. And indeed the very term feign in imagination proves to me my error, for I really do this if

I imagine myself as something, since to imagine is nothing else than to contemplate the figure or image of a corporeal thing. But I already know for certain that I am, and that it may be that all these images, and, speaking generally, all things that relate to the nature of body are nothing but dreams [and chimeras]. For this reason I see clearly that I have as little reason to say, "I shall stimulate my imagination in order to know more distinctly what I am," than if I were to say, "I am now awake, and I perceive somewhat that is real and true: but because I do not yet perceive it distinctly enough, I shall go to sleep of express purpose, so that my dreams may represent the perception with greatest truth and evidence." And, thus, I know for certain that nothing of all that I can understand by means of my imagination belongs to this knowledge which I have of myself, and that it is necessary to recall the mind from this mode of thought with the utmost diligence in order that it may be able to know its own nature with perfect distinctness.

But what then am I? A thing which thinks. What is a thing which thinks? It is a thing which doubts, understands, [conceives], affirms, denies, wills, refuses, which also imagines and feels.

Certainly it is no small matter if all these things pertain to my nature. But why should they not so pertain? Am I not that being who now doubts nearly everything, who nevertheless understands certain things, who affirms that one only is true, who denies all the others, who desires to know more, is averse from being deceived, who imagines many things, sometimes indeed despite his will, and who perceives many likewise, as by the intervention of the bodily organs? Is there nothing in all this which is as true as it is certain that I exist, even though I should always sleep and though he who has given me being employed all his ingenuity in deceiving me? Is there likewise any one of these attributes which can be distinguished from my thought, or which might be said to be separated from myself? For it is so evident of itself that it is I who doubts, who understands, and who desires, that there is no reason here to add anything to explain it. And I have certainly the power of imagining likewise; for although it may happen (as I formerly supposed) that none of the things which I imagine are true, nevertheless this power of imagining does not cease to be really in use, and it forms part of my thought. Finally, I am the same who feels, that is to say, who perceives certain things, as by the organs of sense, since it truth I see light, I hear noise, I feel heat. But it will be said that these phenomena are false and that I am dreaming. Let it be so; still it is at least quite certain that it seems to me that I see light, that I hear noise and that I feel heat. That cannot be false; properly speaking it is what is in me called feeling; and used in this precise sense that is no other thing than thinking.

From this time I begin to know what I am with a little more clearness and distinction than before; but nevertheless it still seems to me, and I cannot prevent myself from thinking, that corporeal things, whose images are framed by thought, which are tested by the senses, are much more distinctly known than that obscure part of me which does not come under the imagination. Although really it is very strange to say that I know and understand more distinctly these things whose existence seems to me dubious, which are unknown to me, and which do not belong to me, than others of the truth of which I am convinced, which are known to me and which pertain to my real nature, in a word, than myself. But I see clearly how the case stands: my mind loves to wander, and cannot yet suffer itself to be retained within the just limits of truth. Very good, let us once more give it the freest rein, so that, when afterwards we seize the proper occasion for pulling up, it may the more easily be regulated and controlled.

Let us begin by considering the commonest matters, those which we believe to be the most distinctly comprehended, to wit, the bodies which we touch and see; not indeed bodies in general, for these general ideas are usually a little more confused, but let us consider one body in particular. Let us take, for example, this piece of wax: it has been taken quite freshly from the hive, and it has not yet lost the sweetness of the honey which it contains; it still retains somewhat of the odour of the flowers from which it has been culled; its colour, its figure, its size are apparent; it is hard, cold, easily handled, and if you strike it with the finger, it will emit a sound. Finally all the things which are requisite to cause us distinctly to recognise a body, are met with in it. But notice that while I speak and approach the fire what remained of the taste is exhaled, the smell evaporates, the colour alters, the figure is destroyed, the size increases, it becomes liquid, it heats, scarcely can one handle it, and when one strikes it, no sound is emitted. Does the same wax remain after this change? We must confess that it remains; none would judge otherwise. What then did I know so distinctly in this piece of wax? It could certainly be nothing of all that the senses brought to my notice, since all these things which fall under taste, smell, sight, touch, and hearing, are found to be changed, and yet the same wax remains.

Perhaps it was what I now think, viz. that this wax was not that sweetness of honey, nor that agreeable scent of flowers, nor that particular whiteness, nor that figure, nor that sound, but simply a body which a little while before appeared to me as perceptible under these forms, and which is now perceptible under others. But what, precisely, is it that I imagine when I form such conceptions? Let us attentively consider this, and, abstracting from all that does not belong to the wax, let us see what remains. Certainly nothing remains excepting a certain extended thing which is flexible and movable. But what is the meaning of flexible and movable? Is it not that I imagine that this piece of wax being round is capable of becoming square and of passing from a square to a triangular figure? No, certainly it is not that, since I imagine it admits of an infinitude of similar changes, and I nevertheless do not know how to compass the infinitude by my imagination, and consequently this conception which I have of the wax is not brought about by the faculty of imagination. What now is this extension? Is it not also unknown? For it becomes greater when the wax is melted, greater when it is boiled, and greater still when the heat increases; and I should not conceive [clearly] according to truth what wax is, if I did not think that even this piece that we are considering is capable of receiving more variations in extension than I have ever imagined. We must then grant that I could not even understand through the imagination what this piece of wax is, and that it is my mind alone which perceives it. I say this piece of wax in particular, for as to wax in general it is yet clearer. But what is this piece of wax which cannot be understood excepting by the [understanding or] mind? It is certainly the same that I see, touch, imagine, and finally it is the same which I have always believed it to be from the beginning. But what must particularly be observed is that its perception is neither an act of vision, nor of touch, nor of imagination, and has never been such although it may have appeared formerly to be so, but only an intuition of the mind, which may be imperfect and confused as it was formerly, or clear and distinct as it is at present, according as my attention is more or less directed to the elements which are found in it, and of which it is composed.

Yet in the meantime I am greatly astonished when I consider [the great feebleness of mind] and its proneness to fall [insensibly] into error; for although without giving expression to my thought I consider all this in my own mind, words often impede me and I am almost deceived by the terms of ordinary language. For we say that we see the same wax, if it is present, and not that we simply judge that it is the same from its having the same colour and figure. From this I should conclude that I knew the wax by means of vision and not simply by the intuition of the mind; unless by chance I remember that, when looking from a window and saying I see men who pass in the street, I really do not see them, but infer that what I see is men, just as I say that I see wax. And yet what do I see from the window but hats and coats which may cover automatic machines? Yet I judge these to be men. And similarly solely by the faculty of judgment which rests in my mind, I comprehend that which I believed I saw with my eyes.

A man who makes it his aim to raise his knowledge above the common should be ashamed to derive the occasion for doubting from the forms of speech invented by the vulgar; I prefer to pass on and consider whether I had a more evident and perfect conception of what the wax was when I first perceived it, and when I believed I knew it by means of the external senses or at least by the common sense as it is called, that is to say by the imaginative faculty, or whether my present conception is clearer now that I have most carefully examined what it is, and in what way it can be known. It would certainly be absurd to doubt as to this. For what was there in this first perception which was distinct? What was there which might not as well have been perceived by any of the animals? But when I distinguish the wax from its external forms, and when, just as if I had taken from it its vestments, I consider it quite naked, it is certain that although some error may still be found in my judgment, I can nevertheless not perceive it thus without a human mind.

But finally what shall I say of this mind, that is, of myself, for up to this point I do not admit in myself anything but mind? What then, I who seem to perceive this piece of wax so distinctly, do I not know myself, not only with much more truth and certainty, but also with much more distinctness and clearness? For if I judge that the wax is or exists from the fact that I see it, it certainly follows much more clearly that I am or that I exist myself from the fact that I see it. For it may be that what I see is not really wax, it may also be that I do not possess eyes with which to see anything; but it cannot be that when I see, or (for I no longer take account of the distinction) when I think I see, that I myself who think am nought. So if I judge that the wax exists from the fact that I touch it, the same thing will follow, to wit, that I am; and if

I judge that my imagination, or some other cause, whatever it is, persuades me that the wax exists, I shall still conclude the same. And what I have here remarked of wax may be applied to all other things which are external to me [and which are met with outside of me]. And further, if the [notion or] perception of wax has seemed to me clearer and more distinct, not only after the sight or the touch, but also after many other causes have rendered it quite manifest to me, with how much more [evidence] and distinctness must it be said that I now know myself, since all the reasons which contribute to the knowledge of wax, or any other body whatever, are yet better proofs of the nature of my mind! And there are so many other things in the mind itself which may contribute to the elucidation of its nature, that those which depend on body such as these just mentioned, hardly merit being taken into account.

But finally here I am, having insensibly reverted to the point I desired, for, since it is now manifest to me that even bodies are not, properly speaking, known" by the senses or by the faculty of imagination, but by the understanding only, and since they are not known from the fact that they are seen or touched, but only because they are understood, I see clearly that there is nothing which is easier for me to know than my mind. But because it is difficult to rid oneself so promptly of an opinion to which one was accustomed for so long, it will be well that I should halt a little at this point, so that by the length of my meditation I may more deeply imprint on my memory this new knowledge.

THIRD MEDITATION

By René Descartes

Of God: that He exists

I shall now close my eyes, I shall stop my ears, I shall call away all my senses, I shall efface even from my thoughts all the images of corporeal things, or at least (for that is hardly possible) I shall esteem them as vain and false; and thus holding converse only with myself and considering my own nature, I shall try little by little to reach a better knowledge of and a more familiar acquaintanceship with myself. I am a thing that thinks, that is to say, that doubts, affirms, denies, that knows a few things, that is ignorant of many [that loves, that hates], that wills, that desires, that also imagines and perceives; for as I remarked before, although the things which I perceive and imagine are perhaps nothing at all apart from me and in themselves, I am nevertheless assured that these modes of thought that I call perceptions and imaginations, inasmuch only as they are modes of thought, certainly reside [and are met with] in me.

And in the little that I have just said, I think I have summed up all that I really know, or at least all that hitherto I was aware that I knew. In order to try to extend my knowledge further, I shall now look around more carefully and see whether I cannot still discover in myself some other things which I have not hitherto perceived. I am certain that I am a thing which thinks; but do I not then likewise know what is requisite to render me certain of a truth? Certainly in this first knowledge there is nothing that assures me of its truth, excepting the clear and distinct perception of that which I state, which would not indeed suffice to assure me that what I say is true, if it could ever happen that a thing which I conceived so clearly and distinctly could be false; and accordingly it seems to me that already I can establish as a general rule that all things which I perceive very clearly and very distinctly are true.

At the same time I have before received and admitted many things to be very certain and manifest, which yet I afterwards recognized as being dubious. What then were these things? They were the earth, sky, stars and all other objects which I apprehended by means of the senses. But what did I clearly [and distinctly] perceive in them? Nothing more than that the ideas or thoughts of these things were presented to my mind. And not even now do I deny that these ideas are met within me. But there was yet another thing which I affirmed, and which, owing to the habit which I had formed of believing it, I thought I perceived very clearly, although in truth I did not perceive it at all, to wit, that there were objects outside of me from which these ideas proceeded, and to which they were entirely similar. And it was in this that I erred, or, if perchance my judgment was correct, this was not due to any knowledge arising from my perception.

But when I took anything very simple and easy in the sphere of arithmetic or geometry into consideration, e.g. that two and three together made five, and other things of the sort, were not these present to my mind so clearly as to enable me to affirm that they were true? Certainly if I judged that since such matters could be doubted, this would not have been so for any other reason than that it came into my mind that perhaps a God might have endowed me with such a nature that I may have been deceived even concerning things which seemed to me most manifest. But every time that this preconceived opinion of the sovereign power of a God presents itself to my thought, I am constrained to confess that it is easy to Him, if He wishes it, to cause me to err, even in matters in which I believe myself to have the best evidence. And, on the other hand, always when I direct my attention to things which I believe myself to perceive very clearly, I am so persuaded of their truth that I let myself break out into words such as these: Let who will deceive me, He can never cause me to be nothing while I think that I am, or some day cause it to be true to say that I have never been, it being true now to say that I am, or that two and three make more or less than five, or any such thing in which I see a manifest contradiction. And, certainly, since I have no reason to believe that there is a God who is a deceiver, and as I have not yet satisfied myself that there is a God at all, the reason for doubt which depends on this opinion alone is very slight, and so to speak metaphysical. But in order to be able altogether to remove it, I must inquire whether there is a God as soon as the occasion presents itself; and if I find that there is a God, I must also inquire whether He may be a deceiver; for without a knowledge of these two truths I do not see that I can ever be certain of anything.

And in order that I may have an opportunity of inquiring into this in an orderly way [without interrupting the order of meditation which I have proposed to myself, and which is little by little to pass from the notions which I find first of all in my mind to those which I shall later on discover in it]. It is requisite that I should here divide my thoughts into certain kinds, and that I should consider in which of these kinds there is, properly speaking, truth or error to be found. Of my thoughts some are, so to speak, images of the things, and to these alone is the title "idea" properly applied; examples are my thought of a man or of a chimera, of heaven, of an angel, or [even] of God. But other thoughts possess other forms as well. For example in willing, fearing, approving, denying, though I always perceive something as the subject of the action of my mind, yet by this action I always add something else to the idea which I have of that thing; and of the thoughts of this kind some are called volitions or affections, and others judgments.

Now as to what concerns ideas, if we consider them only in themselves and do not relate them to anything else beyond themselves, they cannot properly speaking be false; for whether I imagine a goat or a chimera, it is not less true that I imagine the one than the other. We must not fear likewise that falsity can enter into will and into affections, for although I may desire evil things, or even things that never existed, it is not the less true that I desire them. Thus there remains no more than the judgments which we make, in which I must take the greatest care not to deceive myself. But the principal error and the commonest which we may meet with in them, consists in my judging that the ideas which are in me are similar or conformable to the things which are outside me; for without doubt if I considered the ideas only as certain modes of my thoughts, without trying to relate them to anything beyond, they could scarcely give me material for error.

But among these ideas, some appear to me to be innate, some adventitious, and others to be formed [or invented] by myself; for, as I have the power of understanding what is called a thing, or a truth, or a thought, it appears to me that I hold this power from no other source than my own nature. But if I now hear some sound, if I see the sun, or feel heat, I have hitherto judged that these sensations proceeded from certain things that exist outside of me; and finally it appears to me that sirens, hippogryphs, and the like, are formed out of my own mind. But again I may possibly persuade myself that all these ideas are of the nature of those which I term adventitious, or else that they are all innate, or all fictitious: for I have not yet clearly discovered their true origin.

And my principal task in this place is to consider, in respect to those ideas which appear to me to proceed from certain objects that are outside me, what are the reasons which cause me to think them similar to these objects. It seems indeed in the first place that I am taught this lesson by nature; and, secondly, I experience in myself that these ideas do not depend on my will nor therefore on myself—for they often present themselves to my mind in spite of my will. Just now, for instance, whether I will or whether I do not will, I feel heat, and thus I persuade myself that this feeling, or at least this idea of heat, is produced in me by something which is different from me, i.e. by the heat of the fire near which I sit. And nothing seems to me more obvious than to judge that this object imprints its likeness rather than anything else upon me.

Now I must discover whether these proofs are sufficiently strong and convincing. When I say that I am so instructed by nature, I merely mean a certain spontaneous inclination which impels me to believe in this connection, and not a natural light which makes me recognise that it is true. But these two things are very different; for I cannot doubt that which the natural light causes me to believe to be true, as, for example, it has shown me that I am from the fact that I doubt, or other facts of the same kind. And I possess no other faculty whereby to distinguish truth from falsehood, which can teach me that what this light shows me to be true is not really true, and no other faculty that is equally trustworthy. But as far as [apparently] natural impulses are concerned, I have frequently remarked, when I had to make active choice between virtue and vice, that they often enough led me to the part that was worse; and this is why I do not see any reason for following them in what regards truth and error.

And as to the other reason, which is that these ideas must proceed from objects outside me, since they do not depend on my will, I do not find it any the more convincing. For just as these impulses of which I have spoken are found in me, notwithstanding that they do not always concur with my will, so perhaps there is in me some faculty fitted to produce these ideas without the assistance of any external things, even though it is not yet known by me; just as, apparently, they have hitherto always been found in me during sleep without the aid of any external objects.

And finally, though they did proceed from objects different from myself, it is not a necessary consequence that they should resemble these. On the contrary, I have noticed that in many cases there was a great difference between the object and its idea. I find, for example, two completely diverse ideas of the sun in my mind; the one derives its origin from the senses, and should be placed in the category of adventitious ideas; according to this idea the sun seems to be extremely small; but the other is derived from astronomical reasonings, i.e. is elicited from certain notions that are innate in me, or else it is formed by me in some other manner; in accordance with it the sun appears to be several times greater than the earth. These two ideas cannot, indeed, both resemble the same sun, and reason makes me believe that the one which seems to have originated directly from the sun itself, is the one which is most dissimilar to it.

All this causes me to believe that until the present time it has not been by a judgment that was certain [or premeditated], but only by a sort of blind impulse that I believed that things existed outside of, and different from me, which, by the organs of my senses, or by some other method whatever it might be, conveyed these ideas or images to me [and imprinted on me their similitudes].

But there is yet another method of inquiring whether any of the objects of which I have ideas within me exist outside of me. If ideas are only taken as certain modes of thought, I recognise amongst them no difference or inequality, and all appear to proceed from me in the same manner; but when we consider them as images, one representing one thing and the other another, it is clear that they are very different one from the other. There is no doubt that those which represent to me substances are something more, and contain so to speak more objective reality within them [that is to say, by representation participate in a higher degree of being or perfection] than those that simply represent modes or accidents; and that idea again by which I understand a supreme God, eternal, infinite, [immutable], omniscient, omnipotent, and

Creator of all things which are outside of Himself, has certainly more objective reality in itself than those ideas by which finite substances are represented.

Now it is manifest by the natural light that there must at least be as much reality in the efficient and total cause as in its effect. For, pray, whence can the effect derive its reality, if not from its cause? And in what way can this cause communicate this reality to it, unless it possessed it in itself? And from this it follows, not only that something cannot proceed from nothing, but likewise that what is more perfect—that is to say, which has more reality within itself—cannot proceed from the less perfect. And this is not only evidently true of those effects which possess actual or formal reality, but also of the ideas in which we consider merely what is termed objective reality. To take an example, the stone which has not yet existed not only cannot now commence to be unless it has been produced by something which possesses within itself, either formally or eminently, all that enters into the composition of the stone [i.e. it must possess the same things or other more excellent things than those which exist in the stone] and heat can only be produced in a subject in which it did not previously exist by a cause that is of an order [degree or kind] at least as perfect as heat, and so in all other cases. But further, the idea of heat, or of a stone, cannot exist in me unless it has been placed within me by some cause which possesses within it at least as much reality as that which I conceive to exist in the heat or the stone. For although this cause does not transmit anything of its actual or formal reality to my idea, we must not for that reason imagine that it is necessarily a less real cause; we must remember that [since every idea is a work of the mind] its nature is such that it demands of itself no other formal reality than that which it borrows from my thought, of which it is only a mode [i.e. a manner or way of thinking]. But in order that an idea should contain some one certain objective reality rather than another, it must without doubt derive it from some cause in which there is at least as much formal reality as this idea contains of objective reality. For if we imagine that something is found in an idea which is not found in the cause, it must then have been derived from nought; but however imperfect may be this mode of being by which a thing is objectively [or by representation] in the understanding by its idea, we cannot certainly say that this mode of being is nothing, nor consequently, that the idea derives its origin from nothing.

Nor must I imagine that, since the reality that I consider in these ideas is only objective, it is not essential that this reality should be formally in the causes of my ideas, but that it is sufficient that it should be found objectively. For just as this mode of objective existence pertains to ideas by their proper nature, so does the mode of formal existence pertain to the causes of those ideas (this is at least true of the first and principal) by the nature peculiar to them. And although it may be the case that one idea gives birth to another idea, that cannot continue to be so indefinitely; for in the end we must reach an idea whose cause shall be, so to speak, an archetype, in which the whole reality [or perfection] which is so to speak objectively [or by representation] in these ideas is contained formally [and really]. Thus the light of nature causes me to know clearly that the ideas in me are like [pictures or] images which can, in truth, easily fall short of the perfection of the objects from which they have been derived, but which can never contain anything greater or more perfect.

And the longer and the more carefully that I investigate these matters, the more clearly and distinctly do I recognise their truth. But what am I to conclude from it all in the end? It is this, that if the objective reality of any one of my ideas is of such a nature as clearly to make me recognise that it is not in me either formally or eminently, and that consequently I cannot myself be the cause of it. It follows of necessity that I am not alone in the world, but that there is another being which exists, or which is the cause of this idea. On the other hand, had no such an idea existed in me, I should have had no sufficient argument to convince me of the existence of any being beyond myself; for I have made very careful investigation everywhere and up to the present time have been able to find no other ground.

But of my ideas, beyond that which represents me to myself, as to which there can here be no difficulty, there is another which represents a God, and there are others representing corporeal and inanimate things, others angels, others animals, and others again which represent to me men similar to myself.

As regards the ideas which represent to me other men or animals, or angels, I can however easily conceive that they might be formed by an admixture of the other ideas which I have of myself, of corporeal things, and of God, even although there were apart from me neither men nor animals, nor angels, in all the world.

And in regard to the ideas of corporeal objects, I do not recognise in them anything so great or so excellent that they might not have possibly proceeded from myself; for if I consider them more closely, and examine them individually, as I yesterday examined the idea of wax, I find that there is very little in them which I perceive clearly and distinctly. Magnitude or extension in length, breadth, or depth, I do so perceive; also figure which results from a termination of this extension, the situation which bodies of different figure preserve in relation to one another, and movement or change of situation; to which we may also add substance, duration and number. As to other things such as light, colours, sounds, scents, tastes, heat, cold and the other tactile qualities, they are thought by me with so much obscurity and confusion that I do not even know if they are true or false, i.e. whether the ideas which I form of these qualities are actually the ideas of real objects or not [or whether they only represent chimeras which cannot exist in fact]. For although I have before remarked that it is only in judgments that falsity, properly speaking, or formal falsity, can be met with, a certain material falsity may nevertheless be found in ideas, i.e. when these ideas represent what is nothing as though it were something. For example, the ideas which I have of cold and heat are so far from clear and distinct that by their means I cannot tell whether cold is merely a privation of heat, or heat a privation of cold, or whether both are real qualities, or are not such. And inasmuch as [since ideas resemble images] there cannot be any ideas which do not appear to represent some things, if it is correct to say that cold is merely a privation of heat, the idea which represents it to me as something real and positive will not be improperly termed false, and the same holds good of other similar ideas.

To these it is certainly not necessary that I should attribute any author other than myself. For if they are false, i.e. if they represent things which do not exist, the light of nature shows me that they issue from nought, that is to say, that they are only in me so far as something is lacking to the perfection of my nature. But if they are true, nevertheless because they exhibit so little reality to me that I cannot even clearly distinguish the thing represented from non-being, I do not see any reason why they should not be produced by myself.

As to the clear and distinct idea which I have of corporeal things, some of them seem as though I might have derived them from the idea which I possess of myself, as those which I have of substance, duration, number, and such like. For [even] when I think that a stone is a substance, or at least a thing capable of existing of itself, and that I am a substance also, although I conceive that I am a thing that thinks and not one that is extended, and that the stone on the other hand is an extended thing which does not think, and that thus there is a notable difference between the two conceptions—they seem, nevertheless, to agree in this, that both represent substances. In the same way, when I perceive that I now exist and further recollect that I have in former times existed, and when I remember that I have various thoughts of which I can recognise the number, I acquire ideas of duration and number which I can afterwards transfer to any object that I please. But as to all the other qualities of which the ideas of corporeal things are composed, to wit, extension, figure, situation and motion, it is true that they are not formally in me, since I am only a thing that thinks; but because they are merely certain modes of substance [and so to speak the vestments under which corporeal substance appears to us] and because I myself am also a substance, it would seem that they might be contained in me eminently.

Hence there remains only the idea of God, concerning which we must consider whether it is something which cannot have proceeded from me myself. By the name God I understand a substance that is infinite [eternal, immutable], independent, all-knowing, all-powerful, and by which I myself and everything else, if anything else does exist, have been created. Now all these characteristics are such that the more diligently I attend to them, the less do they appear capable of proceeding from me alone; hence, from what has been already said, we must conclude that God necessarily exists.

For although the idea of substance is within me owing to the fact that I am substance, nevertheless I should not have the idea of an infinite substance—since I am finite—if it had not proceeded from some substance which was veritably infinite.

Nor should I imagine that I do not perceive the infinite by a true idea, but only by the negation of the finite, just as I perceive repose and darkness by the negation of movement and of light; for, on the contrary, I see that there is manifestly more reality in infinite substance than in finite, and therefore that in some way I have in me the notion of the infinite earlier then the finite—to wit, the notion of God before that of myself. For how would it be possible that I should know that I doubt and desire, that is to say, that something is lacking to me, and that I am not quite perfect, unless I had within me some idea of a Being more perfect than myself, in comparison with which I should recognise the deficiencies of my nature?

And we cannot say that this idea of God is perhaps materially false and that consequently I can derive it from nought[i.e. that possibly it exists in me because I am imperfect], as I have just said is the case with ideas of heat, cold and other such things; for, on the contrary, as this idea is very clear and distinct and contains within it more objective reality than any other, there can be none which is of itself more true, nor any in which there can be less suspicion of falsehood. The idea, I say, of this Being who is absolutely perfect and infinite, is entirely true; for although, perhaps, we can imagine that such a Being does not exist, we cannot nevertheless imagine that His idea represents nothing real to me, as I have said of the idea of cold. This idea is also very clear and distinct; since all that I conceive clearly and distinctly of the real and the true, and of what conveys some perfection, is in its entirety contained in this idea. And this does not cease to be true although I do not comprehend the infinite, or though in God there is an infinitude of things which I cannot comprehend, nor possibly even reach in any way by thought; for it is of the nature of the infinite that my nature, which is finite and limited, should not comprehend it; and it is sufficient that I should understand this, and that I should judge that all things which I clearly perceive and in which I know that there is some perfection, and possibly likewise an infinitude of properties of which I am ignorant, are in God formally or eminently, so that the idea which I have of Him may become the most true, most clear, and most distinct of all the ideas that are in my mind.

But possibly I am something more than I suppose myself to be, and perhaps all those perfections which I attribute to God are in some way potentially in me, although they do not yet disclose themselves, or issue in action. As a matter of fact I am already sensible that my knowledge increases [and perfects itself] little by little, and I see nothing which can prevent it from increasing more and more into infinitude; nor do I see, after it has thus been increased [or perfected], anything to prevent my being able to acquire by its means all the other perfections of the Divine nature; nor finally why the power I have of acquiring these perfections, if it really exists in me, shall not suffice to produce the ideas of them.

At the same time I recognise that this cannot be. For, in the first place, although it were true that every day my knowledge acquired new degrees of perfection, and that there were in my nature many things potentially which are not yet there actually, nevertheless these excellences do not pertain to [or make the smallest approach to] the idea which I have of God in whom there is nothing merely potential [but in whom all is present really and actually]; for it is an infallible token of imperfection in my knowledge that it increases little by little. And further, although my knowledge grows more and more, nevertheless I do not for that reason believe that it can ever be actually infinite, since it can never reach a point so high that it will be unable to attain to any greater increase. But I understand God to be actually infinite, so that He can add nothing to His supreme perfection. And finally I perceive that the objective being of an idea cannot be produced by a being that exists potentially only, which properly speaking is nothing, but only by a being which is formal or actual.

To speak the truth, I see nothing in all that I have just said which by the light of nature is not manifest to anyone who desires to think attentively on the subject; but when I slightly relax my attention, my mind, finding its vision somewhat obscured and so to speak blinded by the images of sensible objects, I do not easily recollect the reason why the idea that I possess of a being more perfect then I, must necessarily have been placed in me by a being which is really more perfect; and this is why I wish here to go on to inquire whether I, who have this idea, can exist if no such being exists.

And I ask, from whom do I then derive my existence? Perhaps from myself or from my parents, or from some other source less perfect than God; for we can imagine nothing more perfect than God, or even as perfect as He is.

But [were I independent of every other and] were I myself the author of my being, I should doubt nothing and I should desire nothing, and finally no perfection would be lacking to me; for I should have bestowed on myself every perfection of which I possessed any idea and should thus be God. And it must not be imagined that those things that are lacking to me are perhaps more difficult of attainment than those which I already possess; for, on the contrary, it is quite evident that it was a matter of much greater difficulty to bring to pass that I, that is to say, a thing or a substance that thinks, should emerge out of nothing, than it would be to attain to the knowledge of many things of which I am ignorant, and which are only the accidents of this thinking substance. But it is clear that if I had of myself possessed this greater perfection of which I have just spoken [that is to say, if I had been the author of my own existence], I should not at least have denied myself the things which are the more easy to acquire [to wit, many branches of knowledge of which my nature is destitute]; nor should I have deprived myself of any of the things contained in the idea which I form of God, because there are none of them which seem to me specially difficult to acquire: and if there were any that were more difficult to acquire, they would certainly appear to me to be such (supposing I myself were the origin of the other things which I possess) since I should discover in them that my powers were limited.

But though I assume that perhaps I have always existed just as I am at present, neither can I escape the force of this reasoning, and imagine that the conclusion to be drawn from this is, that I need not seek for any author of my existence. For all the course of my life may be divided into an infinite number of parts, none of which is in any way dependent on the other; and thus from the fact that I was in existence a short time ago it does not follow that I must be in existence now, unless some cause at this instant, so to speak, produces me anew, that is to say, conserves me. It is as a matter of fact perfectly clear and evident to all those who consider with attention the nature of time, that, in order to be conserved in each moment in which it endures, a substance has need of the same power and action as would be necessary to produce and create it anew, supposing it did not yet exist, so that the light of nature shows us clearly that the distinction between creation and conservation is solely a distinction of the reason.

All that I thus require here is that I should interrogate myself, if I wish to know whether I possess a power which is capable of bringing it to pass that I who now am shall still be in the future; for since I am nothing but a thinking thing, or at least since thus far it is only this portion of myself which is precisely in question at present, if such a power did reside in me, I should certainly be conscious of it. But I am conscious of nothing of the kind, and by this I know clearly that I depend on some being different from myself.

Possibly, however, this being on which I depend is not that which I call God, and I am created either by my parents or by some other cause less perfect than God. This cannot be, because, as I have just said, it is perfectly evident that there must be at least as much reality in the cause as in the effect; and thus since I am a thinking thing, and possess an idea of God within me, whatever in the end be the cause assigned to my existence, it must be allowed that it is likewise a thinking thing and that it possesses in itself the idea of all the perfections which I attribute to God. We may again inquire whether this cause derives its origin from itself or from some other thing. For if from itself, it follows by the reasons before brought forward, that this cause must itself be God; for since it possesses the virtue of self-existence, it must also without doubt have the power of actually possessing all the perfections of which it has the idea, that is, all those which I conceive as existing in God. But if it derives its existence from some other cause than itself, we shall again ask, for the same reason, whether this second cause exists by itself or through another, until from one step to another, we finally arrive at an ultimate cause, which will be God.

And it is perfectly manifest that in this there can be no regression into infinity, since what is in question is not so much the cause which formerly created me, as that which conserves me at the present time.

Nor can we suppose that several causes may have concurred in my production, and that from one I have received the idea of one of the perfections which I attribute to God, and from another the idea of some other, so that all these perfections indeed exist somewhere in the universe, but not as complete in one unity which is God. On the contrary, the unity, the simplicity or the inseparability of all things which are in god is one of the principal perfections which I conceive to be in Him. And certainly the idea of this unity of all Divine perfections cannot have been placed in me by any cause from which I have not likewise received the ideas of all the other perfections; for this cause could not make me able to comprehend them as joined together in an inseparable unity without having at the same time caused me in some measure to know what they are [and in some way to recognise each one of them].

Finally, so far as my parents [from whom it appears I have sprung] are concerned, although all that I have ever been able to believe of them were true, that does not make it follow that it is they who conserve me, nor are they even the authors of my being in any sense, in so far as I am a thinking being; since what they did was merely to implant certain dispositions in that matter in which the self—i.e. the mind, which alone I at present identify with myself—is by me deemed to exist. And thus there can be no difficulty in their regard, but we must of necessity conclude from the fact alone that I exist, or that the idea of a Being supremely perfect—that is of God—is in me, that the proof of God's existence is grounded on the highest evidence.

It only remains to me to examine into the manner in which I have acquired this idea from God; for I have not received it through the senses, and it is never presented to me unexpectedly, as is usual with the ideas of sensible things when these things present themselves, or seem to present themselves, to the external organs of my senses; nor is it likewise a fiction of my mind, for it is not in my power to take from or to add anything to it; and consequently the only alternative is that it is innate in me, just as the idea of myself is innate in me.

And one certainly ought not to find it strange that God, in creating me, placed this idea within me to be like the mark of the workman imprinted on his work; and it is likewise not essential that the mark shall be something different from the work itself. For from the sole fact that God created me it is most probable that in some way he has placed his image and similitude upon me, and that I perceive this similitude (in which the idea of God is contained) by means of the same faculty by which I perceive myself—that is to say, when I reflect on myself I not only know that I am something [imperfect], incomplete and dependent on another, which incessantly aspires after something which is better and greater than myself, but I also know that He on whom I depend possesses in Himself all the great things towards which I aspire [and the ideas of which I find within myself], and that not indefinitely or potentially alone, but really, actually and infinitely; and that thus He is God. And the whole strength of the argument which I have here made use of to prove the existence of God consists in this, that I recognise that it is not possible that my nature should be what it is, and indeed that I should have in myself the idea of a God, if God did not veritably exist—a God, I say, whose idea is in me, i.e. who possesses all those supreme perfections of which our mind may indeed have some idea but without understanding them all, who is liable to no errors or defect [and who has none of all those marks which denote imperfection]. From this it is manifest that He cannot be a deceiver, since the light of nature teaches us that fraud and deception necessarily proceed from some defect.

But before I examine this matter with more care, and pass on to the consideration of other truths which may be derived from it. It seems to me right to pause for a while in order to contemplate God Himself, to ponder at leisure His marvelous attributes, to consider, and admire, and adore, the beauty of this light so resplendent, at least as far as the strength of my mind, which is in some measure dazzled by the sight, will allow me to do so. For just as faith teaches us that the supreme felicity of the other life consists only in this contemplation of the Divine Majesty, so we continue to learn by experience that a similar meditation, though incomparably less perfect, causes us to enjoy the greatest satisfaction of which we are capable in this life.

THE MIND-BODY PROBLEM

By Richard Popkin and Avrum Stroll

The mind-body problem has been a major concern of metaphysicians, especially since the rise of modern philosophy in the seventeenth century. In the form in which we shall discuss it, this problem has arisen as the result of certain views of the great French philosopher René Descartes. In spite of our increasing knowledge about the behavior of the mental and the physical world, this metaphysical question continues to plague philosophers.

Basically, the problem involves answering the questions **"What is the fundamental nature of mind and body?"** and **"How are mind and body related?"** An elementary consideration of what we know about mental and physical events might well lead one to suspect that the most general characteristics of each are different from the other, and yet that they seem to bear some relation to each other or have some influence upon each other.

Our scientific knowledge would seem to suggest that the physical world is inanimate, purposeless, yet determined or fixed in the order of events within it. The mental world, on the other hand, involves consciousness, planning, willing, desiring, etc. Yet, though these worlds may be different in many respects, our experience appears to indicate that they are interrelated or interconnected. When something happens in the physical world, this affects the mental world and may change one's thoughts, wishes, etc. Similarly, a desire that one may have can alter events in the physical world, as when one decides to strike a match. This decision, an event in the mental world, is then followed by a physical event of a match being struck and a flame being lit. Given the apparent differences between mental and physical events, and their apparent relationships with each other, various metaphysicians have tried to construct theories about the nature of mind and body and the connections between them.

CARTESIAN THEORY

Descartes, who is often blamed for having created the difficulties that arose from this problem, asserted that mind and body are two totally different types of entity. They are different **substances**. From a careful scrutiny of the "clear and distinct" idea that he had of his own mind and of physical objects, he decided that the basic feature of the latter was its geometrical qualities (size, shape, and so on) and the basic feature of the former was thinking. In each case, these seemed to him to be the inseparable properties that accounted for all the other features of these two entities.

In his work *The Principles of Philosophy*, Descartes summed up his theory as follows:

> But although any one attribute is enough to give us knowledge of a substance, there is always one chief property of a substance that constitutes its nature and essence, and upon which all the others depend. Thus extension in length, breadth and depth makes up the nature of physical substance; and thought makes up the nature of thinking substance. For, everything else that may be attributed to bodies presupposes their extension, and is only a form of this extended thing; just as everything that we find in mind is only some form of thinking. Thus, for example, we cannot conceive of a figure except as an extended thing, nor of movement except as taking place in an extended space; and in the same way imagination, feeling and will occur only in a. thinking thing. But, on the other hand, we are able to conceive of extension without figure or action, and of thinking without imagination or sensation, and so on, as is quite clear to anyone who examines the matter carefully.

Thinking and Extension

Thus, according to Descartes, the **essential property of a mind is that it thinks, and the essential property of body is that it is "extended."** All of the forms in which bodies occur involve only various extensional features, never mental ones. Similarly, no form of thought involves extension. The realms of thought and extension are completely different. Then, if all this is accepted, how can mental events have anything to do with physical ones and vice versa, since the one occurs in space and the other is unextended thought with no physical properties whatsoever? To make the question more difficult, Descartes claimed in his physical theories that all physical action occurs by the impact of one extended object upon another. Since mental events are not extended, how can there be any impact or contact between that whose nature it is to occur in space and that which does not occur in space? How can an idea move a hammer, or a hammer strike upon an idea?

Conflicting Evidence

In spite of the complete separation in his theory between mind and body, Descartes was impressed by the commonsensical and scientific evidence that indicated the reciprocal influence of mental and physical events. A pin jabbed into the physical, extended finger is followed by a thought or a pain in the unextended mind. But a studious examination of the medical and psychological evidence convinced Descartes that the mind is only aware of physical events in the brain. Various motions can take place in the body without being followed by mental events, unless the physical motions first cause movements in the nervous system and then in the brain. Similarly, just by producing certain physical motions in the brain, without affecting the rest of the body, one can stimulate thoughts. The example that most impressed Descartes was that persons who had lost a limb could be led to think that this 'limb" was being moved, or pained, merely by stimulating parts of the nervous system. This sort of information led Descartes to the conclusion that there must be some kind of contact between the mental and physical worlds, and that the contact must take place in the brain.

On the basis of this conclusion, Descartes developed a theory that the interaction between mind and body took place in the pineal gland, which is located at the base of the brain. Here, presumably, some sort of impact occurred between the physical, extended brain and the unextended, thinking mind, which allowed physical events to lead to thoughts, and thoughts to alter the direction of the motions of extended objects.

When it was pointed out to him that his solution to this metaphysical problem was quite unsatisfactory, because he had still not explained plausibly how it was possible for mind and body to interact upon each other if they were really of two totally different natures, Descartes became more and more vague about the matter. He insisted that the fact of interaction was known to everybody; we experience it all the time. But how mind and body were united, he admitted, was most difficult to explain. The pineal gland theory actually produced more problems than it solved, since one could ask whether this gland was physical, and if so, how it could be next to something that did not occupy space. If it were mental, how could it be next to any part of the brain? And so on. In a letter written late in his life to one of his admirers, the Princess Elizabeth of the Palatinate, Descartes threw up his hands in despair and told her that the union of mind and body was best understood by not thinking about it, and that it was just one of those mysteries that had to be accepted without being comprehended.

The Materialistic Theory

Other metaphysicians were not willing to give up as easily as Descartes, and they suspected that the difficulties in the problem arose from the initial separation of mind and body in the Cartesian metaphysical system. If one refused to grant that mind and body were really different kinds of entity, then one would not have any trouble accounting for their interrelations. One way of avoiding some pitfalls of the

Cartesian theory was to adopt a completely **materialistic metaphysics** and claim that both mental and physical events could be accounted for in terms of purely physical concepts and laws.

This type of theory, which was advanced in Descartes's time by his belligerent opponent, Thomas Hobbes, and in our own day by some **behaviorist psychologists**, maintains **that what we call mental events are really, like physical events, only various combinations of matter in motion.** The physical movements that occur in the brain are what we call thoughts, and these are produced by other events in the material world, either outside our bodies or inside, and, in turn, can produce further physical motions in ourselves or outside of ourselves. Every idea—of pain, of perception, of memory, and so on—is nothing but a set of physical occurrences in our higher nervous system and brain. When we say that we have a sensation of yellow, for example, this is explained as the result of certain light waves stimulating the optic nerve, which in turn causes a certain pattern of motions in the brain.

The very simplicity of the materialistic solution to the mind-body problem makes it appealing. Moreover, the vast body of evidence accumulated about the physical basis of mental events by psychologists, psychiatrists, physiologists, and other scientists also makes this theory seem most plausible. Recent developments in the treatment of mental conditions, such as depression, disconnected thinking, and mood changes, by biochemical drug treatment strongly suggest some links between the biochemical condition of the nervous system and the mental condition of the individual. Various so-called "brain-washing" techniques also indicate that one's mental content and mental processes can be affected by physical stimuli such as sense deprivation and sleeplessness.

Work on "artificial intelligence" in computers, programming them to do intellectual tasks, suggests that physical events—the circuits in a computer—can resemble the mental processes in human beings.

All of these new developments make the materialist case strong, but they raise fundamental difficulties that have led many metaphysicians either to attempt to modify it or else to abandon it.

If one examines an idea and asks if this is actually the same as what we mean by a physical event, one discovers a problem. The experience of seeing or hearing something, and the bodily events that occur in the nervous system and the brain at the same time, do not seem to be identical. For instance, if a person were watching a television show, and a scientist were at the same time examining the viewer's brain, they each would see different things. The viewer would see a series of pictures, while the scientist would see a series of "readings" of various measuring devices. It is conceivable that our information about the physiology of the brain may reach the point where the scientist can tell what the viewer is seeing, that is, from the physical reactions in the brain, he might be able to construct the sequence of events that comprised the television show. Even so, it would still be the case that each of them would be seeing directly something else.

Computer experts like Marvin Minsky (of the Massachusetts Institute of Technology), who coined the term "artificial intelligence" in 1956, have been working on the possibility of designing self-repairing machines that, once in motion, could keep themselves active without human intervention. They are also working on computer programs that duplicate the way human beings deal with problems. This would involve duplicating not just logical or mathematical activities, but mixed logical and psychological ones as well. Computer programs already exist that can outdo humans in computation and in the solution of certain kinds of mathematical problems. And computer programs are being designed that come closer and closer to winning chess competitions; even against the best experts.

Around 1950 the English logician and computer expert Alan Turing raised the question "Can machines think?" He proposed that it might be possible to build a machine (now called a Turing machine) that would make exactly the same responses a human being would to various questions. If so, then would it not be fair to say that if the human respondent thinks, then the Turing machine also thinks?

All of this would suggest that many of the processes that we relate to what we call "intelligence" in human beings can be artificially created, and that there is artificial intelligence. If intelligence is the ability to solve certain kinds of problems through certain kinds of activities, and if the computer program does what human beings seem to do to reach this end, then isn't it fair to say that the computer program is intelligent? The investigation of this, and how to accomplish it, has become a scientific and technological subject in its own right. Various forms of what we take to be human mental activity are being duplicated in computer programs.

Philosophically, this has led to a new, modernized version of the materialist theory about the mind-body problem—put forth as neurophilosophy by Patricia Smith Churchland—using the latest biochemical and biophysical findings about how the higher processes of the brain operate as the way to explain mental actions and to resolve the questions about mental life and mind-body interaction that philosophers have struggled with for centuries. Churchland identifies mind and brain, and insists that explanations of how the brain works account for mental events. She insists that brain processes are mental processes. Hence scientific knowledge of how the brain operates will yield the knowledge we seek about mental events.

In 1991, an important study by Daniel Dennett, *Consciousness Explained,* appeared and has gotten a lot of attention. In it the author argues that the mind functions as a supercomputer, and *is* in fact a supercomputer. Dennett claims that the understanding of how the mind functions dissolves the consideration of the mind as different from the brain-computer. The brain-computer is an organic machine that uses effects of cultural inheritance to store and utilize information, and to solve problems.

Criticism

The materialistic theory, in its simplest form, denies any distinction between our mental life and the physical developments in our brain. Nevertheless, the critics stress the fact that one's immediate experience seems to belie this claim. One is aware of all sorts of sensations, feelings, etc., and not a series of physical occurrences in the brain. Even if the latter are the cause of the former, it still remains the case that they are different and distinguishable. Hence, the critics claim, the materialists cannot successfully reduce the mental world to the physical world simply by asserting that all mental events are actually nothing but a series of physical occurrences.

Another criticism of the materialistic solution to the mind-body problem is that if it were true, the materialistic theory itself, which presumably is a mental event in somebody's life, would turn out to be nothing but one more set of physical events in the brain. Similarly, any alternative theory would merely be some other physical event. In that case, how can one set of motions in the brain be said to constitute the truth, whereas others would constitute a falsehood? If any metaphysical theory is just a physical occurrence in somebody's head, why should one of these occurrences be taken seriously and the others discounted as wrong?

Finally, the materialistic solution also carries serious implications for ethics. If our thoughts are physical occurrences in the brain, they must be ultimately explicable in scientific terms; it must be theoretically possible to explain our thoughts in the same way as we explain events in the physical world, i.e., in terms of cause and effect. This leaves no room for evaluation of a situation, for consideration of its implications, for decisions reached after careful **thought**. In other words, such a theory must lead to an explanation of human behavior in terms not of **free choices** based on careful appraisal but in terms of **physical cause and effect, stimulus and response.** This is in fact the kind of explanation favored by the behaviorist psychologist, but its implication for ethics is that no such thing as a moral choice is possible. (We shall consider this problem in greater detail later in this chapter.) This would still seem to be the case whether one considers mental life as coming from biochemical and biophysical processes in the brain and the nervous system, or whether one considers it as analogous to some computer programs. The former, in each case, may help explain the mental features. But, it can still be asked, is the former identical with our mental life? In an interesting volume, *Artificial Intelligence: The Case Against,* edited by Rainer Born, a group of philosophers have argued both against the reduction of mental states to physical states and against the possibility of creating artificial intelligence.

EPIPHENOMENOLISM

Because of such problems, a modified form of the materialistic theory of mind and body has been developed—**epiphenomenalism**. This view admits that our thoughts, feelings, etc., are not merely physical states in our brain. Instead, they are adjudged to be a by-product of the sequence of physical occurrences, something like the smoke given off by fire. The significant events that occur in the world are only those of matter in motion. But along with this, for reasons not yet known to us, each time there is a certain sort of physical situation in the brain, a thought occurs, which is caused by material events.

The epiphenomenalistic solution may overcome some of the difficulties in the simple version of materialism, but it does not do justice to our mental life. As we have just suggested, we take our thoughts seriously, are bothered by them, brood about them, seem to initiate actions on the basis of them. If they are nothing but a vague by-product of the material events that occur in our brains, bearing no actual relation to them, it is strange that they should play such an important part in our lives.

IDEALISM

If the materialistic theory in one form or another has its difficulties, the opposite alternative, **idealism, which insists that everything is basically mental rather than physical**, may be even less credible. When applied to the mind-body problem, this metaphysical theory (which will be considered later in this chapter) has the disadvantages of flying in the face of our commonsense beliefs and of being in apparent conflict with scientific evidence. Even before reflecting on these matters, we seem to be convinced that there are physical events that influence our behavior. Scientific data concerning the influence of, say, drugs and surgery on our mental life suggest that a mentalistic, or idealistic, approach to the mind-body problem is difficult to accept unless the arguments in its favor can far overweigh the initial conflicts with our ordinary beliefs.

THE THEORIES OF MALEBRANCHE, LEIBNIZ, AND SPINOZA

In the seventeenth century some interesting alternative theories were offered to resolve the problem of the relationship between mind and body, by some of the great metaphysicians of the period, Nicolas Malebranche, Gottfried Wilhelm von Leibniz, and Baruch Spinoza. Malebranche, a Catholic priest, was a follower of Descartes, but much more consistent than his mentor. Where Descartes accepted apparently conflicting theories in order to avoid denying or challenging our ordinary experience, Malebranche insisted on reaching a *consistent* conclusion, no matter how implausible it might be.

Occasionalism

Malebranche's theory, which is called **"occasionalism,"** insists on the Cartesian distinction between mind and matter. Each is totally different—one is composed of nothing but ideas, the other only of extended events. (In fact, they are so different that Malebranche claimed that mind cannot even know body. All that mind can know are ideas. When we think of bodies, what we are thinking of is something called "intelligible extension," rather than physical extension. Malebranche found the sole evidence that bodies exist in the opening lines of the Book of Genesis, which proclaim that God created a physical world. Were it not for this, we would never even know that there are any material objects.) If these two realms are so distinct, Malebranche insisted, then there cannot be any interaction or connection between them.

What actually happens, according to Malebranche, is that although mental events have nothing to do with physical ones, whenever anything happens in one realm, God makes something corresponding occur in the other. The events in one are not the **causes** of events in the other, they are only the **occasions** of God's actions. Thus, when I hear the ring of the telephone, this is not due to the occurrence of sound waves, which are part of the physical world and have nothing to do with thoughts that I may have. Instead, when the events take place in the mechanism of the telephone, God produces a thought in me of ringing. Since one has nothing to do with the other, He might just as well have produced the taste of a pear in me, or the idea of the number 7. But, through the inscrutable wisdom of God, He has decided to order my mental life and the series of physical events so that when a specific event occurs in one, He makes something else occur in the other.

Criticism

No matter how peculiar Malebranche's theory may appear, it has the advantage that it avoids the difficulties of Descartes's speculations, and no experience can possibly disprove it. Descartes had insisted upon holding both to the complete separation of mind and body and to their interaction. By eliminating the latter, Malebranche is able to hold to the former without encountering contradictions. The theory can be made to account for literally everything. No matter what experiment one might devise to show that mind influences body, or body influences mind, it can always be explained in Malebranchian terms, as God producing a certain effect in one realm when something else happens in the other. On the other hand, no matter how consistent Malebranche's theory may be, it remains extremely unconvincing in light of our ordinary experience, which we naturally interpret in terms of some relation between mental and physical events. Moreover, Malebranche's conception of God as being constantly involved in producing all effects in this world—as engaged in producing sounds, tastes, smells, and motions in the physical world—is hardly in keeping with most "acceptable" concepts of the deity.

A further difficulty arises when we ask how God achieves these effects, how God acts causally on both mind and body. The source of the mind-body problem lies in the fact that physical substance and thinking substance cannot interact. The definition of substance that the Cartesians had used logically precludes the interaction of one substance with another. Two substances must by definition have nothing in common with each other. For if they have anything in common, they cannot be separate substances. Now, as Spinoza tells us, "If two things have nothing in common with one another, then one cannot be the cause of the other; for since there would be nothing in the effect that was also in the cause, everything that was in the effect would have arisen out of nothing." How, then, does God act causally on mind and body, on thinking substance and on physical substance? If God Himself is either thinking substance or physical substance, then there is only one of these substances that He can act causally on. The Cartesians, however, regarded God as neither, but as quite separate from both—in other words, as a third substance. On this account it is logically impossible for Him to act causally on either mind or body. This was one of the inconsistencies in Cartesianism, as developed by Malebranche, that Spinoza seized on, as we shall see.

Leibniz

Leibniz's theory of the relations between mental and physical events is not much more plausible than Malebranche's view. According to Leibniz, every entity, whether characterized as mental or physical, is independent and constitutes a **monad.** Each monad is determined or fixed in its properties according to its nature. Everything that can possibly happen to a monad follows from its own essential characteristics and not from the influence of any other entity.

"Preestablished harmony"

What accounts for the apparent relationships between different monads—in Leibniz's theory—is that though they have no influence on each other, there is a **pre-established harmony** between the monads. They have been so constructed that events occurring in one are harmonious with the others. In the example used earlier, monads of the telephone and of my mind are such that when certain physical occurrences take place in the former, I hear a ringing sound. This is not owing to the fact that the telephone caused me to hear anything, but rather, that our monads are in perfect order. Mine is so set that at a given time, I have the idea of a certain sound, and at just that time a physical clapper is beating on a physical bell in the telephone. The following illustration may clarify this theory: if there were two clocks that kept perfect time so that when one pointed to the hour the other rang a bell, it might be the case that this is because the clocks have some connected mechanism (**Descartes's theory**); or that some outside intervention makes one ring when the hands on the other reach a certain point (**Malebranche's theory**); or that the clocks had been made perfectly at the outset, and although they had no relation whatsoever to each other, they each kept perfect time (**Leibniz's theory**). Thus each monad is so created by God that it is in perfect harmony with every other for all eternity, and the events in the career of one are bound to be in perfect accord with the others. Brutus did not kill Caesar because of anything Caesar did; instead, each monad was so constructed by God that at the same moment that Brutus's monad had certain thoughts, and performed certain actions, Caesar's was such that he was in a certain locale, and dropped dead.

Leibniz's theory, like Malebranche's, overcomes the difficulties in Cartesian metaphysics by giving up any claim that there is a relationship between mind and body. Also, like Malebranche's, Leibniz's view, though it may not contain any inconsistencies, is incredible from the point of view of our ordinary, common experience.

Spinoza

The last of these seventeenth-century accounts of the mind-body problem that we shall consider is somewhat different. Spinoza decided that the difficulty in the Cartesian theory came from its total separation of mind and body and, as we have seen, the total separation of both from God, although this difficulty had not been appreciated by the Cartesians. To overcome this, he did not wish to adopt the materialistic or idealistic solution of subordinating one of these realms to the other; instead, he insisted that they were both aspects of the same thing. This theory, sometimes called the "**dual-aspect theory**," claims that mind and body are both attributes of one and the same entity, which Spinoza named God, substance, or nature.

If the mental world and the physical world are both aspects of the same entity, then what is the relationship between one and the other? According to Spinoza, there is no influence between one and the other, but there is a **parallelism**, so that for everything that happens in one realm, a corresponding event occurs in the other. This is due to the fact that the physical and mental worlds are really two different ways of looking at the same thing, God or nature. Hence, Spinoza contended that the logical order of the mind is identical with the physical order of nature. For every thought there is a corresponding physical event, and vice versa. Thus the ringing of the telephone that I hear and the physical motions that are taking place in the mechanism are not two different things but are two different aspects of the same thing, or two different ways of looking at the same thing, as it occurs in God or nature.

Spinoza's metaphysical solution may not lead to the same kind of unbelievable views as those of Malebranche or Leibniz, or the inconsistencies involved in Descartes's view; however, it led to certain conclusions regarding the nature, of God, which most of his contemporaries found completely unacceptable. (Some of these will be considered in the chapter on the philosophy of religion.) As a result, it was not until the time of the nineteenth-century German metaphysicians that Spinoza's views were treated seriously.

The theories regarding the relationship between mind and body illustrate the difficulty the metaphysician has in trying to develop an explanation of this fundamental feature of our experience. The first metaphysical question that we considered dealt with the general character of the universe, and the second, with the relationship between two of the basic features of it. Before examining some of the major metaphysical theories that have attempted to account for all of the chief characteristics of the cosmos as we know it, we shall look at one further problem that metaphysicians have debated throughout history—**the free will problem**.

DESCARTES' ERROR

By Antonio R. Damasio

PHINEAS P. GAGE

I t is the summer of 1848. We are in New England. Phineas P. Gage, twenty-five years old, construction foreman, is about to go from riches to rags. A century and a half later his downfall will still be quite meaningful.

Gage works for the Rutland & Burlington Railroad and is in charge of a large group of men, a "gang" as it is called, whose job it is to lay down the new tracks for the railroad's expansion across Vermont. Over the past two weeks the men have worked their way slowly toward the town of Cavendish; they are now at a bank of the Black River. The assignment is anything but easy. The terrain is uneven in every direction and is filled with hard, stratified rock. Rather than twist and turn the tracks around every escarpment, the strategy is to blast the stone now and then, to make way for a straighter and more level path. Gage oversees all these tasks and is equal to them in every way. He is five-foot-six and athletic, and his movements are swift and precise. He looks like a young Jimmy Cagney, a Yankee Doodle dandy dancing his tap shoes over ties and tracks, moving with vigor and grace.

In the eyes of his bosses, however, Gage is more than just another able body. They say he is "the most efficient and capable" man in their employ. This is a good thing, because the job takes as much physical prowess as keen concentration, especially when it comes to preparing the detonations. Several steps have to be followed, in orderly fashion. First, a hole must be drilled in the rock. After it is filled about halfway with explosive powder, a fuse must be inserted, and the powder covered with sand. Then the sand must be "tamped in," or pounded with a careful sequence of strokes from an iron rod. Finally, the fuse must be lit. If all goes well, the powder will explode into the rock; the sand is essential, for without its protection the explosion would be directed away from the rock. The shape of the iron and the way it is played are also important. Gage, who has had an iron manufactured to his specifications, is a virtuoso of this thing.

Now for what is going to happen. It is four-thirty on this hot afternoon. Gage has just put powder and fuse in a hole and told the man who is helping him to cover it with sand. Someone calls from behind, and Gage looks away, over his right shoulder, for only an instant. Distracted, and before his man has poured the sand in, Gage begins tamping the powder directly with the iron bar. In no time he strikes fire in the rock, and the charge blows upward in his face.

The explosion is so brutal that the entire gang freezes on their feet. It takes a few seconds to piece together what is going on. The bang is unusual, and the rock is intact. Also unusual is the whistling sound, as of a rocket hurled at the sky. But this is more than fireworks. It is assault and battery. The iron enters Gage's left cheek, pierces the base of the skull, traverses the front of his brain, and exits at high speed through the top of the head. The rod has landed more than a hundred feet away, covered in blood and brains. Phineas Gage has been thrown to the ground. He is stunned, in the afternoon glow, silent but awake. So are we all, helpless spectators.

"Horrible Accident" will be the predictable headline in the Boston *Daily Courier* and *Daily Journal* of September 20, a week later. "Wonderful Accident" will be the strange headline in the *Vermont Mercury* of September 22. "Passage of an Iron Rod Through the Head" will be the accurate headline in the *Boston Medical and Surgical Journal.* From the matter-of-factness with which they tell the story, one would think the writers were familiar with Edgar Allan Poe's accounts of the bizarre and the horrific. And perhaps they were, although this is not likely; Poe's gothic tales are not yet popular, and Poe himself will die the next year, unknown and impecunious. Perhaps the horrible is just in the air.

Noting how surprised people were that Gage was not killed instantly, the Boston medical article documents that "immediately after the explosion the patient was thrown upon his back;" that shortly thereafter he exhibited "a few convulsive motions of the extremities," and "spoke in a few minutes;" that "his men (with whom he was a great favourite) took him in their arms and carried him to the road, only a few rods distant (a rod is equivalent to 5 ½ yards, or 16 ½ feet), and sat him into an ox cart, in which he rode, sitting erect, a full three quarters of a mile, to the hotel of Mr. Joseph Adams;" and that Gage "got out of the cart himself, with a little assistance from his men."

Let me introduce Mr. Adams. He is the justice of the peace for Cavendish and the owner of the town's hotel and tavern. He is taller than Gage, twice as round, and as solicitous as his Falstaff shape suggests. He approaches Gage, and immediately has someone call for Dr. John Harlow, one of the town physicians. While they wait, I imagine, he says, "Come, come, Mr. Gage, what have we got here?" and, why not, "My, my, what troubles we've seen." He shakes his head in disbelief and leads Gage to the shady part of the hotel porch, which has been described as a "piazza." That makes it sound grand and spacious and open, and perhaps it is grand and spacious, but it is not open; it is just a porch. And there perhaps Mr. Adams is now giving Phineas Gage lemonade, or maybe cold cider.

An hour has passed since the explosion. The sun is declining and the heat is more bearable. A younger colleague of Dr. Harlow's, Dr. Edward Williams, is arriving. Years later Dr. Williams will describe the scene: "He at that time was sitting in a chair upon the piazza of Mr. Adams' hotel, in Cavendish. When I drove up, he said, 'Doctor, here is business enough for you.' I first noticed the wound upon the head before I alighted from my carriage, the pulsations of the brain being very distinct; there was also an appearance which, before I examined the head, I could not account for: the top of the head appeared somewhat like an inverted funnel; this was owing, I discovered, to the bone being fractured about the opening for a distance of about two inches in every direction. I ought to have mentioned above that the opening through the skull and integuments was not far from one and a half inch in diameter; the edges of this opening were everted, and the whole wound appeared as if some wedge-shaped body had passed from below upward. Mr. Gage, during the time I was examining this wound, was relating the manner in which he was injured to the bystanders; he talked so rationally and was so willing to answer questions, that I directed my inquiries to him in preference to the men who were with him at the time of the accident, and who were standing about at this time. Mr. G. then related to me some of the circumstances, as he has since done; and I can safely say that neither at that time nor on any subsequent occasion, save once, did I consider him to be other than perfectly rational. The one time to which I allude was about a fortnight after the accident, and then he persisted in calling me John Kirwin; yet he answered all my questions correctly."

The survival is made all the more amazing when one considers the shape and weight of the iron bar. Henry Bigelow, a surgery professor at Harvard, describes the iron so: "The iron which thus traversed the skull weighs thirteen and a quarter pounds. It is three feet seven inches in length, and one and a quarter inches in diameter. The end which entered first is pointed; the taper being seven inches long, and the diameter of the point one quarter of an inch; circumstances to which the patient perhaps owes his life. The iron is unlike any other, and was made by a neighbouring blacksmith to please the fancy of the owner." Gage is serious about his trade and its proper tools.

Surviving the explosion with so large a wound to the head, being able to talk and walk and remain coherent immediately afterward—this is all surprising. But just as surprising will be Gage's surviving the inevitable infection that is about to take over his wound. Gage's physician, John Harlow, is well aware of the role of disinfection. He does not have the help of antibiotics, but using what chemicals are available he will clean the wound vigorously and regularly, and place the patient in a semi-recumbent position so that drainage will be natural and easy. Gage will develop high fevers and at least one abscess, which Harlow will promptly remove with his scalpel. In the end, Gage's youth and strong constitution will overcome the odds against him, assisted, as Harlow will put it, by divine intervention: "I dressed him, God healed him."

Phineas Gage will be pronounced cured in less than two months. Yet this astonishing outcome pales in comparison with the extraordinary turn that Gage's personality is about to undergo. Gage's disposition, his likes and dislikes, his dreams and aspirations are all to change. Gage's body may be alive and well, but there is a new spirit animating it.

GAGE WAS NO LONGER GAGE

Just what exactly happened we can glean today from the account Dr. Harlow prepared twenty years after the accident. It is a trustworthy text, with an abundance of facts and a minimum of interpretation. It makes sense humanly and neurologically, and from it we can piece together not just Gage but his doctor as well. John Harlow had been a schoolteacher before he entered Jefferson Medical College in Philadelphia, and was only a few years into his medical career when he took care of Gage. The case became his life-consuming interest, and I suspect that it made Harlow want to be a scholar, something that may not have been in his plans when he set up his medical practice in Vermont. Treating Gage successfully and reporting the results to his Boston colleagues may have been the shining hours of his career, and he must have been disturbed by the fact that a real cloud hung over Gage's cure.

Harlow's narrative describes how Gage regained his strength and how his physical recovery was complete. Gage could touch, hear, and see, and was not paralyzed of limb or tongue. He had lost vision in his left eye, but his vision was perfect in the right. He walked firmly, used his hands with dexterity, and had no noticeable difficulty with speech or language. And yet, as Harlow recounts, the "equilibrium or balance, so to speak, between his intellectual faculty and animal propensities" had been destroyed. The changes became apparent as soon as the acute phase of brain injury subsided. He was now "fitful, irreverent, indulging at times in the grossest profanity which was not previously his custom, manifesting but little deference for his fellows, impatient of restraint or advice when it conflicts with his desires, at times pertinaciously obstinate, yet capricious and vacillating, devising many plans of future operation, which are no sooner arranged than they are abandoned.... A child in his intellectual capacity and manifestations, he has the animal passions of a strong man." The foul language was so debased that women were advised not to stay long in his presence, lest their sensibilities be offended. The strongest admonitions from Harlow himself failed to return our survivor to good behavior.

These new personality traits contrasted sharply with the "temperate habits" and "considerable energy of character" Phineas Gage was known to have possessed before the accident. He had had "a well balanced mind and was looked upon by those who knew him as a shrewd, smart businessman, very energetic and persistent in executing all his plans of action." There is no doubt that in the context of his job and time, he was successful. So radical was the change in him that friends and acquaintances could hardly recognize the man. They noted sadly that "Gage was no longer Gage." So different a man was he that his employers had to let him go shortly after he returned to work, for they "considered the change in his mind so marked that they could not give him his place again." The problem was not lack of physical ability or skill; it was his new character.

The unraveling continued unabated. No longer able to work as a foreman, Gage took jobs on horse farms. He would work at one place or another briefly, only to quit in a capricious fit or be let go because of poor discipline. As Harlow notes, he was good at "always finding something which did not suit him." Then came his career as a circus attraction. Gage was featured at Barnum's Museum in New York City vaingloriously showing his wounds and the tamping iron. (Harlow states that the iron was a constant companion, and points out Gage's strong attachment to objects and animals, which was new and some-what out of the ordinary. This trait, what we might call "collector's behavior," is something I have seen in patients who have suffered injuries like Gage's, as well as in autistic individuals.)

Then far more than now, the circus capitalized on nature's cruelty. The endocrine variety included dwarfs, the fattest woman on earth, the tallest man, the fellow with the largest jaw; the neurological variety included youths with elephant skin, victims of neurofibromatosis—and now Gage. We can imagine him in such Fellinian company, peddling misery for gold.

Four years after the accident, there was another theatrical coup. Gage left for South America. He worked on horse farms, and eventually was a stagecoach driver in Santiago and Valparaiso. Little else is known about his expatriate life except that in 1859 his health was deteriorating.

In 1860, Gage returned to the United States to live with his mother and sister, who had since moved to San Francisco. At first he was employed on a farm in Santa Clara, but he did not stay long. In fact, he moved around often, occasionally finding work as a laborer in the bay area. It is clear that he was not an independent person and that he could not secure the type of steady, remunerative job that he had once held. The end of the fall was nearing.

In my mind is a picture of 1860s San Francisco as a bustling place, full of adventurous entrepreneurs engaged in mining, farming, and shipping. That is where we can find Gage's mother and sister, the latter married to a prosperous San Francisco merchant (D. D. Shattuck, Esquire), and that is where the old Phineas Gage might have belonged. But that is not where we would find him if we could travel back in time. We would find him drinking and brawling in a questionable district, not conversing with the captains of commerce, as astonished as anybody when the fault would slip and the earth would shake threateningly. He had joined the tableau of dispirited people who, as Nathanael West would put it decades later, and a few hundred miles to the south, "had come to California to die."

The meager documents available suggest that Gage developed epileptic fits (seizures). The end came on May 21, 1861, after an illness that lasted little more than a day Gage had a major convulsion which made him lose consciousness. A series of subsequent convulsions, one coming soon on the heels of another, followed. He never regained consciousness. I believe he was the victim of *status epilepticus*, a condition in which convulsions become nearly continuous and usher in death. He was thirty-eight years old. There was no death notice in the San Francisco newspapers.

WHY PHINEAS GAGE?

Why is this sad story worth telling? What is the possible significance of such a bizarre tale? The answer is simple. While other cases of neurological damage that occurred at about the same time revealed that the brain was the foundation for language, perception, and motor function, and generally provided more conclusive details, Gage's story hinted at an amazing fact: Somehow, there were systems in the human brain dedicated more to reasoning than to anything else, and in particular to the personal and social dimensions of reasoning. The observance of previously acquired social convention and ethical rules could be lost as a result of brain damage, even when neither basic intellect nor language seemed compromised. Unwittingly, Gage's example indicated that something in the brain was concerned specifically with unique human properties, among them the ability to anticipate the future and plan accordingly within a complex social environment; the sense of responsibility toward the self and others; and the ability to orchestrate one's survival deliberately, at the command of one's free will.

The most striking aspect of this unpleasant story is the discrepancy between the normal personality structure that preceded the accident and the nefarious personality traits that surfaced thereafter—and remained for the rest of Gage's life. Gage had once known all he needed to know about making choices conducive to his betterment. He had a sense of personal and social responsibility, reflected in the way he had secured advancement in his job, cared for the quality of his work, and attracted the admiration of employers and colleagues. He was well adapted in terms of social convention and appears to have been ethical in his dealings. After the accident, he no longer showed respect for social convention; ethics were violated; the decisions he made did not take into account his best interest, and he was given to invent tales "without any foundation except in his fancy," in Harlow's words. There was no evidence of concern about his future, no sign of forethought.

The alterations in Gage's personality were not subtle. He could not make good choices, and the choices he made were not simply neutral. They were not the reserved or slight decisions of someone whose mind is diminished and who is afraid to act, but were instead actively disadvantageous. Gage worked hard at his downfall. One might venture that either his value system was now different, or, if it was still the same, there was no way in which the old values could influence his decisions. No evidence exists to tell us which is true, yet my investigation of patients with brain damage similar to Phineas Gage's convinces me that neither explanation captures what really happens in those circumstances. Some part of the value system remains and can be utilized in abstract terms, but it is unconnected to real-life situations. When the Phineas Gage's of this world need to operate in reality, the decision-making process is minimally influenced by old knowledge.

Another important aspect of Gage's story is the discrepancy between the degenerated character and the intactness of the several instruments of mind—attention, perception, memory, language, intelligence. In this type of discrepancy, known in neuropsychology as *dissociation*, one or more performances within a general profile of operations are at odds with the rest. In Gage's case the impaired character was dissociated from the otherwise intact cognition and behavior. In other patients, with lesions elsewhere in the brain, language may be the impaired aspect, while character and all other cognitive aspects remain intact; language is then the "dissociated" ability. Subsequent study of patients similar to Gage has confirmed that his specific dissociation profile occurs consistently.

It must have been hard to believe that the character change would not resolve itself, and at first even Dr. Harlow resisted admitting that the change was permanent. This is understandable, since the most dramatic elements in Gage's story were his very survival, and then his survival without a defect that would more easily meet the eye: paralysis, for example, or a speech defect, or memory loss. Somehow, emphasizing Gage's newly developed social shortcomings smacked of ingratitude to both providence and medicine. By 1868, however, Dr. Harlow was ready to acknowledge the full extent of his patient's personality change.

Gage's survival was duly noted, but with the caution reserved for freakish phenomena. The significance of his behavioral changes was largely lost. There were good reasons for this neglect. Even in the small world of brain science at the time, two camps were beginning to form. One held that psychological functions such as language or memory could never be traced to a particular region of the brain. If one had to accept, reluctantly, that the brain did produce the mind, it did so as a whole and not as a collection of parts with special functions. The other camp held that, on the contrary, the brain did have specialized parts and those parts generated separate mind functions. The rift between the two camps was not merely indicative of the infancy of brain research; the argument endured for another century and, to a certain extent, is still with us today.

Whatever scientific debate Phineas Gage's story elicited, it focused on the issue of localizing language and movement in the brain. The debate never turned to the connection between impaired social conduct and frontal lobe damage. I am reminded here of a saying of Warren McCulloch's: "When I point, look where I point, not at my finger." (McCulloch, a legendary neurophysiologist and a pioneer in the field that would become computational neuroscience, was also a poet and a prophet. This saying was usually part of a prophecy.) Few looked to where Gage was unwittingly pointing. It is of course difficult to imagine anybody in Gage's day with the knowledge *and* the courage to look in the proper direction. It was acceptable that the brain sectors whose damage would have caused Gage's heart to stop pumping and his lungs to stop breathing had not been touched by the iron rod. It was also acceptable that the brain sectors which control wakefulness were far from the iron's course and were thus spared. It was even acceptable that the injury did not render Gage unconscious for a long period. (The event anticipated what is current knowledge from studies of head injuries: The style of the injury is a critical variable. A severe blow to the head, even if no bone is broken and no weapon penetrates the brain, can cause a major disruption of wakefulness for a long time; the forces unleashed by the blow disorganize brain function profoundly. A penetrating injury in which the forces are concentrated on a narrow and steady path, rather than dissipate and accelerate the brain against the skull, may cause dysfunction only where brain tissue is actually destroyed, and thus spare brain function elsewhere.) But to understand Gage's behavioral change would have meant believing that normal social conduct required a particular corresponding brain region, and this concept was far more unthinkable than its equivalent for movement, the senses, or even language.

Gage's case was used, in fact, by those who did not believe that mind functions could be linked to specific brain areas. They took a cursory view of the medical evidence and claimed that if such a wound as Gage's could fail to produce paralysis or speech impairments, then it was obvious that neither motor control nor language could be traced to the relatively small brain regions that neurologists had identified as motor and language centers. They argued—in complete error, as we shall see—that Gage's wound directly damaged those centers.

The British physiologist David Ferrier was one of the few to take the trouble to analyze the findings with competence and wisdom. Ferrier's knowledge of other cases of brain lesion with behavioral changes, as well as his own pioneering experiments on electrical stimulation and ablation of the cerebral cortex in animals, had placed him in a unique position to appreciate Harlow's findings. He concluded that the wound spared motor and language "centers," that it did damage the part of the brain he himself had called the prefrontal cortex, and that such damage might be related to Gage's peculiar change in personality, to which Ferrier referred, picturesquely, as "mental degradation." The only supportive voices Harlow and Ferrier may have heard, in their very separate worlds, came from the followers of phrenology.

A LANDMARK BY HINDSIGHT

There is no question that Gage's personality change was caused by a circumscribed brain lesion in a specific site. But that explanation would not be apparent until two decades after the accident, and it became vaguely acceptable only in this century. For a long time, most everybody, John Harlow included, believed that "the portion of the brain traversed, was, for several reasons, the best fitted of any part of the cerebral substance to sustain the injury": in other words, a part of the brain that did nothing much and was thus expendable. But nothing could be further from the truth, as Harlow himself realized. He wrote in 1868 that Gage's mental recovery "was only partial, his intellectual faculties being decidedly impaired, but not totally lost; nothing like dementia, but they were enfeebled in their manifestations, his mental operations being perfect in kind, but not in degree or quantity." The unintentional message in Gage's case was that observing social convention, behaving ethically, and making decisions advantageous to one's survival and progress require knowledge of rules and strategies *and* the integrity of specific brain systems. The problem with this message was that it lacked the evidence required to make it understandable and definitive. Instead the message became a mystery and came down to us as the "enigma" of frontal lobe function. Gage posed more questions than he gave answers.

To begin with, all we knew about Gage's brain lesion was that it was probably in the frontal lobe. That is a bit like saying that Chicago is probably in the United States—accurate but not very specific or helpful. Granted that the damage was likely to involve the frontal lobe, where exactly was it within that region? The left lobe? The right? Both? Somewhere else too? As you will see in the next chapter, new imaging technologies have helped us come up with the answer to this puzzle.

Then there was the nature of Gage's character defect. How did the abnormality develop? The primary cause, sure enough, was a hole in the head, but that just tells why the defect arose, not how. Might a hole anywhere in the frontal lobe have the same result? Whatever the answer, by what plausible means can destruction of a brain region change personality? If there are specific regions in the frontal lobe, what are they made of, and how do they operate in an intact brain? Are they some kind of "center" for social behavior? Are they modules selected in evolution, filled with problem-solving algorithms ready to tell us how to reason and make decisions? How do these modules, if that is what they are, interact with the environment during development to permit normal reasoning and decision making? Or are there in fact no such modules?

What were the mechanisms behind Gage's failure at decision making? It might be that the knowledge required to reason through a problem was destroyed or rendered inaccessible, so that he no longer could decide appropriately. It is possible also that the requisite knowledge remained intact and accessible but the strategies for reasoning were compromised. If this was the case which reasoning steps were missing? More to the point, which steps are there for those who are allegedly normal? And if we are fortunate enough to glean the nature of some of these steps, what are their neural underpinnings?

Intriguing as all these questions are, they may not be as important as those which surround Gage's status as a human being. May he be described as having free will? Did he have a sense of right and wrong, or was he the victim of his new brain design, such that his decisions were imposed upon him and inevitable? Was he responsible for his acts? If we rule that he was not, does this tell us something about responsibility in more general terms? There are many Gages around us, people whose fall from social grace is disturbingly similar. Some have brain damage consequent to brain tumors, or head injury, or other neurological disease. Yet some have had no overt neurological disease and they still behave like Gage, for reasons having to do with their brains or with the society into which they were born. We need to understand the nature of these human beings whose actions can be destructive to themselves and to others, if we are to solve humanely the problems they pose. Neither incarceration nor the death penalty—among the responses that society currently offers for those individuals—contribute to our understanding or solve the problem. In fact, we should take the question further and inquire about our own responsibility when we "normal" individuals slip into the irrationality that marked Phineas Gage's great fall.

Gage lost something uniquely human, the ability to plan his future as a social being. How aware was he of this loss? Might he be described as self-conscious in the same sense that you and I are? Is it fair to say that his soul was diminished, or that he had lost his soul? And if so, what would Descartes have thought had he known about Gage and had he had the knowledge of neurobiology we now have? Would he have inquired about Gage's pineal gland?

PHYSICALISM OR THE THREE-POUND MIND

By Barbara Montero

Methinks that what they call my shadow here on earth is my true substance. Methinks that in looking at things spiritual, we are too much like oysters observing the sun through the water, and thinking that thick water the thinnest of air.

—HERMAN MELVILLE,
MOBY DICK (1851)

I like nonsense; it wakes up the brain cells.

—DR. SEUSS

In treating people with severe epilepsy, the Canadian neurosurgeon Wilder Penfield (1891–1976) would destroy the area of the brain that he thought was causing the epileptic seizures. To discover what area this was, Penfield would stimulate various parts of the patient's brain with a mild electrical current. Since the brain has no sensory nerves of its own, this was done while the individual was awake. What he found was quite interesting. When certain parts of the brain were stimulated, patients would have very specific memories. For example, each time one group of neurons was stimulated, a patient would remember, say, the smell of her grandmother's attic; each time another group was stimulated, she would recall a certain tune. Does this indicate that memory is just the activity of neurons?

Or more generally, does this present a good case for the view that mental processes are physical, a view philosophers call "physicalism"?

Let's look at another example. Certain people suffer from what is called "obsessive-compulsive disorder" (OCD). These individuals are unable to put certain thoughts out of their minds, and they feel compelled to perform certain actions. All of us sometimes wonder whether we left the stove on and feel compelled to go back and check, but the sufferer of OCD will need to do this perhaps a hundred times. Others with OCD might need to wash their hands over and over again. The disease manifests itself in different ways. I actually knew someone with OCD, and the strange way it manifested itself in him was that while driving, he had to constantly stop and check to see if he had run over anyone; driving along one block, he would need to go back and examine the street for dead bodies at least ten or twenty times. For my friend, as well as for others with this disorder, certain drugs seem to eliminate these obsessive thoughts entirely. Since the drugs act on the brain, and the obsession has to do with the mind, does the effectiveness of such drugs indicate that physicalism must be correct?

These are rather tricky questions. It may be that stimulating a certain group of neurons consistently causes a certain perception, yet this alone does not show that the perception and the neuronal activity are one and the same thing. A thrown rock may cause the breaking of a window, and yet the thrown rock and the breaking window are distinct. Similarly, while it may be that changes in the brain brought about by certain drugs affect the mind, this does not show that the changes in the brain and the changes in the mind are one and the same thing. With OCD, obsessive thoughts may be subdued once the person takes the medication, but this doesn't show that the obsessive thought (for example, that the stove must be checked) is just the activity of the brain area affected by the drug. It could be that the neural activity causes the obsessive thoughts but is not one and the same thing as them. So our evidence that neural processes cause mental processes is not alone evidence that certain mental processes are nothing more than certain neural processes.

Nonetheless, you might think that there is still something telling about these cases. And if so, you may be implicitly assuming a principle of reasoning philosophers call Occam's razor, which in one form states that if we have two different explanations for a phenomenon and both explain all the data, the simpler one is more likely to be true. With the OCD example, the data indicates that certain drugs act on the brain to prevent obsessive thoughts and the compulsive actions that result from these thoughts. One explanation is that the drugs are affecting parts of the brain that are those thoughts. Another explanation is that the drugs are affecting parts of the brain that produce those thoughts, but that the thoughts are distinct from the brain. Which explanation is simpler? Well, the second explanation requires us to posit that neural activity can cause changes in a nonphysical mind, while the first explanation merely identifies the thoughts with neural activity. And so the first would seem to be simpler. Similarly, with the epilepsy example, if we say that when Penfield stimulated various brain regions, what happened was that those stimulations affected the mind, a question remains about just how this causation is supposed to have proceeded. To say that the neural activity and the tune playing through your head are one and the same thing eliminates the need for explaining this causal relation, and so would be a simpler explanation.

There is another form of Occam's razor that leads to a similar conclusion. This version of the principle states that when we have two different explanations that both account for all the data, the explanation that posits the fewest entities ought to be preferred, or as it is often expressed aphoristically: Do not multiply entities beyond necessity. In understanding the relation between obsessive thoughts and OCD drugs, we do not need to posit nonphysical mental processes. Since we don't, the principle implies that such processes do not exist.

Are these arguments for physicalism based on Occam's razor convincing? There are a few things to consider before arriving at an answer to this question. For example, is Occam's razor a reasonable principle? Could it be that sometimes the correct theory is not the simpler theory? The principle in the second form says "don't multiply entities beyond necessity," but perhaps there just are more things in the world than need be. (Thoughts along these lines led my dissertation advisor, Bill Wimsatt, to call Occam's razor "Occam's eraser," since, as he saw it, it led us to try to eliminate things that actually exist.) Moreover, even if we do accept Occam's razor, Occam's razor is only a method for choosing between two explanations that explain all the data. But could it be that there are some kinds of data—concerning, for instance, the nature of thoughts—that we cannot account for when we identify thoughts with activity in the brain? Or could it be that nonphysical minds are needed in the world?

If, however, we accept that the obsessive thoughts are distinct from the brain processes, we need to make sense of how to account for causation between physical brains and nonphysical minds. The question of how to account for causation between the brain and mind given dualism was posed to Descartes (who, as we saw in an earlier chapter, argues for dualism based on the idea that he can clearly and distinctly imagine mind without brain and brain without mind) by Princess Elizabeth of Bohemia. Descartes held that mind is "immaterial," meaning that it is pure conscious experience that, as he saw it, takes up no space at all. Moreover, he held that all material things are extended in space. Princess Elizabeth pointed out, however, that it is difficult to see how there could be causal interaction between the mind and the body if this were so. How, for example, could the pain I feel on pressing my finger against a thorn cause me to pull my hand away, if the arm movement is extended in space and the pain is not? How could my desire for a drink of water cause me to go and find some water? Or how could a blow to the head cause a loss of consciousness? All these causal processes are difficult to understand if the mind takes up no space. This question was especially difficult for Descartes to answer, since he thought that for causation to occur, the cause and effect must be in contact with each other, much as a ball is in contact with a racket; and as you can imagine, a ball that takes up space and a racket that does not would not make for a very good game.

Today the problem of understanding how mind and body can causally affect each other does not appear in quite the same form for dualists, and so Princess Elizabeth's criticism of Descartes does not lead inexorably to physicalism. One reason for this is that we no longer think that causation requires contact. Two magnets, for example, can attract each other even if separated in space, and gravity works to pull a soaring baseball back down to the ground. What does causation require, then, if it doesn't require force on contact? This is another big question that has led to an area of philosophical inquiry all its own. But for our purposes here, we can just note that we should not reject dualism simply because it presents us with a difficult picture of causation between mind and body.

Causation, at least as we now understand it, does not seem to require contact. It is also not clear that dualism must be rejected and physicalism accepted because dualists cannot account for how a non-spatial mind can affect a spatial body. The reason for this is that dualists need not be committed to the idea that the mind takes up no space. Certainly dualists hold that the mind is not physical or material, but what exactly does this mean? Must everything that takes up space be physical? Must anything that does not take up space be nonphysical? It is not obvious that dualists must answer these questions in the affirmative.

Another argument that one comes across for physicalism is that dualism is incompatible with the conservation-of-energy law, the law of physics that states that the total energy of any closed system is always conserved. If this were true, this would be bad news for dualists, since the conservation-of-energy law is a bedrock principle in physics, a principle that has achieved both broad theoretical and experimental support. But is dualism inconsistent with the conservation-of-energy law? The reason some think so is that, as they see it, if dualism is correct, then the mind can affect physical objects in such a way as to violate the conservation of energy; that is, it is thought that nonphysical, mental intervention in the physical world would violate the conservation-of-energy law, since nonphysical, mental intervention would create new energy in the physical world.

Dualists, however, have a ready response to this line of reasoning and that is to say that the mental energy acts conservatively; that is, it doesn't create new energy but is just a new form of energy. Thus, the situation that would result if we were to discover mental energy would not be so different from the situation in 1930 when the German physicist Wolfgang Pauli rectified certain apparent violations of the laws of conservation of energy and momentum by positing a new, virtually unobservable form of energy, the neutrino. Along these lines, if we found that mind-body causal interactions violated the conservation laws, this could lead us to posit a new form of energy, mental energy. So it seems that accepting the conservation-of-energy law does not preclude one from being a dualist.

Fortunately for the physicalist, there are other routes to physicalism apart from the conservation of energy. For example, you might reason that while we are far from understanding the details of how the universe evolved, we are fairly certain that the universe began with fundamental physical particles, which by combining in various ways through chance and natural selection resulted in this amazingly complex yet entirely physical world we live in today. Now, where in this story is there room for the nonphysical mental? It would seem that if there are nonphysical minds, then either they or their basic non-physical parts were there from the start in the big bang or they were inserted somewhere along the line. But, say the physicalists, it seems unlikely that either of these situations occurred. It may be, as is hypothesized by astrophysicists that hydrogen was created in the big bang, but minds were not. And as for mind being inserted somewhere along the line, the physicalists will reject this view, too, arguing perhaps that evidence for this is entirely lacking.

Of course, if minds have evolved out of physical particles, it is also true that at some point, though perhaps a fuzzy one, minds entered the universe. However, this is not the sense of "entering the universe" that the dualist has in mind. The dualistic mind's entrance is rather grander, since it has no precedence. For the dualist, the process of evolution that rearranges physical particles could not account for mind. If mind were constituted entirely of physical particles, it would be physical; but according to the dualist, mind is not physical. And it is the dramatic entrance of mind that the physicalist rejects. So the idea that the mind evolved out of physical particles provides a reason to accept physicalism.

A variation of the argument for physicalism from evolution gets its ammunition from ontogeny rather than phylogeny. For it seems that a human being develops out of the combination of an entirely physical sperm and an entirely physical egg, and that each step along the way from fertilized egg to fully mature adult involves nothing but physical changes. This would seem to imply physicalism, since the alternative explanations for fetal development are unacceptable. (Or they are, at least, according to the physicalists.) What are these alternative explanations? One alternative is the idea that the mind developed from increasingly complex physical components in the sperm and egg, that is, that the mental in a primitive form had to already be in either the sperm or the egg or both. Another alternative is that the mind was inserted at the point of conception. And still another alternative is that it was inserted suddenly (not gradually as would be the case if the mental developed out of physical components) sometime during fetal development. According to physicalists, however, there is no evidence for any of these possibilities.

But does our scientific evidence really comprise evidence against these possibilities? What we seem to have is the absence of evidence for mentality existing in the sperm or egg, for mentality being inserted suddenly into a fetus, for mentality coming out of the big bang, and so forth. But what does the absence of evidence show? Sometimes the absence of evidence is evidence of an absence. For example, we reject the idea that ghosts exist in part because we have never found anything that could be identified as a ghost. On the other hand, there also seem to be cases where failure to find evidence for something should not be interpreted as evidence that that thing does not exist. For example, the fact that I've never seen bats in my cellar is not good evidence that there are none if I've only been in my cellar during the day.

Dualists might think that the lack of evidence for these possibilities is no different: It may be that we merely have been looking for nonphysical minds in the wrong way, or perhaps we just haven't searched long enough. Moreover, since dualists believe that there are good reasons to take the mind to be nonphysical, the mere lack of evidence for non-physical minds does not incline them to accept physicalism. If you have a good reason to think that something must be true, then despite the lack of evidence for it, you hold onto your belief.

The most widely discussed argument for physicalism, however, is not any of the arguments we have just canvassed. Rather, it is an argument called the "causal argument for physicalism," which proceeds like this. If physicalism is false, the mind is like a ghost in a machine, a ghost who flips various switches in the machine, causing our physical bodies to move. However, we have good reason to believe that all these switches are flipped on or off by other physical parts of the machine. We have good reason, for example, to think that if you move your arm forward to reach for a glass of water, your arm moves because of what is going on in your central nervous system. This is the physical story (the machine). And since it is absurd to think that the switches are doubly flipped by both the machine and the ghost, we should conclude that there is no ghost in the machine—that the mental causes of our bodily movements are themselves physical parts of the machine.

Is there a ghost in the machine? That is, is there an immaterial mind or soul, working away doing tasks that do not even need to be done? Some dualists think that there is, claiming that there is no reason to reject the idea that our bodily movements are doubly caused, once by the central nervous system and once by the immaterial mind. Others reject the idea that the machine (that is, the body) is capable of flipping all the switches on its own, so that immaterial mind is needed in order to complete the job. And still others claim that the immaterial mind, although it exists, does no causal work at all, or at least does not cause anything to happen in the physical world.

What then are we to conclude? In this chapter, we have looked at a number of arguments for physicalism, that is, for the view that the mind is a physical part of the body.

PROJECT SUGGESTIONS

Put yourself in the brain surgeon Wilder Penfield's shoes by applying a virtual brain probe to an exposed brain at "Probe the Brain," online at http://www.pbs.org/wgbh/aso/tryit/brain/.

PART VI

Personal Identity

PERSONAL IDENTITY

By Marya Schechtman

I magine the following scenario: I am supposed to meet my friend Mary for lunch in a crowded restaurant. Arriving twenty minutes late, I wonder if she will still be there. She hates to be kept waiting, and told me that she will leave after waiting ten minutes. With some relief I hear her calling my name from a table across the room. "I should have left like I threatened," she says, "but I was too hungry."

There is nothing remarkable in this story, least of all the fact that I am able to tell that the person with whom I finally sit down to eat is my friend, Mary. Many of our everyday activities involve re-identifying other people. Without the capacity to make quick and (usually) accurate judgments about when we are dealing with the same person at two different times, we could not do much of what we do. When we stop to ask what it is that actually *makes* someone the same person at two different times, however, it is surprisingly difficult to find a satisfying answer.

In the story described above various cues indicate that the person with whom I am lunching is the friend with whom I made the plan to lunch. Some of these have to do with evidence that the human being at the table is the same human being with whom I made the plan—her voice sounds like Mary's and she looks like Mary. Other cues have more to do with evidence that the person in the restaurant is psychologically continuous with my friend—this person obviously remembers making a lunch date with me and threatening to leave if I was late; I will undoubtedly also find that she remembers a great deal of Mary's past and in other ways demonstrates a psychological life continuous with the person with whom

I made my plans. All of these factors taken together present me with such strong reasons to believe that this is Mary that it is almost misleading to say that I *judge* this person to be Mary; it will almost certainly never enter my mind that she might not be.

But what if we imagine circumstances in which the various features that reveal this person to be Mary diverge? Suppose, for instance, that upon entering the restaurant I hear Mary's voice, and look over to the table where I see someone I recognize as Mary. When I go over to join her however, she has no idea who I am. Seeing her up-close and getting a good look at the distinctive birthmark on her hand, I am convinced that this human being is the same human being I have known as my friend Mary. But she denies having ever seen me before and acts nothing like Mary.

My immediate reaction would likely be to assume that the individual sitting at the table is Mary, suffering from some terrible psychological disorder. Suppose further, however, that when I leave the restaurant, wondering how to find help for my friend, someone I have never seen before rushes up to me in a panic. She insists that she is Mary and that she and the person now in her body were kidnapped by an evil philosopher-neurosurgeon who subjected them to an experimental brain transplant procedure. Mary's brain was transplanted to the body now speaking to me, while the brain taken from that body was placed in Mary's old body, the one now sitting in the restaurant. Were it not for the strange experience in the restaurant, I would probably dismiss these claims as insane. But the behavior of the person in the restaurant makes me wonder, so I talk to this "stranger" a bit longer and find that she reacts to things just as Mary would, remembers parts of our history that only Mary and I know about, and otherwise convinces me that her inner life is indeed continuous with Mary's. I therefore come to believe that this incredible story is true, and that Mary's psychological life has become decoupled from her body.

This case is highly fanciful and probably impossible. Still, it does seem to reveal something important. It demonstrates the need to distinguish between the criteria we use to *determine* when we are dealing with the same person (*epistemic* criteria of identity) and what actually *makes* the person the same person we encountered before (*metaphysical* criteria of identity). In everyday life the continuation of a single human being and of a psychological life usually coincide. Where we find one we typically find the other, and so we use both (or either) to make our judgments of identity. This leaves it unclear which of these types of continuity is mere evidence of sameness of person and which (if either) is what actually constitutes this sameness.

Hypothetical cases of the sort I have described, where the continuities that usually occur together come apart, can serve as thought experiments to help determine which (if any) of the many kinds of continuity we use to make judgments of personal identity can provide a metaphysical identity criterion. The two most salient possibilities are those mentioned above—psychological continuity and biological continuity. Much of the philosophical discussion of personal identity is thus devoted to investigating these two types of continuity and arguing about which is the relation that constitutes personal identity.

PSYCHOLOGICAL CONTINUITY THEORIES

It is generally (but not universally) agreed that hypothetical cases like the scenario described above provide good evidence that it is psychological and not biological continuity that constitutes personal identity. It is natural to describe such a case as one in which Mary and another person have switched bodies. If my friendship with Mary continues it will continue with the person in the unfamiliar body. It seems fair that this is the person who should have access to Mary's hard-earned savings, live in the house she paid for, and continue in her job. If, after explaining the brain transplant, the evil philosopher-neurosurgeon tells his captives that one of them will be set free and the other kept for further experimentation, Mary will have reason to hope (from a self-interested perspective) that the person with her psychological life and the other woman's body is the person who is released. All in all, then, when biological and psychological continuity diverge in Mary's case, it seems that *Mary* goes with the psychological and not the biological life.

Psychological continuity theories have been the most widely defended theories of this topic, through much of the modern discussion of personal identity, and they are frequently defended using cases such as the one I described. It is important to be clear at the outset, however, that the psychological continuity theory is *not* the view that persons are immaterial souls or that the persistence of a person depends upon the continuation of a single soul. Although historically several philosophers have defined personal identity in terms of sameness of soul, there are few philosophers writing today who defend such a view. One of the reasons for this is that sameness of soul does not seem to guarantee the kind of psychological continuity we are looking for. John Locke (1975), who is taken by most to be the progenitor of modern psychological continuity theories, uses hypothetical cases to reveal that psychological continuity can diverge from sameness of soul as well as from sameness of human body. The soul as it is understood in this context is an immaterial substratum that is the locus of thought and experience. Each experience is the experience of some soul, but as far as we know there is nothing that necessitates that what is experienced as a single stream of consciousness implies the involvement of one and only one soul. The soul that starts a thought might be replaced midway through with another soul who has a memory of the beginning of the thought and goes on to complete it. There would be no way to detect such a change, and for all we know it is happening constantly in what we introspectively experience as a single stream of consciousness. On the other hand, a person's current soul may once have supported a completely different stream of consciousness to which he currently has no access at all—it might, to use Locke's example, have been the soul of Nestor or Thersites at the siege of Troy without him having any consciousness of either of their actions. Psychological continuity is no more clearly coextensive with sameness of soul than it is with sameness of human being.

Psychological continuity theorists thus seek to define personal identity not in terms of the continuity of an immaterial substance, but directly in terms of psychological relations. Those who defend these views thus need to describe in more detail the kinds of psychological relations that constitute personal identity.

A natural starting point for this endeavor is Locke's view. Locke says that it is sameness of consciousness that makes a person at one time the same person as a person at another time. It is generally believed that what he has in mind when he talks about "sameness of consciousness" is the kind of connection built by autobiographical memories. The view, interpreted this way, thus says that it is my remembering past experiences that makes them part of my consciousness and so makes me the person who had those experiences.

It is not entirely clear that this is exactly what Locke meant. What is clear, however, is that a simple memory theory is vulnerable to serious objections that prevent it from providing a viable account of personal identity. One important objection (attributed to Joseph Butler [1975]) charges the memory theory with circularity. This objection points out that the memory theory cannot very well claim that every experience I *think* I remember is my experience. Someone who is delusional might think that she remembers the experiences of Joan of Arc, but she would be mistaken. The memory theory is not even remotely plausible unless it says that in order for a past experience to be mine I must genuinely remember it, and not just have an experience that is phenomenologically *like* a memory. The problem is that the distinction between a genuine memory and a delusional memory-like experience seems to be that in the former case the experience remembered is one I actually experienced and in the latter it is one I wrongly believe myself to have experienced. This means that genuine memory is defined in terms of personal identity, and defining identity in terms of genuine memory is viciously circular.

A second significant objection (attributed to Thomas Reid 1975) is that the memory theory leads to absurdities. This is because we can forget what we once knew. At age thirty, a man may remember well something that he did when he was ten. At age fifty, he may remember well what he did at thirty, but have no recollection whatsoever of what he did at age ten. According to the memory theory, the thirty-year-old's memories of the ten-year-old's experiences make them the same person, and the fifty-year-old's memories of the thirty-year-old's experiences make them the same person. By the transitivity of identity (the rule that if *A* is identical to *B*, and B is identical to *C*, *A* must be identical to *C*), this means that the fifty-year-old and the ten-year-old are the same person. But the fifty-year-old does not remember any of the experiences of the ten-year-old, so the memory theory also says they are not the same person. Since the fifty-year-old and ten-year-old cannot both be and not be the same person, the memory theory is absurd.

These two objections, among others, are generally taken to be deadly to the memory theory. In the last several decades, however, philosofphers convinced by the arguments in favor of a psychological account of identity have attempted to rehabilitate the basic Lockean insights into a more plausible view. To answer Butler's circularity objection, these theorists define a notion of "quasi-memory." Someone has a quasi-memory of a past event if (1) she has a memory-like experience of the event; and (2) the memory-like experience is caused in the right kind of way by the event remembered. The "right kind of cause" is usually defined in terms of the ordinary physical mechanism for laying down memories. All genuine memories are quasi-memories. In principle, however, someone could have a quasi-memory of an experience that was not her own, yet is nonetheless (because of its causal link to the original event) not delusional (e.g. if a neurosurgeon could transplant a single memory trace into another brain, giving the recipient a quasi-memory of someone else's experience). Psychological continuity theorists then define identity in terms of quasi-memories rather than genuine memories, thereby avoiding circularity.

To answer Reid's objection, psychological theorists define identity in terms of overlapping chains of direct memory connections rather than direct connections alone. For a person at time t_2 to be the same person as a person at time t_1 she need not directly remember any experiences of the person at t_1 but only directly remember experiences of a person who directly remembers experiences of a person, etc., who directly remembers experiences of the person at t_1.

THE BIOLOGICAL APPROACH

The psychological approach is not, of course, the only possible approach to questions of personal identity. In everyday life we rely upon both biological and psychological continuity to make judgments of personal identity. Despite the dominance of the psychological approach, there have always been some who have defended the view that it is biological rather than psychological continuity that actually constitutes personal identity.

Early versions of this approach tend to argue that personal identity consists in sameness of *body*. For a variety of reasons, including the difficulty of providing a precise definition of what a body is and of what makes for sameness of body, more recent instances tend to place identity in *biological* rather than *physical* continuity. This means that instead of saying that identity depends upon the continuity of a physical body, these views hold that it consists in the continuity of a single organic life, that "one survives just in case one's purely biological functions—metabolism, the capacity to breath and to circulate one's blood, and the like—continue" (Olson 1997: 16).

Arguments for the biological approach generally focus on the difficulty psychological theories have explaining the relation between persons and human animals. All of the uncontroversial examples of persons are human persons like us, and so biological theorists focus on persons who are also humans. Since the psychological approach tells us that persons and human animals have different persistence conditions, it follows that persons and human animals must be distinct entities; no person can be identical to any human animal. If this is the case, biological theorists say, defenders of psychological views owe us an explanation of exactly what relation a person has to the human animal with which he is associated. When I converse with a human person, who is talking, the animal or the person? If it is the person, something more must be said about how it is that the animal fails to speak when its vocal cords vibrate and air is moving through its lungs. Psychological theories have similar difficulties unpacking such ordinary sentences as "I am 5′ 7″

tall" or "I am an animal," or "I was once a fetus." If the person is not identical to the human animal these sentences must be false, but it seems obvious that they are true.

Eric Olson (1997), one of the foremost defenders of the biological approach, argues that psychological continuity theories fall into these difficulties because they confuse metaphysical and practical questions of personal identity. Hypothetical cases like the brain transplant case do show that moral responsibility, egoistic concern, and other practical matters are associated with psychological rather than biological continuity, but this does not show that *identity* must be associated with psychological continuity. Olson argues that there is no reason to assume that the relation that defines our literal persistence should also be the relation that we find most practically important. If we look at the question of what constitutes the continuity of a human person in purely metaphysical terms, Olson says, the biological view is far more compelling than the psychological view. Not only does the biological view avoid the difficulties the psychological approach encounters, it makes our persistence conditions like those of other animals, and accurately reflects our place in the natural order.

Olson is, however, committed to showing how the intuitions behind the psychological approach can be accommodated within the biological theory. To do this, he makes use of the distinction between "phase sortals" and "substance concepts." A substance concept is, roughly, the description of a concrete particular that must continue to apply if that particular is to continue at all; phase sortals are descriptions that apply during some phase in the existence of a particular continuing substance. Phase sortals include things like "athlete," "mother," "student," and "child." We believe that a single individual can be at one time an athlete, mother, student, or child, and at another time fail to be any of these things, while remaining the same entity. Things are otherwise with substance concepts to borrow an example from P. F. Snowdon (1990), the Monty Python skit in which something is introduced as an "ex-parrot" is comical precisely because we do not believe that something that is a parrot can cease to be a parrot without ceasing to exist. "Parrot" is a substance concept.

The real metaphysical question about our identity, according to Olson, is whether our substance concept is "person" or "human animal." Reflection shows that the former is problematic when taken as a substance concept, and the latter far more viable. The insights generated by the hypothetical cases that support the psychological approach can be respected, however, if we recognize that "personhood," defined in terms of higher order psychological capacities, is a phase sortal of human animals. Most humans enjoy this phase for most of their lives, but some do not. Someone who falls into an irreversible vegetative state, for instance, loses consciousness forever, and so ceases to be a person. Since the basic metabolic functions continue in such a state the human animal continues but is no longer a person, something whose coherence the psychological approach must deny. Calling the question with which we start the "problem of personal identity" is misleading, according to Olson, since this implies that it is the question of what is required for a person at one time to be identical to a *person* at another time. The more interesting metaphysical question is the question of what is required for someone who is a person at one time to be identical to *anything* at another time. "Personal identity" is no more a metaphysical question than "athlete identity" or "president identity;" the question is the question of *our* identity, and this is best answered in biological terms.

Biological views are, naturally, subject to many challenges and objections. Since this approach has only recently come to be widely discussed, the objections and replies are not as systematically developed as in the case of the psychological approach. Nonetheless they are very instructive. Some objections to the biological account are internal to the view. When biological continuity or the persistence conditions for human animals are spelled out in detail biological views have implications which may be just as counterintuitive as those of psychological views. Other responses to the biological approach reject its claim that psychological views are implausible, arguing, for instance, that psychological theorists can provide a perfectly coherent account of the relation between persons and humans by saying that persons are *constituted* by human animals in something very like the way statues are constituted by the marble out of which they are sculpted. Finally, the biological approach depends upon a number of controversial metaphysical positions, including the rejection of four-dimensionalism and the assumption that each concrete particular has exactly one set of persistence conditions. The view can thus be criticized by attacking these presuppositions.

The debate between biological and psychological theorists is likely to continue for some time. The emergence of the biological approach as a powerful competitor to psychological views has, however, added an important dimension to the current debate on personal identity, raising fruitful questions that have been largely neglected in recent years.

There are many aspects of the personal identity debate that crisscross the issues described here. Questions arise, for instance, about what role social and environmental factors play in determining facts about personal identity. Theorists of practical identity engage in discussions of personal identity and its relation to autonomy in work on practical reasoning. These discussions do not claim to be about metaphysical problems of identity, but they do intersect metaphysical concerns at several points, and it is important to gain more clarity about how these two investigations of identity are related.

One theme that runs through almost every aspect of work on personal identity is the need to understand the connection between practical and metaphysical questions of personal identity. As we have seen, some theorists presume that we must start with the practical facts and use them as data against which to test proposed metaphysical accounts. Others argue that the metaphysical question should be settled on its own terms, and that practice must conform to our metaphysical conclusions if it is to be rational. Still others see the practical and metaphysical questions as entirely independent issues which are often confused and must be sharply separated. The challenge from the biological approach to identity has helped to push these issues to the fore, and it is to be expected that an increasing amount of work will focus directly on questions about how metaphysical and practical concerns about identity should interact. The problem of personal identity is so compelling, and so complicated, because judgments of identity play such an important role in everyday life. Understanding this importance and its role in defining identity will undoubtedly be a central part of the ongoing philosophical investigation of personal identity.

REFERENCES

Butler, J. (1975) "of Personal Identity," in J. Perry (ed.) *Personal Identity*, Berkeley: University of California Press, pp. 99–106.

Locke, J. (1975) *An Essay Concerning Human Understanding*, ed. P. Nidditch, Oxford: Clarendon Press.

Olson, E. (1997) *The Human Animal: Personal Identity Without Psychology*, New York: Oxford University Press.

Parfit, D. (1984) *Reasons and Persons*, Oxford: Clarendon Press.

Perry, J. (1976) "The Importance of Being Identical," in A. Rorty, ed., *The Identities of Persons*, Berkeley and Los Angeles: University of California Press, pp. 67–90.

Reid, T. (1975) "of Mr. Locke's Account of Our Personal Identity," in J. Perry (ed.), *Personal Identity*, Berkeley: University of California Press, pp. 113–18.

Snowdon, P. F. (1990) "Person, Animals, and Ourselves," in C. Gill (ed.), *The Person and the Human Mind: Issues in Ancient and Modern Philosophy*, Oxford: Clarendon Press, pp. 83–107.

AN ESSAY CONCERNING HUMAN UNDERSTANDING

By John Locke

CHAPTER XXVII
OF IDENTITY AND DIVERSITY

The identity of the same man consists ... in nothing but a participation of the same continued life, by constantly fleeting particles of matter, in succession vitally united to the same organized body. He that shall place the identity of man in anything else, but, like that of other animals, in one fitly organized body, taken in any one instant, and from thence continued, under one organization of life, in several successively fleeting particles of matter united to it, will find it hard to make an embryo, one of years, mad and sober, the same man, by any supposition, that will not make it possible for Seth, Ismael, Socrates, Pilate, St. Austin, and Caesar Borgia, to be the same man. For if the identity of soul alone makes the same man; and there be nothing in the nature of matter why the same individual spirit may not be united to different bodies, it will be possible that those men, living in distant ages, and of different tempers, may have been the same man: which way of speaking must be from a very strange use of the word man, applied to an idea out of which body and shape are excluded. And that way of speaking would agree yet worse with the notions of those philosophers who allow of transmigration, and are of opinion that the souls of men may, for their miscarriages, be detruded into the bodies of beasts, as fit habitations, with organs suited to the satisfaction of their brutal inclinations. But yet I think nobody, could he be sure that the soul of Heliogabalus were in one of his hogs, would yet say that hog were a man or Heliogabalus....

An animal is a living organized body; and consequently the same animal, as we have observed, is the same continued life communicated to different particles of matter, as they happen successively to be united to that organized living body. And whatever is talked of other definitions, ingenious observation puts it past doubt, that the idea in our minds, of which the sound man in our mouths is the sign, is nothing else but of an animal of such a certain form. Since I think I may be confident, that, whoever should see a creature of his own shape or make, though it had no more reason all its life than a cat or a parrot, would call him still a man; or whoever should hear a cat or a parrot discourse, reason, and philosophize, would call or think it nothing but a cat or a parrot; and say, the one was a dull irrational man, and the other a very intelligent rational parrot.

For I presume it is not the idea of a thinking or rational being alone that makes the idea of a man in most people's sense: but of a body, so and so shaped, joined to it: and if that be the idea of a man, the same successive body not shifted all at once, must, as well as the same immaterial spirit, go to the making of the same man.

This being premised, to find wherein personal identity consists, we must consider what *person* stands for;—which, I think, is a thinking intelligent being, that has reason and reflection, and can consider itself as itself, the same thinking thing, in different times and places; which it does only by that consciousness which is inseparable from thinking, and, as it seems to me, essential to it: it being impossible for any one to perceive without perceiving that he does perceive. When we see, hear, smell, taste, feel, meditate, or will anything, we know that we do so. Thus it is always as to our present sensations and perceptions: and by this every one is to himself that which he calls self: it not being considered, in this case, whether the same self be continued in the same or divers substances. For, since consciousness always accompanies thinking, and it is that which makes every one to be what he calls self, and thereby distinguishes himself from all other thinking things, in this alone consists personal identity, i.e. the sameness of a rational being: and as far as this consciousness can be extended backwards to any past action or thought, so far reaches the identity of that person; it is the same self now it was then; and it is by the same self with this present one that now reflects on it, that that action was done.

But it is further inquired, whether it be the same identical substance. This few would think they had reason to doubt of, if these perceptions, with their consciousness, always remained present in the mind, whereby the same thinking thing would be always consciously present, and, as would be thought, evidently the same to itself. But that which seems to make the difficulty is this, that this consciousness being interrupted always by forgetfulness, there being no moment of our lives wherein we have the whole train of all our past actions before our eyes in one view, but even the best memories losing the sight of one part whilst they are viewing another; and we sometimes, and that the greatest part of our lives, not reflecting on our past selves, being intent on our present thoughts, and in sound sleep having no thoughts at all, or at least none with that consciousness which remarks our waking thoughts,—I say, in all these cases, our consciousness being interrupted, and we losing the sight of our past selves, doubts are raised whether we are the same thinking thing, i.e. the same substance or no. Which, however reasonable or unreasonable, concerns not personal identity at all. The question being what makes the same person; and not whether it be the same identical substance, which always thinks in the same person, which, in this case, matters not at all: different substances, by the same consciousness (where they do partake in it) being united into one person, as well as different bodies by the same life are united into one animal, whose identity is preserved in that change of substances by the unity of one continued life. For, it being the same consciousness that makes a man be himself to himself, personal identity depends on that only, whether it be annexed solely to one individual substance, or can be continued in a succession of several substances. For as far as any intelligent being can repeat the idea of any past action with the same consciousness it had of it at first, and with the same consciousness it has of any present action; so far it is the same personal self For it is by the consciousness it has of its present thoughts and actions, that it is self to itself now, and so will be the same self, as far as the same consciousness can extend to actions past or to come, and would be by distance of time, or change of substance, no more two persons, than a man be two men by wearing other clothes to-day than he did yesterday, with a long or a short sleep between: the same consciousness uniting those distant actions into the same person, whatever substances contributed to their production.

That this is so, we have some kind of evidence in our very bodies, all whose particles, whilst vitally united to this same thinking conscious self, so that we feel when they are touched, and are affected by, and conscious of good or harm that happens to them, as a part of ourselves; i.e. of our thinking conscious self. Thus, the limbs of his body are to every one a part of Himself; he sympathizes and is concerned for them. Cut off a hand, and thereby separate it from that consciousness he had of its heat, cold, and other affections, and it is then no longer a part of that which is himself, any more than the remotest part of matter. Thus, we see the substance whereof personal self consisted at one time may be varied at another, without the change of personal identity; there being no question about the same person, though the limbs which but now were a part of it, be cut off....

And thus may we be able, without any difficulty, to conceive the same person at the resurrection, though in a body not exactly in make or parts the same which he had here,—the same consciousness going along with the soul that inhabits it. But yet the soul alone, in the change of bodies, would scarce to any one but to him that makes the soul the man, be enough to make the same man. For should the soul of a prince, carrying with it the consciousness of the prince's past life, enter and inform the body of a cobbler, as soon as deserted by his own soul, every one sees he would be the same person with the prince, accountable only for the prince's actions: but who would say it was the same man? The body too goes to the making the man, and would, I guess, to everybody determine the man in this case, wherein the soul, with all its princely thoughts about it, would not make another man: but he would be the same cobbler to every one besides himself. I know that, in the ordinary way of speaking, the same person, and the same man, stand for one and the same thing. And indeed every one will always have a liberty to speak as he pleases, and to apply what articulate sounds to what ideas he thinks fit, and change them as often as he pleases. But yet, when we will inquire what makes the same spirit, man, or person, we must fix the ideas of spirit, man, or person in our minds; and having resolved with ourselves what we mean by them, it will not be hard to determine, in either of them, or the like, when it is the same, and when not.

But though the same immaterial substance or soul does not alone, wherever it be, and in whatsoever state, make the same man; yet it is plain, consciousness, as far as ever it can be extended—should it be to ages past—unites existences and actions very remote in time into the same person, as well as it does the existences and actions of the immediately preceding moment: so that whatever has the consciousness of present and past actions, is the same person to whom they both belong. Had I the same consciousness that I saw the ark and Noah's flood, as that I saw an overflowing of the Thames last winter, or as that I write now, I could no more doubt that I who write this now, that saw' the Thames overflowed last winter, and that viewed the flood at the general deluge, was the same self,—place that self in what substance you please—than that I who write this am the same myself now whilst I write (whether I consist of all the same substance, material or immaterial, or no) that I was yesterday. For as to this point of being the same self, it matters not whether this present self be made up of the same or other substances—I being as much concerned, and as justly accountable for any action that was done a thousand years since, appropriated to me now by this self-consciousness, as I am for what I did the last moment.

Self is that conscious thinking thing—whatever substance made up of, (whether spiritual or material, simple or compounded, it matters not)—which is sensible or conscious of pleasure and pain, capable of happiness or misery, and so is concerned for itself, as far as that consciousness extends. Thus every one finds that, whilst comprehended under that consciousness, the little finger is as much a part of himself as what is most so. Upon separation of this little finger, should this consciousness go along with the little finger, and leave the rest of the body, it is evident the little finger would be the person, the same person; and self then would have nothing to do with the rest of the body. As in this case it is the consciousness that goes along with the substance, when one part is separate from another, which makes the same person, and constitutes this inseparable self: so it is in reference to substances remote in time. That with which the consciousness of this present thinking thing can join itself, makes the same person, and is one self with it, and with nothing else; and so attributes to itself, and owns all the actions of that thing, as its own, as far as that consciousness reaches, and no further; as every one who reflects will perceive.

In this personal identity is founded all the right and justice of reward and punishment; happiness and misery being that for which every one is concerned for himself, and not mattering what becomes of any substance, not joined to, or affected with that consciousness. For, as it is evident in the instance I gave but now, if the consciousness went along with the little finger when it was cut off, that would be the same self which was concerned for the whole body yesterday, as making part of itself, whose actions then it cannot but admit as its own now. Though, if the same body should still live, and immediately from the separation of the little finger have its own peculiar consciousness, whereof the little finger knew nothing, it would not at all be concerned for it, as a part of itself, or could own any of its actions, or have any of them imputed to him.

This may show us wherein personal identity consists: not in the identity of substance, but, as I have said, in the identity of consciousness, wherein if Socrates and the present mayor of Queinborough agree, they are the same person: if the same Socrates waking and sleeping do not partake of the same consciousness, Socrates waking and sleeping is not the same person. And to punish Socrates waking for what sleeping Socrates thought, and waking Socrates was never conscious of, would be no more of right, than to punish one twin for what his brother-twin did, whereof he knew nothing, because their outsides were so like, that they could not be distinguished; for such twins have been seen.

But yet possibly it will still be objected,—Suppose I wholly lose the memory of some parts of my life, beyond a possibility of retrieving them, so that perhaps I shall never be conscious of them again; yet am I not the same person that did those actions, had those thoughts that I once was conscious of, though I have now forgot them? To which I answer, that we must here take notice what the word I is applied to; which, in this case, is the man only. And the same man being presumed to be the same person, I is easily here supposed to stand also for the same person. But if it be possible for the same man to have distinct incommunicable consciousness at different times, it is past doubt the same man would at different times make different persons; which, we see, is the sense of mankind in the solemnest declaration of their opinions, human laws not punishing the mad man for the sober man's actions, nor the sober man for what the mad man did—thereby making them two persons: which is somewhat explained by our way of speaking in English when we say such an one is "not himself," or is "beside himself;" in which phrases it is insinuated, as if those who now, or at least first used them, thought that self was changed; the selfsame person was no longer in that man.

Nothing but consciousness can unite remote existences into the same person: the identity of substance will not do it; for whatever substance there is, however framed, without consciousness there is no person: and a carcass may be a person, as well as any sort of substance be so, without consciousness.

—Could we suppose two distinct incommunicable consciousnesses acting the same body, the one constantly by day, the other by night; and, on the other side, the same consciousness, acting by intervals, two distinct bodies: I ask, in the first case, whether the day and the night- man would not be two as distinct persons as Socrates and Plato? And whether, in the second case, there would not be one person in two distinct bodies, as much as one man is the same in two distinct clothings? Nor is it at all material to say, that this same, and this distinct consciousness, in the cases above mentioned, is owing to the same and distinct immaterial substances, bringing it with them to those bodies; which, whether true or no, alters not the case: since it is evident the personal identity would equally be determined by the consciousness, whether that consciousness were annexed to some individual immaterial substance or no. For, granting that the thinking substance in man must be necessarily supposed immaterial, it is evident that immaterial thinking thing may sometimes part with its past consciousness, and be restored to it again: as appears in the forgetfulness men often have of their past actions; and the mind many times recovers the memory of a past consciousness, which it had lost for twenty years together. Make these intervals of memory and forgetfulness to take their turns regularly by day and night, and you have two persons with the same immaterial spirit, as much as in the former instance two persons with the same body. So that self is not determined by identity or diversity of substance, which it cannot be sure of, but only by identity of consciousness.

LOCKE ON PERSONAL IDENTITY

By Raymond Martin and John Barresi

INANIMATE OBJECTS, PLANTS, AND ANIMALS

Fortunately, some things about Locke's account are relatively clear. He proposed separate accounts of the identity conditions for inanimate objects, animate objects, and persons. Setting aside, for a moment, his account of the identity conditions for artifacts, in the case of inanimate objects, Locke's view was that an individual at one time and one at another are the same just if they are composed of exactly the same matter. A heap of sand remains the same heap so long as it does not either gain or lose a grain, even if the grains are rearranged. Apparently, Locke thought of composite inanimate objects, implausibly in our view, as if they were sets, rather than wholes composed of parts.

In the case of plants and animals, Locke held that an individual at one time and one at another are the same just if each has the kind of shape appropriate to that sort of plant or animal and sustains the same life. The shape of an animal, not its mentality, determines what biological kind of thing it is. Unless one recognizes this, Locke thought, one might be tempted to say of a rational parrot, if there were one, that it is a human. The life of a thing is simply a way in which its (perhaps exclusively) material parts are organized so as to promote its functioning in a manner appropriate to the sort of thing it is. And a plant or animal can so function even if the matter (and/or spirit) out of which it is composed at any given time is replaced by different matter (and/or spirit). In sum, still leaving the question of artifacts to one side, in Locke's view, in the case of inanimate objects, composition but not organization matters and, in the case of animate objects, shape and organization but not composition or mentality matters. In the case of artifacts, Locke acknowledged the importance of function and allowed for replacement of matter, but he did this not in his chapter on identity and not systematically, but intermittently, in different parts of the *Essay* (Ibid.: III.vi.40;464. Also, III.vi.41;465).

PERSONS

In the case of persons, Locke is unequivocal: consciousness and only consciousness matters. Thus, although biological kind, in virtue of its relation to shape and life, is essential to *human*hood, it is not essential to *person*hood. In Locke's view, a rational parrot could not be *a* human and, hence, *a fortiori,* could not be the *same* human as an individual at another time. But a rational parrot could be the same person as an individual at another time.

On one interpretation of Locke's account, an individual at one time and one at a later time are the same *person* only if the individual at the later time is conscious of having experienced or done what the individual at the earlier time experienced or did. On what is possibly another interpretation, an additional requirement is that the individual at the later time has the 'same consciousness' as the individual at the earlier time. Whether these seemingly different interpretations collapse into one depends on whether satisfying the requirement of the first guarantees that the individuals in question have the same consciousness. A reason why it might not guarantee this is that, in Locke's view, qualitative *similarity* of consciousness, especially in cases in which the later consciousness simply takes up where the earlier left off, might not guarantee numerical *identity* of consciousness. For instance, when the later individual 'wakes up' from a period of unconsciousness, the mere replication in him of a previous consciousness may not guarantee sameness of consciousness, but only mere similarity of consciousness.

In general, when Locke used the phrase 'is conscious of,' in the context of talking about personal identity over time, he meant 'remembers', which is also ambiguous as between the two interpretations just distinguished. In any case, there is a textual basis for supposing that Locke, in his capacity as a theorist of personal identity over time, was a memory theorist, and a rather simple-minded one at that; that is, there is a basis for supposing that Locke proposed to define or analyze personal identity in terms of memory. For the most part, this is how Locke has been interpreted ever since the publication of the second edition of the *Essay,* but particularly by his eighteenth-century critics.

As far as it goes, the simple memory interpretation of Locke's account of personal identity over time is almost, but not quite, correct. As we shall see, Locke made some allowances for forgetfulness. More importantly, Locke may not have been trying, in the first place, to present a non-circular analysis of personal identity over time. Even aside from such qualifications, however, the simple memory interpretation of Locke is, at best, radically incomplete. For central to Locke's account of the self is the idea that consciousness is reflexive and that it plays a dual role in self-constitution: it is what unifies a person not only *over* time but also *at* a time. Memory interpretations, whether simple or not, do not explain how consciousness plays this dual role.

Even so, it is clear that an important part of what Locke meant by *consciousness* has to do with memory. Most of his eighteenth-century critics seized upon this aspect of his account, while basically ignoring the rest, in order to attribute to Locke the simple memory view. According to that view, a person at one time and one at another have the same consciousness, and hence are the same person, just in case the person at the later time *remembers* having had experiences or having performed actions that were had or performed by the person at the earlier time. As we shall see in a moment, these critics were right in thinking that this simple memory view of personal identity is vulnerable to decisive objections. However, in the eighteenth century almost all of Locke's critics wanted to defeat the simple memory view in order to retain the (immaterial) soul view. But even the simple memory view of personal identity which they attributed to Locke is, in important respects, an advance on the soul view.

According to the soul view, personal identity depends on sameness of soul. As simple, immaterial substances, souls are not part of the natural world. Whatever exists or obtains, but not as part of the natural world, is inherently mysterious. Other peoples' souls cannot be observed either directly or indirectly. And since only the activities and not the substance of the soul is open to empirical investigation, there is no way to detect by observing an individual whether his soul remains the same. Hence, on the soul view, personal identity is inherently mysterious.

On the simple memory interpretation of Locke's account, by contrast, personal identity depends on the presence of a psychological relationship—remembering—that binds together earlier and later stages of a person. Other peoples' rememberings, unlike their souls, can be observed indirectly. For instance, by listening to another talk one may be able to determine that they remember having experienced or done various things. In the case of oneself, each person may observe directly, via introspection, that he or she remembers having experienced and done various things. Only by explaining personal identity in terms of things or relations that are observable can an account of it be developed on the basis of which one can determine empirically whether a person at one time and one at another are the same.

For this reason, Locke's account of personal identity was not just another in a long tradition of such accounts that began with Plato. Rather, his account was an idea whose time had come. As Locke seems to have recognized, the *kind* of view that he was proposing was irresistible. By contrast, his critics, though right in thinking that the simple memory view that they attributed to Locke is deeply flawed, failed to notice that their own views were more deeply flawed. So far as the verdict of history is concerned the soul view was not just a wrong account of personal identity, it was the wrong kind of account. The simple memory view of personal identity, by contrast, was the right kind of account, even if it was not the right account. In short, Locke's critics failed to see that even the simple memory view was riding on the crest of a wave of naturalization that was about to engulf them.

CONSCIOUSNESS

In Locke's actual view of personal identity, as opposed to the one most of his critics attributed to him, consciousness is more inclusive than memory; it is, he said, 'inseparable from thinking' and 'essential to it: It being impossible for any one to perceive, without perceiving that he does perceive.' Locke added that 'When we see, hear, smell, taste, feel, meditate, or will any thing, we know that we do so' (Ibid.: II.xxvii.9;335). It is in, and by, knowing that we 'do so', that is, that we perform one of these typically first-order mental operations, that we are conscious. Hence, consciousness is *any* sort of reflexive awareness (or reflexive knowledge).

It is an implication of this view of consciousness that when you *remember* having had an experience or having performed an action, a reflexivity is involved which is similar to that which is involved when you are merely aware that, in the present, you are having an experience or performing an action. But in the case of memory, it would seem, the reflexivity happens twice over. That is, when you remember having had the experience, say, of being anxious, you are aware that it is you who, in the present, is having the experience of *remembering* and also that it was you who, in the past, had the experience of *being anxious*.

In other words, in Locke's view, if right now you are remembering having experienced being anxious, you are not just aware that an experience of being anxious occurred, you are also aware that it was *you* who had the experience; that is, an ingredient of your remembering of 'the having of an experience' is that it was you who had it. Thereby, you *appropriate* (claim *ownership* of) the having of the experience. It is as if you were to claim of the *experience remembered,* 'That was mine' and of the *current having* of the memory experience, 'And this too is mine'. Of course, normally you do not explicitly claim ownership of either experience; rather, your double claim of ownership is implicit in your remembering having had the original experience.

In adopting from Descartes this view of the self-reflexive nature of consciousness and then wedding it to his own memory analysis of personal identity over time, Locke himself, in effect, originated that objection to the memory analysis for which Bishop Butler is famous but which had surfaced earlier in criticisms of Locke by John Sergeant and Samuel Clarke. The objection is that one cannot analyze personal identity non-circularly in terms of memory because the notion of memory includes the notion of personal identity. That Locke was aware of this, indeed that in his unquestioning, explicit, and up-front commitment to the view that all consciousness is reflexive, he all but insisted on the point, is evidence that, contrary to what is often said, he was not, in fact, trying to analyze personal identity non-circularly in terms of memory.

Locke's objectives were different. Primary among them were his developing an account of personal identity that would satisfy two criteria: first, persons had to be capable of persisting through change of substance (or else it would be impossible to determine observationally whether an individual remained the same person over time, and post-mortem persons might not be identifiable with anyone who had lived on Earth); and, second, persons had to be *accountable* for their thoughts and deeds and, hence, appropriate subjects for the just distribution of rewards and punishments (or else the Christian dogmas of the resurrection and divine judgment would not make sense). These objectives were thrust upon Locke by his epistemology and his religious convictions. That is, since Locke was *officially* agnostic about the soul, the fate of persons could not be tied to that of souls; since he accepted that people survive their bodily deaths and that subsequently they are either justly rewarded or punished for what they had done prior to bodily death the fate of persons could not, then, be tied to material bodies (since after bodily death people may not have them, or at least may not have the same ones they had prior to bodily death); and persons, in Locke's view, had to be entities which after bodily death could be rewarded or punished justly for deeds performed before bodily death.

What sort of entity could possibly satisfy such criteria? Only one that could span the migration from being constituted, prior to bodily death, just of matter, to being constituted, after bodily death, of matter or spirit, or both; and only one so linked throughout its duration to its earlier phases that it is transparently accountable for the thoughts and deeds of its earlier phases. To show that there is such an entity, or at least that there is one prior to bodily death, Locke had to show how persons originate in the process of normal human development. And to show how persons could have originated, he had to show how consciousness could unify a person both over time and at a time, regardless of whether there was a change in the person's underlying substance. Locke did this by explaining how *persons* are by-products of the development in at least normal *humans* of reflexive consciousness.

HUMANS AND PERSONS

Locke distinguished between humans and persons in the first place for two reasons: first, he thought that we have different ideas of *man* (= human) and *person* and, so, need different identity conditions for them. In saying that we have different ideas of human and person, Locke was not making a point about ordinary language. In commenting on his prince and cobbler example, in which overnight the 'souls' (= minds) of a prince and cobbler switch bodies, Locke admitted that 'in the ordinary way of speaking, the same Person, and the same Man, stand for one and the same thing' (Ibid.: II.xxvii.15;340). Locke's point, rather, was that there is one *idea* corresponding to what *he* wants to understand by *man* and another corresponding to what *he* wants to understand by *person*. The word *man,* when it corresponds to Locke's idea of man, is what *we* might call a scientific term. It means, or refers to, a certain biological kind. We assume that individual humans are instances of this kind. The word, *person,* on the other hand, when it corresponds to Locke's idea of person, is, he says, 'a Forensick Term appropriating Actions and their Merit; and so belongs only to intelligent Agents capable of a Law, and Happiness and Misery' (Ibid.: II.xxvii.26;346). What that forensic term means is a separate question, to which we shall return.

Whether Locke thought persons were substances and, if so, how and why, are questions that have been discussed endlessly by commentators. In our opinion, it is impossible to determine what Locke's views on the status of persons as substances actually were. But for present purposes, it does not really matter. What matters, rather, is that as Locke was interpreted by some of his most famous critics and followers, persons, as he accounts for them, could not be genuine substances. Rather, since the nominal essence of person is based on a mode, persons, as we might say, are merely virtual (that is, fictional) substances. In saying of a putative substance that it is virtual, rather than real, we mean, first, that, it is not a substance and, second, that for pragmatic reasons one nevertheless continues to speak of it as if it were a substance.

A second reason Locke distinguished between humans and persons has to do with survival and accountability. As already noted, he was interested that his theory of persons somehow reflect or express the circumstances under which humans should be held responsible for their thoughts and deeds; and he was interested in framing a theory of human and personal identity that would be adequate to the Christian doctrine of the resurrection. Although Locke never said so explicitly, his principal worry in connection with the doctrine of the resurrection may well have been that it is implausible to suppose that the same *humans* who acted on Earth will, on the Day of Judgment, be available to be judged. The reasons Locke may have thought this are, first, that there cannot be more than one beginning to a thing, second, that we do not know whether humans have immaterial souls, and, third, that humans obviously decompose soon after their bodily deaths, the material of which they are made becoming parts of other entities.

In Locke's day, many thinkers believed that the matter out of which (some phase or other of) one's body was composed on Earth would be reassembled in the afterlife. But to Locke, this proposal may have been objectionably speculative. And unless one's body were reassembled immediately, bodily continuity, and perhaps also one's persistence as a human, has been broken. Persons, as Locke proposed that we conceive of them, are free of such obstacles to their potential survival. Yet, to make the trick work, persons have to be connected to their associated humans closely enough and in the right ways so as to make persons appropriate recipients of Divine rewards and punishments.

PERSONS AND SELVES

Locke's idea of *person* may be the same as his idea of *self*. Sometimes he uses the words interchangeably. However, often he seems to use *self* to refer to a momentary entity and *person* to refer to a temporally extended one. And, seemingly for other reasons, he defines the two terms differently. A *person*, he says, 'is a thinking intelligent Being, that has reason and reflection, and can consider it self as it self, the same thinking thing in different times and places' (Ibid.: II.xxvii.9;335). A *self,* on the other hand 'is that conscious thinking thing, (whatever Substance, made up of whether Spiritual, or Material, Simple, or Compounded, it matters not) which is sensible, or conscious of Pleasure and Pain, capable of Happiness or Misery, and so is concerned for it *self,* as far as that consciousness extends' (Ibid.: II.xxvii.17;341). There are important differences, at least in emphasis, between these two definitions. Locke's definition of *person* highlights that persons are *thinkers* and, as such, have reason, reflection, intelligence, and whatever else may be required for trans-temporal self-reference. His definition of *self,* on the other hand, highlights that selves are *sensors* and as such feel pleasure and pain, and are capable of happiness, misery and self-concern.

Such differences reflect disparate concerns that Locke expressed throughout his discussion of personal identity. Primary among these are that persons be appropriately subject both to moral and civil law and that they be things that naturally constitute themselves. Locke's concern that persons be appropriately subject to law raises the possibility that persons might simply be artifacts of theory—like *legal property,* or *legal persons* (where, say, corporations count as persons); however, his concern that persons be things that naturally constitute themselves counts against the idea that persons are merely creatures of theory. It is debatable how this tension in Locke's theory should be resolved.

PATHOLOGIES OF MEMORY

As Locke's critics saw, in his analysis of personal identity there is a problem about his use of the notion of memory. Ironically, though, there is a problem not primarily, as they tended to think, because memory is useless for the purpose of providing a non-circular analysis (or definition) of personal identity but for two other reasons. One of these has to do with forgetfulness, the other with delusions of memory. Locke responded to both problems. However, his responses seem incompatible with his theory of personal identity and, hence, constitute an embarrassment to virtually every interpretation of his theory.

Consider, first, the case in which people are (forgetfully) not conscious of having done things they did do. There are three parts to Locke's response to this seeming possibility. First, he denied that people who are awake and thinking about it ever are not conscious of having done anything they did do since if they are not conscious of having done something, they did not do it. In making this point, Locke first recounted that someone he knew thought he had Socrates' soul. Locke then considered the analogous case of someone who thinks he has the soul either of Nestor or Thersites. Locke asked rhetorically, 'Now having no consciousness of any of the Actions either of *Nestor* or *Thersites,* does, or can he, conceive himself the same Person with either of them? Can he be concerned in either of their Actions? Attribute them to himself, or think them his own more than the Actions of any other Man, that ever existed?' (Ibid.: II.xxvii.14;339). The answer, which Locke apparently thought is too obvious to need saying, is, no. Locke continued, 'But let him [someone who claims to be Nestor] once find himself conscious of any of the Actions of *Nestor,* he then finds himself the same Person with *Nestor*' (Ibid.: II.xxvii.14;340). By implication, we think, Locke also must have been saying of the person he knows who claims to have Socrates' soul, that whatever he might *say* he thinks, he does not *really* think he is Socrates, since if he did think that, he would be 'concerned' in the actions of Socrates, that is, he would own them and hold himself accountable for them, and he does not own them or hold himself accountable for them. Locke's point, then, may have been that if the person in question thinks he is concerned in the actions of Socrates, he is deceiving himself.

If this was Locke's point, then far from its being a blunder or symptom of incoherence in his view, as commentators often suppose, it is quite insightful. For what Locke was saying is that whether we appropriate the actions of someone in the past is *not* a matter of what theories we may have about who we are but, rather, of the nature of our experience. In other words, Locke was making two points: first, that our appropriating the experiences and actions of someone in the past depends on our being actually concerned, in the right way, with those experiences and actions, and not on whether we think we are that person or even on whether we think we are concerned in the right way with that person's experiences and actions; and, second, that whether we are actually concerned, in the right way, with someone's past experiences and actions is determined by our phenomenology.

And what sort of phenomenologically expressed concernment is the right sort of concernment to forge identity between ourselves and people who lived in the past? Why, of course, the sort of concernment that is ingredient in reflexive self-consciousness. And, in order to have that sort of concernment, Locke is saying, at least normally, if not always, I must remember in a first-personal way, that is, 'from the inside', the having of the experiences of someone in the past and the performing of his actions. If I do that, Locke thought, then I not only remember, say, the having of the experiences, but I remember that I had them, and in remembering that I had them, I appropriate—that is, declare ownership of—them. It is such acts of appropriation, not any theory I may have about who I am or what I am concerned about, that makes the previous experiences and actions mine.

The second part of Locke's response to the possibility that some people may not be conscious of having done things they did do was to the supposition that he might wholly lose all memories of some parts of his life, with no possibility of retrieving them. 'Yet', Locke asked, 'am I not the same person, that did those Actions, had those Thoughts, that I was once conscious of, though I have now forgot them?' His answer was that 'we must here take notice what the Word *I* is applied to, which in this case is the Man only'. Locke conceded that since, in common language, the man is presumed to be the person, '*I* is easily here supposed to stand also for the same Person'. But, he continued, 'if it be possible for the same Man to have distinct incommunicable consciousness [*sic*] at different times, it is past doubt the same Man would at different times make different Persons'. Locke said that what he is suggesting here is in accord with 'the Sense of Mankind in the solemnest Declaration of their Opinions, Humane Laws not punishing the *Mad Man* for the *Sober Man's* Actions, nor the *Sober Man* for what the *Mad Man* did, thereby making them two Persons'. He also cited in support of his view 'our way of speaking in *English*, when we say such an one *is not himself,* or is *besides himself*; in which Phrases it is insinuated, as if those who now, or, at least, first used them, thought, that *self* was changed, the *self* same Person was no longer in that Man' (Ibid.: II.xxvii.20;342–3). On a charitable reading, Locke's point here, seemingly about ambiguous self-reference, is just his way of saying that while the man performed the actions, the person, who now does not remember having performed them, did not.

The final part of Locke's answer to the problem that some people may not be conscious of having done something they did is that, if it serves Justice, then eventually they will be conscious of it 'when every one shall *receive according to his doing*' and *'the secrets of all hearts shall be laid open'* (Ibid.: II.xxvii.26; 347). There is an obvious problem with this answer. In so far as reward and punishment is accorded to a person only for what the person does, and God on the day of judgment arranges it so that a person is conscious of everything he does, then there must be some standard by which God determines what a person has done other than that of what the person is conscious of having done. Many commentators think that here also Locke lapses into irretrievable incoherence. However, Locke may here simply be betraying the fact that except for a benign skepticism, he is indifferent to mundane metaphysics. He did not think that we can know the real essences of any substances, either persons or anything else. But he also did not think that it matters. At least he did not think that it matters for the practical conduct of our lives, which for Locke was all that really matters. And, as we shall see in more detail when we consider his response to the next pathology of memory to be considered, one of the reasons that Locke was relatively unconcerned about whether he got the metaphysics right was his belief that if he were to get it wrong, God would set it right (Ibid.: I.i.5;45).

Consider next, people who are (delusionally) conscious of having done things they did not do. Locke's answer to the problem of 'delusions of identity' is in two parts. He began by conceding that, without bringing theology into the picture, there is no way to know that delusions of identity do not occur: '[W]hy one intellectual Substance may not have represented to it, as done by it self, what it never did, and was perhaps done by some other Agent, why I say such a representation may not possibly be without reality of Matter of Fact, as well as several representations in Dreams are, which yet, whilst dreaming, we take for true, will be difficult to conclude from the Nature of things'. Then, Locke brought theology into the picture: 'And that it [such delusions] never is so, will by us, till we have clearer views of the Nature of thinking Substances be best resolved into the Goodness of God, who as far as the Happiness or Misery of any of his sensible Creatures is concerned in it, will not by a fatal Error of theirs transfer from one to another, that consciousness, which draws Reward or Punishment with it' (Ibid.: II.xxvii.13;338). So, in effect, Locke, first, conceded that temporarily and on Earth delusions of identity may occur but, then, denied that in the final analysis there will be any. This would seem to be a problem for Locke, since the view of personal identity he had been developing seems to leave no room for delusions of identity. From Locke's point of view, we suspect, it was much less of a problem.

In our view, to a greater degree than is usually acknowledged by commentators, Locke, in the *Essay*, was a 'theological pragmatist', that is, a pragmatist for whom other-worldly consequences were paramount.

Surprising as it may seem, with the exception of three theses—that God exists, that the Self exists, and that there is an external world with the power to cause our ideas of it—Locke was not nearly as interested in *positive* metaphysics as he is usually portrayed as having been. He had a *negative* interest in metaphysics that grew out of his desire to set strict limits on the possibilities of human knowledge. And he had a *positive* interest in establishing theological pragmatism. But except for a few views about the details of corpuscular mechanism, that is about it. Recognizing this becomes important in understanding Locke's response to the problem of forgetfulness.

As a theological pragmatist, Locke's attitude toward problems to his theory of personal identity posed by faulty memory may well have been this: Based on what we (humans) know, the view I (Locke) am expounding is at least as reasonable as any competing view; perhaps even it is the most reasonable view. However, there is no way to know whether it is the true view. On the day of judgment, God will judge on the basis of the true view. While we do not know what that view will be, we know it will be close enough to maximally reasonable views that our view will have been an adequate basis for conduct. Otherwise God would be a deceiver, and God is not a deceiver. And, insofar as personal identity (or anything else) is concerned, all we really need to know is that our view is an adequate basis for conduct.

ESSAYS ON THE INTELLECTUAL POWERS OF MAN

By Thomas Reid

Essay Three: Of Memory

CHAPTER 4: OF IDENTITY

The conviction which every man has of his identity, as far back as his memory reaches, needs no aid of philosophy to strengthen it; and no philosophy can weaken it, without first producing some degree of insanity.

The philosopher, however, may very properly consider this conviction as a phenomenon of human nature worthy of his attention. If he can discover its cause, an addition is made to his stock of knowledge; if not, it must be held as a part of our original constitution, or an effect of that constitution produced in a manner unknown to us.

We may observe, first of all, that this conviction is indispensably necessary to all exercise of reason. The operations of reason, whether in action or in speculation, are made up of successive parts. The antecedent are the foundation of the consequent, and, without the conviction that the antecedent have been seen or done by me, I could have no reason to proceed to the consequent, in any speculation, or in any active project whatever.

There can be no memory of what is past without the conviction that we existed at the time remembered. There may be good arguments to convince me that I existed before the earliest thing I can remember; but to suppose that my memory reaches a moment farther back than my belief and conviction of my existence, is a contradiction.

The moment a man loses this conviction, as if he had drunk the water of Lethe, past things are done away; and, in his own belief, he then begins to exist. Whatever was thought, or said, or done, or suffered before that period, may belong to some other person; but he can never impute it to himself, or take any subsequent step that supposes it to be his doing.

From this it is evident that we must have the conviction of our own continued existence and identity, as soon as we are capable of thinking or doing anything, on account of what we have thought, or done, or suffered before; that is, as soon as we are reasonable creatures.

That we may form as distinct a notion as we are able of this phenomenon of the human mind, it is proper to consider what is meant by identity in general, what by our own personal identity, and how we are led into that invincible belief and conviction which every man has of his own personal identity, as far as his memory reaches.

Identity in general I take to be a relation between a thing which is known to exist at one time, and a thing which is known to have existed at another time. If you ask whether they are one and the same, or two different things, every man of common sense understands the meaning of your question perfectly. Whence we may infer with certainty, that every man of common sense has a clear and distinct notion of identity.

If you ask a definition of identity, I confess I can give none; it is too simple a notion to admit of logical definition: I can say it is a relation, but I cannot find words to express the specific difference between this and other relations, though I am in no danger of confounding it with any other. I can say that diversity is a contrary relation, and that similitude and dissimilitude are another couple of contrary relations, which every man easily distinguishes in his conception from identity and diversity.

I see evidently that identity supposes an uninterrupted continuance of existence. That which has ceased to exist cannot be the same with that which afterwards begins to exist; for this would be to suppose a being to exist after it ceased to exist, and to have had existence before it was produced, which are manifest contradictions. Continued uninterrupted existence is therefore necessarily implied in identity.

Hence we may infer, that identity cannot, in its proper sense, be applied to our pains, our pleasures, our thought, or any operation of our minds. The pain felt this day is not the same individual pain which I felt yesterday, though they may be *similar* in kind and degree, and have the same cause. The same may be said of every feeling, and of every operation of mind. They are all successive in their nature, like time itself, no two moments of which can be the same moment.

It is otherwise with the parts of absolute space. They always are, and were, and will be the same. So far, I think, we proceed upon clear ground in fixing the notion of identity in general.

It is perhaps more difficult to ascertain with precision the meaning of personality; but it is not necessary in the present subject: it is sufficient for our purpose to observe, that all mankind place their personality in something that cannot be divided or consist of parts.

A part of a person is a manifest absurdity. When a man loses his estate, his health, his strength, he is still the same person, and has lost nothing of his personality. If he has a leg or an arm cut off, he is the same person he was before. The amputated member is no part of his person, otherwise it would have a right to a part of his estate, and be liable for a part of hie engagements. It would be entitled to a share of his merit and demerit, which is manifestly absurd. A person is something indivisible, and is what Leibniz calls a *monad*.

My personal identity, therefore, implies the continued existence of that indivisible thing which I call *myself*. Whatever this self may be, it is something which thinks, and deliberates, and resolves, and acts, and suffers. I am not thought, I am not action, I am not feeling; I am something that thinks, and acts, and suffers. My thoughts, and actions, and feelings, change every moment: they have not continued, but a successive existence; but that *self for I*, to which they belong, is permanent, and has the same relation to all the succeeding thoughts, actions, and feelings which I call mine.

Such are the notions that I have of my personal identity. But perhaps it may be said, this may all be fancy without reality. How do you know-what evidence have you-that there is such a permanent self which has a claim to all the thoughts, actions, and feelings which you call yours?

To this I answer, that the proper evidence I have of all this is remembrance. I remember that twenty years ago I conversed with such a person; I remember several things that passed in that conversation: my memory testifies, not only that this was done, but that it was done by me who now remember it. If it was done by me, I must have existed at that time, and continued to exist from that time to the present: if the identical person whom I call myself had not a part in that conversation, my memory is fallacious; it gives a distinct and positive testimony of what is not true. Every man in his senses believes what he distinctly remembers, and every thing he remembers convinces him that he existed at the time remembered.

Although memory gives the most irresistible evidence of my being the identical person that did such a thing, at such a time, I may have other good evidence of things which befell me, and which I do not remember: I know who bore me, and suckled me, but I do not remember these events.

It may here be observed (though the observation would have been unnecessary, if some great philosophers had not contradicted it), that it is not my remembering any action of mine that makes me to be the person who did it. This remembrance makes me to know assuredly that I did it; but I might have done it, though I did not remember it. That relation to me, which is expressed by saying that I did it, would be the same, though I had not the least remembrance of it. To say that my remembering that I did such a thing, or, as some choose to express it, my being conscious that I did it, makes me to have done it, appears to me as great an absurdity as it would be to say, that my belief that the world was created made it to be created.

When we pass judgment on the identity of other persons than ourselves, we proceed upon other grounds, and determine from a variety of circumstances, which sometimes produce the firmest assurance, and sometimes leave room for doubt. The identity of persons has often furnished matter of serious litigation before tribunals of justice. But no man of a sound mind ever doubted of his own identity, as far as he distinctly remembered.

The identity of a person is a perfect identity: wherever it is real, it admits of no degrees; and it is impossible that a person should be in part the same, and in part different; because a person is a *monad*, and is not divisible into parts. The evidence of identity in other persons than ourselves does indeed admit of all degrees, from what we account certainty, to the least degree of probability. But still it is true, that the same person is perfectly the same, and cannot be so in part, or in some degree only.

For this cause, I have first considered personal identity, as that which is perfect in its kind, and the natural measure of that which is imperfect.

We probably at first derive our notion of identity from that natural conviction which every man has from the dawn of reason of his own identity and continued existence. The operations of our minds are all successive, and have no continued existence. But the thinking being has a continued existence, and we have an invincible belief, that it remains the same when all its thoughts and operations change.

Our judgments of the identity of objects of sense seem to be formed much upon the same grounds as our judgments of the identity of other persons than ourselves.

Wherever we observe great similarity, we are apt to presume identity, if no reason appears to the contrary. Two objects ever so like, when they are perceived at the same time, cannot be the same; but if they are presented to our senses at different times, we are apt to think them the same, merely from their similarity.

Whether this be a natural prejudice, or from whatever cause it proceeds, it certainly appears in children from infancy; and when we grow up, it is confirmed in most instances by experience: for we rarely find two individuals of the same species that are not distinguishable by obvious differences.

A man challenges a thief whom he finds in possession of his horse or his watch, only on similarity. When the watchmaker swears that he sold this watch to such a person, his testimony is grounded on similarity. The testimony of witnesses to the identity of a person is commonly grounded on no other evidence.

Thus it appears, that the evidence we have of our own identity, as far back as we remember, is totally of a different kind from the evidence we have of the identity of other persons, or of objects of sense. The first is grounded on memory, and gives undoubted certainly. The last is grounded on similarity, and on other circumstances, which in many cases are not so decisive as to leave no room for doubt.

It may likewise be observed, that the identity of objects of sense is never perfect. All bodies, as they consist of innumerable parts that may be disjoined from them by a great variety of causes, are subject to continual changes of their substance, increasing, diminishing, changing insensibly. When such alterations are gradual, because language could not afford a different name for every different state of such a changeable being, it retains the same name, and is considered as the same thing. Thus we say of an old regiment, that it did such a thing a century ago, though there now is not a man alive who then belonged to it. We say a tree is the same in the seed-bed and in the forest. A ship of war, which has successively changed her anchors, her tackle, her sails, her masts, her planks, and her timbers, while she keeps the same name, is the same.

The identity, therefore, which we ascribe to bodies, whether natural or artificial, is not perfect identity; it is rather something which, for the convenience of speech, we call identity. It admits of a great change of the subject, providing the change be gradual; sometimes, even of a total change. And the changes which is common language are made consistent with identity differ from those that are thought to destroy it, not in kind, but in number and degree. It has no fixed nature when applied to bodies; and questions about the identity of a body are very often questions about words. But identity, when applied to persons, has no ambiguity, and admits not of degrees, or of more and less. It is the foundation of all rights and obligations, and of all accountableness; and the notion of it is fixed and precise.

CHAPTER 6: OF MR. LOCKE'S ACCOUNT OF OUR PERSONAL IDENTITY

In a long chapter upon Identity and Diversity, Mr. Locke has made many ingenious and just observations, and some which I think cannot be defended. I shall only take notice of the account he gives of our own personal identity. His doctrine upon this subject has been censured by Bishop Butler, in a short essay subjoined to his *Analogy*, with whose sentiments I perfectly agree.

Identity, as was observed (Chap. 4 of this Essay), supposes the continued existence of the being of which it is affirmed, and therefore can be applied only to things which have a continued existence. While any being continues to exist, it is the same being; but two beings which have a different beginning or a different ending of their existence cannot possibly by the same. To this, I think, Mr. Locke agrees.

He observes, very justly, that, to know what is meant by the same person, we must consider what the word *person* stands for; and he defines a person to be an intelligent being, endowed with reason and with consciousness, which last he thinks inseparable from thought.

From this definition of a person, it must necessarily follow, that, while the intelligent being continues to exist and to be intelligent, it must be the same person. To say that the intelligent being is the person, and yet that the person ceases to exist while the intelligent being continues, or that the person continues while the intelligent being ceases to exist, is to my apprehension a manifest contradiction.

One would think that the definition of a person should perfectly ascertain the nature of personal identity, or wherein it consists, though it might still be a question how we come to know and be assured of our personal identity.

Mr. Locke tells us, however, "that personal identity, that is, the sameness of a rational being, consists in consciousness alone, and, as far as this consciousness can be extended backwards to any past action or thought, so far reaches the identity of that person. So that whatever has the consciousness of present and past actions is the same person to whom they belong."

This doctrine has some strange consequences, which the author was aware of. Such as, that if the same consciousness can be transferred from one intelligent being to another, which he thinks we cannot show to be impossible, *then two or twenty intelligent beings may be the same person.* And if the intelligent being may lose the consciousness of the actions done by him, which surely is possible, then he is not the person that did those actions; so that *one intelligent being may be two or twenty different persons,* if he shall so often lose the consciousness of this former actions.

There is another consequence of this doctrine, which follows no less necessarily, though Mr. Locke probably did not see it. It is, *that a man may be, and at the same time not be, the person that did a particular action.*

Suppose a brave officer to have been flogged when a boy at school for robbing an orchard, to have taken a standard from the enemy in his first campaign, and to have been made a general in advanced life; suppose, also, which must be admitted to be possible, that, when he took the standard, he was conscious of his having been flogged at school, and that, when made a general, he was conscious of his taking the standard, but had absolutely lost the consciousness of his flogging.

These things being supposed, it follows, from Mr. Locke's doctrine, that he who was flogged at school is the same person who took the standard, and that he who took the standard is the same person who was made a general. Whence it follows, if there be any truth in logic, that the general is the same person with him who was flogged at school. But the general's consciousness does not reach so far back as his flogging; therefore, according to Mr. Locke's doctrine, he is not the person who was flogged. Therefore the general is, and at the same time is not, the same person with him who was flogged at school.

A TREATISE OF HUMAN NATURE

By David Hume

Book I. Of the Understanding

PART I. OF IDEAS, THEIR ORIGIN, COMPOSITION, CONNEXION, ABSTRACTION, ETC.

Sect. I Of the Origin of Our Ideas.

All the perceptions of the human mind resolve themselves into two distinct kinds, which I shall call impressions and ideas. The difference betwixt these consists in the degrees of force and liveliness, with which they strike upon the mind, and make their way into our thought or consciousness. Those perceptions, which enter with most force and violence, we may name *impressions*: and under this name I comprehend all our sensations, passions and emotions, as they make their first appearance in the soul. By *ideas* I mean the faint images of these in thinking and reasoning; such as, for instance, are all the perceptions excited by the present discourse, excepting only those which arise from the sight and touch, and excepting the immediate pleasure or uneasiness it may occasion. I believe it will not be very necessary to employ many words in explaining this distinction. Every one of himself will readily perceive the difference betwixt feeling and thinking. The common degrees of these are easily distinguished; though it is not impossible but in particular instances they may very nearly approach to each other. Thus in sleep, in a fever, in madness, or in any very violent emotions of soul, our ideas may approach to our impressions. As on the other hand it sometimes happens, that our impressions are so faint and low, that we cannot distinguish them from our ideas. But notwithstanding this near resemblance in a few instances, they are in general so very different, that no-one can make a scruple to rank them under distinct heads, and assign to each a peculiar name to mark the difference.

There is another division of our perceptions, which it will be convenient to observe, and which extends itself both to our impressions and ideas. This division is into simple and complex. Simple perceptions or impressions and ideas are such as admit of no distinction nor separation. The complex are the contrary to these, and may be distinguished into parts. Though a particular colour, taste, and smell, are qualities all united together in this apple, it is easy to perceive they are not the same, but are at least distinguishable from each other.

Having by these divisions given an order and arrangement to our objects, we may now apply ourselves to consider with the more accuracy their qualities and relations. The first circumstance, that strikes my eye, is the great resemblance betwixt our impressions and ideas in every other particular, except their degree of force and vivacity. The one seems to be in a manner the reflexion of the other; so that all the perceptions of the mind are double, and appear both as impressions and ideas. When I shut my eyes and think of my chamber, the ideas I form are exact representations of the impressions I felt; nor is there any circumstance of the one, which is not to be found in the other. In running over my other perceptions, I find still the same resemblance and representation. Ideas and impressions appear always to correspond to each other. This circumstance seems to me remarkable, and engages my attention for a moment.

Upon a more accurate survey I find I have been carried away too far by the first appearance, and that I must make use of the distinction of perceptions into *simple* and *complex*, to limit this general decision, *that all our ideas and impressions are resembling*. I observe, that many of our complex ideas never had impressions, that corresponded to them, and that many of our complex impressions never are exactly copied in ideas. I can imagine to myself such a city as the New Jerusalem, whose pavement is gold and walls are rubies, though I never saw any such. I have seen Paris; but shall I affirm I can form such an idea of that city, as will perfectly represent all its streets and houses in their real and just proportions?

I perceive, therefore, that though there is in general a great, resemblance betwixt our complex impressions and ideas, yet the rule is not universally true, that they are exact copies of each other. We may next consider how the case stands with our simple, perceptions. After the most accurate examination, of which I am capable, I venture to affirm, that the rule here holds without any exception, and that every simple idea has a simple impression, which resembles it, and every simple impression a correspondent idea. That idea of red, which we form in the dark, and that impression which strikes our eyes in sun-shine, differ only in degree, not in nature. That the case is the same with all our simple impressions and ideas, it is impossible to prove by a particular enumeration of them. Every one may satisfy himself in this point by running over as many as he pleases. But if any one should deny this universal resemblance, I know no way of convincing him, but by desiring him to show a simple impression, that has not a correspondent idea, or a simple idea, that has not a correspondent impression. If he does not answer this challenge, as it is certain he cannot, we may from his silence and our own observation establish our conclusion.

Thus we find, that all simple ideas and impressions resemble each other; and as the complex are formed from them, we may affirm in general, that these two species of perception are exactly correspondent. Having discovered this relation, which requires no farther examination, I am curious to find some other of their qualities. Let us consider how they stand with regard to their existence, and which of the impressions and ideas are causes, and which effects.

The full examination of this question is the subject of the present treatise; and therefore we shall here content ourselves with establishing one general proposition, that all our simple ideas in their first appearance are derived from simple impressions, which are correspondent to them, and which they exactly represent.

In seeking for phenomena to prove this proposition, I find only those of two kinds; but in each kind the phenomena are obvious, numerous, and conclusive. I first make myself certain, by a new, review, of what I have already asserted, that every simple impression is attended with a correspondent idea, and every simple idea with a correspondent impression. From this constant conjunction of resembling perceptions I immediately conclude, that there is a great connexion betwixt our correspondent impressions and ideas, and that the existence of the one has a considerable influence upon that of the other. Such a constant conjunction, in such an infinite number of instances, can never arise from chance; but clearly proves a dependence of the impressions on the ideas, or of the ideas on the impressions. That I may know on which side this dependence lies, I consider the order of their first appearance; and find by constant experience, that the simple impressions always take the precedence of their correspondent ideas, but never appear in the contrary order. To give a child an idea of scarlet or orange, of sweet or bitter, I present the objects, or in other words, convey to him these impressions; but proceed not so absurdly, as to endeavour to produce the impressions by exciting the ideas. Our ideas upon their appearance produce not their correspondent impressions, nor do we perceive any colour, or feel any sensation merely upon thinking of them. On the other hand we find, that any impression either of the mind or body is constantly followed by an idea, which resembles it, and is only different in the degrees of force and liveliness. The constant conjunction of our resembling perceptions, is a convincing proof, that the one are the causes of the other; and this priority of the impressions is an equal proof, that our impressions are the causes of our ideas, not our ideas of our impressions.

To confirm this I consider another plain and convincing phenomenon; which is, that, where-ever by any accident the faculties, which give rise to any impressions, are obstructed in their operations, as when one is born blind or deaf; not only the impressions are lost, but also their correspondent ideas; so that there never appear in the mind the least traces of either of them. Nor is this only true, where the organs of sensation are entirely destroyed, but likewise where they have never been put in action to produce a particular impression. We cannot form to ourselves a just idea of the taste of a pine apple, without having actually tasted it.

There is however one contradictory phenomenon, which may prove, that it is not absolutely impossible for ideas to go before their correspondent impressions. I believe it will readily be allowed that the several distinct ideas of colours, which enter by the eyes, or those of sounds, which are conveyed by the hearing, are really different from each other, though at the same time resembling. Now if this be true of different colours, it must be no less so of the different shades of the same colour, that each of them produces a distinct idea, independent of the rest. For if this should be denied, it is possible, by the continual gradation of shades, to run a colour insensibly into what is most remote from it; and if you will not allow any of the means to be different, you cannot without absurdity deny the extremes to be the same. Suppose therefore a person to have enjoyed his sight for thirty years, and to have become perfectly well acquainted with colours of all kinds, excepting one particular shade of blue, for instance, which it never has been his fortune to meet with. Let all the different shades of that colour, except that single one, be placed before him, descending gradually from the deepest to the lightest; it is plain, that he will perceive a blank, where that shade is wanting, said will be sensible, that there is a greater distance in that place betwixt the contiguous colours, than in any other. Now I ask, whether it is possible for him, from his own imagination, to supply this deficiency, and raise up to himself the idea of that particular shade, though it had never been conveyed to him by his senses? I believe there are few but will be of opinion that he can; and this may serve as a proof, that the simple ideas are not always derived from the correspondent impressions; though the instance is so particular and singular, that it is scarce worth our observing, and does not merit that for it alone we should alter our general maxim.

But besides this exception, it may not be amiss to remark on this head, that the principle of the priority of impressions to ideas must be understood with another limitation, viz., that as our ideas are images of our impressions, so we can form secondary ideas, which are images of the primary; as appears from this very reasoning concerning them. This is not, properly speaking, an exception to the rule so much as an explanation of it. Ideas produce the images of themselves in new ideas; but as the first ideas are supposed to be derived from impressions, it still remains true, that all our simple ideas proceed either mediately or immediately, from their correspondent impressions.

This then is the first principle I establish in the science of human nature; nor ought we to despise it because of the simplicity of its appearance. For it is remarkable, that the present question concerning the precedency of our impressions or ideas, is the same with what has made so much noise in other terms, when it has been disputed whether there be any innate ideas, or whether all ideas be derived from sensation and reflexion. We may observe, that in order to prove the ideas of extension and colour not to be innate, philosophers do nothing but show that they are conveyed by our senses. To prove the ideas of passion and desire not to be innate, they observe that we have a preceding experience of these emotions in ourselves. Now if we carefully examine these arguments, we shall find that they prove nothing but that ideas are preceded by other more lively perceptions, from which they are derived, and which they represent. I hope this clear stating of the question will remove all disputes concerning it, and will render this principle of more use in our reasonings, than it seems hitherto to have been.

PART IV. OF THE SCEPTICAL AND OTHER SYSTEMS OF PHILOSOPHY.

Sect. VI. Of Personal Identity

There are some philosophers who imagine we are every moment intimately conscious of what we call our SELF; that we feel its existence and its continuance in existence; and are certain, beyond the evidence of a demonstration, both its perfect identity and simplicity.

Unluckily all these positive assertions are contrary to that very experience, which is pleaded for them, nor have we any idea of self, after the manner it is here explained. For from what impression could this idea be derived? This question it is impossible to answer without a manifest contradiction and absurdity; and yet it is a question, which must necessarily be answered, if we would have the idea of self pass for clear and intelligible, it must be some one impression, that gives rise to every real idea. But self or person is not any one impression, but that to which our several impressions and ideas are supposed to have a reference. If any impression gives rise to the idea of self, that impression must continue invariably the same, through the whole course of our lives; since self is supposed to exist after that manner. But there is no impression constant and invariable. Pain and pleasure, grief and joy, passions and sensations succeed each other, and never all exist at the same time. It cannot, therefore, be from any of these impressions, or from any other, that the idea of self is derived; and consequently there is no such idea.

But farther, what must become of all our particular perceptions upon this hypothesis? All these are different, and distinguishable, and separable from each other, and may be separately considered, and may exist separately, and have no Deed of tiny thing to support their existence. After what manner, therefore, do they belong to self; and how are they connected with it? For my part, when I enter most intimately into what I call myself, I always stumble on some particular perception or other, of heat or cold, light or shade, love or hatred, pain or pleasure. I never can catch myself at any time without a perception, and never can observe any thing but the perception. When my perceptions are removed for any time, as by sound sleep; so long am I insensible of myself, and may truly be said not to exist. And were all my perceptions removed by death, and could I neither think, nor feel, nor see, nor love, nor hate after the dissolution of my body, I should be entirely annihilated, nor do I conceive what is farther requisite to make me a perfect non-entity. If any one, upon serious and unprejudiced reflection thinks he has a different notion of himself, I must confess I can reason no longer with him. All I can allow him is, that he may be in the right as well as I, and that we are essentially different in this particular. He may, perhaps, perceive something simple and continued, which he calls himself; though I am certain there is no such principle in me.

But setting aside some metaphysicians of this kind, I may venture to affirm of the rest of mankind, that they are nothing but a bundle or collection of different perceptions, which succeed each other with an inconceivable rapidity, and are in a perpetual flux and movement. Our eyes cannot turn in their sockets without varying our perceptions. Our thought is still more variable than our sight; and all our other senses and faculties contribute to this change; nor is there any single power of the soul, which remains unalterably the same, perhaps for one moment. The mind is a kind of theatre, where several perceptions successively make their appearance; pass, re-pass, glide away, and mingle in an infinite variety of postures and situations. There is properly no simplicity in it at one time, nor identity in different; whatever natural propension we may have to imagine that simplicity and identity. The comparison of the theatre must not mislead us. They are the successive perceptions only, that constitute the mind; nor have we the most distant notion of the place, where these scenes are represented, or of the materials, of which it is composed.

What then gives us so great a propension to ascribe an identity to these successive perceptions, and to suppose ourselves possessed of an invariable and uninterrupted existence through the whole course of our lives?

We have a distinct idea of an object, that remains invariable and uninterrupted through a supposed variation of time; and this idea we call that of identity or sameness. We have also a distinct idea of several different objects existing in succession, and connected together by a close relation; and this to an accurate view affords as perfect a notion of diversity, as if there was no manner of relation among the objects. But though these two ideas of identity, and a succession of related objects be in themselves perfectly distinct, and even contrary, yet it is certain, that in our common way of thinking they are generally confounded with each other. That action of the imagination, by which we consider the un-interrupted and invariable object, and that by which we reflect on the succession of related objects, are almost the same to the feeling, nor is there much more effort of thought required in the latter case than in the former. The relation facilitates the transition of the mind from one object to another, and renders its passage as smooth as if it contemplated one continued object. This resemblance is the cause of the confusion and mistake, and makes us substitute the notion of identity, instead of that of related objects. However at one instant we may consider the related succession as variable or interrupted, we are sure the next to ascribe to it a perfect identity, and regard it as enviable and uninterrupted. Our propensity to this mistake is so great from the resemblance above-mentioned, that we fall into it before we are aware; and though we incessantly correct ourselves by reflection, and return to a more accurate method of thinking, yet we cannot long sustain our philosophy, or take off this bias from the imagination. Our last resource is to yield to it, and boldly assert that these different related objects are in effect the same, however interrupted and variable. In order to justify to ourselves this absurdity, we often feign some new and unintelligible principle, that connects the objects together, and prevents their interruption or variation. Thus we feign the continued existence of the perceptions of our senses, to remove the interruption: and run into the notion of a soul, and self, and substance, to disguise the variation. But we may farther observe, that where we do not give rise to such a fiction, our propension to confound identity with relation is so great, that we are apt to imagine something unknown and mysterious, connecting the parts, beside their relation; and this I take to be the case with regard to the identity we ascribe to plants and vegetables. And even when this does not take place, we still feel a propensity to confound these ideas, though we are not able fully to satisfy ourselves in that particular, nor find any thing invariable and uninterrupted to justify our notion of identity.

Thus the controversy concerning identity is not merely a dispute of words. For when we attribute identity, in an improper sense, to variable or interrupted objects, our mistake is not confined to the expression, but is commonly attended with a fiction, either of something invariable and uninterrupted, or of something mysterious and inexplicable, or at least with a propensity to such fictions. What will suffice to prove this hypothesis to the satisfaction of every fair enquirer, is to show from daily experience and observation, that the objects, which are variable or interrupted, and yet are supposed to continue the same, are such only as consist of a succession of parts, connected together by resemblance, contiguity, or causation. For as such a succession answers evidently to our notion of diversity, it can only be by mistake we ascribe to it an identity; and as the relation of parts, which leads us into this mistake, is really nothing but a quality, which produces an association of ideas, and an easy transition of the imagination from one to another, it can only be from the resemblance, which this act of the mind bears to that, by which we contemplate one continued object, that the error arises. Our chief business, then, must be to prove, that all objects, to which we ascribe identity, without observing their invariableness and uninterruptedness, are such as consist of a succession of related objects. In order to this, suppose any mass of matter, of which the parts are contiguous and connected, to be placed before us; it is plain we must attribute a perfect identity to this mass, provided all the parts continue uninterruptedly and invariably the same, whatever motion or change of place we may observe either in the whole or in any of the parts. But supposing some very small or inconsiderable part to be added to the mass, or subtracted from it; though this absolutely destroys the identity of the whole, strictly speaking; yet as we seldom think so accurately, we scruple not to pronounce a mass of matter the same, where we find so trivial an alteration. The passage of the thought from the object before the change to the object after it, is so smooth and easy, that we scarce perceive the transition, and are apt to imagine, that it is nothing but a continued survey of the same object.

There is a very remarkable circumstance, that attends this experiment; which is, that though the change of any considerable part in a mass of matter destroys the identity of the whole, yet we must measure the greatness of the part, not absolutely, but by its proportion to the whole. The addition or diminution of a mountain would not be sufficient to produce a diversity in a planet: though the change of a very few inches would be able to destroy the identity of some bodies. It will be impossible to account for this, but by reflecting that objects operate upon the mind, and break or interrupt the continuity of its actions not according to their real greatness, but according to their proportion to each other: And therefore, since this interruption makes an object cease to appear the same, it must be the uninterrupted progress, of the thought, which constitutes the imperfect identity.

This may be confirmed by another phenomenon. A change in any considerable part of a body destroys its identity; but it is remarkable, that where the change is produced gradually and insensibly we are less apt to ascribe to it the same effect. The reason can plainly be no other, than that the mind, in following the successive changes of the body, feels an easy passage from the surveying its condition in one moment to the viewing of it in another, and at no particular time perceives any interruption in its actions. From which continued perception, it ascribes a continued existence and identity to the object.

But whatever precaution we may use in introducing the changes gradually, and making them proportionable to the whole, it is certain, that where the changes are at last observed to become considerable, we make a scruple of ascribing identity to such different objects. There is, however, another artifice, by which we may induce the imagination to advance a step farther; and that is, by producing a reference of the parts to each other, and a combination to some common end or purpose. A ship, of which a considerable part has been changed by frequent reparations, is still considered as the same; nor does the difference of the materials hinder us from ascribing an identity to it. The common end, in which the parts conspire, is the same under all their variations, and affords an easy transition of the imagination from one situation of the body to another.

But this is still more remarkable, when we add a sympathy of parts to their common end, and suppose that they bear to each other, the reciprocal relation of cause and effect in all their actions and operations. This is the case with all animals and vegetables; where not only the several parts have a reference to some general purpose, but also a mutual dependence on, and connexion with each other. The effect of so strong a relation is, that though every one must allow, that in a very few years both vegetables and animals endure a total change, yet we still attribute identity to them, while their form, size, and substance are entirely altered. An oak, that grows from a small plant to a large tree, is still the same oak; though there be not one particle of matter, or figure of its parts the same. An infant becomes a man-, and is sometimes fat, sometimes lean, without any change in his identity.

We may also consider the two following phenomena, which are remarkable in their kind. The first is, that though we commonly be able to distinguish pretty exactly betwixt numerical and specific identity, yet it sometimes happens, that we confound them, and in our thinking and reasoning employ the one for the other. Thus a man, who hears a noise, that is frequently interrupted and renewed, says, it is still the same noise; though it is evident the sounds have only a specific identity or resemblance, and there is nothing numerically the same, but the cause, which produced them. In like manner it may be said without breach of the propriety of language, that such a church, which was formerly of brick, fell to ruin, and that the parish rebuilt the same church of free-stone, and according to modern architecture. Here neither the form nor materials are the same, nor is there any thing common to the two objects, but their relation to the inhabitants of the parish; and yet this alone is sufficient to make us denominate them the same. But we must observe, that in these cases the first object is in a manner annihilated before the second comes into existence; by which means, we are never presented in any one point of time with the idea of difference and multiplicity: and for that reason are less scrupulous in calling them the same.

Secondly, we may remark, that though in a succession of related objects, it be in a manner requisite, that the change of parts be not sudden nor entire, in order to preserve the identity, yet where the objects are in their nature changeable and inconstant, we admit of a more sudden transition, than would otherwise be consistent with that relation. Thus as the nature of a river consists in the motion and change of parts; though in less than four and twenty hours these be totally altered; this hinders not the river from continuing the same during several ages. What is natural and essential to any thing is, in a manner, expected; and what is expected makes less impression, and appears of less moment, than what is unusual and extraordinary. A considerable change of the former kind seems really less to the imagination, than the most trivial alteration of the latter; and by breaking less the continuity of the thought, has less influence in destroying the identity.

We now proceed to explain the nature of personal identity, which has become so great a question in philosophy, especially of late years in England, where all the abstruser sciences are studied with a peculiar ardour and application. And here it is evident, the same method of reasoning must be continued which has so successfully explained the identity of plants, and animals, and ships, and houses, and of all the compounded and changeable productions either of art or nature. The identity, which we ascribe to the mind of man, is only a fictitious one, and of a like kind with that which we ascribe to vegetables and animal bodies. It cannot, therefore, have a different origin, but must proceed from a like operation of the imagination upon like objects.

But lest this argument should not convince the reader; though in my opinion perfectly decisive; let him weigh the following reasoning, which is still closer and more immediate. It is evident, that the identity, which we attribute to the human mind, however perfect we may imagine it to be, is not able to run the several different perceptions into one, and make them lose their characters of distinction and difference, which are essential to them. It is still true, that every distinct perception, which enters into the composition of the mind, is a distinct existence, and is different, and distinguishable, and separable from every other perception, either contemporary or successive. But, as, notwithstanding this distinction and separability, we suppose the whole train of perceptions to be united by identity, a question naturally arises concerning this relation of identity; whether it be something that really binds our several perceptions together, or only associates their ideas in the imagination. That is, in other words, whether in pronouncing concerning the identity of a person, we observe some real bond among his perceptions, or only feel one among the ideas we form of them. This question we might easily decide, if we would recollect what has been already proud at large, that the understanding never observes any real connexion among objects, and that even the union of cause and effect, when strictly examined, resolves itself into a customary association of ideas. For from thence it evidently follows, that identity is nothing really belonging to these different perceptions, and uniting them together; but is merely a quality, which we attribute to them, because of the union of their ideas in the imagination, when we reflect upon them.

As a memory alone acquaints us with the continuance and extent of this succession of perceptions, it is to be considered, upon that account chiefly, as the source of personal identity. Had we no memory, we never should have any notion of causation, nor consequently of that chain of causes and effects, which constitute our self or person. But having once acquired this notion of causation from the memory, we can extend the same chain of causes, and consequently the identity of our persons beyond our memory, and can comprehend times, and circumstances, and actions, which we have entirely forgot, but suppose in general to have existed. For how few of our past actions are there, of which we have any memory? Who can tell me, for instance, what were his thoughts and actions on the 1st of January 1715, the 11th of March 1719, and the 3rd of August 1733? Or will he affirm, because he has entirely forgot the incidents of these days, that the present self is not the same person with the self of that time; and by that means overturn all the most established notions of personal identity? In this view, therefore, memory does not so much produce as discover personal identity, by showing us the relation of cause and effect among our different perceptions. It will be incumbent on those, who affirm that memory produces entirely our personal identity, to give a reason why we can thus extend our identity beyond our memory.

The whole of this doctrine leads us to a conclusion, which is of great importance in the present affair, viz. that all the nice and subtile questions concerning personal identity can never possibly be decided, and are to be regarded rather as grammatical than as philosophical difficulties. Identity depends on the relations of ideas; and these relations produce identity, by means of that easy transition they occasion. But as the relations, and the easiness of the transition may diminish by insensible degrees, we have no just standard, by which we can decide any dispute concerning the time, when they acquire or lose a title to the name of identity. All the disputes concerning the identity of connected objects are merely verbal, except so far as the relation of parts gives rise to some fiction or imaginary principle of union, as we have already observed.

PART VII

Free Will, Determinism, and Compatibilism

ESSAYS ON THE ACTIVE POWERS OF THE HUMAN MIND

By Thomas Reid

Essay IV: Of the Liberty of Moral Agents

CHAPTER 1: THE NOTIONS OF MORAL LIBERTY STATED

By the *liberty* of a moral agent, I understand, a power over the determinations of his own will.

If, in any action, he had power to will what he did, or not to will it, in that action he is free.

But if, in every voluntary action, the determination of his will be the necessary consequence of something involuntary in the state of his mind, or of something in his external circumstances, he is not free; he has not what I call the liberty of a moral agent, but is subject to necessity.

This liberty supposes the agent to have understanding and will; for the determinations of the will are the sole object about which this power is employed; and there can be no will, without, at least, such a degree of understanding as gives the conception of that which we will.

The liberty of a moral agent implies, not only a conception of what he wills, but some degree of practical judgment or reason.

For, if he has not the judgment to discern one determination to be preferable to another, either in itself, or for some purpose which he intends, what can be the use of a power to determine? His determinations must be made perfectly in the dark, without reason, motive, or end. They can neither be right nor wrong, wise nor foolish. Whatever the consequences may be, they cannot be imputed to the agent, who had not the capacity of foreseeing them, or of perceiving any reason for acting otherwise than he did.

We may perhaps be able to conceive a being endowed with power over the determinations of his will, without any light in his mind to direct that power to some end. But such power would be given in vain. No exercise of it could be either blamed or approved. As nature gives no power in vain, I see no ground to ascribe a power over the determinations of the will to any being who has no judgment to apply it to the direction of his conduct, no discernment of what he ought or ought not to do.

For that reason, in this essay, I speak only of the liberty of moral agents, who are capable of acting well or ill, wisely or foolishly, and this, for distinction's sake, I shall call *moral liberty*.

What kind, or what degree of liberty belongs to brute animals, or to our own species, before any use of reason, I do not know. We acknowledge that they have not the power of self-government. Such of their actions as may be called *voluntary*, seem to be invariably determined by the passion or appetite, or affection or habit, which is strongest at the time.

This seems to be the law of their constitution, to which they yield, as the inanimate creation does, without any conception of the law, or any intention of obedience.

But of civil or moral government, which are addressed to the rational powers, and require a conception of the law and an intentional obedience, they are, in the judgment of all mankind, incapable. Nor do I see what end could be served by giving them a power over the determinations of their own will, unless to make them intractable by discipline, which we see they are not.

The effect of moral liberty is, that it is in the power of the agent to do well or ill. This power, like every other gift of God, may be abused. The right use of this gift of God is to do well and wisely, as far as his best judgment can direct him, and thereby merit esteem and approbation. The abuse of it is to act contrary to what he knows, or suspects to be his duty and his wisdom, and thereby justly merit disapprobation and blame.

By *necessity*, I understand the want of that moral liberty which I have above defined.

If there can be a better and a worse in actions on the system of necessity, let us suppose a man necessarily determined in all cases to will and to do what is best to be done, he would surely be innocent and inculpable. But, as far as I am able to judge, he would not be entitled to the esteem and moral approbation of those who knew and believed this necessity. What was, by an ancient author, said of Cato, might indeed be said of him. *He was good because he could not be otherwise.*

But this saying, if understood literally and strictly, is not the praise of Cato, but of his constitution, which was no more the work of Cato, than his existence.

On the other hand, if a man be necessarily determined to do ill, this case seems to me to move pity, but not disapprobation. He was ill, because he could not be otherwise. Who can blame him? Necessity has no law....

Supposing it therefore to be true, that man is a free agent, it may be true, at the same time, that his liberty may be impaired or lost, by disorder of body or mind, as in melancholy, or in madness; it may be impaired or lost by vicious habits; it may, in particular cases, be restrained by divine interposition.

We call man a free agent in the same way as we call him a reasonable agent.

In many things he is not guided by reason, but by principles similar to those of the brutes. His reason is weak at best. It is liable to be impaired or lost, by his own fault, or by other means. In like manner, he may be a free agent, though his freedom of action may have many similar limitations.

CHAPTER 5: LIBERTY INCONSISTENT WITH GOVERNMENT

The arguments to prove that man is endowed with moral liberty, which have the greatest weight with me, are three: *first*, because he has a natural conviction or belief, that, in many cases, he acts freely; *secondly*, because he is accountable; and, *thirdly*, because he is able to prosecute an end by a long series of means adapted to it....

CHAPTER 6: FIRST ARGUMENT FOR LIBERTY

We have, by our constitution a natural conviction or belief that we act freely—a conviction so early, so universal, and so necessary in most of our rational operations, that it must be the result of our constitution, and the work of Him that made us.

Some of the most strenuous advocates for the doctrine of necessity acknowledge that it is impossible to act upon it. They say that we have a natural sense or conviction that we act freely; but that this is a fallacious sense.

This doctrine is dishonorable to our Maker, and lays a foundation for universal skepticism. It supposes the Author of our being to have given us one faculty on purpose to deceive us, and another by which we may detect the fallacy, and find that he imposed upon us.

If any one of our natural faculties be fallacious, there can be no reason to trust to any of them; for He that made one made all....

Passing this opinion, therefore, as shocking to an ingenuous mind, and, in its consequences, subversive of all religion, all morals, and all knowledge, let us proceed to consider the evidence of our having a natural conviction that we have some degree of active power.

The very conception or idea of active power must be derived from something in our own constitution. It is impossible to account for it otherwise. We see events, but we see not the power that produces them. We perceive one event to follow another, but we perceive not the chain that binds them together. The notion of power and causation, therefore, cannot be got from external objects.

Yet the notion of causes, and the belief that every event must have a cause which had power to produce it, is found in every human mind so firmly established, that it cannot be rooted out.

This notion and this belief must have its origin from something in our constitution; and that it is natural to man, appears from the following observations.

First, we are conscious of many voluntary exertions, some easy, others more difficult, some requiring a great effort. These are exertions of power. And, though a man may be unconscious of his power when he does not exert it, he must have both the conception and the belief of it, when he knowingly and willingly exerts it, with intention to produce some effect.

Second, deliberation about an action of movement, whether we shall do it or not, implies a conviction that it is in our power. To deliberate about an end, we must be convinced that the means are in our power; and to deliberate about the means, we must be convinced that we have power to choose the most proper.

Third, suppose our deliberation brought to an issue, and that we resolve to do what appeared proper, can we form such a resolution or purpose, without any conviction of power to execute it? No, it is impossible. A man cannot resolve to lay out a sum of money which he neither has nor hopes ever to have.

Fourth, when I plight my faith in any promise or contract, I must believe that I shall have power to perform what I promise. Without this persuasion, a promise would be downright fraud.

There is a condition implied in every promise, *if we live* and *if God continue with us the power which he has given us.* Our conviction, therefore, of this power derogates not in the least from our dependence upon God. The rudest savage is taught by nature to admit this condition in all promises, whether it be expressed or not. For it is a dictate of common sense, that we can be under no obligation to do what it is impossible for us to do.

If we act upon the system of necessity, there must be another condition implied in all deliberation, in every resolution, and in every promise; and that is, *if we shall be willing.* But the will not being in our power, we cannot engage for it.

If this condition be understood, as it must be understood if we act upon the system of necessity, there can be no deliberation, or resolution, nor any obligation in a promise. A man might as well deliberate, resolve, and promise, upon the actions of other men as upon his own.

It is no less evident that we have a conviction of power in other men, when we advise or persuade, or command, or conceive them to be under obligation by their promises.

Fifth, is it possible for any man to blame himself for yielding to necessity? Then he may blame himself for dying, or for being a man. Blame supposes a wrong use of power; and, when a man does as well as it was possible for him to do, wherein is he to be blamed? Therefore, all conviction of wrong conduct, all remorse and self-condemnation, imply a conviction of our power to have done better. Take away this conviction, and there may be a sense of misery, or a dread of evil to come; but there can be no sense of guilt or resolution to do better.

Many who hold the doctrine of necessity, disown these consequences of it, and think to evade them. To such, they ought not to be imputed; but their inseparable connection with that doctrine appears self-evident; and, therefore, some late patrons of it have had the boldness to avow them. "They cannot accuse themselves of having done anything wrong, in the ultimate sense of the words. In a strict sense, they have nothing to do with repentance, confession, and pardon—these being adapted to a fallacious view of things." Those who can adopt these sentiments, may, indeed, celebrate, with high encomiums, "the great and glorious doctrine of necessity." It restores them, in their own conceit, to the state of innocence. It delivers them from all the pangs of guilt and remorse, and from all fear about their future conduct, though not about their fate. They may be as secure that they shall do nothing wrong as those who have finished their course. A doctrine so flattering to the mind of a sinner, is very apt to give strength to weak arguments.

After all, it is acknowledged, by those who boast of this glorious doctrine, "that every man, let him use what efforts he can, will necessarily feel the sentiments of shame, remorse, and repentance, and, oppressed with a sense of guilt, will have recourse to that mercy of which he stands in need." The meaning of this seems to me to be that, although the doctrine of necessity be supported by invincible arguments, and though it be the most consolatory doctrine in the world; yet no man, in his most serious moments, when he sits himself before the throne of his Maker, can possibly believe it, but must then necessarily lay aside this glorious doctrine, and all its flattering consequences, and return to the humiliating conviction of his having made a bad use of the power which God had given him.

If the belief of our having active power be necessarily implied in those rational operations we have mentioned, it must be coeval with our reason; it must be as universal among men, and as necessary in the conduct of life, as those operations are.

We cannot recollect by memory when it began. It cannot be a prejudice of education, or of false philosophy. It must be a part of our constitution, or the necessary result of our constitution and therefore the work of God.

It resembles, in this respect, our belief of the existence of a material world; our belief that those we converse with are living and intelligent beings; our belief that those things did really happen, which we distinctly remember; and our belief that we continue the same identical persons.

We find difficulty in accounting for our belief of these things; and some philosophers think that they have discovered good reasons for throwing it off.

But it sticks fast, and the greatest skeptic finds that he must yield to it in his practice, while he wages war with it in speculation.

This natural conviction of some degree of power in ourselves and in other men, respects voluntary actions only. For, as all our power is directed by our will, we can form no conception of power, properly so called, that is not under the direction of will. And therefore our exertions, our deliberations, our purposes, our promises are only in things that depend upon our will. Our advices, exhortations, and commands, are only in things that depend upon the will of those to whom they are addressed. We impute no guilt to ourselves, nor to others, in things where the will is not concerned.

But it deserves our notice, that we do not conceive everything, without exception, to be in a man's power which depends upon his will. There are many exceptions to this general rule. The most obvious of these I shall mention, because they both serve to illustrate the rule, and are of importance in the question concerning the liberty of man.

In the rage of madness, men are absolutely deprived of the power of self-government.

They act voluntarily, but their will is driven as by a tempest, which, in lucid intervals, they resolve to oppose with all their might, but are overcome when the fit of madness returns.

Idiots are like men walking in the dark, who cannot be said to have the power of choosing their way, because they cannot distinguish the good road from the bad. Having no light in their understanding, they must either sit still, or be carried on by some blind impulse.

Between the darkness of infancy, which is equal to that of idiots, and the maturity of reason, there is a long twilight, which, by insensible degrees, advances to the perfect day.

In this period of life, man has but little of the power of self-government. His actions, by nature, as well as by the laws of society, are in the power of others more than in his own. His folly and indiscretion, his levity and inconstancy, are considered as the fault of youth, rather than of the man. We consider him as half a man and half a child, and expect that each by turns should play its part. He would be thought a severe and unequitable censor of manners, who required the same cool deliberation, the same steady conduct, and the same mastery over himself, in a boy of thirteen, as in a man of thirty.

It is an old adage that violent anger is a short fit of madness. If this be literally true in any case, a man, in such a fit of passion, cannot be said to have the command of himself. If real madness could be proved, it must have the effect of madness while it lasts, whether it be for an hour or for life. But the madness of a short fit of passion, if it be really madness, is incapable of proof; and therefore is not admitted in human tribunals as an exculpation. And, I believe, there is no case where a man can satisfy his own mind that his passion, both in its beginning and in its progress, was irresistible. The Searcher of hearts alone knows infallibly what allowance is due in cases of this kind.

But a violent passion, though it may not be irresistible, is difficult to be resisted: And a man, surely, has not the same power over himself in passion, as when he is cool. On this account it is allowed by all men to alleviate, when it cannot exculpate; and has its weight in criminal courts, as well as in private judgment.

This natural conviction of our acting freely, which is acknowledged by many who hold the doctrine of necessity, ought to throw the whole burden of proof upon that side; for, by this, the side of liberty has what lawyers call a *jus quaesitum*, or a right of ancient possession, which ought to stand good till it be overturned.

If it cannot be proved that we always act from necessity, there is no need of arguments on the other side to convince us that we are free agents.

To illustrate this by a similar case: If a philosopher would persuade me that my fellow-men with whom I converse are not thinking, intelligent beings, but mere machines, though I might be at a loss to find arguments against this strange opinion, I should think it reasonable to hold the belief which nature gave me before I was capable of weighing evidence, until convincing proof is brought against it.

CHAPTER 7: SECOND ARGUMENT

That there is a real and essential distinction between right and wrong conduct, between just and unjust, that the most perfect moral rectitude is to be ascribed to the Deity, that man is a moral and accountable being, capable of acting right and wrong, and answerable for his conduct to Him who made him, and assigned him a part to act upon the stage of life; are principles proclaimed by every man's conscience— principles upon which the systems of morality and natural religion, as well as the system of revelation, are grounded, and which have been generally acknowledged by those who hold contrary opinions on the subject of human liberty. I shall therefore here take them for granted.

These principles afford an obvious, and, I think, an invincible argument, that man is endowed with moral liberty.

Two things are implied in the notion of a moral and accountable being: *understanding* and *active power.*

First, he must *understand the law to which he is bound, and his obligation to obey it.* Moral obedience must be voluntary, and must regard the authority of the law. I may command my horse to eat when he hungers, and drink when he thirsts. He does so; but his doing it is no moral obedience. He does not understand my command, and therefore can have no will to obey it. He has not the conception of moral obligation, and therefore cannot act from the conviction of it.

In eating and drinking, he is moved by his own appetite only, and not by my authority.

Brute animals are incapable of moral obligation, because they have not that degree of understanding which it implies. They have not the conception of a rule of conduct and of obligation to obey it, and therefore, though they may be noxious, they cannot be criminal.

Man, by his rational nature, is capable both of understanding the law that is prescribed to him, and of perceiving its obligation. He knows what it is to be just and honest, to injure no man, and to obey his Maker. From his constitution, he has an immediate conviction of his obligation to these things. He has the approbation of his conscience when he acts by these rules; and he is conscious of guilt and demerit when he transgresses them. And, without this knowledge of his duty and his obligation, he would not be a moral and accountable being.

Secondly, another thing implied in the notion of a moral and accountable being, is *power to do what he is accountable for.*

That no man can be under a moral obligation to do what it is impossible for him to do, or to forbear what it is impossible for him for forbear, is an axiom as self-evident as any in mathematics. It cannot be contradicted, without overturning all notion of moral obligation; nor can there be any exception to it, when it is rightly understood....

Active power, therefore, is necessarily implied in the very notion of a moral accountable being. And if man be such a being, he must have a degree of active power proportioned to the account he is to make. He may have a model of perfection set before him which he is unable to reach; but, if he does to the utmost of his power, this is all he can be answerable for. To incur guilt, by not going beyond his power, is impossible.

What was said, in the first argument, of the limitation of our power, adds much strength to the present argument. A man's power, it was observed, extends only to his voluntary actions, and has many limitations, even with respect to them.

His accountableness has the same extent and the same limitations.

In the rage of madness he has no power over himself, neither is he accountable, or capable of moral obligation. In ripe age, man is accountable in a greater degree than in non-age, because his power over himself is greater. Violent passions and violent motives alleviate what is done through their influence, in the same proportion as they diminish the power of resistance.

There is, therefore, a perfect correspondence between power, on the one hand, and moral obligation and accountableness, on the other. They not only correspond in general, as they respect voluntary actions only, but every limitation of the first produces a corresponding limitation of the two last. This, indeed, amounts to nothing more than that maxim of common sense, confirmed by Divine authority, "That to whom much is given, of him much will be required." The sum of this argument is: that a certain degree of active power is the talent which God has given to every rational accountable creature, and of which he will require an account. If man had no power, he would have nothing to account for.

All wise and all foolish conduct, all virtue and vice, consist in the right use or in the abuse of that power which God has given us. If man had no power, he could neither be wise nor foolish, virtuous nor vicious.

If we adopt the system of necessity, the terms *moral obligation* and *accountableness*, *praise* and *blame*, *merit* and *demerit*, *justice* and *injustice*, *reward* and *punishment*, *wisdom* and *folly*, *virtue* and *vice*, ought to be disused, or to have new meanings given to them when they are used in religion, in morals, or in civil government; for, upon that system, there can be no such thing as they have been always used to signify.

CHAPTER 8: THIRD ARGUMENT

That man has power over his own actions and volitions appears, because he is capable of carrying on, wisely and prudently, a system of conduct, which he has before conceived in his mind, and resolved to prosecute.

I take it for granted, that, among the various characters of men, there have been some who, after they came to years of understanding, deliberately laid down a plan of conduct, which they resolve to pursue through life; and that of these, some have steadily pursued the end they had in view, by the proper means.

It is of no consequence in this argument, whether one has made the best choice of his main end or not; whether his end be riches, or power, or fame, or the approbation of his Maker. I suppose only, that he has prudently and steadily pursued it; that, in a long course of deliberate actions, he has taken the means that appeared most conducive to his end, and avoided whatever might cross it.

That such conduct in a man demonstrates a certain degree of wisdom and understanding, no man ever doubted; and I say it demonstrates, with equal force, a certain degree of power over his voluntary determinations.

This will appear evident, if we consider, that understanding without power may project, but can execute nothing. A regular plan of conduct, as it cannot be contrived without understanding, so it cannot be carried into execution without power; and, therefore, the execution, as an effect, demonstrates, with equal force, both power and understanding in the cause. Every indication of wisdom, taken from the effect, is equally an indication of power to execute what wisdom planned. And if we have any evidence that the wisdom which formed the plan is in the man, we have the very same evidence that the power which executed it is in him also.

In this argument, we reason from the same principles as in demonstrating the being and perfections of the First Cause of all things.

The effects we observe in the course of nature require a cause. Effects wisely adapted to an end, require a wise cause. Every indication of the wisdom of the Creator is equally an indication of His power. His wisdom appears only in the works done by his power; for wisdom without power may speculate, but it cannot act; it may plan, but it cannot execute its plans.

The same reasoning we apply to the works of men. In a stately palace we see the wisdom of the architect. His wisdom contrived it, and wisdom could do no more. The execution required both a distinct conception of the plan, and power to operate according to that plan.

Let us apply these principles to the supposition we have made: that a man, in a long course of conduct, has determined and acted prudently in the prosecution of a certain end. If the man had both the wisdom to plan this course of conduct, and that power over his own actions that was necessary to carry it into execution, he is a free agent, and used his liberty, in this instance, with understanding.

But, if all his particular determinations, which concurred in the execution of this plan were produced, not by himself, but by some cause acting necessarily upon him, then there is no evidence left that he contrived this plan, or that he ever spent a thought about it.

The cause that directed all these determinations so wisely, whatever it was, must be a wise and intelligent cause; it must have understood the plan, and have intended the execution of it.

If it be said that all this course of determination was produced by motives, motives surely, have not understanding to receive a plan, and intend its execution.

We must, therefore, go back beyond motives to some intelligent being who had the power of arranging those motives, and applying them in their proper order and season, so as to bring about the end.

This intelligent being must have understood the plan, and intended to execute it. If this be so, as the man had no hand in the execution, we have not any evidence left that he had any hand in the contrivance, or even that he is a thinking being.

If we can believe that an extensive series of means may conspire to promote an end without a cause that intended the end, and had power to choose and apply those means for the purpose, we may as well believe that this world was made by a fortuitous concourse of atoms, without an intelligent and powerful cause.

If a lucky concourse of motives could produce the conduct of an Alexander or a Julius Caesar, no reason can be given why a lucky concourse of atoms might not produce the planetary system.

If, therefore, wise conduct in a man demonstrates that he has some degree of wisdom, it demonstrates, with equal force and evidence, that he has some degree of power over his own determinations.

All the reason we can assign for believing that our fellow-men think and reason, is grounded upon their actions and speeches. If they are not the cause of these, there is no reason left to conclude that they think and reason.

Descartes thought that the human body is merely an engine, and that all its motions and actions are produced by mechanism. If such a machine could be made to speak and to act rationally, we might, indeed, conclude with certainty, that the maker of it had both reason and active power; but, if we once knew that all the motions of the machine were purely mechanical, we should have no reason to conclude that the man had reason or thought.

The conclusion of this argument is: that, if the actions and speeches of other men give us sufficient evidence that they are reasonable beings, they give us the same evidence, and the same degree of evidence, that they are free agents.

THE SYSTEM OF NATURE

By Baron d'Holbach

PART I.
CHAPTER XI.

Of the System of Man's free agency. Those who have pretended that the *soul* is distinguished from the body, is immaterial, draws its ideas from its own peculiar source, acts by its own energies without the aid of any exterior object; by a consequence of their own system, have enfranchised it from those physical laws, according to which all beings of which we have a knowledge are obliged to act. They have believed that the foul is mistress of its own conduct, is able to regulate its own peculiar operations; has the faculty to determine its will by its own natural energy; in a word, they have pretended man is a *free agent*.

It has been already sufficiently proved, that the soul is nothing more than the body, considered relatively to some of its functions, more concealed than others: it has been shown that this soul, even when it shall be supposed immaterial, is continually modified conjointly with the body; is submitted to all its motion; that without this it would remain inert and dead: that, consequently, it is subjected to the influence of those material, to the operation those physical causes, which give impulse to the body; of which the mode of existence, whether habitual or transitory, depends upon the material elements by which it is surrounded; that form its texture; that constitute its temperament; that enter into it by the means of the aliments; that penetrate it by their subtility; the faculties which are called intellectual, and those qualities which are styled moral, have been explained in a manner purely physical; entirely natural: in the last place, it has been demonstrated, that all the ideas, all the systems, all the affections, all the opinions, whether true or false, which man forms to himself, are to be attributed to his physical powers; are to be ascribed to his material senses. Thus man is a being purely physical; in whatever manner he is considered, he is connected to universal Nature: submitted to the necessary, to the immutable laws that she imposes on all the beings she contains, according to their peculiar essences; conformable to the respective properties with which, without consulting them, she endows each particular species. Man's life is a line that Nature commands him to describe upon the surface of the earth: without his ever being able to swerve from it even for an instant. He is born without his own consent; his organization doe in no wise depend upon himself; his ideas come to him involuntarily; his habits are in the power of those who cause him to contract them; he is unceasingly modified by causes, whether visible or concealed, over which he has no control; give the hue to his way of thinking, and determine his manner of acting. He is good or bad—happy or miserable—wise or foolish—reasonable or irrational, without his will going for anything in these various states. Nevertheless, in despite of the shackles by which he is bound, it is pretended he is a free agent, or that independent of the causes by which he is moved, he determines his own will; regulates his own condition.

However slender the foundation of this opinion, of which every thing ought to point out to him the error; it is current at this day for an incontestable truth, and believed enlightened; it is the basis of religion, which has been incapable of imagining how man could either merit reward or deserve punishment if he was not a free agent. Society has been believed interested in this system, because an idea has gone abroad, that if all the actions of man were to be contemplated as necessary, the right of punishing those who injure their associates would no longer exist. At length human vanity accommodated itself to an hypothesis which, unquestionable, appears to distinguish man from all other physical beings, by assigning to him the special privilege of a total independence of all other causes; but of which a very little reflection would have shown him the absurdity or even the impossibility.

As a part, subordinate to the great whole, man is obliged to experience its influence. To be a free agent it were needful that each individual was of greater strength than the entire of Nature; or, that he was out of this Nature: who, always in action herself, obliges all the beings she embraces, to act, and to concur to her general motion; or, as it has been said elsewhere, to conserve her active existence, by the motion that all beings produce in consequence of their particular energies, which result from their being submitted to fixed, eternal, and immutable laws. In order that man might be a free agent, it were needful that all beings should lose their essences; it is equally necessary that he himself should no longer enjoy physical sensibility; that he should neither know good nor evil; pleasure nor pain; but if this was the case, from that moment he would no longer be in a state to conserve himself, or render his existence happy; all beings would become indifferent to him; he would no longer have any choice; he would cease to know what he ought to love; what it was right he should fear; he would not have any acquaintance with that which he should seek after; or with that which it is requisite he should avoid. In short, man would be an unnatural being; totally incapable of acting in the manner we behold. It is the actual essence of man to tend to his well-being; to be desirous to conserve his existence; if all the motion of his machine springs as a necessary consequence from this primitive impulse; if pain warns him of that which he ought to avoid; if pleasure announces to him that which he should desire; if it is in his essence to love that which either excites delight, or, that from which he expects agreeable sensations; to hate that which makes him either fear contrary impressions; or, that which afflicts him with uneasiness; it must necessarily be, that he will be attracted by that which he deems advantageous; that his will shall he determined by those objects which he judges useful; that he will be repelled by those beings which he believes prejudicial, either to his habitual, or to his transitory mode of existence; by that which he considers disadvantageous. It is only by the aid of experience, that man acquires the faculty of understanding what he ought to love; of knowing what he ought to fear. Are his organs sound? his experience will he true: are they unsound? it will be false: in the first instance he will have reason, prudence, foresight; he will frequently foresee very remote effects; he will know, that what he sometimes contemplates as a good, may possibly become an evil, by its necessary or probable consequences: that what must be to him a transient evil, may by its result procure him a solid and durable good. It is thus experience enables him to foresee that the amputation of a limb will cause him painful sensation, he consequently is obliged to fear this operation, and he endeavours to avoid the pain; but if experience has also shown him, that the transitory pain this amputation will cause him may be the means of saving his life; the preservation, of his existence being of necessity dear to him, he is obliged to submit himself to the momentary pain with a view to procuring a permanent good, by which it will be overbalanced.

The will, as we have elsewhere said, is a modification of the brain, by which it is disposed to action or prepared to give play to the organs. This will is necessarily determined by the qualities, good or bad, agreeable or painful, of the object or the motive that acts upon his senses; or of which the idea remains with him, and is resuscitated by his memory. In consequence, he acts necessarily; his action is the result of the impulse he receives either from the motive, from the object, or from the idea, which has modified his brain, or disposed his will. When he does not act according to this impulse, it is because there comes some new cause, some new motive, some new idea, which modifies his brain in a different manner, gives him a new impulse, determines his will in another way; by which the action of the former impulse is suspended: thus, the sight of an agreeable object, or its idea, determines his will to set him in action to procure it; but if a new object or a new idea more powerfully attracts him, it gives a new direction to his will, annihilates the effect of the former, and prevents the action by which it was to be procured. This is the mode in which reflection, experience, reason, necessarily arrests or suspends the action of man's will; without this, he would, of necessity, have followed the anterior impulse which carried him towards a then desirable object. In all this he always acts according to necessary laws, from which he has no means of emancipating himself.

If, when tormented with violent thirst, he figures to himself an idea, or really perceives a fountain, whose limpid streams might cool his feverish habit, is he sufficient master of himself to desire or not to desire the object competent to satisfy so lively a want? It will no doubt be conceded, that it is impossible he should not be desirous to satisfy it; but it will be said,—If at this moment it is announced to him, the water he so ardently desires is poisoned, he will, notwithstanding his vehement thirst, abstain from drinking it; and it has, therefore, been falsely concluded that he is a free agent. The fact, however, is, that the motive in either case is exactly the same: his own conservation. The same necessity that determined him to drink, before he knew the water was deleterious, upon this new discovery, equally determines him not to drink; the desire of conserving himself, either annihilates or suspends the former impulse; the second motive becomes stronger than the preceding; that is, the fear of death, or the desire of preserving himself, necessarily prevails over the painful sensation caused by his eagerness to drink. But, (it will be said) if the thirst is very parching, an inconsiderate man, without regarding the danger, will risque swallowing the water. Nothing is gained by this remark: in this case, the anterior impulse only regains the ascendency; he is persuaded, that life may possibly be longer preserved, or that he shall derive a greater good by drinking the poisoned water, than by enduring the torment, which, to his mind, threatens instant dissolution: thus, the first becomes the strongest, and necessarily urges him on to action. Nevertheless, in either case, whether he partakes of the water, or whether he does not, the two actions will be equally necessary; they will be the effect of that motive which finds itself most puissant; which consequently acts in a most coercive manner upon his will.

This example will serve to explain the whole phenomena of the human will. This will, or rather the brain, finds itself in the same situation as a ball, which although it has received an impulse that drives it forward in a straight line, is deranged in its course, whenever a force, superior to the first, obliges it to change its direction. The man who drinks the poisoned water, appears a madman; but the actions of fools are as necessary as those of the most prudent individuals. The motives that determine the voluptuary, that actuate the debauchee to risk their health, are as powerful, their actions are as necessary, as those which decide the wise man to manage his. But, it will be insisted, the debauchee may be prevailed on to change his conduct; this does not imply that he is a free agent; but, that motives may be found sufficiently powerful to annihilate the effect of those that previously acted upon him; then these new motives determine his will to the new mode of conduct he may adopt, as necessarily as the former did to the old mode.

Man is said to *deliberate* when the action of the will is suspended; this happens when two opposite motives act alternately upon him. To deliberate, is to hate and to love in succession; it is to be alternately attracted and repelled; it is to be moved sometimes by one motive, sometimes by another. Man only deliberates when he does not distinctly understand the quality of the objects from which he receives impulse, or when experience has not sufficiently apprised him of the effects, more or less remote, which his actions will produce. He would take the air, but the weather is uncertain; he deliberates in consequence;

he weighs the various motives that urge his will to go out or to stay at home; he is at length determined by that motive which is most probable; this removes his indecision, which necessarily settles his will either to remain within or to go abroad: this motive is always either the immediate or ultimate advantage he finds or thinks he finds in the action to which he is persuaded.

Man's will frequently fluctuates between two objects, of which either the presence or the ideas move him alternately: he waits until he has contemplated the objects or the ideas they have left in his brain; which solicit him to different actions; he then compares these objects or ideas: but even in the time of deliberation, during the comparison, pending these alternatives of love and hatred, which succeed each other sometimes with the utmost rapidity, he is not a free agent for a single instant; the good or the evil which he believes he finds successively in the objects, are the necessary motives of these momentary wills; of the rapid motion of desire or fear that he experiences as long as his uncertainty continues. From this it will be obvious, that deliberation is necessary; that uncertainty is necessary; that whatever part he takes, in consequence of this deliberation, it will always necessarily be that which he has judged, whether well or ill, is most probable to turn to his advantage.

When the soul is assailed by two motives that act alternately upon it, or modify it successively, it deliberates; the brain is in a sort of equilibrium, accompanied with perpetual oscillations, sometimes towards one object, sometimes towards the other, until the most forcible carries the point, and thereby extricates it, from this state of suspense, in which consists the indecision of his will. But when the brain is simultaneously assailed by causes equally strong, that move it in opposite directions; agreeable to the general law of all bodies, when they are struck equally by contrary powers, it stops, it is in *nisu*; it is neither capable to will nor to act; it waits until one of the two causes has obtained sufficient force to overpower the other, to determine its will, to attract it in such a manner that it may prevail over the efforts of the other cause.

Choice by no means proves the free-agency of man; he only deliberates when he does not yet know which to choose of the many objects that move him, he is then in an embarrassment, which does not terminate, until his will as decided by the greater advantage he believes he shall find in the object he chooses, or the action he undertakes. From whence it may be seen that choice is necessary, because he would not determine for an object, or for an action, if he did not believe that he should find in it some direct advantage. That man should have free-agency, it were needful that he should he able to will or choose without motive; or, that he could prevent motives coercing his will. Action always being the effect of his will once determined, as his will cannot be determined but by a motive, which is not in his own power, it follows that he is never the master of the determination of his own peculiar will; that consequently he never acts as a free agent. It has been believed that man was a free agent, because he had a will with the power of choosing; but attention has not been paid to the fact, that even his will is moved by causes independent of himself, is owing to that which is inherent in his own organization, or which belongs to the nature of the beings acting on him. Indeed, man passes a great portion of his life without even willing. His will attends the motive by which it is determined. If he was to render an exact account of every thing he does in the course of each day, from rising in the morning to lying down at night, he would find, that not one of his actions have been in the least voluntary; that they have been mechanical, habitual, determined by causes he was not able to foresee, to which he was either obliged to, yield, or with which he was allured to acquiesce; he would discover, that all the motives of his labours, of his amusements, of his discourses, of his thoughts, have been necessary; that they have evidently either seduced him or drawn him along. Is he the master of willing, not to withdraw his hand from the fire when he fears it will be burnt? Or has he the power to take away from fire the property which makes him fear it? Is he the master of not choosing a dish of meat which he knows to be agreeable, or analogous to his palate; of not preferring it to that which he knows to be disagreeable or dangerous? It is always according to his sensations, to his own peculiar experience, or to his suppositions, that he judges of things either well or ill; but whatever way be his judgment, it depends necessarily on his mode of feeling, whether habitual or accidental, and the qualities he finds in the causes that move him, which exist in despite of himself.

All the causes which by his will is actuated, must act upon him in a manner sufficiently marked, to give him some sensation, some perception, some idea, whether complete or incomplete, true or false; as soon as his will is determined, he must have felt, either strongly or feebly; if this was not the case he would have determined without motive: thus, to speak correctly, there are no causes which are truly indifferent to the will: however faint the impulse he receives, whether on the part of the objects themselves, or on the part of their images or ideas, as soon as his will acts, the impulse has been competent to determine him. In consequence of a slight, of a feeble impulse, the will is weak, it is this weakness of the will that is called *indifference*. His brain with difficulty perceives the sensation, it has received; it consequently acts with less vigour, either to obtain or remove the object or the idea that has modified it. If the impulse is powerful, the will is strong, it makes him act vigorously, to obtain or to remove the object which appears to him either very agreeable or very incommodious.

It has been believed man was a free agent, because it has been imagined that his soul could at will recall ideas, which sometimes suffice to check his most unruly desires. Thus, the idea of a remote evil frequently prevents him from enjoying a present and actual good: thus, remembrance, which is an almost insensible, a slight modification of his brain, annihilates, at each instant, the real objects that act upon his will. But he is not master of recalling to himself his ideas at pleasure; their association is independent of him; they are arranged in his brain, in despite of him, without his own knowledge, where they have made an impression more or less profound; his memory itself depends upon his organization;. its fidelity depends upon the habitual or momentary state in which he finds himself; when his will is vigorously determined to some object or idea that excites a very lively passion in him, those objects or ideas that would be able to arrest his action no longer present themselves to his mind; in those moments his eyes are shut to the dangers that menace him, of which the idea ought to make him forbear; he marches forward headlong towards the object by whose image he is hurried on; reflection cannot operate upon him in any way; he sees nothing but the object of his desires; the salutary ideas which might be able to arrest his progress disappear, or else display themselves either too faintly or too late to prevent his acting. Such is the case with all those who, blinded by some strong passion, are not in a condition to recall to themselves those motives, of which the idea alone, in cooler moments, would be sufficient to deter them from proceeding; the disorder in which they are, prevents their judging soundly; render them incapable of foreseeing the consequence of their actions; precludes them from applying to their experience; from making use of their reason; natural operations, which suppose a justness in the manner of associating their ideas; but to which their brain is then not more competent, in consequence of the momentary delirium it suffers, than their hand is to write whilst they are taking violent exercise.

Man's mode of thinking is necessarily determined by his manner of being; it must, therefore, depend on his natural organization, and the modification his system receives independently of his will. From this we are obliged to conclude, that his thoughts, his reflections, his manner of viewing things, of feeling, of judging, of combining ideas, is neither voluntary nor free. In a word, that his soul is neither mistress of the motion excited in it, nor of representing to itself, when wanted, those images or ideas that are capable of counterbalancing the impulse it receives. This is the reason why man, when in a passion, ceases to reason; at that moment reason is as impossible to be heard, as it is during an extacy, or in a fit of drunkenness. The wicked are never more than men who are either drunk or mad: if they reason, it is not until tranquillity is re-established in their machine; then, and not till then, the tardy ideas that present themselves to their mind, enable them to see the consequence of their actions, and give birth to ideas, that bring on them that trouble, which is designated *shame, regret, remorse.*

The errors of philosophers on the free-agency of man, have arisen from their regarding his will as the *primum mobile*, the original motive of his actions; for want of recurring back, they have not perceived the multiplied, the complicated causes, which, independently of him, give motion to the will itself, or which dispose and modify his brain, whilst he himself is purely passive in the motion he receives. Is he the master of desiring or not desiring an object that appears desirable to him? Without doubt it will be answered, No: but he is the master of resisting his desire, if he reflects on the consequences. But, I ask, is he capable of reflecting on these consequences when his soul is hurried along by a very lively passion, which entirely depends upon his natural organization, and the causes by which he is modified? Is it in his power to add to these consequences all the weight necessary to counterbalance his desire? Is he the master of preventing the qualities which render an object desirable from residing in it? I shall be told, he ought to have learned to resist his passions; to contract a habit of putting a curb on his desires. I agree to it without any difficulty: but in reply, I again ask, Is his nature susceptible of this modification? Does his boiling blood, his unruly imagination, the igneous fluid that circulates in his veins, permit him to make, enable him to apply true experience in the moment when it is wanted? And, even when his temperament has capacitated him, has his education, the examples set before him, the ideas with which he has been inspired in early life, been suitable to make him contract this habit of repressing his desires? Have not all these things rather contributed to induce him to seek with avidity, to make him actually desire those objects which you say he ought to resist.

In short, the actions of man are never free; they are always the necessary consequence of his temperament, of the received ideas, of the notions, either true or false, which he has formed to himself of happiness: of his opinions, strengthened by example, forfeited by education, consolidated by daily experience. So many crimes are witnessed on the earth, only because every thing conspires to render man vicious, to make him criminal; very frequently the superstitions he has adopted, his government, his education, the examples set before him, irresistibly drive him on to evil: under these circumstances morality preaches virtue to him in vain. In those societies where vice is esteemed, where crime is crowned, where venality is constantly recompenced, where the most dreadful disorders are punished, only in those who are too weak to enjoy the privilege of committing them with impunity; the practice of virtue is considered nothing more than a painful sacrifice of fancied happiness. Such societies chastise, in the lower orders, those excesses which they respect in the higher ranks; and frequently have the injustice to condemn those in penalty of death, whom public prejudices, maintained by constant example, have rendered criminal.

Man, then, is not a free agent in any one instant of his life; he is necessarily guided in each step by those advantages, whether real or fictitious, that he attaches to the objects by which his passions are roused: these passions themselves are necessary in a being who, unceasingly tends towards his own happiness; their energy is necessary, since that depends on his temperament; his temperament is necessary, because it depends on the physical elements which enter into his composition; the modification of this temperament is necessary, as it is the infallible result, the inevitable consequence of the impulse he receives from the incessant action of moral and physical beings.

In despite of these proofs of the want of free-agency in man, so clear to unprejudiced minds, it will, perhaps, be insisted upon with no small feeling of triumph, that if it be proposed to any one to move or not to move his hand, an action in the number of those called *indifferent*, he evidently appears to be the master of choosing; from which it is concluded, evidence has been offered of his free-agency. The reply is, this example is perfectly simple; man in performing some action which he is resolved on doing, does not by any means prove his free-agency: the very desire of displaying this quality, excited by the dispute, becomes a necessary motive which decides his will either for the one or the other of these actions: what deludes him in this instance, or that which persuades him he is a free agent at this moment, is, that he does not discern the true motive which sets him in action; which is neither more nor less than the desire of convincing his opponent: if in the heat of the dispute he insists and asks, "Am I not the master of throwing myself out of the window?" I shall answer him, no; that whilst he preserves his reason, there is not even a probability that the desire of proving his free-agency, will become a motive sufficiently powerful, to make him sacrifice his life to the attempt; if, notwithstanding this, to prove he is a free agent, he should actually precipitate himself from the window, it would not be a sufficient warrantry to conclude he acted freely, but rather that it was the violence of his temperament which spurred him on to this folly. Madness is a state that depends upon the heat of the blood, not upon the will. A fanatic or a hero, braves death as necessarily as a more phlegmatic man or a coward flies from it. There is, in point of fact, no difference between the man who is cast out of the window by another, and the man who throws himself out of it, except that the impulse in the first instance comes immediately from without, whilst that which determines the fall in the second case, springs from within his own peculiar machine, having its more remote cause also exterior.

The partizans of the system of free-agency appear ever to have confounded constraint with necessity. Man believes he acts as a free agent, every time he does not see any thing that places obstacles to his actions; he does not perceive that the motive which causes him to will is always necessary, is ever independent of himself. A prisoner loaded with chains is compelled to remain in prison, but he is not a free agent, he is not able to resist the desire to emancipate himself; his chains prevent him from acting, but they do not prevent him from willing; he would save himself if they would loose his fetters, but he would not save himself as a free agent, fear or the idea of punishment would be sufficient motives for his action.

Man may therefore cease to be restrained, without, for that reason, becoming a free agent: in whatever manner he acts, he will act necessarily; according to motives by which he shall be determined. He may be compared to a heavy body, that finds itself arrested in its descent by any obstacle whatever: take away this obstacle, it will gravitate or continue to fall; but who shall say this dense body is free to fall or not? Is not its descent the necessary effect of its own specific gravity? The virtuous Socrates submitted to the laws of his country, although they were unjust; notwithstanding the doors of his gaol were left open to him he would not save himself; but in this he did not act as a free agent; the invisible chains of opinion, the secret love of decorum, the inward respect for the laws, even when they were iniquitous, the fear of tarnishing his glory, kept him in his prison: they were motives sufficiently powerful, with this enthusiast for virtue, to induce him to wait death with tranquillity; it was not in his power to save himself, because he could find no potential motive to bring him to depart, even for an instant, from those principles to which his mind was accustomed.

Man, says he, frequently acts against his inclination, from whence he has falsely concluded he is a free agent; when he appears to act contrary to his inclination, he is determined to it by some motive sufficiently efficacious to vanquish this inclination. A sick man, with a view to his cure, arrives at conquering his repugnance to the most disgusting remedies: the fear of pain, the dread of death, then become necessary and intelligent motives; consequently, this sick man cannot be said, with truth, by any means, to act freely.

When it is said, that man is not a free agent, it is not pretended to compare him to a body moved by a simple impulsive cause: he contains within himself causes inherent to his existence; he is moved by an interior organ, which has its own peculiar laws; which is itself necessarily determined, in consequence of ideas formed from perceptions, resulting from sensations, which it receives from exterior objects. As the mechanism of these sensations, of these perceptions, and the manner they engrave ideas on the brain of man, are not known to him, because he is unable to unravel all these motions; because he cannot perceive the chain of operations in his soul, or the motive-principle that acts within him, he supposes himself a free agent; which, literally translated, signifies that he moves himself by himself; that he determines himself without cause; when he rather ought to say, he is ignorant how or for why he acts in the manner he does. It is true the soul enjoys an activity peculiar to itself, but it is equally certain that this activity would never be displayed if some motive or some cause did not put it in a condition to exercise itself, at least it will not be pretended that the soul is able either to love or to hate without being moved, without knowing the objects, without having some idea of their qualities. Gunpowder has unquestionably a particular activity, but this activity will never display itself, unless fire be applied to it; this, however, immediately sets in motion.

It is the great complication of motion in man, it is the variety of his action, it is the multiplicity of causes that move him, whether simultaneously or in continual succession, that persuades him he is a free agent: if all his motions were simple, if the causes that move him did not confound themselves with each other, if they were distinct, if his machine was less complicated, he would perceive that all his actions were necessary, because he would be enabled to recur instantly to the cause that made him act.

It is, then, for want of recurring to the causes that move him, for want of being able to analyze, from not being competent to decompose the complicated motion of his machine, that man believes himself a free agent; it is only upon his own ignorance that he founds the profound yet deceitful notion he has of his free-agency, that he builds those opinions which he brings forward as a striking proof of his pretended freedom of action. If, for a short time, each man was willing to examine his own peculiar actions, to search out their true motives, to discover their concatenation, he would remain convinced that the sentiment he has of his natural free-agency is a chimera that must speedily be destroyed by experience.

From all that has been advanced in this chapter, it results, that in no one moment of his existence man is a free agent: he is not the architect of his own conformation; this he holds from Nature, he has no control over his own ideas, or over the modification of his brain; these are due to causes, that, in despite of him, very frequently without his own knowledge, unceasingly act upon him; he is not the master of not loving that which he finds amiable; of not coveting that which appears to him desirable; he is not capable of refusing to deliberate, when he is uncertain of the effects certain objects will produce upon him; he cannot avoid choosing that which he believes will be most advantageous to him: in the moment when his will is determined by his choice, he is not competent to act otherwise than he does: in what instance, then, is he the master of his own actions? In what moment is he a free agent?

In the moral as well as in the physical world, every thing that happens is a necessary consequence of causes, either visible or concealed; which are, of necessity, obliged to act after their peculiar essences. *In man, free-agency is nothing more than necessity contained within himself.*

THE DILEMMA OF
DETERMINISM

By William James

Acommon opinion prevails that the juice has ages ago been pressed out of the free-will controversy, and that no new champion can do more than warm up stale arguments which everyone has heard. This is a radical mistake. I know of no subject less worn out, or in which inventive genius has a better chance of breaking open new ground—not, perhaps, of forcing a conclusion or of coercing assent, but of deepening our sense of what the issue between the two parties really is, of what the ideas of fate and of free will imply....

To begin, then, I must suppose you acquainted with all the usual arguments on the subject. I cannot stop to take up the old proofs from causation, from statistics, from the certainty with which we can foretell one another's conduct, from the fixity of character, and all the rest. But there are two *words* which usually encumber these classical arguments, and which we must immediately dispose of if we are to make any progress. One is the eulogistic word *freedom,* and the other is the opprobrious word *chance.* The word "chance" I wish to keep, but I wish to get rid of the word "freedom." Its eulogistic associations have so far overshadowed all the rest of its meaning that both parties claim the sole right to use it, and determinists today insist that they alone are freedom's champions. Old-fashioned determinism was what we may call *hard* determinism. It did not shrink from such words as fatality, bondage of the will, necessitation, and the like. Nowadays, we have a *soft* determinism which abhors harsh words, and, repudiating fatality, necessity, and even predetermination, says that its real name is freedom; for freedom is only necessity understood, and bondage to the highest is identical with true freedom....

Now, all this is a quagmire of evasion under which the real issue of fact has been entirely smothered. Freedom in all these senses presents simply no problem at all. No matter what the soft determinist means by it, whether he means the acting without external constraint; whether he means the acting rightly, or whether he means the acquiescing in the law of the whole, who cannot answer him that sometimes we are free and sometimes we are not? But there *is* a problem, an issue of fact and not of words, an issue of the most momentous importance, which is often decided without discussion in one sentence,—nay, in one clause of a sentence,—by those very writers who spin out whole chapters in their efforts to show what "true" freedom is; and that is the question of determinism, about which we are to talk tonight.

Fortunately, no ambiguities hang about this word or about its opposite, indeterminism. Both designate an outward way in which things may happen, and their cold and mathematical sound has no sentimental associations that can bribe our partiality either way in advance. Now, evidence of an external kind to decide between determinism and indeterminism is … strictly impossible to find. Let us look at the difference between them and see for ourselves. What does determinism profess?

It professes that those parts of the universe already laid down absolutely appoint and decree what the other parts shall be. The future has no ambiguous possibilities hidden in its womb; the part we call the present is compatible with only one totality. Any other future complement than the one fixed from eternity is impossible. The whole is in each and every part, and welds it with the rest into an absolute unity, an iron block, in which there can be no equivocation or shadow of turning.

> With earth's first clay they did the last man knead,
> And there of the last harvest sowed the seed.
> And the first morning of creation wrote
> What the last dawn of reckoning shall read.

Indeterminism, on the contrary, says that the parts have a certain amount of loose play on one another, so that the laying down of one of them does not necessarily determine what the others shall be. It admits that possibilities may be in excess of actualities, and that things not yet revealed to our knowledge may really in themselves be ambiguous. Of two alternative futures which we conceive, both may now be really possible; and the one becomes impossible only at the very moment when the other excludes it by becoming real itself. Indeterminism thus denies the world to be one unbending unit of fact. It says there is a certain ultimate pluralism in it; and, so saying, it corroborates our ordinary unsophisticated view of things. To that view, actualities seem to float in a wider sea of possibilities from out of which they are chosen; and, *somewhere,* indeterminism says, such possibilities exist, and form a part of truth.

Determinism, on the contrary, says they exist *nowhere,* and that necessity on the one hand and impossibility on the other are the sole categories of the real. Possibilities that fail to get realized are, for determinism, pure illusions: they never were possibilities at all. There is nothing inchoate, it says, about this universe of ours, all that was or is or shall be actual in it having been from eternity virtually there. The cloud of alternatives our minds escort this mass of actuality withal is a cloud of sheer deceptions, to which "impossibilities" is the only name that rightfully belongs.

The issue, it will be seen, is a perfectly sharp one, which no eulogistic terminology can smear over or wipe out. The truth *must* lie with one side or the other, and its lying with one side makes the other false.

The question relates solely to the existence of possibilities, in the strict sense of the term, as things that may, but need not, be. Both sides admit that a volition, for instance, has occurred. The indeterminists say another volition might have occurred in its place: the determinists swear that nothing could possibly have occurred in its place. Now, can science be called in to tell us which of these two point-blank contradictors of each other is right? Science professes to draw no conclusions but such as are based on matters of fact, things that have actually happened; but how can any amount of assurance that something actually happened give us the least grain of information as to whether another thing might or might not have happened in its place? Only facts can prove facts. With things that are possibilities and not facts, facts have no concern. If we have no other evidence than the evidence of existing facts, the possibility-question must remain a mystery never to be cleared up.

And the truth is that facts practically have hardly anything to do with making us either determinists or indeterminists. Sure enough, we make a flourish of quoting facts this way or that; and if we are determinists, we talk about the infallibility with which we can predict one another's conduct; while if we are indeterminists, we lay great stress on the fact that it is just because we cannot foretell one another's conduct, either in war or statecraft or in any of the great and small intrigues and businesses of men, that life is so intensely anxious and hazardous a game. But who does not see the wretched insufficiency of this so-called objective testimony on both sides? What fills up the gaps in our minds is something not objective, not external. What divides us into *possibility* men and *anti-possibility* men is different faiths or postulates,—postulates of rationality. To this man the world seems more rational with possibilities in it,—to that man more rational with possibilities excluded; and talk as we will about having to yield to evidence, what makes us monists or pluralists, determinists or indeterminists, is at bottom always some sentiment like this.

The stronghold of the deterministic sentiment is the antipathy to the idea of chance. As soon as we begin to talk indeterminism to our friends, we find a number of them shaking their heads. This notion of alternative possibilities, they say, this admission that any one of several things may come to pass, is, after all, only a roundabout name for chance; and chance is something the notion of which no sane mind can for an instant tolerate in the world. What is it, they ask, but barefaced crazy unreason, the negation of intelligibility and law? And if the slightest particle of it exists anywhere, what is to prevent the whole fabric from falling together, the stars from going out, and chaos from recommencing her topsy-turvy reign?

Remarks of this sort about chance will put an end to discussion as quickly as anything one can find. I have already told you that "chance" was a word I wished to keep and use. Let us then examine exactly what it means, and see whether it ought to be such a terrible bugbear to us. I fancy that squeezing the thistle boldly will rob it of its sting.

The sting of the word "chance" seems to lie in the assumption that it means something positive, and that if anything happens by chance, it must needs be something of an intrinsically irrational and preposterous sort. Now, chance means nothing of the kind. It is a purely negative and relative term, giving us no information about that of which it is predicated, except that it happens to be disconnected with something else-not controlled, secured, or necessitated by other things in advance of its own actual presence. As this point is the most subtile one of the whole lecture, and at the same time the point on which all the rest hinges, I beg you to pay particular attention to it. What I say is that it tells us nothing about what a thing may be in itself to call it "chance." It may be a bad thing, it may be a good thing. It may be lucidity, transparency, fitness incarnate, matching the whole system of other things, when it has once befallen, in an unimaginably perfect way. All you mean by calling it "chance" is that this is not guaranteed, that it may also fall out otherwise. For the system of other things has no positive hold on the chance-thing. Its origin is in a certain fashion negative: it escapes, and says, "Hands off!" coming, when it comes, as a free gift, or not at all....

Nevertheless, many persons talk as if the minutest dose of disconnectedness of one part with another, the smallest modicum of independence, the faintest tremor of ambiguity about the future, for example, would ruin everything, and turn this goodly universe into a sort of insane sand-heap or nulliverse, no universe at all. Since future human volitions are as a matter of fact the only ambiguous things we are tempted to believe in, let us stop for a moment to make ourselves sure whether their independent and accidental character need be fraught with such direful consequences to the universe as these.

What is meant by saying that my choice of which way to walk home after the lecture is ambiguous and matter of chance as far as the present moment is concerned? It means that both Divinity Avenue and Oxford Street are called; but that only one, and that one *either* one, shall be chosen. Now, I ask you seriously to suppose that this ambiguity of my choice is real; and then to make the impossible hypothesis that the choice is made twice over, and each time falls on a different street. In other words, imagine that I first walk through Divinity Avenue, and then imagine that the powers governing the universe annihilate ten minutes of time with all that it contained, and set me back at the door of this hall just as I was before the choice was made. Imagine then that, everything else being the same, I now make a different choice and traverse Oxford Street. You, as passive spectators, look on and see the two alternative universes,—one of them with me walking through Divinity Avenue in it, the other with the same me walking through Oxford Street. Now, if you are determinists you believe one of these universes to have been from eternity impossible: you believe it to have been impossible because of the intrinsic irrationality or accidently somewhere involved in it. But looking outwardly at these universes, can you say which is the impossible and accidental one, and which the rational and necessary one? I doubt if the most ironclad determinist among you could have the slightest glimmer of light on this point. In other words, either universe *after the fact* and once there would, to our means of observation and understanding, appear just as rational as the other. There would be absolutely no criterion by which we might judge one necessary and the other matter of chance. Suppose now we relieve the gods of their hypothetical task and assume my choice, once made, to be made forever. I go through Divinity Avenue for good and all. If, as good determinists, you now begin to affirm, what all good determinists punctually do affirm, that in the nature of things I *couldn't* have gone through Oxford Street,—had I done so it would have been chance, irrationality, insanity, a horrid gap in nature,—I simply call your attention to this, that your affirmation is what the Germans call a *Machtspruch,* a mere conception fulminated as a dogma and based on no insight into details. Before my choice, either street seemed as natural to you as to me. Had I happened to take Oxford Street, Divinity Avenue would have figured in your philosophy as the gap in nature; and you would have so proclaimed it with the best deterministic conscience in the world.

But what a hollow outcry, then, is this against a chance which, if it were presented to us, we could by no character whatever distinguish from a rational necessity!…

And this at last brings us within sight of our subject. We have seen what determinism means: we have seen that indeterminism is rightly described as meaning chance; and we have seen that chance, the very name of which we are urged to shrink from as from a metaphysical pestilence, means only the negative fact that no part of the world, however big, can claim to control absolutely the destinies of the whole. But although, in discussing the word "chance," I may at moments have seemed to be arguing for its real existence, I have not meant to do so yet. We have not yet ascertained whether this be a world of chance or no; at most, we have agreed that it seems so. And I now repeat what I said at the outset, that, from any strict theoretical point of view, the question is insoluble. To deepen our theoretic sense of the *difference* between a world with chances in it and a deterministic world is the most I can hope to do; and this I may now at last begin upon, after all our tedious clearing of the way.

I wish first of all to show you just what the notion that this is a deterministic world implies. The implications I call your attention to are all bound up with the fact that it is a world in which we constantly have to make what I shall, with your permission, call judgments of regret. Hardly an hour passes in which we do not wish that something might be otherwise; and happy indeed are those of us whose hearts have never echoed the wish of Omar Khayam:

That we might clasp, ere closed, the book of fate,
And make the writer on a fairer leaf
Inscribe our names, or quite obliterate.

Ah! Love, could you and I with fate conspire
To mend this sorry scheme of things entire,
Would we not shatter it to bits, and then
Remold it nearer to the heart's desire?

Now, it is undeniable that most of these regrets are foolish, and quite on a par in point of philosophic value with the criticisms on the universe of that friend of our infancy, the hero of the fable "The Atheist and the Acorn,"

Fool! had that bough a pumpkin bore,
Thy whimsies would have worked no more, etc.

Even from the point of view of our own ends, we should probably make a botch of remodeling the universe. How much more then from the point of view of ends we cannot see! Wise men therefore regret as little as they can. But still some regrets are pretty obstinate and hard to stifle,—regrets for acts of wanton cruelty or treachery, for example, whether performed by others or by ourselves. Hardly any one can remain *entirely* optimistic after reading the confession of the murderer at Brockton the other day: how, to get rid of the wife whose continued existence bored him, he inveigled her into a desert spot, shot her four times, and then, as she lay on the ground and said to him, "You didn't do it on purpose, did you, dear?" replied, "No, I didn't do it on purpose," as he raised a rock and smashed her skull. Such an occurrence, with the mild sentence and self-satisfaction of the prisoner, is a field for a crop of regrets, which one need not take up in detail. We feel that, although a perfect mechanical fit to the rest of the universe, it is a bad moral fit, and that something else would really have been better in its place.

But for the deterministic philosophy the murder, the sentence, and the prisoner's optimism were all necessary from eternity; and nothing else for a moment had a ghost of a chance of being put in their place. To admit such a chance, the determinists tell us, would be to make a suicide of reason; so we must steel our hearts against the thought. And here our plot thickens, for we see the first of those difficult implications of determinism and monism, which it is my purpose to make you feel. If this Brockton murder was called for by the rest of the universe, if it had to come at its pre appointed hour, and if nothing else would have been consistent with the sense of the whole, what are we to think of the universe? Are we stubbornly to stick to our judgment of regret, and say, though it *couldn't* be, yet it *would* have been a better universe with something different from this Brockton murder in it? That, of course, seems the natural and spontaneous thing for us to do; and yet it is nothing short of deliberately espousing a kind of pessimism. The judgment of regret calls the murder bad. Calling a thing bad means, if it means anything at all, that the thing ought not to be, that something else ought to be in its stead. Determinism, in denying that anything else can be in its stead, virtually defines the universe as a place in which what ought to be is impossible,—in other words, as an organism whose constitution is afflicted with an incurable taint, an irremediable flaw.... Regret for the murder must transform itself, if we are determinists and wise, into a larger regret. It is absurd to regret the murder alone. Other things being what they are, *it* could not be different. What we should regret is that whole frame of things of which the murder is one member. I see no escape whatever from this pessimistic conclusion if, being determinists, our judgment of regret is to be allowed to stand at all.

The only deterministic escape from pessimism is everywhere to abandon the judgment of regret. That this can be done, history shows to be not impossible. The devil, *quoad existentiam,* may be good. That is, although he be a *principle* of evil, yet the universe, with such a principle in it, may practically be a better universe than it could have been without. On every hand, in a small way, we find that a certain amount of evil is a condition by which a higher form of good is brought. There is nothing to prevent anybody from generalizing this view, and trusting that if we could but see things in the largest of all ways, even such matters as this Brockton murder would appear to be paid for by the uses that follow in their train. An optimism *quand même,* a systematic and infatuated optimism like that ridiculed by Voltaire in his *Candide,* is one of the possible ideal ways in which a man may train himself to look on life. Bereft of dogmatic hardness and lit up with the expression of a tender and pathetic hope, such an optimism has been the grace of some of the most religious characters that ever lived.

> Throb thine with Nature's throbbing breast,
> And all is clear from east to west.

Even cruelty and treachery may be among the absolutely blessed fruits of time, and to quarrel with any of their details may be blasphemy. The only real blasphemy, in short, may be that pessimistic temper of the soul which lets it give way to such things as regrets, remorse, and grief.

Thus, our deterministic pessimism may become a deterministic optimism at the price of extinguishing our judgments of regret.

But does not this immediately bring us into a curious logical predicament? Our determinism leads us to call our judgments of regret wrong, because they are pessimistic in implying that what is impossible yet ought to be. But how then about the judgments of regret themselves? If they are wrong, other judgments, judgments of approval presumably, ought to be in their place. But as they are necessitated, nothing else *can* be in their place; and the universe is just what it was before,—namely, a place in which what ought to be appears impossible. We have got one foot out of the pessimistic bog, but the other one sinks all the deeper. We have rescued our actions from the bonds of evil, but our judgments are now held fast. When murders and treacheries cease to be sins, regrets are theoretic absurdities and errors. The theoretic and the active life thus play a kind of see-saw with each other on the ground of evil. The rise of either sends the other down. Murder and treachery cannot be good without regret being bad: regret cannot be good without treachery and murder being bad. Both, however, are supposed to have been foredoomed; so something must be fatally unreasonable, absurd, and wrong in the world. It must be a place of which either sin or error forms a necessary part....

The only consistent way of representing a pluralism and a world whose parts may affect one another through their conduct being either good or bad is the indeterministic way. What interest, zest, or excitement can there be in achieving the right way, unless we are enabled to feel that the wrong way is also a possible and a natural way,—nay, more, a menacing and an imminent way? And what sense can there be in condemning ourselves for taking the wrong way, unless we need have done nothing of the sort, unless the right way was open to us as well? I cannot understand the willingness to act, no matter how we feel, without the belief that acts are really good and bad. I cannot understand the belief that an act is bad, without regret at its happening. I cannot understand regret without the admission of real, genuine possibilities in the world. Only *then* is it other than a mockery to feel, after we have failed to do our best, that an irreparable opportunity is gone from the universe, the loss of which it must forever after mourn....

The world is enigmatical enough in all conscience, whatever theory we may take up toward it. The indeterminism I defend, the free-will theory of popular sense based on the judgment of regret, represents that world as vulnerable, and liable to be injured by certain of its parts if they act wrong. And it represents their acting wrong as a matter of possibility or accident, neither inevitable nor yet to be infallibly warded off. In all this, it is a theory devoid either of transparency or of stability. It gives us a pluralistic, restless universe, in which no single point of view can ever take in the whole scene; and to a mind possessed of the love of unity at any cost, it will, no doubt, remain forever unacceptable. A friend with such a mind once told me that the thought of my universe made him sick, like the sight of the horrible motion of a mass of maggots in their carrion bed.

But while I freely admit that the pluralism and the restlessness are repugnant and irrational in a certain way, I find that every alternative to them is irrational in a deeper way. The indeterminism with its maggots, if you please to speak so about it, offends only the native absolutism of my intellect,—an absolutism which, after all, perhaps, deserves to be snubbed and kept in check. But the determinism with its necessary carrion, to continue the figure of speech, and with no possible maggots to eat the latter up, violates my sense of moral reality through and through. When, for example, I imagine such carrion as the Brockton murder, I cannot conceive it as an act by which the universe, as a whole, logically and necessarily expresses its nature without shrinking from complicity with such a whole. And I deliberately refuse to keep on terms of loyalty with the universe by saying blankly that the murder, since it does flow from the nature of the whole, is not carrion. There are *some* instinctive reactions which I, for one, will not tamper with....

Make as great an uproar about chance as you please, I know that chance means pluralism and nothing more. If some of the members of the pluralism are bad, the philosophy of pluralism, whatever broad views it may deny me, permits me, at least, to turn to the other members with a clean breast of affection and an unsophisticated moral sense. And if I still wish to think of the world as a totality, it lets me feel that a world with a *chance* in it of being altogether good, even if the chance never come to pass, is better than a world with no such chance at all. That "chance" whose very notion I am exhorted and conjured to banish from my view of the future as the suicide of reason concerning it, that "chance" is—what? Just this,—the chance that in moral respects the future may be other and better than the past has been. This is the only chance we have any motive for supposing to exist. Shame, rather, on its repudiation and its denial! For its presence is the vital air which lets the world live, the salt which keeps it sweet, the air that fills its lungs.

FREEDOM OF THE WILL AND THE CONCEPT OF A PERSON

By Harry G. Frankfurt

W

hat philosophers have lately come to accept as analysis of the concept of a person is not actually analysis of *that* concept at all. Strawson, whose usage represents the current standard, identifies the concept of a person as "the concept of a type of entity such that *both* predicates ascribing states of consciousness *and* predicates ascribing corporeal characteristics ... are equally applicable to a single individual of that single type."[1] But there are many entities besides persons that have both mental and physical properties. As it happens-though it seems extraordinary that this should be so-there is no common English word for the type of entity Strawson has in mind, a type that includes not only human beings but animals of various lesser species as well. Still, this hardly justifies the misappropriation of a valuable philosophical term.

Whether the members of some animal species are persons is surely not to be settled merely by determining whether it is correct to apply to them, in addition to predicates ascribing corporeal characteristics, predicates that ascribe states of consciousness. It does violence to our language to endorse the application of the term 'person' to those numerous creatures which do have both psychological and material properties but which are manifestly not persons in any normal sense of the word. This misuse of language is doubtless innocent of any theoretical error. But although the offense is "merely verbal," it does significant harm. For it gratuitously diminishes our philosophical vocabulary, and it increases the likelihood that we will overlook the important area of inquiry with which the term 'person' is most naturally associated. It might have been expected that no problem would be of more central and persistent concern to philosophers than that of understanding what we ourselves essentially are. Yet this problem is so generally neglected that it has been possible to make off with its very name almost without being noticed and, evidently, without evoking any widespread feeling of loss. There is a sense in which the word 'person' is merely the singular form of 'people' and in which both terms connote no more than membership in a certain biological species. In those senses of the word which are of greater philosophical interest, however, the criteria for being a person do not serve primarily to distinguish the members of our own species from the members of other species. Rather, they are designed to capture those attributes which are the subject of our most humane concern with ourselves and the source of what we regard as most important and most problematical in our lives. Now these attributes would be of equal significance to us even if they were not in fact peculiar and common to the members of our own species. What interests us most in the human condition would not interest us less if it were also a feature of the condition of other creatures as well.

Our concept of ourselves as persons is not to be understood, therefore, as a concept of attributes that are necessarily species-specific. It is conceptually possible that members of novel or even of familiar nonhuman species should be persons; and it is also conceptually possible that some members of the human species are not persons. We do in fact assume, on the other hand, that no member of another species is a person. Accordingly, there is a presumption that what is essential to persons is a set of characteristics that we generally suppose-whether rightly or wrongly-to be uniquely human.

It is my view that one essential difference between persons and other creatures is to be found in the structure of a person's will. Human beings are not alone in having desires and motives, or in making choices. They share these things with the members of certain other species, some of whom even appear to engage in deliberation and to make decisions based upon prior thought. It seems to be peculiarly characteristic of humans, however, that they are able to form what I shall call "second-order desires" or "desires of the second order."

Besides wanting and choosing and being moved *to do* this or that, men may also want to have (or not to have) certain desires and motives. They are capable of wanting to be different, in their preferences and purposes, from what they are. Many animals appear to have the capacity for what I shall call "first-order desires" or "desires of the first order," which are simply desires to do or not to do one thing or another. No animal other than man, however, appears to have the capacity for reflective self-evaluation that is manifested in the formation of second-order desires.[2]

I

The concept designated by the verb 'to want' is extraordinarily elusive. A statement of the form "*A* wants to X"-taken by itself, apart from a context that serves to amplify or to specify its meaning-conveys remarkably little information. Such a statement may be consistent, for example, with each of the following statements: (a) the prospect of doing X elicits no sensation or introspectible emotional response in A; (b) A is unaware that he wants to X; A believes that he does not want to X; (d) A wants to refrain from X-ing; (e) A wants to Y and believes that it is impossible for him both to Y and to X; (f) A does not "really" want to X; (g) A would rather die than X; and so on. It is therefore hardly sufficient to formulate the distinction between first-order and second-order desires, as I have done, by suggesting merely that someone has a first-order desire when he wants to do or not to do such-and-such, and that he has a second-order desire when he wants to have or not to have a certain desire of the first order.

As I shall understand them, statements of the form "A wants to X" cover a rather broad range of possibilities.[3] They may be true even when statements like (a) through (g) are true: when A is unaware of any feelings concerning X-ing, when he is unaware that he wants to X, when he deceives himself about what he wants and believes falsely that he does not want to X, when he also has other desires that conflict with his desire to X, or when he is ambivalent. The desires in question may be conscious or unconscious, they need not be univocal, and A may be mistaken about them. There is a further source of uncertainty with regard to statements that identify someone's desires, however, and here it is important for my purposes to be less permissive.

Consider first those statements of the form "A wants to X" which identify first-order desires-that is, statements in which the term 'to X' refers to an action. A statement of this kind does not, by itself, indicate the relative strength of A's desire to X. It does not make it clear whether this desire is at all likely to play a decisive role in what A actually does or tries to do. For it may correctly be said that A wants to X even when his desire to X is only one among his desires and when it is far from being paramount among them. Thus, it may be true that A wants to X when he strongly prefers to do something else instead; and it may be true that he wants to X despite the fact that, when he acts, it is not the desire to X that motivates him to do what he does. On the other hand, someone who states that A wants to X may mean to convey that it is this desire that is motivating or moving A to do what he is actually doing or that A will in fact be moved by this desire (unless he changes his mind) when he acts.

It is only when it is used in the second of these ways that, given the special usage of 'will' that I propose to adopt, the statement identifies A's will. To identify an agent's will is either to identify the desire (or desires) by which he is motivated in some action he performs or to identify the desire (or desires) by which he will or would be motivated when or if he acts. An agent's will, then, is identical with one or more of his first-order desires. But the notion of the will, as I am employing it, is not coextensive with the notion of first-order desires. It is not the notion of something that merely inclines an agent in some degree to act in a certain way. Rather, it is the notion of an *effective* desire-one that moves (or will or would move) a person all the way to action. Thus the notion of the will is not coextensive with the notion of what an agent intends to do. For even though someone may have a settled intention to do X, he may nonetheless do something else instead of doing X because, despite his intention, his desire to do X proves to be weaker or less effective than some conflicting desire.

Now consider those statements of the form *"A wants to X"* which identify second-order desires-that is, statements in which the term 'to X' refers to a desire of the first order. There are also two kinds of situation in which it may be true that A wants to want to X. In the first place, it might be true of A that he wants to have a desire to X despite the fact that he has a univocal desire, altogether free of conflict and ambivalence, to refrain from X-ing. Someone might want to have a certain desire, in other words, but univocally want that desire to be unsatisfied.

Suppose that a physician engaged in psychotherapy with narcotics addicts believes that his ability to help his patients would be enhanced if he understood better what it is like for them to desire the drug to which they are addicted. Suppose that he is led in this way to want to have a desire for the drug. If it is a genuine desire that he wants, then what he wants is not merely to feel the sensations that addicts characteristically feel when they are gripped by their desires for the drug. What the physician wants, insofar as he wants to have a desire, is to be inclined or moved to some extent to take the drug.

It is entirely possible, however, that, although he wants to be moved by a desire to take the drug, he does not want this desire to be effective. He may not want it to move him all the way to action. He need not be interested in finding out what it is like to take the drug. And insofar as he now wants only to *want* to take it, and not to *take it,* there is nothing in what he now wants that would be satisfied by the drug itself. He may now have, in fact, an altogether univocal desire *not* to take the drug; and he may prudently arrange to make it impossible for him to satisfy the desire he would have if his desire to want the drug should in time be satisfied.

It would thus be incorrect to infer, from the fact that the physician now wants to desire to take the drug, that he already does desire to take it. His second-order desire to be moved to take the drug does not entail that he has a first-order desire to take it. If the drug were now to be administered to him, this might satisfy no desire that is implicit in his desire to want to take it. While he wants to want to take the drug, he may have *no* desire to take it; it may be that *all* he wants is to taste the desire for it. That is, his desire to have a certain desire that he does not have may not be a desire that his will should be at all different than it is.

Someone who wants only in this truncated way to want to X stands at the margin of preciosity, and the fact that he wants to want to X is not pertinent to the identification of his will. There is, however, a second kind of situation that may be described by 'A wants to want to X'; and when the statement is used to describe a situation of this second kind, then it does pertain to what A wants his will to be. In such cases the statement means that A wants the desire to X to be the desire that moves him effectively to act. It is not merely that he wants the desire to X to be among the desires by which, to one degree or another, he is moved or inclined to act. He wants this desire to be effective-that is, to provide the motive in what he actually does. Now when the statement that A wants to want to X is used in this way, it does entail that A already has a desire to X. It could not be true both that A wants the desire to X to move him into action and that he does not want to X. It is only if he does want to X that he can coherently want the desire to X not merely to be one of his desires but, more decisively, to be his will.[4] Suppose a man wants to be motivated in what he does by the desire to concentrate on his work. It is necessarily true, if this supposition is correct, that he already wants to concentrate on his work. This desire is now among his desires. But the question of whether or not his second-order desire is fulfilled does not turn merely on whether the desire he wants is one of his desires. It turns on whether this desire is, as he wants it to be, his effective desire or will. If, when the chips are down, it is his desire to concentrate on his work that moves him to do what he does, then what he wants at that time is indeed (in the relevant sense) what he wants to want. If it is some other desire that actually moves him when he acts, on the other hand, then what he wants at that time is not (in the relevant sense) what he wants to want. This will be so despite the fact that the desire to concentrate on his work continues to be among his desires.

II

Someone has a desire of the second order either when he wants simply to have a certain desire or when he wants a certain desire to be his will. In situations of the latter kind, I shall call his second-order desires "second-order volitions" or "volitions of the second order." Now it is having second-order volitions, and not having second-order desires generally, that I regard as essential to being a person. It is logically possible, however unlikely, that there should be an agent with second-order desires but with no volitions of the second order. Such a creature, in my view, would not be a person. I shall use the term 'wanton' to refer to agents who have first-order desires but who are not persons because, whether or not they have desires of the second order, they have no second-order volitions.[5]

The essential characteristic of a wanton is that he does not care about his will. His desires move him to do certain things, without its being true of him either that he wants to be moved by those desires or that he prefers to be moved by other desires. The class of wantons includes all nonhuman animals that have desires and all very young children. Perhaps it also includes some adult human beings as well. In any case, adult humans may be more or less wanton; they may act wantonly, in response to first-order desires concerning which they have no volitions of the second order, more or less frequently.

The fact that a wanton has no second-order volitions does not mean that each of his first-order desires is translated heedlessly and at once into action. He may have no opportunity to act in accordance with some of his desires. Moreover, the translation of his desires into action may be delayed or precluded either by conflicting desires of the first order or by the intervention of deliberation. For a wanton may possess and employ rational faculties of a high order. Nothing in the concept of a wanton implies that he cannot reason or that he cannot deliberate concerning how to do what he wants to do. What distinguishes the rational wanton from other rational agents is that he is not concerned with the desirability of his desires themselves. He ignores the question of what his will is to be. Not only does he pursue whatever course of action he is most strongly inclined to pursue, but he does not care which of his inclinations is the strongest.

Thus a rational creature, who reflects upon the suitability to his desires of one course of action or another, may nonetheless be a wanton. In maintaining that the essence of being a person lies not in reason but in will, I am far from suggesting that a creature without reason may be a person. For it is only in virtue of his rational capacities that a person is capable of becoming critically aware of his own will and of forming volitions of the second order. The structure of a person's will presupposes, accordingly, that he is a rational being.

The distinction between a person and a wanton may be illustrated by the difference between two narcotics addicts. Let us suppose that the physiological condition accounting for the addiction is the same in both men, and that both succumb inevitably to their periodic desires for the drug to which they are addicted. One of the addicts hates his addiction and always struggles desperately, although to no avail, against its thrust. He tries everything that he thinks might enable him to overcome his desires for the drug. But these desires are too powerful for him to withstand, and invariably, in the end, they conquer him. He is an unwilling addict, helplessly violated by his own desires.

The unwilling addict has conflicting first-order desires: he wants to take the drug, and he also wants to refrain from taking it. In addition to these first-order desires, however, he has a volition of the second order. He is not a neutral with regard to the conflict between his desire to take the drug and his desire to refrain from taking it. It is the latter desire, and not the former, that he wants to constitute his will; it is the latter desire, rather than the former, that he wants to be effective and to provide the purpose that he will seek to realize in what he actually does.

The other addict is a wanton. His actions reflect the economy of his first-order desires, without his being concerned whether the desires that move him to act are desires by which he wants to be moved to act. *H* he encounters problems in obtaining the drug or in administering it to himself, his responses to his urges to take it may involve deliberation. But it never occurs to him to consider whether he wants the relations among his desires to result in his having the will he has. The wanton addict may be an animal, and thus incapable of being concerned about his will. In any event he is, in respect of his wanton lack of concern, no different from an animal.

The second of these addicts may suffer a first-order conflict similar to the first-order conflict suffered by the first. Whether he is human or not, the wanton may (perhaps due to conditioning) both want to take the drug and want to refrain from taking it. Unlike the unwilling addict, however, he does not prefer that one of his conflicting desires should be paramount over the other; he does not prefer that one first-order desire rather than the other should constitute his will. It would be misleading to say that he is neutral as to the conflict between his desires, since this would suggest that he regards them as equally acceptable. Since he has no identity apart from his first-order desires, it is true neither that he prefers one to the other nor that he prefers not to take sides.

It makes a difference to the unwilling addict, who is a person, which of his conflicting first-order desires wins out. Both desires are his, to be sure; and whether he finally takes the drug or finally succeeds in refraining from taking it, he acts to satisfy what is in a literal sense his own desire. In either case he does something he himself wants to do, and he does it not because of some external influence whose aim happens to coincide with his own but because of his desire to do it. The unwilling addict identifies himself, however, through the formation of a second-order volition, with one rather than with the other of his conflicting first-order desires. He makes one of them more truly his own and, in so doing, he withdraws himself from the other. It is in virtue of this identification and withdrawal, accomplished through the formation of a second-order volition, that the unwilling addict may meaningfully make the analytically puzzling statements that the force moving him to take the drug is a force other than his own, and that it is not of his own free will but rather against his will that this force moves him to take it.

The wanton addict cannot or does not care which of his conflicting first-order desires wins out. His lack of concern is not due to his inability to find a convincing basis for preference. It is due either to his lack of the capacity for reflection or to his mindless indifference to the enterprise of evaluating his own desires and motives.[6] There is only one issue in the struggle to which his first-order conflict may lead: whether the one or the other of his conflicting desires is the stronger. Since he is moved by both desires, he will not be altogether satisfied by what he does no matter which of them is effective. But it makes no difference *to him* whether his craving or his aversion gets the upper hand. He has no stake in the conflict between them and so, unlike the unwilling addict, he can neither win nor lose the struggle in which he is engaged. When a *person* acts, the desire by which he is moved is either the will he wants or a will he wants to be without. When a *wanton* acts, it is neither.

III

There is a very close relationship between the capacity for forming second-order volitions and another capacity that is essential to persons-one that has often been considered a distinguishing mark of the human condition. It is only because a person has volitions of the second order that he is capable both of enjoying and of lacking freedom of the will. The concept of a person is not only, then, the concept of a type of entity that has both first-order desires and volitions of the second order. It can also be construed as the concept of a type of entity for whom the freedom of its will may be a problem. This concept excludes all wantons, both infrahuman and human, since they fail to satisfy an essential condition for the enjoyment of freedom of the will. And it excludes those supra-human beings, if any, whose wills are necessarily free.

Just what kind of freedom is the freedom of the will? This question calls for an identification of the special area of human experience to which the concept of freedom of the will, as distinct from the concepts of other sorts of freedom, is particularly germane. In dealing with it, my aim will be primarily to locate the problem with which a person is most immediately concerned when he is concerned with the freedom of his will.

According to one familiar philosophical tradition, being free is fundamentally a matter of doing what one wants to do. Now the notion of an agent who does what he wants to do is by no means an altogether clear one: both the doing and the wanting, and the appropriate relation between them as well, require elucidation. But although its focus needs to be sharpened and its formulation refined, I believe that this notion does capture at least part of what is implicit in the idea of an agent who *acts* freely. It misses entirely, however, the peculiar content of the quite different idea of an agent whose *will* is free.

We do not suppose that animals enjoy freedom of the will, although we recognize that an animal may be free to run in whatever direction it wants. Thus, having the freedom to do what one wants to do is not a sufficient condition of having a free will. It is not a necessary condition either. For to deprive someone of his freedom of action is not necessarily to undermine the freedom of his will. When an agent is aware that there are certain things he is not free to do, this doubtless affects his desires and limits the range of choices he can make. But suppose that someone, without being aware of it, has in fact lost or been deprived of his freedom of action. Even though he is no longer free to do what he wants to do, his will may remain as free as it was before. Despite the fact that he is not free to translate his desires into actions or to act according to the determinations of his will, he may still form those desires and make those determinations as freely as if his freedom of action had not been impaired.

When we ask whether a person's will is free we are not asking whether he is in a position to translate his first-order desires into actions. That is the question of whether he is free to do as he pleases. The question of the freedom of his will does not concern the relation between what he does and what he wants to do. Rather, it concerns his desires themselves. But what question about them is it?

It seems to me both natural and useful to construe the question of whether a person's will is free in close analogy to the question of whether an agent enjoys freedom of action. Now freedom of action is (roughly, at least) the freedom to do what one wants to do. Analogously, then, the statement that a person enjoys freedom of the will means (also roughly) that he is free to want what he wants to want. More precisely, it means that he is free to will what he wants to will, or to have the will he wants. Just as the question about the freedom of an agent's action has to do with whether it is the action he wants to perform, so the question about the freedom of his will has to do with whether it is the will he wants to have.

It is in securing the conformity of his will to his second-order volitions, then, that a person exercises freedom of the will. And it is in the discrepancy between his will and his second-order volitions, or in his awareness that their coincidence is not his own doing but only a happy chance, that a person who does not have this freedom feels its lack. The unwilling addict's will is not free. This is shown by the fact that it is not the will he wants. It is also true, though in a different way, that the will of the wanton addict is not free. The wanton addict neither has the will he wants nor has a will that differs from the will he wants. Since he has no volitions of the second order, the freedom of his will cannot be a problem for him. He lacks it, so to speak, by default.

People are generally far more complicated than my sketchy account of the structure of a person's will may suggest. There is as much opportunity for ambivalence, conflict, and self-deception with regard to desires of the second order, for example, as there is with regard to first-order desires. If there is an unresolved conflict among someone's second-order desires, then he is in danger of having no second-order volition; for unless this conflict is resolved, he has no preference concerning which of his first-order desires it to be his will. This condition, if it is so severe that it prevents him from identifying himself in a sufficiently decisive way with *any* of his conflicting first-order desires, destroys him as a person. For it either tends to paralyze his will and to keep him from acting at all, or it tends to remove him from his will so that his will operates without his participation. In both cases he becomes, like the unwilling addict though in a different way, a helpless bystander to the forces that move him.

Another complexity is that a person may have, especially if his second-order desires are in conflict, desires and volitions of a higher order than the second. There is no theoretical limit to the length of the series of desires of higher and higher orders; nothing except common sense and, perhaps, a saving fatigue prevents an individual from obsessively refusing to identify himself with any of his desires until he forms a desire of the next higher order. The tendency to generate such a series of acts of forming desires, which would be a case of humanization run wild, also leads toward the destruction of a person.

It is possible, however, to terminate such a series of acts without cutting it off arbitrarily. When a person identifies himself *decisively* with one of his first-order desires, this commitment "resounds" throughout the potentially endless array of higher orders. Consider a person who, without reservation or conflict, wants to be motivated by the desire to concentrate on his work. The fact that his second-order volition to be moved by this desire is a decisive one means that there is no room for questions concerning the pertinence of desires or volitions of higher orders. Suppose the person is asked whether he wants to want to want to concentrate on his work. He can properly insist that this question concerning a third-order desire does not arise. It would be a mistake to claim that, because he has not considered whether he wants the second-order volition he has formed, he is indifferent to the question of whether it is with this volition or with some other that he wants his will to accord. The decisiveness of the commitment he has made means that he has decided that no further question about his second-order volition, at any higher order, remains to be asked. It is relatively unimportant whether we explain this by saying that this commitment implicitly generates an endless series of confirming desires of higher orders, or by saying that the commitment is tantamount to a dissolution of the pointedness of all questions concerning higher orders of desire.

Examples such as the one concerning the unwilling addict may suggest that volitions of the second order, or of higher orders, must be formed deliberately and that a person characteristically struggles to ensure that they are satisfied. But the conformity of a person's will to his higher-order volitions may be far more thoughtless and spontaneous than this. Some people are naturally moved by kindness when they want to be kind, and by nastiness when they want to be nasty, without any explicit forethought and without any need for energetic self-control. Others are moved by nastiness when they want to be kind and by kindness when they intend to be nasty, equally without forethought and without active resistance to these violations of their higher-order desires. The enjoyment of freedom comes easily to some. Others must struggle to achieve it.

IV

My theory concerning the freedom of the will accounts easily for our disinclination to allow that this freedom is enjoyed by the members of any species inferior to our own. It also satisfies another condition that must be met by any such theory, by making it apparent why the freedom of the will should be regarded as desirable. The enjoyment of a free will means the satisfaction of certain desires-desires of the second or of higher orders-whereas its absence means their frustration. The satisfactions at stake are those which accrue to a person of whom it may be said that his will is his own. The corresponding frustrations are those suffered by a person of whom it may be said that he is estranged from himself, or that he finds himself a helpless or a passive bystander to the forces that move him.

A person who is free to do what he wants to do may yet not be in a position to have the will he wants. Suppose, however, that he enjoys both freedom of action and freedom of the will. Then he is not only free to do what he wants to do; he is also free to want what he wants to want. It seems to me that he has, in that case, all the freedom it is possible to desire or to conceive. There are other good things in life, and he may not possess some of them. But there is nothing in the way of freedom that he lacks.

It is far from clear that certain other theories of the freedom of the will meet these elementary but essential conditions: that it be understandable why we desire this freedom and why we refuse to ascribe it to animals. Consider, for example, Roderick Chisholm's quaint version of the doctrine that human freedom entails an absence of causal determination.[7] Whenever a person performs a free action, according to Chisholm, it's a miracle. The motion of a person's hand, when the person moves it, is the outcome of a series of physical causes; but some event in this series, "and presumably one of those that took place within the brain, was caused by the agent and not by any other events" (18). A free agent has, therefore, "a prerogative which some would attribute only to God: each of us, when we act, is a prime mover unmoved" (23).

This account fails to provide any basis for doubting that animals of subhuman species enjoy the freedom it defines. Chisholm says nothing that makes it seem less likely that a rabbit performs a miracle when it moves its leg than that a man does so when he moves his hand. But why, in any case, should anyone *care* whether he can interrupt the natural order of causes in the way Chisholm describes? Chisholm offers no reason for believing that there is a discernible difference between the experience of a man who miraculously initiates a series of causes when he moves his hand and a man who moves his hand without any such breach of the normal causal sequence. There appears to be no concrete basis for preferring to be involved in the one state of affairs rather than in the other.[8]

It is generally supposed that, in addition to satisfying the two conditions I have mentioned, a satisfactory theory of the freedom of the will necessarily provide an analysis of one of the conditions of moral responsibility. The most common recent approach to the problem of understanding the freedom of the will has been, indeed, to inquire what is entailed by the assumption that someone is morally responsible for what he has done. In my view, however, the relation between moral responsibility and the freedom of the will has been very widely misunderstood. It is not true that a person is morally responsible for what he has done only if his will was free when he did it. He may be morally responsible for having done it even though his will was not free at all.

A person's will is free only if he is free to have the will he wants. This means that, with regard to any of his first-order desires, he is free either to make that desire his will or to make some other first-order desire his will instead. Whatever his will, then, the will of the person whose will is free could have been otherwise; he could have done otherwise than to constitute his will as he did. It is a vexed question just how 'he could have done otherwise' is to be understood in contexts such as this one. But although this question is important to the theory of freedom, it has no bearing on the theory of moral responsibility. For the assumption that a person is morally responsible for what he has done does not entail that the person was in a position to have whatever will he wanted.

This assumption *does* entail that the person did what he did freely, or that he did it of his own free will. It is a mistake, however, to believe that someone acts freely only when he is free to do whatever he wants or that he acts of his own free will only if his will is free. Suppose that a person has done what he wanted to do, that he did it because he wanted to do it, and that the will by which he was moved when he did it was his will because it was the will he wanted. Then he did it freely and of his own free will. Even supposing that he could have done otherwise, he would not have done otherwise; and even supposing that he could have had a different will, he would not have wanted his will to differ from what it was. Moreover, since the will that moved him when he acted was his will because he wanted it to be, he cannot claim that his will was forced upon him or that he was a passive bystander to its constitution. Under these conditions, it is quite irrelevant to the evaluation of his moral responsibility to inquire whether the alternatives that he opted against were actually available to him.[9]

In illustration, consider a third kind of addict. Suppose that his addiction has the same physiological basis and the same irresistible thrust as the addictions of the unwilling and wanton addicts, but that he is altogether delighted with his condition. He is a willing addict, who would not have things any other way. If the grip of his addiction should somehow weaken, he would do whatever he could to reinstate it; if his desire for the drug should begin to fade, he would take steps to renew its intensity.

The willing addict's will is not free, for his desire to take the drug will be effective regardless of whether or not he wants this desire to constitute his will. But when he takes the drug, he takes it freely and of his own free will. I am inclined to understand his situation as involving the over-determination of his first-order desire to take the drug. This desire is his effective desire because he is physiologically addicted. But it is his effective desire also because he wants it to be. His will is outside his control, but, by his second-order desire that his desire for the drug should be effective, he has made this will his own. Given that it is therefore not only because of his addiction that his desire for the drug is effective, he may be morally responsible for taking the drug.

My conception of the freedom of the will appears to be neutral with regard to the problem of determinism. It seems conceivable that it should be causally determined that a person is free to want what he wants to want. If this is conceivable, then it might be causally determined that a person enjoys a free will. There is no more than an innocuous appearance of paradox in the proposition that it is determined, ineluctably and by forces beyond their control, that certain people have free wills and that others do not. There is no incoherence in the proposition that some agency other than a person's own is responsible (even *morally* responsible) for the fact that he enjoys or fails to enjoy freedom of the will. It is possible that a person should be morally responsible for what he does of his own free will and that some other person should also be morally responsible for his having done it.[10]

On the other hand, it seems conceivable that it should come about by chance that a person is free to have the will he wants. If this is conceivable, then it might be a matter of chance that certain people enjoy freedom of the will and that certain others do not. Perhaps it is also conceivable, as a number of philosophers believe, for states of affairs to come about in a way other than by chance or as the outcome of a sequence of natural causes. If it is indeed conceivable for the relevant states of affairs to come about in some third way, then it is also possible that a person should in that third way come to enjoy the freedom of the will.

HARRY G. FRANKFURT
The Rockefeller University

NOTES

1. P. F. Strawson, *Individuals* (London: Methuen, 1959), pp. 101–102. Ayer's usage of 'person' is similar: "it is characteristic of persons in this sense that besides having various physical properties ... they are also credited with various forms of consciousness" [A. J. Ayer, *The Concept of a Person* (New York: St. Martin's, 196!), p. 82]. What concerns Strawson and Ayer is the problem of understanding the relation between mind and body, rather than the quite different problem of understanding what it is to be a creature that not only has a mind and a body but is also a person.

2. For the sake of simplicity, I shall deal only with what someone wants or desires, neglecting related phenomena such as choices and decisions. I propose to use the verbs 'to want' and 'to desire' interchangeably, although they are by no means perfect synonyms. My motive in forsaking the established nuances of these words arises from the fact that the verb 'to want', which suits my purposes better so far as its meaning is concerned, does not lend itself so readily to the formation of nouns as does the verb 'to desire'. It is perhaps acceptable, albeit graceless, to speak in the plural of someone's "wants." But to speak in the singular of someone's "want" would be an abomination.

3. What I say in this paragraph applies not only to cases in which 'to X' refers to a possible action or inaction. It also applies to cases in which 'to X' refers to a first-order desire and in which the statement that 'A wants to X' is therefore a shortened version of a statement "A wants to want to X" that identifies a desire of the second order.

4. It is not so clear that the entailment relation described here holds in certain kinds of cases, which I think may fairly be regarded as nonstandard, where the essential difference between the standard and the nonstandard cases lies in the kind of description by which the first-order desire in question is identified. Thus, suppose that A admires B so fulsomely that, even though he does not know what B wants to do, he wants to be effectively moved by whatever desire effectively moves B; without knowing what B's will is, in other words, A wants his own will to be the same. It certainly does not follow that A already has, among his desires, a desire like the one that constitutes B's will. I shall not pursue here the questions of whether there are genuine counterexamples to the claim made in the text or of how, if there are, that claim should be altered.

5. Creatures with second-order desires but no second-order volitions differ significantly from brute animals, and, for some purposes, it would be desirable to regard them as persons. My usage, which withholds the designation 'person' from them, is thus somewhat arbitrary. I adopt it largely because it facilitates the formulation of some of the points I wish to make. Hereafter, whenever I consider statements of the form "A wants to want to X," I shall have in mind statements identifying second-order volitions and not statements identifying second-order desires that are not second-order volitions.

6. In speaking of the evaluation of his own desires and motives as being characteristic of a person, I do not mean to suggest that a person's second-order volitions necessarily manifest a *moral* stance on his part toward his first-order desires. It may not be from the point of view of morality that the person evaluates his first-order desires. Moreover, a person may be capricious and irresponsible in forming his second-order volitions and give no serious consideration to what is at stake. Second-order volitions express evaluations only in the sense that they are preferences. There is no essential restriction on the kind of basis, if any, upon which they are formed.

7. "Freedom and Action," in K. Lehrer, ed., *Freedom and Determinism* (New York: Random House, 1966), pp. 11–44.

8. I am not suggesting that the alleged difference between these two states of affairs is unverifiable. On the contrary, physiologists might well be able to show that Chisholm's conditions for a free action are not satisfied, by establishing that there is no relevant brain event for which a sufficient physical cause cannot be found.

9. For another discussion of the considerations that cast doubt on the principle that a person is morally responsible for what he has done only if he could have done otherwise, see my "Alternate Possibilities and Moral Responsibility," this JOURNAL, LXVI, 23 (Dec. 4, 1969): 829–839.

10. There is a difference between being *fully* responsible and being *solely* responsible. Suppose that the willing addict has been made an addict by the deliberate and calculated work of another. Then it may be that both the addict and this other person are fully responsible for the addict's taking the drug, while neither of them is solely responsible for it. That there is a distinction between full moral responsibility and sole moral responsibility is apparent in the following example. A certain light can be turned on or off by flicking either of two switches, and each of these switches is simultaneously flicked to the "on" position by a different person, neither of whom is aware of the other. Neither person is solely responsible for the light's going on, nor do they share the responsibility in the sense that each is partially responsible; rather, each of them is fully responsible.

FREEDOM, DETERMINISM, AND RESPONSIBILITY

By Quentin Smith and Nathan L. Oaklander

SOPHIA: So far we have presented two different kinds of challenge to the reality of freedom. The first is based on logic and the law of excluded middle, and the second is based on religion and the nature of divine foreknowledge. There is, however, a third challenge to freedom that is equally interesting.

IVAN: What challenge do you have in mind?

SOPHIA: It is a challenge that comes not from logic or religion, but from nature, or more specifically, from the connections most people believe exist among events in nature. Most people believe events have causes, and the causes of events "necessitate" the occurrence of those events. That is, given certain laws and initial conditions, then what happens is determined.

ALICE: Could you give me an example of laws and initial conditions determining something?

SOPHIA: Well, it is a law that if under laboratory conditions water is cooled to a temperature of or below 32 degrees Fahrenheit then water freezes. Thus, if the conditions are such that the environment of a cup of water is below 32 degrees then its freezing is determined. Now, although science has not discovered all the laws governing human actions, it would appear human behavior, like non-human behavior, is causally determined. In other words, we believe that people's character and motives, together with the circumstances in which they are placed, will cause them to behave in a certain way.

PHIL: That might be true in general, but the most basic laws of modern physics are not all deterministic. It is a feature of quantum mechanics that, in the micro-world, some events are random (or certain initial conditions do not necessitate specific later states). For example, the behavior of an isolated micro-particle cannot always be predicted with certainty because its position and velocity are not both determinate.

SOPHIA: True, but these quantum indeterminacies do not usually affect the behavior of large collections of particles like human bodies and brains. Human bodies and brains could be causally deterministic, even if events in the micro-world are random. If, then, human actions are causally determined, it might seem, contrary to common beliefs, that people are not free.

IVAN: The issue of whether our intuitive belief that we are free conflicts with our belief in determinism connects with the question we raised at the end of our last discussion. Remember, we were then wondering whether freedom should be understood solely in terms of doing what one wants or wishes to do or whether, in addition, a truly free act must be one that could have been otherwise. It should not surprise us if the question of the compatibility or incompatibility of causal determinism and human freedom hinges largely on which conception of freedom is correct. For example, those who maintain that the ability to do otherwise is a necessary condition of freedom also typically believe that free will and determinism are incompatible. Others, like Hume, thought that the entire free will versus determinism debate was a verbal dispute that could be resolved or dissolved once we properly defined our terms. That is, Hume thought that if we define "freedom" in terms of acting in accordance with one's will, then freedom and determinism are compatible.

SOPHIA: Metaphysical disputes about freedom have important practical and ethical implications as well. We often praise or blame and reward or punish people for their actions. Philosophical theories about what makes it right to do this involve the notion of responsibility, and the idea of responsibility is usually tied to a person's being free. For example, punishment in the form of retribution is clearly wrong if we are not free but are compelled or forced to act as we do.

IVAN: There is an interesting legal case that can serve as a starting point for a discussion of determinism, freedom and responsibility. The case involves two young students (Nathan Leopold Jr. and Richard Loeb) at the University of Michigan who, in 1924, unsuccessfully attempted to commit the "perfect crime." They did, in fact, kidnap and murder a 15-year-old boy, but were caught. They both came from wealthy families who retained the services of the most famous lawyer of the day, Clarence Darrow. Since there was no question but that Leopold and Loeb committed the crime, Darrow's plea was that although guilty as charged, they should be spared their lives.

ALICE: Given the different attitudes concerning the death penalty in the 1920s, and given the hideous nature of their crime, how did Darrow argue his case?

IVAN: He tried to convince the jury, through a consideration of the childhood, boyhood and youth of Leopold and Loeb that their behavior was the inevitable result of forces over which they had no control. In other words, he argued, in effect, that the environment, upbringing and heredity of the two boys, together with the circumstances in which they found themselves, *determined* their actions, the implication being that if their actions were determined, then they were unfree. Since freedom is a precondition of responsibility, Darrow concluded that the boys should not be held responsible for their actions. In one part of his defense Darrow said:

> "Nature is strong and she is pitiless. She works in her own mysterious way, and we are her victims. We have not much to do with it ourselves.... What had this boy to do with it? He was not his own father; he was not his own mother; he was not his own grandparents. All of this was handed to him.... If there is responsibility anywhere, it is back of him; somewhere in the infinite number of his ancestors, or in his surroundings, or in both. And I submit, Your Honor, that under every principle of natural justice, under every principle of conscience, of right, and of law, he should not be made responsible for the acts of someone else...."[1]

PHIL: That is the most ridiculous argument I ever heard in my life. It's just a cop-out, a way of avoiding responsibility. Anybody can literally get away with murder by committing a crime and saying that they were caused to do it by events in their past.

IVAN: It does seem to be rather outlandish, but Darrow did succeed in keeping his clients out of the electric chair. I raise this case, not because I am sympathetic with the argument, but because it brings to light some of the crucial issues surrounding the topics we are considering.

ALICE: What are they?

IVAN: Darrow's argument reflects a position known as *hard determinism*. According to this position, if our actions are causally determined by antecedent events, then they are not free. Since, however, hard determinists believe our actions are determined, they conclude that human freedom is an illusion and consequently, we are not responsible for our actions.

PHIL: But why do they believe that if an action is causally determined, then it is not free?

IVAN: This is where the incompatibilist definition of freedom comes in. Hard determinists, like incompatibilists in general, maintain that the power to do otherwise is a necessary condition of freedom. They also believe that if an action is caused by prior events then, given those events, it could not have been otherwise. Thus, they conclude that freedom and determinism are incompatible.

ALICE: Let me make sure I understand the line of reasoning so far. The hard determinist maintains that an action A is a free action only if instead of action A, action B could have occurred.

IVAN: Yes.

ALICE: It is then argued that if action A is determined or caused or necessitated by prior circumstances then it couldn't be otherwise. The idea is that if an action is *caused* then given the cause the action *must* follow; there could not have been any other action. However, if an action could not be otherwise, then it is not free. And, of course, if an action is not free then we cannot be held responsible for it.

IVAN: Yes, that's the logic, but we can get at the intuitive idea behind their position in a slightly different way. We ordinarily believe that an action is performed freely only if it originates with us. Aristotle once said that an action is voluntary when the moving principle is in the agent and so it is in the power of the person himself or herself to do or not to do the action. If however, our actions are caused by our constitution (e.g., our character and motives) and the external circumstances in which we find ourselves, and our being in those circumstances and having that constitution can be traced back to causes that be outside us, e.g., our parents, grandparents, teachers, genetic make-up and the like, then ultimately, the cause of our action does not lie within us (the moving principle is not in the agent). But then the person does not have it within his or her power to do other than what in fact he or she does do, and so is unfree.

ALICE: So, since Darrow accepts determinism, he denies both human freedom and responsibility.

IVAN: Yes, but I disagree.

ALICE: Why?

IVAN: I believe that determinism is a frame of reference for understanding the world and that determinism can be reconciled with human freedom.

PHIL: What do you mean by saying that "determinism is a frame of reference for understanding the world"?

IVAN: Well, we do believe, concerning things that we experience in nature, that there is a cause for why they are so and not otherwise. For example, if I see water boiling I believe that its being heated caused it to boil. Of course there are many cases when we do not *know* the cause. For example, we do not know what caused the AIDS virus to first appear, but we do believe that there was a cause, and scientists are hard at work to find it out. Furthermore, there is every reason to believe that the same is true of human actions. Of course, you might think you know what a person will do in a given situation and that person may surprise you. But even when that happens we still believe that there is some reason, in the sense of cause, for why the person acts differently. We don't believe that such unusual behavior has no cause, a complete accident without rhyme or reason.

ALICE: Given that determinism is a frame of reference that most of us implicitly assume in our daily dealings with the world and people around us, why are so many philosophers convinced that determinism is incompatible with freedom?

IVAN: In response to your first question I suggest that the very word "determined," and the claim that if determinism is true then every event is "necessary," gives rise to the impression of its incompatibility with human freedom. For the words "necessarily determined" suggest that the cause *compels* or *forces* the effect to occur whether one wants it to occur or not. But I think that these suggestions are misleading. If we base our understanding of causation and necessity on our experience, then we see, as Hume argued, that there is no compulsion involved. Hume said that "A causes B," or that "A determines B," are statements whose truth involves nothing more than the constant conjunction of events of a certain type A being followed by events of type B. Upon having observed many instances of similar causes being followed by similar effects, (e.g., seeing a baby first fall and then cry) we conclude that falling caused this baby to cry. A further basis for the idea of necessity comes from the repeated experience of a constant conjunction which gives rise to a transition in the mind from the cause to the effect (when I see a baby fall I immediately think that it will cry). We should not conclude, however, that there is a necessary connection in nature, or a power in the cause that forces the effect to occur. If we think of causality as just describing lawful relations among the properties of individual things (e.g., whenever water has the property of being heated to 212 degrees then it has the property of boiling), then there should be no temptation to think of causation as compulsion, i.e., the picture that if our choices are caused then we are somehow overwhelmed by the past.

SOPHIA: It would take us too far afield to get into an extended discussion of causation, but I must point out that the Humean view of causation is questionable. For one thing, as it stands, it fails to distinguish between accidental generalities (or constant conjunctions that do not reflect causal connections) and lawful connections. For example, although night always follows day, it is not the case that night and day are causally connected. Leaving that issue aside, how do you propose to render freedom and determinism compatible?

IVAN: I was getting to that. Let's look at an example. Consider my present action. At this moment I am sitting before you and talking about the free will-determinism issue. As I see it, I am now acting freely. Why? Because last night I thought about coming to the office this morning to talk philosophy, and on the basis of such deliberation I made the choice to be here. Thus my being in the office right now is a *conscious choice* or decision that I made. No one forced me to choose to come here, and obviously no one prevented me from coming to the office because here I am. In short, if my action results from a conscious choice that I make, then my action is free, whereas if it results from a conscious choice that someone else makes then it is unfree. Alternatively, we could say, following Hume, that if I do as I will, then my action is free, whereas if my action is compelled by some external circumstance, or I am constrained to perform an action against my will, then it is unfree. Liberty or freedom is not to be contrasted with necessity or determinism, but with compulsion or constraint. Thus, even if my action is causally determined it may still be free.

PHIL: I think I understand you: it is not *that* our actions are caused but rather it is *how* they are caused that is relevant to whether or not they are free. If they are caused by me, i.e., by a conscious choice that I make, then they are free, whereas if they are caused by you or something external to me, then they are unfree. Since a free action is one for which we can be held responsible, on your view, freedom is compatible with both determinism and responsibility.

IVAN: I would go further and say that not only are determinism and responsibility compatible, but that without determinism no person can be held responsible for his or her actions. For if determinism is false, and our actions are not caused by our character and motives together with the circumstances in which we find ourselves, then our actions just happen for no reason. They are, as it were, arbitrary and capricious. But then, they can hardly be considered free. Since, however, freedom is a condition of moral responsibility, such indeterministic acts are ones for which we cannot be held responsible.

SOPHIA: I do not find this argument all that convincing, and will explain why when I discuss my own libertarian view. But before we turn to that, let me say I am still not satisfied with your attempt to reconcile freedom and determinism.

IVAN: Why not? What is wrong with it?

SOPHIA: There are two problems. First of all, you put a lot of weight on the idea that we make choices, and our actions are free if they flow from a conscious choice. But I don't understand how determinism is compatible with there being genuine choices at all. If your "choice" is determined by antecedent events, then how can you say you really have a choice? I believe that we do make genuine choices and for that reason reject determinism.

IVAN: So your argument amounts to this: (1) if determinism is true then none of us make *genuine choices.* (2) Since, however, we do make choices, (3) determinism must be false.

SOPHIA: Exactly.

IVAN: Your argument is based upon a confusion of two different meanings of the word "choice" or the idea of a "genuine choice." By "choice" I mean a certain process or state of events which occurs in human beings from time to time. This is a process that involves making a decision based on prior deliberation. In that sense it is clear and unproblematic that we do make choices, genuine choices. Moreover, in this sense of the term, determinism is compatible with our making genuine choices, for there is nothing in the nature of choices which implies that they are or are not caused by prior events. On the other hand, if by "genuine choice" you mean a choice that is not causally determined, then it is not clear that we do make genuine choices. That is, if you just assert that a necessary condition of an event being a choice is that it is not causally determined, then you are simply assuming that the existence of choices is incompatible with determinism and so are begging the question. Thus, given either understanding of "choice" your argument rests upon a doubtful premise.

SOPHIA: I think you are missing the point of my argument, as will become apparent by considering a second argument against your view.

IVAN: What is it?

SOPHIA: My argument goes like this. An action is free only if it could have been otherwise. But if determinism is true, then we could never do anything other than what we do. Therefore, if we are free then determinism must be false. Look at it this way. There are really two components in an action. There is the determination of the will to do X, and there is the actual event of doing X. In order for an action to be free, it is not enough that the event of doing X is the result of doing what one wills. It must also be the case that the will is free. But when is a will free? We have freedom of the will only when it is in our power to will to do X or to will not to do X. However, if determinism is the case, then given our motives, character and circumstances, we could not will or choose anything other than what we do will or choose, and therefore, we could not do anything other than what we actually do. Thus, if determinism is true, we are neither free nor responsible for our actions. Since, however, we are free and are responsible for our actions, determinism must be false. I just don't see how freedom and determinism can be reconciled, and since I affirm freedom I am a *libertarian*.

IVAN: As I shall suggest later, I doubt that the ability to do otherwise is a necessary condition of freedom or responsibility, but I will let that pass for the time being. What I now wish to question is the thesis that determinism is incompatible with the idea that we could do otherwise, for I don't think that they are incompatible.

SOPHIA: Could you please explain your reasoning to me?

IVAN: There is an ambiguity in the word "could" when we say that if an individual has free will then he or she could have done otherwise. In one sense of the word "could," if determinism is the case, and I did action A, then I could not have done otherwise. In another sense of the word, however, even though I performed action A, I could have done otherwise.

SOPHIA: What are the two senses of "could"?

IVAN: Suppose we say of a cat that did not climb the tree that she *could* have climbed the tree, but that a dog who did not climb the tree that she *could not* have climbed it. The notion of "could" in this context refers to what is causally possible. Given the physical constitution of the dog, she could not climb the tree; it is causally impossible. Since the cat could climb the tree, it is causally possible for the cat. On one interpretation, then, to say of an event X (my walking to school this morning) which did not happen (because I drove), that it *could* have happened means that it is causally possible. On this understanding, only what is causally possible could have been otherwise.

In this sense of the word, to say that "An event X which did not happen, could have happened," means that "X would have happened, if so-and-so had chosen or willed it to happen." Thus, for example, although I didn't walk to school this morning, I could have walked to school this morning, meaning that I would have walked to school, if I had chosen to do so.

SOPHIA: What is the second sense of "could"?

IVAN: In a second sense, an event X which did not happen could have happened if and only if not all events are determined by a cause that precedes it. Thus, if X occurs, then to say that something else could have happened means that X was not caused to happen by prior events. Clearly, in this sense of "could," if determinism is the case, then we could not do otherwise.

SOPHIA: How does that distinction help avoid my problem with your account of freedom and responsibility?

IVAN: Well, you are claiming that determinism is incompatible with freedom and responsibility, because a condition of freedom, namely, the ability to do otherwise, is not fulfilled if determinism is the case. What I am maintaining is that there is a sense in which I could have done other than what I do even if determinism is the case. For even if action A is determined, I could have done otherwise in that I *would* have done otherwise, had I made a different choice. It was causally possible for me to act differently if I chose differently.

SOPHIA: The problem with your argument is that your interpretation of "could have done otherwise" is inadequate. You say that "She could have done otherwise" means that "She would have done otherwise, if she had so chosen." I agree that if she had chosen differently then she would have acted differently, but that is a moot point because she couldn't have chosen differently. Since our choices are causally determined, they couldn't be otherwise, and if they couldn't be otherwise it hardly makes a difference to our freedom to say that if our choices had been different we would have acted differently.

IVAN: But I deny your claim that if determinism is the case, we could not have chosen or acted differently. To say that "She could have done otherwise" means that "She would have done otherwise, if she had made a different choice," and that is compatible with the action that one in fact performs being caused.

SOPHIA: But could she have chosen to act differently? I don't think so, if determinism is the case.

IVAN: But I do. To say that a person could have chosen to act differently means that a person would have acted differently, if the deliberation and reflection that led to the choice was different. You are simply assuming that if our actions are caused, then they could not be otherwise, but that just reflects the confusion between the two senses of "could" that we have been discussing.

SOPHIA: I still don't see how a determined action could ever be other than what it is, if it is determined to be just that action.

IVAN: I can see that you don't agree with this analysis of "could have done otherwise," but perhaps we could move on since later I will suggest that the ability to do otherwise should not be a necessary condition of human freedom and responsibility anyway. So, rather than try to continue defending the compatibilist approach now, I want to know what you would say about the alleged dilemma of freedom and determinism that we have been considering.

ALICE: I am afraid that I have lost sight of why exactly there is a dilemma concerning these two notions. Could you explain it again?

SOPHIA: Certainly. As I understand the issue, there is a prima facie problem with maintaining that determinism is false, and it is precisely the same problem as that which arises if determinism is true. As you know, I believe that if various events, such as a person's wants, beliefs and desires are the cause of a person's action, then we cannot hold that person responsible for the action since the person did not bring the action about. Of course, if the person brought about his or her wants, desires and wishes, then he or she could be held responsible, but if determinism is the case then our wants, desires and beliefs are caused by other events and not by the agent. So, it seems that freedom and responsibility require indeterminism.

Unfortunately, it does not help to maintain that actions are not caused by people's character and circumstances since if actions are totally uncaused, happening out of the blue, then once again no individual person is the cause of them and so no individual can be held responsible. If my left arm suddenly jerks up in the air, without being caused to do so, *I* cannot be held responsible for that event. Thus, the dilemma is that if every event is caused by some other event, then we are not free and hence not responsible. And if human actions are not caused, then our freedom is beyond our control, utterly spontaneous and so once again we cannot be held responsible.

IVAN: As you know, I believe that determinism and responsibility are compatible, but I agree the problem you pose does arise for the indeterminist. How do you propose to resolve it?

SOPHIA: It seems to me that to solve the problem we must adopt a certain conception of personal identity, namely, the substantialist conception. Persons are substances, not necessarily immaterial Cartesian substances, but substances nonetheless. Since I am a substance, and not an event or a succession of events, it is within my power to bring about or cause an event or action to take place without myself being caused to do so. If we ourselves bring about an action without being determined to do so by any prior cause, then the action is free and one for which we are wholly responsible. Each of us, on occasion, is an uncaused cause. Sometimes when we act we cause certain events to happen, and nothing or no one causes us to cause those events to happen.

PHIL: Your view does have important implications for the nature of personal identity. If we are a succession of events somehow related, as the relational view maintains, and if determinism is the case, so that every event is caused by some other event, then the chain of causes extends outside our selves and the individual agent is not the cause of his or her actions. On the other hand, if a person is a substance which has experiences, then this substance which lies outside the causal network can originate action without being caused to act by any event, or any other substance. When this happens we are free and we are responsible for our actions. Thus, the libertarian view avoids determinism, since some events are not caused by prior events, but it also avoids the strong form of indeterminism according to which some events occur uncaused, or occur for no reason whatsoever. Both freedom and responsibility are presented.

SOPHIA: That is a good summary of my position.

IVAN: Perhaps, but then I do not see how your view really avoids the problem facing the indeterminist; it just pushes the problem one step back. Admittedly, an action performed by a substantialist agent is not purely spontaneous, since it is caused by the agent who chooses it. But what of the agent's choice to bring about one action rather than another? Presumably that is an uncaused choice. How then can we hold an agent responsible for the actions he or she causes if the agent bringing about or choosing or causing one action rather than another is itself uncaused? If the doing of A and the doing otherwise are not causally determined, then either might occur given all the same past circumstances and laws of nature. But then we are left with the question: "Why did the agent do A rather than do otherwise?" If the agent's choice of A rather than B is just an arbitrary, spontaneous choice, then it would appear that it is not one for which the agent can be held ultimately responsible and the entire motivation for the libertarian view seems to collapse. How would you attempt to resolve this difficulty?

SOPHIA: Good question. I can just hint at the outlines of a solution now. I think what is necessary is some account of how there can be reasons for our final choice, without those reasons *determining* our final choice. Suppose a man is faced with an important choice. His girlfriend is pregnant and wants to give up the baby for adoption unless he agrees to marry her. He has to make a decision. Where does free will come in? Suppose that in this case there is real conflict. Given the man's character there is a pull toward both sides. He has reasons for marrying her, e.g., he wants to have a child, but he also has reasons for not marrying her, e.g., he is not sure that she is the person for him. To make a decision, an effort of will is going to be necessary. That is, whatever he chooses will involve an inner struggle and effort of will which must be exercised against opposing inclinations. The result of this effort is a decision to marry her or not marry her.

The opposing desires and beliefs make an effort of will necessary to make a choice between one set of reasons rather than another. But the effort of will which terminates in the choice is not causally determined. In other words, his wants, desires and beliefs can provide reasons for either choice he makes, and yet these reasons do not determine his choice; he is capable of choosing differently. Thus his decision is free, and one for which he can be held responsible.

IVAN: I agree that sometimes we can give a teleological explanation of why people act by appealing to the end or goal they hope to achieve, but as I see it, if we can supply reasons for why people act the way they do, those reasons are still causal.

SOPHIA: And, of course, I disagree.

IVAN: Even so, our discussion certainly has helped to bring some of the central issues into clearer focus. Before going to class I want to touch on a point I suggested earlier, namely, that the ability to do otherwise should not be thought of as necessary for freedom and responsibility.

PHIL: What is your reasoning for that claim?

IVAN: It is based on a rather hypothetical situation, but sometimes a consideration of such situations is a useful technique to bring out the nature of a certain concept. Suppose, then, that a mad neuro-surgeon has created a machine that is attached to my brain. This machine, when turned on, ensures that whenever I want a piece of fruit I will choose an apple. Suppose further that I go to the farmer's market and having looked over the fruit I decide *of my own free will* that I want an apple. Following my want, I reach for an apple, buy it and begin to eat it. In this case, I couldn't have done other than buy an apple since the machine would have interceded and prevented me from buying a pear. But I didn't want a pear, I wanted an apple, and that is why we would not hesitate to say that my eating the apple was a free action even though I could not do anything else. We say this because I did not get any help from the mechanism, i.e., the mechanism played no role in my choice to buy an apple. Rather I decided to have an apple, and that is why the action is free; my being unable to do otherwise has nothing to do with it.

SOPHIA: The question of whether or not the "could not do otherwise" principle deserves our future philosophical allegiance is highly debatable. But since I have to teach, perhaps we can pursue that question further some other time.

IVAN: Sounds good.

NOTE

1. Clarence Darrow (1957) "The Crime of Compulsion," in Arthur Weinberg (ed.) *Attorney for the Damned,* New York: Simon and Schuster, reprinted in Victor Grassian (1984) *Perennial Issues in Philosophy,* Englewood Cliffs, NJ: Prentice Hall, p. 427.

GLOSSARY OF TERMS

Compatibilism There is human freedom and determinism is the case. This view is also called "soft determinism."

Hard determinism Since determinism is true we are neither free nor responsible for our actions.

Incompatibilism The view that human freedom and causal determinism cannot both be true. *See* libertarianism and hard determinism.

Initial conditions A set of circumstances which, together with laws, imply that a certain event will occur.

Law of nature A law is a generality (of the form, for every X if X has the property F_1, then X has the property F_2) that describes a relation between the properties of things.

Libertarianism Determinism is false, and therefore we are free and responsible for our actions.

Quantum mechanics A theory of the structure and behavior of particles. In this theory there is an element of unpredictability and randomness in the behavior of micro-particles because particles no longer have separate, well-defined positions and velocities.

PART VIII

Modern Theories of Human Nature

ON HUMAN NATURE

By Arthur Schopenhauer
Trans. by T. Bailey Saunders

Truths of the physical order may possess much external significance, but internal significance they have none. The latter is the privilege of intellectual and moral truths, which are concerned with the objectivation of the will in its highest stages, whereas physical truths are concerned with it in its lowest.

For example, if we could establish the truth of what up till now is only a conjecture, namely, that it is the action of the sun which produces thermoelectricity at the equator; that this produces terrestrial magnetism; and that this magnetism, again, is the cause of the *aurora borealis*, these would be truths externally of great, but internally of little, significance. On the other hand, examples of internal significance are furnished by all great and true philosophical systems; by the catastrophe of every good tragedy; nay, even by the observation of human conduct in the extreme manifestations of its morality and immorality, of its good and its evil character. For all these are expressions of that reality which takes outward shape as the world, and which, in the highest stages of its objectivation, proclaims its innermost nature.

To say that the world has only a physical and not a moral significance is the greatest and most pernicious of all errors, the fundamental blunder, the real perversity of mind and temper; and, at bottom, it is doubtless the tendency which faith personifies as Anti-Christ. Nevertheless, in spite of all religions—and they are systems which one and all maintain the opposite, and seek to establish it in their mythical way—this fundamental error never becomes quite extinct, but raises its head from time to time afresh, until universal indignation compels it to hide itself once more.

Yet, however certain we may feel of the moral significance of life and the world, to explain and illustrate it, and to resolve the contradiction between this significance and the world as it is, form a task of great difficulty; so great, indeed, as to make it possible that it has remained for me to exhibit the true and only genuine and sound basis of morality everywhere and at all times effective, together with the results to which it leads. The actual facts of morality are too much on my side for me to fear that my theory can ever be replaced or upset by any other.

However, so long as even my ethical system continues to be ignored by the professorial world, it is Kant's moral principle that prevails in the universities. Among its various forms the one which is most in favour at present is "the dignity of man." I have already exposed the absurdity of this doctrine in my treatise on the *Foundation of Morality*. Therefore I will only say here that if the question were asked on what the alleged dignity of man rests, it would not be long before the answer was made that it rests upon his morality. In other words, his morality rests upon his dignity, and his dignity rests upon his morality.

But apart from this circular argument it seems to me that the idea of dignity can be applied only in an ironical sense to a being whose will is so sinful, whose intellect is so limited, whose body is so weak and perishable as man's. How shall a man be proud, when his conception is a crime, his birth a penalty, his life a labour, and death a necessity!—

> *Quid superbit homo? cujus conceptio culpa, Nasci poena, labor vita, necesse mori!*

Therefore, in opposition to the above-mentioned form of the Kantian principle, I should be inclined to lay down the following rule: When you come into contact with a man, no matter whom, do not attempt an objective appreciation of him according to his worth and dignity. Do not consider his bad will, or his narrow understanding and perverse ideas; as the former may easily lead you to hate and the latter to despise him; but fix your attention only upon his sufferings, his needs, his anxieties, his pains. Then you will always feel your kinship with him; you will sympathise with him; and instead of hatred or contempt you will experience the commiseration that alone is the peace to which the Gospel calls us. The way to keep down hatred and contempt is certainly not to look for a man's alleged "dignity," but, on the contrary, to regard him as an object of pity.

•••

Fundamental disposition towards others, assuming the character either of Envy or of Sympathy, is the point at which the moral virtues and vices of mankind first diverge. These two diametrically opposite qualities exist in every man; for they spring from the inevitable comparison which he draws between his own lot and that of others. According as the result of this comparison affects his individual character does the one or the other of these qualities become the source and principle of all his action. Envy builds the wall between *Thee* and *Me* thicker and stronger; Sympathy makes it slight and transparent; nay, sometimes it pulls down the wall altogether; and then the distinction between self and not-self vanishes.

...

Every human perfection is allied to a defect into which it threatens to pass; but it is also true that every defect is allied to a perfection. Hence it is that if, as often happens, we make a mistake about a man, it is because at the beginning of our acquaintance with him we confound his defects with the kinds of perfection to which they are allied. The cautious man seems to us a coward; the economical man, a miser; the spendthrift seems liberal; the rude fellow, downright and sincere; the foolhardy person looks as if he were going to work with a noble self-confidence; and so on in many other cases.

No one can live among men without feeling drawn again and again to the tempting supposition that moral baseness and intellectual incapacity are closely connected, as though they both sprang direct from one source.... That it seems to be so is merely due to the fact that both are so often found together; and the circumstance is to be explained by the very frequent occurrence of each of them, so that it may easily happen for both to be compelled to live under one roof. At the same time it is not to be denied that they play into each other's hands to their mutual benefit; and it is this that produces the very unedifying spectacle which only too many men exhibit, and that makes the world to go as it goes. A man who is unintelligent is very likely to show his perfidy, villainy and malice; whereas a clever man understands how to conceal these qualities. And how often, on the other hand, does a perversity of heart prevent a man from seeing truths which his intelligence is quite capable of grasping!

Nevertheless, let no one boast. Just as every man, though he be the greatest genius, has very definite limitations in some one sphere of knowledge, and thus attests his common origin with the essentially perverse and stupid mass of mankind, so also has every man something in his nature which is positively evil. Even the best, nay the noblest, character will sometimes surprise us by isolated traits of depravity; as though it were to acknowledge his kinship with the human race, in which villainy—nay, cruelty—is to be found in that degree. For it was just in virtue of this evil in him, this bad principle, that of necessity he became a man. And for the same reason the world in general is what my clear mirror of it has shown it to be.

But in spite of all this the difference even between one man and another is incalculably great, and many a one would be horrified to see another as he really is. Oh, for some Asmodeus of morality, to make not only roofs and walls transparent to his favorites, but also to lift the veil of dissimulation, fraud, hypocrisy, pretence, falsehood and deception, which is spread over all things! to show how little true honesty there is in the world, and how often, even where it is least to be expected, behind all the exterior outwork of virtue, secretly and in the innermost recesses, unrighteousness sits at the helm! It is just on this account that so many men of the better kind have four-footed friends: for, to be sure, how is a man to get relief from the endless dissimulation, falsity and malice of mankind, if there were no dogs into whose honest faces he can look without distrust?

For what is our civilised world but a big masquerade? where you meet knights, priests, soldiers, men of learning, barristers, clergymen, philosophers, and I don't know what all! But they are not what they pretend to be; they are only masks, and, as a rule, behind the masks you will find money makers. One man, I suppose, puts on the mask of law, which he has borrowed for the purpose from a barrister, only in order to be able to give another man a sound drubbing; a second has chosen the mask of patriotism and the public welfare with a similar intent; a third takes religion or purity of doctrine. For all sorts of purposes men have often put on the mask of philosophy, and even of philanthropy, and I know not what besides. Women have a smaller choice. As a rule they avail themselves of the mask of morality, modesty, domesticity, and humility. Then there are general masks, without any particular character attaching to them like dominoes. They may be met with everywhere; and of this sort is the strict rectitude, the courtesy, the sincere sympathy, the smiling friendship, that people profess. The whole of these masks as a rule are merely, as I have said, a disguise for some industry, commerce, or speculation. It is merchants alone who in this respect constitute any honest class. They are the only people who give themselves out to be what they are; and therefore they go about without any mask at all, and consequently take a humble rank.

It is very necessary that a man should be apprised early in life that it is a masquerade in which he finds himself. For otherwise there are many things which he will fail to understand and put up with, nay, at which he will be completely puzzled, and that man longest of all whose heart is made of better clay—

Et meliore luto finxit praecordia Titan.[1]

Such for instance is the favour that villainy finds; the neglect that merit, even the rarest and the greatest, suffers at the hands of those of the same profession; the hatred of truth and great capacity; the ignorance of scholars in their own province; and the fact that true wares are almost always despised and the merely specious ones in request. Therefore let even the young be instructed betimes that in this masquerade the apples are of wax, the flowers of silk, the fish of pasteboard, and that all things—yes, all things—are toys and trifles; and that of two men whom he may see earnestly engaged in business, one is supplying spurious goods and the other paying for them in false coin.

But there are more serious reflections to be made, and worse things to be recorded. Man is at bottom a savage, horrible beast. We know it, if only in the business of taming and restraining him which we call civilization. Hence it is that we are terrified if now and then his nature breaks out. Wherever and whenever the locks and chains of law and order fall off and give place to anarchy, he shows himself for what he is. But it is unnecessary to wait for anarchy in order to gain enlightenment on this subject. A hundred records, old and new, produce the conviction that in his unrelenting cruelty man is in no way inferior to the tiger and the hyaena. A forcible example is supplied by a publication of the year 1841 entitled *Slavery and the Internal Slave Trade in the United States of North America: being replies to questions transmitted by the British Anti-slavery Society to the American Anti-slavery Society.* This book constitutes one of the heaviest indictments against the human race. No one can put it down with a feeling of horror, and few without tears. For whatever the reader may have ever heard, or imagined, or dreamt, of the unhappy condition of slavery, or indeed of human cruelty in general, it will seem small to him when he reads of the way in which those devils in human form, those bigoted, church-going, strictly Sabbatarian rascals—and in particular the Anglican priests among them—treated their innocent black brothers, who by wrong and violence had got into their diabolical clutches.

Other examples are furnished by Tshudi's *Travels in Peru*, in the description which he gives of the treatment of the Peruvian soldiers at the hands of their officers; and by Macleod's *Travels in Eastern Africa*, where the author tells of the cold-blooded and truly devilish cruelty with which the Portuguese in Mozambique treat their slaves. But we need not go for examples to the New World, that obverse side of our planet. In the year 1848 it was brought to life that in England, not in one, but apparently in a hundred cases within a brief period, a husband had poisoned his wife or *vice versâ*, or both had joined in poisoning their children, or in torturing them slowly to death by starving and ill-treating them, with no other object than to get the money for burying them which they had insured in the Burial Clubs against their death. For this purpose a child was often insured in several, even in as many as twenty clubs at once.

Details of this character belong, indeed, to the blackest pages in the criminal records of humanity. But, when all is said, it is the inward and innate character of man, this god *par excellence* of the Pantheists, from which they and everything like them proceed. In every man there dwells, first and foremost, a colossal egoism, which breaks the bounds of right and justice with the greatest freedom, as everyday life shows on a small scale, and as history on every page of it on a large. Does not the recognized need of a balance of power in Europe, with the anxious way in which it is preserved, demonstrate that man is a beast of prey, who no sooner sees a weaker man near him than he falls upon him without fail? and does not the same hold good of the affairs of ordinary life?

But to the boundless egoism of our nature there is joined more or less in every human breast a fund of hatred, anger, envy, rancour and malice, accumulated like the venom in a serpent's tooth, and waiting only for an opportunity of venting itself, and then, like a demon unchained, of storming and raging. If a man has no great occasion for breaking out, he will end by taking advantage of the smallest, and by working it up into something great by the aid of his imagination; for, however small it may be, it is enough to rouse his anger—

Quantulacunque adeo est occasio, sufficit irae—[2]

and then he will carry it as far as he can and may. We see this in daily life, where such outbursts are well known under the name of "venting one's gall on something." It will also have been observed that if such outbursts meet with no opposition the subject of them feels decidedly the better for them afterwards. That anger is not without its pleasure is a truth that was recorded even by Aristotle[3]; and he quotes a passage from Homer, who declares anger to be sweeter than honey. But not in anger alone—in hatred too, which stands to anger like a chronic to an acute disease, a man may indulge with the greatest delight:

Now hatred is by far the longest pleasure, Men love in haste, but they detest at leisure[4]

Gobineau in his work *Les Races Humaines* has called man *l'animal méchant par excellence*. People take this very ill, because they feel that it hits them; but he is quite right, for man is the only animal which causes pain to others without any further purpose than just to cause it. Other animals never do it except to satisfy their hunger, or in the rage of combat. If it is said against the tiger that he kills more than eats, he strangles his prey only for the purpose of eating it; and if he cannot eat it, the only explanation is, as the French phrase has it, that *ses yeux sont plus grands que son estomac*. No animal ever torments another for the mere purpose of tormenting, but man does it, and it is this that constitutes the diabolical feature in his character which is so much worse than the merely animal. I have already spoken of the matter in its broad aspect; but it is manifest even in small things, and every reader has a daily opportunity of observing it. For instance, if two little dogs are playing together—and what a genial and charming sight it is—and a child of three or four years joins them, it is almost inevitable for it to begin hitting them with a whip or stick, and thereby show itself, even at that age, *l'animal méchant par excellence*. The love of teasing and playing tricks, which is common enough, may be traced to the same source. For instance, if a man has expressed his annoyance at any interruption or other petty inconvenience, there will be no lack of people who for that very reason will bring it about: *animal méchant par excellence*! This is so certain that a man should be careful not to express any annoyance at small evils. On the other hand he should also be careful not to express his pleasure at any trifle, for, if he does so, men will act like the jailer who, when he found that his prisoner had performed the laborious task of taming a spider, and took a pleasure in watching it, immediately crushed it under his foot: *l'animal méchant par excellence*! This is why all animals are instinctively afraid of the sight, or even of the track of a man, that *animal méchant par excellence*! nor does their instinct play them false; for it is man alone who hunts game for which he has no use and which does him no harm.

It is a fact, then, that in the heart of every man there lies a wild beast which only waits for an opportunity to storm and rage, in its desire to inflict pain on others, or, if they stand in his way, to kill them. It is this which is the source of all the lust of war and battle. In trying to tame and to some extent hold it in check, the intelligence, its appointed keeper, has always enough to do. People may, if they please, call it the radical evil of human nature—a name which will at least serve those with whom a word stands for an explanation. I say, however, that it is the will to live, which, more and more embittered by the constant sufferings of existence, seeks to alleviate its own torment by causing torment in others. But in this way a man gradually develops in himself real cruelty and malice. The observation may also be added that as, according to Kant, matter subsists only through the antagonism of the powers of expansion and contraction, so human society subsists only by the antagonism of hatred, or anger, and fear. For there is a moment in the life of all of us when the malignity of our nature might perhaps make us murderers, if it were not accompanied by a due admixture of fear to keep it within bounds; and this fear, again, would make a man the sport and laughing stock of every boy, if anger were not lying ready in him, and keeping watch.

But it is *Schadenfreude*, a mischievous delight in the misfortunes of others, which remains the worst trait in human nature. It is a feeling which is closely akin to cruelty, and differs from it, to say the truth, only as theory from practice. In general, it may be said of it that it takes the place which pity ought to take—pity which is its opposite, and the true source of all real justice and charity.

...

We have been taking a look at the *depravity* of man, and it is a sight which may well fill us with horror. But now we must cast our eyes on the *misery* of his existence; and when we have done so, and are horrified by that too, we must look back again at his depravity. We shall then find that they hold the balance to each other. We shall perceive the eternal justice of things; for we shall recognise that the world is itself the Last Judgment on it, and we shall begin to understand why it is that everything that lives must pay the penalty of its existence, first in living and then in dying. Thus the evil of the penalty accords with the evil of the sin—*malum poenae* with *malum culpae*. From the same point of view we lose our indignation at that intellectual incapacity of the great majority of mankind which in life so often disgusts us. In this *Sansara*, as the Buddhists call it, human misery, human depravity and human folly correspond with one another perfectly, and they are of like magnitude. But if, on some special inducement, we direct our gaze to one of them, and survey it in particular, it seems to exceed the other two. This, however, is an illusion, and merely the effect of their colossal range.

All things proclaim this *Sansara*; more than all else, the world of mankind; in which, from a moral point of view, villainy and baseness, and from an intellectual point of view, incapacity and stupidity, prevail to a horrifying extent. Nevertheless, there appear in it, although very spasmodically, and always as a fresh surprise, manifestations of honesty, of goodness, nay, even of nobility; and also of great intelligence, of the thinking mind of genius. They never quite vanish, but like single points of light gleam upon us out of the great dark mass. We must accept them as a pledge that this *Sansara* contains a good and redeeming principle, which is capable of breaking through and of filling and freeing the whole of it.

The readers of my *Ethics* know that with me the ultimate foundation of morality is the truth which in the *Vedas* and the *Vedanta* receives its expression in the established, mystical formula, *Tat twam asi* (*This is thyself*), which is spoken with reference to every living thing, be it man or beast, and is called the *Mahavakya*, the great word.

Actions which proceed in accordance with this principle, such as those of the philanthropist, may indeed be regarded as the beginning of mysticism. Every benefit rendered with a pure intention proclaims that the man who exercises it acts in direct conflict with the world of appearance; for he recognizes himself as identical with another individual, who exists in complete separation from him. Accordingly, all disinterested kindness is inexplicable; it is a mystery; and hence in order to explain it a man has to resort to all sorts of fictions. When Kant had demolished all other arguments for theism, he admitted one only, that it gave the best interpretation and solution of such mysterious actions, and of all others like them. He therefore allowed it to stand as a presumption unsusceptible indeed of theoretical proof, but valid from a practical point of view. I may, however, express my doubts whether he was quite serious about it. For to make morality rest on theism is really to reduce morality to egoism; although the English, it is true, as also the lowest classes of society with us, do not perceive the possibility of any other foundation for it.

The above-mentioned recognition of a man's own true being in another individual objectively presented to him, is exhibited in a particularly beautiful and clear way in the cases in which a man, already destined to death beyond any hope of rescue, gives himself up to the welfare of others with great solicitude and zeal, and tries to save them. Of this kind is the well-known story of a servant who was bitten in a courtyard at night by a mad dog. In the belief that she was beyond hope, she seized the dog and dragged it into a stable, which she then locked, so that no one else might be bitten. Then again there is the incident in Naples, which Tischbein has immortalized in one of his *aquarelles*. A son, fleeing from the lava which is rapidly streaming toward the sea, is carrying his aged father on his back. When there is only a narrow strip of land left between the devouring elements, the father bids the son put him down, so that the son may save himself by flight, as otherwise both will be lost. The son obeys, and as he goes casts a glance of farewell on his father. This is the moment depicted. The historical circumstance which Scott represents in his masterly way in *The Heart of Midlothian*, chap, ii., is of a precisely similar kind; where, of two delinquents condemned to death, the one who by his awkwardness caused the capture of the other happily sets him free in the chapel by overpowering the guard after the execution-sermon, without at the same time making any attempt on his own behalf. Nay, in the same category must also be placed the scene which is represented in a common engraving, which may perhaps be objectionable to western readers—I mean the one in which a soldier, kneeling to be shot, is trying by waving a cloth to frighten away his dog who wants to come to him.

In all these cases we see an individual in the face of his own immediate and certain destruction no longer thinking of saving himself, so that he may direct the whole of his efforts to saving some one else. How could there be a clearer expression of the consciousness that what is being destroyed is only a phenomenon, and that the destruction itself is only a phenomenon; that, on the other hand, the real being of the man who meets his death is untouched by that event, and lives on in the other man, in whom even now, as his action betrays, he so clearly perceives it to exist? For if this were not so, and it was his real being which was about to be annihilated, how could that being spend its last efforts in showing such an ardent sympathy in the welfare and continued existence of another?

There are two different ways in which a man may become conscious of his own existence. On the one hand, he may have an empirical perception of it, as it manifests itself externally—something so small that it approaches vanishing point; set in a world which, as regards time and space, is infinite; one only of the thousand millions of human creatures who run about on this planet for a very brief period and are renewed every thirty years. On the other hand, by going down into the depths of his own nature, a man may become conscious that he is all in all; that, in fact, he is the only real being; and that, in addition, this real being perceives itself again in others, who present themselves from without, as though they formed a mirror of himself.

Of these two ways in which a man may come to know what he is, the first grasps the phenomenon alone, the mere product of *the principle of individuation*; whereas the second makes a man immediately conscious that he is *the thing-in-itself*. This is a doctrine in which, as regards the first way, I have Kant, and as regards both, I have the *Vedas*, to support me.

There is, it is true, a simple objection to the second method. It may be said to assume that one and the same being can exist in different places at the same time, and yet be complete in each of them. Although, from an empirical point of view, this is the most palpable impossibility—nay, absurdity—it is nevertheless perfectly true of the thing-in-itself. The impossibility and the absurdity of it, empirically, are only due to the forms which phenomena assume, in accordance with the principle of individuation. For the thing-in-itself, the will to live, exists whole and undivided in every being, even in the smallest, as completely as in the sum-total of all things that ever were or are or will be. This is why every being, even the smallest, says to itself, So long as I am safe, let the world perish—*dum ego salvus sim, pereat mundus.* And, in truth, even if only one individual were left in the world, and all the rest were to perish, the one that remained would still possess the whole self-being of the world, uninjured and undiminished, and would laugh at the destruction of the world as an illusion. This conclusion *per impossible* may be balanced by the counter-conclusion, which is on all fours with it, that if that last individual were to be annihilated in and with him the whole world would be destroyed. It was in this sense that the mystic Angelas Silesius declared that God could not live for a moment without him, and that if he were to be annihilated God must of necessity give up the ghost:

> *Ich weiss dass ohne mich Gott nicht ein Nun kann leben; Werd' ich zunicht, er muss von Not den Geist aufgeben.*[5]

But the empirical point of view also to some extent enables us to perceive that it is true, or at least possible, that our self can exist in other beings whose consciousness is separated and different from our own. That this is so is shown by the experience of somnambulists. Although the identity of their ego is preserved throughout, they know nothing, when they awake, of all that a moment before they themselves said, did or suffered. So entirely is the individual consciousness a phenomenon that even in the same ego two consciousness can arise of which the one knows nothing of the other.

NOTES

1. Juvenal, *Sat.* 14, 34.
2. Juvenal, *Sat*, 13, 183.
3. *Rhet.*, i., 11; ii., 2.
4. Byron, *Don Juan*, c. xiii, 6.
5. Translator's Note—Angelus Silesius, see *Counsels and Maxims*, p. 39, note.

HUMAN ALL TOO HUMAN

By Friedrich Nietzsche

SELECTIONS FROM *HUMAN, ALL TOO HUMAN*

[...]

At the waterfall. When we see a waterfall, we think we see freedom of will and choice in the innumerable turnings, windings, breaking of the waves; but everything is necessary; each movement can be calculated mathematically. Thus it is with human actions; if one were omniscient, one would be able to calculate each individual action in advance, each step in the progress of knowledge, each error, each act of malice. To be sure, the acting man is caught in his illusion of volition; if the wheel of the world were to stand still for a moment and an omniscient, calculating mind were there to take advantage of this interruption, he would be able to tell into the farthest future of each being and describe every rut that wheel will roll upon. The acting man's delusion about himself, his assumption that free will exists, is also part of the calculable mechanism.

Irresponsibility and innocence.[1] Man's complete lack of responsibility, for his behavior and for his nature, is the bitterest drop which the man of knowledge must swallow, if he had been in the habit of seeing responsibility and duty as humanity's claim to nobility. All his judgments, distinctions, dislikes have thereby become worthless and wrong: the deepest feeling he had offered a victim or a hero was misdirected; he may no longer praise, no longer blame, for it is nonsensical to praise and blame nature and necessity. Just as he loves a good work of art, but does not praise it, because it can do nothing about itself, just as he regards a plant, so he must regard the actions of men and his own actions. He can admire their strength, beauty, abundance, but he may not find any earned merit in them: chemical processes, and the clash of elements, the agony of the sick man who yearns for recovery, these have no more earned merit than do those inner struggles and crises in which a man is torn back and forth by various motives until he finally decides for the most powerful as is said (in truth until the most powerful motive decides about us). But all these motives, whatever great names we give them, have grown out of the same roots which are thought to hold the evil poisons. Between good and evil actions there is no difference in type; at most, a difference in degree. Good actions are sublimated evil actions; evil actions are good actions become coarse and stupid. The individual's only demand, for self-enjoyment (along with the fear of losing it), is satisfied in all circumstances: man may act as he can, that is, as he must, whether in deeds of vanity, revenge, pleasure, usefulness, malice, cunning, or in deeds of sacrifice, pity, knowledge. His powers of judgment determine where a man will let this demand for self-enjoyment take him. In each society, in each individual, a hierarchy of the good is always present, by which man determines his own actions and judges other people's actions. But this standard is continually in flux; many actions are called evil, and are only stupid, because the degree of intelligence which chose them was very low. Indeed, in a certain sense *all* actions are stupid even now, for the highest degree of human intelligence which can now be attained will surely be surpassed. And then, in hindsight, all *our* behavior and judgments will appear as inadequate and rash as the behavior and judgments of backward savage tribes now seem to us inadequate and rash. To understand all this can cause great pain, but afterwards there is consolation. These pains are birth pangs. The butterfly wants to break through his cocoon; he tears at it, he rends it: then he is blinded and confused by the unknown light, the realm of freedom. Men who are *capable* of that sorrow (how few they will be!) will make the first attempt to see if mankind *can transform itself* from a *moral* into a *wise* mankind. In those individuals, the sun of a new gospel is casting its first ray onto the highest mountaintop of the soul; the fog is condensing more thickly than ever, and the brightest light and cloudiest dusk lie next to each other. Everything is necessity: this is the new knowledge, and this knowledge itself is necessity. Everything is innocence: and knowledge is the way to insight into this innocence. If pleasure, egoism, vanity are *necessary* for the generation of moral phenomena and their greatest flower, the sense for true and just knowledge; if error and confusion of imagination were the only means by which mankind could raise itself gradually to this degree of self-illumination and self-redemption-who could scorn those means? Who could be sad when he perceives the goal to which those paths lead? Everything in the sphere of morality[2] has evolved; changeable, fluctuating, everything is fluid, it is true: but *everything is also streaming onward* to one goal. Even if the inherited habit of erroneous esteeming, loving, hating continues to govern us, it will grow weaker under the influence of growing knowledge: a new habit, that of understanding, non-loving, non-hating, surveying is gradually being implanted in us on the same ground, and in thousands of years will be powerful enough perhaps to give mankind the strength to produce wise, innocent (conscious of their innocence)[3] men as regularly as it now produces unwise, unfair men, conscious of their guilt[4]—*these men are the necessary first stage, not the opposite of those to come.*

SELECTIONS FROM *THE GAY SCIENCE*

The madman.—Have you not heard of that madman who lit a lantern in the bright morning hours, ran to the market place, and cried incessantly: "I seek God! I seek God!"—As many of those who did not believe in God were standing around just then, he provoked much laughter. Has he got lost? asked one. Did he lose his way like a child? asked another. Or is he hiding? Is he afraid of us? Has he gone on a voyage? emigrated?—Thus they yelled and laughed. The madman jumped into their midst and pierced them with his eyes. "Whither is God?" he cried; "I will tell you. *We have killed him*—you and I. All of us are his murderers. But how did we do this? How could we drink up the sea? Who gave us the sponge to wipe away the entire horizon? What were we doing when we unchained this earth from its sun? Whither is it moving now? Whither are we moving? Away from all suns? Are we not plunging continually? Backward, sideward, forward, in all directions? Is there still any up or down? Are we not straying as through an infinite nothing? Do we not feel the breath of empty space? Has it not become colder? Is not night continually closing in on us? Do we not need to light lanterns in the morning? Do we hear nothing as yet of the noise of the grave diggers who are burying God? Do we smell nothing as yet of the divine decomposition? Gods, too, decompose. God is dead. God remains dead. And we have killed him. "How shall we comfort ourselves, the murderers of all murderers? What was holiest and mightiest of all that the world has yet owned has bled to death under our knives: who will wipe this blood off us? What water is there for us to clean ourselves? What festivals of atonement, what sacred games shall we have to invent? Is not the greatness of this deed too great for us? Must we ourselves not become gods simply to appear worthy of it? There has never been a greater deed; and whoever is born after us for the sake of this deed he will belong to a higher history than all history hitherto." Here the madman fell silent and looked again at his listeners; and they, too, were silent and stared at him in astonishment. At last he threw his lantern on the ground, and it broke into pieces and went out. "I have come too early," he said then; "my time is not yet. This tremendous event is still on its way, still wandering; it has not yet reached the ears of men. Lightning and thunder require time; the light of the stars requires time; deeds, though done, still require time to be seen and heard. This deed is still more distant from them than the most distant stars—*and yet they have done it themselves.* It has been related further that on the same day the madman forced his way into several churches and there struck up his *requiem aetemam deo.*[5] Led out and called to account, he is said always to have replied nothing but: "What after all are these churches now if they are not the tombs and sepulchers of God?"

The dying Socrates.—I admire the courage and wisdom of Socrates in everything he did, said—and did not say. This mocking and enamored monster and pied piper of Athens, who made the most overweening youths tremble and sob, was not only the wisest chatterer of all time: he was equally great in silence. I wish he had remained taciturn also at the last moment of his life; in that case he might belong to a still higher order of spirits. Whether it was death or the poison or piety or malice—something loosened his tongue at that moment and he said: "O Crito, I owe Asclepius a rooster." This ridiculous and terrible "last word" means for those who have ears: "O Crito, *life is a disease.*" Is it possible that a man like him, who had lived cheerfully and like a soldier in the sight of everyone, should have been a pessimist? He had merely kept a cheerful mien while concealing all his life long his ultimate judgment, his inmost feeling. Socrates, Socrates *suffered life!* And then he still revenged himself—with this veiled, gruesome, pious, and blasphemous saying. Did a Socrates need such revenge? Did his overrich virtue lack an ounce of magnanimity?—Alas, my friends, we must overcome even the Greeks![6]

The greatest weight.—What, if some day or night a demon were to steal after you into your loneliest loneliness and say to you: "This life as you now live it and have lived it, you will have to live once more and innumerable times more; and there will be nothing new in it, but every pain and every joy and every thought and sigh and everything unutterably small or great in your life will have to return to you, all in the same succession and sequence—even this spider and this moonlight between the trees, and even this moment and I myself. The eternal hourglass of existence is turned upside down again and again, and you with it, speck of dust!" Would you not throw yourself down and gnash your teeth and curse the demon who spoke thus? Or have you once experienced a tremendous moment when you would have answered him: "You are a god and never have I heard anything more divine." If this thought gained possession of you, it would change you as you are or perhaps crush you. The question in each and everything, "Do you desire this once more and innumerable times more?" would lie upon your actions as the greatest weight. Or how well disposed would you have to become to yourself and to life *to crave nothing more fervently* than this ultimate eternal confirmation and seal?—

Incipit tragoedia.[7]—When Zarathustra was thirty years old, he left his home and Lake Urmi and went into the mountains. There he enjoyed his spirit and his solitude, and for ten years did not tire of that. But at last his heart changed-and one morning he rose with the dawn, stepped before the sun, and spoke to it thus: "You great star, what would your happiness be if you did not have those for whom you shine? For ten years you have climbed up to my cave: You would have become weary of your light and of the journey had it not been for me and my eagle and my serpent; but we waited for you every morning, took your overflow from you, and blessed you for it. Behold, I am sick of my wisdom, like a bee that has gathered too much honey; I need hands outstretched to receive it; I want to give away and distribute until the wise among men enjoy their folly once again and the poor their riches. For that I must descend to the depths, as you do in the evening when you go behind the sea and still bring light to the underworld, you over-rich star. Like you I must *go under,* as men put it to whom I wish to descend. Bless me then, you calm eye that can look without envy even upon an all too great happiness. Bless the cup that wants to overflow in order that the water may flow from it golden and carry the reflection of your rapture everywhere. Behold, this cup wants to become empty again, and Zarathustra wants to become man again.—Thus Zarathustra began to go under.

SELECTIONS FROM *THUS SPOKE ZARATHUSTRA*

What do you think, you Higher Men? Am I a prophet? A dreamer? A drunkard? An interpreter of dreams? A midnight bell?

A drop of dew? An odour and scent of eternity? Do you not hear it? Do you not smell it? My world has just become perfect, midnight is also noonday, pain is also joy, a curse is also a blessing, the night is also a sun—be gone, or you will learn: a wise man is also a fool.

Did you ever say Yes to one joy? O my friends, then you said Yes to *all* woe as well. All things are chained and entwined together, all things are in love;

if ever you wanted one moment twice, if ever you said: 'You please me, happiness, instant, moment!' then you wanted *everything* to return!

you wanted everything anew, everything eternal, everything chained, entwined together, everything in love, O that is how you *loved* the world,

you everlasting men, loved it eternally and for all time: and you say even to woe: 'Go, but return!' *For all joy wants eternity!*

All joy wants the eternity of all things, wants honey, wants dregs, wants intoxicated midnight, wants graves, wants the consolation of grave side tears, wants gilded sunsets,

what does joy not want! it is thirstier, warmer, hungrier, more fearful, more secret than all woe, it wants *itself;* it bites into *itself,* the will of the ring wrestles within it,

it wants love, it wants hatred, it is superabundant, it gives, throws away, begs for someone to take it, thanks him who takes, it would like to be hated;

so rich is joy that it thirsts for woe, for Hell, for hatred, for shame, for the lame, for the *world*—for it knows, oh it knows this world!

You Higher Men, joy longs for you, joy the intractable, blissful-for your woe, you ill-constituted! All eternal joy longs for the ill-constituted.

For all joy wants itself, therefore it also wants heart's agony! O happiness! O pain! Oh break, heart! You Higher Men, learn this, learn that joy wants eternity,

joy wants the eternity of *all* things, *wants deep, deep, deep eternity!*

Have you now learned my song? Have you divined what it means? Very well! Come on! You Higher Men, now sing my roundelay!

Now sing yourselves the song whose name is 'Once more', whose meaning is 'To all eternity!'—sing, you Higher Men, Zarathustra's roundelay!

O *Man! Attend!*
What does deep midnight's voice contend?
'I slept my sleep,
'And now awake at dreaming's end:
'The world is deep,
'Deeper than day can comprehend.
'Deep is its woe,
'Joy—deeper than heart's agony:
'Woe says: Fade! Go!
'But all joy wants eternity,
'Wants deep, deep, deep eternity!'

SELECTIONS FROM *TWILIGHT OF THE IDOLS*
The Four Great Errors

1

The error of confusing cause and consequence.—There is no more dangerous error than that of *mistaking the consequence for the cause*: I call it reason's intrinsic form of corruption. None the less, this error is among the most ancient and most recent habits of mankind: it is even sanctified among us, it bears the names 'religion' and 'morality'. *Every* proposition formulated by religion and morality contains it; priests and moral legislators are the authors of this corruption of reason.—I adduce an example. Everyone knows the book of the celebrated Cornaro in which he recommends his meagre diet as a recipe for a long and happy life—a virtuous one, too. Few books have been so widely read; even now many thousands of copies are printed in England every year. I do not doubt that hardly any book (the Bible rightly excepted) has done so much harm, has shortened so many lives, as this curiosity, which was so well meant. The reason: mistaking the consequence for the cause. The worthy Italian saw in his diet the *cause* of his long life: while the prerequisite of long life, an extraordinarily slow metabolism, a small consumption, was the cause of his meagre diet. He was not free to eat much *or* little as he chose, his frugality was *not* an act of "free will": he became ill when he ate more. But if one is not a bony fellow of this sort one does not merely do well, one positively needs to eat *properly*. A scholar of *our* day, with his rapid consumption of nervous energy, would kill himself with Cornaro's regimen. *Credo experto.* *

2

The most general formula at the basis of every religion and morality is: 'Do this and this, refrain from this and this—and you will be happy! Otherwise....' Every morality, every religion *is* this imperative—I call it the great original sin of reason, *immortal unreason.* In my mouth this formula is converted into its reverse—*first* example of my 'revaluation of all values:' a well-constituted human being, a 'happy one,' *must* perform certain actions and instinctively shrinks from other actions, he transports the order of which he is the physiological representative into his relations with other human beings and with things. In a formula: his virtue is the *consequence* of his happiness.... Long life, a plentiful posterity is *not* the reward of virtue, virtue itself is rather just that slowing down of the metabolism which also has, among other things, a long life, a plentiful posterity, in short *Cornarism*, as its outcome.—The Church and morality say: 'A race, a people perishes through vice and luxury.' My *restored* reason says: when a people is perishing, degenerating physiologically, vice and luxury (that is to say the necessity for stronger and stronger and more and more frequent stimulants, such as every exhausted nature is acquainted with) *follow* therefrom. A young man grows prematurely pale and faded. His friends say: this and that illness is to blame. I say: *that* he became ill, *that* he failed to resist the illness, was already the consequence of an impoverished life, an hereditary exhaustion. The newspaper reader says: this party will ruin itself if it makes errors like this. My *higher* politics says: a party which makes errors like this is already finished—it is no longer secure in its instincts. Every error, of whatever kind, is a consequence of degeneration of instinct, disgregation of will: one has thereby virtually defined the *bad*. Everything *good* is instinct—and consequently easy, necessary, free. Effort is an objection, the *god* is typically distinguished from the hero (in my language: *light* feet are the first attribute of divinity).

3

The error of a false causality.—We have always believed we know what a cause is: but whence did we derive our knowledge, more precisely our belief we possessed this knowledge? From the realm of the celebrated 'inner facts', none of which has up till now been shown to be factual. We believed ourselves to be causal agents in the act of willing; we at least thought we were there *catching causality in the act.* It was likewise never doubted that all the *antecedentia* of an action, its causes, were to be sought in the consciousness and could be discovered there if one sought them—as 'motives': for otherwise one would not have been *free* to perform it, *responsible* for it. Finally, who would have disputed that a thought is caused? that the ego causes the thought? ... Of these three 'inner facts' through which causality seemed to be guaranteed the first and most convincing was that of *will as cause*; the conception of a consciousness ('mind') as cause and later still that of the ego (the 'subject') as cause are merely after-products after causality had, on the basis of will, been firmly established as a given fact, as *empiricism....* Meanwhile, we have thought better. Today we do not believe a word of it. The 'inner world' is full of phantoms and false lights: the will is one of them. The will no longer moves anything, consequently no longer explains anything—it merely accompanies events, it can also be absent. The so-called 'motive': another error. Merely a surface phenomenon of consciousness, an accompaniment to an act, which conceals rather than exposes the *antecedentia* of the act. And as for the ego! It has become a fable, a fiction, a play on words: it has totally ceased to think, to feel and to will! ... What follows from this? There are no spiritual causes at all! The whole of the alleged empiricism which affirmed them has gone to the devil! *That* is what follows!—And we had made a nice misuse of that 'empiricism', we had *created* the world on the basis of it as a world of causes, as a world of will, as a world of spirit. The oldest and longest-lived psychology was at work here—indeed it has done nothing else: every event was to it an action, every action the effect of a will, the world became for it a multiplicity of agents, an agent ('subject') foisted itself upon every event. Man projected his three 'inner facts', that in which he believed more firmly than in anything else, will, spirit, ego, outside himself—he derived the concept 'being' only from the concept 'ego', he posited 'things' as possessing being according to his own image, according to his concept of the ego as cause. No wonder he later always discovered in things only *that which he had put into them!*—The thing itself, to say it again, the concept 'thing' is merely a reflection of the belief in the ego as cause.... And even your atom, *messieurs* mechanists and physicists, how much error, how much rudimentary psychology, still remains in your atom!—To say nothing of the 'thing in itself',[8] that *horrendum pudendum*[9] of the metaphysicians! The error of spirit as cause mistaken for reality! And made the measure of reality! And called *God!*—

The error of imaginary causes.—To start from the dream: on to a certain sensation, the result for example of a distant cannon-shot, a cause is subsequently foisted (often a whole little novel in which precisely the dreamer is the chief character). The sensation, meanwhile, continues to persist, as a kind of resonance: it waits, as it were, until the cause-creating drive permits it to step into the foreground—now no longer as a chance occurrence but as 'meaning'. The cannon-shot enters in a *causal* way, in an apparent inversion of time. That which comes later, the motivation, is experienced first, often with a hundred details which pass like lightning, the shot *follows*.... What has happened? The ideas *engendered* by a certain condition have been misunderstood as the cause of that condition.—We do just the same thing, in fact, when we are awake. Most of our general feelings—every sort of restraint, pressure, tension, explosion in the play and counter-play of our organs, likewise and especially the condition of the *nervus sympathicus*—excite our cause-creating drive: we want to have a *reason* for feeling *as we do*—for feeling well or for feeling ill. It never suffices us simply to establish the mere fact *that* we feel as we do: we acknowledge this fact—become *conscious* of it—only *when* we have furnished it with a motivation of some kind.—The memory, which in such a case becomes active without our being aware of it, calls up earlier states of a similar kind and the causal interpretations which have grown out of them—*not* their causality. To be sure, the belief that these ideas, the accompanying occurrences in the consciousness, were causes is also brought up by the memory. Thus there arises an *habituation* to a certain causal interpretation which in truth obstructs and even prohibits an *investigation* of the cause.

Psychological explanation.—To trace something unknown back to something known is alleviating, soothing, gratifying and gives moreover a feeling of power. Danger, disquiet, anxiety attend the unknown—the first instinct is to *eliminate* these distressing states. First principle: any explanation is better than none. Because it is at bottom only a question of wanting to get rid of oppressive ideas, one is not exactly particular about what means one uses to get rid of them: the first idea which explains that the unknown is in fact the known does so much good that one 'holds it for true'. Proof by *pleasure* ('by potency') as criterion of truth.—The cause-creating drive is thus conditioned and excited by the feeling of fear. The question 'why?' should furnish, if at all possible, not so much the cause for its own sake as a *certain kind of cause*—a soothing, liberating, alleviating cause. That something already *known*, experienced, inscribed in the memory is posited as cause is the first consequence of this need. The new, the unexperienced, the strange is excluded from being cause.—Thus there is sought not only some kind of explanation as cause, but a *selected* and *preferred* kind of explanation, the kind by means of which the feeling of the strange, new, unexperienced is most speedily and most frequently abolished—the *most common* explanations.—Consequence: a particular kind of cause-ascription comes to preponderate more and more, becomes concentrated into a system and finally comes to *dominate* over the rest, that is to say simply to exclude *other* causes and explanations.—The banker thinks at once of 'business', the Christian of 'sin', the girl of her love.

6

The entire realm of morality and religion falls under this concept of imaginary causes.—'Explanation' *of unpleasant* general feelings. They arise from beings hostile to us (evil spirits: most celebrated case—hysterics misunderstood as witches). They arise from actions we cannot approve of (the feeling of 'sin', of 'culpability' foisted upon a physiological discomfort—one always finds reasons for being discontented with oneself). They arise as punishments, as payment for something we should not have done, should not have *been* (generalized in an impudent form by Schopenhauer into a proposition in which morality appears for what it is, the actual poisoner and calumniator of life: 'Every great pain, whether physical or mental, declares what it is we deserve; for it could not have come upon us if we had not deserved it.' *World as Will and Idea* II 666). They arise as the consequences of rash actions which have turned out badly (—the emotions, the senses assigned as 'cause', as 'to blame'; physiological states of distress construed, with the aid of *other* states of distress, as 'deserved').—'Explanation' of *pleasant* general feelings. They arise from trust in God. They arise from the consciousness of good actions (the so-called 'good conscience', a physiological condition sometimes so like a sound digestion as to be mistaken for it). They arise from the successful outcome of undertakings (—naïve fallacy: the successful outcome of an undertaking certainly does not produce any pleasant general feelings in a hypochondriac or a Pascal). They arise from faith, hope and charity—the Christian virtues.—In reality all these supposed explanations are *consequential* states and as it were translations of pleasurable and unpleasurable feelings into a false dialect: one is in a state in which one can experience hope *because* the physiological basic feeling is once more strong and ample; one trusts in God *because* the feeling of plenitude and strength makes one calm.—Morality and religion fall entirely under the *psychology of error*, in every single case cause is mistaken for effect; or the effect of what is *believed* true is mistaken for the truth; or a state of consciousness is mistaken for the causation of this state.

7

The error of free will.—We no longer have any sympathy today with the concept of 'free will': we know only too well what it is—the most infamous of all the arts of the theologian for making mankind 'accountable' in his sense of the word, that is to say for *making mankind dependent on him*.... I give here only the psychology of making men accountable.—Everywhere accountability is sought, it is usually the instinct for *punishing and judging* which seeks it. One has deprived becoming of its innocence if being in this or that state is traced back to will, to intentions, to accountable acts: the doctrine of will has been invented essentially for the purpose of punishment, that is of *finding guilty.* The whole of the old-style psychology, the psychology of will, has as its precondition the desire of its authors, the priests at the head of the ancient communities, to create for themselves a *right* to ordain punishments—or their desire to create for God a right to do so.… Men were thought of as 'free' so that they could become *guilty*: consequently, every action *had* to be thought of as willed, the origin of every action as lying in the consciousness (—whereby the most *fundamental* falsification *in psychologicis* was made into the very principle of psychology).… Today, when we have started to move in the *reverse* direction, when we immoralists especially are trying with all our might to remove the concept of guilt and the concept of punishment from the world and to purge psychology, history, nature, the social institutions and sanctions of them, there is in our eyes no more radical opposition than that of the theologians, who continue to infect the innocence of becoming with 'punishment' and 'guilt' by means of the concept of the 'moral world-order'. Christianity is a hangman's metaphysics.…

8

What alone can *our* teaching be?—That no one *gives* a human being his qualities: not God, not society, not his parents or ancestors, not he *himself* (—the nonsensical idea here last rejected was propounded, as 'intelligible freedom', by Kant, and perhaps also by Plato before him). *No one* is accountable for existing at all, or for being constituted as he is, or for living in the circumstances and surroundings in which he lives. The fatality of his nature cannot be disentangled from the fatality of all that which has been and will be. He is *not* the result of a special design, a will, a purpose; he is *not* the subject of an attempt to attain to an 'ideal of man' or an 'ideal of happiness' or an 'ideal of morality'—it is absurd to want to *hand over* his nature to some purpose or other. *We* invented the concept 'purpose': in reality purpose is *lacking*, … One is necessary, one is a piece of fate, one belongs to the whole, one is in the whole—there exists nothing which could judge, measure, compare, condemn our being, for that would be to judge, measure, compare, condemn the whole.… *But nothing exists apart from the whole!*—That no one is any longer made accountable, that the kind of being manifested cannot be traced back to a *causa prima*,[10] that the world is a unity neither as sensorium nor as 'spirit', this alone is the great liberation—thus alone is the innocence of becoming restored.… The concept 'God' has hitherto been the greatest objection to existence.… We deny God; in denying God, we deny accountability: only by doing that do we redeem the world.

SELECTIONS FROM *THE ANTI-CHRIST*

Foreword

This book belongs to the very few. Perhaps none of them is even living yet. Possibly they are the readers who understand my *Zarathustra*: how *could* I confound myself with those for whom there are ears listening today?—Only the day after tomorrow belongs to me. Some are born posthumously.

The conditions under which one understands me and then *necessarily* understands—I know them all too well. One must be honest in intellectual matters to the point of harshness to so much as endure my seriousness, my passion. One must be accustomed to living on mountains —to seeing the wretched ephemeral chatter of politics and national egoism *beneath* one. One must have become indifferent, one must never ask whether truth is useful or a fatality…. Strength which prefers questions for which no one today is sufficiently daring; courage for the *forbidden*; predestination for the labyrinth. An experience out of seven solitudes. New ears for new music. New eyes for the most distant things. A new conscience for truths which have hitherto remained dumb. *And* the will to economy in the grand style: to keeping one's energy, one's *enthusiasm* in bounds…. Reverence for oneself; love for oneself; unconditional freedom with respect to oneself….

Very well! These alone are my readers, my rightful readers, my predestined readers: what do the *rest* matter?—The rest are merely mankind.—One must be superior to mankind in force, in *loftiness* of soul— in contempt….

FRIEDRICH NIETZSCHE

I

—Let us look one another in the face. We are Hyperboreans[11]—we know well enough how much out of the way we live. 'Neither by land nor by sea shalt thou find the road to the Hyperboreans': Pindar already knew that of us. Beyond the North, beyond the ice, beyond death—*our* life, *our* happiness…. We have discovered happiness, we know the road, we have found the exit out of whole millennia of labyrinth. Who *else* has found it?—Modern man perhaps?—'I know not which way to turn; I am everything that knows not which way to turn'—sighs modern man…. It was from *this* modernity that we were ill—from lazy peace, from cowardly compromise, from the whole virtuous uncleanliness of modern Yes and No. This tolerance and *largeur* of heart which 'forgives' everything because it 'Understands' everything is sirocco to us. Better to live among ice than among modern virtues and other south winds! … We were brave enough, we spared neither ourselves nor others: but for long we did not know *where* to apply our courage. We became gloomy, we were called fatalists. *Our* fatality—was the plenitude, the tension, the blocking-up of our forces. We thirsted for lightning and action, of all things we kept ourselves furthest from the happiness of the weaklings, from 'resignation'.... There was a thunderstorm in our air, the nature which we are grew dark—*for we had no road.* Formula of our happiness: a Yes, a No, a straight line, a *goal* ...

2

What is good?—All that heightens the feeling of power, the will to power, power itself in man.

What is bad?—All that proceeds from weakness.

What is happiness?—The feeling that power *increases* that a resistance is overcome.

Not contentment, but more power; *not* peace at all, but war; *not* virtue, but proficiency (virtue in the Renaissance style, *virtù*, virtue free of moralic acid).

The weak and ill-constituted shall perish: first principle of *our* philanthropy. And one shall help them to do so.

What is more harmful than any vice?—Active sympathy for ill-constituted and weak—Christianity ...

3

The problem I raise here is not what ought to succeed mankind in the sequence of species (—the human being is a *conclusion*—): but what type of human being one ought to *breed* ought to *will*, as more valuable, more worthy of life, more certain of the future.

This more valuable type has existed often enough already: but as a lucky accident, as an exception, never as *willed*. *He* has rather been the most feared, he has hitherto been virtually *the* thing to be feared—and out of fear the reverse type has been willed, bred, *achieved*: the domestic animal, the herd animal, the sick animal man—the Christian ...

4

Mankind does *not* represent a development of the better or the stronger or the higher in the way that is believed today. 'Progress' is merely a modern idea, that is to say a false idea. The European of today is of far less value than the European of the Renaissance; onward development is not by *any* means, by any necessity the same thing as elevation, advance, strengthening.

In another sense there are cases of individual success constantly appearing in the most various parts of the earth and from the most various cultures in which a *higher type* does manifest itself: something which in relation to collective mankind is a sort of superman. Such chance occurrences of great success have always been possible and perhaps always will be possible. And even entire races, tribes, nations can under certain circumstances represent such a *lucky hit.*

5

One should not embellish or dress up Christianity: it has waged a *war to the death* against this *higher* type of man, it has excommunicated all the fundamental instincts of this type, it has distilled evil, the *Evil One*, out of these instincts—the strong human being as the type of reprehensibility, as the 'outcast'. Christianity has taken the side of everything weak, base, ill-constituted, it has made an ideal out of *opposition* to the preservative instincts of strong life; it has depraved the reason even of the intellectually strongest natures by teaching men to feel the supreme values of intellectuality as sinful, as misleading, as *temptations*. The most deplorable example: the depraving of Pascal, who believed his reason had been depraved by original sin while it had only been depraved by his Christianity!—

6

It is a painful, a dreadful spectacle which has opened up before me: I have drawn back the curtain on the *depravity of* man. In my mouth this word is protected against at any rate one suspicion: that it contains a moral accusation of man. It is—I should like to underline the fact again—free of any *moralic acid*: and this to the extent that I find that depravity precisely where hitherto one most consciously aspired to virtue', to 'divinity'. I understand depravity, as will already have been guessed, in the sense of *décadence*: my assertion is that all the values in which mankind at present summarizes its highest desideratum are *décadence values*.

I call an animal, a species, an individual depraved when it loses its instincts, when it chooses, when it *prefers* what is harmful to it. A history of the 'higher feelings', of the 'ideals of mankind'—and it is possible I shall have to narrate it—would almost also constitute an explanation of *why* man is so depraved. I consider life itself instinct for growth, for continuance, for accumulation of forces, for *power*, where the will to power is lacking there is decline. My assertion is that this will is *lacking* in all the supreme values of mankind—that values of decline, *nihilistic* values hold sway under the holiest names.

7

Christianity is called the religion of *pity*.—Pity stands in antithesis to the tonic emotions which enhance the energy of the feeling of life: it has a depressive effect. One loses force when one pities. The loss of force which life has already sustained through suffering is increased and multiplied even further by pity. Suffering itself becomes contagious through pity; sometimes it can bring about a collective loss of life and life-energy which stands in an absurd relation to the quantum of its cause (—the case of the death of the Nazarene). This is the first aspect; but there is an even more important one. If one judges pity by the value of the reactions which it usually brings about, its mortally dangerous character appears in a much clearer light. Pity on the whole thwarts the law of evolution, which is the law of *selection*. It preserves what is ripe for destruction; it defends life's disinherited and condemned; through the abundance of the ill-constituted of all kinds which it *retains* in life it gives life itself a gloomy and questionable aspect. One has ventured to call pity a virtue (—in every *noble* morality it counts as weakness—); one has gone further, one has made of it *the* virtue, the ground and origin of all virtue—only, to be sure, from the viewpoint of a nihilistic philosophy which inscribed *Denial of Life* on its escutcheon—a fact always to be kept in view. Schopenhauer was within his rights in this: life is denied, made *more worthy of denial* by pity—pity is *practical* nihilism. To say it again, this depressive and contagious instinct thwarts those instincts bent on preserving and enhancing the value of life: both as a *multiplier* of misery and as a *conservator* of everything miserable it is one of the chief instruments for the advancement of *décadence*—pity persuades to *nothingness*! ... One does not say 'nothingness': one says 'the Beyond'; or 'God' or '*true* life'; or Nirvana, redemption, blessedness.... This innocent rhetoric from the domain of religio-moral idiosyncrasy at once appears *much less innocent* when one grasps *which* tendency is here draping the mantle of sublime words about itself: the tendency *hostile to life*. Schopenhauer was hostile to life: *therefore* pity became for him a virtue.... Aristotle, as is well known, saw in pity a morbid and dangerous condition which one did well to get at from time to time with a purgative: he understood tragedy as a purgative. From the instinct for life one would indeed have to seek some means of puncturing so morbid and dangerous an accumulation of pity as that represented by the case of Schopenhauer (and unfortunately also by our entire literary and artistic *décadence* from St. Petersburg to Paris, from Tolstoy to Wagner), so that it might *burst*.... Nothing in our unhealthy modernity is more unhealthy than Christian pity. To be physician *here*, to be inexorable *here*, to wield the knife *here*—that pertains to *us*, that is *our* kind of philanthropy, with that are *we* philosophers, we Hyperboreans!—

8

It is necessary to say *whom* we feel to be our antithesis—the theologians and all that has theologian blood in its veins—our entire philosophy.... One must have seen the fatality from close up, better still one must have experienced it in oneself, one must have almost perished by it, no longer to find anything funny here (the free-thinking of our naturalists and physiologists is to my mind *funny*—they lack passion in these things, they do not *suffer* from them—). That poison extends much further than one thinks: I have discovered the arrogant theologian-instinct wherever anyone today feels himself to be an 'idealist'—wherever anyone assumes, by virtue of a higher origin, a right to cast strange and superior looks at actuality.... Just like the priest, the idealist has all the great concepts in his hand (—and not only in his hand!), he plays them out with a benevolent contempt against the 'understanding', the 'senses', 'honours', 'luxury', 'science', he sees these things as *beneath* him, as harmful and seductive forces above which 'the spirit' soars in pure self-sufficiency—as though humility, chastity, poverty, in a word *holiness*, had not hitherto done life unutterably more harm than any sort of frightfulness or vice whatever.... Pure spirit is pure lie ... So long as the priest, that denier, calumniator and poisoner of life by *profession*, still counts as a *higher* kind of human being, there can be no answer to the question: what is truth? One *has* already stood truth on its head when the conscious advocate of denial and nothingness counts as the representative of 'truth' ...

9

I make war on this theologian instinct: I have found traces of it everywhere. Whoever has theologian blood in his veins has a wrong and dishonest attitude towards all things from the very first. The pathos that develops out of this is called *faith*: closing one's eyes with respect to oneself for good and all so as not to suffer from the sight of incurable falsity. Out of this erroneous perspective on all things one makes a morality, a virtue, a holiness for oneself, one unites the good conscience with seeing *falsely*—one demands that no *other* kind of perspective shall be accorded any value after one has rendered one's own sacrosanct with the names 'God', 'redemption', 'eternity.' I have dug out the theologian instinct everywhere: it is the most widespread, peculiarly *subterranean* form of falsity that exists on earth. What a theologian feels to be true *must* be false: this provides almost a criterion of truth. It is his deepest instinct of self-preservation which forbids any part of reality whatever to be held in esteem or even spoken of. Wherever the influence of the theologian extends, *value judgement* is stood on its head, the concepts 'true' and 'false' are necessarily reversed: that which is most harmful to life is here called 'true', that which enhances, intensifies, affirms, justifies it and causes it to triumph is called 'false'.... If it happens that, by way of the 'conscience' of princes (*or* of nations—), theologians stretch out their hands after *power*, let us be in no doubt *what* at bottom is taking place every time: the will to the end, the *nihilistic* will wants power ... actuality means to be an abortive actuality.... The preponderance of feelings of displeasure over feelings of pleasure is the *cause* of a fictitious morality and religion: such a preponderance, however, provides the *formula* for *décadence* ...

14

We have learned better. We have become more modest in every respect. We no longer trace the origin of man in the 'spirit', in the 'divinity', we have placed him back among the animals. We consider him the strongest animal because he is the most cunning: his spirituality is a consequence of this. On the other hand, we guard ourselves against a vanity which would like to find expression even here: the vanity that man is the great secret objective of animal evolution. Man is absolutely not the crown of creation: every creature stands beside him at the same stage of perfection.... And even in asserting that we assert too much:

man is, relatively speaking, the most unsuccessful animal, the sickliest, the one most dangerously strayed from its instincts—with all that, to be sure, the most *interesting*!—As regards the animals, Descartes was the first who, with a boldness worthy of reverence, ventured to think of the animal as a *machine*: our whole science of physiology is devoted to proving this proposition, Nor, logically, do we exclude man, as even Descartes did: our knowledge of man today is real knowledge precisely to the extent that it is knowledge of him as a machine. Formerly man was presented with 'free will' as a dowry from a higher order: today we have taken even will away from him, in the sense that will may no longer be understood as a faculty. The old word 'will' only serves to designate a resultant, a kind of individual reaction which necessarily follows a host of partly contradictory, partly congruous stimuli—the will no longer 'effects' anything, no longer 'moves' anything.... Formerly one saw in man's consciousness, in his 'spirit', the proof of his higher origin, his divinity; to make himself *perfect* man was advised to draw his senses back into himself in the manner of the tortoise, to cease to have any traffic with the earthly, to lay aside his mortal frame: then the chief part of him would remain behind, 'pure spirit'. We have thought better of this too: becoming-conscious, 'spirit', is to us precisely a symptom of a relative imperfection of the organism, as an attempting, fumbling, blundering, as a toiling in which an unnecessarily large amount of nervous energy is expended—we deny that anything can be made perfect so long as it is still made conscious. 'Pure spirit' is pure stupidity: if we deduct the nervous system and the senses, the 'mortal frame', *we miscalculate*—that's all! ...

SELECTIONS FROM *BEYOND GOOD AND EVIL*

260

Wandering through the many subtler and coarser moralities which have so far been prevalent on earth, or still are prevalent, I found that certain features recurred regularly together and were closely associated—until I finally discovered two basic types and one basic difference.

There are *master morality and slave morality*—I add immediately that in all the higher and more mixed cultures there also appear attempts at mediation between these two moralities, and yet more often the interpenetration and mutual misunderstanding of both, and at times they occur directly alongside each other—even in the same human being, within a *single* soul. The moral discrimination of values has originated either among a ruling group whose consciousness of its difference from the ruled group was accompanied by delight—or among the ruled, the slaves and dependents of every degree.

In the first case, when the ruling group determines what is "good," the exalted, proud states of the soul are experienced as conferring distinction and determining the order of rank. The noble human being separates from himself those in whom the opposite of such exalted, proud states finds expression: he despises them. It should be noted immediately that in this first type of morality the opposition of "good" and *"bad"* means approximately the same as "noble" and "contemptible." (The opposition of "good" and *"evil"* has a different origin.) One feels contempt for the cowardly, the anxious, the petty, those intent on narrow utility; also for the suspicious with their unfree glances, those who humble themselves, the doglike people who allow themselves to be maltreated, the begging flatterers, above all the liars: it is part of the fundamental faith of all aristocrats that the common people lie. "We truthful ones"—thus the nobility of ancient Greece referred to itself.

It is obvious that moral designations were everywhere first applied to *human beings* and only later, derivatively, to actions. Therefore it is a gross mistake when historians of morality start from such questions as: why was the compassionate act praised? The noble type of man experiences *itself* as determining values; it does not need approval; it judges, "what is harmful to me is harmful in itself;" it knows itself to be that which first accords honor to things; it is *value-creating*. Everything it knows as part of itself it honors: such a morality is self-glorification. In the foreground there is the feeling of fullness, of power that seeks to overflow, the happiness of high tension, the consciousness of wealth that would give and bestow: the noble human being, too, helps the unfortunate, but not, or almost not, from pity, but prompted more by an urge begotten by excess of power. The noble human being honors himself as one who is powerful, also as one who has power over himself who knows how to speak and be silent, who delights in being severe and hard with himself and respects all severity and hardness. "A hard heart Wotan put into my breast," says an old Scandinavian saga: a fitting poetic expression, seeing that it comes from the soul of a proud Viking. Such a type of man is actually proud of the fact that he is *not* made for pity, and the hero of the saga therefore adds as a warning: "If the heart is not hard in youth it will never harden." Noble and courageous human beings who think that way are furthest removed from that morality which finds the distinction of morality precisely in pity, or in acting for others, or in *désintéressement*; faith in oneself, pride in oneself, a fundamental hostility and irony against "selflessness" belong just as definitely to noble morality as does a slight disdain and caution regarding compassionate feelings and a "warm heart."

It is the powerful who *understand* how to honor; this is their art, their realm of invention. The profound reverence for age and tradition—all law rests on this double reverence—the faith and prejudice in favor of ancestors and disfavor of those yet to come are typical of the morality of the powerful; and when the men of "modern ideas," conversely, believe almost instinctively in "progress" and "the future" and more and more lack respect for age, this in itself would sufficiently betray the ignoble origin of these "ideas."

A morality of the ruling group, however is most alien and embarrassing to the present taste in the severity of its principle that one has duties only to one's peers; that against beings of a lower rank, against everything alien, one may behave as one please or "as the heart desires," and in any case "beyond, good and evil"—here pity and like feelings may find their place. The capacity for, and the duty of, long gratitude and long revenge—both only among one's peers—refinement in repaying, the sophisticated concept of friendship, a certain necessity for having enemies (as it were, as drainage ditches for the affects of envy, quarrelsomeness, exuberance—at bottom, in order to be capable of being good *friends*): all these are typical characteristics of noble morality which, as suggested, is not the morality of "modern ideas" and therefore is hard to empathize with today, also hard to dig up and uncover.

It is different with the second type of morality, *slave morality.* Suppose the violated, oppressed, suffering, unfree, who are uncertain of themselves and weary, moralize: what will their moral valuations have in common? Probably, a pessimistic suspicion about the whole condition of man with his condition. The slave's eye is not favorable to the virtues of the powerful: he is skeptical and suspicious, *subtly* suspicious, of all the "good" that is honored there—he would like to persuade himself that even their happiness is not genuine. Conversely, those qualities are brought out and flooded with light which serve to ease existence for those who suffer: here pity, the complaisant and obliging hand, the warm heart, patience, industry, humility, and friendliness are honored—for here these are the most useful qualities and almost the only means for enduring the pressure of existence. Slave morality is essentially a morality of utility.

Here is the place for the origin of that famous opposition of "good" and "evil": into evil one's feelings project power and dangerousness, a certain terribleness, subtlety, and strength that does not permit contempt to develop. According to slave morality, those who are "evil" thus inspire fear; according to master morality it is precisely those who are "good" that, inspire, and wish to inspire, fear, while the "bad" are felt to be contemptible.

The opposition reaches its climax when, as a logical consequence of slave morality, a touch of disdain is associated also with the "good" of this morality—this may be slight and benevolent—because the good human being has to be *undangerous* in the slaves' way of thinking: he is good-natured, easy to deceive, a little stupid perhaps, *un bonhomme.*[12] Wherever slave morality becomes preponderant, language tends to bring the words "good" and "stupid" closer together.

One last fundamental difference: the longing for. *Freedom,* the instinct for happiness and the subtleties of the feeling of freedom belong just as necessarily to slave morality and morals as artful and enthusiastic reverence and devotion are the regular symptom of an aristocratic way of thinking and evaluating.

This makes plain why love *as passion*—which is our European specialty—simply must be of noble origin: as is well known, its invention must be credited to the Provençal knight-poets, those magnificent and inventive human beings of the *"gai saber"* to whom Europe owes so many things and almost owes itself. —

SELECTIONS FROM *GENEALOGY OF MORALS*

The slave revolt in morality begins when *ressentiment*[13] itself becomes creative and gives birth to values: the *ressentiment* of natures that are denied the true reaction, that of deeds, and compensate themselves with an imaginary revenge. While every noble morality develops from a triumphant affirmation of itself, slave morality from the outset says No to what is "outside," what is "different," what is "not itself;" and this No is its creative deed. This inversion of the value-positing eye—this *need* to direct one's view outward instead of back to oneself—is of the essence of *ressentiment*: in order to exist, slave morality always first needs a hostile external world; it needs, physiologically speaking, external stimuli in order to act at all—its action is fundamentally reaction.

The reverse is the case with the noble mode of valuation: it acts and grows spontaneously, it seeks its opposite only so as to affirm itself more gratefully and triumphantly—its negative concept "low," "common," "bad" is only a subsequently-invented pale, contrasting image in relation to its positive basic concept—filled with life and passion through and through—"we noble ones, we good, beautiful, happy ones!" When the noble mode of valuation blunders and sins against reality, it does so in respect to the sphere with which it is *not* sufficiently familiar, against a real knowledge of which it has indeed inflexibly guarded itself: in some circumstances it misunderstands the sphere it despises, that of the common man, of the lower orders; on the other hand, one should remember that, even supposing that the affect of contempt, of looking down from a superior height, *falsifies* the image of that which it despises, it will at any rate still be a much less serious falsification than that perpetrated on its opponent—*in effigie* of course—by the submerged hatred, the vengefulness of the impotent. There is indeed too much carelessness, too much taking lightly, too much looking away and impatience involved in contempt, even too much joyfulness, for it to be able to transform its object into a real caricature and monster.

One should not overlook the almost benevolent nuances that the Greek nobility, for example, bestows on all the words it employs to distinguish the lower orders from itself; how they are continuously mingled and sweetened with a kind of pity, consideration, and forbearance, so that finally almost all the words referring to the common man have remained as expressions signifying "unhappy," "pitiable" (campore *deilos*,[14] *deilaios*,[15] *ponēros*,[16] *mochthēros*,[17] the last two of which properly designate the common man as work-slave and beast of burden)—and how on the other hand "bad," "low," "unhappy" have never ceased to sound to the Greek ear as one note with a tone-color in which "unhappy" preponderates: this as an inheritance from the ancient nobler aristocratic mode of evaluation, which does not belie itself even in its contempt (—philologists should recall the sense in which *oïzyros*,[18] *anolbos*,[19] *tlēmōn*,[20] *dystychein*,[21] *xymphora*[22] are employed). The "well-born" *felt* themselves to be the "happy;" they did not have to establish their happiness artificially by examining their enemies, or to persuade themselves, *deceive* themselves, that they were happy (as all men of *ressentiment* are in the habit of doing); and they likewise knew, as rounded men replete with energy and therefore *necessarily* active, that happiness should not be sundered from action—being active was with them necessarily a part of happiness (whence *eu prattein*[23] takes its origin)—all very much the opposite of "happiness" at the level of the impotent, the oppressed, and those in whom poisonous and inimical feelings are festering, with whom it appears as essentially narcotic, drug, rest, peace, "sabbath," slackening of tension and relaxing of limbs, in short *passively*.

While the noble man lives in trust and openness with himself (*gennaios*[24] "of noble descent" underlines the nuance "upright" and probably also "naïve"), the man of *ressentiment* is neither upright nor naive nor honest and straightforward with himself. His soul *squints*; his spirit loves hiding places, secret paths and back doors, everything covert entices him as *his* world, *his* security, *his* refreshment; he understands how to keep silent, how not to forget, how to wait, how to be provisionally self-deprecating and humble. A race of such men of *ressentiment* is bound to become eventually *cleverer* than any noble race; it will also honor cleverness to a far greater degree: namely, as a condition of existence of the first importance; while with noble men cleverness can easily acquire a subtle flavor of luxury and subtlety—for here it is far less essential than the perfect functioning of the regulating *unconscious* instincts or even than a certain imprudence, perhaps a bold recklessness whether in the face of danger or of the enemy, or that enthusiastic impulsiveness in anger, love, reverence, gratitude, and revenge by which noble souls have at all times recognized one another. *Ressentiment* itself, if it should appear in the noble man, consummates and exhausts itself in an immediate reaction, and therefore does not *poison*: on the other hand, it fails to appear at all on countless occasions on which it inevitably appears in the weak and impotent.

To be incapable of taking one's enemies, one's accidents, even one's misdeeds seriously for very long—that is the sign of strong, full natures in whom there is an excess of the power to form, to mold, to recuperate and to forget (a good example of this in modern times is Mirabeau,[25] who had no memory for insults and vile actions done him and was unable to forgive simply because he—forgot). Such a man shakes off with a *single* shrug many vermin that eat deep, into others; here alone genuine "love of one's enemies" is possible—supposing it to be possible at all on earth. How much reverence has a noble man for his enemies!—and such reverence is a bridge to love.—For he desires his enemy for himself, as his mark of distinction; he can endure no other enemy than one in whom there is nothing to despise and *very much* to honor! In contrast to this, picture "the enemy" as the man of *ressentiment* conceives him—and here precisely is his deed, his creation: he has conceived "the evil enemy," *"the Evil One,"* and this in fact is his basic concept, from which he then evolves, as an afterthought and pendant, a "good one"—himself!

11

This, then, is quite the contrary of what the noble man does, who conceives the basic concept "good" in advance and spontaneously out of himself and only then creates for himself an idea of "bad!" This "bad" of noble origin and that "evil" out of the cauldron of unsatisfied hatred—the former an after-production, a side issue, a contrasting shade, the latter on the contrary the original thing, the beginning, the distinctive *deed* in the conception of a slave morality—how different these words "bad" and "evil" are, although they are both apparently the opposite of the same concept "good." But it is *not* the same concept "good": one should ask rather precisely *who* is "evil" in the sense of the morality of *ressentiment*. The answer, in all strictness, is: *precisely* the "good man" of the other morality, precisely the noble, powerful man, the ruler, but dyed in another color, interpreted in another fashion, seen in another way by the venomous eye of *ressentiment*.

Here there is one thing we shall be the last to deny: he who knows these "good men" only as enemies knows only *evil enemies*, and the same men who are held so sternly in check *inter pares*[26] by custom, respect, usage, gratitude, and even more by mutual suspicion and jealousy, and who on the other hand in their relations with one another show themselves so resourceful in consideration, self-control, delicacy, loyalty, pride, and friendship—once they go outside, where the strange, the *stranger* is found, they are not much better than uncaged beasts of prey. There they savor a freedom from all social constraints, they compensate themselves in the wilderness for the tension engendered by protracted confinement and enclosure within the peace of society, they go *back* to the innocent conscience of the beast of prey, as triumphant monsters who perhaps emerge from a disgusting[27] procession of murder, arson, rape, and torture, exhilarated and undisturbed of soul, as if it were no more than a students' prank, convinced they have provided the poets with a lot more material for song and praise. One cannot fail to see at the bottom of all these noble races the beast of prey, the splendid *blond beast*[28] prowling about avidly in search of spoil and victory; this hidden core needs to erupt from time to time, the animal has to get out again and go back to the wilderness: the Roman, Arabian, Germanic, Japanese nobility, the Homeric heroes, the Scandinavian Vikings—they all shared this need.

It is the noble races that have left behind them the concept "barbarian" wherever they have gone; even their highest culture betrays a consciousness of it and even a pride in it (for example, when Pericles says to his Athenians in his famous funeral oration "our boldness has gained access to every land and sea, everywhere raising imperishable monuments to its goodness *and wickedness*"). This "boldness" of noble races, mad, absurd, and sudden in its expression, the incalculability, even incredibility of their undertakings—Pericles specially commends the *rhathymia*[29] of the Athenians—their indifference to and contempt for security, body, life, comfort, their hair-raising[30] cheerfulness and profound joy in all destruction, in all the voluptuousness of victory and cruelty—all this came together, in the minds of those who suffered from it, in the image of the "barbarian," the "evil enemy," perhaps as the "Goths," the "Vandals." The deep and icy mistrust the German still arouses today whenever he gets into a position of power is an echo of that inextinguishable horror with which Europe observed for centuries that raging of the blond Germanic beast (although between the old Germanic tribes and us Germans there exists hardly a conceptual relationship, let alone one of blood).

I once drew attention to the dilemma in which Hesiod found himself when he concocted his succession of cultural epochs and sought to express them in terms of gold, silver, and bronze: he knew no way of handling the contradiction presented by the glorious but at the same time terrible and violent world of Homer except by dividing one epoch into two epochs, which he then placed one behind the other—first the epoch of the heroes and demigods of Troy and Thebes, the form in which that world had survived in the memory of the noble races who were those heroes' true descendants; then the bronze epoch, the form in which that same world appeared to the descendants of the downtrodden, pillaged, mistreated, abducted, enslaved: an epoch of bronze, as aforesaid, hard, cold, cruel, devoid of feeling or conscience, destructive and bloody.

Supposing that what is at any rate believed to be the "truth" really is true, and the *meaning of all culture* is the reduction of the beast of prey "man" to a tame and civilized animal, a *domestic animal*, then one would undoubtedly have to regard all those instincts of reaction and *ressentiment* through whose aid the noble races and their ideals were finally confounded and overthrown as the actual *instruments of culture*; which is not to say that the *bearers* of these instincts themselves represent culture. Rather is the reverse not merely probable—no! today it is *palpable!* These bearers of the oppressive instincts that thirst for reprisal, the descendants of every kind of European and non-European slavery, and especially of the entire pre-Aryan populace—they represent the *regression* of mankind! These "instruments of culture" are a disgrace to man and rather an accusation and counterargument against "culture" in general! One may be quite justified in continuing to fear the blond beast at the core of all noble races and in being on one's guard against it: but who would not a hundred times sooner fear where one can also admire than *not* fear but be permanently condemned to the repellent sight of the ill-constituted, dwarfed, atrophied, and poisoned?[6] And is that not *our* fate? What today constitutes *our* antipathy to "man"?—for we suffer from man, beyond doubt.

Not fear; rather that we no longer have anything left to fear in man; that the maggot "man" is swarming in the foreground; that the "tame man," the hopelessly mediocre and insipid man, has already learned to feel himself as the goal and zenith, as the meaning of history, as "higher man"—that he has indeed a certain right to feel thus, insofar as he feels himself elevated above the surfeit of ill-constituted, sickly, weary and exhausted people of which Europe is beginning to stink today, as something at least relatively well-constituted, at least still capable of living, at least affirming life.

NOTES

1. In German: *Unveerantwortlichkeit und Unschuld.*

2. In German: *Moral.*

3. In German: *unschuld-bewussten.*

4. In German: *schuldbewussten.*

5. Latin: grant God eternal rest. Parody of the Order of Mass for the Dead: "Grant [the dead] eternal rest, O Lord."

6. Asclepius was the god of healing or medicine, and in Athenian custom people would make a sacrifice to him in hope of a cure. See Plato, Phaedo 118; see also TIII. 1. Hugh Tredennick interprets Socrates' final words as follows: "The cock is either a preliminary offering such as sufferers made before sleeping the night in his precincts with the hope of waking up cured, or (more probably) a thank-offering for cure effected. In either case Socrates implies—with a characteristic mixture of humor, paradox and piety-that death is the cure for life" (Plato, The Last Days of Socrates, ed. and trans. Tredennick, 3rd edn [Harmondsworth: Penguin, 1969], p. 199). Nietzsche interprets the last words as Socrates' revealing a spirit of revenge towards the time of life. The desire is for the liberation of the soul from its mortal coil and for release from empirical life into a realm of timeless being.

7. Latin: the tragedy begins.

8. In Kant's philosophy the causes of sensations are called 'things in themselves'. The thing in itself is unknowable: the sensations we actually experience are produced by the operation of our subjective mental apparatus.

9. Ugly shameful part.

10. first cause.

11. In Greek mythology a race dwelling beyond the north wind (Boreas) in a country of warmth and plenty.

12. Literally "a good human being," the term is used for precisely she type described here.

13. Resentment.

14. All of the footnoted words in this section are Greek. The first four mean wretched, but each has a separate note to suggest some of its other connotations. Deilos: cowardly, worthless, vile.

15. Paltry.

16. Oppressed by toils, good for nothing, worthless, knavish, base, cowardly.

17. Suffering hardship, knavish.

18. Woeful, miserable, toilsome; wretch.

19. Unblest, wretched, luckless, poor.

20. Wretched, miserable.

21. To be unlucky, unfortunate.

22. Misfortune.

23. To do well in the sense of faring well.

24. High-born, noble, high-minded.

25. Honoré Gabriel Riqueti, Comte de Mirabeau (1749–1791), was a celebrated French Revolutionary statesman and writer.

26. Among equals.

27. *Scheusslichen.*

28. This is the first appearance in Nietzsche's writings of the notorious "blond beast." It is encountered twice more in the present section; a variant appears in section 17 of the second essay; and then the blonde Bestie appears once more in Twilight; "The 'Improvers' of Mankind," section 2 (*Portable Nietzsche*, p. 502). That is all. For a detailed discussion of these passages see Kaufmann's Nietzsche, Chapter 7, section III: "… The 'blond beast' is not a racial concept and does not refer to the 'Nordic race' of which the Nazis later made so much. Nietzsche specifically refers to Arabs and Japanese …—and the 'blondness' presumably refers to the beast, the lion."

    Francis Golffing, in his free translation of the *Genealogy*, deletes the blond beast three times out of four; only where it appears the second time in the original text, he has "the blond Teutonic beast." This helps to corroborate the myth that the blondness refers to the Teutons. Without the image of the lion, however, we lose not only some of Nietzsche's poetry as well as any chance to understand one of his best known coinages; we also lose an echo of the crucial first chapter of *Zarathustra*, where the lion represents the second stage in "The Three Metamorphoses" of the spirit—above the obedient camel but below the creative child (*Portable Nietzsche*, pp. 138f).

    Arthur Danto has suggested that if lions were black and Nietzsche had written "Black Beast," the expression would "provide support for African instead of German nationalists" (*Nietzsche as Philosopher*, New York, Macmillan, 1965, p. 170). Panthers are black and magnificent animals, but anyone calling Negroes black beasts and associating them with "a disgusting procession of murder, arson, rape, and torture," adding that "the animal has to get out again and go back to the wilderness," and then going on to speak of "their hair-raising cheerfulness and profound joy in all destruction," would scarcely be taken to "provide support for … nationalists." On the contrary, he would be taken for a highly prejudiced critic of the Negro.

    No other German writer of comparable stature has been a more extreme critic of German nationalism than Nietzsche. For all that, it is plain that in this section he sought to describe the behavior of the ancient Greeks and Romans, the Goths and the Vandals, not that of nineteenth-century Germans.

29. Thucydides, 2.39. In *A Historical Commentary on Thucydides*, vol. II (Oxford, Clarendon Press, 1956; corrected imprint of 1966), p. 118, A. W, Gomme comments on this word: "in its original sense, 'ease of mind,' 'without anxiety' … But ease of mind can in certain circumstances become carelessness, remissness, frivolity: Demosthenes often accused the Athenians of rhathymia …"

30. *Entsetzliche.*

FREUD AND PSYCHOANALYSIS

By Stephen P. Thornton

Sigmund Freud (1856–1939), the father of psychoanalysis, was a physiologist, medical doctor, psychologist and influential thinker of the early twentieth century. Working initially in close collaboration with Joseph Breuer, Freud elaborated the theory that the mind is a complex energy-system, the structural investigation of which is the proper province of psychology. He articulated and refined the concepts of the unconscious, infantile sexuality and repression, and he proposed a tripartite account of the mind's structure—all as part of a radically new conceptual and therapeutic frame of reference for the understanding of human psychological development and the treatment of abnormal mental conditions. Notwithstanding the multiple manifestations of psychoanalysis as it exists today, it can in almost all fundamental respects be traced directly back to Freud's original work.

Freud's innovative treatment of human actions, dreams, and indeed of cultural artifacts as invariably possessing implicit symbolic significance has proven to be extraordinarily fruitful, and has had massive implications for a wide variety of fields including psychology, anthropology, semiotics, and artistic creativity and appreciation. However, Freud's most important and frequently re-iterated claim, that with psychoanalysis he had invented a successful science of the mind, remains the subject of much critical debate and controversy.

LIFE

Freud was born in Frieberg, Moravia in 1856, but when he was four years old his family moved to Vienna where he was to live and work until the last years of his life. In 1938 the Nazis annexed Austria, and Freud, who was Jewish, was allowed to leave for England. For these reasons, it was above all with the city of Vienna that Freud's name was destined to be deeply associated for posterity, founding as he did what was to become known as the 'first Viennese school' of psychoanalysis from which flowed psychoanalysis as a movement and all subsequent developments in this field. The scope of Freud's interests, and of his professional training, was very broad. He always considered himself first and foremost a scientist, endeavoring to extend the compass of human knowledge, and to this end (rather than to the practice of medicine) he enrolled at the medical school at the University of Vienna in 1873. He concentrated initially on biology, doing research in physiology for six years under the great German scientist Ernst Brücke, who was director of the Physiology Laboratory at the University, and thereafter specializing in neurology. He received his medical degree in 1881, and having become engaged to be married in 1882, he rather reluctantly took up more secure and financially rewarding work as a doctor at Vienna General Hospital. Shortly after his marriage in 1886, which was extremely happy and gave Freud six children—the youngest of whom, Anna, was to herself become a distinguished psychoanalyst—Freud set up a private practice in the treatment of psychological disorders, which gave him much of the clinical material that he based his theories and pioneering techniques on.

In 1885–86, Freud spent the greater part of a year in Paris, where he was deeply impressed by the work of the French neurologist Jean Charcot who was at that time using hypnotism to treat hysteria and other abnormal mental conditions. When he returned to Vienna, Freud experimented with hypnosis but found that its beneficial effects did not last. At this point he decided to adopt instead a method suggested by the work of an older Viennese colleague and friend, Josef Breuer, who had discovered that when he encouraged a hysterical patient to talk uninhibitedly about the earliest occurrences of the symptoms, they sometimes gradually abated. Working with Breuer, Freud formulated and developed the idea that many neuroses (phobias, hysterical paralysis and pains, some forms of paranoia, and so forth) had their origins in deeply traumatic experiences which had occurred in the patient's past but which were now forgotten—hidden from consciousness. The treatment was to enable the patient to recall the experience to consciousness, to confront it in a deep way both intellectually and emotionally, and in thus discharging it, to remove the underlying psychological causes of the neurotic symptoms. This technique, and the theory from which it is derived, was given its classical expression in *Studies in Hysteria*, jointly published by Freud and Breuer in 1895.

Shortly thereafter, however, Breuer found that he could not agree with what he regarded as the excessive emphasis which Freud placed upon the sexual origins and content of neuroses and the two parted company, with Freud continuing to work alone to develop and refine the theory and practice of psychoanalysis. In 1900, after a protracted period of self-analysis, he published *The Interpretation of Dreams*, which is generally regarded as his greatest work. This was followed in 1901 by *The Psychopathology of Everyday Life*; and in 1905 by *Three Essays on the Theory of Sexuality*. Freud's psychoanalytic theory was initially not well received—when its existence was acknowledged at all it was usually by people who were, as Breuer had foreseen, scandalized by the emphasis placed on sexuality by Freud. It was not until 1908, when the first International Psychoanalytical Congress was held at Salzburg that Freud's importance began to be generally recognized. This was greatly facilitated in 1909, when he was invited to give a course of lectures in the United States, which were to form the basis of his 1916 book *Five Lectures on Psycho-Analysis*. From this point on Freud's reputation and fame grew enormously and he continued to write prolifically until his death, producing in all more than twenty volumes of theoretical works and clinical studies. He was also not averse to critically revising his views, or to making fundamental alterations to his most basic principles when he considered that the scientific evidence demanded it—this was most clearly evidenced by his advancement of a completely new tripartite (id, ego, and super-ego) model of the mind in his 1923 work *The Ego and the Id*. He was initially greatly heartened by attracting followers of the intellectual caliber of Adler and Jung, and was correspondingly disappointed when they both went on to found rival schools of psychoanalysis—thus giving rise to the first two of many schisms in the movement—but he knew that such disagreement over basic principles had been part of the early development of every new science. After a life of remarkable vigor and creative productivity, he died of cancer while exiled in England in 1939.

BACKDROP TO HIS THOUGHT

Although a highly original thinker, Freud was also deeply influenced by a number of diverse factors which overlapped and interconnected with each other to shape the development of his thought. As indicated above, both Charcot and Breuer had a direct and immediate impact upon him, but some of the other factors, though no less important than these, were of a rather different nature. First of all, Freud himself was very much a Freudian—his father had two sons by a previous marriage, Emmanuel and Philip, and the young Freud often played with Philip's son John, who was his own age. Freud's self-analysis, which forms the core of his masterpiece *The Interpretation of Dreams*, originated in the emotional crisis which he suffered on the death of his father and the series of dreams to which this gave rise. This analysis revealed to him that the love and admiration which he had felt for his father were mixed with very contrasting feelings of shame and hate (such a mixed attitude he termed 'ambivalence'). Particularly revealing was his discovery that he had often fantasized as a youth that his half-brother Philip (who was of an age with his mother,) was really his father, and certain other signs convinced him of the deep underlying meaning of this fantasy—that he had wished his real father dead because he was his rival for his mother's affections.

This was to become the personal (though by no means exclusive) basis for his theory of the Oedipus complex.

Secondly, and at a more general level, account must be taken of the contemporary scientific climate in which Freud lived and worked. In most respects, the towering scientific figure of nineteenth century science was Charles Darwin, who had published his revolutionary *Origin of Species* when Freud was four years old. The evolutionary doctrine radically altered the prevailing conception of man—whereas before, man had been seen as a being different in nature to the members of the animal kingdom by virtue of his possession of an immortal soul, he was now seen as being part of the natural order, different from non-human animals only in degree of structural complexity. This made it possible and plausible, for the first time, to treat man as an object of scientific investigation, and to conceive of the vast and varied range of human behavior, and the motivational causes from which it springs, as being amenable in principle to scientific explanation. Much of the creative work done in a whole variety of diverse scientific fields over the next century was to be inspired by, and derive sustenance from, this new world-view, which Freud with his enormous esteem for science, accepted implicitly.

An even more important influence on Freud however, came from the field of physics. The second 50 years of the nineteenth century saw monumental advances in contemporary physics, which were largely initiated by the formulation of the principle of the conservation of energy by Helmholz. This principle states, in effect, that the total amount of energy in any given physical system is always constant, that energy quanta can be changed but not annihilated, and that consequently when energy is moved from one part of the system, it must reappear in another part. The progressive application of this principle led to monumental discoveries in the fields of thermodynamics, electromagnetism and nuclear physics which, with their associated technologies, have so comprehensively transformed the contemporary world. As we have seen, when he first came to the University of Vienna, Freud worked under the direction of Ernst Brücke who in 1874 published a book setting out the view that all living organisms, including humans, are essentially energy-systems to which, no less than to inanimate objects, the principle of the conservation of energy applies. Freud, who had great admiration and respect for Brücke, quickly adopted this new "dynamic physiology" with enthusiasm. From there it was but a short conceptual step—but one which Freud was the first to take, and on which his claim to fame is largely grounded—to the view that there is such a thing as "psychic energy," that the human personality is also an energy-system, and that it is the function of psychology to investigate the modifications, transmissions and conversions of psychic energy within the personality which shape and determine it. This latter conception is the very cornerstone of Freud's psychoanalytic theory.

THE THEORY OF THE UNCONSCIOUS

Freud's theory of the unconscious, then, is highly deterministic—a fact which, given the nature of nineteenth century science, should not be surprising. Freud was arguably the first thinker to apply deterministic principles systematically to the sphere of the mental, and to hold that the broad spectrum of human behavior is explicable only in terms of the (usually hidden) mental processes or states which determine it. Thus, instead of treating the behavior of the neurotic as being causally inexplicable—which had been the prevailing approach for centuries—Freud insisted, on the contrary, on treating it as behavior for which it is meaningful to seek an explanation by searching for causes in terms of the mental states of the individual concerned. Hence the significance which he attributed to slips of the tongue or pen, obsessive behavior and dreams—all, he held, are determined by hidden causes in the person's mind, and so they reveal in covert form what would otherwise not be known at all. This suggests the view that freedom of the will is, if not completely an illusion, certainly more tightly circumscribed than is commonly believed, for it follows from this that whenever we make a choice we are governed by hidden mental processes of which we are unaware and over which we have no control.

The postulate that there are such things as unconscious mental states at all is a direct function of Freud's determinism, his reasoning here being simply that the principle of causality requires that such mental states should exist, for it is evident that there is frequently nothing in the conscious mind which can be said to cause neurotic or other behavior. An 'unconscious' mental process or event, for Freud, is not one which merely happens to be out of consciousness at a given time, but is rather one which cannot, except through protracted psychoanalysis, be brought to the forefront of consciousness. The postulation of such unconscious mental states entails, of course, that the mind is not, and cannot be, either identified with consciousness, or an object of consciousness. To employ a much-used analogy, it is rather structurally akin to an iceberg, the bulk of it lying below the surface, exerting a dynamic and determining influence upon the part which is amenable to direct inspection—the conscious mind.

Deeply associated with this view of the mind is Freud's account of instincts or drives. Instincts, for Freud, are the principal motivating forces in the mental realm, and as such they 'energise' the mind in all of its functions. There are, he held, an indefinitely large number of such instincts, but these can be reduced to a small number of basic ones, which he grouped into two broad generic categories, Eros (the life instinct), which covers all the self-preserving and erotic instincts, and Thanatos (the death instinct), which covers all the instincts towards aggression, self-destruction, and cruelty. Thus it is a mistake to interpret Freud as asserting that all human actions spring from motivations which are sexual in their origin, since those which derive from Thanatos are not sexually motivated—indeed, Thanatos is the irrational urge to destroy the source of all sexual energy in the annihilation of the self. Having said that, it is undeniably true that Freud gave sexual drives an importance and centrality in human life, human actions, and human behavior which was new (and to many, shocking), arguing as he does that sexual drives exist and can be discerned in children from birth (the theory of infantile sexuality), and that sexual energy (libido) is the single most important motivating force in adult life. However, a crucial qualification has to be added here—Freud effectively redefined the term "sexuality" to make it cover any form of pleasure which is or can be derived from the body. Thus his theory of the instincts or drives is essentially that the human being is energized or driven from birth by the desire to acquire and enhance bodily pleasure.

INFANTILE SEXUALITY

Freud's theory of infantile sexuality must be seen as an integral part of a broader developmental theory of human personality. This had its origins in, and was a generalization of, Breuer's earlier discovery that traumatic childhood events could have devastating negative effects upon the adult individual, and took the form of the general thesis that early childhood sexual experiences were the crucial factors in the determination of the adult personality. From his account of the instincts or drives it followed that from the moment of birth the infant is driven in his actions by the desire for bodily/sexual pleasure, where this is seen by Freud in almost mechanical terms as the desire to release mental energy. Initially, infants gain such release, and derive such pleasure, from the act of sucking. Freud accordingly terms this the "oral" stage of development. This is followed by a stage in which the locus of pleasure or energy release is the anus, particularly in the act of defecation, and this is accordingly termed the 'anal' stage. Then the young child develops an interest in its sexual organs as a site of pleasure (the "phallic" stage), and develops a deep sexual attraction for the parent of the opposite sex, and a hatred of the parent of the same sex (the "Oedipus complex"). This, however, gives rise to (socially derived) feelings of guilt in the child, who recognizes that it can never supplant the stronger parent. A male child also perceives himself to be at risk. He fears that if he persists in pursuing the sexual attraction for his mother, he may be harmed by the father; specifically, he comes to fear that he may be castrated. This is termed "castration anxiety." Both the attraction for the mother and the hatred are usually repressed, and the child usually resolves the conflict of the Oedipus complex by coming to identify with the parent of the same sex. This happens at the age of five, whereupon the child enters a "latency" period, in which sexual motivations become much less pronounced. This lasts until puberty when mature genital development begins, and the pleasure drive refocuses around the genital area.

This, Freud believed, is the sequence or progression implicit in normal human development, and it is to be observed that at the infant level the instinctual attempts to satisfy the pleasure drive are frequently checked by parental control and social coercion. The developmental process, then, is for the child essentially a movement through a series of conflicts, the successful resolution of which is crucial to adult mental health. Many mental illnesses, particularly hysteria, Freud held, can be traced back to unresolved conflicts experienced at this stage, or to events which otherwise disrupt the normal pattern of infantile development. For example, homosexuality is seen by some Freudians as resulting from a failure to resolve the conflicts of the Oedipus complex, particularly a failure to identify with the parent of the same sex; the obsessive concern with washing and personal hygiene which characterizes the behavior of some neurotics is seen as resulting from unresolved conflicts/repressions occurring at the anal stage.

NEUROSES AND THE STRUCTURE OF THE MIND

Freud's account of the unconscious, and the psychoanalytic therapy associated with it, is best illustrated by his famous tripartite model of the structure of the mind or personality (although, as we have seen, he did not formulate this until 1923). This model has many points of similarity with the account of the mind offered by Plato over 2,000 years earlier. The theory is termed 'tripartite' simply because, again like Plato, Freud distinguished three structural elements within the mind, which he called id, ego, and super-ego. The id is that part of the mind in which are situated the instinctual sexual drives which require satisfaction; the super-ego is that part which contains the "conscience," namely, socially-acquired control mechanisms which have been internalized, and which are usually imparted in the first instance by the parents; while the ego is the conscious self that is created by the dynamic tensions and interactions between the id and the super-ego and has the task of reconciling their conflicting demands with the requirements of external reality. It is in this sense that the mind is to be understood as a dynamic energy-system. All objects of consciousness reside in the ego; the contents of the id belong permanently to the unconscious mind; while the super-ego is an unconscious screening-mechanism which seeks to limit the blind pleasure-seeking drives of the id by the imposition of restrictive rules. There is some debate as to how literally Freud intended this model to be taken (he appears to have taken it extremely literally himself), but it is important to note that what is being offered here is indeed a theoretical model rather than a description of an observable object, which functions as a frame of reference to explain the link between early childhood experience and the mature adult (normal or dysfunctional) personality.

Freud also followed Plato in his account of the nature of mental health or psychological well-being, which he saw as the establishment of a harmonious relationship between the three elements which constitute the mind. If the external world offers no scope for the satisfaction of the id's pleasure drives, or more commonly, if the satisfaction of some or all of these drives would indeed transgress the moral sanctions laid down by the super-ego, then an inner conflict occurs in the mind between its constituent parts or elements. Failure to resolve this can lead to later neurosis. A key concept introduced here by Freud is that the mind possesses a number of 'defense mechanisms' to attempt to prevent conflicts from becoming too acute, such as repression (pushing conflicts back into the unconscious), sublimation (channeling the sexual drives into the achievement socially acceptable goals, in art, science, poetry, and so forth), fixation (the failure to progress beyond one of the developmental stages), and regression (a return to the behavior characteristic of one of the stages).

Of these, repression is the most important, and Freud's account of this is as follows: when a person experiences an instinctual impulse to behave in a manner which the super-ego deems to be reprehensible (for example, a strong erotic impulse on the part of the child towards the parent of the opposite sex), then it is possible for the mind to push this impulse away, to repress it into the unconscious. Repression is thus one of the central defense mechanisms by which the ego seeks to avoid internal conflict and pain, and to reconcile reality with the demands of both id and super-ego. As such it is completely normal and an integral part of the developmental process through which every child must pass on the way to adulthood. However, the repressed instinctual drive, as an energy-form, is not and cannot be destroyed when it is repressed—it continues to exist intact in the unconscious, from where it exerts a determining force upon the conscious mind, and can give rise to the dysfunctional behavior characteristic of neuroses. This is one reason why dreams and slips of the tongue possess such a strong symbolic significance for Freud, and why their analysis became such a key part of his treatment—they represent instances in which the vigilance of the super-ego is relaxed, and when the repressed drives are accordingly able to present themselves to the conscious mind in a transmuted form. The difference between 'normal' repression and the kind of repression which results in neurotic illness is one of degree, not of kind—the compulsive behavior of the neurotic is itself a manifestation of an instinctual drive repressed in childhood. Such behavioral symptoms are highly irrational (and may even be perceived as such by the neurotic), but are completely beyond the control of the subject because they are driven by the now unconscious repressed impulse. Freud positioned the key repressions for both, the normal individual and the neurotic, in the first five years of childhood, and of course, held them to be essentially sexual in nature; since, as we have seen, repressions which disrupt the process of infantile sexual development in particular, according to him, lead to a strong tendency to later neurosis in adult life. The task of psychoanalysis as a therapy is to find the repressions which cause the neurotic symptoms by delving into the unconscious mind of the subject, and by bringing them to the forefront of consciousness, to allow the ego to confront them directly and thus to discharge them.

PSYCHOANALYSIS AS A THERAPY

Freud's account of the sexual genesis and nature of neuroses led him naturally to develop a clinical treatment for treating such disorders. This has become so influential today that when people speak of psychoanalysis they frequently refer exclusively to the clinical treatment; however, the term properly designates both the clinical treatment and the theory which underlies it. The aim of the method may be stated simply in general terms—to re-establish a harmonious relationship between the three elements which constitute the mind by excavating and resolving unconscious repressed conflicts. The actual method of treatment pioneered by Freud grew out of Breuer's earlier discovery, mentioned above, that when a hysterical patient was encouraged to talk freely about the earliest occurrences of her symptoms and fantasies, the symptoms began to abate, and were eliminated entirely when she was induced to remember the initial trauma which occasioned them. Turning away from his early attempts to explore the unconscious through hypnosis, Freud further developed this "talking cure," acting on the assumption that the repressed conflicts were buried in the deepest recesses of the unconscious mind. Accordingly, he got his patients to relax in a position in which they were deprived of strong sensory stimulation, and even keen awareness of the presence of the analyst (hence the famous use of the couch, with the analyst virtually silent and out of sight), and then encouraged them to speak freely and uninhibitedly, preferably without forethought, in the belief that he could thereby discern the unconscious forces lying behind what was said. This is the method of free-association, the rationale for which is similar to that involved in the analysis of dreams—in both cases the super-ego is to some degree disarmed, its efficiency as a screening mechanism is moderated, and material is allowed to filter through to the conscious ego which would otherwise be completely repressed. The process is necessarily a difficult and protracted one, and it is therefore one of the primary tasks of the analyst to help the patient recognize, and overcome, his own natural resistances, which may exhibit themselves as hostility towards the analyst. However, Freud always took the occurrence of resistance as a sign that he was on the right track in his assessment of the underlying unconscious causes of the patient's condition. The patient's dreams are of particular interest, for reasons which we have already partly seen. Taking it that the super-ego functioned less effectively in sleep, as in free association, Freud made a distinction between the manifest content of a dream (what the dream appeared to be about on the surface) and its latent content (the unconscious, repressed desires or wishes which are its real object). The correct interpretation of the patient's dreams, slips of tongue, free-associations, and responses to carefully selected questions leads the analyst to a point where he can locate the unconscious repressions producing the neurotic symptoms, invariably in terms of the patient's passage through the sexual developmental process, the manner in which the conflicts implicit in this process were handled, and the libidinal content of the patient's family relationships. To effect a cure, the analyst must facilitate the patient himself to become conscious of unresolved conflicts buried in the deep recesses of the unconscious mind, and to confront and engage with them directly.

In this sense, then, the object of psychoanalytic treatment may be said to be a form of self-understanding—once this is acquired it is largely up to the patient, in consultation with the analyst, to determine how he shall handle this newly-acquired understanding of the unconscious forces which motivate him. One possibility, mentioned above, is the channeling of sexual energy into the achievement of social, artistic or scientific goals—this is sublimation, which Freud saw as the motivating force behind most great cultural achievements. Another possibility would be the conscious, rational control of formerly repressed drives—this is suppression. Yet another would be the decision that it is the super-ego and the social constraints which inform it that are at fault, in which case the patient may decide in the end to satisfy the instinctual drives. But in all cases the cure is effected essentially by a kind of catharsis or purgation—a release of the pent-up psychic energy, the constriction of which was the basic cause of the neurotic illness.

CRITICAL EVALUATION OF FREUD

It should be evident from the foregoing why psychoanalysis in general, and Freud in particular, have exerted such a strong influence upon the popular imagination in the Western World, and why both the theory and practice of psychoanalysis should remain the object of a great deal of controversy. In fact, the controversy which exists in relation to Freud is more heated and multi-faceted than that relating to virtually any other post-1850 thinker (a possible exception being Darwin), with criticisms ranging from the contention that Freud's theory was generated by logical confusions arising out of his alleged long-standing addiction to cocaine (see Thornton, E.M. *Freud and Cocaine: The Freudian Fallacy*) to the view that he made an important, but grim, empirical discovery, which he knowingly suppressed in favour of the theory of the unconscious, knowing that the latter would be more socially acceptable (see Masson, J. *The Assault on Truth*).

It should be emphasized here that Freud's genius is not (generally) in doubt, but the precise nature of his achievement is still the source of much debate. The supporters and followers of Freud (and Jung and Adler) are noted for the zeal and enthusiasm with which they espouse the doctrines of the master, to the point where many of the detractors of the movement see it as a kind of secular religion, requiring as it does an initiation process in which the aspiring psychoanalyst must himself first be analyzed. In this way, it is often alleged, the unquestioning acceptance of a set of ideological principles becomes a necessary precondition for acceptance into the movement—as with most religious groupings. In reply, the exponents and supporters of psychoanalysis frequently analyze the motivations of their critics in terms of the very theory which those critics reject. And so the debate goes on.

Here we will confine ourselves to: (a) the evaluation of Freud's claim that his theory is a scientific one, (b) the question of the theory's coherence, (c) the dispute concerning what, if anything, Freud really discovered, and (d) the question of the efficacy of psychoanalysis as a treatment for neurotic illnesses.

The Claim to Scientific Status

This is a crucially important issue since Freud saw himself first and foremost as a pioneering scientist, and repeatedly asserted that the significance of psychoanalysis is that it is a new science, incorporating a new scientific method of dealing with the mind and with mental illness. There can, moreover, be no doubt but that this has been the chief attraction of the theory for most of its advocates since then—on the face of it, it has the appearance of being not just a scientific theory but an enormously strong one, with the capacity to accommodate, and explain, every possible form of human behavior. However, it is precisely this latter which, for many commentators, undermines its claim to scientific status. On the question of what makes a theory a genuinely scientific one, Karl Popper's criterion of demarcation, as it is called, has now gained very general acceptance: namely, that every genuine scientific theory must be testable, and therefore falsifiable, at least in principle. In other words, if a theory is incompatible with possible observations, it is scientific; conversely, a theory which is compatible with all possible observations is unscientific (see Popper, K. *The Logic of Scientific Discovery*). Thus the principle of the conservation of energy (physical, not psychic), which influenced Freud so greatly, is a scientific one because it is falsifiable—the discovery of a physical system in which the total amount of physical energy was not constant would conclusively show it to be false. It is argued that nothing of the kind is possible with respect to Freud's theory—it is not falsifiable. If the question is asked: "What does this theory imply which, if false, would show the whole theory to be false?," the answer is "Nothing" because the theory is compatible with every possible state of affairs. Hence it is concluded that the theory is not scientific, and while this does not, as some critics claim, rob it of all value, it certainly diminishes its intellectual status as projected by its strongest advocates, including Freud himself.

The Coherence of the Theory

A related (but perhaps more serious) point is that the coherence of the theory is, at the very least, questionable. What is attractive about the theory, even to the layman, is that it seems to offer us long sought-after and much needed causal explanations for conditions which have been a source of a great deal of human misery. The thesis that neuroses are caused by unconscious conflicts buried deep in the unconscious mind in the form of repressed libidinal energy would appear to offer us, at last, an insight in the causal mechanism underlying these abnormal psychological conditions as they are expressed in human behavior, and further show us how they are related to the psychology of the 'normal' person. However, even this is questionable, and is a matter of much dispute. In general, when it is said that an event X causes another event Y to happen, both X and Y are, and must be, independently identifiable. It is true that this is not always a simple process, as in science causes are sometimes unobservable (sub-atomic particles, radio and electromagnetic waves, molecular structures, and so forth), but in these latter cases there are clear 'correspondence rules' connecting the unobservable causes with observable phenomena. The difficulty with Freud's theory is that it offers us entities (for example repressed unconscious conflicts), which are said to be the unobservable causes of certain forms of behavior But there are no correspondence rules for these alleged causes—they cannot be identified except by reference to the behavior which they are said to cause (that is, the analyst does not demonstratively assert: "This is the unconscious cause, and that is its behavioral effect;" rather he asserts: "This is the behavior, therefore its unconscious cause must exist"), and this does raise serious doubts as to whether Freud's theory offers us genuine causal explanations at all.

Freud's Discovery?

At a less theoretical, but no less critical level, it has been alleged that Freud did make a genuine discovery which he was initially prepared to reveal to the world. However, the response he encountered was so ferociously hostile that he masked his findings and offered his theory of the unconscious in its place (see Masson, J. *The Assault on Truth*). What he discovered, it has been suggested, was the extreme prevalence of child sexual abuse, particularly of young girls (the vast majority of hysterics are women), even in respectable nineteenth century Vienna. He did in fact offer an early "seduction theory" of neuroses, which met with fierce animosity, and which he quickly withdrew and replaced with the theory of the unconscious. As one contemporary Freudian commentator explains it, Freud's change of mind on this issue came about as follows:

> Questions concerning the traumas suffered by his patients seemed to reveal [to Freud] that Viennese girls were extraordinarily often seduced in very early childhood by older male relatives. Doubt about the actual occurrence of these seductions was soon replaced by certainty that it was descriptions about childhood fantasy that were being offered. (MacIntyre).

In this way, it is suggested, the theory of the Oedipus complex was generated.

This statement begs a number of questions, not least, what does the expression 'extraordinarily often' mean in this context? By what standard is this being judged? The answer can only be: By the standard of what we generally believe—or would like to believe—to be the case. But the contention of some of Freud's critics here is that his patients were not recalling childhood fantasies, but traumatic events from their childhood which were all too real. Freud, according to them, had stumbled upon and knowingly suppressed the fact that the level of child sexual abuse in society is much higher than is generally believed or acknowledged. If this contention is true—and it must at least be contemplated seriously—then this is undoubtedly the most serious criticism that Freud and his followers have to face.

Further, this particular point has taken on an added and even more controversial significance in recent years, with the willingness of some contemporary Freudians to combine the theory of repression with an acceptance of the widespread social prevalence of child sexual abuse. The result has been that in the United States and Britain in particular, many thousands of people have emerged from analysis with 'recovered memories' of alleged childhood sexual abuse by their parents; memories which, it is suggested, were hitherto repressed. On this basis, parents have been accused and repudiated, and whole families have been divided or destroyed. Unsurprisingly, this in turn has given rise to a systematic backlash in which organizations of accused parents, seeing themselves as the true victims of what they term 'False Memory Syndrome', have denounced all such memory-claims as falsidical —the direct product of a belief in what they see as the myth of repression. (see Pendergast, M. *Victims of Memory*). In this way, the concept of repression, which Freud himself termed "the foundation stone upon which the structure of psychoanalysis rests," has come in for more widespread critical scrutiny than ever before. Here, the fact that, unlike some of his contemporary followers, Freud did not himself ever countenance the extension of the concept of repression to cover actual child sexual abuse, and the fact that we are not necessarily forced to choose between the views that all "recovered memories" are either veridical or falsidical are, perhaps understandably, frequently lost sight of in the extreme heat generated by this debate.

The Efficacy of Psychoanalytic Therapy

It does not follow that, if Freud's theory is unscientific, or even false, it cannot provide us with a basis for the beneficial treatment of neurotic illness because the relationship between a theory's truth or falsity and its utility-value is far from being an isomorphic one. (The theory upon which the use of leeches to bleed patients in eighteenth century medicine was based was quite spurious, but patients did sometimes actually benefit from the treatment!). And of course even a true theory might be badly applied, leading to negative consequences. One of the problems here is that it is difficult to specify what counts as a cure for a neurotic illness as distinct, say, from a mere alleviation of the symptoms. In general, however, the efficiency of a given method of treatment is usually clinically measured by means of a control group—the proportion of patients suffering from a given disorder who are cured by treatment X is measured by comparison with those cured by other treatments, or by no treatment at all. Such clinical tests as have been conducted indicate that the proportion of patients who have benefited from psychoanalytic treatment does not diverge significantly from the proportion who recover spontaneously or as a result of other forms of intervention in the control groups used. So, the question of the therapeutic effectiveness of psychoanalysis remains an open and controversial one.

SELECTION FROM *AN OUTLINE OF PSYCHOANALYSIS* BY SIGMUND FREUD

Chapter V
DREAM-INTERPRETATION AS AN ILLUSTRATION

An investigation of normal, stable states, in which the frontiers of the ego are safeguarded against the id by resistances (anticathexes) and have held firm, and in which the super-ego is not distinguished from the ego, because they work together harmoniously—an investigation of that kind would teach us little. The only thing that can help us are states of conflict and uproar, when the contents of the unconscious id have a prospect of forcing their way into the ego and into consciousness and the ego puts itself once more on the defensive against this invasion. It is only under these conditions that we can make such observations as will confirm or correct our statements about the two partners. Now, our nightly sleep is precisely a state of this sort, and for that reason psychical activity during sleep, which we perceive as dreams, is our most favorable object of study. In that way, too, we avoid the familiar reproach that we base our constructions of normal mental life on pathological findings; for dreams are regular events in the life of a normal person, however much their characteristics may differ from the productions of our waking life. Dreams, as everyone knows, may be confused, unintelligible or positively nonsensical, what they say may contradict all that we know of reality, and we behave in them like insane people, since, so long as we are dreaming, we attribute objective reality to the contents of the dream.

We find our way to the understanding ('interpretation') of a dream by assuming that what we recollect as the dream after we have woken up is not the true dream-process but only a façade behind which that process lies concealed. Here we have our distinction between the *manifest* content of a dream and the *latent* dream-thoughts. The process which produces the former out of the latter is described as the dream-work. The study of the *dream-work* teaches us by an excellent example the way in which unconscious material from the id (originally unconscious and repressed unconscious alike) forces its way into the ego, becomes preconscious and, as a result of the ego's opposition, undergoes the changes which we know as dream-distortion. There are no features of a dream which cannot be explained in this way.

It is best to begin by pointing out that the formation of a dream can be provoked in two different ways. Either, on the one hand, an instinctual impulse which is ordinarily suppressed (an unconscious wish) finds enough strength during sleep to make itself felt by the ego, or, on the other hand, an urge left over from waking life, a preconscious train of thought with all the conflicting impulses attached to it, finds reinforcement during sleep from an unconscious element. In short, dreams may arise either from the id or from the ego. The mechanism of dream-formation is in both cases the same and so also is the necessary dynamic precondition. The ego gives evidence of its original derivation from the id by occasionally ceasing its functions and allowing a reversion to an earlier state of things. This is logically brought about by its breaking off its relations with the external world and withdrawing its cathexes from the sense organs. We are justified in saying that there arises at birth an instinct to return to the intra-uterine life that has been abandoned—an instinct to sleep. Sleep is a return of this kind to the womb. Since the waking ego governs motility, that function is paralysed in sleep, and accordingly a good part of the inhibitions imposed on the unconscious id become superfluous. The withdrawal or reduction of these 'anticathexes' thus allows the id what is now a harmless amount of liberty.

The evidence of the share taken by the unconscious id in the formation of dreams is abundant and convincing. (*a*) Memory is far more comprehensive in dreams than in waking life. Dreams bring up recollections which the dreamer has forgotten, which are inaccessible to him when he is awake. (*b*) Dreams make an unrestricted use of linguistic symbols, the meaning of which is for the most part unknown to the dreamer. Our experience, however, enables us to confirm their sense. They probably originate from earlier phases in the development of speech. (*c*) Memory very often reproduces in dreams impressions from the dreamer's early childhood of which we can definitely assert not only that they had been forgotten but that they had become unconscious owing to repression. That explains the help—usually indispensable—given us by dreams in the attempts we make during the analytic treatment of neuroses to reconstruct the dreamer's early life. (*d*) Furthermore, dreams bring to light material which cannot have originated either from the dreamer's adult life or from his forgotten childhood. We are obliged to regard it as part of the *archaic heritage* which a child brings with him into the world, before any experience of his own, influenced by the experiences of his ancestors. We find the counterpart of this phylogenetic material in the earliest human legends and in surviving customs. Thus dreams constitute a source of human prehistory which is not to be despised.

But what makes dreams so invaluable in giving us insight is the circumstance that, when the unconscious material makes its way into the ego, it brings its own modes of working along with it. This means that the preconscious thoughts in which the unconscious material has found its expression are handled in the course of the dream-work as though they were unconscious portions of the id; and, in the case of the alternative method of dream-formation, the preconscious thoughts which have obtained reinforcement from an unconscious instinctual impulse are brought down to the unconscious state. It is only in this way that we learn the laws which govern the passage of events in the unconscious and the respects in which they differ from the rules that are familiar to us in waking thought. Thus the dream-work is essentially an instance of the unconscious working-over of preconscious thought-processes. To take an analogy from history: invading conquerors govern a conquered country, not according to the judicial system which they find in force there, but according to their own. It is, however, an unmistakable fact that the outcome of the dream-work is a compromise. The ego-organization is not yet paralysed, and its influence is to be seen in the distortion imposed on the unconscious material and in what are often very ineffective attempts at giving the total result a form not too unacceptable to the ego (*secondary revision*). In our analogy this would be an expression of the continued resistance of the defeated people.

The laws that govern the passage of events in the unconscious, which come to light in this manner, are remarkable enough and suffice to explain most of what seems strange to us about dreams. Above all there is a striking tendency to *condensation*, an inclination to form fresh unities out of elements which in our waking thought we should certainly have kept separate. As a consequence of this, a single element of the manifest dream often stands for a whole number of latent dream-thoughts as though it were a combined allusion to all of them; and in general the compass of the manifest dream is extraordinarily small in comparison with the wealth of material from which it has sprung. Another peculiarity of the dream-work, not entirely independent of the former one, is the ease with which psychical intensities[1] (cathexes) are displaced from one element to another, so that it often happens that an element which was of little importance in the dream-thoughts appears as the clearest and accordingly most important feature of the manifest dream, and, *vice versa*, that essential elements of the dream-thoughts are represented in the manifest dream only by slight allusions. Moreover, as a rule the existence of quite insignificant points in common between two elements is enough to allow the dream-work to replace one by the other in all further operations. It will easily be imagined how greatly these mechanisms of condensation and displacement can increase the difficulty of interpreting a dream and of revealing the relations between the manifest dream and the latent dream-thoughts. From the evidence of the existence of these two tendencies to condensation and displacement our theory infers that in the unconscious id the energy is in a freely mobile state and that the id sets more store by the possibility of discharging quantities of excitation than by any other consideration;[2] and our theory makes use of these two peculiarities in defining the character of the primary process we have attributed to the id.

The study of the dream-work has taught us many other characteristics of the processes in the unconscious which are as remarkable as they are important; but we must only mention a few of them here. The governing rules of logic carry no weight in the unconscious; it might be called the Realm of the Illogical. Urges with contrary aims exist side by side in the unconscious without any need arising for an adjustment between them. Either they have no influence whatever on each other, or, if they have, no decision is reached, but a compromise comes about which is nonsensical since it embraces mutually incompatible details. With this is connected the fact that contraries are not kept apart but treated as though they were identical, so that in the manifest dream any element may also have the meaning of its opposite. Certain philologists have found that the same held good in the most ancient languages and that contraries such as 'strong-weak', 'light-dark' and 'high-deep' were originally expressed by the same roots, until two different modifications of the primitive word distinguished between the two meanings. Residues of this original double meaning seem to have survived even in a highly developed language like Latin in its use of words such as '*altus*' ('high' and 'deep') and '*sacer*' ('sacred' and 'infamous'). [Cf. p. 65 below.]

In view of the complication and ambiguity of the relations between the manifest dream and the latent content lying behind it, it is of course justifiable to ask how it is at all possible to deduce the one from the other and whether all we have to go on is a lucky guess, assisted perhaps by a translation of the symbols that occur in the manifest dream. It may be said in reply that in the great majority of cases the problem can be satisfactorily solved, but only with the help of the associations provided by the dreamer himself to the elements of the manifest content. Any other procedure is arbitrary and can yield no certain result. But the dreamer's associations bring to light intermediate links which we can insert in the gap between the two [between the manifest and latent content] and by aid of which we can reinstate the latent content of the dream and 'interpret' it. It is not to be wondered at if this work of interpretation (acting in a direction opposite to the dream-work) fails occasionally to arrive at complete certainty.

It remains for us to give a dynamic explanation of why the sleeping ego takes on the task of the dream-work at all. The explanation is fortunately easy to find. With the help of the unconscious, every dream that is in process of formation makes a demand upon the ego—for the satisfaction of an instinct, if the dream originates from the id; for the solution of a conflict, the removal of a doubt or the forming of an intention, if the dream originates from a residue of preconscious activity in waking life. The sleeping ego, however, is focused on the wish to maintain sleep; it feels this demand as a disturbance and seeks to get rid of the disturbance. The ego succeeds in doing this by what appears to be an act of compliance: it meets the demand with what is in the circumstances a harmless *fulfilment of a wish* and so gets rid of it. This replacement of the demand by the fulfilment of a wish remains the essential function of the dream-work. It may perhaps be worth while to illustrate this by three simple examples—a hunger dream, a dream of convenience and a dream prompted by sexual desire. A need for food makes itself felt in a dreamer during his sleep: he has a dream of a delicious meal and sleeps on. The choice, of course, was open to him either of waking up and eating something or of continuing his sleep. He decided in favour of the latter and satisfied his hunger by means of the dream—for the time being, at all events, for if his hunger had persisted he would have had to wake up nevertheless. Here is the second example. A sleeper had to wake up so as to be in time for his work at the hospital. But he slept on, and had a dream that he was already at the hospital—but as a patient, who has no need to get up. Or again, a desire becomes active during the night for the enjoyment of a forbidden sexual object, the wife of a friend of the sleeper. He has a dream of sexual intercourse—not, indeed, with this person but with someone else of the same name to whom he is in fact indifferent; or his struggle against the desire may find expression in his mistress remaining altogether anonymous.

Naturally, every case is not so simple. Especially in dreams which have originated from undealt-with residues of the previous day, and which have only obtained an unconscious reinforcement during the state of sleep, it is often no easy task to uncover the unconscious motive force and its wish-fulfilment; but we may assume that it is always there. The thesis that dreams are the fulfilments of wishes will easily arouse scepticism when it is remembered how many dreams have an actually distressing content or even wake the dreamer in anxiety, quite apart from the numerous dreams without any definite feeling-tone. But the objection based on anxiety dreams cannot be sustained against analysis. It must not be forgotten that dreams are invariably the product of a conflict, that they are a kind of compromise-structure. Something that is a satisfaction for the unconscious id may for that very reason be a cause of anxiety for the ego.

As the dream-work proceeds, sometimes the unconscious will press forward more successfully and sometimes the ego will defend itself with greater energy. Anxiety dreams are mostly those whose content has undergone the least distortion. If the demand made by the unconscious is too great for the sleeping ego to be in a position to fend it off by the means at its disposal, it abandons the wish to sleep and returns to waking life. We shall be taking every experience into account if we say that a dream is invariably an *attempt* to get rid of a disturbance of sleep by means of a wish-fulfilment, so that the dream is a guardian of sleep. The attempt may succeed more or less completely; it may also fail, and in that case the sleeper wakes up, apparently woken precisely by the dream. So, too, there are occasions when that excellent fellow the night-watchman, whose business it is to guard the little township's sleep, has no alternative but to sound the alarm and waken the sleeping townspeople.

I will close this discussion with a comment which will justify the length of time I have spent on the problem of the interpretation of dreams. Experience has shown that the unconscious mechanisms which we have come to know from our study of the dream-work and which gave us the explanation of the formation of dreams also help us to understand the puzzling symptoms which attract our interest to neuroses and psychoses. A conformity of such a kind cannot fail to excite high hopes in us.

NOTES

1. [A term very often used by Freud from the earliest times as an equivalent to psychical energy. See the Editor's Appendix to the first paper on the neuro-psychoses of defence (1894a), *Standard Ed.*, 3, 66–7; also an Editor's footnote near the end of the paper on 'Female Sexuality' (1931b), ibid., 21, 242–3.]

2. An analogy may be seen in the behaviour of a non-commissioned officer who accepts a reprimand from his superior in silence but vents his anger on the first innocent private he comes across. [In this insistance by the id on discharging quantities of excitation we have an exact replica of what Freud in his *Project* of 1895 (Part I, Section 1) had described in quasi-neurological terms as the primary principle of neuronal activity: 'neurones tend to divest themselves of quantity'. (1950a, S.E., 1, 296.)]

EXISTENTIALISM, HUMANISM, AND BAD FAITH

By Jean-Paul Sartre

SELECTION FROM *EXISTENTIALISM AND HUMANISM*

My purpose here is to offer a defense of existentialism against several reproaches that have been laid against it.

First, it has been reproached as an invitation to people to dwell in quietism of despair. For if every way to a solution is barred, one would have to regard any action in this world as entirely ineffective, and one would arrive finally at a contemplative philosophy. Moreover, since contemplation is a luxury, this would be only another bourgeois philosophy. This is, especially, the reproach made by the Communists.

From another quarter we are reproached for having underlined all that is ignominious in the human situation, for depicting what is mean, sordid or base to the neglect of certain things that possess charm and beauty and belong to the brighter side of human nature: for example, according to the Catholic critic, Mlle. Mercier, we forget how an infant smiles. Both from this side and from the other we are also reproached for leaving out of account the solidarity of mankind and considering man in isolation. And this, say the Communists, is because we base our doctrine upon pure subjectivity—upon the Cartesian "I think": which is the moment in which solitary man attains to himself; a position from which it is impossible to regain solidarity with other men who exist outside of the self. The *ego* cannot reach them through the *cogito*.

Jean-Paul Sartre, *Being and Nothingness*; trans. Hazel Barnes, pp. 47-61, 86-90, 96-98, 101-103. Copyright © 1956 by Philosophical Library. Reprinted with permission.

From the Christian side, we are reproached as people who deny the reality and seriousness of human affairs. For since we ignore the commandments of God and all values prescribed as eternal, nothing remains but what is strictly voluntary. Everyone can do what he likes, and will be incapable, from such a point of view, of condemning either the point of view or the action of anyone else.

It is to these various reproaches that I shall endeavor to reply today; that is why I have entitled this brief exposition "Existentialism is a Humanism." Many may be surprised at the mention of humanism in this connection, but we shall try to see in what sense we understand it. In any case, we can begin by saying that existentialism, in our sense of the word, is a doctrine that does render human life possible; a doctrine, also, which affirms that every truth and every action imply both an environment and a human subjectivity. The essential charge laid against us is, of course, that of over-emphasis upon the evil side of human life. I have lately been told of a lady who, whenever she lets slip a vulgar expression in a moment of nervousness, excuses herself by exclaiming, "I believe I am becoming an existentialist." So it appears that ugliness is being identified with existentialism. That is why some people say we are "naturalistic," and if we are, it is strange to see how much we scandalize and horrify them, for no one seems to be much frightened or humiliated nowadays by what is properly called naturalism. Those who can quite well keep down a novel by Zola such as *La Terre* are sickened as soon as they read an existentialist novel. Those who appeal to the wisdom of the people—which is a sad wisdom—find ours sadder still. And yet, what could be more disillusioned than such sayings as "Charity begins at home" or "Promote a rogue and he'll sue you for damage, knock him down and he'll do you homage"? We all know how many common sayings can be quoted to this effect, and they all mean much the same—that you must not oppose the powers that be; that you must not fight against superior force; must not meddle in matters that are above your station. Or that any action not in accordance with some tradition is mere romanticism; or that any undertaking which has not the support of proven experience is foredoomed to frustration; and that since experience has shown men to be invariably inclined to evil, there must be firm rules to restrain them, otherwise we shall have anarchy. It is, however, the people who are forever mouthing these dismal proverbs and, whenever they are told of some more or less repulsive action, say "How like human nature!"—it is these very people, always harping upon realism, who complain that existentialism is too gloomy a view of things. Indeed their excessive protests make me suspect that what is annoying them is not so much our pessimism, but, much more likely, our optimism. For at bottom, what is alarming in the doctrine that I am about to try to explain to you is—is it not?—that it confronts man with a possibility of choice. To verify this, let us review the whole question upon the strictly philosophic level. What, then, is this that we call existentialism?

Most of those who are making use of this word would be highly confused if required to explain its meaning. For since it has become fashionable, people cheerfully declare that this musician or that painter is "existentialist." A columnist in *Clartés* signs himself "The Existentialist," and, indeed, the word is now so loosely applied to so many things that it no longer means anything at all. It would appear that, for the lack of any novel doctrine such as that of surrealism, all those who are eager to join in the latest scandal or movement now seize upon this philosophy in which, however, they can find nothing to their purpose. For in truth this is of all teachings the least scandalous and the most austere: it is intended strictly for technicians and philosophers. All the same, it can easily be defined.

The question is only complicated because there are two kinds of existentialists. There are, on the one hand, the Christians, amongst whom I shall name Karl Jaspers and Gabriel Marcel, both professed Catholics; and on the other the existential atheists, amongst whom we must place Heidegger as well as the French existentialists and myself. What they have in common is simply the fact that they believe that *existence* comes before *essence*—or, if you will, that we must begin from the subjective. What exactly do we mean by that?

If one considers an article of manufacture as, for example, a book or a paper-knife—one sees that it has been made by an artisan who had a conception of it; and he has paid attention, equally, to the conception of a paper-knife and to the pre-existent technique of production which is a part of that conception and is, at bottom, a formula. Thus the paper-knife is at the same time an article producible in a certain manner and one which, on the other hand, serve a definite purpose, for one cannot suppose that a man would produce a paper-knife without knowing what it was for. Let us say, then, of the paperknife that its essence that is to say the sum of the formulae and the qualities which made its production and its definition possible—precedes its existence. The presence of such—and—such a paper-knife or book is thus determined before my eyes. Here, then, we are viewing the world from a technical standpoint, and we can say that production precedes existence.

When we think of God as the creator, we are thinking of him, most of the time, as a supernal artisan. Whatever doctrine we may be considering, whether it be a doctrine like that of Descartes, or of Leibniz himself, we always imply that the will follows, more or less, from the understanding or at least accompanies it, so that when God creates he knows precisely what he is creating. Thus, the conception of man in the mind of God is comparable to that of the paper-knife in the mind of the artisan: God makes man according to a procedure and a conception, exactly as the artisan manufactures a paper-knife, following a definition and a formula. Thus each individual man is the realization of a certain conception which dwells in the divine understanding. In the philosophic atheism of the eighteenth century, the notion of God is suppressed, but not, for all that, the idea that essence is prior to existence; something of that idea we still find everywhere, in Diderot, in Voltaire and even in Kant. Man possesses a human nature; that "human nature," which is the conception of human being, is found in every man; which means that each man is a particular example of a universal conception, the conception of Man. In Kant, this universality goes so far that the wild man of the woods, man in the state of nature and the bourgeois are all contained in the same definition and have the same fundamental qualities. Here again, the essence of man precedes that historic existence which we confront in experience.

Atheistic existentialism, of which I am a representative, declares with greater consistency that if God does not exist there is at least one being whose existence comes before its essence, a being which exists before it can be defined by any conception of it. That being is man or, as Heidegger has it, the human reality. What do we mean by saying that existence precedes essence? We mean that man first of all exists, encounters himself, surges up in the world—and defines himself afterwards. If man as the existentialist sees him is not definable, it is because to begin with he is nothing. He will not be anything until later, and then he will be what he makes of himself. Thus, there is no human nature, because there is no God to have a conception of it. Man simply is. Not that he is simply what he conceives himself to be, but he is what he wills, and as he conceives himself after already existing—as he wills to be after that leap towards existence.

Man is nothing else but that which he makes of himself. That is the first principle of existentialism. And this is what people call its "subjectivity," using the word as a reproach against us. But what do we mean to say by this, but that man is of a greater dignity than a stone or a table? For we mean to say that man primarily exists—that man is, before all else, something which propels itself towards a future and is aware that it is doing so. Man is, indeed, a project which possesses a subjective life, instead of being a kind of moss, or a fungus or a cauliflower. Before that projection of the self nothing exists; not even in the heaven of intelligence: man will only attain existence when he is what he purposes to be. Not, however, what he may wish to be. For what we usually understand by wishing or willing is a conscious decision taken—much more often than not—after we have made ourselves what we are. I may wish to join a party, to write a book or to marry—but in such a case what is usually called my will is probably a manifestation of a prior and more spontaneous decision. If, however, it is true that existence is prior to essence, man is responsible for what he is. Thus, the first effect of existentialism is that it puts every man in possession of himself as he is, and places the entire responsibility for his existence squarely upon his own shoulders. And, when we say that man is responsible for himself, we do not mean that he is responsible only for his own individuality, but that he is responsible for all men.

The word "subjectivism" is to be understood in two senses, and our adversaries play upon only one of them. Subjectivism means, on the one hand, the freedom of the individual subject and, on the other, that man cannot pass beyond human subjectivity. It is the latter which is the deeper meaning of existentialism. When we say that man chooses himself, we do mean that every one of us must choose himself; but by that we also mean that in choosing for himself he chooses for all men. For in effect, of all the actions a man may take in order to create himself as he wills to be, there is not one which is not creative, at the same time, of an image of man such as he believes he ought to be. To choose between this or that is at the same time to affirm the value of that which is chosen; for we are unable ever to choose the worse. What we choose is always the better; and nothing can be better for us unless it is better for all.

If, moreover, existence precedes essence and we will to exist at the same time as we fashion our image, that image is valid for all and for the entire epoch in which we find ourselves. Our responsibility is thus much greater than we had supposed, for it concerns mankind as a whole. If I am a worker, for instance, I may choose to join a Christian rather than a Communist trade union. And if, by that membership, I choose to signify that resignation is, after all, the attitude that best becomes a man, that man's kingdom is not upon this earth, I do not commit myself alone to that view. Resignation is my will for everyone, and my action is, in consequence, a commitment on behalf of all mankind. Or if, to take a more personal case, I decide to marry and to have children, even though this decision proceeds simply from my situation, from my passion or my desire, I am thereby committing not only myself, but humanity as a whole, to the practice of monogamy. I am thus responsible for myself and for all men, and I am creating a certain image of man as I would have him to be. In fashioning myself I fashion man.

This may enable us to understand what is meant by such terms—perhaps a little grandiloquent—as anguish, abandonment and despair. As you will soon see, it is very simple. First, what do we mean by anguish?—The existentialist frankly states that man is in anguish. His meaning is as follows: When a man commits himself to anything, fully realizing that he is not only choosing what he will be, but is thereby at the same time a legislator deciding for the whole of mankind—in such a moment a man cannot escape from the sense of complete and profound responsibility. There are many, indeed, who show no such anxiety. But we affirm that they are merely disguising their anguish or are in flight from it. Certainly, many people think that in what they are doing they commit no one but themselves to anything: and if you ask them, "What would happen if everyone did so?" they shrug their shoulders and reply, "Everyone does not do so." But in truth, one ought always to ask oneself what would happen if everyone did as one is doing; nor can one escape from that disturbing thought except by a kind of self-deception. The man who lies in self-excuse, by saying "Everyone will not do it" must be ill at ease in his conscience, for the act of lying implies the universal value which it denies. By its very disguise his anguish reveals itself. This is the anguish that Kierkegaard called "the anguish of Abraham." You know the story: An angel commanded Abraham to sacrifice his son: and obedience was obligatory, if it really was an angel who had appeared and said, "Thou, Abraham, shalt sacrifice thy son." But anyone in such a case would wonder, first, whether it was indeed an angel and secondly, whether I am really Abraham. Where are the proofs? A certain mad woman who suffered from hallucinations said that people were telephoning to her, and giving her orders. The doctor asked, "But who is it that speaks to you?" She replied: "He says it is God." And what, indeed, could prove to her that it was God? If an angel appears to me, what is the proof that it is an angel; or, if I hear voices, who can prove that they proceed from heaven and not from hell, or from my own subconsciousness or some pathological condition? Who can prove that they are really addressed to me?

Who, then, can prove that I am the proper person to impose, by my own choice, my conception of man upon mankind? I shall never find any proof whatever; there will be no sign to convince me of it. If a voice speaks to me, it is still I myself who must decide whether the voice is or is not that of an angel. If I regard a certain course of action as good, it is only I who choose to say that it is good and not bad. There is nothing to show that I am Abraham: nevertheless I also am obliged at every instant to perform actions which are examples. Everything happens to every man as though the whole human race had its eyes fixed upon what he is doing and regulated its conduct accordingly. So every man ought to say, "Am I really a man who has the right to act in such a manner that humanity regulates itself by what I do." If a man does not say that, he is dissembling his anguish. Clearly, the anguish with which we are concerned here is not one that could lead to quietism or inaction. It is anguish pure and simple, of the kind well known to all those who have borne responsibilities. When, for instance, a military leader takes upon himself the responsibility for an attack and sends a number of men to their death, he chooses to do it and at bottom he alone chooses. No doubt under a higher command, but its orders, which are more general, require interpretation by him and upon that interpretation depends the life of ten, fourteen or twenty men. In making the decision, he cannot but feel a certain anguish. All leaders know that anguish. It does not prevent their acting, on the contrary it is the very condition of their action, for the action presupposes that there is a plurality of possibilities, and in choosing one of these, they realize that it has value only because it is chosen. Now it is anguish of that kind which existentialism describes, and moreover, as we shall see, makes explicit through direct responsibility towards other men who are concerned. Far from being a screen which could separate us from action, it is a condition of action itself.

And when we speak of "abandonment"—a favorite word of Heidegger—we only mean to say that God does not exist, and that it is necessary to draw the consequences of his absence right to the end. The existentialist is strongly opposed to a certain type of secular moralism which seeks to suppress God at the least possible expense. Towards 1880, when the French professors endeavored to formulate a secular morality, they said something like this: God is a useless and costly hypothesis, so we will do without it. However, if we are to have morality, a society and a law-abiding world, it is essential that certain values should be taken seriously; they must have an *a priori* existence ascribed to them. It must be considered obligatory *a priori* to be honest, not to lie, not to beat one's wife, to bring up children and so forth; so we are going to do a little work on this subject, which will enable us to show that these values exist all the same, inscribed in an intelligible heaven although, of course, there is no God. In other word—and this is, I believe, the purport of all that we in France call radicalism—nothing will be changed if God does not exist; we shall rediscover the same norms of honesty, progress and humanity, and we shall have disposed of God as an out-of-date hypothesis which will die away quietly of itself. The existentialist, on the contrary, finds it extremely embarrassing that God does not exist, for there disappears with Him all possibility of finding values in an intelligible heaven. There can no longer be any good *a priori*, since there is no infinite and perfect consciousness to think it. It is nowhere written that "the good" exists, that one must be honest or must not lie, since we are now upon the plane where there are only men. Dostoievsky once wrote "If God did not exist, everything would be permitted;" and that, for existentialism, is the starting point. Everything is indeed permitted if God does not exist, and man is in consequence forlorn, for he cannot find anything to depend upon either within or outside himself. He discovers forthwith, that he is without excuse. For if indeed existence precedes essence, one will never be able to explain one's action by reference to a given and specific human nature; in other words, there is no determinism—man is free, man *is* freedom. Nor, on the other hand, if God does not exist, are we provided with any values or commands that could legitimize our behavior. Thus we have neither behind us, nor before us in a luminous realm of values, any means of justification or excuse.—We are left alone, without excuse. That is what I mean when I say that man is condemned to be free. Condemned, because he did not create himself, yet is nevertheless at liberty, and from the moment that he is thrown into this world he is responsible for everything he does. The existentialist does not believe in the power of passion. He will never regard a grand passion as a destructive torrent upon which a man is swept into certain actions as by fate, and which, therefore, is an excuse for them. He thinks that man is responsible for his passion. Neither will an existentialist think that a man can find help through some sign being vouchsafed upon earth for his orientation: for he thinks that the man himself interprets the sign as he chooses. He thinks that every man, without any support or help whatever, is condemned at every instant to invent man. As Ponge has written in a very fine article, "Man is the future of man." That is exactly true. Only, if one took this to mean that the future is laid up in Heaven, that God knows what it is, it would be false, for then it would no longer even be a future. If, however, it means that, whatever man may now appear to be, there is a future to be fashioned, a virgin future that awaits him—then it is a true saying. But in the present one is forsaken.

As an example by which you may the better understand this state of abandonment, I will refer to the case of a pupil of mine, who sought me out in the following circumstances. His father was quarrelling with his mother and was also inclined to be a "collaborator;" his elder brother had been killed in the German offensive of 1940 and this young man, with a sentiment somewhat primitive but generous, burned to avenge him. His mother was living alone with him, deeply afflicted by the semi-treason of his father and by the death of her eldest son, and her one consolation was in this young man. But he, at this moment, had the choice between going to England to join the Free French Forces or of staying near his mother and helping her to live. He fully realized that this woman lived only for him and that his disappearance—or perhaps his death—would plunge her into despair. He also realized that, concretely and in fact, every action he performed on his mother's behalf would be sure of effect in the sense of aiding her to live, whereas anything he did in order to go and fight would be an ambiguous action which might vanish like water into sand and serve no purpose. For instance, to set out for England he would have to wait indefinitely in a Spanish camp on the way through Spain; or, on arriving in England or in Algiers he might be put into an office to fill up forms. Consequently, he found himself confronted by two very different modes of action; the one concrete, immediate, but directed towards only one individual; and the other an action addressed to an end infinitely greater, a national collectivity, but for that very reason ambiguous—and it might be frustrated on the way. At the same time, he was hesitating between two kinds of morality; on the one side the morality of sympathy, of personal devotion and, on the other side, a morality of wider scope but of more debatable validity. He had to choose between those two.

What could help him to choose? Could the Christian doctrine? No. Christian doctrine says: Act with charity, love your neighbor, deny yourself for others, choose the way which is hardest, and so forth. But which is the harder road? To whom does one owe the more brotherly love, the patriot or the mother? Which is the more useful aim, the general one of fighting in and for the whole community, or the precise aim of helping one particular person to live? Who can give an answer to that *a priori*? No one. Nor is it given in any ethical scripture. The Kantian ethic says, Never regard another as a means, but always as an end. Very well; if I remain with my mother, I shall be regarding her as the end and not as a means: but by the same token I am in danger of treating as means those who are fighting on my behalf; and the converse is also true, that if I go to the aid of the combatants I shall be treating them as the end at the risk of treating my mother as a means.

If values are uncertain, if they are still too abstract to determine the particular, concrete case under consideration, nothing remains but to trust in our instincts. That is what this young man tried to do; and when I saw him he said, "In the end, it is feeling that counts; the direction in which it is really pushing me is the one I ought to choose. If I feel that I love my mother enough to sacrifice everything else for her—my will to be avenged, all my longings for action and adventure then I stay with her. If, on the contrary, I feel that my love for her is not enough, I go." But how does one estimate the strength of a feeling? The value of his feeling for his mother was determined precisely by the fact that he was standing by her. I may say that I love a certain friend enough to sacrifice such or such a sum of money for him, but I cannot prove that unless I have done it. I may say, "I love my mother enough to remain with her," if actually I have remained with her. I can only estimate the strength of this affection if I have performed an action by which it is defined and ratified. But if I then appeal to this affection to justify my action, I find myself drawn into a vicious circle.

Moreover, as Gide has very well said, a sentiment which is play-acting and one which is vital are two things that are hardly distinguishable one from another. To decide that I love my mother by staying beside her, and to play a comedy the upshot of which is that I do so—these are nearly the same thing. In other words, feeling is formed by the deeds that one does; therefore I cannot consult it as a guide to action. And that is to say that I can neither seek within myself for an authentic impulse to action, nor can I expect, from some ethic, formulae that will enable me to act. You may say that the youth did, at least, go to a professor to ask for advice. But if you seek counsel—from a priest, for example you have selected that priest; and at bottom you already knew, more or less, what he would advise. In other words, to choose an adviser is nevertheless to commit oneself by that choice. If you are a Christian, you will say, Consult a priest; but there are collaborationists, priests who are resisters and priests who wait for the tide to turn: which will you choose? Had this young man chosen a priest of the resistance, or one of the collaboration, he would have decided beforehand the kind of advice he was to receive. Similarly, in coming to me, he knew what advice I should give him, and I had but one reply to make. You are free, therefore choose that is to say, invent. No rule of general morality can show you what you ought to do: no signs are vouchsafed in this world.

SELECTION FROM *BEING AND NOTHINGNESS*
CHAPTER TWO: BAD FAITH

I. BAD FAITH AND FALSEHOOD

One does not undergo his bad faith; one is not infected with it; it is not a *state*. But consciousness affects itself with bad faith. There must be an original intention and a project of bad faith; this project implies a comprehension, of bad faith as such and a pre-reflective apprehension (of) consciousness as affecting itself with bad faith. It follows first that the one to whom the lie is told and the one who lies are one and the same person, which means that I must know in my capacity as deceiver the truth which is hidden from me in my capacity as the one deceived. Better yet I must know the truth very exactly *in order* to conceal it more carefully—and this not at two different moments, which at a pinch would allow us to reestablish a semblance of duality—but in the unitary structure of a single project. How then can the lie subsist if the duality which conditions it is suppressed?

To this difficulty is added another which is derived from the total translucency of consciousness. That which affects itself with bad faith must be conscious (of) its bad faith since the being of consciousness is consciousness of being. It appears then that I must, be in good faith, at least to the extent that I am conscious of my bad faith. But then this whole psychic system is annihilated. We must agree in fact that if I deliberately and cynically attempt to lie to myself, I fail completely in this undertaking; the lie falls back and collapses beneath my look; it is ruined *from behind* by the very consciousness of lying to myself which pitilessly constitutes itself well within my project as its very condition. We have here an *evanescent* phenomenon which exists only in and through its own differentiation. To be sure, these phenomena are frequent and we shall see that there is in fact an "evanescence" of bad faith, which, it is evident, vacillates continually between good faith and cynicism: Even though the existence of bad faith is very precarious, and though it belongs to the kind of psychic structures which we might call "metastable,"[1] it presents nonetheless an autonomous and durable form. It can even be the normal aspect of life for a very great number of people. A person can *live* in bad faith, which does not mean that he does not have abrupt awakenings to cynicism or to good faith, but which implies a constant and particular style of life. Our embarrassment then appears extreme since we can neither reject nor comprehend bad faith.

···

II. PATTERNS OF BAD FAITH

If we wish to get out of this difficulty, we should examine more closely the patterns of bad faith and attempt a description of them. This description will permit us perhaps to fix more exactly the conditions for the possibility of bad faith; that is, to reply to the question we raised at the outset: "What must be the being of man if he is to be capable of bad faith?"

Take the example of a woman who has consented to go out with a particular man for the first time. She knows very well the intentions which the man who is speaking to her cherishes regarding her. She knows also that it will be necessary sooner or later for her to make a decision. But she does not want to realize the urgency; she concerns herself only with what is respectful and discreet in the attitude of her companion. She does not apprehend this conduct as an attempt to achieve what we call "the first approach;" that is, she does not want to see possibilities of temporal development which his conduct presents. She restricts this behavior to what is in the present; she does not wish to read in the phrases which he addresses to her anything other than their explicit meaning. If he says to her, "I find you so attractive!" she disarms this phrase of its sexual background; she attaches to the conversation and to the behavior of the speaker, the immediate meanings, which she imagines as objective qualities. The man who is speaking to her appears to her sincere and respectful as the table is round or square, as the wall coloring is blue or gray. The qualities thus attached to the person she is listening to are in this way fixed in a permanence like that of things, which is no other than the projection of the strict present of the qualities into the temporal flux. This is because she does not quite know what she wants. She is profoundly aware of the desire which she inspires, but the desire cruel and naked would humiliate and horrify her. Yet she would find no charm in a respect which would be only respect. In order to satisfy her, there must be a feeling which is addressed wholly to her *personality*—*i.e.*, to her full freedom—and which would be a recognition of her freedom. But at the same time this feeling must be wholly desire; that is, it must address itself to her body as object. This time then she refuses to apprehend the desire for what it is; she does not even give it a name; she recognizes it only to the extent that it transcends itself toward admiration, esteem, respect and that it is wholly absorbed in the more refined forms which it produces, to the extent of no longer figuring anymore as a sort of warmth and density. But then suppose he takes her hand. This act of her companion risks changing the situation by calling for an immediate decision. To leave the hand there is to consent in herself to flirt, to engage herself. To withdraw it is to break the troubled and unstable harmony which gives the hour its charm. The aim is to postpone the moment of decision as long as possible. We know what happens next; the young woman leaves her hand there, but she *does not notice* that she is leaving it. She does not notice because it happens by chance that she is at this moment all intellect. She draws her companion up to the most lofty regions of sentimental speculation; she speaks of Life, of her life, she shows herself in her essential aspect—a personality, a consciousness. And during this time the divorce of the body from the soul is accomplished; the hand rests inert between the warm hands of her companion—neither consenting nor resisting—a thing.

We shall say that this woman is in bad faith. But we see immediately that she uses various procedures in order to maintain herself in this bad faith. She has disarmed the actions of her companion by reducing them to being only what they are; that is, to existing in the mode of the in-itself. But she permits herself to enjoy his desire, to the extent that she will apprehend it as not being what it is, will recognize its transcendence. Finally while sensing profoundly the presence of her own body—to the degree of being disturbed perhaps—she realizes herself as *not being* her own body, and she contemplates it as though from above as a passive object to which events can *happen* but which can neither provoke them nor avoid them because all its possibilities are outside of it. What unity do we find in these various aspects of bad faith? It is a certain art of forming contradictory concepts which unite in themselves both an idea and the negation of that idea. The basic concept which is thus engendered, utilizes the double property of the human being, who is at once a *facticity* and a *transcendence*. These two aspects of human reality are and ought to be capable of a valid coordination. But bad faith does not wish either to coordinate them nor to surmount them in a synthesis. Bad faith seeks to affirm their identity while preserving their differences. It must affirm facticity as *being* transcendence and transcendence as *being* facticity, in such a way that at the instant when a person apprehends the one, he can find himself abruptly faced with the other.

•••

If man is what he is, bad faith is for ever impossible and candor ceases to be his ideal and becomes instead his being. But is man what he is? And more generally, how can he *be* what he is when he exists as consciousness of being? If candor or sincerity is a universal value, it is evident that the maxim "one must be what one is" does not serve solely as a regulating principle for judgments and concepts by which I express what I am. It posits not merely an ideal of knowing but an ideal of *being*; it proposes for us an absolute equivalence of being with itself as a prototype of being. In this sense it is necessary that *we make ourselves* what we are. But what *are we* then if we have the constant obligation to make ourselves what we are, if our mode of being is having the obligation to be what we are?

Let us consider this waiter in the café. His movement is quick and forward, a little too precise, a little too rapid. He comes toward the patrons with a step a little too quick. He bends forward a little too eagerly; his voice, his eyes express an interest a little too solicitous for the order of the customer. Finally there he returns, trying to imitate in his walk the inflexible stiffness of some kind of automaton while carrying his tray with the recklessness of a tight-rope-walker by putting it in a perpetually unstable, perpetually broken equilibrium which he perpetually reestablishes by a light movement of the arm and hand. All his behavior seems to us a game. He applies himself to chaining his movements as if they were mechanisms, the one regulating the other; his gestures and even his voice seem to be mechanisms; he gives himself the quickness and pitiless rapidity of things. He is playing, he is amusing himself. But what is he playing? We need not watch long before we can explain it: he is playing *at being* a waiter in a café. There is nothing there to surprise us. The game is a kind of marking out and investigation. The child plays with his body in order to explore it, to take inventory of it; the waiter in the café plays with his condition in order to *realize* it. This obligation is not different from that which is imposed on all tradesmen. Their condition is wholly one of ceremony. The public demands of them that they realize it as a ceremony; there is the dance of the grocer, of the tailor, of the auctioneer, by which they endeavour to persuade their clientele that they are nothing but a grocer, an auctioneer, a tailor. A grocer who dreams is offensive to the buyer, because such a grocer is not wholly a grocer. Society demands that he limit himself to his function as a grocer, just as the soldier at attention makes himself into a soldier-thing with a direct regard which does not see at all, which is no longer meant to see, since it is the rule and not the interest of the moment which determines the point he must fix his eyes on (the sight "fixed at ten paces"). There are indeed many precautions to imprison a man in what he is, as if we lived in perpetual fear that he might escape from it, that he might break away and suddenly elude his condition.

In a parallel situation, from within, the waiter in the café can not be immediately a café waiter in the sense that this inkwell *is* an inkwell, or the glass is a glass. It is by no means that he can not form reflective judgments or concepts concerning his condition. He knows well what it "means:" the obligation of getting up at five o'clock, of sweeping the floor of the shop before the restaurant opens, of starting the coffee pot going, etc. He knows the rights which it allows: the right to the tips, the right to belong to a union, etc. But all these concepts, all these judgments refer to the transcendent. It is a matter of abstract possibilities, of rights and duties conferred on a "person possessing rights." And it is precisely this person *who I have to be* (if I am the waiter in question) and who I am not. It is not that I do not wish to be this person or that I want this person to be different. But rather there is no common measure between his being and mine. It is a "representation" for others and for myself, which means that I can be he only in *representation*. But if I represent myself as him, I am not he; I am separated from him as the object from the subject, separated *by nothing*, but this nothing isolates me from him. I can not be he, I can only play *at being* him; that is, imagine to myself that I am he. And thereby I affect him with nothingness. In vain do I fulfill the functions of a café waiter. I can be he only in the neutralized mode, as the actor is Hamlet, by mechanically making the *typical gestures* of my state and by aiming at myself as an imaginary café waiter through those gestures taken as an "analogue."[2] What I attempt to realize is a being-in-itself of the café waiter, as if it were not just in my power to confer their value and their urgency upon my duties and the rights of my position, as if it were not my free choice to get up each morning at five o'clock or to remain in bed, even though it meant getting fired. As if from the very fact that I sustain this role in existence I did not transcend it on every side, as if I did not constitute myself as one *beyond* my condition. Yet there is no doubt that I *am* in a sense a café waiter—otherwise could I not just as well call myself a diplomat or a reporter? But if I am one, this can not be in the mode of being in-itself. I am a waiter in the mode of *being what I am not*.

Furthermore we are dealing with more than mere social positions; I am never any one of my attitudes, any one of my actions. The good speaker is the one who *plays* at speaking, because he can not *be speaking*. The attentive pupil who wishes to *be* attentive, his eyes riveted on the teacher, his ears open wide, so exhausts himself in playing the attentive role that he ends up by no longer hearing anything. Perpetually absent to my body, to my acts, I am despite myself that "divine absence" of which Valéry speaks. I can not say either that I *am* here or that I *am* not here, in the sense that we say "that box of matches *is* on the table;" this would be to confuse my "being-in-the-world" with a "being-in the midst of the world." Nor that I *am* standing, nor that I *am* seated; this would be to confuse my body with the idiosyncratic totality of which it is only one of the structures. On all sides I escape being and yet—I am.

But take a mode of being which concerns only myself: I am sad. One might think that surely I am the sadness in the mode of being what I am. What is the sadness, however, if not the intentional unity which comes to reassemble and animate the totality of my conduct? It is the meaning of this dull look with which I view the world, of my bowed shoulders, of my lowered head, of the listlessness in my whole body. But at the very moment when I adopt each of these attitudes, do I not know that I shall not be able to hold on to it? Let a stranger suddenly appear and I will lift up my head, I will assume a lively cheerfulness. What will remain of my sadness except that I obligingly promise it an appointment for later after the departure of the visitor? Moreover is not this sadness itself a conduct? Is it not consciousness which affects itself with sadness as a magical recourse against a situation too urgent?[3] And in this case even, should we not say that being sad means first to make oneself sad? That may be, someone will say, but after all doesn't giving oneself the being of sadness mean to receive-this being? It makes no difference from where I receive it. The fact is that a consciousness which affects itself with sadness *is* sad precisely for this reason. But it is difficult to comprehend the nature of consciousness; the being-sad is not a ready-made being which I give to myself as I can give this book to my friend. I do not possess the property of *affecting myself with being*. If I make myself sad, I must continue to make myself sad from beginning to end. I can not treat my sadness as an impulse finally achieved and put it on file without recreating it, nor can I carry it in the manner of an inert body which continues its movement after the initial shock. There is no inertia in consciousness. If I make myself sad, it is because I *am* not sad—the being of the sadness escapes me by and in the very act by which I affect myself with it. The being-in-itself of sadness perpetually haunts my consciousness (of) being sad, but it is as a value which I can not realize; it stands as a regulative meaning of my sadness, not as its constitutive modality.

NOTES

1. Sartre's own word, meaning subject to sudden changes or transitions. Tr.
2. Cf. *L'Imaginaire*. Conclusion.
3. *Esquisse d'une théorie des émotions.* Herman Paul. In English. *The Emotions. Outline of a Theory.* Philosophical Library. 1948.

DARWINISM AND THE
SELFISH GENE

By Richard Dawkins

Intelligent life on a planet comes of age when it first works out the reason for its own existence. If superior creatures from space ever visit earth, the first question they will ask, in order to assess the level of our civilization, is: 'Have they discovered evolution yet?' Living organisms had existed on earth, without ever knowing why, for over three thousand million years before the truth finally dawned on one of them. His name was Charles Darwin. To be fair, others had had inklings of the truth, but it was Darwin who first put together a coherent and tenable account of why we exist. Darwin made it possible for us to give a sensible answer to the curious child whose question heads this chapter. We no longer have to resort to superstition when faced with the deep problems: Is there a meaning to life? What are we for? What is man? After posing the last of these questions, the eminent zoologist G. G. Simpson put it thus: "The point I want to make now is that all attempts to answer that question before 1859 are worthless and that we will be better off if we ignore them completely."

Today the theory of evolution is about as much open to doubt as the theory that the earth goes round the sun, but the full implications of Darwin's revolution have yet to be widely realized. Zoology is still a minority subject in universities, and even those who choose to study it often make their decision without appreciating its profound philosophical significance. Philosophy and the subjects known as 'humanities' are still taught almost as if Darwin had never lived. No doubt this will change in time. In any case, this book is not intended as a general advocacy of Darwinism. Instead, it will explore the consequences of the evolution theory for a particular issue. My purpose is to examine the biology of selfishness and altruism.

Apart from its academic interest, the human importance of this subject is obvious. It touches every aspect of our social lives, our loving and hating, fighting and cooperating, giving and stealing, our greed and our generosity. These are claims that could have been made for Lorenz's *On Aggression*, Ardrey's *The Social Contract*, and Eibl-Eibesfeldt's *Love and Hate*. The trouble with these books is that their authors got it totally and utterly wrong. They got it wrong because they misunderstood how evolution works. They made the erroneous assumption that the important thing in evolution is the good of the *species* (or the group) rather than the good of the individual (or the gene). It is ironic that Ashley Montagu should criticize Lorenz as a 'direct descendant of the "nature red in tooth and claw" thinkers of the nineteenth century....' As I understand Lorenz's view of evolution, he would be very much at one with Montagu in rejecting the implications of Tennyson's famous phrase. Unlike both of them, I think 'nature red in tooth and claw' sums up our modern understanding of natural selection admirably.

Before beginning on my argument itself, I want to explain briefly what sort of an argument it is, and what sort of an argument it is not. If we were told that a man had lived a long and prosperous life in the world of Chicago gangsters, we would be entitled to make some guesses as to the sort of man he was. We might expect that he would have qualities such as toughness, a quick trigger finger, and the ability to attract loyal friends. These would not be infallible deductions, but you can make some inferences about a man's character if you know something about the conditions in which he has survived and prospered. The argument of this book is that we, and all other animals, are machines created by our genes. Like successful Chicago gangsters, our genes have survived, in some cases for millions of years, in a highly competitive world. This entitles us to expect certain qualities in our genes. I shall argue that a predominant quality to be expected in a successful gene is ruthless selfishness. This gene selfishness will usually give rise to selfishness in individual behaviour. However, as we shall see, there are special circumstances in which a gene can achieve its own selfish goals best by fostering a limited form of altruism at the level of individual animals, 'Special' and 'limited' are important words in the last sentence. Much as we might wish to believe otherwise, universal love and the welfare of the species as a whole are concepts that simply do not make evolutionary sense.

This brings me to the first point I want to make about what this book is *not*. I am not advocating a morality based on evolution. I am saying how things have evolved. I am not saying how we humans morally ought to behave. I stress this, because I know I am in danger of being misunderstood by those people, all too numerous, who cannot distinguish a statement of belief in what is the case from an advocacy of what ought to be the case. My own feeling is that a human society based simply on the gene's law of universal ruthless selfishness would be a very nasty society in which to live. But unfortunately, however much we may deplore something, it does not stop it being true. This book is mainly intended to be interesting, but if you would extract a moral from it, read it as a warning. Be warned that if you wish, as I do, to build a society in which individuals cooperate generously and unselfishly towards a common good, you can expect little help from biological nature. Let us try to *teach* generosity and altruism, because we are born selfish. Let us understand what our own selfish genes are up to, because we may then at least have the chance to upset their designs, something that no other species has ever aspired to.

As a corollary to these remarks about teaching, it is a fallacy—incidentally a very common one—to suppose that genetically inherited traits are by definition fixed and unmodifiable. Our genes may instruct us to be selfish, but we are not necessarily compelled to obey them all our lives. It may just be more difficult to learn altruism than it would be if we were genetically programmed to be altruistic. Among animals, man is uniquely dominated by culture, by influences learned and handed down. Some would say that culture is so important that genes, whether selfish or not, are virtually irrelevant to the understanding of human nature. Others would disagree. It all depends where you stand in the debate over 'nature versus nurture' as determinants of human attributes. This brings me to the second thing this book is not: it is not an advocacy of one position or another in the nature/nurture controversy. Naturally I have an opinion on this, but I am not going to express it, except insofar as it is implicit in the view of culture that I shall present in the final chapter. If genes really turn out to be totally irrelevant to the determination of modern human behaviour, if we really are unique among animals in this respect, it is, at the very least, still interesting to inquire about the rule to which we have so recently become the exception. And if our species is not so exceptional as we might like to think, it is even more important that we should study the rule.

The third thing this book is not is a descriptive account of the detailed behaviour of man or of any other particular animal species. I shall use factual details only as illustrative examples. I shall not be saying: "If you look at the behaviour of baboons you will find it to be selfish; therefore the chances are that human behaviour is selfish also." The logic of my 'Chicago gangster' argument is quite different. It is this: Humans and baboons have evolved by natural selection. If you look at the way natural selection works, it seems to follow that anything that has evolved by natural selection should be selfish. Therefore we must expect that when we go and look at the behaviour of baboons, humans, and all other living creatures, we shall find it to be selfish. If we find that our expectation is wrong, if we observe that human behaviour is truly altruistic, then we shall be faced with something puzzling, something that needs explaining.

Before going any further, we need a definition. An entity, such as a baboon, is said to be altruistic if it behaves in such a way as to increase another such entity's welfare at the expense of its own. Selfish behaviour has exactly the opposite effect. 'Welfare' is defined as 'chances of survival', even if the effect on actual life and death prospects is so small as to *seem* negligible. One of the surprising consequences of the modern version of the Darwinian theory is that apparently trivial tiny influences on survival probability can have a major impact on evolution. This is because of the enormous time available for such influences to make themselves felt.

It is important to realize that the above definitions of altruism and selfishness are *behavioural*, not subjective. I am not concerned here with the psychology of motives. I am not going to argue about whether people who behave altruistically are 'really' doing it for secret or subconscious selfish motives. Maybe they are and maybe they aren't, and maybe we can never know, but in any case that is not what this book is about. My definition is concerned only with whether the *effect* of an act is to lower or raise the survival prospects of the presumed altruist and the survival prospects of the presumed beneficiary.

It is a very complicated business to demonstrate the effects of behaviour on long-term survival prospects. In practice, when we apply the definition to real behaviour, we must qualify it with the word 'apparently'. An apparently altruistic act is one that looks, superficially, as if it must tend to make the altruist more likely (however slightly) to die, and the recipient more likely to survive. It often turns out on closer inspection that acts of apparent altruism are really selfishness in disguise. Once again, I do not mean that the underlying motives are secretly selfish, but that the real effects of the act on survival prospects are the reverse of what we originally thought.

I am going to give some examples of apparently selfish and apparently altruistic behaviour. It is difficult to suppress subjective habits of thought when we are dealing with our own species, so I shall choose examples from other animals instead. First some miscellaneous examples of selfish behaviour by individual animals.

Blackheaded gulls nest in large colonies, the nests being only a few feet apart. When the chicks first hatch out they are small and defenceless and easy to swallow. It is quite common for a gull to wait until a neighbour's back is turned, perhaps while it is away fishing, and then pounce on one of the neighbour's chicks and swallow it whole. It thereby obtains a good nutritious meal, without having to go to the trouble of catching a fish, and without having to leave its own nest unprotected.

More well known is the macabre cannibalism of female praying mantises. Mantises are large carnivorous insects. They normally eat smaller insects such as flies, but they will attack almost anything that moves. When they mate, the male cautiously creeps up on the female, mounts her, and copulates. If the female gets the chance, she will eat him, beginning by biting his head off, either as the male is approaching, or immediately after he mounts, or after they separate. It might seem most sensible for her to wait until copulation is over before she starts to eat him. But the loss of the head does not seem to throw the rest of the male's body off its sexual stride. Indeed, since the insect head is the seat of some inhibitory nerve centres, it is possible that the female improves the male's sexual performance by eating his head. If so, this is an added benefit. The primary one is that she obtains a good meal.

The word 'selfish' may seem an understatement for such extreme cases as cannibalism, although these fit well with our definition. Perhaps we can sympathize more directly with the reported cowardly behaviour of emperor penguins in the Antarctic. They have been seen standing on the brink of the water, hesitating before diving in, because of the danger of being eaten by seals. If only one of them would dive in, the rest would know whether there was a seal there or not. Naturally nobody wants to be the guinea pig, so they wait, and sometimes even try to push each other in.

More ordinarily, selfish behaviour may simply consist of refusing to share some valued resource such as food, territory, or sexual partners. Now for some examples of apparently altruistic behaviour.

The stinging behaviour of worker bees is a very effective defence against honey robbers. But the bees who do the stinging are kamikaze fighters. In the act of stinging, vital internal organs are usually torn out of the body, and the bee dies soon afterwards. Her suicide mission may have saved the colony's vital food stocks, but she herself is not around to reap the benefits. By our definition this is an altruistic behavioural act. Remember that we are not talking about conscious motives. They may or may not be present, both here and in the selfishness examples, but they are irrelevant to our definition.

Laying down one's life for one's friends is obviously altruistic, but so also is taking a slight risk for them. Many small birds, when they see a flying predator such as a hawk, give a characteristic 'alarm call', upon which the whole flock takes appropriate evasive action. There is indirect evidence that the bird who gives the alarm call puts itself in special danger, because it attracts the predator's attention particularly to itself. This is only a slight additional risk, but it nevertheless seems, at least at first sight, to qualify as an altruistic act by our definition.

The commonest and most conspicuous acts of animal altruism are done by parents, especially mothers, towards their children. They may incubate them, either in nests or in their own bodies, feed them at enormous cost to themselves, and take great risks in protecting them from predators. To take just one particular example, many ground-nesting birds perform a so-called 'distraction display' when a predator such as a fox approaches. The parent bird limps away from the nest, holding out one wing as though it were broken. The predator, sensing easy prey, is lured away from the nest containing the chicks. Finally the parent bird gives up its pretence and leaps into the air just in time to escape the fox's jaws. It has probably saved the life of its nestlings, but at some risk to itself.

I am not trying to make a point by telling stories. Chosen examples are never serious evidence for any worthwhile generalization. These stories are simply intended as illustrations of what I mean by altruistic and selfish behaviour at the level of individuals. This book will show how both individual selfishness and individual altruism are explained by the fundamental law that I am calling *gene selfishness*. But first I must deal with a particular erroneous explanation for altruism, because it is widely known, and even widely taught in schools.

This explanation is based on the misconception that I have already mentioned, that living creatures evolve to do things 'for the good of the species' or 'for the good of the group'. It is easy to see how this idea got its start in biology. Much of an animal's life is devoted to reproduction, and most of the acts of altruistic self-sacrifice that are observed in nature are performed by parents towards their young. 'Perpetuation of the species' is a common euphemism for reproduction, and it is undeniably a *consequence* of reproduction. It requires only a slight over-stretching of logic to deduce that the 'function' of reproduction is 'to' perpetuate the species. From this it is but a further short false step to conclude that animals will in general behave in such a way as to favour the perpetuation of the species. Altruism towards fellow members of the species seems to follow.

This line of thought can be put into vaguely Darwinian terms. Evolution works by natural selection, and natural selection means the differential survival of the 'fittest'. But are we talking about the fittest individuals, the fittest races, the fittest species, or what? For some purposes this does not greatly matter, but when we are talking about altruism it is obviously crucial. If it is species that are competing in what Darwin called the struggle for existence, the individual seems best regarded as a pawn in the game, to be sacrificed when the greater interest of the species as a whole requires it. To put it in a slightly more respectable way, a group, such as a species or a population within a species, whose individual members are prepared to sacrifice themselves for the welfare of the group, may be less likely to go extinct than a rival group whose individual members place their own selfish interests first. Therefore the world becomes populated mainly by groups consisting of self-sacrificing individuals. This is the theory of 'group selection', long assumed to be true by biologists not familiar with the details of evolutionary theory, brought out into the open in a famous book by V. C. Wynne-Edwards, and popularized by Robert Ardrey in *The Social Contract*. The orthodox alternative is normally called 'individual selection', although I personally prefer to speak of gene selection.

The quick answer of the 'individual selectionist' to the argument just put might go something like this. Even in the group of altruists, there will almost certainly be a dissenting minority who refuse to make any sacrifice. If there is just one selfish rebel, prepared to exploit the altruism of the rest, then he, by definition, is more likely than they are to survive and have children. Each of these children will tend to inherit his selfish traits. After several generations of this natural selection, the 'altruistic group' will be over-run by selfish individuals, and will be indistinguishable from the selfish group. Even if we grant the improbable chance existence initially of pure altruistic groups without any rebels, it is very difficult to see what is to stop selfish individuals migrating in from neighbouring selfish groups, and, by inter-marriage, contaminating the purity of the altruistic groups.

The individual-selectionist would admit that groups do indeed die out, and that whether or not a group goes extinct may be influenced by the behaviour of the individuals in that group. He might even admit that *if only* the individuals in a group had the gift of foresight they could see that in the long run their own best interests lay in restraining their selfish greed, to prevent the destruction of the whole group. How many times must this have been said in recent years to the working people of Britain? But group extinction is a slow process compared with the rapid cut and thrust of individual competition. Even while the group is going slowly and inexorably downhill, selfish individuals prosper in the short term at the expense of altruists. The citizens of Britain may or may not be blessed with foresight, but evolution is blind to the future.

Although the group-selection theory now commands little support within the ranks of those professional biologists who understand evolution, it does have great intuitive appeal. Successive generations of zoology students are surprised, when they come up from school, to find that it is not the orthodox point of view. For this they are hardly to be blamed, for in the *Nuffield Biology Teachers' Guide*, written for advanced level biology school teachers in Britain, we find the following: 'In higher animals, behaviour may take the form of individual suicide to ensure the survival of the species.' The anonymous author of this guide is blissfully ignorant of the fact that he has said something controversial. In this respect he is in Nobel Prize-winning company. Konrad Lorenz, in *On Aggression*, speaks of the 'species preserving' functions of aggressive behaviour, one of these functions being to make sure that only the fittest individuals are allowed to breed. This is a gem of a circular argument, but the point I am making here is that the group selection idea is so deeply ingrained that Lorenz, like the author of the *Nuffield Guide*, evidently did not realize that his statements contravened orthodox Darwinian theory.

I recently heard a delightful example of the same thing on an otherwise excellent B.B.C. television programme about Australian spiders. The 'expert' on the programme observed that the vast majority of baby spiders end up as prey for other species, and she then went on to say: 'Perhaps this is the real purpose of their existence, as only a few need to survive in order for the species to be preserved'!

Robert Ardrey, in *The Social Contract*, used the group-selection theory to account for the whole of social order in general. He clearly sees man as a species that has strayed from the path of animal righteousness. Ardrey at least did his homework. His decision to disagree with orthodox theory was a conscious one, and for this he deserves credit.

Perhaps one reason for the great appeal, of the group-selection theory is that it is thoroughly in tune with the moral and political ideals that most of us share. We may frequently behave selfishly as individuals, but in our more idealistic moments we honour and admire those who put the welfare of others first. We get a bit muddled over how widely we want to interpret the word 'others', though. Often altruism within a group goes with selfishness between groups. This is a basis of trade unionism. At another level the nation is a major beneficiary of our altruistic self-sacrifice, and young men are expected to die as individuals for the greater glory of their country as a whole. Moreover, they are encouraged to kill other individuals about whom nothing is known except that they belong to a different nation. (Curiously, peace-time appeals for individuals to make some small sacrifice in the rate at which they increase their standard of living seem to be less effective than war-time appeals for individuals to lay down their lives.)

Recently there has been a reaction against racialism and patriotism, and a tendency to substitute the whole human species as the object of our fellow feeling. This humanist broadening of the target of our altruism has an interesting corollary, which again seems to buttress the 'good of the species' idea in evolution. The politically liberal, who are normally the most convinced spokesmen of the species ethic, now often have the greatest scorn for those who have gone a little further in widening their altruism, so that it includes other species. If I say that I am more interested in preventing the slaughter of large whales than I am in improving housing conditions for people, I am likely to shock some of my friends.

The feeling that members of one's own species deserve special moral consideration as compared with members of other species is old and deep. Killing people outside war is the most seriously-regarded crime ordinarily committed. The only thing more strongly forbidden by our culture is eating people (even if they are already dead). We enjoy eating members of other species, however. Many of us shrink from judicial execution of even the most horrible human criminals, while we cheerfully countenance the shooting without trial of fairly mild animal pests. Indeed we kill members of other harmless species as a means of recreation and amusement. A human foetus, with no more human feeling than an amoeba, enjoys a reverence and legal protection far in excess of those granted to an adult chimpanzee. Yet the chimp feels and thinks and—according to recent experimental evidence—may even be capable of learning a form of human language. The foetus belongs to our own species, and is instantly accorded special privileges and rights because of it. Whether the ethic of 'speciesism', to use Richard Ryder's term, can be put on a logical footing any more sound than that of 'racism', I do not know. What I do know is that it has no proper basis in evolutionary biology.

The muddle in human ethics over the level at which altruism is desirable—family, nation, race, species, or all living things—is mirrored by a parallel muddle in biology over the level at which altruism is to be expected according to the theory of evolution. Even the group-selectionist would not be surprised to find members of rival groups being nasty to each other: in this way, like trade unionists or soldiers, they are favouring their own group in the struggle for limited resources. But then it is worth asking how the group-selectionist decides *which* level is the important one. If selection goes on between groups within a species, and between species, why should it not also go on between larger groupings? Species are grouped together into genera, genera into orders, and orders into classes. Lions and antelopes are both members of the class Mammalia, as are we. Should we then not expect lions to refrain from killing antelopes, 'for the good of the mammals'? Surely they should hunt birds or reptiles instead, in order to prevent the extinction of the class. But then, what of the need to perpetuate the whole phylum of vertebrates?

It is all very well for me to argue by *reductio ad absurdum*, and to point to the difficulties of the group-selection theory, but the apparent existence of individual altruism still has to be explained. Ardrey goes so far as to say that group selection is the only possible explanation for behaviour such as 'stotting' in Thomson's gazelles. This vigorous and conspicuous leaping in front of a predator is analogous to bird alarm calls, in that it seems to warn companions of danger while apparently calling the predator's attention to the stotter himself. We have a responsibility to explain slotting Tommies and all similar phenomena, and this is something I am going to face in later chapters.

Before that I must argue for my belief that the best way to look at evolution is in terms of selection occurring at the lowest level of all. In this belief I am heavily influenced by G. C. Williams's great book

Adaptation and Natural Selection. The central idea I shall make use of was foreshadowed by A. Weismann in pre-gene days at the turn of the century—his doctrine of the 'continuity of the germ-plasm'. I shall argue that the fundamental unit of selection, and therefore of self-interest, is not the species, nor the group, nor even, strictly, the individual. It is the gene, the unit of heredity. To some biologists this may sound at first like an extreme view. I hope when they see in what sense I mean it they will agree that it is, in substance, orthodox, even if it is expressed in an unfamiliar way. The argument takes time to develop, and we must begin at the beginning, with the very origin of life itself.

GLOSSARY

By Stuart Brown

absolutism: (a) In political philosophy, an 'absolute' government is one whose rule is subject to no (human) restraint, for instance by a parliament or a constitution, and answerable (if at all) only to God. Contrasted with 'bounded' government (q.v.). (b) Elsewhere 'absolutism' is contrasted with some form of 'relativism'. For instance an absolutist about space will hold that it exists independently of matter.

a posteriori: what is knowable, if at all, through experience. Contrasted with 'a priori' (q.v.).

a priori: what is known, if at all, independently of experience. Contrasted with 'a posteriori' (q.v.).

bounded government: bounded government is government that is limited by human laws. Belief in bounded government is contrasted with 'absolutism' (q.v.).

Cabala: literally 'tradition', specifically an esoteric tradition of interpreting Scripture supposed to have been handed down in secret by Moses to certain select disciples and by them in turn. There was considerable Christian interest in the Cabala during the Renaissance and, though it was discouraged by the Catholic Reformation, this continued to be expressed by Neoplatonists in Protestant countries into the eighteenth century.

Calvinism: the theology of the French Protestant theologian John Calvin (1509–64) which was influential in England in the seventeenth century and in Scotland throughout the period covered by this volume. Calvin subscribed to an austere doctrine of predestination according to which the future salvation or damnation of any individual soul has been predetermined for all time. The Calvinistic emphasis on the corruption of human nature led to a stress on faith rather than fallible human reason. It was opposed by those who believed in natural theology or rational religion.

Cartesianism: the doctrines associated with the philosophy of René Descartes: especially, in the context of this volume, the belief that events in the natural world are determined by invariant mechanical laws. Descartes claimed to know a priori that the essence of matter consisted in extension and Cartesianism was associated with a physics that was partly a priori. Descartes's radical separation of the material world from that of the mind and his endorsement of innate ideas encouraged some to interpret him as sympathetic to Christian Platonism.

cause: a cause has often been understood to mean that, in the presence of which some event *must* occur. If, however, this means that there would be a contradiction in supposing that the cause occurred but not its effect, it seems there are few causes in this sense. As the occasionalists (q.v.) recognized it was only in the case of God willing something to happen that there would be a contradiction (since God is by definition omnipotent) in supposing it not to happen. From this it seems as if a natural cause is nothing more than a phenomenon that is regularly found to be followed by events of the kind in question. Empiricist (q.v.) accounts of causation stress this regularity or, in Hume's phrase, 'constant conjunction.'

certainty, moral: what is morally certain had the highest degree of probability and is certain for the purposes of practical life. It is distinguished from theoretical certainty or *scientia*. (q.v.).

common notions: these are notions that are universally imprinted on humans and make possible a universal consent to certain propositions. The existence of such notions was a matter of controversy during the period covered by this volume. See 'innate ideas'.

consensus gentium: a mode of argument for the truth of a proposition from the existence of universal consent to it. This mode of argument was attractive to those who believed in common notions (q.v.).

constructivism: opposed, for example to realism in mathematics, those who hold this view argue that truths are not so much discovered as constructed. This view was advocated by Vico.

contract, original: the obligation to obey the ruler was supposed by some theorists to be based upon a contract made at the founding of political society. In return for the promise of the people to obey the sovereign, the ruler undertook for his part to protect the people and their rights.

contradiction, principle of: every self-contradictory statement must be false and its denial must be true.

corpuscular philosophy: the view, associated with Gassendi, Boyle and Locke, that the world is made up of tiny particles of matter.

correspondence theory of truth: the theory that a proposition is true if, and only if, there is some (corresponding) state of affairs or set of facts in the objective world in virtue of which it is so.

deism: a point of view embracing belief in a Creator but hostile to revealed religion. Deists characteristically disbelieved in miracles and tended to be anti-clerical. Though they sometimes believed in a general Providence and even in a deity who punishes the wicked and rewards the virtuous, they did not regard the sacraments as necessary to salvation.

demonstration: a logical term for an argument whose conclusion follows from its premisses, i.e. where it would be inconsistent to accept the premisses and reject the conclusion. Demonstrations, so defined, have been admired as the strongest possible form of argument. Deductive logic is concerned with valid forms of demonstrative or deductive inference.

deontology: the science of duty, usually associated with the view that we are bound by certain absolute duties, which we can know, and which are not affected by circumstances.

design, argument from: an argument based upon the orderliness observed in nature which is intended to establish the existence of an intelligent and purposive cause of the natural world. This argument became very popular in the eighteenth century, though it was severely criticized in Hume's *Dialogues Concerning Natural Religion*.

determinism: the view that every event (including every human action) has a cause and that there is no chance in the universe. Determinists usually interpret the existence of a cause as meaning the event could not fail to occur and that human actions, when caused, are not 'free'. Some determinists, however, have claimed not to deny free will and have maintained, on the contrary, that the absence of a cause of a human action would bring free will into question in a way that the presence of a cause does not.

divine right (of kings): an absolutist (q.v.) doctrine according to which kings are appointed by God and are not answerable to their people for their actions.

eclecticism: a term used of the tendency of some philosophers to take elements from several different sects or schools rather than adhere consistently to a single one. Eclectics are usually liberal and anti-sectarian.

egoism, ethical: the view that what I morally ought to do is to promote my own interests.

egoism, psychological: a theory according to which individuals are motivated to action only by concern for their own interests.

egoism, rational: the view that I only have good reason to do those actions which promote my own interests.

emanation: a characteristically Neoplatonic (q.v.) doctrine in which the world is conceived as a kind of over-flowing of the divine nature. Everything that is of the spirit, comes from the divine light, thus emanates from God. Evil is simply the privation of this and so is present in anything which is not pure divinity. Evil and good, darkness and light, matter and spirit, passivity and activity, are all treated in analogous ways. So the material world, though it is fundamentally spirit-like, was conceived as having fallen into a torpid state from which, according to some, it will eventually be restored to its true nature.

empiricism: the view that all our knowledge about the nature of things is derived from experience. Usually contrasted with rationalism (q.v.).

Enlightenment: the name given to a period in European history which was marked by an emphasis on reason and a distrust of mystery and authority. Though there were many connections across national boundaries, the circumstances of the intellectual élite in each country were different and so what may be true of the Enlightenment in one country may not be in another.

epistemology: theory of knowledge. Concern with the nature of human knowledge and its limitations became, as a result of Locke's *Essay,* a major concern of eighteenth-century philosophy.

fideism: from the Latin word for 'faith', this term is used to refer to the view that there is no basis in reason for religion and that its basis can only be that of faith.

final cause: that for the sake of which something is done. In that sense the final cause or 'end' of taking exercise may be health. The term goes back to Aristotle. According to the mechanical philosophy final causes were not to be used in physics.

form, substantial: a scholastic (q.v.) term deriving ultimately from Aristotle. The substantial form of a thing is what makes it the kind of thing it is. Any change in the state of a thing which is not caused externally is referred to its substantial form.

general will: a term of French social thought, signifying the collective will of society or the will of an individual insofar as that person is public-spirited. The term is probably theological in origin, deriving from a contrast between God's general will (which results, for example in the laws of nature) and His particular wills (on specified occasions, for example in performing a miracle). As applied to individual humans a general will contrasts with a self-regarding 'particular will.'

gnoseology: another term for epistemology (q.v.).

hedonism: the view that pleasure is the greatest good.

hedonism, psychological: a theory according to which human beings are primarily motivated by the prospect of their own pleasure.

humanism (Renaissance): the movement is associated with the *studia humanitatis* and with promoting the 'humanities' through the recovery and establishment of the classical texts—particularly of ancient Roman but also of Greek authors. The humanities, so understood, included grammar, rhetoric, poetics, moral philosophy and history. Humanists were opposed to the scholastic curricula which predominated in universities until the end of the seventeenth century. But their ideas influenced the education of the aristocratic laity and remained influential throughout our period.

humanism (Erasmian): usually associated with the project of applying humanistic disciplines to the texts of the Bible. This was opposed, on the one hand, to the authoritarian view that the Bible meant what the Church determined that it meant and, on the other hand, to the subjective interpretations of 'enthusiasts'. Erasmian humanism may be seen as paving the way for the more rational approaches to religion that emerged in the seventeenth century.

idea: the term originates with Plato for whom the ideas or forms constituted a transcendent realm of archetypes. Christian Platonists located these ideas in the mind of God. Descartes extended this use to allow that the human mind is also furnished with 'ideas' and the use of the term to refer to what is before our minds when we think, imagine, dream, etc., became established in the writings of later philosophers, such as Locke and Berkeley.

idealist: originally contrasted with 'materialist' and used of philosophers such as Plato, the term is readily applicable to philosophers like Berkeley who denied the existence of 'matter' and who affirmed that the sensible world was dependent on (the divine) mind. It was not until after Kant that 'idealist' came to be contrasted with 'realist' and to be associated with the view that the physical world is in some way the product of (the human) mind.

indiscernibles, identity of: a principle of Leibniz's, that there are no two things in the universe that differ only numerically, hence if A and B are exactly alike then A is identical with B. Leibniz inferred this principle from the principle of sufficient reason (q.v.) since God could have no reason to create A and B as separate individuals.

induction: a process of arguing from particulars to an a posteriori (q.v.) conclusion, characteristically a statement about the future, a generalization or a claim about an unobserved member of a class.

innate ideas: these are ideas (such as the idea of God) with which human beings were supposed to have been born and in virtue of which they are able to have a priori knowledge of how things are. Locke's *Essay* played an important part in bringing innate ideas into disfavour during the eighteenth century and in encouraging explanations of ideas in terms of origins in sense experience.

intuition/intuitive knowledge: commonly regarded as the highest form of knowledge by seventeenth-century philosophers, intuitive knowledge involves a total understanding of why something that is so, has to be so. This kind of knowledge, rare in humans, was thought to be characteristic of God's knowledge of the world. See also under *scientia*.

materialism: the view that, the basic metaphysical entities of the universe are material and that there is no independent world of mind or spirit. Hobbes and Spinoza were read as materialists, Locke was suspected of it and a number of the French *philosophes* openly advocated materialism.

mechanical philosophy: the view that all the interactions in the physical universe are to be understood as like the interactions of parts of a mechanism such as a clock. Advocates of the mechanical philosophy rejected explanations in terms of 'occult qualities' (q.v.) or unintelligible 'influences'. Their rejection of action 'at a distance' led the mechanical philosophers to develop their own theories of gravitation, magnetic attraction, etc. They also rejected the use of final causes in physics.

metaphysics: the supposed a priori (q.v.) science of what really exists. Metaphysics goes beyond what can be discovered by the empirical sciences. It purports to demonstrate, for instance, the immortality of the soul or the existence of God and perhaps even the nature of a 'hidden' world beyond the world of phenomena. What is generally called 'rationalism' (q.v.) by philosophers is favourable to metaphysics, whereas empiricism (q.v.) is generally ami-metaphysical.

microcosm/macrocosm: the view that Man is a microcosm of the Cosmos (the macrocosm) was quite widely held in the sixteenth century and persisted through the seventeenth. It is associated with Renaissance Neoplatonism (q.v.) and had a range of applications from design to medicine. In a scientific context it assumed interactions that were excluded by the mechanical philosophy (q.v.).

monad: Neoplatonic term for 'one'. In the seventeenth century some Neoplatonists used the term 'monad' to describe the equivalent in their system of atoms in materialistic systems. Their monads were, however, never merely material and were sometimes conceived of (for example by Leibniz) as essentially non-extended, albeit always having some connection to matter.

moral sense (theory): the view that the ability of human beings to distinguish right from wrong depends, not on their reason, but on the fact that they are disposed to find certain actions (and characters) pleasing and others displeasing.

naturalism: a word with a wide range of variously related meanings but used (in connection with Hume) to refer to the view that our beliefs are arrived at by natural processes rather than by the operation of abstract Reason.

natural law: a moral code, laid down by God but based on created human nature, for instance on the urge for self preservation and the need to live in society. Natural law was supposed to be known through human reason.

Neoplatonism: this term is used in the first place of the revival of an eclectic Platonism between the third and sixth centuries AD. The most important figure of this movement was Plotinus. During the Renaissance there was a revival of this Neoplatonism when Ficino produced Latin editions from Plato, Plotinus and others.

occasionalism: a theory according to which God is the only true cause, hence that the apparent causes of the changes in the world should be regarded as no more than 'occasions' for God's acting to bring the changes about. On this view we should not say, strictly speaking, that striking a match is the cause of its lighting but that it is the 'occasion' on which God causes the match to light.

occult qualities: scholastic philosophers regarded certain qualities such as attraction as 'occult'. Adherents of the mechanical philosophy sought to do away with such 'occult qualities' and the phrase became, for them, a term of abuse.

ontological argument: one kind of argument for the existence of God, according to a classification that derives from Kant. Such arguments begin with a premiss about the nature or essence of God or definition of 'God' and seek to demonstrate that such a being must exist. Some of these arguments are still found impressive, as they were by Descartes, Spinoza and Leibniz. Such a priori arguments were not in favour in the eighteenth century, however, when the argument from design (q.v.) became the main argument used to support belief in God.

parsimony, principle of: the principle that, other things being equal, simpler hypotheses should be preferred to more complex ones.

peripatetics: Aristotle was reputed to have walked around whilst lecturing and the term 'peripatetics' (literally, 'those who walk round and round') came to be used in an uncomplimentary way of his followers, eventually of the scholastics (q.v.).

philosophe: French word for 'philosopher' but used especially of the intellectual figures of the French Enlightenment.

philosophia perennis: literally 'perennial philosophy'. It is a reference to that body of ancient wisdom in which Renaissance philosophers believed and which they sought to revive. See also under *prisca theologia*.

pietism: a devotional movement within the Lutheran Church in Germany. Founded by P.J. Spener (1635–1705), pietism encouraged Bible Study and advocated love rather than argument in dealing with dissenters and unbelievers.

positivism: the view that there is no knowledge to be obtained of the nature of things except by following the methods of the natural sciences.

predestinarianism: the theological theory that each individual's capacity for good or ill (and destiny of salvation or damnation) is totally dependent upon a divine grace whose distribution has been determined for all eternity. This theory is part and parcel of the Calvinist (q.v.) view of human nature as wholly 'fallen' and corrupt. It was opposed by those who thought human nature was basically good, as for instance did the Cambridge Platonists.

pre-established harmony: Leibniz, like the occasionalists, rejected the idea of an external causal action by one substance on another. He proposed instead that each substance had been so designed from the Creation that everything that would happen to it would emerge spontaneously from its own 'nature' but in perfect harmony with what was taking place in other substances. Leibniz himself referred to his proposal as a 'hypothesis' or, more commonly, as his 'system' of 'pre-established harmony.'

premiss: a logical term for a proposition put forward at the beginning of an argument, particularly in a formal demonstration (q.v.).

prisca theologia: literally 'ancient theology'. Renaissance Neoplatonists such as Ficino sought to recover the wisdom of ancient sages such as Hermes Trismegistus (a legendary Egyptian priest), Zoroaster and Orpheus. They assumed that the thoughts of the ancient theologians were harmonious with one another and with both Platonism and Christianity.

qualities, primary and secondary: an old distinction certain seventeenth-century philosophers took over in order to separate those qualities of bodies that were essential from those that were not. The exact formulation of the distinction varied and was controversial. Locke, for instance, characterized primary qualities (like shape) as ones which produced ideas in us that resembled their causes as they are in bodies. In the case of secondary qualities (like colour), on the other hand, there is no resemblance between the ideas they produce in us and their causes in bodies. For Locke these qualities are all powers in bodies, whereas

Berkeley offered a radically different account of qualities which rejected such powers and material bodies (so understood).

rationalism: a term used in a number of senses, for instance to signify opposition to any reliance on mystery or the arbitrary will of God in religion. Its main use is for the view, as opposed to empiricism (q.v.), that true certainty is grounded in reason ('intuition', q.v.) and that we can have a priori knowledge of the nature of things, of our duties, etc.

realism, moral: a theory in ethics according to which there are distinctively moral facts.

relativism: (a) in ethics, the view that there are no absolute moral standards but that these vary from one society to another, (b) about space and time, that they are nothing ('absolute') in themselves, but ways in which phenomena and events are ordered.

scepticism: most generally the view that knowledge of any sort is unobtainable. Commonly used for the view that knowledge of an objective world is unobtainable.

scepticism (moral): strictly the view that we have no knowledge of objective moral truth but often also for the view that there is no objective moral truth, in the sense of moral realism (q.v.), and that moral distinctions are conventional or subjective.

scholasticism: the style of philosophy associated with the Church schools and universities of the medieval period. The status according to Aristotle by the scholastics is indicated by their referring to him simply as 'the philosopher'. But, although they operated within a broadly Aristotelian framework, the scholastics elaborated a technical vocabulary of their own. The humanists attacked the 'barbarity' and the Moderns the 'obscurity' of this language. Scholasticism lost its dominance in universities around the end of the seventeenth century.

scientia: the term means 'knowledge' but is used to refer to an Aristotelian ideal of knowledge widely shared by philosophers in the seventeenth century. According to this view *scientia* is of 'that which is necessary' and 'cannot be otherwise'. Ultimately knowledge depends upon 'intuition' (q.v.), on this view, but demonstration (q.v.) was seen as the key process for arriving at new knowledge.

sensationalism: the view that all human knowledge derives from the senses.

sentimentalism: an ethical theory according to which moral distinctions are discerned not by reason but by feeling or sentiment.

Stoicism: one of the ancient Greek Schools of philosophy which spread to Rome, where it was adopted by Cicero and other figures who were widely admired during the seventeenth and eighteenth centuries. Stoics tended to pantheism, believing that events in the natural world are part of an interconnected whole. Though it was sometimes liberally interpreted as a Christian philosophy the Stoic virtue of steadfastness in the face of necessity did not sit easily with belief in a personal providence or in a God who acts freely. At the same time philosophers with a tendency to deism (q.v.) were not necessarily deterred from accepting Stoic ideas by such a consideration.

subjectivism: in ethics, the view that a moral judgement does no more than express the speaker's feelings, for example of approval.

sufficient reason, principle of: a favourite principle of Leibniz's, admitting of many formulations, including: for every statement that is true there is a sufficient reason (though not always know to us) why it is true. Leibniz denied that there could be any two things in the universe that were exactly alike since God would not have a sufficient reason to create both of them.

system: a theory such as the Copernican theory but also a speculative a priori metaphysical theory. It is in the latter sense that the term 'system' was often used during the Enlightenment in a disparaging way, especially by Condillac.

utilitarianism: a view according to which the rightness or wrongness of an action was to be decided by reference to question whether its consequences were beneficial or harmful. The term was first adopted by J.S. Mill in the nineteenth century but utilitarian thinking had become more common during the eighteenth century. Earlier theological utilitarians had credited God with a commitment to securing the greatest amount of human happiness possible in the long term. But utilitarian thinking in Hume, Helvétius, Bentham and others was distinctly secular and often anti-religious.

verstehen: a cognitive empathy or imaginative understanding peculiar to human understanding of personal activities, for example of motives, etc. This view is associated with the rejection of attempts to model the human on the natural sciences.

voluntarism (theological): any of several views that stress the will of God, among them (a) the view (endorsed, for instance by Descartes) that the so-called 'eternal truths' depend for their truth upon the will of God, who could have willed that they are false. On this view the natural order is good simply because God created it. God did not create the world the way He did in conformity with some standard of goodness that is independent of His will: (b) the view (held by Berkeley among others) that the continuing existence of the sensible world depends on God's continuing causation and that the constancy of the laws of nature are dependent on the constancy of the divine will.

CPSIA information can be obtained
at www.ICGtesting.com
Printed in the USA
LVHW100450250119
605158LV00002B/7/P